# Semantics, Pragmatics, Philo

Semantics and pragmatics – the st... ...context, respectively – are two fundamental area... ..., and as such are crucial to our understanding of how meaning is created. However, their theoretical ideas are often introduced without making clear connections between views, theories, and problems. This pioneering volume is both a textbook and a research guide, taking the reader on a journey through language in progressively ordered stages and ultimately enabling them to think about meaning as linguists and philosophers would. Assuming no prior knowledge of linguistics, it introduces semantics, pragmatics, and the philosophy of language, showing how all three fields can address the 'big questions' that run through the study of meaning. It covers key theories and approaches, while also enabling increasingly more sophisticated questions about the interconnected aspects of meaning, with the end goal of preparing the reader to make their own, original contributions to ideas about meaning.

**Kasia M. Jaszczolt** (pronounced Yashchout) is Professor of Linguistics and Philosophy of Language at the University of Cambridge and Professorial Fellow of Newnham College, Cambridge. Notable publications include *Meaning in Linguistic Interaction* (2016, Oxford University Press), *Representing Time* (2009, Oxford University Press), *Default Semantics* (2005, Oxford University Press) and *The Cambridge Handbook of Pragmatics* (co-edited with Keith Allan, 2012, Cambridge University Press).

# Semantics, Pragmatics, Philosophy

A Journey through Meaning

KASIA M. JASZCZOLT
*University of Cambridge*

Shaftesbury Road, Cambridge CB2 8EA, United Kingdom

One Liberty Plaza, 20th Floor, New York, NY 10006, USA

477 Williamstown Road, Port Melbourne, VIC 3207, Australia

314–321, 3rd Floor, Plot 3, Splendor Forum, Jasola District Centre,
New Delhi – 110025, India

103 Penang Road, #05–06/07, Visioncrest Commercial, Singapore 238467

Cambridge University Press is part of Cambridge University Press & Assessment,
a department of the University of Cambridge.

We share the University's mission to contribute to society through the pursuit of
education, learning and research at the highest international levels of excellence.

www.cambridge.org
Information on this title: www.cambridge.org/highereducation/isbn/9781108499651

DOI: 10.1017/9781108589338

© Kasia M. Jaszczolt 2023

This publication is in copyright. Subject to statutory exception and to the provisions
of relevant collective licensing agreements, no reproduction of any part may take
place without the written permission of Cambridge University Press & Assessment.

First published 2023

Printed in the United Kingdom by TJ Books Limited, Padstow Cornwall

*A catalogue record for this publication is available from the British Library.*

*Library of Congress Cataloging-in-Publication Data*
Names: Jaszczolt, Katarzyna, author.
Title: Semantics, pragmatics, philosophy : a journey through meaning / Kasia M. Jaszczolt.
Description: Cambridge, United Kingdom ; New York, NY : Cambridge University Press, 2023. |
Includes bibliographical references.
Identifiers: LCCN 2022043148 | ISBN 9781108499651 (hardback) | ISBN 9781108589338 (ebook)
Subjects: LCSH: Semantics. | Pragmatics. | Meaning (Philosophy)
Classification: LCC P325 .J338 2023 | DDC 401/.43–dc23/eng/20221018
LC record available at https://lccn.loc.gov/2022043148

ISBN 978-1-108-49965-1 Hardback
ISBN 978-1-108-73104-1 Paperback

Cambridge University Press & Assessment has no responsibility for the persistence
or accuracy of URLs for external or third-party internet websites referred to in this
publication and does not guarantee that any content on such websites is, or will
remain, accurate or appropriate.

**To all past, present, and future meaning hunters**

# Contents

| | | |
|---|---|---|
| *List of Figures* | | *page* xi |
| *List of Tables* | | xiii |
| *Preface and Tips on How to Read This Book* | | xv |
| *Acknowledgements* | | xviii |
| *List of Abbreviations and Symbols* | | xx |

| Stage 1 | **Introduction: Meaning – What It Is and Where to Find It** | 1 |
|---|---|---|
| | 1.1 How (Not) to Study Meaning | 1 |
| | 1.2 Semantics, Pragmatics, and Philosophy (and Why They Are Best Done Together) | 3 |
| | 1.3 Proposition: A Flexible Unit for Studying Meaning? | 6 |
| | 1.4 Meaning and Its Correlates | 11 |

| Stage 2 | **Word Meaning and Concepts** | 18 |
|---|---|---|
| | 2.1 Harnessing Word Meaning | 18 |
| | 2.2 The 'Concept' Commotion | 21 |
| | 2.3 Language and Thought | 33 |
| | 2.4 Lexicon and Pragmatics | 36 |
| | 2.5 The Role of Reference | 39 |

| Stage 3 | **Composing Sentence Meaning: Tools and Their Purpose** | 44 |
|---|---|---|
| | 3.1 Truth in Service of Meaning: Truth Conditions and Truth-Value Judgements | 44 |
| | 3.2 The Metalanguage for the Logical Form | 48 |
| | 3.3 Possible Worlds and Models | 57 |
| | 3.4 Semantic Composition and Semantic Types | 63 |
| | 3.5 Type-Theoretic Metalanguage and Lambda Abstraction | 72 |
| | 3.6 Formal Tools and Cognitive Reality | 74 |

| Stage 4 | **Operations on Sentences** | 77 |
|---|---|---|
| | 4.1 Sentential Connectives and Propositional Logic | 77 |
| | 4.2 Conjunction | 79 |
| | 4.3 Disjunction | 88 |
| | 4.4 Conditional and Biconditional | 92 |

|         |       |                                                                 |     |
|---------|-------|-----------------------------------------------------------------|-----|
|         | 4.5   | Negation                                                        | 97  |
|         |       | 4.5.1 Negation and Opposition                                   | 97  |
|         |       | 4.5.2 Objecting to 'The Way of Putting It'                      | 99  |
|         |       | 4.5.3 Negation vis-à-vis the Semantic Ambiguity/ Underspecification Debate | 103 |
|         | 4.6   | Linguistic Diversity: Snakes and Ladders, Cluedo, and Monopoly  | 108 |
| Stage 5 | **Inside the Sentence**                                                | 112 |
|         | 5.1   | Limitations of the Metalanguage                                 | 112 |
|         | 5.2   | Quantification                                                  | 116 |
|         |       | 5.2.1 Quantifiers as Relations between Sets                     | 116 |
|         |       | 5.2.2 Quantifiers and Quirks of Interpretation                  | 122 |
|         |       | 5.2.3 Number Terms and Counting                                 | 124 |
|         | 5.3   | Representing Time                                               | 130 |
|         |       | 5.3.1 Eventualities and Their Types                             | 130 |
|         |       | 5.3.2 Tense and Aspect                                          | 133 |
|         |       | 5.3.3 Tense Logic?                                              | 135 |
|         |       | 5.3.4 Logical Form and Events                                   | 139 |
|         |       | 5.3.5 Time: Semantics, Pragmatics, and Metaphysics              | 142 |
|         | 5.4   | Modality                                                        | 146 |
|         |       | 5.4.1 Types of Modality and Modal Logic                         | 146 |
|         |       | 5.4.2 Modals as Relational Expressions                          | 148 |
|         |       | 5.4.3 Modality and Mood                                         | 149 |
|         |       | 5.4.4 Modality and Temporality                                  | 151 |
|         | 5.5   | Propositional Attitude Reports                                  | 154 |
|         | 5.6   | Interim Conclusions: Semantic Tools for Formal Cognitive Representations? | 164 |
| Stage 6 | **Conveying Information**                                             | 167 |
|         | 6.1   | From Sentences to Discourses: Dynamic Semantics for Dynamic Meaning | 167 |
|         |       | 6.1.1 Donkey Sentences                                          | 168 |
|         |       | 6.1.2 Multi-Sentence Discourses                                 | 172 |
|         |       | 6.1.2.1 Multi-Sentence Discourses in DRT                        | 173 |
|         |       | 6.1.2.2 Multi-Sentence Discourses in DPL                        | 178 |
|         | 6.2   | Referring and Its Tools                                         | 180 |
|         |       | 6.2.1 Types and Hierarchies of Referring                        | 180 |
|         |       | 6.2.2 Proper Names                                              | 185 |
|         |       | 6.2.3 Definite and Indefinite Descriptions                      | 189 |
|         |       | 6.2.4 Indexical Expressions                                     | 197 |
|         |       | 6.2.4.1 Indexicality or Deixis?                                 | 197 |
|         |       | 6.2.4.2 Deixis and Traditional-Descriptive Classifications      | 198 |

|  |  | 6.2.4.3 | Indexicality: Two-Dimensional Semantics and the Roles of Context | 202 |
|  |  | 6.2.4.4 | From Monster Contexts to Indexicals as Functions of Expressions | 208 |
|  | 6.3 | Organizing Information in Discourse | | 215 |
|  |  | 6.3.1 | Topic and Coherence | 215 |
|  |  | 6.3.2 | Focus and Truth Conditions | 220 |
|  |  | 6.3.3 | Presupposition and Projective Content | 223 |
|  |  | 6.3.4 | At-Issue Content vis-à-vis Projective Content | 232 |

**Stage 7 Utterance Meaning, or What Lurks under the Surface** — 236

|  | 7.1 | Saying, Implicating, and Inferring | | 236 |
|  |  | 7.1.1 | Beginning with Grice: From Intentions to Utterance Meaning | 236 |
|  |  | 7.1.2 | The Cooperative Principle and Maxims of Conversation | 240 |
|  |  | 7.1.3 | Intentions and Conventions | 249 |
|  |  | 7.1.4 | Post-Gricean Principles and Heuristics | 251 |
|  | 7.2 | Truth-Conditional vs. Non-Truth-Conditional, Semantic vs. Pragmatic: What to Include and What to Leave Out | | 260 |
|  |  | 7.2.1 | The Point of Departure | 260 |
|  |  | 7.2.2 | Making Truth Conditions Intuitive: Relevance Theory and Truth-Conditional Pragmatics | 262 |
|  |  | 7.2.3 | Making Truth Conditions Functional: Default Semantics | 272 |
|  |  | 7.2.4 | Cancellability Revisited | 279 |
|  | 7.3 | Keeping Semantics and Pragmatics Apart | | 281 |
|  |  | 7.3.1 | Minimalism without Propositions | 281 |
|  |  | 7.3.2 | 'Minimal' and 'Insensitive' Semantics | 284 |
|  |  | 7.3.3 | Semantic 'Indexicalisms' | 286 |
|  |  | 7.3.4 | Semantics or Pragmatics? Or, Who Cares? | 288 |

**Stage 8 Meaning in Service of Its Makers** — 291

|  | 8.1 | Who Needs Literal Meanings? | | 291 |
|  | 8.2 | What Makes a Metaphor | | 296 |
|  |  | 8.2.1 | Objectivism and Subjectivism Revisited | 296 |
|  |  | 8.2.2 | Metaphor: Comparison and Interaction | 299 |
|  |  | 8.2.3 | Towards a Contextualist-Semantic/Pragmatic Account | 301 |
|  |  | 8.2.4 | Metaphor in Cognition | 307 |
|  |  | 8.2.5 | The Demise of 'Metaphor'? | 312 |
|  | 8.3 | Speech and Action | | 316 |
|  |  | 8.3.1 | Speech Acts and Mental States | 316 |
|  |  | 8.3.2 | Harnessing Illocutionary Force | 321 |
|  |  | 8.3.3 | Indirect Speech Acts? | 327 |

| | | | | |
|---|---|---|---|---|
| 8.4 | At a Crossroads with Ethical and Social Debates | | | 330 |
| | 8.4.1 | Commitment and Accountability | | 331 |
| | | 8.4.1.1 | Negotiation of Meaning and Taking Responsibility | 331 |
| | | 8.4.1.2 | Lying, Misleading, and Liability | 338 |
| | 8.4.2 | Social Persona | | 341 |
| | | 8.4.2.1 | Being Polite and Being Proper | 341 |
| | | 8.4.2.2 | 'Forbidden Words' and 'Bad Language': Semantics, Pragmatics, or Neither? | 349 |

**Stage 9   Conclusion: The Future of Meaning?**     360

*References*     364
*Index*     399

# Figures

| | | |
|---|---|---|
| 1.1 | Relation between language, the world, and thought (adapted from Ogden and Richards 1960 [1923]: 11) | *page* 16 |
| 3.1 | Syntactic composition of sentence (3.52) ('Daniel sneezed loudly.') in categorial grammar, using basic categories N and S and derived categories | 68 |
| 3.2 | Composition of the meaning of sentence (3.52) ('Daniel sneezed loudly.') in intensional semantics | 70 |
| 5.1 | Partial DRS for (5.18) ('Few dogs like cats.') | 118 |
| 5.2 | Duplex condition | 118 |
| 5.3 | Partial DRS for the distributive reading of (5.48) ('Three boys ordered a pizza.') | 125 |
| 5.4 | Partial DRS for the collective reading of (5.48) ('Three boys ordered a pizza.') | 126 |
| 5.5 | Partial DRS for the collective reading of (5.49) ('Three boys ordered a pizza. They were hungry.') | 127 |
| 5.6 | A possible representation of time flow | 135 |
| 5.7 | A possible representation of branching future | 135 |
| 5.8 | Representation of tenses using S, R, E (adapted from Reichenbach 1948: 290) | 137 |
| 5.9 | Representation of progressive aspect/extended event (adapted from Reichenbach 1948: 290) | 138 |
| 5.10 | DRS for (5.90) ('Anna gave a lecture on Monday.') | 141 |
| 5.11 | DRS for (5.91) ('Bill was ill on Monday.') | 141 |
| 5.12 | DRS for (5.93) ('Anna has given a lecture.') | 142 |
| 5.13 | DRS for (5.94) ('Bill is sleeping.') | 142 |
| 5.14 | Partial DRS for (5.132) ('Max believes that the king of France is bald.') | 160 |
| 6.1 | Partial DRS for (6.1) ('Every farmer who owns a donkey is fond of it.') | 171 |
| 6.2 | Partial DRS for (6.18) ('Bill owns a donkey.') | 174 |
| 6.3 | Mental structure of (6.18) ('Bill owns a donkey.') | 174 |
| 6.4 | Triggering configurations for proper name (adapted from Kamp and Reyle 1993: 65) | 175 |
| 6.5 | Triggering configurations for indefinite description (adapted from Kamp and Reyle 1993: 75) | 175 |

| | | |
|---|---|---|
| 6.6 | Partial DRS for (6.19) ('Bill owns a donkey. He is fond of it.') | 176 |
| 6.7 | Partial DRS for (6.20) ('Bill doesn't own a horse$_j$. He is fond of *it$_j$.') | 177 |
| 6.8 | Restrictor and scope for (6.100) ('Paula isn't registered in PARIS.') (adapted from Kuboň 2004: 211) | 221 |
| 7.1 | Components of Grice's meaning$_{NN}$ (modelled on Horn 1988: 121) | 260 |
| 7.2 | Merger representation for a possible primary meaning of (7.42) ('Bill will not get a job with the London Symphony Orchestra.') | 276 |
| 7.3 | Merger representation for a possible primary meaning of (7.43) ('Antoni Gaudí was an eccentric.') | 277 |
| 8.1 | Typology of literalness modelled on Recanati (2004: 68–78 and Fig. 5.1) | 293 |

# Tables

| | | |
|---|---|---:|
| 4.1 | Truth table for conjunction in propositional logic | *page* 79 |
| 4.2 | Truth table for disjunction in propositional logic | 89 |
| 4.3 | Truth table for material implication in propositional logic | 93 |
| 4.4 | Truth table for equivalence in propositional logic | 93 |
| 4.5 | Truth table for negation in propositional logic | 98 |
| 4.6 | Truth table for the relation of presupposition | 100 |
| 4.7 | Truth table for the relation of entailment | 101 |
| 6.1 | Givenness Hierarchy (adapted from Gundel et al. 1993: 275) | 184 |

# Preface and Tips on How to Read This Book

This is a journey through *thinking about meaning like a linguist and a philosopher*. It provides introductions to ideas and approaches, like a textbook should, but it is not merely a conventional textbook. Conventional textbooks tend to contain lots of pieces of information ready to be picked up. But one can't pick them up without first knowing what one wants to do with them. Instead, this is a structured journey through meaning that aims to prepare the reader for their own journey. It reaches to advanced readers too, in that they can follow my voyage assessing the choices of landmarks and perhaps pause at what is marked as 'food for thought'. As such, it can also serve as a guide to how one can conduct research on meaning – a guide that spans semantics, pragmatics, and philosophy, sometimes with their other interfaces. Read this preface, the table of contents, and the final, short stage of the journey (Stage 9) to see if you want to join in.

In 2002 I published *Semantics and Pragmatics: Meaning in Language and Discourse* for the Longman Linguistics Library – seventeen chapters, a comprehensive, wide-scope introduction, but still a conventional textbook. In spite of my initial plan that what follows would be a new edition of that book, I couldn't bring myself to do so. I don't really like conventional textbooks. I like a hands-on approach to what authors of theories themselves really thought and wrote. But guidebooks of some sort are necessary: starting with primary sources without help can be a daunting task. Moreover, we all need tips on how to arrange all these bits of knowledge and ideas from brilliant linguists and philosophers into a full picture. We need to know which theories have become timeless landmarks, which views are controversial and how, and we need suggestions on which ideas might be adaptable for specific purposes. There is no need always to agree with such suggestions but they provide a start for thinking about meaning like a linguist and a philosopher.

So, after three decades of experience of teaching semantics, pragmatics, and philosophy of language to many bright and enthusiastic students (most of the time at the University of Cambridge), it was time to write up a focused journey in which pieces of information are arranged in search of an answer to such questions as what meaning in language is, how it works, and how to represent it. Hence, what follows is a *journey through meaning*. I hope that it will not only inform but also invoke thoughts, judgements, and emotions about this whimsical beast: Meaning in Language and Meaning in Language Use. The views in the journey are, of course, opinionated, like any honest and authentic assessment must be. But textbook information is not. It is given in a way that allows the reader to make a choice between continuing to travel with me or picking up the textbook material (the introductions to theories, approaches, and methods included here) at any stage and starting their own journey alongside mine. It is always possible to adopt some views but reject others, carrying along some of the toys (building blocks and tools that make up meaning) but leaving others behind. The whole excitement and fun about inquiring into meaning in language is finding one's own way through it from the very beginning, rather than leaving it to ageing scholars. But this can only be done when their old ways are well understood, appreciated, and thought through. Then they are not shackles but wings for new ideas. And this was the rationale behind this 'textbook +' project.

Each of the nine chapters, called *stages* of the journey, has to be taken slowly rather than read in one go – they are not lecture-length units (unlike those of my 'textbooky' textbook of twenty years ago). They organize the journey into stages in thinking about meaning and they get longer as the journey progresses. But they get *easier to read* as the journey progresses: Stage 1 may still be daunting because it lays out what it means to think about meaning. But from Stage 2, it should be a pleasant, informative, and rewarding run (if it isn't, let me know!). Less ephemerally, this is what I mean: before embarking on any journey, one must decide where one wants to go and how to get there. In what follows, we start with the desiderata that we want to end the journey with understanding (i) cognitively real meaning, meaning that speakers intend, addressees recover, but also meaning that they partly jointly construct and agree on in the process of conversation. We also want to travel there using (ii) reliable, precise, formal tools. We will carry along with us whatever brilliant, ground-breaking ideas and theories can help achieve that. It will soon appear that semantics, pragmatics, and philosophy of language are full of such exciting ideas, on all sides of what is often seen as disputes or even insurmountable divisions. The field is rife with such treasures, and instead of asking who is right, we will often be asking *what* they are *right* about and *what* they may be *wrong* about in order to learn from them all, as long as they can help with our desiderata (i) and (ii). We will also point backward and forward to different stages in the journey, showing how a different path could have been taken and how different roadmaps can result in different meaning experiences.

We will be quite greedy for getting to the bottom of meaning in language, so we cover a lot in this journey. We start with words and concepts, move to sentences, utterances, and then to what 'lurks under the surface' – dynamically emerging meanings, non-literal meanings – and go further into practical effects and consequences that acts of speech produce, focusing on accountability, lying and misleading, politeness, and use of bad and offensive language. So, the journey covers what is usually split into different textbooks: in Semantics, Pragmatics, and Philosophy of Language. As such, it has to be taken at one's own pace: stop where you wish and go to the sources recommended in the footnotes if you wish. I kept the text free from bibliographical references (apart from referencing quotations), putting them all in the footnotes. But this is all that the footnotes contain: additional pointers and references. So, they can be ignored outright if one wants a more introductory, flowing, evenly paced journey. Or they can be inspected as you go along, dipping into them whenever the particular topic grips you. As such, **the book can be read in many different ways**: (i) as a free-flowing discussion of various phenomena and approaches in the study of meaning; (ii) as a journey towards a comprehensive theory of cognitively real meaning that picks up different views and approaches on the way and makes use of them; or as (iii) a shopper's guide to whatever interests you – stop and follow the select references as you see fit, creating your own roadmap. And there are probably some other ways of reading it too.

By necessity, a journey through meaning leads along a meandering path. It is also a path with many crossroads, so there will still be many facets and types of meaning that this book is *not* about. Some examples of this are animal communication, non-linguistic communication, such as the semantics of gestures, or particular theories of meaning in language and discourse that would fit with the topics covered here but had to be left out. We will also largely leave out meaning in artificial intelligence (AI) and cross-cultural communication, although we will have recourse to these areas from time to time. As I said, every journey is a selective and somewhat opinionated journey, or else it becomes a list of meaningless filing cards. Since it is a progressing journey, a flow of ideas, divided into stages rather than disconnected chapters, there are ample cross-references to earlier sections and a detailed index to make travelling as comfortable as possible. For example, the discussion of semantic ambiguity will unavoidably crop up again and again, but with ample pointers. To reiterate, the flow of argumentation is based on two foundational desiderata: cognitive reality and formalizability. And, of course, the assumption that they are compatible: that it is possible to get to the bottom, to the very blueprints of how meaning really works.

In short, the aim is to encourage thinking about meaning in ways that will enable the reader to make informed judgements about views, theories, and methods, to acquire confidence to agree or disagree with the authorities, and, most importantly, *to feel empowered to pursue semantics and pragmatics in a new, different way.* In short, by the end, *my* journey will not be *your* journey. But I hope this journey will inform, inspire, and encourage.

# Acknowledgements

First and foremost, I owe gratitude to all my mentors, teachers, colleagues, as well as my students who, throughout the decades, shared with me their thoughts and enthusiasm for semantic, pragmatic, and philosophical questions about meaning. Thinking about the subject and discussing it is not a job, it is a passion. I have to start here with Barbara Lewandowska-Tomaszczyk, my first teacher of semantics, who opened my mind and heart to big questions about meaning in language at the tender age of nineteen, and to whom I owe my personal lifetime journey through meaning. What follows are merely highlights from a long list of those to whom I owe thanks for helping me shape my views on various aspects of what follows: Keith Allan, Jay Atlas, Johan van der Auwera, Paul Dekker, Michael Dummett, Chi-Hé Elder, Thorstein Fretheim, Michael Haugh, Larry Horn, Hans Kamp, Eleni Kapogianni, Sławoj Olczyk, Louis de Saussure, Stephen Schiffer, Roberto Sileo, Jiranthara Srioutai, Barbara Tuchańska, Deirdre Wilson, Maciej Witek, Henk Zeevat, and many, many others – there is no obvious cut-off point.

My warmest and heartfelt thank you goes to three people who read the entire draft of this rather long book: my two colleagues in the field, Keith Allan and Chi-Hé Elder, who commented on the contents as well as editorial issues, and my husband Charles Berthon, who provided careful and thoughtful copy-editing. Thank you all for tracking ambiguities, convoluted sentences, missing premises in presenting arguments, as well as missing articles – a nemesis of most non-native speakers of English. Needless to say, all remaining follies are mine.

Helen Barton, my Cambridge University Press editor, has been encouraging, patient, and an ideal editor to work with. Then, the book benefited from an excellent, professional, and thoughtful production team: Lisa Carter, the Cambridge University Press content manager, Sue Browning, the copy-editor, and Kim Birchall, the indexer. It was a pleasure to work with them all. I also owe thanks to the Theoretical and Applied Linguistics Section of the University of Cambridge and to Newnham College for supporting my research with regular grants. To Newnham College, I also owe gratitude for providing a calm but stimulating ambience and collegiality.

Some of the sections include material adapted from my 2002 textbook *Semantics and Pragmatics* published in the Longman Linguistics Library Series. I owe thanks to Longman/Pearson Education for granting me copyright reversal so that I could use it. In critical discussions of the presented approaches, I have also used some ideas from my previous publications, in particular Jaszczolt 2009b, 2019a, 2021a, 2023 and Jaszczolt and Berthon, in press, as referenced in the text.

## Acknowledgements

Last but not least, to my husband Charles Berthon and my daughter Lidia Berthon I owe immense gratitude for their patience, understanding, love, and for various forms of assistance, including answering my endless questions about the quirks of English idiomatic phrases. And, finally, to Melford, our Siamese cat, for keeping me company, sleeping on the piles of notes and guarding them lovingly. Sadly, he died in Stage 7 of what follows, having given us fourteen years of wonderful companionship. After a period of mourning, a working cocker spaniel Roddy arrived at the stage of copy-editing, so I owe him thanks too for the (sometimes) welcome, (usually) needed, and (always) enjoyable distractions.

# Abbreviations and Symbols

| | |
|---|---|
| ∧, & | truth-functional conjunction |
| ∨ | truth-functional disjunction |
| → | truth-functional implication (material implication) |
| ↔ | truth-functional equivalence |
| ¬ | truth-functional negation |
| ⊢ | 'it is the case that' |
| ∀ | universal quantifier (*all*, *every*) |
| ∃ | existential quantifier (*some*, *a*) |
| < > | ordered *n*-tuple (ordered pair, triple ...) |
| {...} | set; extension |
| {$x \mid f(x)$} | set of elements on the left (here: $x$) satisfy properties on the right (here: $f(x)$) |
| ⇒ | implication (consequence, inferential link, as distinguished from material implication) |
| \|...\| | cardinality of a set |
| ∈ | membership of a set ('belongs to', 'is a member of') |
| ∩ | intersection (common part) of sets |
| − | difference between sets |
| ∅ | 1. empty set; 2. truth-value gap |
| ≥ | greater than or equal to |
| > | 1. greater than; 2. temporal sequence ('later than'); 3. sequence of categories in any principled ordering |
| < | 1. smaller than; 2. temporal precedence ('earlier than') |
| ⊃⊂ | temporal contiguity |
| $e$ ⊃⊂ $s$ | '$s$ starts at the moment $e$ ends' |
| ⊆ | 1. set inclusion ('is a subset of'); 2. temporal inclusion |
| $e \subseteq t$ | 'event $e$ is temporally included within time $t$' |
| ○ | temporal overlap |
| $s$ o $t$ | 'state $s$ overlaps with time $t$' |
| ⟦...⟧ | intension |
| □ | necessity operator |
| ◊ | possibility operator |
| λ | abstraction operator (lambda operator) |

# List of Abbreviations and Symbols

| | |
|---|---|
| * | ungrammatical |
| ? | awkward/pragmatically ill-formed |
| ≫ | communicates |
| = | 1. equals; 2. clitic boundary |
| ≠ | does not equal |
| [...]$_f$ | material in focus position |
| $\phi, \varphi$ | metalinguistic sentential variables |
| $\Phi$ | metalinguistic predicate variable |
| $\Phi*m$ | type of mode of presentation |
| $\Delta$ | degree of acceptability (in ACC$_\Delta$) |
| $\Sigma$ | summation of information |
| *1/2/3 Sg/Pl* | 1st/2nd/3rd person singular/plural number |
| $a, b, c \ldots$ | individual constants in predicate logic |
| A, B, C | sets |
| ACC | acceptability operator |
| ANCH | anchor |
| Att | attitude |
| Bel | belief operator |
| $c$ | context |
| CA | Conversation Analysis |
| CD | cognitive default |
| *Class* | classifier |
| CMT | Conceptual Metaphor Theory |
| CPI | conscious pragmatic inference |
| DET | determiner |
| DPL | Dynamic Predicate Logic |
| DRS | discourse representation structure |
| DRT | Discourse Representation Theory |
| DS | Default Semantics |
| E | event point (Reichenbach) |
| e | nominal category ('entity') in intensional (t/e) semantics |
| *e* | event |
| epp | epistemic possibility past |
| f | truth value 'false' |
| *f* | function |
| F | 1. future-tense operator; 2. illocutionary force |
| *F* | feminine gender |
| FTA | face-threatening act |
| *g* | 1. assignment function; 2. a variable defined for a specific discussion |
| GCI | generalized conversational implicature |
| Gen | grammatical gender |
| *Gen* | genitive case |
| GIIN | generalized invited inference |

# List of Abbreviations and Symbols

| | |
|---|---|
| HWAM | Hey, wait a minute! |
| I | I-principle/heuristic |
| *I* | interpretation |
| ICE-GB | International Corpus of English, British component |
| ICM | Idealized Cognitive Model |
| IEM | immunity to error through misidentification |
| iff | if and only if |
| *Imperf* | imperfective aspect |
| *Ind* | indicative mood |
| IS | properties of the human inferential system |
| ISA | indirect speech act |
| m | mode of presentation |
| M | M-principle/heuristic |
| *M* | 1. model; 2. masculine gender |
| *mod* | modulation |
| mon↑ | monotone increasing |
| mon↓ | monotone decreasing |
| N | 1. noun; 2. nominal category (bearer of reference) in categorial grammar |
| *Nom* | nominative case |
| NP | noun phrase |
| *p* | proposition (in semi-formal representations) |
| P | past-tense operator |
| *p, q, r* | sentential variables |
| *P, Q* | predicate variables |
| *Past* | past tense |
| PCI | particularized conversational implicature |
| PE | proposition expressed |
| *Perf* | perfective aspect |
| PIIN | particularized invited inference |
| PM | proposition meant |
| PN | proper noun |
| *Poss* | possessive |
| *Pres* | present tense |
| *Pron* | pronoun |
| *Prosp* | prospective marker |
| Q | 1. quantifier; 2. Q-principle/heuristic |
| QUD | question under discussion |
| R | 1. relation; 2. R-principle/heuristic; 3. reference point (Reichenbach); 4. restrictor (alternative semantics) |
| *Refl* | reflexive marker |
| rf | regular future (in $ACC_\Delta^{rf}$) |
| rn | regular present ('now') |
| rp | regular past (in $ACC_\Delta^{rp}$) |

| | |
|---|---|
| s | intension |
| *s* | state |
| S | 1. sentence; 2. sentential category (bearer of truth value) in categorial grammar; 3. 'since' operator (DRT); 4. speech point (Reichenbach); 5. scope (alternative semantics) |
| SAT | Speech Act Theory |
| SC | stereotypes and presumptions about society and culture |
| SCWD | social, cultural, or world-knowledge default |
| SD | situation of discourse |
| SDRT | Segmented Discourse Representation Theory |
| *Seq* | sequential marker |
| SG | speaker's grounds |
| *Sg* | singular |
| SM | semantic meaning |
| *Subj* | subjunctive mood |
| t | 1. truth value 'true'; 2. proposition ('truth-evaluable category') in intensional (t/e) semantics |
| *t* | time |
| U | 'until' operator (DRT) |
| V | verb |
| VP | verb phrase |
| *W* | possible world |
| WK | world knowledge |
| WS | word meaning and sentence structure |
| *x, y, z* | individual variables in predicate logic |

SMALL CAPITALS stand for concepts (e.g. DOG)
LARGE CAPITALS in examples stand for intonational focus

# Stage 1   Introduction
### *Meaning – What It Is and Where to Find It*

> This is the primary commandment humanism has given us: create meaning for a meaningless world.
>
> (Harari 2017: 259)

## 1.1   How (Not) to Study Meaning

This book is about meaning – not the meaning of certain concepts such as the meaning of life or the meaning of freedom but about what it means for linguistic expressions to *mean* something. It is also a book about *meaning for humans*. The qualification 'human meaning' is not yet common in linguistics book titles but it is increasingly important to add it. We are already experiencing fundamental differences in *how*, and *what kind of*, meaning is approached in computational linguistics and computer science in general on the one hand, and in philosophy of language or sociopragmatics on the other. 'Semantics' sits in the middle and tends to be approached either (i) philosophically, through questions such as 'What are concepts and where can we find them?' and sociopragmatically, through questions such as 'What meaning does this utterance have in this context and what effect does it have on the addressee?'. This is the 'top-down' approach, from ideas and theories to the practice of use. Or it can be approached (ii) starting with databases of language use and distilling meanings, that is 'bottom-up'. Using (ii), we can distil patterns that can also be useful for producing algorithms and training data processors for human–machine or machine–machine interaction, as in deep learning in AI. That is how (ii) may prove to go beyond (i) and apply to other than human ways of carving and conceptualizing reality.

   This book is about the first kind of meaning – human meaning, meaning that we want to better understand in order to understand the systems of natural languages we employ in communication and the language(s) in which we convey our thoughts (more about this soon). 'Bottom-up' and 'top-down' methods may meet in the middle but only if they prove to be about the same *kind* of meaning: meaning that humans make out of reality and externalize through language. We don't know if they do meet, and that is why the book is only about the 'top-down' methods and human meaning.

Non-biological intelligence that humans invent may develop our human feelings, thoughts, and ideas as emergent features of data processing, like, for example, in Ian McEwan's (2019) novel *Machines Like Me and People Like You*. But this is fantasy – we simply don't know yet. And until we do, this is to be read as a book about human meaning, in human natural languages and human discourse.

It focuses on language as a means of conveying and expressing meaning, although it will also on occasion touch upon non-linguistic vehicles such as actions, gestures, or employing context and shared assumptions. It will also focus on human communication – on people and linguistic communities (in that the latter are a source of some useful generalizations about meaning), almost totally to the exclusion of animal and human–machine communication. The field delimited by human languages is vast enough without including these as well.

'To mean' is a notoriously vague predicate. For example, it can figure in the following expressions:

(1.1)   Dark spots on the leaves mean a deficiency of iron.

(1.2)   The beep means that you are parking too close to the wall.

(1.3)   'Divertirsi' means 'to have fun'.

As mid-twentieth-century philosopher Paul Grice famously remarked in his seminal paper 'Meaning',[1] these meanings of 'meaning' are of little interest to a student of intentional communication.[2] Likewise, they will be of little interest to us. In (1.1), 'means' stands for a natural sign of a plant disease; in (1.2), it stands for a conventional symbol; and in (1.3), it functions to provide a translation from one natural language (Italian) to another (English). This book is about a much more nuanced connection between a sign that is used to perform the task of meaning something (a sign that an early-twentieth-century linguist, Ferdinand de Saussure, called a 'signifier'[3]) and the thing that is meant ('signified'). It is about meaning that is associated with, and arises from the use of, expressions of natural language – all of them, that is the lexical items that belong to the system of a given language, the sentences that speakers can produce by combining them, and the physical utterances that they can produce using such sentences. As such, it concerns the kind of meaning where the relation between the sign (a word) and the meant content is arbitrary, but the relation between the combinations of words (sentences or their fragments) is much less so. It strives to discuss explanations of this relation that account for the *productivity* of these linguistic devices (the power of the language system to produce expressions and meanings never produced before) and their *systematicity* (the property of being organized into rules, or a system,

---

[1] See Grice 1989a [1957].

[2] To reiterate, the book can be read either without the footnotes, as a conceptual journey through meaning – a journey through ideas – or with consulting the footnotes that provide detailed references to sources and recommendations for a more in-depth study. General recommendations for further reading follow at the end of each stage.

[3] See de Saussure's (1983) [1916] *Course in General Linguistics* that consists of a translation of his lectures delivered at the University of Geneva between 1906 and 1911.

that guide the derivation of meaning). The explanations we are going to consider tend to be *normative* – not in the sense of laying down the rules of how we ought to use language (that would be the long-abandoned prescriptivism) but rather in the descriptive sense of capturing regularities (or norms) of how the language works and how speakers use it. These explanations often have the status of *theories*. So, theories usually contain rules that capture the properties of the devices used for communication in a system of a particular language and/or conversational behaviour of the users of this system. I say 'usually' because this depends on the philosophical stance towards language: on some views, vagaries of language use are foregrounded, while regularities are downplayed. Most of this book will concern theories that do assume some regularity of linguistic behaviour, both in the behaviour of the linguistic devices and their users, and the ensuing normativity of theories. But I will also say a little more about 'the rebels' in Section 8.3.

## 1.2 Semantics, Pragmatics, and Philosophy (and Why They Are Best Done Together)

The four terms in the title of this book delimit what we are going to focus on. 'Meaning' in the sense just discussed is analysed from three perspectives: (a) devices of the language system and the primary output they express (semantics); (b) meaning-producing activities of the users of this system in their contextual settings (pragmatics); and (c) the 'overlay' of higher-level questions to do with how to define and delimit meaning, as well as related concepts such as referring, intending, inference, and semantics and pragmatics. The latter are the domain of philosophy – and within it, mostly, but not exclusively, philosophy of language. All of the above definitions are debatable, which reflects the state of the art in meaning research and, on a more positive note, testifies to the buoyancy of discussions on these matters. Where the boundary exactly lies between semantics and pragmatics has been a matter of fierce 'border wars' (to use the apt term by the American pragmaticist Laurence Horn[4]) since the late 1970s, and the disputes are not abating, although more and more linguists and philosophers opt to practise meaning theory 'without borders'. More recently, the debates have tended to focus on *metasemantics* and *metapragmatics* that ask foundational questions such as what facts endow a theory with meaning (I go into more detail in Stage 9), and, on the other hand, inroads into practical concerns that belong to the domains of ethics, sociology, social anthropology, or theory of social justice. Examples of the latter include the study of lying and misleading, language and humour, politeness and impoliteness, hate speech and within it the use of racial and ethnic slurs, to name but a few. A pertinent area here is research into *conceptual engineering* – attempts to affect the use of existing lexical items to express novel or updated concepts, for example concepts that better reflect attitudes to gender and ethnicity that are currently regarded as politically, socially, and morally correct. I introduce the semantics/

[4] See Horn 2006.

pragmatics boundary disputes in Stage 7 of the journey (although they are also implicit in the discussions throughout the book), and refer to some of these more practical, including ethical and social, concerns to do with language use in Stage 8.

The fluid and contentious boundary between semantics and pragmatics, and the associated meta-level inquiries into what the disciplines entail in the first place, demonstrate that separating them, even (or especially!) for the purpose of introducing the subject, would be a non-starter. Studying pragmatics without studying semantics is notoriously difficult if one wants to get to the bottom of the 'big questions' about meaning. One might argue that this is so because the study of what conversation interactants *do* with language presupposes understanding of how the linguistic tools they use actually work. But then, arguably, studying semantics without studying pragmatics is also very limiting, or even a non-starter to the same degree, in that it would somewhat dogmatically fix the boundary beyond which semantic concerns turn into pragmatic concerns and leave semantics helpless, unable to deal with the meaning of a vast bulk of natural-language sentences. As I try to demonstrate throughout this book, fixing such a boundary at the start takes away all the excitement and all the raison d'être from studying meaning. Language as a tool is extremely flexible – to the degree that many linguists and philosophers now argue whether words do indeed have any core meaning instead of merely functioning as 'pointers' to the meanings they help express in different contexts. Likewise, it is highly debatable whether the concept of *sentence meaning* stands up to scrutiny or, rather, whether it ought to be replaced with *utterance meaning*, in that both the lexical items and the structure in which they are used are so overwhelmingly underdetermined. Naturally, the debate concerning the feasibility of maintaining the traditional literal/non-literal meaning distinction is also under close scrutiny. I say more about the flexibility of word meaning in Stage 2 and in Sections 8.1–8.2.

The great fun of studying meaning in this way is that one can question the bulk of long-established assumptions and fixed core concepts, such as 'word meaning', 'literal meaning', or 'semantics' and 'pragmatics', and keep asking oneself what meaning really is – meaning which the devices we have at our disposal (words and structures) allow us to communicate. As was said, the meaning of the devices themselves (which is the traditional understanding of the scope of semantics) and the meaning as it is intended and conveyed in the context of discourse (which is one of the core traditional understandings of pragmatics) are, arguably, inseparable, in view of the overwhelming flexibility of words and structures. And, of course, in view of the related fact that pragmatic devices of communication are devices on a par with the lexicon and structure.

No one who writes about these topics can ever produce an objective account. This is so for various reasons. First, it is because covering all existing approaches is impossible and one has to make informed but subjective choices as to which ones are at the forefront of research, or historically important and still produce valuable explanations – or which ones are promising and sufficiently advanced as theories in progress to be included. Second, it is because every linguist starts with some initial assumptions. Some of these assumptions foreground regularity, that is finding universal rules and patterns on which human language is founded, others focus on linguistic diversity. If regularity is aimed at, then a theorist will strive to fit meaning into the mould of theories and then provide a separate account that explains the departures and exceptions. If diversity is foregrounded, then generalizations might be sought on the level of mental representations (conceptual structures) or/and social norms rather than a theory of systematic linguistic meaning. The importance of such desiderata will be attended to throughout this journey. Another important assumption concerns the relation between meaning and structure, where the generative tradition follows Noam Chomsky in treating semantics as a component of generative grammar[5] and the tradition of truth-conditional, model-theoretic, possible-world semantics follows the outlook popularized in linguistics by Richard Montague in conceptualizing semantics as a mirror of syntax.[6] I will have much more to say about the latter than the first, beginning with Stage 3. And third, every journey through meaning reflects a personal journey through meaning. This one is mine, but its aim is to inspire the reader's own experience with meaning that will be different from this one. There will be no exercises and no memorizing of rules – just a lot of thinking about meaning.

One may ask here: what about the *objective truth* about meaning? What about meaning as an objective reflection of reality? Or meaning that is stored and processed by the human mind? Let us begin with the latter: what about the cognitive reality of the theories, views about meaning that are in the minds of the users of the language? In my view, psychological reality ought to be one of the foremost concerns of a theory of meaning, but there are limitations. First, in spite of overwhelming progress in the neuroscience of meaning in the relatively newly emerged sub-disciplines of neurosemantics and neuropragmatics, we are still quite a long way from being able to correlate neuronal structures and images of brain activity with meanings and with processing meaning.[7] And if we can't map them onto meanings, they cannot act as reliable evidence for or against many core tenets of theories of meaning ('for' and 'against' because both corroboration and falsification of theories play a part).[8]

Next, we move to 'objective meaning' as reflection of reality. That there *is* a relation is a truism and as such does not require defending, in that language either *describes* the world or *acts on* the world: meanings are always grounded in reality, be it social or that of an individual. But to understand the form this relation takes, and justify calling it 'objective', is not an easy quest. I will say more about the reasons for this in Section 1.4, and about the solutions in the rest of the book.

Semantics and pragmatics strive to understand such mappings, so the excitement of critically assessing existing theories, and the even greater fun of proposing new, more explanatorily adequate theories (especially in view of growing empirical evidence) can

---

[5] One such introduction to semantic theory is aptly entitled *Semantics in Generative Grammar* (Heim and Kratzer 1998). See also the debate between Ludlow (2003) and Chomsky (2003) on the properties of such a semantics, and notably whether it can link meanings and the world (i.e. whether it can be *referential* – a label to be discussed shortly).
[6] See de Swart 1998, p. 26; Dowty, Wall, and Peters 1981, p. 41.
[7] See Pulvermüller 2010 and further discussion in Stage 2.
[8] The best source for the methodology of scientific inquiry and the importance of falsification is Popper 1959 [1934].

continue. The concerns of philosophical semantics and pragmatics are the richer for it – just as they are enriched (rather than made obsolete, as some might naively think) by various experimental approaches to meaning. This book is about such philosophical approaches to meaning and the semantic and pragmatic theories they endorse. It is also a guide to how to go about finding one's own stance on meaning: what to question and how, and what principles to follow in making one's own theoretical choices. As I said, every journey is different but this is as it should be: inspiration for new journeys follows whenever something makes you jump and think: 'This can't be right!'

## 1.3 Proposition: A Flexible Unit for Studying Meaning?

As I have just pointed out, in the light of the semantics/pragmatics boundary disputes that permeate pretty much every topic to do with meaning in language, the best bet seems to be to think about semantics as the study of relations between (i) linguistic units such as words and sentences on the one hand, and on the other (ii) some *correlates* that give them meaning. Although, strictly speaking, asking about the correlates belongs to a higher level of inquiry that we have just mentioned, that is metasemantics or the investigation about the *foundations* of meaning, it is important to think about these questions in tandem. These correlates could be concepts or objects *for words* and situations in the world, or complex mental representations *for sentences*. In other words, in semantics, we are interested in (a) how sentences of a natural language such as English reflect reality – be it objects, people, states, events, processes, as well as in (b) how sentences relate to our mental representations of reality. As we will see, some approaches are only concerned with (a) or (b) and some with both.

The units of the analysis of meaning in semantics are *propositions*. In pragmatics, to reiterate, we talk about *utterances* and, more and more often, *discourses*. The terms *proposition*, *sentence*, and *utterance* require closer attention. Utterances are concrete products of speech and writing that occur in discourse. They come with information as to who the speaker is, as well as information about the time, place, and other circumstances of the performed act of speaking. Sentences are abstract grammatical units that can be extracted from utterances. The meaning of a sentence is a proposition (at least on the standard understanding of 'proposition', but read on). Propositions are probably the most recalcitrant constructs to define. They can be thought of as descriptions of situations, or what philosophers refer to as states of affairs, or, on a more fine-grained conception, as the contents of beliefs and other mental states. They do not bear a one-to-one relation to sentence types. For example, (1.4) said by me and (1.5) said to me by someone else express the same proposition that Kasia Jaszczolt is happy.

(1.4)   I am happy writing about meaning.

(1.5)   You are happy writing about meaning.

(1.6) and the Italian translation in (1.7) also express the same proposition, insofar as they are accurate translations of each other.

(1.6)   I am happy.

(1.7)   Sono felice.

Similarly, (1.8) and (1.9) express the same proposition.

(1.8)   The dog has eaten the roast.

(1.9)   The roast has been eaten by the dog.

This is so in spite of the fact that a sentence in the active voice and its passive equivalent are not identical in meaning.

Now, when a proposition is thought of as a description of states of affairs, it does not exhaust the meaning of the sentence. It is even less successful in capturing the meaning of utterances of that sentence in their respective contexts. It constitutes the core, but there is more to meaning than the proposition. This concept is now known as a Russellian proposition. The more 'fine-grained' option is that of a Fregean proposition. Fregean proposition is sensitive to the *way* the speaker (or holder of the belief) can think about the entities referred to in the sentence. But Frege's proposition is not a thought in a speaker's mind either: it is an abstract concept, which, apparently confusingly, he called *Thought* (*Gedanke*) – apparently because this is in accord with his concept of Thought.[9] Such a proposition pertains to the way of thinking about the situation but it can be shared by different speakers and as such inhabits a Platonic 'third realm': neither a physical nor a mental world. While for Frege the way of thinking about an object is an important component, Russellian propositions, so to speak, 'have the objects in them'. The importance of the 'way of thinking' or the 'sense' will be made clear very shortly when we discuss belief reports and example (1.21). The third major stance on propositions is that they can be thought of as those possible worlds in which the sentence is true. This (Carnapian) proposition[10] will become relevant when we discuss the tools of possible-word truth-conditional semantics in Stage 3.

The main recent criticism of such theoretical constructs is that they are abstract: they do not reflect the meaning held by the actual individual speaker. So, Scott Soames, for example, proposes in his recent work a new concept of a *cognitive proposition*: propositions are cognitive event types.[11] The tokens of these types are *instances of speakers'/thinkers' representing things*. By representing he means here an act of ascribing properties to objects (act of predication that we will focus on in Stage 3). Such propositions come closer to accounting for semantic and pragmatic content that is conveyed in discourse in that they are generalizations over what speakers themselves do. But his overall approach to meaning in language is still Russellian in that, according to Soames, we predicate something of objects rather than of their 'mental equivalents'. As a result, what is true or false is not sensitive to such ways of thinking.

---

[9] See Frege 1956 [1918–19].
[10] See Szabó and Thomason 2019, Section 5.3 on controversies about propositions and for more background on the Fregean, Russellian, and Carnapian propositions.
[11] See Soames 2014 and 2019. See also a discussion in King, Soames, and Speaks 2014 and in Jaszczolt 2021a.

So, his cognitive propositions are the 'extra' layer, so to speak. They are 'cognitive', and 'naturalized', in the sense of not being abstract, but what is true or false applies only to their 'objective' equivalents. But even as cognitive propositions they are very sentence-bound: they are 'naturalized', in the sense of being about people and their meanings, but they cannot capture human patterns of reasoning when what is said is expressed indirectly or non-literally, for example.

So, the question to ask next is whether we want semantics to capture the ways speakers conceptualize states of affairs. We want to ask what kind of meaning semantic theory should be about in that different answers to this question will trigger different requirements of what a proposition ought to be. Linguists are happy to treat proposition as a functional, technical construct and choose the concept of it that does the best job for explaining meaning. If semantics is to include more nuanced meanings that the speaker, or the addressee, or both have in the mind(s), then proposition as the unit of meaning will follow suit and reflect it too.

And we have a lot to choose among – from proposition as (i) the meaning of a sentence, through (ii) the bearer of a truth value ('true' or 'false', on which more in Stage 3), to proposition as (iii) an object of beliefs and other mental attitudes. They pull us in different directions: should a proposition be the meaning of the sentence or a mental state the sentence is about? If the latter, do we construe it in terms of abstract, intersubjective *types* of mental states or in terms of *tokens*: the actual states? Stephen Schiffer[12] opts for propositions as objects of beliefs. He calls them *pleonastic propositions*, in that they are constructed, so to speak, 'out of nothing', simply in virtue of the general characteristics of our cognition and our use of language. They capture the nuances of meaning that a cognitively plausible semantic theory ought to capture but the pay-off is that they do not capture the *structure* of the natural-language *that*-clauses. This is important because *A believes that* ... construction linguistically represents the content of beliefs. His propositions are 'unstructured', as philosophers say. This reflects Schiffer's questioning of the compositionality of natural languages, that is the assumed property of languages that their meaning is given by the meanings of the lexical items and the structure of the sentence (more about this principle shortly). But as will be seen in Section 5.5 where I discuss the meaning of belief and other propositional attitude reports and Schiffer's contribution to the debate, his stance need not lead to such a drastic denial. For now, suffice it to say that our functional propositions introduced immediately below do better in this respect: they are also cognitive and naturalized, and they are sufficiently finely grained to capture the required nuances of thought. They are also paired with a semantic theory that allows for such nuances to be included. Details will have to wait until Section 7.2.3.

All in all, propositions are flexible and controversial beasts. No wonder that McGrath and Frank (2018: 1) call 'proposition' a 'quasi-technical word'. And yet, propositions have proven to be indispensable in most theories of meaning that strive for some formalization and predictive power. So, equipped with Fregean, Russellian, and various naturalized propositions, let us ask now how much content, and what kinds

---

[12] See Schiffer 2003.

## 1.3 Proposition: A Flexible Unit?

of content, a proposition ought to contain to serve the purpose on this journey through meaning – that is, to serve a cognitively real theory of natural-language meaning. If semantics is to rely only on the words and structures of the sentences, we may have to do without a proposition. (1.10) does not correlate with specific situations, or even with situation types: who is 'ready', for what, and what time does 'is' refer to?

(1.10)   He is ready.

If we want to adopt propositions as units of meaning and if they are to describe states of affairs, don't they have to be embellished, filled in sometimes, when the sentence itself does not pick out a situation uniquely or when it picks out *no* situation without such an embellishment? Yes, they do, unless we opt for some very general propositions that would pick out a range of different situations or even different situation types and as such be of little use in explaining meaning. At the very least, the route from a sentence containing essentially context-dependent expressions (*indexicals*), such as *I*, *here*, and *now* in (1.11), to propositions has to involve filling in the referents (here, the speaker, the place, and the time of the utterance).

(1.11)   I am here now.

This resolution of indexicals is a pragmatic, situation-driven process, but it is pretty much uniformly accepted as part of semantics too: we need to resolve them to obtain a proposition. The semantic roles of *I*, *here*, and *now* are almost always fixed: they stand for, respectively, the speaker/writer, the place, and the time of the current act of speaking/writing (*pace* a handful of interesting cases that I discuss in Section 6.2.4). Indexicals that require a greater recourse to context, such as *he* or *then*, are the first tier on which opinions begin to diverge: is their resolution part of semantics as well, or does it belong to the pragmatic overlay? In other words, do the processes of assigning referents to such highly context-sensitive words contribute to the semantics of the sentences in which they occur, and as such to the proposition that is their meaning? Well, yes, if we pin down a particular utterance of this sentence. And when we do, we enter the territory of pragmatics. On the other hand, to reiterate, notice that when we don't fill the indexicals in with referents, we either have to relinquish propositions as objects of study or make propositions so general that *he* and *then* pick out, say, 'a conversationally salient male' or 'a contextually salient time', nothing more. So, it appears that we are still on the territory of semantics after all. To move to the next tier, if we want our semantics to be strongly guided by the criterion of cognitive reality, we can allow even more contextual resolution of referents: filling in slots provided by indexicals of any kind. For this purpose we can arguably include *ready* in (1.10) in this category, as it is in need of filling in 'ready for what?'[13] But we can also include expanding propositions where there are no such slots to be filled, as in (1.12), analysed as (1.13). Indexicals in (1.11) provided obvious 'slots' in the syntactic structure that require filling in. On the other hand, in (1.12), the quantifying expression 'everybody'

---

[13] The membership of the category of indexicals is a moot topic. I discuss it in Section 6.2.4. See also Kaplan 1989a; Cappelen and Lepore 2005; Borg 2004, 2012.

does not come with a syntactic slot but comes with a domain of quantification that requires a restriction in a given context (everybody *in what category/group of people?*), for example as in (1.13).

(1.12)  Everybody signed up for the *Semantics, Pragmatics and Philosophy* seminar.

(1.13)  Every linguistics student at Cambridge signed up for the *Semantics, Pragmatics and Philosophy* seminar.

Next, there are sentences that, in spite of being syntactically complete, do not provide enough information to identify a corresponding situation without help from context. Here, again, there is no syntactic slot to be filled, but, unlike in (1.12), there is no 'wrong proposition' ('Every person *in the world* signed up for the *Semantics, Pragmatics and Philosophy* seminar.') either: the hearer has to complete the speaker's thought in order to find it, as for example in (1.15) corresponding to the uttered (1.14). Or like (1.10) above.

(1.14)  Pyjamas are not interesting enough.

(1.15)  Pyjamas are not interesting enough to be given as a birthday present.

So, if the hearer has to 'find it', what does the semanticist do? They have to find it too, or else resort to the kind of semantics that has something to say only about the meaning of the tools we are using for expressing meaning in language (that is, words and structures of the language system) but rather little about the meaning itself – at least little of cognitive validity. If we allow the filling in of indexicals, then wouldn't there be tension in not allowing the resolution of meaning in (1.14) as well?

But we can go a bit further. As I said earlier, we can 'amend' Frege's fine-grained propositions and make them less abstract. And make them stand for the meaning that the holder of the belief actually has in mind – and, importantly for us, the meaning that the speaker and the addressee home in on as the primary message of the utterance. (I discuss joint construction of meaning by the interlocutors in Section 7.1.4.) But first, we can adopt the view that there is a need in theory of meaning for different kinds of propositions, corresponding to different aspects of meaning. Then, if we need propositions to account for conceptual structures, we can even go as far as adopting the stance that it is the proposition that corresponds to the *main message* (covertly or overtly expressed, no matter!) that is intended and conveyed by the speaker that constitutes the object of study of semantics. I call it 'intended' and 'conveyed' in agreement with the desideratum discussed earlier that the theory of meaning looks out for regularities and descriptive norms. Miscommunication then falls outside the scope of the theory of meaning but is firmly placed in the study of language processing in psycholinguistics and sociolinguistics. The kind of proposition that we will have to make use of then will have to have the status of what I call a *functional proposition*:[14] its content is delimited by the informative intentions of the speaker, not by the structure of what the speaker actually says. Depending on one's interests, say, in what the tools can do or what the

---

[14] See Jaszczolt 2021a.

meaning on an occasion of using the language is, one can adopt different concepts of a proposition. By choosing functional proposition, and with it a radically pragmatics-rich semantics, we can proceed directly from the utterance to the proposition, as in (1.16). (1.17) is likely to be the strongly conveyed message, or the main meaning, of 'I went vegan in 1987' in the given context, captured by the functional proposition.

(1.16)  A:  Why do you think it's OK to eat animals?
        B:  I went vegan in 1987. You're preaching to the converted here.[15]

(1.17)  B doesn't think it's OK to eat animals.

All in all, we have a spectrum of options here. At one end, there is very 'minimal' semantics that correlates sentences with a range of situation types, or sometimes doesn't even do that, and enjoys little cognitive reality as far as the actual meaning associated with the use of the sentence is concerned. At the other, there is correlating utterances with the main message on the occasion of use, even if the message is conveyed indirectly. The latter is a logically viable (and existing) option for semantics (some use the term 'semantics of utterances').[16] I include this option here, putting it on the table to propound that propositions and cognitive reality of meaning can perhaps be reconciled by adopting a functional proposition. (Remember that you can disagree with any suggestions at any stage and still continue with the textbook!) The overall message is that, concerning the scope of semantic theory, there are options galore. Proposition is a flexible conceptual tool that can stand for any kind of meaning, from the 'minimal' to the 'maximal'. I frequently refer to this abundance of choice throughout this book, whenever it helps see a bigger picture of the discussed problem or expression type. The theories that the options listed here represent, from the 'minimal' to the 'maximal' meaning, are introduced and discussed in Sections 7.2–7.3.

## 1.4 Meaning and Its Correlates

We have identified the world and the mind as the main correlates of meaning in language (or, more properly: correlates *for* linguistic expressions, to explain their meaning) and said that some theories opt for one of them, others assume that they are both necessary. On the 'mind side', we have theories that identify semantic representations with some form of mental (conceptual) structures. That is, semantics operates *not* on the level of sentences in natural language but on the level of thoughts, structures in which concepts participate. These are *mentalistic* or *representational* theories. Various strands of cognitive linguistics belong to this orientation.[17] Others stay clear of mental objects and correlate linguistic expressions with the world – or

---

[15] https://answers.yahoo.com/question/index?qid=20200913065657AAehFpV [accessed 15 September 2020].
[16] For a particular theory, see Default Semantics in Section 7.2.3 below and Jaszczolt 2005, 2010, 2021b.
[17] For comprehensive surveys on different theories and topics in cognitive linguistics, see articles in Geeraerts and Cuyckens 2007.

with formal models of possible worlds. This is the referential approach that gave rise to the truth-conditional, model-theoretic, possible-world semantic tradition. I introduce this orientation in Stage 3 but suffice it to say that on the truth-conditional approach, the meaning of an expression equals its contribution to the truth conditions of the sentence, where truth conditions are the conditions the world has to fulfil for the sentence to be true. As we will see, truth-conditional representations can also be considered to be mental representations and as such can combine what is best in both traditions.

Needless to say, the first orientation has been more successful in attaining cognitive reality, whereas the latter group of theories have been more successful in formalizing meaning and as such in attaining predictive power. We will have to say more about this latter orientation for two good reasons: first, because it employs analytical tools that allow for a formal approach to meaning and assume a fair degree of its objectivity, and, second, because it constitutes a 'skeleton' into which aspects of the cognitive outlook can be fitted, producing, as I have indicated, the best of the two worlds, so to speak – if done with care and attention to maintaining their commensurability. Throughout this book, we will try to avail ourselves of the most efficient tools to study meaning and ask how they can be reconciled to achieve the goals we want to achieve: descriptive normativity and cognitive reality, where the latter also subsumes social reality of discourses. Many of the tools come from formal, truth-conditional methods of analysis used for objectivist semantics with world as correlate. But since we are adopting both correlates of meaning, the tools will have to be adapted. I introduce the tools in the following stages of the journey and point out some ways in which they have been, or can be, adapted. After all, 'objective meaning in the void' is only of interest at most to a handful of theoreticians who inquire into the power and workings of the language system, and who assume that the workings of this system can be studied in isolation from how this system is put to use. On the other hand, meaning in the mind, and meaning as it emerges from the use of language in society, by members of a linguistic community, are of theoretical as well as practical interest to us all. In short, adopting the world and the mind as the necessary correlates (or *explanantia*) will allow us to pursue meaning with paying due attention to context, speaker's intentions, conventions, and addressee's inferences. It will allow us to maintain the necessary rigour in explaining how meaning is composed – that is, how it is put together from smaller components and ends up as a semantic qua conceptual representation – the meaning of an utterance that reflects the speaker's intended and conveyed thought. If the semantics/pragmatics boundary disappears in the process, so much the better: pursuing meaning may not need strict shackles after all.

A terminological note is in order at this point. Throughout the book, I refer to the thing (object, term, concept) that is to be explained as an *explanandum* (plural: *explananda*) and the tool that explains it as an *explanans* (plural: *explanantia*). These Latin terms may seem a little obsolete but they capture succinctly the essence of 'the thing (concept) to be explained' and 'the thing that does the explaining'.

To sum up, we have argued here that there is a good reason for combining 'objectivism' with 'mentalism' in that, whatever we do, the pursuit of meaning will remain the pursuit of human meaning, the sense that human organisms, with specific mental architecture and mental operations, make of the world. This is an important caveat – much more important than it was in the times of Enlightenment philosophy because, arguably, it is no longer a matter of philosophical persuasion but a matter of embracing science: human consciousness is increasingly more frequently explained as an emergent property, something that does not belong to the stuff from which the universe is built. Just as our human time flows because our mental processes and the finiteness of our earthly lives make us conceptualize it as such (while in physics it is a static dimension of spacetime) so the human *ego* itself emerges on what Jenann Ismael describes in her mind-boggling *How Physics Makes Us Free*[18] as a macro-level of human reality. This is contrasted with the micro-level of physical processes that do not contain the *ego*, the self, consciousness, human time, or human way of rationalizing reality through meanings. So, the traditional divisions between 'objectivist' formal truth-conditional semantics and the 'subjectivist' cognitive semantics are beginning to dissolve: there is no 'objective' with human consciousness in it. At most, 'objective' can now refer to the universal, cross-cultural mental, meaning-giving processes, while 'subjective' refers to their language- and culture-specific 'precisification'. And even then, one would have to subscribe to the view that there are semantic and pragmatic universals. This journey through meaning will help with answering the question as to whether such universals are justified: it will give a positive answer, as long as the universals are understood as universal tendencies in reasoning and conceptualizing reality. Crucially, in Stage 9, it will also end with the question as to whether it makes sense to talk about a 'post-meaning world'.

Now, the choice of the correlate is pivotal in addressing the question of what meaning is, and each of the three options listed above (the mind, the world, or both together) has given rise to multiple solutions. Let us now unpack the labels further. The *mentalistic theory* claims that meaning is a concept in the speaker's mind. The *referential theory* says that the meaning of an expression is what the expression refers to or denotes. 'Lidia' means the individual called 'Lidia'; 'cat' means the property of cathood or the (imaginary) class (*denotation*) of all the cats in the world. There are good arguments in support of the view that neither of them will suffice alone. To begin with, Gottlob Frege, in his seminal paper, 'On sense and reference',[19] addressed the question of expressions that refer to the same entity and yet, when substituted for one another, may differ in meaning in some contexts. According to a by now well clichéd example, the ancients thought that what they called the Morning Star and the Evening

---

[18] See Ismael 2016. On her view, the macro-level on which humans operate, with its laws of causation, has a status of reality – is as real as the micro-level of physical laws:

When a system develops an internal point of view and starts making judgments and decisions, the unity that emerges is a real unity, not the as-if unity attributed to the anthill by the curious spectator. (Ismael 2016: 45)

So it is a position that is not as strong as Dennett's celebrated view that consciousness is an illusion (see e.g. Dennett 1993).

[19] Frege 1997a [1892]. For an introduction to compositionality see e.g. Szabó and Thomason 2019, Chapter 2. On the importance of Frege for philosophy of language see also Chapter 1 there.

Star were two different celestial bodies, while, unbeknownst to them, they were different occurrences of one and the same planet, Venus. Hence, the ancients would consent to (1.18) as a *tautology* (a sentence always true, in virtue of its form) – not that they are likely to have heard it since it is not informative) – but deny (1.19). Clearly, these two sentences in turn differ in meaning from (1.20).

(1.18)   The Morning Star is the Morning Star.

(1.19)   The Morning Star is the Evening Star.

(1.20)   Venus is Venus.

In other words, *The Morning Star* and *The Evening Star* are *coreferential*, i.e. refer to the same object, and yet they differ in meaning, as the failure of substitutivity of one for the other in sentences such as the above demonstrates. The substitution of the asterisked expression in (1.21) results in a false statement in this situation.

(1.21)   The ancients believed that the Morning Star/*the Evening Star is the Morning Star.

The substitutivity is not truth-preserving (or, not *salva veritate*). Then, there must be more to meaning than the reference: the referent remains the same and yet a substitution is not always meaning-preserving. Now, Frege built his argument on the assumption that is now known as the *principle of compositionality*, saying that meaning is structured and compositional; that is, that the meaning of the sentence amounts to the meanings of the words and the structure in which they are immersed. So, in order to 'save' compositionality, he had to introduce another component of meaning, called *sense*, that can take the place of the referent in meaning composition. Sense is the way the holder of the belief thinks about the object or situation, or a *mode of presentation* of the referent. But at the same time, Frege's sense is objective: it can be shared between the speakers, just as informed stargazers can share thoughts about Venus as a planet that is visible in the morning and, during other parts of the year, in the evening. Meaning as reference, when combined with sense and some other devices introduced in the following stages of this journey (such as reference in counterfactual, imaginary worlds), is a relatively successful view. Not only does it combine the two useful correlates, the mind and the world, in explaining word meaning, but it allows us to tackle the problem of semantic composition and as such, sentence meaning.

Belief reports such as (1.21) clearly show that there is more to meaning than reference alone. They are examples of *propositional attitude reports*, sentences reporting on an attitude, such as belief, thought, fear, doubt, etc., towards a proposition. They are also examples of so-called *intensional contexts*, i.e. contexts in which *intensions* matter for the meaning (NB: not to be confused with 'intentional' and 'intentions'). I say more about intensions during the next two stages of this journey but suffice it to say that intensions stand for concepts, or even mental representations, and as such side with senses and modes of presentation. They are contrasted in formal semantics with *extensions* that stand for referents – objects or sets of objects that delimit the meaning of an expression in the world (or, as we shall see, in 'a world' – one of endless possible worlds that we have to abstract over in order to arrive at intensions as the meaning of expressions). Intensional contexts are notoriously difficult to account for in formal theories of meaning in that they require some concept that pertains to a mental representation, such as sense, or mode of presentation, and these are still largely obscure to theorists. Propositional attitude reports are not only a sub-class of such intensional contexts but also, so to speak, their advocate: providing a semantics of such expressions has often been regarded as a criterion of adequacy of semantic theories.

We have just looked at a scenario of a mismatch between concepts and referents where one referent, the planet Venus, corresponds to two different concepts. Let us now take the opposite case: two objects associated with one concept. Here Hilary Putnam's paper 'The meaning of "meaning"'[20] provides another overused but memorable example, and at the same time a compelling argument in favour of the world as a necessary correlate of meaning. Putnam devised a thought experiment in which there is a planet called Twin-Earth, which is just like Earth except for the fact that the liquid that is in its rivers, its rain, the liquid that the Twin-Earthlings drink and bathe in, has a chemical composition different from $H_2O$ – say, XYZ. They call it 'water', just as we call $H_2O$ 'water'. Their thoughts about what they call 'water' are indistinguishable from our thoughts about what we call 'water'. The thought experiment was put forward as a challenge to the claim that meaning is a purely mental entity: here mental processes alone cannot differentiate between two different substances. It follows that the substance, $H_2O$ or XYZ, has to be, so to speak, part of the content of thought. Put simply, *meanings are not in the head; they are in the world*.

Needless to say, this point of view, called *externalism*, has triggered arguments on both sides of the debate.[21] But, as we have just seen, meaning as mental representation and meaning as reference are compatible. And it appears that they need each other. Ogden and Richards, in their early-twentieth-century book *The Meaning of Meaning*,[22] aptly summarized the relation between language, the world, and thought as a triangle (see Figure 1.1), where the relation between the word (a linguistic unit) and the object (in the world) is indirect, mediated by the concept (as a unit of thought).

Although Ogden and Richards emphasize that the word (as an arbitrary symbol) and the object it refers to (referent) are related only indirectly,[23] there are various ways of approaching such a diagram. On the standard reading, its implication for the referential theories of meaning is that in using words we never perform any direct reference to things in the world – not even when we use pronouns or proper names. The concept is always involved. On another reading, words do refer to reality, but in problematic cases, such as *The Morning Star–The Evening Star*, we can resort to mental representations or concepts as 'mediators'. And the latter, as we shall see, is the most promising direction for semantics: to merge referential and mentalistic (representational) approaches to meaning, including truth-conditional and cognitive, in a 'positively eclectic' view that applies the most suitable resources required. The advantages of such a merger will become apparent when I introduce truth-conditional semantics in Stages 3–5 and discuss solutions to the

---

[20] See Putnam 1975. For an introduction to the problem, see Szabó and Thomason 2019, Chapter 12.
[21] See e.g. Stalnaker 1999a, 2008, and Ludlow 2014 for its defence and Segal 2000 for criticism.
[22] Ogden and Richards 1960 [1923].   [23] See Ogden and Richards 1960, p. 11.

```
            thought (concept)
                  /\
                 /  \
                /    \
               /      \
              /        \
             /_____\
          word           object
```

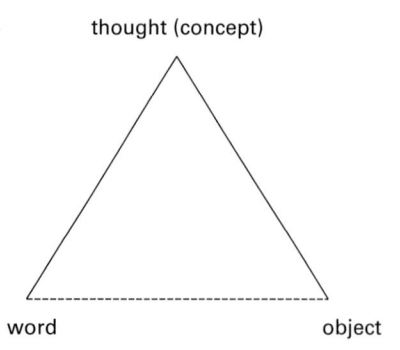

**Figure 1.1** Relation between language, the world, and thought (adapted from Ogden and Richards 1960 [1923]: 11)

semantics of propositional attitude reports in Section 5.5. Put simply, when the context is extensional, we need not overburden the semantic representation with needless detail of what the speaker has in the mind; but when it is intensional and nuances such as ways of thinking about the referent make a mark on semantic properties as they do in (1.20), we wheel them into the representation.

In addition to the referential and the mentalistic approach, *use theory* deserves attention. It says that the meaning of an expression is its use in language activities or language games. This view was put forward by so-called *ordinary language philosophers* in the 1950s and 1960s and is discussed in Section 8.3.[24] As will become apparent, all these theories are best seen as interconnected, where there is no real choice involved. Moreover, as we shall see in the analyses of some troublesome English constructions, various devices may be needed in order to account for their meaning.

To sum up, for the most part, we will resort to the truth-conditional method of analysing meaning. But we will use it somewhat eclectically, to remain true to our desideratum to combine (i) employing the most successful formal devices that semantic theories have to offer with (ii) striving for cognitive reality, whereby semantic representations reflect the thoughts of language users. The journey through different approaches will aim at this task in that, arguably, this is the best way to come as close as possible to answering the question 'What is meaning?'

There are numerous other approaches to meaning which have either fallen out of favour among semanticists or attained a lesser degree of explanatory adequacy, or are limited in their application. We shall not be concerned with them or will merely refer to them in passing.[25] For example, the noble tradition of structuralism, in which meaning was derived from the relations between linguistic signs in a system of the language, will concern us only when some foundational questions need to be addressed, such as whether signs (and concepts as their facets) have meaning in isolation or only as part of the system (known as the *meaning atomism–holism* debate addressed in Stage 2). Particular approaches within cognitive semantics, with their advocated meaning

---

[24] See Wittgenstein 1958 [1953]; Austin 1975 [1962]; for an introduction Section 8.3 below.
[25] See e.g. Lyons 1995, p. 40.

## 1.4 Meaning and Its Correlates

subjectivism, will come into the picture when the literal/non-literal distinction is called into question in Sections 8.1–8.2 and when we attempt to calibrate their tools with those used in truth-conditional semantics. In this spirit, we start with words and their two correlates, the mind and the world, in that more has to be said about what it is in the world and what it is in the mind that make the answer to 'What is meaning?' sufficiently informative; we would not want to explain an unknown by an unknown. We will focus in Stage 2 on the top corner of Figure 1.1, in that different takes on concepts will come with different answers as to how, and whether, the world is a viable correlate in the first place.

**Suggested General Reference for This Journey**
I recommend the following two encyclopedic resources for specialist terminology and theoretical concepts. Concerning philosophical background to natural-language meaning, try *Stanford Encyclopedia of Philosophy* edited by Edward Zalta (https://plato.stanford.edu/, free access), and for linguistic aspects, *Elsevier Encyclopedia of Language and Linguistics* edited by Keith Brown (book and online).

**Suggested Further Reading for Stage 1**
Among accessible readings that introduce the field with some flair, enthusiasm, and informed selectivity are Elbourne's (2011) *Meaning: A Slim Guide to Semantics*, Chapters 1–3; Portner's (2005) *What Is Meaning?*, Chapters 1–2; Birner's (2018) *Language and Meaning*, Chapters 1–3; Allan's (2001) *Natural Language Semantics*, Chapters 1–3; and Saeed's (2016) *Semantics*, Chapter 1. I also recommend reading primary sources – they can be challenging but they provide first-hand knowledge of the author's view, without any conscious or unconscious bias introduced by those who write about them (remember: no textbook is objective!). On meaning in the mind vs. meaning in the world some of the classics are Frege's (1997a) [1892] 'On sense and reference' and Putnam's (1975) 'The meaning of "meaning"'. For introductions to these topics, see also Chapters 1 and 12 of Szabó and Thomason's (2019) *Philosophy of Language*. On speaker meaning, intentions, and inferences, one of the classics is Grice's (1989a) [1957] 'Meaning'. Semantics/pragmatics boundary disputes are succinctly covered in Jaszczolt 2019a [2012]. The topic of functional propositions is introduced in Jaszczolt 2021a and the distinctions between semantics and pragmatics on the one hand and metasemantics and metapragmatics on the other in Jaszczolt 2022.

Detailed, including advanced, reading suggestions for particular problems and ideas were given in the footnotes as we moved along.

# Stage 2  Word Meaning and Concepts

## 2.1 Harnessing Word Meaning

In the course of this journey we will be trying to establish connections between word meaning, sentence meaning, and utterance meaning and draw on their extant analyses to produce one coherent view of meaning in language and discourse. First, we will consider word meaning: what does it mean to know the meaning of the word? Which of the two correlates, the mind or the world, if either and if not both, should we employ to harness word meaning? We can surmise that to know the meaning of a word is to be in a position to provide the definition. But this intuitively plausible view is untenable for various reasons, the most important of which being infinite regress or, alternatively, circularity. When we provide a definition of a word (or a *lexeme*, the semantic word rather than a word form) we do so in terms of other words (lexemes) which in turn have to be defined . . . and so on, ad infinitum – unless we use the same word as definiens (the defining concept) and definiendum (the word being defined) and reach circularity. It would be bad practice if a lexicographer defined, for example, *courgette* as 'zucchini' and *zucchini* as 'courgette' in a dictionary. I will say more about meaning as definitions in discussing the so-called classical theory of concepts in Section 2.2.

A further problem consists of specifying where these definitions come from and what criteria we can muster to guarantee they are exact and correct: are they speaker-relative or objective? Are they language-specific or universal? If objective or universal, what makes them objective or universal? Moreover, we want to know how much detail enters into linguistic meaning. If you believe that penguins are birds and I believe that penguins are mammals, we still share some basic meaning of the word *penguin* that enables us to communicate: we agree on what it looks like, and perhaps where it lives and what it eats. In other words, there is linguistic knowledge on the one hand and encyclopedic knowledge on the other, but the problem is to specify the boundary between the two (this is known in semantics as the *lexicon–encyclopedia interface*). Further, how do we decide 'whose meaning' is the correct one? Do we refer to experts in relevant disciplines or rather to common folk wisdom? Finally, words are used differently in different contexts. In (2.1), the speaker does not normally mean that they are likely to die but rather that the task is particularly difficult and demanding.

(2.1)   This essay is killing me.

## 2.1 Harnessing Word Meaning

Instead of placing all these various uses of the word *kill* in its definition, it is more plausible and economical to resort to the study of the contribution of context to meaning. The role of context in defining meaning is standardly approached by separating (i) literal aspects of meaning from (ii.a) non-literal but conventional and (ii.b) non-literal and context-dependent aspects of meaning. But, separating context-free from context-dependent, or conventional from non-conventional aspects of meaning amounts to a mere redefining of the problem rather than solving it: the task is just as difficult as the original one. We have to go further and ask what nature word meanings have. Do they have a fixed, stable core? I mean 'fixed' in the synchronic rather than diachronic sense – we are not interested in semantic change but rather in meaning in a *synchronic state* of a language. If there is a core, then how does this core yield itself to contextual alterations when we use the expression non-literally or just in a very specific sense?

Here views differ, and we encounter terminological and conceptual complications. What is word meaning in the first place? Are word meanings concepts? If so, what are concepts? If we assume that concepts are mental representations that users of the language have (a view that is by no means shared by everyone – we will see shortly that concepts can be construed as abstract constructs), then, surely, concepts contain more information than word meanings. Meanings are shared, they belong to the language system and can be employed as tools for communication. If one accepts the hypothesis that we think in natural language rather than in some form of a language of thought (or what American philosopher Jerry Fodor called *Mentalese*[1]), then we also use them in our thought processes. But even if we do think in Mentalese, then its units of meaning must bear some systematic resemblance to the units of natural language. So, returning to the lexicon–encyclopedia interface, we could settle for the view that word meanings constitute the core of concepts – the core that corresponds to the lexical (linguistic) information, where the overlay is encyclopedic (non-linguistic) knowledge.[2] On the other hand, concepts need not be construed as private mental representations that contain an overlay of information from personal experience. They can be more akin to Frege's objective, shared senses. But perhaps this would be overkill as well? Perhaps the meaning of the word is as simple as its referent, as the referential theory has it, and the rest is the social or psychological overlay that deserves a separate treatment? In other words, the meaning of *dog* is the class (extension) of dogs in the world? Or, as in possible-world semantics introduced in Stage 3, in any *possible* world, where, to reiterate, all these possible extensions make up a concept, an intension? Then, word meaning could be that component of a proposition that enters into a compositional analysis. But we have already seen problems with this simplification during Stage 1 in the example of reports on beliefs about the Morning Star and the Evening Star (example (1.21)).

We are not going to have final answers to these questions. The great attraction of lexical semantics is that we have theoretical choices that can be assessed through

---

[1] See e.g. Fodor's (1975) classic *The Language of Thought*, followed by Fodor 2008. For arguments against Fodor's Mentalese and in favour of the view that we use natural language in thinking, see e.g. Carruthers 1996. The question is further discussed in Section 2.3.

[2] For an overview of different stances on the interface between lexical and encyclopaedic knowledge, see Peeters 2000 or, for a very brief introduction, Section 3.3 of Riemer 2010.

logical argumentation. This argumentation is always checked against evidence, for example from neurosemantics. It is known that patterns of brain activation and areas of activation correlate with comprehension of specific clusters of words related by semantic features such as, for example, words that refer to objects or words standing for actions.[3] But as I pointed out in Stage 1, one has to remember that empirical evidence from patterns of neuronal activation does not lead to the answer to the 'What is word meaning?' question. One has to make a decision on what to use as the mapping relation. Once such a relation is justified, one can have a theory of meaning where 'meaning is in the mind' – meaning as a human-specific take on the world:

> The aim of the neuroscience of language is to find the brain correlates of linguistic processes and representations. Correlates of linguistic representations are sought in neuronal structures, that is, nerve cell circuits, and correlates of linguistic processes are sought in patterns of neuronal activation. (Pulvermüller 2010: 255)[4]

Although neurosemantics and neuropragmatics are progressing fast, they are still far from achieving this objective.

On an even higher level, one has to justify what counts as appropriate empirical data. For example, computational linguists adopt statistical, distributional approaches to meaning. Using big corpora, they investigate how words co-occur in texts. Such information is quantitatively analysed and leads to what can be called word meaning.[5] This orientation is instantiated in current *vector semantics* that represents words as points in multidimensional semantic spaces. It exploits the finding dating back to the 1950s and John Firth that one can compute the meaning of a word from the distribution of the words in its immediate context.[6] The representation of the quantitative values in the distribution is called a vector. In other words, a vector is a distributional model in which information is presented in the form of a co-occurrence matrix. Like the idea itself, vectors date back to the 1950s but their recent success was engendered by combining the distributional methods with logic-based approaches to meaning.[7] On this approach, the explanans (introduced in Section 1.4) is not 'in the mind'; it is 'in the world': evidence from existing corpora allows us to extract word meaning.

Choices of empirical data and method of analysis notwithstanding, the concept of a 'concept' has to be scrutinized so that we can either adopt it as a possible meaning of 'word meaning' or reject it as redundant. We have briefly encountered 'concept' as a mental entity in the mentalistic theory introduced in Stage 1 and as an abstraction over extensions, originating in the referential theory, that is open to different ontologies. But there are many ideas to choose from.

---

[3] For evidence and discussion, see e.g. Pulvermüller 2012.
[4] Pulvermüller (2010) also discusses concrete examples of brain activation associated with particular lexical items and clusters of items. Or, for a simpler introduction, see Chapter 4 of Pulvermüller 2002.
[5] See e.g. Jurafsky and Martin 2014, 2016; Coecke, Sadrzadeh, and Clarke 2010; and for discussion Liang and Potts 2015.
[6] See Harris 1954 and Firth 1957.
[7] See Liang and Potts 2015. Vectors are also used, for example, to measure the similarity of texts with reference to a particular word, the similarity of words with respect to sources, or to measure the co-occurrence of a selection of words in a selection of contexts.

## 2.2 The 'Concept' Commotion

First, I discuss several versions of the mentalistic/representational approach to word meaning and assess them for candidacy for our general theory of meaning in language that, as we saw, covers words, sentences, utterances, and discourses. In the process we will bear in mind the caveats discussed during the previous stage of this journey, such as the question of the relative scope of word meaning as lexical content vis-à-vis mental representation that may also include encyclopedic content. According to the mentalistic/representational approach, speakers and hearers use the set of concepts they possess to construct representations of the world. While in the referential approach meaning is defined by relating language to the world, in the representational approach meaning is defined by relating language to concepts and conceptual structures, i.e. constructions made out of these simple concepts. Let us assume that the representations we are interested in have to have cognitive reality: they have to be located in the mind of the speaker. This common version of representationalism is then called mentalism, hence I called it a mentalistic/representational approach. In order to understand the function of mental representations, we can think of the relation between sentences and the world and then substitute the mental correlate for the world. Words can denote objects in the world only *because* they are associated with representations in the speaker's and in the hearer's minds. But merely postulating a theoretical construct called 'mental representation' will not do: we have to say what these representations are and how they work.

The simplest (but not very informative) answer is to say that the meaning of a word is an image in the speaker's or the hearer's mind. But what is an image of, say, *dog*? And do all members of a linguistic community share the same image? If they do not, can they still communicate? What is it that they share and that delineates the meaning of *dog*? Moreover, a speaker may have more than one image corresponding to an expression, or two expressions may correspond to one image. Finally, there are words which do not have obvious images, such as abstract words *serendipity*, *integrity*, and many others. Visual images seem to be bad candidates for mental representations; other sensory experiences fare no better. Concepts are better candidates, if we can unpack the term. Concepts need not be related to perception, they can be sets of characteristics, for example, and they can be derived from culture. The task then becomes to assess different views on what concepts are, so as not to define unknown by unknown. First, on the one hand, a concept is something shared that can be learned or acquired *because* the word is used in this way by other members of the linguistic community, and on the other, qua mental representation, it is private, located in the person's mind. Alternatively, concepts have been contrasted with *ideas* and it is an idea that is private, while a concept is shared by users of a language. But this is just terminology: merely adopting it makes us no wiser as to what a concept or an idea really is and how they are related.

What information do concepts contain? Let us take, for example, the concept TIGER.[8] Does the concept have to contain ANIMAL, FELINE, HAS FOUR LEGS, IS STRIPED? Is this a set of its necessary and sufficient characteristics? While these features are useful, they

---

[8] Expressions in SMALL CAPITALS stand for concepts.

would exclude from the class membership all tigers that lost a leg or, due to, say, genetic manipulation, have no stripes. In the past, it was generally accepted that the meaning of such natural (and cultural) kinds is given by their defining properties. This is the essence of the classical theory that we have already referred to: it holds that concepts are definitions. On this view, concepts are structured (rather than primitive, indivisible) and come with necessary and sufficient conditions, such as ANIMAL, FELINE, HAS FOUR LEGS, IS STRIPED above, for something to fall under this definition. Selecting such essential properties, however, has occupied philosophers from antiquity onwards and has proven to be a non-starter, unless one adopts a more flexible approach, takes the 'necessary' and 'sufficient' as, say, 'prototypical' and 'default', or combines the view with some other view that better accounts for the processing of word meanings.[9]

It goes without saying that an entity can fall under a concept even if the definition does not properly apply to it. Think again of a tiger without stripes or a tiger that lost a leg in a fight. Or about the concept of the SUN when geocentrism was the accepted doctrine: the definition, a celestial body that revolves around the Earth, would not lead to the correct referent. Did the concept SUN change when geocentrism was replaced by heliocentrism, or is the concept not the same thing as the definition? When 'concept' means 'necessary and sufficient characteristics', then the answer logically follows.

There is more to be found in the pool of proposals. Since sometimes there is nothing that is shared by *all* the members of the category, we can talk about *family resemblance*. Ludwig Wittgenstein gives here an example of the concept GAME: neither competition, nor skill, nor luck, nor even physical activity are necessary to all games.[10] (Lexical ambiguity between birds and sports can be ignored in the current discussion as they are two different lexemes and two different concepts.) But if concepts are so fuzzy and elusive, we can only presume that humans communicate as successfully as they do thanks to the general assumption that the hearer understands the words in the same way as the speaker. The discrepancies are only attended to when a deviant use is obvious in the context, to quote an anecdotal exchange of a parent with a child:

(2.2)  PARENT:  Why are you so pensive?
       CHILD:   I am not pensive, I am just thinking.

But let us for a moment engage in some conditional reasoning: *if* we could identify such definitional components of meaning, that is, if the approach of lexical decomposition in the classical theory (to refer to it by its name) could plausibly be assumed, could this help address other big questions about meaning? It would, and it did. The lexical decomposition approach addresses the big debate between meaning universalism and relativity. Concepts have been variously regarded as generally universal or generally language- and culture-specific. According to universalism, thought and cognition determine the language of our thinking and this common language of mental operations underlies natural languages. This

---

[9] Both have been attempted. The neo-classical theory relaxes the conditions to allow for their different strength and as such allow for border cases and exceptions. Ray Jackendoff's approach, referred to in fn 12 below, belongs to this category. Next, in *theory-theory*, classical theory has been combined with prototype theory. See Laurence and Margolis 1999 for further discussion and references.

[10] See Wittgenstein 1958, pp. 31–32.

is because the architecture of the human brain and brain processes are universal. The idea that language structure and semantics are based on universal principles is the dominant standpoint nowadays, although evidence of incommensurable differences between concepts and conceptual structures of different languages keeps being discovered by anthropological linguists, undermining the tenets of universal concepts and universal grammar. This leads to the revival of linguistic relativity. According to linguistic relativity popularized by Sapir and Whorf in the first half of the twentieth century,[11] language determines, at least to some extent, our thoughts. But once we adopt decomposing the meaning of lexemes into semantic components (lexical decomposition), a conciliatory position becomes available, namely that languages differ superficially in their semantics, but on the level of the *conceptual components of lexemes*, they are all the same. These components have also been dubbed *semantic primitives*, and lexical decomposition is sometimes called *componential analysis*.

Components help describe relations between words. For example, they explain why *dead* and *alive* are incompatible, or why *tulip* includes, or entails, *flower*. In order to work as the 'middle solution' just mentioned, they also have to be cognitively real: they are concepts in the mind. For the sake of economy, elegance, and psychological plausibility, instead of MALE and FEMALE, MARRIED and UNMARRIED, ADULT and NON-ADULT we can use binary features: +/− MALE, +/− ADULT, and so on. However, it is often difficult to decide which of the two terms, for example *male* or *female*, is more basic. Componential analysis has been developed in various directions by linguists and philosophers such as Rudolf Carnap; Jerrold Katz, Jerry Fodor (in his early work), and Paul Postal; Ray Jackendoff; Leonard Talmy; and Anna Wierzbicka, among others, all of whom extended it to the analysis of conceptual structures.[12] But, as I have pointed out, among the main difficulties theorists encountered was specifying how many components, or 'atoms', there are and what their cognitive status is. Empirical support is lacking: comprehension of words does not appear to be founded on the recognition of such components, so it is doubtful that the claim has psychological validity. If words were composed from

---

[11] Linguistic relativity still engenders lively debates in that it is disputable what counts as linguistic universals and, relatedly, whether universals ought to be sought on the level of linguistic or conceptual structure. For an example of a 'first-hand' exposition of the Sapir-Whorf hypothesis, see e.g. Whorf 1956. For a discussion, see Gumperz and Levinson 1996, especially Introduction (Chapter 1) and Part I (Chapters 2–5). Elbourne 2011, Chapter 8 contains a critical introduction. For an empirically grounded defence of a version of relativity, see Levinson 1996, 1997, or parts of Levinson 2003, especially Sections 7.2 on the relation between linguistic and conceptual categories and 7.3 on neo-Whorfianism. For interesting experiments, move on to Pederson et al. 1998 and Levinson et al. 2002. For an excellent defence of foregrounding linguistic diversity and arguments that universals belong to conceptual structure, see Evans and Levinson 2009. On what universals mean for semantics and pragmatics, see von Fintel and Matthewson 2008.

[12] These historically important accounts cannot be covered in our 'shoppers' guide' search for the meaning of meaning. But to introduce the gist, Katz and Fodor (1963) and Katz and Postal (1964) developed a conceptual analysis account within generative grammar; Jackendoff (e.g. 1990) has a semantics of conceptual structures (for a brief introduction, see Culicover and Jackendoff 2005, Section 5.2); Talmy (1985, 2000) developed a conceptual analysis within the cognitive linguistics tradition; Wierzbicka's (1996) Natural Semantic Metalanguage has a set of universal semantic primes and a theory of their composition.

components, they should be stored as 'molecules' and processing a more complex molecule should take longer – a hypothesis for which there is no empirical support.

So, do concepts that correspond to lexical items have such compositional structure? Complex concepts, that is concepts that correspond to complex expressions such as phrases or sentences, arguably have to have compositional structure. This is because, as was discussed in Section 1.1, the devices of natural language are productive (the infinity of possible complex concepts can be traced back to a finite set of primitive concepts and their grammar) and systematic (if we can grasp the thought that John loves Mary, we can grasp the thought that Mary loves John, etc.). But as regards concepts that are supposed to stand for word meanings, the opposing view is that they are instead indivisible primitives. Jerry Fodor, the main advocate of this view, calls it *conceptual atomism*.[13] He claims that simple lexical concepts don't have internal structure. Semantic content arises through experience – a relation between the mind and the world, or 'locking' on the property expressed by the concept. He calls it *nomological locking*. But this comes at a price: as Fodor (1998: 162) says, 'we *make things be of a kind* by being disposed to *take them to be of a kind* '; we conceptualize a doorknob as DOORKNOB because our mental architecture and mental activities are as they are. Extraterrestrials with different meaning-processing systems (or different 'kinds of minds') might do it differently.

In older introductions to concepts one may encounter criticism of Fodor in that the early version of his conceptual atomism came with the idea that concepts were innate. But he weakened his innateness claim by saying that 'locking on properties of objects' proceeds through experience. What *is* innate is not the concepts themselves but rather having the kinds of mind (unlike those of imaginary extraterrestrials) that allows this kind of experience. Views differ among philosophers as to what exactly is innate. We can date this discussion at least to the eighteenth-century German philosopher Immanuel Kant, who developed a theory of mind on which the mind imposes its own way of seeing objects. The concepts that the mind has at its disposal on the one hand, and our perceptions on the other, are necessary for each other and both are necessary for experience, but what we see are not 'things in themselves' but things that conform to our kind of cognition.[14] Kant's ideas permeate many recent accounts of concepts. In contemporary cognitive semantics, linguists such as George Lakoff and Mark Johnson adopt the idea of embodied experience: embodied concepts are neural structures, formed through experience. Children's early spatial concepts such as FRONT, BACK, UP, or DOWN affect the conceptualization of reality, as evidenced, for example, in conceptual metaphors, such as *I'm feeling down*.[15] 'Embodiment' means here

the realization that scientific understanding of mind and language entails detailed modeling of the human brain and how it evolved to control a physical body in a social community. (Feldman 2010: 385)

---

[13] The best defence of conceptual atomism can be found in Fodor 1998.
[14] The main exposition of these ideas is in Kant's (1990) [1781]).
[15] I discuss the approach to conceptualization in cognitive semantics in Section 8.2. Seminal references here are Lakoff and Johnson 1980 and 1999. For an introduction to embodied cognition, see also Wilson and Foglia 2015.

In other words,

> [o]ur sense of what is real begins with and depends crucially upon our bodies, especially our sensorimotor apparatus, which enables us to perceive, move, and manipulate, and the detailed structures of the brains, which have been shaped by both evolution and experience. (Lakoff and Johnson 1999: 17)

However, embodiment is not used in the literature with much consistency. As Tim Rohrer points out, it can mean the direction of conceptual (such as metaphorical) mappings, from body to mind, the direction in which we explain them, or the premise that body and mind ought not to be studied in isolation. It can also refer to the social and cultural context in which the body is immersed, to the evolutionary perspective, to the subjective, 'embodied' perspective, among other things. As he says, '[by] my latest count, the term "embodiment" can be used in at least twelve different important senses with respect to our cognition' (Rohrer 2007: 28).

Now, speakers quite often lack sufficient knowledge to distinguish one concept from another, while still using them both in conversation. Let us take another oft-quoted example: *beech* and *elm*. A speaker may not be able to tell the difference between a beech tree and an elm tree or specify the necessary and sufficient conditions for either, and yet they may use both words, relying on expert botanists' knowledge. This is what Hilary Putnam (whom we have already encountered in discussing the $H_2O - XYZ$ thought experiment in Section 1.4), called the *division of linguistic labour*: experts know the definitions, so ordinary speakers don't have to. Next, as we saw in earlier examples, speakers may have two concepts for one object (THE MORNING STAR and THE EVENING STAR for the planet Venus) or one concept for two objects (as in WATER for $H_2O$ and hypothetical XYZ). But why are we interested in these uncommon scenarios? Do they actually happen? In his apt contribution to the debate, Jerry Fodor concluded that the world allows us to pretty much presume that there is a one-to-one correspondence (bi-uniqueness) between concepts and objects. That is, if there is ELM and BEECH, then there are elms and beeches, this is what the world is like. The cases of *The Morning Star* and *The Evening Star*, on the one hand, and $H_2O$ and XYZ, on the other, don't occur very often. They are not the norm. This is so because the world acts like a 'cop', to use Fodor's metaphor, preventing the cases where thought (computations) and meaning (content, relating the thought to the world) get unstuck.[16]

Some philosophers, among them Bertrand Russell, believed that concepts are acquired individually, one by one. On this view, a person can learn the meaning of *red* without having an idea of the meaning of *yellow* or *green*. According to this view, some words are learned by observing an act of pointing at an object and hearing *that is X*, i.e. by an *ostensive definition*. It can now be seen that Fodor's atomism and his idea of nomological locking also belong to this view. But, as was aptly pointed out by an American philosopher, W. V. O. Quine, in order to know that what was uttered was a name for this object rather than, for example, a name of a part of the object,

---

[16] By 'content' Fodor means here so-called *broad content*, relating the thought processes to the world – contrasted with *narrow* (mental) *content*. On how to reconcile thinking as computation and meaning as information (where semantics is referential, with broad content), see Fodor 1994.

a comment on the nuisance the object causes, or a warning about the danger the object poses, *we already have to know the language*. So, atomism is contrasted with meaning *holism*, according to which, like in the structuralist approach I have already mentioned while discussing Ferdinand de Saussure in Section 1.1, only whole languages and whole belief systems have meaning.[17] Structuralism is a movement that affected all of the social sciences in the early decades of the twentieth century in the form of a search for underlying patterns of behaviour (here: patterns of language). Saussure[18] developed a theory around the claim that the relations into which words enter in the language system give them their sense. Sense is created between words. (Reference on the other hand, holds between a word and entities in the world.) For example, *cat* means CAT because we can oppose it to DOG, COW, or HAMSTER (and to *dog*, *cow*, or *hamster*), follow it by the predicate *miaowed*, and so on. Saussure exemplifies the idea of sense as follows. Words in a language (linguistic signs) have two aspects: a *concept* and a *sound pattern* – the latter being the way in which they are pronounced. The concept is delimited by other concepts that can be found in the particular language. So, the scope of meaning of a sign depends on the way the signs of the language system divide, so to speak, the available meanings among themselves. This concept of sense also allows us to investigate relations between words based on sameness, opposition, and inclusion (or *synonymy*, *antonymy*, and *hyponymy*, such as *to buy* and *to purchase*; *big* and *small*; *tulip* and *flower*, respectively, some of which were mentioned in the discussion of lexical decomposition).[19] It is for analysing such relations that sense is utilized in structuralism – very different (a note of caution) from 'sense' in Frege's distinction between sense and reference discussed in Section 1.4, where sense stood for a shared, objective mode of presentation of the referent. Focusing on these language-specific divisions of the 'totality of meaning', so to speak, structuralism well explains why in a language that has, say, only two colour terms, *black* does not equal in value the English term *black* but instead has a much wider scope of meaning. In such a language, it covers the whole spectrum of dark colours, meaning something akin to *dark* as opposed to *light*.[20]

---

[17] See Fodor and Lepore 1992; L. J. Cohen 1999.    [18] See de Saussure 1983 [1916].
[19] Since this is not an introduction to the history of semantics, I will not elaborate on the properties of sense relations. Introductions are ample. But I want to mention a special kind of inclusion that points to interesting cross-linguistic differences: *meronymy*. Meronymy is a part–whole relation between lexical items, for example *hand–finger*; *house–chimney*. Meronymy forms a hierarchy, as can be seen from the body-to-nail example. It is an *optional* relation: the part is not a necessary constituent of the whole, for example not all houses have chimneys. In some languages, meronymy is distinguished grammatically as *inalienable possessives*. For example, in Hawaiian, *Mary's picture* can have two grammatical forms and meanings: picture *belonging to* Mary and, for inalienable possessives, the picture *of* Mary. Similarly, *dog's bones* acquires two grammatical forms corresponding to the two meanings. Similar to the part–whole relation is the *member–collection* relation, such as in *tree–forest*; *sheep–flock,* and the *portion–mass* relation, such as in *grain of–sand*; *sheet of–paper*.
[20] Needless to say, more finely grained distinctions are still available to speakers of such a language and so is the ability to acquire colour terms distinguished in other languages. On the universal principles on which the language-specific sets of colour terms are organized, see Berlin and Kay's (1969) classic *Basic Colour Terms: Their Universality and Evolution*.

One implication of the structuralist outlook is that words are stored in the mind in clusters – a tenet that has received empirical support. They are related mainly by associations, formed by habits, as in *black–white, hammer–nail, grass–green*. Such words are usually in the same semantic field. Typical mental links utilize the relationships of coordination (*salt–pepper*), collocation (*salt–water*), superordination (*red–colour*), and synonymy (*hungry–starving*). Some concepts are formed gradually, as a response to the environment. Small children often use concepts too narrowly or too widely, that is, they *underdetermine* them or *overextend* them, for example using the word *dog* either (i) only for the pet Fido or (ii) to refer to dogs but also to cats or furry slippers. So, children's concepts can be different from those of adults. But like those of adults, they sum up to the system of the 'totality of meaning' that the child adopts at a particular stage of development.

We can now move on, bearing in mind, first, the inadequacy of defining meaning as a set of characteristic features (at least when the constraints that the classical theory imposes are not weakened) and next, that structuralism advocates meaning holism but has rather little to offer as far as concepts qua components of linguistic signs are concerned: they are just deemed to be abstractions, shareable by members of a linguistic community. We can probably also be slightly wary of conceptual atomism in that it leaves so much to *fiat*: the explanation that the human mind 'grasps something as something' in virtue of being a human mind leaves a lot of room for questions. But there is more to browse through in the pool of existing proposals. Let us go back to the camp that advocates an attenuated and cognitively real version of characteristic features (classical theory) approach.

One of the principal problems with concepts is that they have fuzzy boundaries. In other words, it can be difficult to determine whether some individuals fall under a certain label. For example, for most of us, penguins are less typical representatives of birds than pigeons, whales are less typical members of the class of mammals than dogs, celeriac is a less typical vegetable than a carrot. Some people attempted to build a theory of word meaning on this observation. But as we shall see, although such a theory has an intuitive appeal, it is not without problems. While using a word, speakers usually have a stereotype in mind – that is, types of examples, amounting to a set of features, which fall in the focus of a category. Back in the 1970s, Eleanor Rosch and William Labov concluded from experimental evidence they collected that speakers have no difficulty with naming or classifying typical members of a class, whereas they have increasing difficulty the more atypical the member is. Rosch called this structuring of a concept a *typicality effect* and the best examples *prototypes*:

Think of dogs. You all have some notion of what a 'real dog', 'a doggy dog' is. To me a retriever or a German shepherd is a very doggy dog while a Pekinese is a less doggy dog. Notice that this kind of judgment has nothing to do with how well you like the thing. (Rosch 1975: 198)

Rosch's students performed the task of rating of goodness (typicality) of examples according to which, for instance, chair and sofa are among the best examples of the concept FURNITURE, lamp and piano are in the middle ranks, while picture and fan are among the worst.[21] In a broadly similar vein, Labov experimented with people's ability

---

[21] See Rosch 1975.

to name containers which can be classed somewhere between a bowl and a cup, and a cup and a vase.[22] Additional functional clues were provided, such as filling the container with flowers, potatoes, or coffee, or adding one or two handles. Depending on these clues, a container was classed as a bowl (of potatoes) or a vase (with flowers). So, we can conclude that categorization makes use of the cognitive capacities of the human mind, and these categories, particularly of natural and cultural kinds, are founded on conceptually salient prototypes that can also make use of functional characteristics, such as in the bowl/cup/vase example. The prototypes, in turn, allow for rating examples on a typicality scale. But the boundaries of these categories are fuzzy.

Prototypes also come with other theoretical insights. Rosch investigated relations between concepts, in particular hierarchies of concepts. For example, ANIMAL, FISH, and SALMON constitute a hierarchy: SALMON inherits the attributes of ANIMAL (such as *eats* or *breathes*) and of FISH (such as *can swim* or *has fins*), adding some more specific ones (such as 'is pink'). Rosch calls FISH a *basic level category*, ANIMAL a superordinate one, and SALMON a subordinate category. Basic level categories are the most conspicuous ones, easily learned and easily used for classification on a perceptual basis. They are not the same for everybody: fishing experts are more likely to hold SALMON as a basic level category because what appear to be the most natural features will differ with expertise, preferences, and experience.

But what exactly are prototypes? Are their cores mental images, real, existing exemplars, or abstract sets of characteristic features? Remember that a prototype will vary with cultural and personal experience. George Lakoff called this experience *Idealized Cognitive Models* (ICMs): a frame is built from encyclopedic knowledge about entities and from cultural knowledge that leads to construction of a view about the world.[23] To use another popular example, BACHELOR will capture the standard meaning of the term but will not capture every unmarried adult man; the Pope or Tarzan do not quite fit in. And,

the worse the fit between the background conditions of the ICM and our knowledge, the less appropriate it is for us to apply the concept. The result is a gradience – a simple kind of prototype effect. (Lakoff 1987: 71)

*Radial structures*, such as MOTHER, where there is a central member of the category and variations are conventionalized, not predictable by rules (e.g. FOSTER MOTHER or COLLEGE MOTHER – at Cambridge, a female mentor of a student, usually from the year above), are the most interesting source of prototype effects: there is no single cognitive model that would represent the entire category.[24] Similar views are held by other cognitive linguists, ICMs being more or less equivalent to *frames*, *mental models* (in a theory-internal sense), or *mental spaces*.[25] Prototypes so understood allow us to see them as stereotypical situations – frames into which we try to fit newly encountered situations.

---

[22] See Labov 1973.  [23] See Lakoff 1987, p. 70.  [24] See Lakoff 1999, p. 406.
[25] Fillmore 1985; Johnson-Laird 1983; and Fauconnier 1985, 1997 respectively.

## 2.2 The 'Concept' Commotion

Next, a prototype will also vary as a result of conscious revision of concepts that takes place when some influential members of a group, for example philosophers, journalists, or lawyers, begin to ask the question whether the concepts we have are the concepts we *ought to* have. Concepts such as WOMAN, MISOGYNY or SEXISM, for example, have engendered debates in different waves of feminism and gender studies. The topic is at the forefront of research spanning philosophy, linguistics, and ethics. Debates include political correctness and the question of the dynamism of concepts, including the conceptual engineering introduced in Section 1.2.[26]

Further, the main problem with prototypes appears to be that they lack the property of combining into new prototypes. In other words, they are not compositional. As we have already established, concepts can only function as word meanings if they are compositional: putting together the concepts associated with words using the principles of mental combinations (some form of grammar of such conceptual structures) ought to result in complex concepts, such as those corresponding to sentences or phrases. At this point we can return to Jerry Fodor's view of concepts. Fodor starts with the assumption that concepts are constituents of thoughts and that complex concepts are compositional. They are compositional, and hence productive and systematic (the characteristics discussed earlier in this section). And these are exactly the properties of natural-language meaning that make us search for compositional units. So far so good: such concepts fit the bill as word meanings. So, in accordance with compositionality, if one has the concept FISH and the concept PET, one should also have the concept PET FISH. But neither the prototypical fish, say, trout or tuna, nor the prototypical pet, say, a dog, will lead us to a prototypical pet fish, say, a goldfish or a guppy. This is why, the criticism goes, concepts cannot be prototypes.[27]

But, to reiterate, we have to be careful here in that there is a danger in conflating two very different questions: what concepts qua mental representations *are* and what concepts qua word meanings *ought to be*. Note again that we are asking here a conditional question: *if* concepts are assumed to be mental representations (that is, have cognitive reality) and *if* they are at the same time to function as word meanings, what theory of concepts would best fulfil such a task? Whatever framework for sentential concepts we adopt, we want prototypes to follow the principle of compositionality (introduced briefly in Section 1.4 and in more detail in Stage 3) as it is the essential principle of any successful theory of meaning. Arguably, meaning without some form of compositionality is inconceivable.

Fodor's conclusion seems to be pretty definitive. So, can compositionality be salvaged as a property of prototypes? There have been some sophisticated attempts to do so but they appear to add an unnecessary complication. First, one can postulate different combinatorial principles for prototypes. In particular, Hans Kamp and Barbara Partee[28] proposed a so-called context-sensitive *recalibration* of an adjective in the context of a noun to account for, for example, STRIPED APPLE. Recalibration

---

[26] Cappelen 2018 contains a thought-provoking discussion of conceptual engineering. On redefining these particular two concepts, see Manne 2019.
[27] For a bracing critique of prototypes as concepts, see Fodor 1998, especially Chapter 5.
[28] Kamp and Partee 1995.

means an adjustment of meaning in context and is a result of an interaction between concepts – here, STRIPED and APPLE. But one size doesn't fit all. In combining concepts, one has to bear in mind that component concepts may have different characteristics: they (i) can be vague or sharp; (ii) can, but need not, have a prototype, and if they do, (iii) the prototype can, but need not, determine the extension.[29] For example, TALL or INANIMATE do not have a prototype, and although ADOLESCENT or GRANDMOTHER do, the prototype is not helpful in determining class membership. Distinguishing *types of concept combination* is a difficult task. In any case, as we can see from (i)–(iii), prototype theory only applies to a subset of concepts, so it would need supplementing by a separate account for words that are left out.

In particular, the observation that the characteristics of the compound may not bear any obvious relation to those of its constituents has been tested in an interesting experiment by Connolly, Fodor, Gleitman, and Gleitman. They observed that complex concepts with modifiers do not inherit the stereotypical characteristics associated with their heads (unmodified nouns). (2.3) contains one example from their questionnaire.

(2.3)  A: Ducks have webbed feet.
       B: Quacking ducks have webbed feet.
       C: Baby ducks have webbed feet.
       D: Baby Peruvian ducks have webbed feet.

(from Connolly et al. 2007: 10)

In B, a stereotypical modifier (*quacking*) was added; in C, it was replaced by a non-stereotypical modifier (*baby*), and in D, a second non-stereotypical modifier was added (*baby Peruvian*). The consultants' judgement of the likelihood that the statement is true progressively diminished between A and D. The fact that it was not carried through to the complex concepts shows that prototype inheritance is not a default reasoning strategy.

On the defence side, if we allow for some context-sensitivity of prototypes, then it is possible to 'save' prototypes as word meanings in that what enters into the composition process is the meaning that fits the situation of discourse. So, perhaps prototypes and compositionality can be reconciled. Various ways to reconcile them have been proposed. Del Pinal, for example, makes lexical prototypes flexible by allowing them to contain very different kinds of information, including not only perceptual but also functional information or information about salience.[30] Combined with the assumption that compositionality allows for some context-sensitivity because of the influence the lexical items exert on the choice of the appropriate structure, this gives us a possible reconciliation of prototypes and compositionality and as such allows us to treat prototypes as word meanings. However, one has to be wary of some tension here: if we start with the question as to whether prototypes could be made to fit the purpose as word meanings, then, surely, their assumed properties can be adjusted to fit the task. But then prototypes

---

[29] See Kamp and Partee 1995, p. 172.
[30] See e.g. Del Pinal 2016 and references there to other similar proposals. On compositionality of prototypes, see also Hampton and Jönsson 2012; Prinz 2012; and Schurz 2012.

## 2.2 The 'Concept' Commotion

are defended only if they are made sufficiently malleable to be defended and the burden of explanation is only shifted from one mysterious term to another.

Finally, the role we assign to prototypes can be channelled in such a way that compositionality is no longer a necessary requirement. If we accept, as in the neo-classical theory, that concepts are definitions, sets of necessary and sufficient characteristics, but assign to prototypes a more 'practical' role of identifying the right exemplars, then both theories can be salvaged: the strict characteristics give us the core, while prototypes provide a cognitive overlay. In other words, concepts are sets of characteristics that allow for exceptions (neo-classical theory) paired with the way they are processed, and the latter relies on typicality effects (prototype theory).[31] Such a rich conception of concepts, the so-called *dual theory*, is currently gaining currency in that it also addresses problems on the semantics/pragmatics boundary: how much information in an utterance comes from its semantic content and how much is contributed by pragmatic processes. If we make word meaning rich and flexible and allow the compositional process to operate on such context-dependent meanings, then there is less to defer to the pragmatics of utterances. Perhaps, even, like on Rayo's *grab-bag localist*[32] approach, we can adopt the view that there is no context-shifting of the meaning of words to explain because, so to speak, there is nothing to 'shift from': there is no fixed semantic meaning, no semantic rules; there is only a metaphorical 'grab bag' of samples of use:

With each expression of the basic lexicon, the subject associates a 'grab bag' of mental items: memories, mental images, pieces of encyclopedic information, pieces of anecdotal information, mental maps, and so forth.

So,

A grab bag for 'elephant', for example, might consist of a mental image of an elephant, a few encyclopedic entries ('elephants are animals', 'elephants are big and grey, and have trunks'), and a few memories ('I once rode an elephant when I was a child'). (Rayo 2013: 648, 657)

Speakers' 'grab bags' can differ but they calibrate and become commensurate through mutual accommodation as people speak. Next, 'localist' in the name of the view contrasts with 'globalist' and refers to the view that meaning distinctions are made among the candidates for meaning in this particular context rather than 'globally'. Needless to say, the literal/non-literal distinction is obliterated in that the 'grab bag' contains a variety of memories of use of a lexical item, including metaphors, for example. While this is not yet a complete theory, neither have the assumptions been properly tested, the promise lies in its intuitive appeal and in providing equally intuitive answers to some big questions that have occupied linguists for a very long time: the semantics/pragmatics distinction and the literal/non-literal distinction, to be pursued in Stages 7 and 8. The debate concerning the lexicon–encyclopedia interface has, no doubt, paved the way, but there is still a long way to go.[33]

---

[31] For a discussion of dual theory and pertinent references, see Laurence and Margolis 1999, pp. 42–43.
[32] See Rayo 2013.
[33] For the lexicon–encyclopedia interface see Peeters 2000; Allan 2000, and other contributors to that collection. Allan, for example, argues that lexical meaning arises out of encyclopaedic information. For other discussions of context-dependent lexical semantics, see Carston 2012a or Del Pinal 2018.

To return to our earlier quandary, the problem is that during the attempt to adopt concepts as word meanings we have to reconcile questions from different levels of inquiry. One is, what is a concept if it is to function as word meaning, and the other, a meta-level question, what is a concept in the first place. The latter contains the debate about the ontology of concepts, that is whether they are abstract objects of some kind or mental representations.[34] But should linguists be interested in the ontology of concepts, or are they merely looking for a theoretical construct of a concept that fits the bill as word meaning? I hope to have shown that they should be, and are, interested. While most linguists define concepts as mental objects, there are also views that they are abstractions over bodies of knowledge, for example that they are constituents of propositions – just as Fregean senses discussed in Section 1.4 were public, shared modes of presentation and at the same time components of propositions in belief reports and in other propositional attitude constructions.[35] Throughout this discussion, we treated them as mental representations, following our working assumption, in that our question was whether the relation between the mind and the world can lead to understanding word meaning. But the abstract objects view has to be kept in mind because the discussion will re-emerge when we ask about the components of propositions in discussing sentence and utterance meaning.

Now, if concepts do compose, do we have theories of such concept composition? Yes, we do. But concept composition can mean very different things. Earlier in this section, I mentioned theories of conceptual structure that originated in the formal 'objectivist' tradition. The truth-conditional approach to sentence meaning, which will constitute the leading thread in our journey through meaning, functions as a theory of concept composition in that intensions are construals that give us word meaning (and as such, by our assumption, concepts). We will see that when truth-conditional semantics is supplemented with a good account of context- and mind-dependence, it might be able to explain various vagaries of meaning while at the same time benefiting from the rigour of the formal method of analysis. I use the word 'might' because the journey is not about making decisions but about flagging some viable opportunities.[36] We will be reviewing this possibility while pointing out the strengths and limitations of truth-conditional semantics during the following stages of this journey. But it has to be remembered that there are various grammars of conceptual constructs whose assumptions about compositionality and the kinds of units that compose vary substantially from those adopted here. Most notably, in cognitive linguistics, human language is said to consist of *constructions* understood as units of meaning of pretty much any kind, as long as their meaning cannot be predicted from their constituent parts.[37] We won't be

---

[34] Margolis and Laurence (2007) also discuss the possibility of a mixed view in which concepts are mental representations compatible with abstract objects. They find this position coherent but provide arguments against it, defending the mental representations view.

[35] For an introduction to propositional attitudes, see Section 5.5.

[36] On my own proposal of how it *can* account for various nuances of meaning, see my *Default Semantics* (Jaszczolt 2005) or, for a brief overview, Jaszczolt 2010.

[37] In the broad sense, the term covers approaches by such cognitive linguists as Charles Fillmore, George Lakoff, Ronald Langacker, or William Croft. Writing about these orientations would mean a journey through meaning with a very different trajectory, adopting a different perspective on the units of meaning

using the term but some points of convergence will become clear while we discuss cognitive representations.

## 2.3 Language and Thought

The picture that is beginning to emerge is that it is quite expedient to think of concepts as our sought explanantia for word meaning but the correlation is not without problems. It is also beginning to emerge that concepts are best thought of as mental representations, with the proviso that some form of word–object relation also enters the theory to avoid Putnam's $H_2O$–XYZ scenarios. But in order to go further, we must say more about the relation between natural language and thought.

First, there are forms of human thought that are independent of speech, just as there are forms of conceptual representation that are independent of linguistic representation. In other words, thought can use a non-linguistic medium.[38] For example, in manufacturing an object, sensorimotor representations dominate.[39] Information from sensorimotor, visual, and linguistic domains associates with the appropriate physical processes of producing the object. Or, to take artistic achievement, Beethoven's music or Picasso's art, for example, give evidence for such complex, languageless thought processes. It has also been empirically demonstrated that natural language is not necessary for thinking. Children born without hearing who do not begin to acquire language until later in life play and act just as hearing children do.[40] If it were true that grammar determines how we think and analyse nature, presumably these children would behave differently. Conversely, language can exist without thought. For example, in Williams syndrome, people can use advanced vocabulary without using it for reasoning. The problem of the relative priority of language and thought has many aspects to it and is still unresolved. But although it is clear that thought is possible without language, people normally use language (or *a* language, depending on one's stance on the Mentalese vs. natural-language debate) for thinking. Moreover, there is evidence from the study of cognitively impaired children that language aids mental development.[41]

It can now be seen why the idea of linguistic relativity is contentious. If the structure and operations of the brain determine language, we are justified in holding the view that there is a uniform language or computational system used by all people for thinking – the idea attributed to Alan Turing. With the rise of Noam Chomsky's

---

and their composition. See relevant chapters of Geeraerts and Cuyckens 2007 for comprehensive introductions.

[38] See e.g. Dummett 1991; Jaszczolt 1999, pp. 244–249. NB: I will not discuss here the debates that the issue of animal thought engenders.

[39] See Keller and Keller 1996. [40] See Goldin-Meadow and Zheng 1998.

[41] One widely quoted case is that of a girl, Genie, who was brought up in isolation, without learning to speak, until she was discovered at the age of thirteen. She had no language when she was discovered and her mental age was estimated to be between one and two years. Once she acquired language, her intelligence level rose rapidly. Previously, she had lacked basic human concepts which can only be acquired through language. See Curtiss 1977. See also Aitchison 1989, p. 86; Carruthers 1996, pp. 42–43.

universal grammar, linguists modelled the mind as an information-processing device that is genetically pre-programmed and thus the same for all speakers of all languages. According to Jerry Fodor, this device uses the Mentalese that I discussed in Section 2.1. A good way to conceptualize the relation between language of thought and languages in which we speak may be the following snippet related by Daniel Dennett (1993: 302–303):

> Fodor and others who defend the idea of the language of thought typically insist that they are *not* talking about the level at which *human* languages do their constraining work. They are talking about a deeper, less accessible level of representation. Fodor once made the point with the aid of an amusing confession: he acknowledged that when he was thinking his hardest, the only sort of linguistic items he was conscious of were snatches along the lines of 'C'mon, Jerry, you can do it!'

We won't manage to have recourse to Daniel Dennett's own celebrated ideas here, but suffice it to say that he defends the view that there is no single 'stream of consciousness', a single process in the brain, or a moment where all 'comes together'. As he says, '[s]ince cognition and control – and hence consciousness – is distributed around in the brain, no moment can count as the precise moment at which each conscious event happens' (p. 169). His controversial *Consciousness Explained* and the follow-up popular cognitive science books are highly commendable but somewhat tangential to our current journey (although we will have more to say about a related debate over connectionism and parallel architecture of the brain in a moment).

Now, since natural languages are full of vagueness and ambiguity and their use relies on recovering implied information, they are not very plausible candidates for a medium of mental computations. But Mentalese is also a contentious postulate rather than a fact. For some philosophers, it is merely a metaphor for a neural state of belief. This neural state is supposed to have a structure resembling that of natural language. Fodor argues in favour of computations that resemble sentence processing, and hence the syntax and semantics of Mentalese arguably resemble natural-language syntax and semantics. But Mentalese, as the medium of thought, has the 'advantage' over natural languages such as English, French, or Mandarin in that problems such as that of *The Morning Star* and *The Evening Star* discussed in Section 1.4 (see examples 1.18–1.21) do not arise: Mentalese, as a language of conceptual representations, is fully compositional. Fodor (2008: 219) compares these languages as follows:

> There may be no good reason for supposing that English has a semantics at all; perhaps the only thing that does is Mentalese. If that's right, then what are usually called 'semantic level' representations of English sentences ... are really no such things. Rather, they should be taken as representing translations of English into Mentalese. The translation of a sentence in Mentalese is, of course, no more a representation of that sentence than is its translation in French.

In the following stages of this journey through meaning we will question what kind of meaning representation is to be regarded as compositional.[42] For now, what interests us is the debate over the language of thought in which the sides are the defenders of Mentalese on one hand, and the defenders of natural language as a language of mental

---

[42] See also Schiffer 1993, p. 245. Cohen (1986) points out problems with the semantics of such a language.

representations on the other. An intuitive argument in favour of natural language as a medium of thought comes from Peter Carruthers.[43] He proposes that using natural languages for thinking has some survival value:

> when early hominids debated with one another about the best way to hunt an elephant, for example, and one of them said, 'We should attack from both flanks', there would have been some advantage in this statement figuring immediately as an item in practical reasoning, to be considered, manipulated, accepted, or rejected, without having to be translated into a wholly different system of representation (Mentalese). (Carruthers 1996: 232)

Next, Wittgenstein's view was that there is no language of mental representations because there are no mental representations separate from the expressions of thoughts.[44] There are no mental states and no meanings that would accompany expressions; beliefs are not hidden behind, so to speak, *expressions* of belief. The main argument goes that if there were mental states and private objects of thought, anything could count as their description. The discussion of private language has occupied many generations of philosophers at least from Thomas Aquinas, and doing it justice would require a different, historical journey through meaning.

Whatever language of thought turns out to be (assuming there *are* thoughts and mental states separate from their neuronal vignettes!), it seems that it has to be compatible with the universal operations of the human mind, as well as with the diversity of natural languages used for communication. A detailed discussion of universality and relativity also goes beyond our quest for meaning but its gist is essential to it. With evidence pointing in both directions, we will tentatively assume that, on the level of *conceptual operations*, universalism prevails. If elements of linguistic structures prove not to be mutually translatable on any level, then in order to understand meaning, we can use the idea of what I called elsewhere the 'lexicon–grammar–pragmatics trade-offs' (Jaszczolt 2012a: 118). The idea is that when a language does not communicate a certain kind of meaning through one of these media, it resorts to another. If it lacks grammatical tenses, for example, it can resort to temporal adverbials, cultural conventions, or pragmatic inference from context. Meaning composition will go on, it will just be 'kicked one level up', so to speak, to the level of conceptual structures. To do that, concepts have to be mental representations, but also have the property of being shareable and compositional – the features that various approaches discussed here take on board in different ways. The debate continues.

Now, Fodor's view, called the *representational theory of mind*, is that the mind resembles a digital computer used to manipulate symbols. It is composed of *modules*, specialized input–output devices that process various types of information, including visual and auditory. The output of this processing is submitted to the central processing system that is the domain of thinking. But there are other possibilities for conceptualizing the mind. For *connectionists*, the mind *means* the brain and the brain consists of a network of electrical processing units that stimulate and inhibit each other. Connectionists model the brain as artificial *neural networks*. According to this view,

---

[43] See Carruthers 1996.   [44] See Wittgenstein 1988, p. 11; 1984, p. 131; 1958: §318, 329; 1980: §585.

learning takes place through strengthening of the connections between units. This strength of connections can be measured by weights attached to the units that are supposed to model the working of synapses connecting neurons in the brain.[45] Connectionist models are also called *parallel distributed processing* models in that they model the brain as performing activities at the same time, in parallel to each other, rather than in a series. Connectionism first became popular in the 1940s and was revived in the 1980s.[46] It constitutes a challenge to the view that cognition means storing propositions and processing them according to rules of logic. It is an alternative way of modelling the mind.

On the other hand, as we have seen in Section 1.3, proposition is a useful construct for 'top-down' approaches to meaning, as long as we delimit it in such a way that it captures all the important aspects of meaning as it is conveyed in linguistic communication. We are not going to resolve the debate on language processing, but suffice it to say that connectionism has been steadily gaining ground thanks to growing empirical support. As is often the case, the most explanatorily successful approach to meaning in language may have to draw in both orientations. To reiterate, this means rethinking the status of propositions and representations on the one hand, and, relatedly, understanding what mapping procedure to use from images of brain activation to meanings in linguistic communications. Both are works in progress, and are at the forefront of research in linguistics, philosophy, and cognitive science.

Arguably, proposition-based approaches to meaning are the best worked-out and most successful ones to date, on the proviso that we make propositions malleable to account for cognitively real, intended and recovered, discourse meaning. Various strands of the representational approach to meaning presented here will prove useful when we unify the views of sentence meaning and word meaning into one coherent theory that uses the most rigid available tools (the truth-conditional method) but at the same time delivers cognitively viable results. In short, concepts have to have their rightful place in truth-conditional semantics and we have to be clear on what they are. The fun of doing semantics begins when one (i) can see a lot of different fish in the pool but also (ii) knows the reason why one wants to catch only some of them and (iii) tries to put them in one pie when they apparently don't fit in one recipe.

## 2.4 Lexicon and Pragmatics

During the past few decades, semantic theories, perhaps with the exception of computational linguistics, tended to focus on sentences, having no satisfactory accounts of word meaning – or even no particular interest in developing one. However, lexical semantics is being brought back to the fore, primarily as a result of the assumption that

---

[45] For an introduction, see Buckner and Garson 2019. [46] See Rumelhart and McClelland 1986.

much structural information about a sentence is traceable to the lexicon. Accounts of conceptual structures that developed from componential analysis rely on meaning components such as Agent, Goal, or Path; Del Pinal's prototypes compose because compositionality is context-sensitive; Rayo's 'grab bag' helps direct the syntactic composition, so his theory of meaning incorporates a good dose of pragmatics. In Pustejovsky's *generative lexicon*, a set of word senses is said to generate a larger set of senses when the words are combined in larger expressions. The syntactic patterns in which the word participates are important for assigning them to semantic classes. Word senses are approached through a number of rather detailed distinctions. For example, the sense of the verb *to bake* only appears to be problematic when we distinguish between *change-of-state* and *creation* verbs as in *bake the potatoes* vs. *bake a cake*.[47] This distinction allows for several observations concerning word senses. Firstly, the boundary between senses is unclear and depends on how finely grained our approach is. Secondly, words can be used creatively with respect to some of these fine distinctions and senses may not be fixed and yielding to enumeration. Therefore, more recent approaches, such as that of Nicholas Asher, foreground questions such as how meanings differ from context to context, how context can fix what look like category mismatches, and how to incorporate this dynamic nature of the lexicon into a formal account of sentence or utterance meaning, or even the meaning of longer discourses.[48]

On such approaches, lexical semantics interacts with pragmatics because word senses will have to be selected and sometimes modified. This caveat replaces the need for a precise specification of senses. World knowledge, also known as *knowledge base*, is indispensable for drawing inferences. Computational semanticists standardly invoke such fine-grained senses, and hence they make use of *ambiguous semantic representations* because on this level of detail, some information can be missing. This ambiguity on the level of lexical meaning results in the representations of whole sentences that lack some specification of detailed senses. In other words, they are *underspecified*. It has been argued, and evidenced, that complete disambiguation of such representations is not always necessary: as long as it is possible to reason using ambiguous premises, the specification of detailed senses may be superfluous. This approach to sentence/utterance interpretation is called a logic for underspecified representations or *ambiguous logic*.[49] The approach seems plausible as far as the processing of polysemous words is concerned because their senses are related (e.g. two senses of *press*: printing press and publishing house): not all aspects of their senses are always relevant. However, for homonyms, the situation is more complicated: there may not be any common core on which we can rely in reasoning from ambiguous premises (e.g. two separate lexemes *bank* as financial institution and *bank* as river bank).[50] We may have to resort to contextual and encyclopedic knowledge and to rules for selecting from among meaning alternatives, such as the

---

[47] See Pustejovsky 1995, p. 47. For a very brief introduction, see Section 8.2.3 of Riemer 2010.
[48] See here Asher 2011. For a formal theory that focuses on coherence relations in discourse, see Asher and Lascarides 2003 and Section 6.3 below. For a philosophical essay on fluid word meanings, see Ludlow 2014.
[49] See e.g. Deemter 1998.
[50] I say 'may not' because there are also unclear cases, straddling the boundary between polysemy and homonymy, where there is a historical link between the senses that is now obscure.

appeal to coherence[51] or to principles of rational, cooperative conversational behaviour. Suffice it to say, the process of disambiguation of homonyms and polysemous expressions is 'pragmaticized', moved to the domain of contextual clues or, on some approaches, to the domain of hearer's inference and heuristics that capture its regularities.[52] The question whether disambiguation is pragmatic *sensu stricto* or, rather, pragmatic qua context-sensitive meaning but at the same time semantic or even pre-semantic in that it is necessary in the process of identifying the proposition, is addressed when I summarize the semantics/pragmatics boundary disputes in Sections 7.2–7.3.

The interface between lexicon and pragmatics has many facets. An important facet that I haven't discussed is vagueness: *big, bald, heap,* or *rich* are examples of vague words. The first question to ask (since we are not doing semantics without doing philosophy) is whether vagueness resides in language, in the mind, in the world, or in any subset of these. Then, one has to ask how to harness vagueness: whether all vague words are alike or rather there are different kinds. Are all vague words relative, like *small* or *tall*, where small in *a small egg* differs from small in *a small house*? Do they all have borderline cases? Do they all come with a way of counting the degrees, say, in centimetres or inches? These are just a few aspects with respect to which vague words can differ. Theories abound. Even the ancient Sorites ('heap') paradox still engenders different solutions; if I take one grain of sand away from a heap, is it still a heap? If so, where is the boundary? And if there is no clear boundary, and not a boundary of a boundary, then how is it that we use these words without getting into difficulty? They often come with perfectly clear prototypes and unproblematic conditions of use. So, we are back to the intuitive conclusion that it is the pragmatics, the use of words in discourse, that ultimately makes up the semantic content, that is their meaning.[53,54]

The lexicon/pragmatics interface comes with a twist: what if we cannot find a suitable concept of a 'concept' that fulfils the requirement of being a mental object, a mental representation? We have seen this question in the example of dual theory: concepts can be prototypes but only if they are supplemented with the classical theory. Perhaps, as Edouard Machery has recently argued, concepts are even more heterogeneous: they can be prototypes, or exemplars, or theories.[55] They are also supposed to be 'stable bodies of knowledge', which they clearly are not: people's categorization differs with circumstances and purposes, and it changes when, say, new scientific evidence is uncovered. For example, a person's judgement will vary with circumstances as to whether a tomato is a fruit. To use a real historical event, even learning

---

[51] Literature in coherence-based approaches is vast. For our purposes, it is useful to consult Asher and Lascarides 2003.
[52] Such as Grice's maxims of conversation or their post-Gricean developments discussed in Stage 7. See Blutner 1998 for an example of an application to computational linguistics.
[53] Or, as Ludlow (2014) says, language provides the 'skeleton' for constructing the lexicon but the lexicon is dynamic: conversation adjusts the meaning to a much greater degree than is traditionally assumed.
[54] For different philosophical approaches to vagueness, try e.g. Fine 2020; Raffman 2014; Szabó and Thomason 2019, Chapter 13; Williamson 1994; Shapiro 2006; Smith 2008. All are rather advanced, but Chapter 1 of Raffman and Chapter 1 of Fine provide good introductions.
[55] For the best exposition, see Machery 2009. See also Machery 2015 and for criticism Pino and Aguilera 2018.

that whales are not fish does not necessarily lead to a stable body of knowledge. In the celebrated story of an 1818 New York court case Maurice *v* Judd, brilliantly discussed by Mark Sainsbury in his short squib 'Fishy business',[56] judges were asked for a verdict as to whether not paying taxes for dealing in whale oil falls under the regulations concerning 'gauging, inspecting and branding' fish oil. After hearing evidence from scientists that whales are mammals, and from fishermen that whales are fish, they gave the verdict that tax ought to be paid: whales are fish. Now, Sainsbury points out that this does not feel like merely a *verbal* disagreement; the disagreement was *substantive*: all evidence was presented in the case. To contrast, the celebrated example where the Earth used to be conceptualized by the ancients as flat makes an imaginary disagreement with a contemporary person a *verbal* disagreement: they disagree about the *definitions*. Sainsbury leaves the problem open. But we can perhaps say that the solution lies in a functional approach to concepts: depending on the function, the context, and the purpose (such as, here, making a judgement on tax avoidance), whales are either mammals or fish! Or, perhaps, complex concepts such as FISH OIL use functional characteristics for concept composition? Food for thought.

So, if concepts are not definable as a category, then, Machery concludes, they should be eradicated from psychology. But this is linguistics and philosophy: in talking about word meanings, we have no reason to lump together all these diversified facets and even categories of concepts, as long as they fulfil the condition of having cognitive reality. And, also, as long as they provide links to reference, since, as we have seen, meaning cannot be *only* in the mind.

## 2.5 The Role of Reference

Most approaches to sentence and utterance meaning that we are going to move to in the following stages of this journey make some use of the referential theory of meaning. On the referential approach that I introduced in Section 1.4, on a crude approximation, nouns refer to individuals or denote classes of individuals, adjectives and adverbs denote properties, and verbs denote actions, which can also be properties (*A dog barks*) or they can be relations (*A dog chases a cat*). The founding of meaning on reference seems intuitively plausible. It even has empirical support from an unusual domain in that it is said to be displayed by vervet monkeys and other primates that often have conventional signs for 'referents' that pose danger, such as eagles, snakes, or tigers. Referring to entities in the world is an important component of their communication.

Problematic fringes of this common-sense proposal are vast, though: *a unicorn* and *the present king of France* have no existing referents, and yet, surely, they have meaning. They have sense, the way of thinking about some counterfactual entity, and sense is, arguably, part of their meaning. On the other hand, where a referent *does* exist, it may not exhaust the meaning. There is intuitively more to meaning than denoting the object, and in some contexts this sense, mode of presentation, or

---

[56] Sainsbury 2014.

connotational overlay seems essential to the meaning – say, thinking of the planet Venus as the celestial body observed in the morning in example (1.21) in Section 1.4.

For the above reasons, referential theory in this strict sense, in which the meaning of a word is the object or entity it stands for, will be of little use to us in the remainder of this book. It can be said that in general terms, the theory suffers from a lack of explanatory power: correlating a lexeme with its referent makes a poor explanation. But when it is built into an approach where reference is conceptualized as reference in possible situations/worlds, it becomes useful in addressing the question as to what counts as meaning. Assessing the truth value of the sentence or utterance with respect to *any* such imaginary world gives us a concept of meaning that is powerful enough for the meaning of *unicorn* or *Santa* and even makes inroads into the meaning of abstract words such as *freedom* or *serendipity*. Since the meaning is given by the intension, that is, the generalization, so to speak, over extensions in all abstract possible worlds, rather than by the extension in the real world, then, arguably, referential theory so adapted can be called *conceptual*. However, the term 'concept' has to be understood then as an abstract construct that can only contingently be given an interpretation as a mental object. We will address this in more detail in Stage 3.

We now have to take a closer look at reference. Speakers use language to talk about the world. When the speaker utters (2.4), they use the proper names *Ludwig Wittgenstein* and *Cambridge* to refer to an individual and a location respectively.

(2.4)   Ludwig Wittgenstein lived in Cambridge.

Reference is a technical term in semantics but it is not used uniformly across approaches. The referent is an entity to which the expression refers. Words refer to entities but also speakers refer to entities in the world by using them. Hence, we have to distinguish *reference* from the *act of referring*, just as we have to distinguish sentence meaning and speaker meaning. There is another term in semantics that has a similar role to play and that was used in Section 1.4, namely denotation. A word *refers* to an object or a person, but it also *denotes* a class of entities. In some cases, this class can have one member or can be empty. For example, *dog* denotes all dogs in the world (that is, describes anything that can be called a dog), but is *used* to refer to a particular dog, or to the property of doghood if no particular dog is meant (this is what we call *generic* use: *Dog is a domestic animal*). So, an expression denotes a class and refers to an entity, a property, or a relation. To reiterate, the class denoted is called the expression's extension. In the case of proper names, the class is assumed to contain one member, that is the particular person, city, and so on. (The fact that there is more than one city called 'Cambridge' can be put aside for now – we are talking about disambiguated lexemes.) Denotation does not depend on the context; it is stable, whereas reference is context-dependent: *the dog* refers to different dogs on different occasions. (I return to semantic properties of definite descriptions in Section 6.2.3.) Similarly, on the referential approach, meanings of sentences are situations which they describe. According to this view, normally, matching words with the world gives their meaning. But as we have seen in the example of belief reports, for some types of expressions, reference is not sufficient and we have to employ sense, or mode of presentation. This is where

## 2.5 The Role of Reference

reference and mental representations meet: we need them both (not that everyone has to agree!).

Not all linguistic expressions that speakers use to refer fall under the technical term 'referring expression'. Standardly proper names (*Ludwig Wittgenstein*), definite descriptions – although not all definite noun phrases[57] – (*the author of* Philosophical Investigations), referentially (rather than anaphorically) used pronouns (*he*), including demonstratives (*that*), and demonstrative noun phrases (*this man*), are referring expressions. This reference can be either constant, context-independent (as in *Ludwig Wittgenstein*, with the earlier disclaimer in place) or context-dependent (as in *that man* or *he*). Not all semanticists are unanimous concerning the membership of the category of referring expressions, but the above definition will be accepted as a springboard for our inquiries in the remainder of the book.

A proper name refers because it names an entity. But how exactly this reference takes place is a matter of dispute. Perhaps it refers because it abbreviates a description of some entity, as Bertrand Russell suggested.[58] Or it refers because there has been social practice inaugurated in the initial act of naming which spread through a chain of referring acts performed by various people – a view due to Saul Kripke.[59] Some semanticists say that proper names and pronouns, including demonstrative pronouns, refer by picking out the object and they convey no other meaning in addition to this 'pointing at' an object. So, 'David Kaplan' refers to the person David Kaplan and this reference exhausts its semantic role. This view is defended by David Kaplan, among others (although it goes back further in history of philosophy of language), and the property is called *direct reference*.[60] Kaplan also held the view that such terms have a constant referent across possible worlds (more about this property in Section 6.2.4.3). There are good arguments for keeping such directly referring expressions separate from, say, definite descriptions, and I will discuss them briefly in Section 6.2.3. Intuitively, however, it is easy to argue that there is more to the meaning of proper names than the referent: proper names, like descriptions, also convey sense, the way of thinking about the object or person, and since sense is needed to get the meaning of propositional attitude reports and other intensional contexts right, then why not go the whole hog and admit it into semantics? The discussion will have to wait until Section 5.5 but suffice it to say that it is still contentious what the exact meaning content of proper names is.[61] I will come back to this question having first laid out the principles of truth-conditional semantics.

Definite descriptions also refer, but this need not mean that the speaker refers to an entity by using them. In (2.5), the definite noun phrase 'the architect of this church', used as a definite description, has a referent. But the speaker may have used it either to refer to a particular individual, say, Antoni Gaudí, or, alternatively, having just seen the

---

[57] See Section 6.2.3.  [58] See Russell 1962 [1912].  [59] See Kripke 1980 [1972].
[60] For the best account, see Kaplan 1989a.  [61] See e.g. Neale 1990 and Elbourne 2005, Chapter 6.

unusual design of La Sagrada Família in Barcelona, may have meant that whoever the architect was, they were insane.

(2.5)   The architect of this church was mad.

In other words, the definite description may have been used *referentially*, referring to Antoni Gaudí, or *attributively*, attributing the property of madness to whoever satisfies the description. The status of this ambiguity will occupy us in Sections 6.2 and 7.2–7.3.

To sum up, *Antoni Gaudí* and *the architect of this church* may refer to the same person but they differ in meaning. So, in order to make any good use of the idea of a referent, we have to move from extensions to intensions; after all, there are imaginary worlds in which La Sagrada Família was designed by someone else, say, Simon Guggenheim, and worlds in which unicorns exist! (This is fun until it gets to the formal aspects in Stage 3 where the experience of fun with imaginary worlds is replaced by the experience of enthusiasm, awe, or disbelief in formal methods! Keep on with the journey and see in which camp you end up.) Or, perhaps, we have to go further and combine referents with a more psychologically real story about concepts – concepts as mental representations? Arguably the best of the two worlds is to retain formal methods of analysis, or, in any case, rigid methods that result in normativity and as such in predictive power, without sacrificing cognitive reality. Semantic theory is not quite there yet but the concept–object mismatches show clearly that this is what is needed. Even if I know and you know that we don't have the same concept of, say, the mountain Snowdon if I have climbed it and you haven't, or if you know it under its Welsh name 'Yr Wyddfa' and I know it as 'Snowdon', it is not so easy to generalize what it is that we share and where we differ, and how much, if any, of these differences are relevant for the theory of meaning.

**Suggested Further Reading**
For a survey of theories of word meaning that focuses on structuralist and cognitive approaches, see Geeraerts's (2010) *Theories of Lexical Semantics*. On cognitive approaches, see also various chapters in Geeraerts and Cuyckens' (2007) *The Oxford Handbook of Cognitive Linguistics*. For an overview of approaches to concepts, see Laurence and Margolis 1999 – Chapter 1 of Margolis and Laurence's *Concepts: Core Readings* (it is a comprehensive introduction, although a bit compact at times). Also, browse through the rest of that book, depending on your interests: it contains seminal articles on various approaches and various questions pertaining to concepts. But beware that Fodor's views on the innateness of concepts have changed – read up on that in Fodor's (1998) *Concepts*, especially towards the end of Chapter 7. On compositionality of prototypes see Chapter 5 there, especially on the PET FISH example. Remember that Fodor's view has been disputed – some recent rebuttals were introduced in fn 30 (in that they make rather advanced reading). For an introduction to language and thought, see Elbourne's (2011) *Meaning*, Chapter 8. Saeed's (2016) *Semantics*, Chapter 2 is also a comprehensive introduction to language and thought, and Chapter 3 to various aspects of word meaning. For reading on concepts across

disciplines (and species), see Margolis and Laurence's (2015) *The Conceptual Mind*. For a thought-provoking introduction to the relation between language, thoughts, and concepts, see Jackendoff's (2012) *A User's Guide to Thought and Meaning*. Think which tenets you agree with and which you disagree with and why – as I said, all books, even introductions, present the subject from the author's point of view (which is as it should be!).

Detailed, including advanced, reading suggestions for particular problems and ideas were given in the footnotes as we moved along.

# Stage 3  Composing Sentence Meaning
*Tools and Their Purpose*

> Objectivity is a method of understanding. It is beliefs and attitudes that are objective in the primary sense. Only derivatively do we call objective the truths that can be arrived at in this way.
>
> (Nagel 1986: 4)

## 3.1  Truth in Service of Meaning: Truth Conditions and Truth-Value Judgements

One of the lessons learned from our journey so far has been that meaning connects language with the mind and with the world. We say 'language' rather than 'a language' or, say, 'the English language' because the desideratum is that the tools and principles of composition of meaning we search for ought to apply to all languages alike, with only superficial adjustments to cater for the structure and lexicon of a particular language. Remember that we may choose to use it only as a step towards the composition of conceptual structures – mental representations, if there are good reasons for analysing meaning on that level instead. Sentences are constructed and used to communicate something about the world and about the minds of their users. Declarative sentences often describe situations in the world, correctly or incorrectly. That is, they can be true or false. Before we move to non-declaratives, let us explore the utility of 'being true' and 'being false' for understanding and explaining meaning. Truth means different things to different philosophers: there are different conceptions of truth. We will explore the traditional, common-sense approach according to which truth means correspondence with facts in the world. This is called the *correspondence theory of truth*. 'True' and 'false', when predicated of sentences (and, as we will see later, also of utterances), are called the *truth values* of the sentence (or utterance).

This notion of truth is used in semantics in the following way. *We know the meaning of the sentence when we know what the world would have to be like for this sentence to be true*. The facts that would have to be the case for the sentence to be true are the *truth conditions* of the sentence. For example, for (3.1) to be true, there would have to exist a person called Kate Manne who wrote a book entitled *Down Girl: The Logic of Misogyny*.

(3.1)   Kate Manne wrote a book *Down Girl: The Logic of Misogyny.*

The sentence is true in the actual world: this brilliant book appeared in 2018. But *knowing that it is true* is not the explanatory concept we need; we need *truth conditions*, not the *truth value*. To be able to explain what 'meaning' means, we have to know under what conditions, in principle, this sentence would be true. This is the explanatory concept we need because it allows us to link any sentence, even ones never produced before, with situations, even ones never encountered before. There has to be a set of rules that pairs each sentence with a set of conditions. Otherwise, we could not account for the infinite number of sentences that can be generated using the devices of natural languages.

This means that we can truly map language and reality (and also the mind, as we will see later in this journey). Alfred Tarski developed this matching procedure between sentences and sets of conditions for artificial languages (deductive systems), proposing what is known as the semantic definition of truth. This procedure can be briefly stated as in (3.2), where $p$ is a set of conditions, S is a sentence, and 'iff' stands for 'if and only if'. S can be any sentence of the analysed language.

(3.2)   S is true iff $p$

The best known formulation of the idea is the so-called T-sentence, as in (3.3), where '...' contains the sentence whose meaning is to be analysed, or what we called earlier an explanandum, also called a 'name' of the sentence, or an *uninterpreted string*. We will see shortly that what follows 'iff' has to be spelled out in an unambiguous, formal language of description, that is a *metalanguage*.

(3.3)   'Snow is white' is true iff snow is white.

Linguists, and most notably Donald Davidson and Richard Montague, borrowed this explanatory relation between meaning and truth but used it for their own purpose: *not* to explain truth using meaning, but to explain meaning using truth. And they used it for meaning in natural languages – systems we use for communication.[1]

Truth-conditional semantics focuses on sentence meaning and does not bear a straightforward relation to either the referential or the mentalistic approaches to word meaning discussed during the preceding stages. Truth conditions make use of correspondence with facts in the world, so the natural correlate in lexical semantics is the referential approach. But, as I have mentioned, referents or sets of referents (denotations) are not where the explanation ends: we have to have a generalization over denotations (extensions) in possible worlds in order to get to a concept that would be of use as word meaning. Assessing the sentence for truth value in the actual world does not yet give us a satisfactory answer to what meaning is. More on this below.

Mapping sentences onto truth values is only an idealization. First, as we have seen, there are many types of constructions, such as propositional attitude reports, for which

---

[1] See Tarski 1952 [1944]. His first seminal work in Polish on this topic is Tarski 1933. For applications to natural-language semantics, see e.g. Davidson 1984a and Dowty, Wall, and Peters 1981.

we have to resort to mental representations. If a simple link with the referent will not suffice, mental representations are invoked. Second, the theory is an idealization in that the truth conditions of the sentence may prove rather counterintuitive when speaker meaning differs from sentence meaning. Third, as we have seen, some sentences may not be sufficiently informative to allow for the identification of their truth conditions and we have to resort to contextual clues, including speaker intentions. So, semantics is never 'pure': pragmatic aspects of meaning, that is meaning that comes from the context of utterance, including the recognition of speaker intentions, as well as various conventions of use, frequently (if not always) enter into the truth-conditional analysis.

Now, one may wonder what notion of context would suffice to provide all the necessary information. There are scenarios in which the speaker and the referent remain the same, and yet common-sense truth-value judgement will differ. This is so in the scenario thought up by Charles Travis about Pia and a Japanese maple tree. The tree has naturally russet leaves but imagine that she paints the leaves green (which is her preferred colour for leaves) and then utters (3.4) to herself.

(3.4)   The leaves are green.

(from Travis 2008a [1997]: 111)

What she says appears to be true. But now imagine she is uttering it to a botanist who is searching for trees with green leaves for their research. Now our judgement differs: what Pia says appears to be false – simply because the purpose, the circumstances in which the sentence is evaluated, affect the outcome.[2] So, truth conditions are very sensitive indeed.

Arguably, the semantics of conceptual representations has more practical utility than the semantics of sentences, especially, as we have seen, because so often sentences need embellishment from pragmatics to be truth-evaluable anyway. But, of course, one can do either, or both: one can apply truth conditions to the 'minimal' units or to the 'maximal', cognitively real units, as was discussed in Section 1.3. Truth conditions are just a flexible tool. One can think of them as utensils – say, a knife and a fork, that we can use to eat either the main, substantial meal, or a smaller, much less substantial meal. The first translates into the main, psychologically real, intuitively plausible meaning of a sentence uttered in context, while the other translates into the meaning of the sentence, that is the 'minimalist' meaning as it was conceived of in traditional formal semantics – sentence meaning composed out of the lexicon and structure of the language system, *tout court*.

Now, normally, in standard truth-conditional semantics, truth value is provided by the relation between the sentence and the world and the truth is empirical truth. But some sentences are true or false in virtue of their form and there is no need to 'check' their value, so to speak, against situations in the world. We call such sentences *analytic* sentences: sentences whose truth or falsehood follows from the structure of the sentence alone. We contrast them with *synthetic* sentences. Sentences (3.5) and (3.6) are always true – they are true in virtue of their form. They are *tautologies*.

[2] Adapted from Travis 2008a [1997].

(3.5)   London is London.

(3.6)   The bus will come or it won't come.

These sentences are informationally empty, although in specific contexts they can communicate something indirectly, such as, for example, (3.7) and (3.8) respectively.

(3.7)   London is not Paris: there is no point comparing the two cities.

(3.8)   City buses are unreliable here.

Sentence (3.9) can also be called a tautology if we recognize that MAMMAL is part of the definition of WHALE, or one of its components of meaning (in other words, WHALE entails MAMMAL). In other words, we can classify it as a case of tautology if the adopted approach to word meaning allows us to do so.

(3.9)   Whales are mammals.

Example (3.9) shows that the truth of some analytic sentences is not known a priori, prior to observation or experience: a discovery must have been made that whales belong to the class Mammalia. So, it is truth a posteriori: post-observation or post-experience – just as example (1.19) repeated below is a tautology (*Venus is Venus*) but is based on an astronomical discovery.

(1.19)   The Morning Star is the Evening Star.

Similarly, *contradictions* such as (3.10) and (3.11) are false in virtue of their form: they are always false. Again, including (3.11) will depend on the definition of word meaning we adopt. Unlike (3.10), (3.11) is not a contradiction in virtue of the grammatical structure alone; we have to consider the lexical opposition of the adjectives *dead* and *alive*.

(3.10)   It is raining and it is not raining.

(3.11)   My cat is dead but it is alive.

It is sometimes possible to use adjectives such as *dead* and *alive* 'as if they were gradable', so to speak, in order to express non-literal meanings such as, for example, that one is 'more alive' after a stimulating lecture or 'more dead' after jogging than after yoga exercises. But, typically, they are classified as non-gradable and as such as mutually exclusive. On the other hand, proper gradable adjectives such as *tall* or *rich* lead to what we can call a weaker form of incongruence: while *rich* and *poor* in (3.12) cannot normally be juxtaposed because the context would not make the evaluation standards clear and the sentence appears to be a contradiction, they can be juxtaposed when the standards are clarified, as in (3.13).

(3.12)   ?He is rich but also poor.

(3.13)   Among his friends, he is rich, but compared with fellow club members, he is poor.

Understanding (3.12) does not require invoking non-literality; it merely requires an explanation of the evaluation standard. But non-gradable antonyms as in (3.11) are different: they are true *contradictories*, while gradable ones are what we call *contraries*. Moreover, contraries, unlike contradictories, can be both false: a person can be neither tall nor short; neither poor nor rich.

The truth of 'pure' analytic sentences, such as (3.5), (3.6), or (3.10), can be predicted from their form called the *logical form*. This is the notion to which we now turn.

## 3.2 The Metalanguage for the Logical Form

It goes without saying that the natural language that is the object of analysis has to be different from the language that we use for its description; otherwise we would be analysing the language whose ambiguities, vagueness, and other vagaries we want to get to the bottom of using the same 'imperfect' or at least 'informal' system as a tool. We would also be running the risk of circularity of explanation (discussed while assessing candidates for word meaning in Section 2.1). So, we need a language that can be used for talking about natural-language meaning – we need a *metalanguage*, referred to briefly in the discussion of the T-sentence in (3.3). This is where formal languages of logic come to the rescue. In order to capture principles of valid reasoning, logicians devised artificial languages which are characterized by their precision and lack of ambiguity. Linguists use some of them as a natural-language-semantics metalanguage into which they translate sentences in order to dispel their ambiguity and vagueness. This allows them to assign truth conditions to natural-language sentences by analogy because the structure of the sentence is clearly represented in the translation. Logic is the study of inference, of constructing a valid argument, where the conclusion follows from the premises not because of what the sentences mean but because of the rules of logical inference that operate on the structures alone. In what follows, I will present the utility of such languages of logic in their role of metalanguage, but I will also expose their limitations.

Logical form is a representation of a proposition in a precise, unambiguous, logically 'perfect' language. It proves very useful for providing truth conditions of complex sentences. We translate a sentence from a natural language such as English into a language of logic. Then, by looking at the form, we are able to tell under what conditions this sentence is true. Similarly, by looking at the logical form of analytic sentences, we can easily tell they are analytic without thinking about what they mean: the principles of logical deduction allow us to do so.

For example, it is intuitively obvious how the forms, that is, the structures alone, of (3.14) and (3.15) help in the judgements of analyticity.

(3.14)   If the cat is black and furry, then it is black.

(3.15)   All black cats are cats.

Sentence (3.14), with its full meaning spelled out as simple sentences in (3.16), has the approximate logical form in (3.17). The logical form tells us that the sentence is always true.

(3.16) If the cat is black and the cat is furry then the cat is black.

(3.17) if $p$ and $q$ then $p$

Similarly, we can translate synthetic sentences into a language of logic. In (3.18), the first thing we will notice is that the relation between the two simple sentences, marked as *conjunction* by the word *and*, comes with fixed truth conditions: for (3.18) to be true both conjuncts will have to be true. They are fixed, in that the truth conditions are such in virtue of the form alone: $p$ and $q$, where 'p' and 'q' stand for any declarative sentences.

(3.18) It is Friday and we are going to a concert.

But for (3.19) to be true, it is enough for one simple sentence to be true: *Charles went to a concert* or *Charles went to an opera*. This is an example of *disjunction*, marked by the word *or*.

(3.19) Charles went to a concert or to an opera.

Such relations between simple sentences are the subject of *propositional logic*: the logic of sentences. In addition to conjunction ('$p$ and $q$', or using the standard symbols of the metalanguage, '$p \land q$') and disjunction ('$p$ or $q$', that is '$p \lor q$'), the language of propositional logic that we use in natural-language semantics also includes *implication* (to be precise: *material implication*) or *conditional* ('if $p$ then $q$', written as '$p \rightarrow q$'), *equivalence* or *biconditional* ('$p$ if and only if $q$', or '$p \leftrightarrow q$'), and sentential *negation* ('It is not true that $p$', '$\neg p$'). In Stage 4, I say more about such relations and about rather significant limitations of propositional logic in handling their English (and other natural-language) equivalents.

In propositional logic, '$p$', '$q$', '$r$', and so on conventionally stand for simple sentences. But then, these simple sentences also have their logical forms that reveal their structure and as such allow us to assign truth conditions. Translation into *predicate logic* tells us what this form of simple sentences is. For example, the translation of (3.20) into predicate logic reveals the logical form that gives us information in (3.21). It reveals that being happy is predicated of Anna.

(3.20) Anna is happy.

(3.21) Happy (Anna)

It also allows us to assign a truth condition: sentence (3.20) is true *if and only if* there is a unique individual called Anna and this individual has a property of being happy. When sentences become more complicated, this translation into a metalanguage is a saviour in that it allows us to assign truth conditions on the basis of a clear, unambiguous logical form alone. There is no circularity, no talking about meanings of the components before we answer what their meaning is. It is so in that the language of description (the metalanguage) dispels the ambiguities of the object language (natural language whose semantics we want to pursue) and the truth conditions are clearly 'visible' from the form alone.

So, where do ambiguities go? How do they disappear? If it is lexical ambiguity, as in the case of *bank – bank*, the translations will be marked as different: they will be treated as two separate lexemes, translated as two separate predicates; something can have the property Bank$_1$ and another thing a property Bank$_2$. If the ambiguity is syntactic (structural), as in (3.22), then there will be two different structures when the sentence is translated into the metalanguage: one where *beautiful* is predicated of a dog and the other where it is predicated of the dog's house. In other words, ambiguous sentences have as many different logical forms as there are ways in which they are ambiguous.

(3.22)   A beautiful dog's house attracted my attention.

In addition, sentences that on the surface do not seem to be structurally ambiguous also may have to be given different logical forms. Pertinent examples here are the referential and attributive readings of the definite description *the architect of this church* in (2.5), discussed in Section 2.5 and repeated below; group reference that can be either *distributive* or *collective*, as in (3.23); and possibly also indefinite reference that can be either *specific* or *non-specific*, as in (3.24).

(2.5)    The architect of this church was mad.
         (a particular individual or whoever designed this church)

(3.23)   These books cost £50.
         (each or the set)

(3.24)   Every evening a hedgehog appears in the garden.
         (the same one or any)

Next, plural nouns as in (3.25) can have a universal quantifier reading ('all') or a generic reading ('as a kind'). I say more about the universal quantifier later in this section.

(3.25)   Horses are friendly.
         (all horses or normally, as a species)

Now, just as in the case of translations into propositional logic, translations into predicate logic reveal validity of arguments. That is, we can tell that the conclusion is true in virtue of the logical form (the structure) alone. A translation into the metalanguage reveals that (3.26) is a valid argument: (3.27) tells us that the inference is valid.

(3.26)   Melford is a cat. All cats are mammals. Therefore, Melford is a mammal.

(3.27)   Premise 1:      Cat (Melford)
         Premise 2:      For all $\Delta$s: If $\Delta$ is a cat, then $\Delta$ is a mammal.
         ──────────────────────────────────────────────────────────
         Conclusion:     Mammal (Melford)

## 3.2 The Metalanguage for the Logical Form

'Δ' stands here for a 'slot holder', a 'dummy' for which one can substitute an individual. It allows us to write a pattern, a general rule of inference that will apply to any individual object that occupies this slot.

Let us now start using predicate logic. A simple sentence in predicate logic can look as in (3.28). The letter '*a*' marks an *individual constant* that stands for a referent. Lower-case letters from the beginning of the alphabet are standardly used as individual constants. We can stipulate that it stands for Anna and now rewrite (3.21) as (3.28). We will see in a moment, while discussing possible worlds and models, what assigning individuals to constants means.

(3.28)    Happy ($a$)

'Happy' is a *predicate* and '*a*' is its *argument*. Predicates are expressions such as adjectives, verbs, or common nouns – they predicate something about various individuals. A *one-place predicate* (e.g. an adjective, a common noun, or an intransitive verb) describes a property: it predicates something of an argument.

Next, *a two-place predicate*, such as a transitive verb *like*, is a relation between two arguments. It is interpreted as a set of all the pairs of individuals related in a particular way. For example, *Anna likes Bill* can be translated as in (3.29). It has to be an *ordered pair*: Anna's liking Bill doesn't mean that Bill also likes Anna. 'Likes ($a, b$)' differs from 'Likes ($b, a$)'.

(3.29)    Likes ($a, b$)

A three-place predicate such as *to be located between* acquires an analogous translation, as, for example, in (3.30).

(3.30)    Between ($b, a, c$)

These simple formulae can be joined by using logical connectives as in (3.31).

(3.31)    Likes ($a, b$) ∧ Happy ($a$)

But some English sentences are not so straightforward to translate. For example, (3.32) is not satisfactorily translated as (3.33).

(3.32)    Some students are happy.

(3.33)    *Happy (Some Students)

It is not satisfactory because 'some students' is not an individual that can be represented by an individual constant on a par with *a* for Anna. In order to translate it, we need a device that will allow us to use a 'slot holder' for individuals and say there are some of them – just as we used 'Δ' in for 'all Δs' in (3.27). We need an *existential quantifier* ('∃') that translates the English quantifier expression 'some' and its equivalents. We will see in Stage 5 that there are better methods to render quantification in our metalanguage but the traditional quantifiers of predicate logic will do for now. They are important to understand at this point because they allow us to differentiate between individuals marked as individual constants and the 'slot holders'. Sentence (3.32) can now be represented as in (3.34).

(3.34)   ∃x (Student (x) ∧ Happy (x))

'∃x' is read in these formulae as 'there is an *x* such that ... ', 'there is at least one *x* such that ... ', 'some', 'someone', or 'something'. In other words, at least one member of the universe of discourse satisfies the formula (also called an *open sentence*) that follows the quantifier. The quantifier transforms an *open sentence* (a *well-formed formula* but not yet a *sentence*) into a sentence. The letter '*x*' stands for an *individual variable* or what we earlier marked as 'Δ' – a slot into which various referents can fit ('some students' could be Anna, Bill, Cesar, and so on). Variables are normally marked by lower-case letters from the end of the alphabet, '*x*', '*y*', '*z*'. The outer brackets in (3.34) indicate the expression to which the quantifier applies. In other words, the variables within the outer brackets are *bound* by the quantifier, so they stand for the same individual. The outer brackets indicate the *scope* of the quantifier. In short, because quantifiers bind the variables, they make it possible to specify what the truth conditions of the sentence are.

We will see in a moment, while discussing models, how the difference between individual variables and individual constants works in assigning referents. They are called 'individual' because they stand for individuals, although, as we will see in Section 5.2.3, the metalanguage can be modified to account for groups in order to capture the collective (as opposed to distributive) reading of plurals. This is exemplified in (3.35) that allows for both readings: the collective, that they own one car between them (the more natural reading of the two), and the distributive, that they own one car each (say, in answer to the question who among a group of friends owns a car). For the distributive reading we can simply use two quantified expressions: ∃x ∃y and specify that $x \neq y$.

(3.35)   Anna and Bill own a car.

Variables are only slot holders, so there is nothing in the symbols *x* and *y* themselves that tells us they are different. 'Individual variable' is also contrasted with 'predicate variable' where we can quantify over a property ('∃P' – 'there is a property *P* such that ... '). But the metalanguage that is standardly used in natural-language semantics only quantifies over individuals – it is called for this reason *first-order logic*. Quantifying over properties belongs to a higher-order language, to be introduced briefly in Section 5.1.

Now, 'for all Δs' in example (3.27), properly symbolized as '∀x', is the *universal quantifier* of predicate logic, translating as 'for all *x*s it is the case that ... ', 'all *x*s', 'every *x*', and other related expressions. Analogous to the existential quantifier, sentence (3.36) is not satisfactorily translated as (3.37) because 'all students', unlike 'Anna' or 'Bill', is not an entity – it does not correspond to an individual constant.

(3.36)   All students are happy.

(3.37)   *Happy (All Students)

Instead, we have to translate it to capture the following sense about *x*: if we consider any entity (*x*) such that this entity is a student, then this entity is happy (or, 'If *x* is a student, then *x* is happy'), as in (3.38).

(3.38)   $\forall x \, (\text{Student}\,(x) \rightarrow \text{Happy}\,(x))$

While in the case of formulae with the existential quantifier we used conjunction ('∧') between the predicates, in the case of the universal quantifier we have to use implication ('→') instead. The use of conjunction with the existential quantifier would result in very different meaning: every entity (in the universe of discourse) is both a student and happy.

Quantifiers have occupied logicians from Aristotle, through medieval scholars, Frege, to contemporary projects in generalized quantifier theory and dynamic logic that we will encounter later in this journey. Aristotle can be credited with observing relations between quantifiers, such as that 'Not all individuals (*x*s) are dogs (*P*s)' equals 'Some individuals are not dogs (*P*s)'; 'No *x*s are *P*s' equals 'All *x*s are not *P*s'. These equivalences, summarized in (3.39), are logical truths (tautologies), introduced in Section 3.1. We will find them useful in discussing rules of pragmatic inference in discourse in Section 7.1.

(3.39)   $\exists x \, P(x) \leftrightarrow \neg \forall x \, \neg P(x)$
$\neg \exists x \, P(x) \leftrightarrow \forall x \, \neg P(x)$
$\exists x \, \neg P(x) \leftrightarrow \neg \forall x \, P(x)$
$\neg \exists x \, \neg P(x) \leftrightarrow \forall x \, P(x)$

This is not a manual of predicate logic, so we will only focus, in rather general terms, on the rationale behind such translations into an artificial language. Moreover, traditional quantifiers are not the best way to account for natural-language quantifying expressions in that many quantifying expressions are left out. Traditional propositional logic would not handle expressions such as *most*, *many*, or *few*, and is very limited in handling number terms as well. Nowadays we mostly use the traditional quantifiers in discussing natural-language meaning for specific illustrative purposes, especially in philosophy of language.

Let us take stock. Natural languages are full of vagueness and ambiguity and it would not make a satisfactory theory of meaning to speculate or intuitively predict what the world would have to be like for such English, Mandarin, etc. sentences to be true. Neither would it give us a theory with predictive power. Instead, we translate each English sentence into an artificial, unambiguous language and this translation gives us the logical form of the sentence. The advantage of this translation is precision and perspicuity of the structure of the sentence. For example, English sentences with more than one quantified expression tend to be ambiguous – at least potentially, if not also in context. (3.40) can mean that everyone has some person or other whom he or she likes or that everyone likes one single person.

We can only see it with clarity when we provide separate translations for these readings. These readings are represented by two distinct logical forms, arrived at through varying the relative order of the quantifiers, as in (3.41a)–(3.41b). They make it clear that each comes with its own truth conditions.

(3.40)   Everyone likes someone.

(3.41a)   $\forall x \, \exists y \, \text{Like}\,(x, y)$   ('Everyone has someone whom he/she likes.')

(3.41b)   $\exists y \, \forall x \, \text{Like}\,(x, y)$   ('There is someone whom everybody likes.')

To some extent, we can remedy this ambiguity in English by the ordering of the constituents, as in the glosses above or in (3.42a) and (3.42b).

(3.42a)   Everyone in this room speaks two languages.

(3.42b)   Two languages are spoken by everyone in this room.

However, although the order of the constituents suggests one interpretation more strongly than the other, the sentences still remain ambiguous. In other words, (3.42a) and (3.42b) have two logical forms each. Now, (3.43) is many-ways ambiguous. The general idea as to why and how is clear but if one wants to list all of the readings, logical forms undoubtedly help!

(3.43)   Three boys sent five Christmas presents to four friends.

All in all, lexical and syntactic ambiguities are relatively easy to eradicate in such translations because they lead to different logical forms. So-called 'semantic ambiguity', on the other hand, is more akin to underdeterminacy or vagueness as the forms are not totally unrelated. This is the case with sentences involving the English connective *and* that can mean either a straightforward logical conjunction, or temporal, causal, or other discourse-inferential connection. I discuss English sentential connectives at length in the next stage of this journey.

To sum up, quantifiers of predicate logic, albeit not perfect as a tool, allow us to provide representations of natural-language sentences that display their internal relations. Then, an unambiguous logical form allows for truth conditions to be stated automatically, without invoking the meaning of the sentence. Logical form makes the rules of logical inference accessible for this purpose. We will see the need for some additions to this metalanguage in further stages of this journey. In Stage 5, we will attend to the additions that will allow us to represent, among other things, modality and time in natural language, as well as more natural-language quantifiers such as *many*, *few*, or *most* already mentioned.

Next, in Sections 3.4–3.5, I introduce a different language, called type-theoretic, used among others in Montague's influential intensional logic. This is a different metalanguage but this general introduction to the principles of a formal analysis in predicate logic will help us understand it. Understanding the rationale behind using such formal languages will allow us to proceed in this philosophical journey through meaning, repeatedly reassessing the assumption that the semantics of such a formal metalanguage will give us a springboard to the semantics of the object language for which they provide translations.

Two questions are likely to arise at this point. First, what if the logical form does not capture the 'whole meaning', so to speak, or does not capture the 'right kind of meaning', the meaning that is intended by the particular use of a sentence? Semantic theories offer different answers, and all of them come with advantages and limitations. Since, as was discussed in Section 1.3, semantics can be 'minimal' and capture only (or almost only) the meaning of the sentence, or it can capture more cognitively real meaning, all the way to the 'maximal', primary intended (and/or recovered) message, the object of study of semantics is up for grabs. Some semanticists are attracted to a formal analysis that either (i) mirrors or (ii) falls within the domain of, syntactic analysis, depending on whether we follow the tradition of Richard Montague or of Noam Chomsky, respectively. Such analyses have the attraction of being almost free from the 'contamination' by muddying, fuzzy context dependence, conjectures about intentions, unspecified intended meaning, and so forth. Others, those placed towards the 'maximalist' (or strongly contextualist, to give it the proper label) end of the spectrum, want the semantic representation to be a conceptual representation, a cognitively real representation that draws on the logical form of the sentence but also on myriad other sources of information in discourse. They can still use a formal metalanguage to represent the conceptual structure. The formal representation will incorporate various pragmatic components of meaning and the composition of meaning will be assumed to take place on the level of this conceptual structure, rather than on the level of sentence structure. On that view, it is emphasized that language is only one of the vehicles of meaning and that semantics ought to respect that fact. After all, the metalanguage is just a tool, a language of description, so in principle we should be able to represent in it all aspects of meaning – even unexpressed, implied thoughts. In short, using the tools from formal logic, one can pursue either a 'narrow' semantics of sentences as in standard truth-conditional semantics, or a cognitively real semantics of conceptual structures. Food for thought.

To proceed towards the cognitively real meaning, we can reason as follows. Although we can easily write down two logical forms corresponding to an ambiguous sentence, this won't yet give us an answer to the question as to what meaning was intended and conveyed by the speaker. Moreover, addressees don't go through all these possible meanings in their minds before settling on one. Instead, if the common ground (shared assumptions) was correctly gauged, they jump to the meaning that was intended. So, it has to be remembered that the listing of the possible logical forms is not cognitively real; normally only one of these forms will represent the actual meaning that is shared in conversation (although not in the case of puns of course!). Sometimes the possible meanings are even logically related: one may simply be more specific and entail the other. This will be discussed during Stages 5 and 6 of this journey when we use existential quantifiers to depict different readings of definite descriptions – the referential and attributive reading introduced in Section 2.5 in the context of La Sagrada Família scenario (example 2.5). The journey through such meanings will be completed in Section 7.2.3 when we discuss default interpretations. Suffice it to say at this point that using the metalanguage of first-order logic must not remain merely an exercise in translating sentences into logical formulae. If the logical form of the sentence has no psychological plausibility, that is, does not reflect a real step in utterance processing, we may as well use our powerful metalanguage to represent *contextually enriched*, cognitively real meanings instead if this is what we want our kind of semantics to do. Either way, the powerful tool of a formal metalanguage is definitely worth having. Food for thought again.

Now, if cognitively real meanings are to be pursued, leaving aside the 'big question' of the language of thought will be difficult. But this need not necessarily trouble us at the moment. To follow up on the discussion from Stage 2, one can opt for one of the following three stances: (i) the natural-language system is different from the conceptual system; (ii.a) they are the same: we speak and think in the same sentences; or (ii.b) they are the same and there is a mapping from utterances to sentences of the inner speech. So, if one is a 'maximalist' about semantics, one may want to ask oneself the question as to whether the semantics one is pursuing is the semantics of natural language, as in (ii), or is different from it, as in (i). On the other hand, what appears to be complicated is adopting (ii) and being a 'minimalist' at the same time. One will want to say that sentences of natural language are compositional by themselves, without being able to count on more 'pragmaticky' and 'cognitive' aspects of meaning that appear to be necessary for the semantics of, say, belief reports (*The Morning Star – The Evening Star* example). But some journeys through meaning *are* minimalist and in spite of this, they *do* have their own solutions to such problems. For example, one will stipulate then that the meaning of *The Morning Star* is the same as the meaning of *The Evening Star*, no matter what the ancients believed and no matter that intuitively they invoke different truth conditions. Truth conditions will then be insensitive to people's judgements. In a nutshell, one can then banish any psychologism, any cognitive reality, from the pure, formal, minimalist-semantic theory. It is all a matter of adopting some or other sets of assumptions that the researcher deems important, and rejecting others. As I have pointed out, truth conditions are a tool that can be used for analysing either intuitive meanings or very 'coarse' ones. And it has to be remembered that historically formal tools were employed in the service of the latter kind.

The second question that may spring to mind is, how do we analyse non-declaratives? What would it mean for interrogatives or imperatives to have truth conditions? Interrogative and imperative sentences do indeed pose a problem for truth-conditional semantics. Generally, declaratives express statements, interrogatives express questions, and imperatives are used to give commands – although there are different communicative acts we can perform in conversation using them, as is discussed in Section 8.3. The difficulties they pose are not insurmountable though. It has been proposed that the semantics of a question is given by the meanings of sets of correct, or correct and exhaustive, answers to the question. In other words, the sets of propositions that correspond to true, or true and exhaustive, answers to the question, across imaginable possible worlds (on whose utility I say more shortly in this discussion of 'tools'), provide the meaning. 'Exhaustive' means here 'not partial'. For example, when I answer the question about who passed the exam by saying 'Anna did', while in fact Anna, Bill, and Daniel all did, my answer is not an exhaustive answer. The first proposal was developed in the 1950s by C. L. Hamblin and in the 1970s by Lauri Karttunen, and the latter in the 1980s by Jeroen Groenendijk and Martin Stokhof. According to a more recent proposal by Jonathan Ginzburg, what counts as an answer that *resolves a question* varies with context and is sensitive to such parameters as goals and inference in context.[3] Next, according to another recent formal theory called Inquisitive Semantics, we need a new theoretical notion of *issues*, understood in relation to context and to agents' information states:

the standard notion of semantic content does not seem applicable to interrogative sentences. Rather, what we need for interrogatives is a notion of content that directly captures the issues that they raise. (Ciardelli, Groenendijk, and Roelofsen 2019: 4)

Another option is to include information about the communicative act, such as a question, order, request, and so on, in the formal representation of the sentence. Then, the truth conditions will pertain to the situation that is asked about or desired (requested, ordered) but the overall representation will not be truth-conditional: the structure will reveal instead what this act of communication means by placing it against some social and conventional norms for what counts as its successful performance. But this route is lined with difficulties in that, say, a question beginning with *could you* is more likely to convey a request and *I promise* can in fact mean 'I warn you', depending on the proposition that follows and on the context, so formalization is rife with difficulties. More about it in Section 8.3.

## 3.3 Possible Worlds and Models

It is important to understand why truth conditions, not just truth values 'true' or 'false' about some real-world situation, are necessary tools. What the world *would* have to be like for the sentence to be true (the truth condition(s)) allows us to dissociate meaning from factual truth, from having to know what the situations really are like – that is, from knowing the facts. It is this generalization, this being able to tell what the facts would have to be, and being able to tell from the structurally clear, unambiguous logical form alone, that gives a semantic theory that uses these tools a formidable predictive power. We can analyse every declarative sentence using these tools, and even tweak them for analysing non-declaratives and sentence fragments. Such tweaking of the tools makes the history of contemporary semantics. It is also what this particular journey emphasizes, considering our initial desiderata. If some aspects of meaning that we want the semantic theory to capture are not accounted for, we can still use the theory as a springboard and think *how* to account for these aspects. This is how approaches of the contextualist orientation use it. To reiterate, if the English (or other object language) sentence does not obviously translate into a logical form in the metalanguage from which truth conditions can be gleaned, we can always go progressively 'deeper into context and intentions'. That is, we can go deeper into pragmatics:

---

[3] The seminal sources for the first proposal (knowing what counts as a true answer) are Hamblin 1958 and Karttunen 1977, and for the second (true exhaustive answers) Groenendijk and Stokhof 1982. See also Asher and Lascarides 2003 (sections on questions) for a discussion; Ginzburg 1995; Ginzburg and Sag 2000 and Dayal 2016 for a functional, goal-based approach, as well as Ciardelli et al. 2019. See also Dayal 2016 for an accessible survey of different approaches. Next, Cremers and Chemla (2016) report interesting experimental evidence that sentences with questions embedded under *know* (as in *John knows who called*) don't necessarily have the exhaustive reading.

disambiguating, filling in pronouns, completing subsentential strings by assessing context or speaker intentions – or, alternatively, starting from the other end and assessing what meaning the addressee recovered from such an incomplete string. Every journey through meaning can make different assumptions as to 'whose meaning' to study and 'how pragmatically rich', how cognitively real, this object of study ought to be, as long as such choices are well justified and consistently followed through. I anticipate here what will be the topic of Sections 7.2–7.3.

Returning to our tools, another way of looking at the 'would' in 'what the world would have to be like for the sentence to be true' is to employ a concept of different *possible worlds*, or possible scenarios, situations. Possible worlds, which we have already encountered briefly, can be intuitively invoked when we think of constructions such as *If I were a man, ...,* or *If it hadn't rained, ...* – 'the ways the world could have been'. But they are even more abstract than that. Possible worlds are theoretical constructs and as such have nothing to do with the feasibility of such a possibility. They are technical constructs: counterfactual worlds, imaginary and infinite alternatives to the actual world that allow us to obtain formal models of such possibilities and then, through obtaining such a 'bird's eye' view over worlds, get a big picture of what meaning is. So, we know what the meaning of a sentence, say, *All dogs are black* is when we can 'tell apart' the worlds in which it is true and the ones in which it is false. Then, truth conditions are the conditions which must hold in any possible world in which the sentence is true. Notice, again, that this has nothing to do with the facts in the actual world (where the sentence happens to be false). The bunch of worlds in which the sentence is true gives us the intension, the meaning of the sentence. This is so because the extension of a sentence is its truth value in a given world, and extensions from such a bunch of worlds sums up to an intension. Likewise, we know what a word *dog* means when we can have an imaginary, abstract, 'bird's eye' view over the sets of objects that can be called 'dog' (the extensions) in all such imaginary, abstract possible worlds. The totality of such extensions, again, will give us the intension: the meaning, the concept DOG. It follows that intension can be thought of simply as meaning. Dowty, Wall, and Peters (1981: 145) sum it up admirably clearly:

the intension of an expression is nothing more than all the varying extensions (denotations) the expression can have, put together and 'organized', as it were, as a function with all possible states of affairs as arguments and the appropriate extensions arranged as values.

For every sentence there is a set of possible situations (worlds) in which the sentence is true. Let us imagine a set of possible worlds (not to worry how many – we can continue adding them ad infinitum by tweaking their inhabitants, properties, and activities!). Then, let us remember that we have two truth values at our disposal: 'true' and 'false'. In other words, our logic is binary, two-valued logic, without any uncertainties, gaps ('neither true nor false'), or degrees of probability. Then, let us imagine that the proposition, the meaning of the sentence, is a connector, a link that we can draw (or a mapping that we can imagine) between each of such endless worlds and one of the truth values – because in each of these worlds the sentence is either true or false. One has grasped this way of doing semantics when one can imagine this abstract principle of having a 'bunch' of worlds in which the sentence is true and separating it from a bunch in which it is false. *A proposition, the meaning of the sentence, is then a mapping (in other words, a function) from possible worlds to truth values.* So, here is another useful definition of the ubiquitous 'proposition' in semantics.

This is the gist of, the concept behind, truth-conditional possible-world semantics. And we have to remember that it can be done either on 'minimal' assumptions, staying close to the structure of the sentence, without adding any 'contamination' from pragmatic aspects of meaning, or it can be done in a more 'maximal', contextualist way, by allowing more, or less, context-dependent and/or conventions- and intentions-dependent aspects of meaning. The minimal way is the standard way and is easier to formalize but does not give us the cognitive reality of the conceptual structure. It separates utterance meaning, even of the kind that can be predicted from contextual parameters, from sentence meaning: it keeps pragmatics at bay. The contextualist way is more difficult, since we have to appeal to the murky territory of thoughts, intentions, and contexts, but it gives us practical answers to what meaning is for the users of the language, including 'occasion-sensitive' meaning, meaning in context that depends on the circumstances of evaluation.[4] We can use truth conditions for both, remembering that a broad spectrum of journeys through meaning is viable and semanticists have taken many different paths while pursuing these journeys. Moreover, choices on the 'minimal–maximal' spectrum are compatible because, as I mentioned in Section 1.3, the semanticist's objectives may differ, and a greater, or lesser, dose of contextualism will be compatible with these objectives. Arguably, tools such as representations in a logical metalanguage, truth conditions, and possible worlds are worth having whatever the stance on the 'minimal–maximal' meaning is.

Having captured the gist of possible worlds, we can move to models. Just as the logical form allows us to see the structure of the sentence clearly, so formal *models* of some relevant parts (situations) in possible worlds let us see the correlates of words and sentences clearly. In truth-conditional semantics, in order to specify the meaning of simple sentences, we have to glean from the logical form how these expressions are related to the world, or, in other words, how they are *interpreted*. The *interpretation* relates the sentences of the metalanguage (logical forms), and as such, also the sentences of natural language of which the logical forms are translations, to the world. Or, at least, this is the semanticist's starting point – the springboard, whereby any incompatibilities between the logical form and the sentence in the object language such as English can be patched up later, by supplementing this analysis with something else (to wit, most likely, a rule-governed account of the speaker's intended meaning). The interpretation relates the logical forms and the natural-language sentences from which they originated by providing extensions of the expressions, i.e. the objects in the possible world, in configurations that are about to be explained. The interpretation is called a *model*. If a sentence is true in a certain *interpretation*, the interpretation is a *model* of that sentence.

---

[4] See Travis 2008b.

It is important to understand what role such models play in truth-conditional semantics. The idea in its current form derives from the work of a logician, Richard Montague, who worked in the 1960s and 1970s. His approach is still the foundation stone of cutting-edge formal semantic theories. But now, several decades later, we have progressed to having relatively satisfactory accounts of context-dependent aspects of meaning and its dynamic nature – that is, how meaning 'grows' as conversation progresses. These newer developments are discussed in Section 6.1 on dynamic semantics.

A model is a formal representation of a discourse situation. Approaches that make use of such representations are called *model-theoretic semantics*. So, Montague's approach to meaning is a truth-conditional, model-theoretic, possible-world semantics. Those following in his footsteps, taking the approach further, represent Montagovian semantics.

This is how it works. Having obtained an unambiguous logical form, we have to provide formal models of situations that sentences of the metalanguage describe and then lay out a set of procedures for checking whether they are true or false of the modelled situations. The best way to comprehend the idea behind this method is to think of an example of such a model. Let us think of one small model of a part of a possible world. It is one example of endless constructs we need in order to comprehend the 'bird's eye view' – that is, to get from extensions to intensions. First, one has to associate with each individual in a model a name which uniquely identifies that individual, as in (3.44). The individual then is the interpretation of the name.

(3.44)    Anna = $a$; Bill = $b$; Cesar = $c$; Daniel = $d$

As we know, the letters '$a$', '$b$', '$c$', and so on stand for individual constants. Next, one must also provide an interpretation for the predicates. To reiterate, a one-place predicate (e.g. an adjective or an intransitive verb) describes a property: it predicates something of an argument. For example, it predicates sneezing of Daniel or being a cat of Cesar. It is interpreted as a set of all the individuals in that world that have the property it describes. These individuals constitute the extension of the predicate. For example, 'Sneeze' is true in our model about Anna and Daniel, as part of the model in (3.45) shows. Curly brackets stand for a group – a set, an extension.

(3.45)    Sneeze:    {a, d}

This part of the model will let us check if sentences such as *Anna sneezed* or *Cesar sneezed* are true in the world which this model formally represents. While $a$ is in the extension of 'Sneeze', $c$ is not; so, the first sentence is true and the other is false. We can now add other models to formally represent parts of this particular sample world and evaluate other sentences. Then, we can check the truth value of various other English sentences against the relevant models (strictly speaking, we are checking their translations into the metalanguage, that is logical forms). Let us say that the extension of the predicate 'Happy' is as in (3.46) and the extension of 'Cat' as in (3.47).

(3.46)　Happy:　　{a, b, c, d}

(3.47)　Cat:　　{c}

Is Anna happy in this world? Yes, she is because 'Happy (a)' is true in the model if and only if a refers to an individual in the model which is an element in the extension of Happy in this model. We can also check that that world has one cat in it and that cat is called Cesar.

Next, a two-place predicate, such as a transitive verb 'Like', is interpreted as a set of all the ordered pairs of individuals. For example, *Cesar likes Anna* is true in every model in every world in which Cesar and Anna are an ordered pair in the extension of 'Like'. So, the extension of 'Like' in a model (where 'Like' stands, in the metalanguage of predicate logic, for the English two-place predicate, that is transitive verb, *to like*) is a set of all ordered pairs of individuals where the first likes the other. This is then the interpretation of the two-place predicate 'Like' and we put it in the model as in (3.48). The angle brackets around the pairs of individual constants show that these are ordered pairs.

(3.48)　Like:　　{<a, b>, <c, a>, <d, c>}

The model that consists of (3.44) and (3.48) allows us to assign a truth value to the sentence *Cesar likes Anna* in the world which this model is 'modelling': there is a pair <c, a> in the extension of 'Like', so the sentence is true. We also know that Anna likes Bill because 'Like (a, b)' is true iff <a, b> refers to a pair which is an element of the extension of 'Like'. We check and find out that it indeed is part of the extension. We can then move to three-place predicates such as 'Between'. If our model consists of (3.44) and (3.49), then we can tell that *Daniel is between Anna and Cesar* is true, while, say, *Bill is between Anna and Daniel* is not.

(3.49)　Between:　　{<c, d, b>, <d, a, c>}

It is important not to lose track of what this exercise of assigning models to imaginary worlds is for. When we grasp, and formally represent, the 'bird's eye' view over endless extensions of 'Like' that we can find in endless possible worlds, then we have reached the meaning of 'Like' in our metalanguage. Then, what remains is to step back from the logical form to the original English sentence and acknowledge that the meaning of *to like* is given to us by the meaning of 'Like' in predicate logic. After all, we have chosen predicate logic as our best available metalanguage, the language of description. Or we can be sceptical and admit that there is more to the meaning of English *to like* because it is so dynamic, dependent on the flow of conversation. Then, models would have to be tweaked by differentiating between the nuances of meaning in drawing up the extensions and by updating information content at every step as conversation progresses. Be that as it may, possible worlds, and models as their formal 'vignettes' for evaluating sentences, are a pretty good springboard for such pragmatic tweaking.

Let us now go back to the famous T-sentence in (3.3), repeated below, that captures the gist of Tarski's semantic theory of truth, to better understand how linguists 'flipped it' to use it for their own purpose – that is, to develop a truth-driven theory of natural-language meaning. Recall that the expression inside the quotation marks is an uninterpreted string, that is, the expression of the object language whose semantics linguists want to provide, while the material that follows it is its interpretation – as it is understood with reference to possible worlds and models.

(3.3)   'Snow is white' is true iff snow is white.

We can now unpack it. To know the truth value is to know whether the particular individual or an ordered pair, triple, or, in theory, *n*-tuple is in the extension of a particular predicate, where '*n*' stands for a cardinal number. So, the sentence is true with respect to a model if and only if there is something in that model that is both in the extension of 'Snow' and in the extension of 'White'.

Regarding *n*-tuples, it is worth pointing out that in natural languages we rarely go beyond three-place predicates. However, it all depends on how finely grained an ontology of a 'predicate' we adopt. We may want to stipulate that some of the arguments of the predicate are conceptual entities such as senses, modes of presentation. This would help with the semantics of belief reports in the *Morning Star – Evening Star*-type scenarios. But the semantics of propositional attitude reports will have to wait until Section 5.5 where it receives more attention.

It is not easy to grasp the significance of such toy models. Their strength lies in clearly demonstrating the importance of the world as a correlate of linguistic expressions. We have to grasp what the worldly correlates (extensions) of a word or a sentence are in each imaginary world. The procedure to do so is to consult the clear, unambiguous 'vignettes' of these worlds in the form of models of situations and follow the method introduced above. Extensions of the expressions relate the logical form, that is, the sentence in predicate logic, to a possible world. And then, we extrapolate from the meaning of this sentence to the meaning of the English, or French, or Mandarin, etc. sentence of which it is a translation.

A model is just an abstraction. Likewise, a possible world is an abstraction. But we need those abstractions because, as we have seen, extension alone will not give us meaning. It only shows contingent correlations between words and sentences on the one hand, and objects and their configurations (pairs or *n*-tuples) on the other. So, we have to stretch incredibly the capacity for abstract thinking and conceptualize meaning as the 'bird's eye' view over such contingent extensions. At that point, models themselves can be thrown away – like a ladder that we used in order to climb to obtain this 'bird's eye' view. Models have no cognitive reality – their only reality is that of a theoretical tool. Model-theoretic semantics is not in the business of building mental models; it provides a conceptual tool for understanding *what meaning is*.

Let us now sum up the method that the tools such as truth conditions, possible worlds, and models provide. Semantics is envisaged here as a mirror of syntax, and truth conditions are generated by using the syntactic structure of the sentence, clearly represented in the logical form, mirrored in the relations between entities in the world. These relations are given in a model that is a formal representation of a situation in a world, where the 'bird's eye' view over such models provides the meaning, the intension. Intension can be thought of as a concept – a simple concept for word meaning and a complex concept (a proposition) for sentence meaning. So, to relate this semantics to the discussion of concepts from Stage 2 of this journey, concepts are understood here as abstract objects, theoretical constructs. We can only endow them with mental reality when they can be said to correspond to representations in the mind. But this is a question best left to empirical inquiry such as those in neurosemantics and neuropragmatics.

## 3.4  Semantic Composition and Semantic Types

The summary of the overall procedure with which we finished the preceding section shows the importance of selecting a suitable formal metalanguage. We must remember that just as English has its syntax and semantics, so does the metalanguage. The translation gives us a syntactic representation. Then we interpret the formula, the logical form – we move from the syntactic representation to the semantic representation, associating the truth conditions with the formula using an automatic procedure. Extensions in possible worlds tell us whether the sentence is true in that world, and a conceptual abstracting over all possible worlds gives us the meaning – the intensions.

The power of intensions does not end there. The way they work in the composition of meaning requires a better conceptual grasp. Montague's intensional logic is a language that allows us to do precisely this. His semantics uses the tools we have just introduced but it uses a specific intensional language. It is a so-called higher-order type-theoretic language and it is based on Russell's theory of types.[5] I briefly discuss type-theoretic metalanguage here, in spite of the fact that we will not use it in the later stages of this journey, because it is important to appreciate the overall conception behind it: it gives an unrivalled insight into the principles of composition of natural-language meaning. It avails itself in the process of a method of composing an endless, in principle, number of syntactic and semantic categories (*syntactic types* and *semantic types*). Then it associates intensional semantic categories, modelled on Frege's senses, with each type to cater for vagaries of meaning.

But first things first. We start with the observation that the principles of semantic composition can be seen as mirroring those of syntactic composition. Next, we move to semantic types, in order to understand the power (and beauty!) with which they capture composing meaning, and extend the discussion to intensional types. Finally, I introduce the tool of lambda abstraction and explain its utility.

To discuss the composition of meaning, we have to first establish what 'kind of meaning' we want to discuss the composition of. To reiterate, in Montague semantics,

---

[5] For an introduction see Jacobson 2014 or the classic, Dowty et al. 1981. Montague's intensional logic is applied to a fragment of English in his seminal article 'The proper treatment of quantification in ordinary English' (Montague 2002 [1973]). It makes advanced reading but Dowty et al. offers a step-by-step introduction. For a selection of seminal articles in formal semantics that make advanced reading across different approaches and periods, see also other papers in Portner and Partee 2002. I refer to some of them in the course of this journey.

semantics is the mirror of syntax of natural-language sentences; it 'reads off', so to speak, the meaning from their structure. But, by incorporating intensions (we will see shortly how), it also attempts to mirror conceptual structure – the syntax of mental equivalents of the sentences we utter. For example, *The ancients believed that The Morning Star is the Morning Star*, the example analysed as (1.18)–(1.21) in Section 1.4, will render a counterintuitive truth value without recourse to concepts: it will come out as true in virtue of the tautological embedded sentence, while it is unlikely that such a belief was actually ever held (just as we don't *believe*, in the sense of having a mental state of such a belief, that dogs are dogs). When we include in the logical form the way of thinking about the planet Venus, the truth value comes up as cognitively real: it mirrors the structure of *thought* rather than the structure of the uttered or written English *sentence*. Compositionality is still there. Without it, meaning (of sentences and thoughts alike) is inconceivable: we have to be able to provide a procedure for composing meaning from units (words or their mental equivalents respectively) and structures. Without it, a theory has no predictive power and does not account for the productivity and systematicity of language. So, it is time to say more about compositionality because the tools presented in the previous section were all developed in its aid – to understand and systematize compositionality of meaning. And in this philosophical journey, we want to be able to use them for whatever kind of meaning we choose to analyse, as long as these tools do the job, following, and going beyond, Davidson's, Montague's, and other great masters' original intent.

In short, we are going to unpack the principle of compositionality. As a principle of meaning composition it is normally attributed to Gottlob Frege, although there are many different versions of it. The principle says that the meaning of a complex expression, such as a sentence, is determined by the meanings of its constituents, such as words, and the structure in which they are immersed. For our current purpose, it is used as follows. The structure of the sentence in the metalanguage is taken to mirror that of an English sentence. (Remember at this point that on newer, contextualist construals of semantics it can mirror the structure of an unuttered but 'meant' sentence instead. The principle of compositionality does not favour any particular theory of meaning, as long as the theory assumes that meaning *is* compositional. But let us continue with mirroring of the sentence.) This structure is given in the logical form that provides crucial insight into how the meaning of the sentence is composed. It goes without saying that juxtaposing words in a random order does not result in a meaningful structure. Neither can changing the order be relied on if we want to preserve the meaning – if it does so, it does it contingently. (3.50) and (3.51) clearly express different propositions. Needless to say, languages with more free word order will obey some other restrictions, such as, say, obligatory case markings.

(3.50)   The cat ate the mouse.

(3.51)   The mouse ate the cat.

## 3.4 Semantic Composition and Semantic Types

Compositionality is not only a principle about syntactic theories and meaning theories. It is also a principle that governs human and machine learning of language. As Liang and Potts (2015: 362) put it, compositionality and learning '[b]oth concern the ability of a system (human or artificial) to generalize from a finite set of experiences to a creative capacity, and to come to grips with new inputs and experiences effectively. From this perspective, compositionality is a claim about the nature of this ability when it comes to linguistic interpretation.'[6] The importance of structure for the meaning of the sentence is well exemplified in the phenomenon of structural ambiguity – to reiterate, sentence (3.22) repeated below has two meanings and two corresponding structures, giving rise to two different logical forms.

(3.22) A beautiful dog's house attracted my attention.

We have also observed that compositionality, although arguably absolutely necessary for any semantics as an assumption about possible languages, is not easy to capture. Propositional attitude reports either show compositionality but yield intuitively wrong truth values or 'can be made to' show compositional structure when we add some hidden constituents to that structure such as Frege's sense, or a mode of presentation, a way of thinking about the referent. Idioms also create problems for compositionality as they appear to be non-compositional, although their meaning is not totally opaque. We still process the phrase, for example *kick the bucket*, and are able to assign to it a compositional interpretation – though this is not necessarily a step through which the understanding of the utterance has to proceed, in that idioms are highly conventional and as such are normally grasped automatically.

All in all, getting to the bottom of the composition of meaning is not a simple task. There are also difficulties involved in combining the meaning of adjectives and nouns, as was mentioned in Section 2.2. For example, *a possible solution* is not necessarily a solution; *an alleged thief* is not necessarily a thief; *a fake Rembrandt* is definitely not a Rembrandt; *an occasional passer-by* refers to various people on various occasions who happen to pass by some contextually salient spot. Kamp and Partee's recalibration discussed in Section 2.2 is one of the attempts to bridge this gap and save compositionality on the level of adjective–noun combinations. Barbara Partee discusses the problems with compositionality of adjectives by first dividing them into classes.[7] There are *intersective adjectives*, as, for example, in *a vegetarian student*, where the set of vegetarians combines with the set of students and renders the extension which is an intersection of these two sets. There are also *subsective adjectives*, as, for example, in *a skilful dentist*, where the adjective *skilful* has meaning specific for dentists and would have a different meaning when combined, for example, with *butcher*. The set of skilful dentists is a *subset* of dentists. Finally, there are adjectives which are not even subsective, such as *former* in *a former prime minister* or the examples listed at the beginning of this paragraph. It has been pointed out by Terence Parsons and Richard Montague that discussing these combinations in terms of denotation (in extensional

---

[6] Readers with background in computational semantics may be interested in Liang and Potts 2015.
[7] See Partee 1995.

terms) is inadequate. Instead, we should consider sense, intensions, or map the semantic value of the noun onto the semantic value of the adjective–noun combination. Alternatively, Barbara Partee suggests 'type-shifting', where a syntactic rule corresponds to several rules of semantic interpretation. We will say more about types in a moment.

Solutions to problems like these are vital because we have nothing better than uncovering compositionality on some or other level of analysis of meaning. Complex expressions are indefinite in number and we could not learn their meanings one by one. Similarly, we could not account for their meanings one by one. Compositionality is a well-justified assumption: a methodological assumption about semantic theory, and an ontological assumption about the language this semantic theory is about. As such, it is an empirical assumption: Zoltán Szabó,[8] in his 'Compositionality as supervenience', proposes that compositionality should be regarded as much more than a methodological assumption that a theory of meaning ought to adopt. For him, it is a necessary characteristic of all human languages:

If it is accepted that the principle of compositionality is an intricate thesis about the nature of possible human languages, one will be less inclined to think of it as a triviality or as a mere methodological assumption. It will more likely be taken as a significant, though extremely general empirical assumption. (Szabó 2000: 503)

Whether it has to be an assumption about the meaning of sentences as they are uttered or written, or it can be an assumption about the meaning of mental representations that underlie them, is a bone of contention to which we will keep returning throughout this journey. In Jaszczolt's (2005: 81) theory of Default Semantics (discussed in Section 7.2.3), 'it is assumed that there is some level or other of representing meaning that is compositional'. The principles of composition proposed there acknowledge various linguistic and non-linguistic sources of information that combine to compose meaning – 'real meaning', as intended, recovered, and often to some extent jointly constructed by the interlocutors (or *co-constructed*, see mainly Section 8.4.1.1). We don't yet have a fully worked-out compositional theory of multimodal semantics but it is a start. Likewise, David Dowty (2007: 27) suggests that we should not ask *whether* a natural language is compositional but *how* it is compositional:

I propose that we let the term NATURAL LANGUAGE COMPOSITIONALITY refer to *whatever strategies and principles we discover that natural languages actually do employ to derive the meanings of sentences, on the basis of whatever aspects of syntax and whatever additional information (if any) research shows that they do in fact depend on*. Since we do not know what all those are, we do not at this point know what 'natural language compositionality' is really like; it is our goal to figure that out by linguistic investigation. Under this revised terminology, there can be no such things as 'counterexamples to compositionality', but there will surely be counterexamples to many particular hypotheses we contemplate as to the form that it takes.

But what if the semantics of conceptual structures is compositional, but the semantics of the written or spoken natural-language structures is not? Recall the discussion of

---

[8] See Szabó 2000.

## 3.4 Semantic Composition and Semantic Types

Stephen Schiffer's proposal in Section 1.3, who tentatively suggests that a mode of presentation (say, a way of thinking about the planet Venus as The Morning Star or The Evening Star in our examples (1.18)–(1.21)) be added to the logical form of belief reports. But having suggested this, he makes a sharp U-turn in his argument and says that it is like adding something unknown, and hence it is not a solution: we don't know what such modes of presentation are. English language may not have a compositional semantics after all (more about this in Section 5.5). Now, if the natural-language system is at the same time the language of thought, then all is well: we go 'higher up' and represent what is in these thoughts. But if it is not, or if we have to rely on some additional modalities that supplement it, such as images or memories of actions, then we are in trouble. Equally, on the level of spoken and written natural-language sentences, we may attain compositional semantics only if we incorporate information from gestures, mental representations of objects, that is ways of thinking about these objects (like in the 'Venus' example). The semantics has to be compositional to capture the productivity of language and its systematicity but it may have to be sought 'higher up', where language meets other modalities, other 'vehicles' through which thoughts are conducted and expressed. So, compositionality may have to be sought on the level of thoughts, or on the level of the use of language in discourse, or on the level of situations in the world that language relates to. But then, if other modalities participate in the composition of meaning, the sentence merely reflects compositionality to some degree, as one of the participants of a bigger pool of 'meaning makers'. So we are left with a big question: the semantics of *what*? More about this in Section 7.2.3, where such compositionality will be assumed in the theory of Default Semantics.[9] Be that as it may, I have already argued that the tools we are assessing during this stage of the journey can in principle be utilized for compositional meaning on any level, regardless of the initial intent of its inventors. After all, this is a journey to discover meaning and not just to trace its historical footprints.

Having discussed the philosophy behind the compositionality of meaning, let us now proceed with type-theoretic language and with the question as to how it caters for the composition of meaning. I have already pointed out that semantic types mirror syntactic types here. We begin by introducing *categorial grammars* where the principle of compositionality is particularly conspicuous. We owe the concept of categorial grammar to the German philosopher Edmund Husserl and his *Logical Investigations*.[10] There are different versions of such grammars currently on the market but here is the gist. First, we introduce two entities: a name, the bearer of reference (N) and a sentence, the bearer of truth value (S), as the two basic categories. We take N as an argument for a function that produces S as its value. For example, the analysis of (3.52) is presented in Figure 3.1.

(3.52)    Daniel sneezed loudly.

---

[9] See also Jaszczolt 2005 and 2010 for a full exposition of this view. See Recanati 2004 (esp. p. 132) for the idea of pragmatic compositionality.

[10] In addition to Husserl (1970) [1900–1901], other important figures in the development of categorial grammar are Leśniewski, Ajdukiewicz, Bar-Hillel, and Cresswell, among others.

## 3 Composing Sentence Meaning

```
        Daniel sneezed loudly.
                 S
             /       \
            /         \
           N          S/N
                    /     \
                   /       \
                 S/N      (S/N)/(S/N)
        Daniel  sneezed    loudly
```

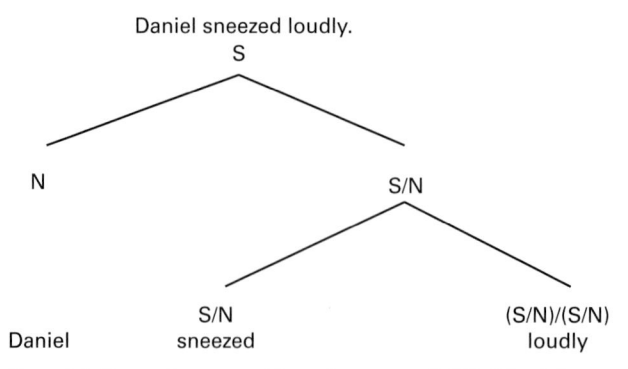

**Figure 3.1** Syntactic composition of sentence (3.52) ('Daniel sneezed loudly.') in categorial grammar, using basic categories N and S and derived categories

The *basic categories* (basic syntactic types) are S and N. Other categories are *derived categories* (derived syntactic types). Some of the most common ones are listed in (3.53), with examples.

(3.53)  S/S           necessarily, possibly, not
        S/SS          and, or, if ... then, iff
        S/N           runs, sneezed
        (S/N)/(S/N)   fast, carefully, slowly, loudly
        S/(S/N)       someone, everyone
        (S/N)/N       likes

We read them from right to left. For example, 'runs' takes a name as its argument and renders a sentence; 'and' takes two sentences and renders one sentence; 'fast' takes a derived category (S/N) and renders a derived category of the same type (S/N). In other words, 'fast' takes an intransitive verb and renders a verb phrase. In this way we can show the structure of the sentence exceptionally clearly by using only two basic notions: S and N – much more clearly than in traditional grammars of natural language with their many somewhat arbitrarily named category labels and their not so perspicuous rules of combination. In categorial grammar, just two basic categories, S and N, are all we need to build the entire edifice of sentence structure – there is no need for adding VPs, APs, and so forth – and as such no need to learn what such category labels mean. The labels themselves tell us everything we need to know about composition: 'runs' is of a category that requires a nominal category to make up a sentence. So, it is S/N. For 'likes', we have a category label that says 'combines with a nominal category to render a category that itself needs a nominal category to make up a sentence', or (S/N)/N. In traditional parsing, a noun in the subject position combines with a verb phrase which itself is a combination of a noun in the object position with a verb. The latter sounds simple because this is the traditional parsing we are used to. But it does not give us as good an insight into the composition of meaning as the system where there are only two categories N and S popping up throughout the analysis.

## 3.4 Semantic Composition and Semantic Types

These are examples of syntactic types. Then, their semantic equivalents, the semantic types, tell us about the composition of meaning equally clearly: the label provides all the information we need. Here we have the following types: $<t>$ (truth value) as a semantic equivalent of S, $<e>$ for N, $<e,t>$ for S/N (a verbal category), and so forth, including $<e,<e,t>>$ for a two-place predicate (transitive verb), say, 'like', a semantic mirror image of (S/N)/N, and $<<e,t>,<e,t>>$ for an adverb that modifies the verbal category, such as 'loudly' (like in the case of its syntactic equivalent, it does not change the type: both 'sneezed' and 'sneezed loudly' require an expression of the $e$ type to make up the $t$ type. Quantifiers are of the type $<<e,t>,t>$ – they require an expression of the type $<e,t>$, i.e. a verbal category, to make up an expression of the type $t$ (a sentence). (Note that in the case of semantic types, we read from left to right.)

But we can go further. This is an extensional semantics, where meanings equal extensions, and we know already that truth value in a given world (model) won't yet give us all we need to get to the meaning. In (3.54), for example, or in reports on beliefs discussed earlier, we clearly require intensions.

(3.54)   Lidia thinks that the architect of La Sagrada Família was Catalan.

To reuse our scenario of La Sagrada Família from Section 2.5, Lidia can be thinking about Antoni Gaudí or about whoever happened to design that church. Or Lidia may be thinking about Gaudí but not know that he designed La Sagrada Família.

So, let us now unpack intensional semantics. Intensional semantics was first developed for artificial languages by Rudolf Carnap[11] and was brought to the fore of natural-language semantics by Richard Montague and his successors. It was Frege's idea of sense that gave rise to the concept of intension in the way that was described above as a 'bird's eye' view over possible worlds. It can be thought of as a formalization of Frege's sense applied to a range of syntactic categories. But, several decades on, we are implementing it more broadly than the original Fregean–Montagovian intent. We can make intension stand not just for objective senses, but also for personal ways of thinking or psychological modes of presentation just discussed. 'Intension' is a flexible construct: like truth conditions, it can be adapted and reused for different kinds of meaning that a semanticist chooses to pursue.

But let us go back to the basics. First, let us summarize the relation between extensions and intensions discussed in Section 3.3. Intensions are functions from possible worlds to extensions. The extension of a common noun (*dog*) is a set of individuals (dogs); the intension is a mapping from possible worlds to such sets of individuals. The extension of a sentence is a truth value (true, false), while the intension of a sentence is a proposition – where a proposition is a mapping (a function) from possible worlds to truth values. If we mark truth value by the extensional type (i.e. category) $t$, and entities by the type $e$, then intensions of sentences are marked by $<s, t>$, where $s$ is the intensional type corresponding to the extensional type $t$. Intensions of names are marked by $<s, e>$. Similarly, intensional types are added to other derived categories. Needless to say, the derivation can get complicated when

---

[11] In Carnap's (1956) [1947] *Meaning and Necessity*.

we want to represent this need for intensions – and we want to do it for the reasons just discussed with the help of example (3.54). Then, we have to stipulate that arguments of derived types are not extensions but intensions. In other words, they are mappings (functions) from intensions rather than extensions. (The 'Superman' example in (3.57) later in this section demonstrates why it can be important to use <s,e> rather than <e>.)

Intensions percolate through the tree. Introducing intensions of names in lieu of their extensions has the consequence of altering other derived categories, like a domino effect in the semantic analysis tree. For example, 'sneezed' now has the extension ≪s, e>, t> instead of the basic extension <e, t>, i.e. it incorporates the intension of the name (<s,e>). Its own intensional type is now <s, ≪s, e>, t≫, following the 'percolation' of intensions (adding 's' at the beginning). But even when intensions are added, the mirroring of syntactic types is still transparent, as can be observed from comparing Figure 3.1 with Figure 3.2. The historical legacy that *syntactic* types are read from right to left, while semantic types are read from left to right, is a nuisance. At least *semantic* types (and we need only these in semantics) are more intuitive; they can be read as tracking the composition 'towards the sentence as a unit' so to speak – that is, what we need, from left to right, to make up a sentence.

The top category remains the extensional <t> rather than <s, t> when the sentence is straightforwardly extensional. In other words, when taken in isolation, S corresponds to <t> and N to <e>. But if we prefix sentence (3.52) with a modal adverb as in (3.55), or embed it in a propositional attitude construction, as in (3.56), we obtain an intensional construction and with it all the problems of *The Morning Star–The Evening Star* kind. So, we need to bring intension, <s,t>, to the rescue.

(3.55)  Possibly, Daniel sneezed loudly.

(3.56)  Anna believes that Daniel sneezed loudly.

'Possibly' and 'Anna believes that' operate on the intension of the following sentence. The adverb 'possibly' makes us think of a possible world or state of affairs in which Daniel sneezed. In other words, it relativizes the sentence to possible worlds rather than to one actual world. Likewise, the belief operator in (3.56) relativizes the sentence to possible (belief) worlds. In other words again, the intension (the proposition) serves in lieu of an extension (the truth value) in these contexts. Other categories follow suit.

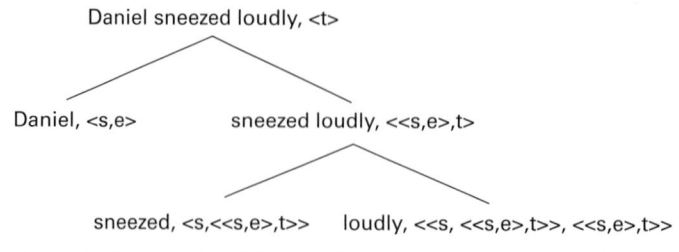

```
              Daniel sneezed loudly, <t>
                       /\
                      /  \
          Daniel, <s,e>    sneezed loudly, <<s,e>,t>
                                   /\
                                  /  \
                     sneezed, <s,<<s,e>,t>>   loudly, <<s, <<s,e>,t>>, <<s,e>,t>>
```

**Figure 3.2** Composition of the meaning of sentence (3.52) ('Daniel sneezed loudly.') in intensional semantics

## 3.4 Semantic Composition and Semantic Types

In fact, even simple sentences ascribing properties may require intensions. I can utter (2.5), repeated below (still reusing the same scenario), in the full knowledge that I am speaking about Antoni Gaudí or about whoever the architect of that church was. And we may want our semantics to be sensitive to this fact.

(2.5)   The architect of this church was mad.

Moreover, proper names, often regarded as labels with constant extensions across possible words (for the reasons we will go into in Stage 6), may require intensions as well, as was convincingly argued by Jennifer Saul with the help of her example (3.57). For readers unfamiliar with the story: Superman, who has supernatural powers, is the alter ego of Clark Kent, who is an ordinary, inconspicuous man. The names refer to the same person. This is a more intuitive instantiation of *The Morning Star–The Evening Star* story but, crucially, there is no context of a belief report here.

(3.57)   Clark Kent went into the phone booth and Superman came out.

(from Saul 2007: viii)[12]

Intensional semantics allows us to represent the meaning of *any* sentence as an intension ($<s,t>$) – a proposition, a mapping from possible worlds to extensions ($<t>$). Intensional contexts are not just a structurally delimited category. Standardly, they are sentences that either use specific intensional verbs such as *think* or sentences in the scope of a propositional attitude verb ('A believes that *p*') or a modal or temporal adverbial ('Possibly, *p*'; 'In 1963, *p*'). Selecting them as 'special' keeps senses and intensions at bay and keeps the rest of the semantics simple. Intensional semantics delivers what Frege suggested in his seminal nineteenth-century paper 'On sense and reference': senses replace referents in belief and other propositional attitude reports, as well as in other constructions where substitution is not truth-preserving (*salva veritate*) – that is, in intensional contexts. But, as we have seen, it also does much more: any context can be an intensional context, and intensional semantics has devices to capture this. This complication of added intensions makes the semantics more powerful in that it now accounts for all contexts in which the 'routes to the extensions' are as important as the extensions themselves.[13] But intensional semantics can do even more than that. Arguably, formal semantic tools, such as those that we trace back to Frege, Carnap, or Montague, could meet the demands of cognitively real semantic objects of study. Intensions are even more powerful and important than the great masters allowed them to be. Not only is there no clear extensional context/intensional context distinction, as we can see from (3.57), but neither is there a need to stipulate that intensions are some objective, magical constituents of semantic composition that give us objectivist semantics. We

---

[12] First argued by Saul in her 1997 and more extensively in Saul 2007.
[13] Type theory has inspired various novel approaches. Fox and Lappin 2005 offers their own theory, with their own take on intensions and types (this is advanced reading with a computational linguistics angle).

can very well use them to reflect people's modes of presentation of referents and people's truth-value judgements. Food for thought.

## 3.5 Type-Theoretic Metalanguage and Lambda Abstraction

As I said, Montague semantics makes use of truth conditions, possible worlds, and model theory as its tools, so we have already discussed the benefits of that aspect of it. We have also discussed the benefits of intensional semantics for semantic composition. What we have left to discuss for the purpose of this journey is the gist of how Montague's intensional language works in practice, and in particular one important tool it has at its disposal, namely an operator on sets.

First of all, expressions such as 'happy'', 'sneeze'', or 'like'' are translations of natural-language expressions into the language used in Montague's intensional logic. To reiterate, what we gain by it is being able to generalize about truth conditions. More specifically, we can generalize that, say, 'Someone sneezes' is true of a (any given) model and on an (any given) assignment function (about which there will be more shortly) if and only if there is at least one individual in the extension of 'sneeze'' in that model. The models, that is, the 'vignettes' of relevant parts of possible worlds, allow for an automatic application of such a procedure, envisaged over models of any number and any content. The basics of the notation are as follows. For example, $[\![\text{sneeze}']\!]^{M,g}$ stands for the interpretation of 'sneeze'' (our earlier 'Sneeze') in model $M$ under the assignment $g$. The assignment function starts with the domain of all variables *in the language* (that is, expressions whose extensions we provide for each model in which they are instantiated) and maps them onto entities in a particular model. As such, it will also have in its domain expressions whose extension is empty on some models. This allows us to specify the truth conditions in a formal manner, as in (3.58): 'Somebody sneezes' is true (represented as '1') in a model $M$ if and only if there is a $g$ of which it is true for at least one member in that model – that is, if and only if there is at least one individual in the extension of sneeze' in $M$.

(3.58)  $\exists x\,[\text{sneeze}'(x)]^{M} = 1$ iff, for some $g$, $\exists x\,[\text{sneeze}'(x)]^{M,g}$ is true

Assigning individuals from the model $M$ to $x$ is then an automatic procedure: we do so for all individuals in the model $\{a, b, c, d\}$ until we find an assignment function $g$ that renders the value 'true'. The assignment function $g$ on which $x$ is substituted with $a$, that is, $[\![x]\!]^{M,g} = a$, or with $d$, that is, $[\![x]\!]^{M,g} = d$, shows that $\exists x\,[\text{sneeze}'(x)]$ is true in $M$.

Now we can introduce one more important tool that, as we shall see, makes the metalanguage more adequate for representing the logical structure of natural-language sentences. This tool allows us to abstract over sets. While quantifiers bind individuals, the *lambda operator* ($\lambda$) binds sets. For this reason, it is also called an *abstraction operator* or a *set operator*. For example, in (3.59), $\lambda$ binds the variable $x$ and it reads 'the set of happy individuals', 'the property of being happy', or, better reflecting the structure, 'the set of $x$s such that $x$ is happy'. We also say that $\lambda$ 'abstracts over $x$' here.

## 3.5 Type-Theoretic Metalanguage and Lambda Abstraction

(3.59)    $\lambda x\,[\text{happy}'(x)]$

The lambda operator is not part of first-order predicate logic. It belongs to type theory whose utility in representing the composition of meaning we discussed in the previous section. It was introduced to logic by Alonzo Church.[14] It is part of type-theoretic metalanguage in that it is used for representing properties as abstract sets and as such showing different layers of structure. So, (3.59) is a way of writing formally 'the property of being happy'. It also shows what its extensional type is: it is a predicate that requires one argument in order to become a sentence. In other words, this functional type is a mapping, or a function, from entities to truth values – the semantic type <e,t> familiar from the last section, also sometimes written as $e \rightarrow t$. For example, from our model in Section 3.3, where the extension of 'happy', that is, $[\![\text{happy}']\!]^M$, was given in (3.46), now written as (3.60), we can choose, say, the individual constant $a$ (Anna) as in (3.61a) to say that Anna is happy – that is, that $a$ instantiates the property of being happy.

(3.60)    $[\![\text{happy}']\!]^M$:    $\{a, b, c, d\}$

(3.61a)   $\lambda x\,[\text{happy}'(x)]\,(a)$

This is de facto an operation of substituting $a$ for $x$ that is in the scope of the lambda operator: from a general property of being happy we get to predicating it of a particular individual (Anna), as in (3.61b). This operation is called *lambda conversion*.

(3.61b)   $\text{happy}'(a)$

Next, lambda abstraction allows us to represent a two-place predicate, such as the transitive verb *like*, as in (3.62).

(3.62)    $\lambda x\,\lambda y\,[\text{like}'(x,y)]$

The semantic type is <e, <e,t>>, also sometimes written as $e \rightarrow (e \rightarrow t)$. It requires an entity ($e$) to make up a category ($e,t$). In more familiar terms of grammatical parsing, a verb requires a nominal element (an object) to make up a verb phrase, which in turn requires a nominal element (a subject) to make up a sentence. But, as we have seen, composing meaning in terms of types that use only $e$ and $t$ as basic categories gives us a much better insight into compositionality than the standard myriad grammatical categories with their obscured rules of combination.

To use our model from Section 3.3 again, and in particular the extension for like' as in (3.63), modified from (3.48), we can get to a true sentence, for example *Anna likes Bill*, by performing lambda conversion as in (3.64). First we set out the scene: we want to substitute $x$ with $a$ (for Anna) and $y$ with $b$ (for Bill). In Step 1, we perform abstracting over $x$ and obtain 'the property of Anna's liking someone/something' (semantic type <e,t>). In other words, the expression is of a type that requires an entity ($e$) to render a sentence. The sentence is marked by '$t$' in that in the semantic analysis it renders a truth value, and the truth value (extension) allows us to get to the meaning of

---

[14] See Church 1940.

the sentence (the intension, the proposition). In Step 2, we abstract over $y$ and obtain 'the property of Bill's being liked by someone' (type $<e, <e,t>>$). In other words, we fill in the entity (the first $e$) in the object position ('likes Bill') to obtain a type $<e,t>$ that requires another entity (the subject, Anna, the second $e$) to render a sentence ($t$). (We have done the latter in Step 1 – which shows that the order of the steps is optional: we could have started with Step 2, followed by Step 1). Put together, the result is the last line of (3.64).

(3.63)    $[\![like']\!]^M$:    $\{<a, b>, <c, a>, <d, c>\}$

(3.64)    $\lambda x \lambda y [like'(x,y)] (a)(b)$
          Result of Step 1:    $\lambda y [like'(a,y)] (b)$
          Result of Step 2:    $like'(a,b)$

The lambda operator also allows us to go 'higher' in that it also operates on properties: $\lambda P \lambda x [P(x)]$, where '$P$' is a variable over properties, and $x$, as usual, an individual variable, says 'the set of $x$s that have property $P$'. As before, through lambda conversion (first for $P$, and then for $x$) we can get to a sentence – say, to use our model again, *Cesar is a cat*. Using the theory of types, and as such introducing steps in the conversion, brings us closer to representing how the structure of the language (here: English) works. It shows that the structure is hierarchical: we have the subject ('Anna') that is required by the verb phrase to make up a sentence. In a separate operation of lambda conversion, we provide an object that is required by the verb to make up a verb phrase, which then is ready to take that subject to make up the sentence – a semantics mirroring natural-language syntax.

We shall not be 'doing semantics hands-on' in this philosophical journey through meaning; all that matters is understanding the gist of it, the idea behind these proposals so that, in the more 'pragmaticky' stages of the journey, we can build on the assumption that compositional theories of meaning do indeed take us considerably far towards the end point. The composition of types out of just two simple semantic categories $e$ and $t$ (or three, including $s$ for intensional types) allows for an exceptional insight into the composition of meaning.

## 3.6 Formal Tools and Cognitive Reality

On the flipside, the proposals discussed here are not very informative about word meaning. The edifice of such a semantics simply gives us intensions, or bunches of extensions across worlds, to answer what word meaning is. And here is where the journey through sentence meaning meets up with the journey through word meaning pursued in Stage 2. If we want cognitive reality, we need to adjust and reapply the tools. We need to apply them to cognitive structures, often multimodal, and as such also to their units – mental equivalents of words. Concepts understood as mental representations (that is, cognitively real units) will then paradoxically be given a semantics that boasts little cognitive reality: concepts, intensions, are bunches of extensions across endless imaginary worlds and endless formal models. But at least the tools are so powerful that we obtain an overwhelmingly precise answer to the question as to what concepts so construed are – once we have climbed the edifice and got the 'bird's eye' view. Then we can, arguably, start doing grassroots semantics of conceptual structures rather than just semantics of sentences as abstract units. And we have to combine it with doing lexical semantics if compositionality is to be sought there, on the level of conceptual structures. Food for thought. Meaning hunters are not there yet and they won't be there for some time. There is a lot left to think about and to do.

Needless to say, attempts to combine cognitive semantics with formal methods of semantics of sentences are not common. Such eclecticism may even be frowned upon as 'picking and choosing', mixing different sets of assumptions, such as that of objectivism and subjectivism. But these are not mixed at random. Recalling my earlier knife and fork metaphor, we are simply proposing to eat a big, 'real' meal, a meal that people are likely to want (viz. psychologically real, intuitive meaning) with the tools that were originally designed for a smaller, 'minimalist' meal, consisting only of the elements of the language *system*. But, according to this journey, the tools are likely to be strong enough to be bent and reused in this way – reused for the 'right' kind of meaning, the meaning that one wants to pursue.

We can do so because, while composition of meaning is a fact without which we would not be able to use languages for any purpose, the composition of meanings in a language *system* alone is not there unless we are prepared to sacrifice cognitive plausibility. As was very aptly summarized by Ray Jackendoff (2012: 63), '[t]he meaning of a compound expression (a phrase, sentence, or discourse) is a function of the meanings of its parts, of the grammatical rules by which they are combined – and of other stuff'. And this 'other stuff' is quite diversified, but at the same time quite typical of natural languages. As Jackendoff adds, 'these things aren't blemishes on language, they're integral to its texture' (p. 64). This 'stuff' is not merely needed in modal and propositional attitude contexts but also, for example, in (3.57) above or in reference transfer as in (3.65). The symbol '≫' stands for 'communicates'.

(3.65)     Kasia likes Ian McEwan.
        ≫ Kasia likes books by Ian McEwan.

Arguably, it is also needed for propositions that are indirectly communicated, as for example B's response in (3.66) in that the main intended (and recovered) message, or the functional proposition, is often communicated indirectly. Notice that in (3.66), the logical form for that main message is not a translation of B's sentence into the metalanguage but of what was indirectly communicated by B and inferred by the addressee. The concept of a functional proposition we entertained in Section 1.3 can capture such meanings as primary messages.

(3.66)   A:     Do you want to go to Starbucks and have some coffee?
        B:     I have a lecture in five minutes.
             ≫ B can't go to Starbucks.

And if there is such a structured proposition, so there can be compositionality and the tools can be adapted to work on it. As I mentioned earlier, this 'other stuff' will also have to include dynamic meaning – meaning that 'grows' as discourse progresses and meaning that is negotiated between the interlocutors rather than intended and passively recovered (these are attended to in Stages 6 and 7). The remainder of this journey through semantics and pragmatics will show that the tools we have accumulated through formal approaches are sufficiently strong and flexible. But we have to remember that having such a cognitively real formal semantics/pragmatics is still far from being an accomplished task. Looking on the bright side, the philosophy behind it is there already, for various journeys through meaning to build on.

**Suggested Further Reading**
Since this is not an introduction to first-order logic, nor even to any particular formal semantic theory of natural language, we are only trying to capture here the gist of powerful tools that can eventually, when the journey is complete, take us to answers to such questions as (i) what *kinds of meaning* are worth distinguishing in semantics and (ii) *what meaning is* when delimited in these ways. For a more in-depth introduction to these tools, see e.g. Jacobson's (2014) *Compositional Semantics: An Introduction to the Syntax/Semantics Interface* or Henriëtte de Swart's (1998) still staple *Introduction to Natural Language Semantics*. These books offer self-contained courses through formal semantic methods. Also, Chapters 1–4 of Cann, Kempson, and Gregoromichelaki's (2009) *Semantics: An Introduction to Meaning in Language* offer a concise introduction. On truth conditions, see also Kearns' (2011) *Semantics*, Section 1.3. For a philosophical introduction to compositionality, see Szabó 2020. To think about compositionality of meaning from different perspectives see also articles in Werning, Hinzen, and Machery's (2012) *The Oxford Handbook of Compositionality* and in Barker and Jacobson's (2007) *Direct Compositionality*. Pragmatic, conceptual composition of meaning is also discussed in Section 7.2.3 and in more depth in Jaszczolt's (2005) *Default Semantics*. For an introduction to type theory see Chapter 4 of Dowty et al.'s (1981) classic *Introduction to Montague Semantics*. The book is still an unbeatable, step-by-step, in-depth introduction to Montague's intensional semantics. Also, Chapters 4 and 5 of Cann's (1993) *Formal Semantics: An Introduction*; again Chapter 6 of Jacobson (2014); Chapter 3 of Cann et al. (2009); or, for a brief and user-friendly summary of the idea behind types, Chapter 7.6 of Allan's (2001) *Natural Language Semantics*.

Detailed, including advanced, reading suggestions for particular problems and ideas were given in the footnotes as we moved along, following the 'two-tier' template for this journey through meaning.

# Stage 4   Operations on Sentences

## 4.1   Sentential Connectives and Propositional Logic

We now move to an example of how employing a formal metalanguage helps with analysing, and as such also often precisifying, the meaning of natural-language expressions. As was indicated in Stage 3 of the journey, we will now continue introducing and employing the devices of standard first-order logic for this purpose. The connectives of propositional logic are a good example to start with here. (We can also in the process assess the adequacy of first-order logic as a source of metalanguage for natural-language semantics.) Their meaning is constant and can be specified precisely. So, if they fitted as translations of English (and other natural-language) operations on sentences, then their adequacy would be formidable. They do not, but, arguably, they fit sufficiently well to provide a springboard for their semantics – a pragmatics-rich, contextualist semantics. This fit and misfit are what this stage of our journey through meaning is about. Among others, we will have to assess how close logical conjunction $p \land q$ takes us to the meaning of '$S_1$ and $S_2$', '$S_1$ but $S_2$', sentence-initial 'But $S_1$', or a juxtaposition of sentences '$S_1$. $S_2$', where '$S_1$' and '$S_2$' stand for sentences of English (or clauses, when conjoined). As was said in Section 3.2, in addition to conjunction (approximately corresponding to 'and'), the metalanguage of propositional logic that is standardly used for this purpose also contains disjunction (approximately corresponding to 'or'), implication (approximately corresponding to 'if ... then'), equivalence (approximately corresponding to 'only if'), and, perhaps surprisingly, also negation ('not', 'it is not the case that'). I will discuss these operators one by one, assessing their utility for their English equivalents. We are going to look at relations between simple sentences and see how the truth value of a complex sentence is determined by the truth values of its constituent sentences and the sentential connective that joins them. I say 'sentence' but, of course, in contextualist semantics we will also use this tool to join utterances or conceptual structures. To use the correct semantic terminology, we can join minimal propositions that sentences express or, alternatively, propositions that they actually convey in the context. Predictably, the analysis will show that while logical connectives help illuminate the meaning of their English counterparts, there are also aspects of meaning of the latter that are 'lost in translation'.

First, there are many more connectives in natural languages than in the metalanguage. To name a few, *but, therefore, because, since, after all, moreover, so, before, as, even though* do not have obvious equivalents. At best, we can render their meaning periphrastically: '$S_1$ but $S_2$', for example, can be translated as '$(p \land q) \land$ Contrast $(p, q)$'. There is no direct translation of a contrastive conjunction *but*. This caveat is the result of the fact that we are borrowing a formal language and using it for a task for which it was not designed. Logicians are interested in finding a perfect artificial language to capture the rules of inference, whereas linguists are adopting (and adapting!) these languages to serve their own purpose: to pursue meaning in natural language and elucidate its composition. The truth conditions that are automatically associated with formulae containing these connectives provide linguists with a way of analysing the meaning of English sentences for which they serve as translations. But, to reiterate, this takes us only part of the way; English connectives don't translate that easily.

As I have indicated, some instances of *but* or *and* are sentence-initial or even discourse-initial. These are *discourse connectives* and belong to a larger category of *discourse markers*:[1] expressions that are commonly used in the initial position of an utterance and are syntactically detachable from a sentence, such as in (4.1) and (4.2).

(4.1)   Lidia has moved to Oxford. *But* she promised to visit often.

(4.2)   The library at Trinity College, Cambridge is impressive. *After all*, it was designed by Christopher Wren.

While we normally think of their meaning in terms of the *concepts* they convey, according to one view they signal *procedures* for interpreting the oncoming sentence. In fact, they are likely to do both: convey a concept as well as direct the addressee to the correct path for recovering the meaning of the sentence that they introduce.[2] As their meaning cannot be captured by translating them directly into operators of propositional logic, they will not concern us here as a category. But (no pun intended!) they will pop up when we ask the 'higher-level' question as to what the logical connectives translate and what they leave behind.

I focus here on English as an example of a natural language (or object language to which the metalanguage is applied) simply because sentential connectives are most widely researched for the English language. But it will be easy to apply the same method to any other natural language and analyse the meaning of whatever connectives that language has – remembering that the inventory of connectives can differ from language to language and that the sense conveyed by a lexical item such as *if* or *and* in one language can be conveyed in another by some different means such as, respectively, modal verbs or the ordering of sentences. I return to the intra-linguistic differences in their meaning in Sections 4.2–4.4 and to cross-linguistic differences in expressing such connections in Section 4.6.

We can now start using the metalanguage of propositional logic introduced in Section 3.2 and see how far it will take us with the meaning of English sentential connectives. The five connectives in the metalanguage are translated as follows: conjunction ('$S_1$ *and* $S_2$') as $p \land q$; disjunction ('$S_1$ *or* $S_2$') as $p \lor q$;

---
[1] See e.g. Schiffrin 1987; Fraser 1990a, 1999.
[2] For the procedural vis-à-vis conceptual meaning of selected discourse markers, see e.g. Blakemore 2002.

implication (or conditional, '*If* S$_1$ *then* S$_2$') as $p \rightarrow q$; equivalence (or biconditional, 'S$_1$ *if and only if* S$_2$') as $p \leftrightarrow q$; and negation ('*It is not the case that* S') as $\neg p$. If the English sentence is composed of two or more constituent sentences (clauses), the first step in the translation procedure is to identify them and the connective which links them. Negation is an odd one out here. It is included because it is *sentential* negation; it attaches itself, so to speak, to the entire proposition, and hence it is an operator of propositional logic. These connectives have constant meaning in logic: they are *truth-functional*. This is what makes them somewhat different from their English counterparts, whose meaning is not so rigidly fixed. So, let us see how far the translation can take us and judge if it takes us sufficiently far to adopt this language of propositional logic as an adequate metalanguage.

## 4.2 Conjunction

Propositional logic stipulates that the meaning of conjunction is constant: it is a logical constant whereby $p \wedge q$ is true when both of its conjuncts, $p$ and $q$, are true. Truth tables are the simplest way to show this constant meaning. Table 4.1 makes it clear that the truth value of the compound depends only on the truth values of its conjuncts, nothing else, as long as $p$ and $q$ stand for propositions. Letters '$t$' and '$f$' stand for 'true' and 'false' (sometimes symbolized as 1 and 0 respectively). Conjunction is also sometimes written in a different notation, most commonly in linguistics as $p \mathbin{\&} q$.

So, sentence (4.3a) is true only if both (4.3b) and (4.3c) are true.

(4.3a)  Bill wrote a novel and posted it on the Internet.   $p \wedge q$

(4.3b)  Bill wrote a novel.   $p$

(4.3c)  Bill posted the novel on the Internet.   $q$

In addition to *and*, other connectives, such as *but*, are also translated as '$\wedge$'. However, the fit is not as good with *but* as with *and*: the meaning of contrast is lost in translation. If we want our translation into the metalanguage to be faithful, we will have to add this meaning somehow or other, using a different method. We can do so by translating it as '$(p \wedge q) \wedge \text{Contrast}\,(p, q)$', as in the previous section, or by accepting that the translation '$p \wedge q$' is fine but imperfect and has to be enhanced by a separate pragmatic analysis.

**Table 4.1** Truth table for conjunction in propositional logic

| $p$ | $q$ | $p \wedge q$ |
|---|---|---|
| t | t | t |
| t | f | f |
| f | t | f |
| f | f | f |

Moreover, English *and* can itself have a richer meaning than that of the logical conjunction. For example, (4.3a) above says not only that two events happened, but it also strongly suggests that they happened in the order in which they were stated: Bill wrote the novel first and then put in on the Internet. So, there is a sense of 'and then' there. Example (4.4a)–(4.4b) shows this clearly: Bill may strongly object to (4.4a) because he would never drink alcohol before driving, while accepting (4.4b).

(4.4a)   Bill had a G&T and drove home.

(4.4b)   Bill drove home and had a G&T.

In (4.5), there is a sense of a causal link: it is *because* Bill forgot to water the plant that it withered; there is a sense of 'and therefore' or 'and as a result'.

(4.5)   Bill forgot to water the plant and it withered.

But where do these meanings 'and then' and 'and as a result' come from? Are they just different meanings of the English *and*? It is unlikely: *and* itself does not strike us as ambiguous. Neither is it good practice to succumb to ambiguity of lexical items when more economical principles are available, as one of the gurus of Western pragmatics, Paul Grice (1989c: 47), reminds us in what he called a Modified Occam's Razor: 'Senses are not to be modified beyond necessity.'[3] And, according to Grice, a simpler explanation is to go along with propositional-logic analysis part of the way and give the temporal or causal 'add-ons' the status of *pragmatically implied* meanings. As post-Griceans later suggested, these are pragmatic meanings but at the same time meanings to which truth conditions are sensitive, to account for differences such as that between (4.4a) and (4.4b) or any other case of reversing the order $p \wedge q$ to $q \wedge p$, where the swap of the conjuncts produces differences in meaning. But I anticipate – there will be much more about such pragmatic 'add-ons' in Sections 7.2–7.3.

On the other hand, there are cases of clear ambiguity as in (3.35), repeated below.

(3.35)   Anna and Bill own a car.

The choice between the collective and the distributive reading, discussed in Section 3.2, is a case of a genuine ambiguity because it is only on the second, distributive, reading that *and* behaves like a sentential connective: Anne owns a car ($p$) and Bill owns a car ($q$). On the collective reading, we have only one simple sentence with a plural subject.

So, conjunction may sometimes lead to genuine ambiguity between sentential conjunction and conjunction within the noun phrase[4] as in (3.35). But even when it

---

[3] In Grice's (1989c) [1978] 'Further notes on logic and conversation'. The original Occam's razor is a principle in medieval scholastic philosophy saying that beings or entities should not be multiplied beyond necessity. More generally, William of Ockham (or Occam) proposed that where a simpler explanation is available, it is the preferred one, 'cutting' (by the metaphorical 'razor') the unnecessary assumptions or entities.

[4] My use of the term 'noun phrase' is non-committal: I don't invoke any particular syntactic theory at this point but merely use an explicit label that is in wide circulation.

doesn't, it does not appear to be uniformly truth-functional, as (4.4a)–(4.4b) and (4.5) seem to suggest. The logical form requires a great deal of adjustment or supplementing with pragmatic information in order to account for the meaning of these English sentences. It requires even more twisting to translate (4.6), which we normally understand as a conditional, as in (4.7), with a logical form in (4.8).

(4.6)   Touch me and I will hit you.

(4.7)   If you touch me, I will hit you.

(4.8)   $p \rightarrow q$

Or, we can even understand it as an act of threatening, as in (4.9).

(4.9)   Don't touch me! I can defend myself.

Since imperatives, unlike declaratives, do not have a straightforward translation into propositional or predicate logic and are better treated by different accounts, we will have to leave (4.9) until Section 8.3 and only note that *and* is not always what it seems to be.

There is an abundance of proposals concerning the semantics of English sentential connectives and an increasing number of works on connectives in other languages, as well as cross-linguistic accounts. I am going to say a little more about conjunction here than about disjunction or conditional (negation will detain us for other reasons) because I have already flagged here an overarching question that, *mutatis mutandis*, applies to them all: where do these extra meanings come from? If we try to go part-way towards solving the 'What is meaning?' question by applying a formal language, and by 'pretending' (this is what it feels like, doesn't it?) that semantics mirrors syntax and all is well, then it would only be fair to take a step back and ask: 'Perhaps the senses of temporal sequence ('and then') and causation ('and as a result') are in fact independent from the meaning of sentential *and*? Perhaps they come from somewhere else altogether? Let us look at (4.10) and (4.11) as slightly altered variants of (4.3a) and (4.5).

(4.10)   Bill wrote a novel. He posted it on the Internet.

(4.11)   Bill forgot to water the plant. It withered.

There is no 'and' there but the sense of temporal order and causal link remain. So, perhaps the metalanguage is not so bad after all? There is no unique, correct answer to this question. The aim of this journey through meaning agrees with the humanist outlook, that is, it opens up questions that lead to more questions and points out that there are many possible (and plausible) answers.

Examples (4.10) and (4.11) suggest that the semantics of sentential coordination using the English *and* may be best approached in the context of a wider phenomenon, in that the source of the temporal reading may lie outside the lexical item *and* itself. There are several approaches available on the market and the best way to address the question is to assess them briefly, in a 'shopper's guide' manner, taking into consideration not only the power and simplicity of the solutions but also how well they are grounded in empirical data.

It goes without saying that (4.3a), repeated below, says, or at least strongly suggests, that the second event took place after the first.

(4.3a)   Bill wrote a novel and posted it on the Internet.

While it can be argued that writing a novel has to logically precede publishing it, examples such as (4.12) also carry this sense of temporal ordering.

(4.12)   Anna and Bill had a baby and got married.

Likewise, there is no need for empirical testing in order to claim that (4.5), repeated below, says, or at least strongly suggests, that the second event is the consequence of the first. There is an asymmetrical, common-sense relation of dependence between the two events.

(4.5)   Bill forgot to water the plant and it withered.

We can often manipulate this dependence by providing a specific context, but such manipulation is difficult: the default reading where the second event temporally or causally depends on the first is quite entrenched. In the case of (4.3a), the situation evolves and an object (novel) is created: it cannot be put online before it is written. In the case of (4.12), it is likely that the sequence of events was foregrounded by this ordering of the conjuncts. In the case of (4.5), the situation also evolves: a living plant is now dead or nearly dead. We can perhaps try (4.13a), but then shortening (4.13a) to (4.5) would still be extremely misleading. Even a simple reversal of the order of the conjuncts as in (4.13b) would be better.

(4.13a)   ?Bill's favourite plant withered. He promised himself to rescue it by watering it immediately. But he forgot.

(4.13b)   Bill's plant withered and (even then) he forgot to water it (in order to rescue it).

On the other hand, a reversal of the order of simple sentences and juxtaposing them as in (4.14) retains the previous causal order in that the second sentence functions as an explanation of why the plant withered.

(4.14)   Bill's plant withered. He forgot to water it.

Since the 1970s and Grice's Modified Occam's Razor just mentioned, the temporal and causal meanings of *and* have frequently been ascribed not to what is said but to what is conversationally implied – a *conversational implicature* (which will be the topic of Section 7.1). To reiterate, post-Griceans attempted to reconcile our intuitions that, say, (4.4a) can be false and (4.4b) true – Bill can strongly object to the first while confirming the latter. So, the next move was to ask whether the temporal ordering, the 'and then' meaning was an entirely pragmatic 'top layer', so to speak, as Grice suggested, or rather a kind of pragmatic content that *does* make a difference to the truth conditions. In other words, it would be pragmatic but at the same time part of semantic, truth-conditional content.

Another question concerned the provenance of these rich readings of sentential *and*: are they inferred by the addressee in specific contexts or, rather, are they there due to some social, cultural, or linguistic conventions? Grice deemed temporal and causal senses to be derived from general principles of rationality of human conversational behaviour.[5] In neo-Gricean pragmatics, Stephen Levinson makes the relevant enriched meanings strongly dependent on the *system* of language:

Utterance-type meanings are matters of preferred interpretations ... which are carried by the structure of utterances, given the structure of the language, and not by virtue of the particular contexts of utterance. (Levinson 2000: 1)

Among these meanings are '$p$ and then $q$', '$p$ caused $q$', 'John intended $p$ to cause $q$'.[6] In a similar spirit, in his recent work 'First things first: The pragmatics of "natural order"', Laurence Horn discerns different patterns of coordination that follow conventional, or sometimes natural, principles for how ideas are ordered.[7] Going back to the works of Aristotle, Dionysius, and Quintilian, he discusses ordering with respect to (i) temporal order; (ii) causation or some other inherent order; (iii) attributed worth or value; and (iv) implication or presupposition of existence (such as what is backgrounded, what sets the stage comes before what is foregrounded and newly affirmed). (4.12) above exemplifies (i) and (4.5) exemplifies (ii). Examples of categories (iii) and (iv) are given in (4.15) and (4.16) respectively.

(4.15)  Take it or leave it.
         (cf. ?Leave it or take it.)

(from Horn 2019: 267)

(4.16)  Last but not least, ...
         (cf. ?Least but not last, ...)

(adapted from Horn 2019: 277)

This systematicity of ordering also permeates other accounts, such as Robyn Carston's in which she invokes stereotypical situations or scripts.[8]

Another solution comes from lexical semantics and advocates that the content of *and* is rich in the first place. According to the proposal by Jonathan Cohen from the 1970s, the meaning of the lexical item *and* comprises all of the standard richer senses which are then 'subtracted' from the interpretation whenever they are not relevant.[9]

In spite of some similarities, *and*-conjunction is not semantically identical with the juxtaposition of sentences; there are heavier restrictions on *and*. Although they are not as strong as those proposed in the so-called semantic command principle[10] whereby the second conjunct is claimed not to be prior to the first conjunct chronologically or

---

[5] See his 'Logic and conversation' (Grice 1989b [1975]).  [6] Adapted from Levinson 2000, p. 38.
[7] See Horn 2019.  [8] See e.g. Carston 1993, 1994, esp. pp. 41, 697; 2002, esp. p. 226.
[9] See Cohen 1971.
[10] See Bar-Lev and Palacas 1980, p. 141. For a discussion of counterexamples, see Bar-Lev and Palacas 1980 and Carston, e.g. 1993.

causally, there are many types of coordination where conjoining separate sentences with *and* does not normally work very well, as in (4.17a).

(4.17a)   Bill went for a walk and it was sunny.

It appears to sound natural only in the context where being sunny is focused on as, say, in a remark that contradicts someone's prediction – for example in emphasizing 'was' in (4.17b).

(4.17b)   Bill went for a walk and it *was* sunny after all.

So, perhaps it is *and* after all that should be credited with this extra meaning? Carston, in this context, points out that a '*p* and *q*' construction is a single syntactic unit and '[t]he simplest assumption to make here, surely, is that an utterance unit is in some fairly direct correspondence with a grammatical unit' (Carston 1993: 41). Juxtaposing two sentences does not create a single syntactic unit and as such will have different properties.

But there are other theories that foreground some other sources of this temporal ordering. Some focus on the aspectual class of the connected eventualities: whether they are, say, events, or rather static eventualities (states) or processes (eventualities without clear completion). Others emphasize the role of grammatical tenses in forming default interpretations. Yet others stay away from default, context-free interpretations and focus on listing the available readings. So, let us look at some more seminal approaches to propositional *and* coordination and see how they cater for different examples and problems. From now on, I will call it 'propositional' rather than 'sentential' coordination because one proposition can correspond to different stylistic variants of the sentence due to, say, anaphora (*he* for 'Bill', or *it* for 'Bill's plant') or ellipsis (' ... and [Bill] posted it on the Internet').

The temporal order of events such as that in (4.10) is often derived from the assumption of rationality of human communication and the maximization of coherence in discourse. Nicholas Asher and Alex Lascarides in their Segmented Discourse Representation Theory (SDRT) formalize coherence as so-called *rhetorical structure rules*.[11] (4.10) is explained by the rule of *Narration* that accounts for the temporal ordering of events: '[i]f narration ($\alpha$, $\beta$) holds, and $\alpha$ and $\beta$ describe the eventualities $e_1$ and $e_2$ respectively, then $e_1$ occurs before $e_2$' (Lascarides and Asher 1993: 443). The rule states only a strong but defeasible regularity: it can be overridden by the requirements of a particular context, or one can cancel the assumption of a temporal order by explicitly denying it or by some other clarification. Next, the rule *Result* caters for the causal connection as in (4.11). If there is no such dependence, we apply the rule *Parallel* that signals parallel events.[12] These three rules are then labelled 'coordinators'. For Asher and Lascarides, these temporal, causal, and other readings originate between pragmatics and grammar, in what they call *glue logic*. Glue logic captures

---

[11] See their *Logics of Conversation* (Asher and Lascarides 2003).
[12] See also Gómez Txurruka (2003), who proposes that Coordinated Discourse Topic is what underlies the functioning of these rules.

## 4.2 Conjunction

rules of defeasible (*non-monotonic*) reasoning – or, simply, 'if *p* then *normally q*'. Human reasoning uses glue language for connecting what is given as *information content* to *information packaging*. In other words, there is a logic of information content (of the juxtaposed propositions) and the logic of *how* they are presented in discourse. There are also rules that allow us to put together the content and the way it is presented – *Narration* and *Parallel* belong to the set of such rules. So does *Explanation*: this accounts for example for the order of events in (4.14). Next, when one of the juxtaposed sentences does not describe an event but, say, a state, we may have to resort to the rule of *Background*, as in (4.18). The state described in the second sentence temporally overlaps with the event in the first.

(4.18)   Anna went for a walk. It was sunny.

This view belongs to the group of theories of discourse coherence grounded in the objectives of computational linguistics.[13] They offer a mixed semantic/pragmatic solution in that they appeal to discourse participants' expectations of coherence. Various heuristics can lead to interpretative preferences that jointly result in coherence of discourse. But since these sometimes clash, common sense, world knowledge, and context may have to be invoked to explain the choices of interpretation. Asher and Lascarides' approach offers one of such proposals of a systematization of heuristics.

Understanding how this theory represents discourses will require foundations in dynamic semantics that are discussed in Section 6.1. What matters at the moment is to observe that ordering sentences carries meaning, and one of these orderings, that of events joined by *Narration*, carries the same meaning as one of those enriched senses of *and*: 'and then'. It follows that it would be methodologically prudent, and economical, to find an umbrella explanation for (4.3a) and (4.10) in spite of somewhat tighter restrictions on *and*-conjunction, as discussed in example (4.17a). It also follows that it is unlikely that we would want to ditch our metalanguage of propositional logic because *and* sometimes means 'and then'. Contrary to the mainstream tradition in semantics and pragmatics, it may not mean it after all: the culprit may be simply the ordering of the conjuncts.

Or, perhaps, we *should* ditch the metalanguage because it does not account for the meaning of the ordering? After all, $p \wedge q$ means the same in propositional logic as $q \wedge p$. But then, so it does in the case of some English sentences such as (4.19).

(4.19)   Bill swam the English Channel and climbed Snowdon.

When we enumerate Bill's various endeavours, the temporal ordering is likely to be neither intended nor recovered from the utterance. So, the take-home messages seem to be that (i) English conjunction can be, but need not be, richer in meaning than conjunction of propositional logic, but (ii) these additional aspects of meaning need not necessarily be pegged to the lexical item *and*; it is likely that they are derived from the assumption of rationality of human communication. If the order matters to events, then

---

[13] See e.g. Hobbs 1979, 1990; Kehler 2002; Kehler et al. 2008.

the order in which they are narrated is likely to mirror the order in which they occurred. The causal link is also likely to originate in rationality of communication: if the event types are by default linked as a cause and effect, then we can expect that this is what the speaker intended to communicate. Otherwise it would be misleading, and as such, irrational, to utter such a sentence, except for the very purpose of misleading itself. The final take-home message appears then to be that (iii) the metalanguage of propositional logic is a useful springboard but we have to supplement the logical form it throws up with an explanation that comes from rationality of human communication, following Grice and post-Griceans. In Stage 7 we will do precisely that.

Another way of explaining the temporal reading of *and*-conjunction is to ascribe it to linguistic conventions, and in particular to grammar. In their recent and much debated proposal, Ernie Lepore and Matthew Stone[14] suggest that in examples such as (4.20), the past tense of the verbs produces, by linguistic convention, the temporal succession reading of *and*.

(4.20)    Oil prices doubled and demand for consumer goods plunged.

(from Lepore and Stone 2015: 115)

As they say, Simple Past in English 'draws attention to the interval immediately afterwards' (p. 124). They also appeal to attention theory, according to which there is a ranking of candidates for interpretation by what is called the attentional state of discourse, and this ranking is reflected in the structure.[15] The attribution of the sequential reading to the grammatical tense becomes then a sub-case of a more general rule of ordering conjuncts. Like Asher and Lascarides, they appeal to the theories of coherence. But we have to remember that coherence theorists attribute a very small role to grammatical regularities in their overall lists of factors.

Lepore and Stone's proposal takes a lot on trust, and leaves a lot out. First, even if the past tense does indeed have a role to play, this can't simply be assumed without proper testing. (4.21) appears to have an equally strong default 'and then' and 'as a result' interpretation in spite of deploying future tense.

(4.21)    Bill will get a job in the City of London and make a lot of money.

Even if we argue that the proposed readings are due to the default scenarios or sociocultural knowledge, we could argue analogously about (4.20). In the case of (4.20), we could equally appeal to non-linguistic conventions, such as social or cultural conventions, to report events in the order in which they occurred, or to rationality of human cognition and communication. So, Lepore and Stone's proposal does not appear to generalize seamlessly. Jaszczolt and Sileo have recently demonstrated that non-past verb forms can also easily trigger temporal ordering readings even in context-free environments.[16] Their theoretical discussion of the phenomenon, supported with

---

[14] In Lepore and Stone 2015.
[15] See especially Centering Theory: Grosz, Joshi, and Weinstein 1995; Grosz and Sidner 1998, and other contributions to Walker, Joshi, and Prince 1998.
[16] See Jaszczolt and Sileo 2021.

several case studies of *and*-conjunction, lead them to the conclusion that the 'and then' reading ought to be captured on a higher level of generalization, in that although grammatical tense plays some part, it does not provide the full picture of the phenomenon. They studied consultants' judgements when sentences with propositional *and*-conjunction were placed in different context conditions (biasing to temporal reading, biasing to atemporal reading, and context-free) and concluded that there are many different factors that sway the judgement to the default temporal interpretation, even out of context. Apart from the default scenarios just mentioned, they tentatively propose that the degree of eventhood affects the probability of the temporal or causal interpretation of *and* coordination. This claim is compatible with the differences in the application of rhetorical structure rules in SDRT when (a) two events or (b) an event and a state are juxtaposed. (See examples (4.10) and (4.18) above and further discussion in the context of dynamic semantics in Section 6.1.)

Now, the fact is that what looks like a battle of opposing views is in fact working towards a more or less uniform explanation, in that pragmatic and grammatical solutions are not entirely separable; it is only a matter of different emphasis and the scope with which their proponents approach the phenomenon. Back in the 1970s, Barbara Partee[17] proposed that tenses are structurally analogous to pronouns in that they contain information about how eventualities are ordered in relation to one another in conjoined sentences. If the temporal reading can be explained by invoking variables pertaining to tense in the syntactic representation, then saying that it is the connective *and* that carries this meaning becomes superfluous: at most, the 'and then' meaning of *and* is an emergent property – emerging from the syntactic properties of the conjoined sentence.

While Lepore and Stone focus on the role of grammar to see how far one can go with linguistic conventions, Gricean pragmatics focuses on situations of discourse, embracing a wide spectrum of uses of propositional *and*. Without entirely discrediting grammar as a source of generalizations, Griceans take a 'bird's eye' view to see whether, from a higher vantage point – a vantage point pertaining to the activities of discourse interactants – there is a broader picture to be had. At the same time, it has to be remembered that a direct comparison would not do justice to either of the views in that, as has already been emphasized, they set their objectives somewhat differently: investigating the power of grammar and investigating rationality of discourse 'top-down', respectively. These differences also reflect their respective stances on the question of ambiguity. Griceans remain faithful to Modified Occam's Razor and do not postulate multiple meanings of *and* – not only because they can be pragmatically explained but, more importantly, because hearers do not go through a list of options before settling on one sense in the process of utterance interpretation. On the other hand, proponents of the grammatical-convention view belong to the computational-linguistic tradition, whereby listing meanings extracted from big data, from large corpora of language use, is what is needed. Multiple senses of *and*, regularities that

---

[17] See her seminal 'Some structural analogies between tenses and pronouns in English' (Partee 2004 [1973]).

a machine can learn, take preference over the psychological reality of human discourse interactants. And this is as it should be: different objectives justify different assumptions and different emphases.

The purpose of this detour through the vagaries of sentential *and* was to demonstrate that there are lots of different generalizations one can arrive at when one looks at how speakers use sentential conjunction in discourse and asks what exactly they mean by it. To take our journey back to the main track, we have to ask again whether the logical conjunction of the metalanguage, with its fixed, truth-functional meaning, is of sufficient use in this enterprise. Arguably, on this journey, it is – and so is it in most state-of-the-art journeys through meaning that aim at normativity. It provides a logical form that either elucidates the truth conditions, and as such the meaning that we search for, or at least provides a springboard for some richer meanings of an expression with sentential coordination. As to whether this sense resides in the lexical item *and*, or rather in the grammatical structure, or else in some rules of rational communicative behaviour, this detour allows us to appreciate that there are a myriad different answers that appeal to different levels of generalization and aim at eating a bigger or a smaller pie – that is, they aim at rules that apply to a bigger or a smaller sample of uses. The rules can apply either (i) only to sentence meaning as guaranteed by the lexicon and grammar of the language, or (ii) also to meanings that are conveyed by these sentences in discourse where *and*-conjunction can be put to very different uses. That is as it should be, and is reassuring. When we ask about the meaning of *and*, we may overlook sentence juxtaposition '$S_1.S_2$'; when we ask about how we narrate events in conversation, we consider various ways of doing so – with, and without, the connective. When we search for a psychologically real account of conversation, we go to a 'bird's eye' view and seek rules that tell us what speakers do. When we want to train machines, we start with listing the interpretations encountered in the corpora. Whatever we want to search, the metalanguage can provide the representation: a representation of the English sentence where '$S_1$ and $S_2$' is translated as '$p \wedge q$', or a representation of some other construction where the concept conveyed is that of '$p$ and $q$'. Propositional logic is a flexible tool that we can apply to structures of English but also to structures of thought – conceptual structures that sometimes match the structure of English sentences and at other times depart from them a little, or a lot – a progression that the 'and then', 'and as a result', but also 'if ... then' interpretations (in example (4.6)) demonstrate.

## 4.3 Disjunction

The properties of disjunction in propositional logic are summarized in the truth Table 4.2.

Disjunction is false when both simple sentences (disjuncts) are false. Notice that logical disjunction is true not only when one of the disjuncts is true but also when both are true.

We sometimes use *or* in English in this way, as in (4.22), where both disjuncts can be true. We call it *inclusive disjunction*.

## 4.3 Disjunction

**Table 4.2** Truth table for disjunction in propositional logic

| $p$ | $q$ | $p \vee q$ |
|---|---|---|
| t | t | t |
| t | f | t |
| f | t | t |
| f | f | f |

(4.22)  Bill must be extravagant or [Bill must be] rich to spend so much on a holiday.

But the most common use of the English *or* is different: it is *exclusive*, as in (4.23).

(4.23)  Lima is the capital of Peru or [Lima is the capital] of Argentina.

There is a good reason for the predominant exclusive use: if the speaker knew which alternative was true, they would state only that one instead of making a disjunctive statement, unless they intended to mislead. That is why an inclusive disjunction may require clarification, as in (4.24).

(4.24)  You may have fish or [you may have] meat for the main course – or both if you prefer.

So, like *and*, *or* can also depart from the meaning of its propositional-logic counterpart. It is often 'stronger', so to speak: saying, or at least implying, 'but not both', for reasons to do with rationality of discourse, such as the expectation of being informative and not misleading. In some instances, such as (4.23), the 'not both' reading is obvious: a city cannot be a capital of two different countries at the same time. At other times, it is strongly suggested, as in (4.24), where it may appear cheeky or impolite to ask 'Can I have both of them?' unless the inclusive meaning is explicitly stated. Yet in others, different parties arrive at different interpretations, or even go into legal battles over the 'correct' interpretation, as in the case that took place in 1957, between the Department of Welfare in New York City and a Mrs Siebel, who was sued for her share of the correction school fees to which her son was sent. The regulation said that, to quote after Noveck (2018:78):

If in the opinion of the department of welfare such parent or legal custodian is able to contribute ... the commissioner of welfare shall thereupon institute a proceeding ... to compel such parent or other person legally chargeable to contribute.

The disjunction in 'parent or legal custodian' was intended as inclusive – as it is in most rules and regulations (cf. *citizen or permanent resident*). But Mrs Siebel battled her grounds for not being obliged to pay, using the more standard, exclusive meaning of disjunction. Her argument was accepted in court (although, as Noveck points out, she lost the case on some other independent grounds). Noveck uses the case to highlight the need for an experimental approach. While he is absolutely correct on this, we will see by the end of this journey that the problem is in fact much broader than the question as to whether logical, inclusive *or* always figures in utterance processing (and if so, how). First, there is a metasemantic question to answer as to whether logical disjunction is the right concept to use in the first place to look at natural-language disjunction. Next, even more importantly, there is a question as to whether there is *the concept of disjunction* as such – as we could see from our journey through concepts in Stage 2, with the ever-progressing contextualism, or even nihilism, about concepts per se. Food for thought.

English *or* can also be used not to present disjoint propositions but rather to contrast different ways of expressing a thought, as in (4.25).

(4.25) Shit happens – or, should I say, life is unpredictable.

While superficially simple, disjunction in English can be quite complex semantically and pragmatically. The '$S_1$ or $S_2$' construction can convey various messages, such as that (i) the speaker is giving the addressee a choice from a set of alternatives; (ii) the speaker is unable to make a stronger claim due to lack of information; (iii) the states of affairs conveyed by $S_1$ and $S_2$ are equally possible; or, in the case of incomplete disjunctive statements ending with 'or ... ', (iv) the speaker wants the addressee to think of possible alternatives.[18] Again, the properties of logical disjunction give us a springboard, while rules of communication do the rest and allow us to assume that the speaker is as cooperative – informative, relevant, and clear – as the situation requires. And again, as in the case of conjunction, we can either (a) use the metalanguage of propositional logic to represent sentences of natural language, like in the standard formal semantics, or (b) use it in the spirit of more recent accounts which aim at representing the conceptual structure – the structure of underlying thoughts. For example, Mira Ariel and Caterina Mauri[19] have recently proposed that the core meaning of *or* is subjective. It points to the existence of alternatives on some level, whereby the speaker need not be committed to either of them – for example while trying to find a correct answer to a question, 'thinking aloud' about various solutions, only to reject them later. So, any truth-conditional conceptual-semantic analysis will have to resolve the status of the disjunction first.

Application of the metalanguage to represent conceptual structure has an additional advantage in that it allows us to represent incomplete disjunctive sentences such as (4.26a) and their complete intended (and recovered) but 'unsaid' meaning as, say, in (4.26b) or (4.26 c) – bearing in mind options (i)–(iv) above.

(4.26a) We can go to the seaside or ...

(4.26b) We can go to the seaside or to the lakes.

(4.26c) We can go to the seaside or, I don't know, I want you to suggest something else.

Another possible reading is that *or* does not signal disjunction but rather functions as a politeness marker, gauging whether the addressee welcomes the idea or considers it an imposition. Moreover, remembering that there are truth-conditional semantic

---

[18] See Jaszczolt, Savva, and Haugh (2016) for a discussion of the semantic and pragmatic properties of disjunction. The article focuses on incomplete disjunctive questions.

[19] See Ariel and Mauri 2019.

theories of questions (introduced briefly in Section 3.2), we can also cater for the meaning of incomplete disjunctive questions such as (4.27). Incomplete questions are quite common in discourse. (4.27) is an example of using an interrogative form to convey a polite request.

(4.27)    Will you be able to help me with this project or ... ?

Incomplete utterances are a viable strategy in discourse, frequently used for reasons to do with politeness or other social considerations. They are viable because of the assumption of rationality of conversation appealed to by Paul Grice and his followers: the speaker would not produce an incomplete sentence if the corresponding complete thought, or at least the reason for the incompleteness, were not expected to be clear to the addressee. The discussion of the exact workings of Grice's explanation will have to wait until Section 7.1 and the discussion of the semantics/pragmatics interplay in conveying meanings until Sections 7.2–7.3. But the gist should be clear: there is a 'backbone' of conveying alternatives and the exact significance of juxtaposing these disjuncts may have to be worked out as any of the categories (i)–(iv) above, or perhaps some others. In the case of incomplete disjunction, some of the alternatives may also have to be worked out by applying one's knowledge of social or cultural conventions or by inferring them from context. Propositional logic simply allows for representing them in a perspicuous form that enables the assignment of truth conditions and as such pursuing their meaning – in the case of this journey, the meanings of conceptual structures.

Incomplete, subsentential utterances have generated quite a lot of discussion in the literature, where they were given either pragmatic or syntactic solutions. The topic would be tangential to the issue of sentential connectives if not for the fact that both incomplete disjunction and incomplete conditional (which I mention in the next section) are a common, conventional strategy in communication. The syntactic take on their meaning assumes that there is a hidden 'unsaid' part of the structure.[20] However, it is clear even from the brief distinction between categories (i)–(iv) above that there may not be such one, unique structure. Neither does *or* have to always yield a statement where a disjunction of two propositions is intended; as we have seen, *or* may be used as a conventional politeness marker at the end of the sentence. As such,

subsentential utterances provide an ideal testing ground for an unprejudiced analysis of the extent to which the sentence should be the centre of attention in the analyses of meaning. (Jaszczolt, Savva, and Haugh 2016: 252)

As Jaszczolt et al. (2016: 255) claim, the second disjunct is often not only unpronounced, but even 'unthought':

In the case of *incomplete disjunctive statements*, the status of $q$ varies. By saying '$p$ or ... ', the speaker may intend to indicate that the alternative ($q$) is (i) salient in his/her mind but best left unuttered because (i.a) it can easily be inferred, or because (i.b) it would be potentially

---

[20] For a pragmatic solution, see e.g. Stainton 2006; Savva 2017. For a syntactic solution, appealing to ellipsis, see Merchant 2004, 2010. For incomplete utterances in modelling dialogue, see e.g. Ginzburg 2012; Gregoromichelaki and Kempson 2016.

face-threatening to utter it. Alternatively, (ii) the speaker may intend to indicate that he/she has no clear alternative in mind. Here, the utterance can convey (ii.a) a complete open-endedness of the possibilities of completion, even going beyond the usual constraints of common ground or (ii.b) that 'or' does not play its customary role of disjunction but instead is used as a discourse marker, signalling hesitation ...: an attitude to the expressed proposition such as uncertainty as to whether this was the correct way to phrase the assertion, whether it was appropriate to raise in that context, and so forth. Next, given that in the case of option (i), the speaker evidently has in mind a distinct set of alternatives, such examples also interact with the (α) polar ('or not') vs. (β) non-polar (or what we can call a 'local alternative') distinction, and within (β), and sometimes also in (α), the (α/β.1) exclusive vs. (α/β.2) inclusive distinction. In addition, (β) can be instantiated as (β′) a local closed set of alternatives or (β′′) a local open set.[21] Both (β′) and (β′′) permit exclusive and inclusive interpretation.

(4.28) exemplifies category (i.a. α.1) on the scenario where the inferred completion is as suggested.[22]

(4.28)   I could tell her the whole truth or ...
≫ I could tell her the whole truth or (I could) not (tell her the truth).

As in the case of conjunction earlier on, so this detour into the vagaries of English disjunction exposed differences between its use and the truth-functional meaning of its logical equivalent. But the differences do not appear to discredit propositional logic as the metalanguage – far from it. Arguably, again, they show its flexibility as a tool that can be used not only for the semantics of English sentences but also for the semantics of conceptual structures.

## 4.4 Conditional and Biconditional

Conditional sentences are standardly translated into the metalanguage of propositional logic using the connective of implication. Implication (properly: material implication) expresses a causal connection between an *antecedent* and a *consequent*. Table 4.3 summarizes its truth-functional meaning: implication is false only if the antecedent is true and the consequent is false.

In English, conditionals make use of such expressions as *if*, *if ... then*, *provided*, *whenever*, or *unless*, among others, as in (4.29).

(4.29)   If you cook the main course, I'll make a dessert.

One immediately obvious difference between natural-language conditionals and implication in the metalanguage is that implication is true when the antecedent is false and the consequent is true. It appears counterintuitive but it is so because the system of this formal language dictates it. That would mean that $p$ is a sufficient condition for $q$ but may not be a necessary one: I may also make a dessert if you order a takeaway for the main course but clean the house or do some other onerous

---

[21] Not to be confused with the category (ii.a).
[22] See Jaszczolt et al. 2016 for naturally occurring examples of other categories, taken from corpora of British and Australian English conversation.

**Table 4.3** Truth table for material implication in propositional logic

| $p$ | $q$ | $p \rightarrow q$ |
|---|---|---|
| t | t | t |
| t | f | f |
| f | t | t |
| f | f | t |

**Table 4.4** Truth table for equivalence in propositional logic

| $p$ | $q$ | $p \leftrightarrow q$ |
|---|---|---|
| t | t | t |
| t | f | f |
| f | t | f |
| f | f | t |

chores instead. Further, looking at the properties of the translation into propositional logic, if you don't make the main course, then the conditional cannot be made false, no matter whether I make the dessert or not. But we simply would not use the English conditional in this way without the risk of misleading: when I single out cooking the main course as a condition, I normally make it *the* condition – albeit possibly open to negotiation in the subsequent turns of the conversation.

Looked at with this relevance of the antecedent in mind, we conclude that people rarely use conditionals in the sense of logical implication. We normally use *if*-constructions and their ilk to mean a stronger relation, something like 'only if', 'if and only if', 'exactly when', 'only when' – a *biconditional*. We have already encountered 'only if' (*iff*) in propositional logic – it is the relation of equivalence. Equivalence is true only when both sentences have the same truth value, as demonstrated in Table 4.4.

The term 'biconditional' comes from its property of being a 'two-way conditional', so to speak, as unpacked in (4.30).

(4.30) $(p \leftrightarrow q) \leftrightarrow ((p \rightarrow q) \land (q \rightarrow p))$

English *if* can be difficult to distinguish from *only if*. While (4.29) is likely to communicate the stronger biconditional, at least prior to further negotiation (say, 'What if I cleaned the whole house instead?'), sometimes the antecedent is a necessary condition for the consequent. Intuitions vary, and so do intentions and contexts, but (4.31), for example, strongly suggests the 'only if' interpretation.

(4.31)   I will help you if you are too busy to do it yourself.

On the other hand, saying that (4.29) and (4.31) are semantically biconditionals would be too strong as well: sometimes the speaker issues a conditional with an added disclaimer, as for example in (4.32).

(4.32)   I'll make a dessert if you cook the main course *or if you do some of the other chores*.

Even what appears to be a default, strongly entrenched reading in (4.31) is defeasible, as in (4.33).

(4.33)   I will help you if you are too busy to do it yourself *or have some other good reason to ask for help*.

The assumption of a biconditional reading may be not only cancellable but may not even arise in the first place when (4.29) or (4.31) are uttered with an intonation pattern that signals continuation into the *or* disjunction.

So, this strengthening to a biconditional is at most pragmatic, and as such optional. This is the gist of the solution proposed in the early 1970s by Michael Geis and Arnold Zwicky, known as *conditional perfection* – a pragmatic strengthening of a conditional to a biconditional.[23] As they say, (4.29) 'invites an inference' to (4.34).

(4.34)   If you don't cook the main course, I won't make a dessert.

Analogous to the cases of conjunction and disjunction, it is best to think that the strengthening of *if* to 'iff' does not mean that *if* is ambiguous in English. It is simply pragmatically enriched – or strengthened, just as *some* is often strengthened pragmatically to 'not all', as in (4.35).

(4.35)   I can play some nocturnes by Chopin. (≫ I can't play them all.)

The exact status of such strong pragmatic meanings will be the topic of Stage 7 in this journey. What matters now is that this is how we use *if* – somewhere in between, so to speak, logical implication and logical equivalence.[24]

Another, albeit perhaps less immediately obvious, difficulty is that some conditionals, such as (4.29), are about the future, so it is not so easy to determine truth values of $p$ and $q$ in them. In fact, even counterfactuals such as *If I were a man, . . .* or *If only I had known it then, . . .* are difficult to think of in terms of truth-functional implication because their antecedent is false. Different theories of conditionals have attempted to overcome the difficulty, for example by proposing that what makes (4.29) true (its 'truth-makers') are in the future, or by looking at (4.29) in terms of pragmatic restrictions, also by employing possible worlds or probabilities. Some views apply both to possible (indicative) conditionals and to counterfactual ones, others concern only one or the other.

---

[23] See Geis and Zwicky 1971 and compare with the view in Grice 1989d. For discussion see van der Auwera 1997a. See also van der Auwera 1997b and Horn 2000 for a discussion of approaches to conditionals and the history of conditional perfection.

[24] In a cognitive-semantic framework, instead of conditional perfection, conditionals are represented as mental representations (or mental spaces) whereby, say, making the dessert is *conditionally predicted* (Dancygier and Sweetser 1997). Alternative mental spaces of making and not making the dessert by the speaker are set up by the addressee and are linked to the cooking and not cooking of the main course by the addressee respectively. The predictive nature of the conditional explains why epistemic and speech act conditionals such as (4.37) and (4.40) below are not normally strengthened to biconditionals. In this way conditional perfection obtains a plausible cognitive explanation (*pace* alleged counterexamples in Horn 2000, p. 319).

## 4.4 Conditional and Biconditional

Moreover, in natural-language discourse, the antecedent and the consequent are normally meaningfully (and even causally) tied together. So, sentence (4.36) is pragmatically ill-formed, in spite of coming out as true.

(4.36)  ?If dolphins are mammals, then semantics is a study of meaning.

Pragmatic accounts, such as those of Paul Grice and Robert Stalnaker, emphasize that $p$ has to provide a reason for $q$ – or, in other words, if $p$ is accepted in discourse as a premise, then so should $q$, as a conclusion. In other words, as Stalnaker (1999b: 68) puts it, 'a conditional statement is an assertion that the consequent is true, not necessarily in the world as it is, but in the world as it would be if the antecedent were true'.[25]

Now, like other sentential connectives, conditionals are used for a variety of purposes. There are, for example, epistemic conditionals, such as (4.37), where the link between the antecedent and the consequent pertains to inference in reasoning.

(4.37)  If the car is in the garage, then Bill must be in.

This example is a good place to introduce a seminal analysis of conditionals by Angelika Kratzer, who denies that they constitute a separate semantic category.[26] She claims that *if*-clauses are simply adverbial clauses: they restrict the operators such as *must* in (4.37), the so-called adverb of quantification such as *usually* in (4.38) (also, for example, *sometimes*, *always*, *rarely* or *never*), or the quantifier, such as *most* in (4.39) (also *some*, *all*, *no*, or *few*).

(4.38)  If a train comes from London, it is usually full.

(4.39)  Most dogs bite.

The idea is this. The adverb *usually*, or the quantifier *most*, apply, so to speak, to the predicate of *being full* or *biting*, respectively, but on the condition that it is predicated of the train from London or of a dog. More formally: for most $x$s, if $x$ is a dog, then $x$ bites. The antecedent then *restricts* the application of *bite* to dogs. As such, she famously claims, '[t]he history of the conditional is the story of a syntactic mistake' (Kratzer 2012a [1991]: 106). This analysis thus overcomes the need to translate conditionals as implication altogether, subsuming them under a larger phenomenon:

Semantically, conditionals are no longer much of a topic in their own right, then. We can only truly understand them in connection with the operators they restrict. (Kratzer 2012a [1991]: 94)

The concept of a restrictor deserves more attention and we will encounter it again in more detail while discussing generalized quantifiers in Section 5.2.

The preferred analysis of conditionals notwithstanding, the simple fact is that there are conditional sentences in English that at least appear to look isomorphic with (that is, have an analogous form to) logical implication, and these sentences can serve a plethora of different functions. Instead of signalling some causal, or restricting, link, they can also

---

[25] See also Stalnaker 2011 on conditional assertion.
[26] See Kratzer 2012a [1991] – best read after the introduction to general quantifiers in Section 5.2 below.

serve a purely sociopragmatic function. In these cases the consequent is not conditional upon the antecedent. In (4.40), *if you don't mind me saying so* does not refer to a state of affairs that can be translated as a proposition $p$ to which $q$ is directly related. It is used to hedge the speaker's critical remark and as such it functions as a politeness device.

(4.40)  You are not without blame, if you don't mind me saying so.

In a similar vein, (4.41) is an example of a polite conventional offer. This is known in the literature as a so-called 'biscuit conditional', after J. L. Austin's analogous example of an invitation.

(4.41)  If you are hungry, there is food in the fridge.[27]

Likewise, non-conditional sentences such as (4.42)–(4.44) can express conditional thoughts.

(4.42)  You call the cops, I break her legs.
≫ If you call the cops, I'll break her legs.

(4.43)  No pain, no gain.
≫ If you don't endure pain, you can't expect gains.

(4.44)  You like it? It's yours.
If you like it, you can have it.

(adapted from Elder and Jaszczolt 2016: 45)

Applying the metalanguage to sentences, as was done in traditional truth-conditional semantics, would not take us very far towards the meanings that these sentences have in particular contexts. These examples demonstrate that implication in propositional logic is a useful way of translating the cognitive structures in that the underlying conveyed thoughts *are* conditional. Elder and Jaszczolt[28] do precisely that: they represent conceptual structures of conditional thoughts conveyed in non-conditional structures, conditional structures that convey non-conditional thoughts, biscuit conditionals, as well as incomplete conditionals that consist only of an antecedent, and present these pragmatics-rich representations as truth-conditional representations in that the metalanguage applies equally well to thoughts as to linguistic constructions themselves. They employ the contextualist theory of Default Semantics already mentioned (introduced in more detail in Section 7.2.3).

Applying the metalanguage on the level of conceptual structure also fares better with incomplete conditionals. These are normally heavily context-dependent and range from cases that look like straightforward ellipsis, as in (4.45), to cases where the completion can be pragmatically supplied but is not entirely determinate, as in (4.46).

(4.45)  A: It's obligatory, is it, to have something in a company report?
B: If you've got more than a hundred in the workforce.
[≫ It's obligatory to have something in a company report if you've got more than a hundred in the workforce.]

(from ICE-GB, adapted from Elder and Savva 2018: 52)

---

[27] For a recent pragmatic account of biscuit conditionals, see e.g. Elder 2019.
[28] See Elder and Jaszczolt 2016 and Elder 2019.

(4.46)  (Casual conversation about operations)
A: But a friend of mine pulled some cartilage in her leg when she was playing squash, and she had that done under local. And it was awful because they had to give her uh uh uh injection in her back. It was apparently really dangerous because *if they get the wrong point there* ...
(from ICE-GB, adapted from Elder and Savva 2018: 55)

(4.46) might be resolved as suggested in (4.47) but also in some other ways.

(4.47)  ≫ ? ... if they get the wrong point there, there could be negative effects.

There are also standalone *if*-antecedents that conventionally express requests or wishes, as in (4.48) and (4.49)

(4.48)  If you'd like to sit over there.

(4.49)  If only Bill would stop smoking ...

All in all, it is clear that material implication in logic does not in itself fit all the uses of conditionals in English. Nevertheless, it remains a good starting point for their analysis. As in the case of the other two connectives (as well as negation discussed in the following section), differences can be accounted for by adding a pragmatic overlay such as strengthening, completion, or specifying the exact relation that '→' introduces. And, even if Kratzer makes a good point against conditionals in English being a self-contained category, intuitively, it appears to be one: the *if*-clause restricts, semantically or at least sociopragmatically, what the consequent states. Conceptualizing conditionals in terms of logical implication provides a springboard for an insight into their meaning and use: we start on the level of English sentences, see the misfits or incomplete fits, and progress towards thoughts and conceptual structures. Then we can see how to incorporate what we observe through this analysis into a broader view of such restrictors. We will do so when we move to generalized quantifiers in Section 5.2. They pertain to yet another concept that the original metalanguage (predicate logic) lacked but semanticists found a need to incorporate, on loan from mathematicians, to make truth-conditional semantics more explanatorily adequate.

## 4.5 Negation

### 4.5.1 Negation and Opposition

Negation, as I have mentioned, is the odd one out among connectives of propositional logic in that it does not link two sentences. Instead, it attaches itself to a sentence to form another sentence – its negation. In this sense, like the other connectives, it is a sentential operator. In the standard two-valued logic that we are employing here, the truth value of the negated sentence is opposite to that of the original sentence, as in Table 4.5.

**Table 4.5** Truth table for negation in propositional logic

| $p$ | $\neg p$ |
|---|---|
| t | f |
| f | t |

In English, sentential negation takes various forms, including *it is false that, it is not the case that, it is incorrect that, it is not true that, it is wrong that*, and *not* preceding the predicate. Like the other sentential connectives in English, it does not fit the mould of truth-functional negation very well. First, it has to be noticed that not all negation is sentential negation. For example, (4.50) contains negation of only a constituent of the sentence (a property of being a smoker) that cannot be rendered by $\neg p$ in propositional logic.

(4.50)  Non-smokers can stay inside.

Next, although (4.51) appears to be an example of sentential negation, it is normally interpreted as negation of the subordinate clause and, as such, stronger.

(4.51)  I don't think Bill and Oti will win *Strictly Come Dancing*.
  ≫ I think Bill and Oti won't win *Strictly Come Dancing*.

This is so because people have a tendency to produce higher-clause negation and assign to it lower-clause reading.[29] This psychological trait is dubbed the *Neg*-raising (negative raising) phenomenon. In general, using Aristotle's categories of oppositions, contradictories can be interpreted as stronger contraries. Laurence Horn (2020a: 201) in his comprehensive account of the phenomenon quotes here a nineteenth-century work by Bernard Bosanquet: 'The essence of negation is to invest the contrary with the character of the contradictory.'[30] *Contradictories* are propositions where if one is true, the other must be false – that is, cases of standard sentential negation $p$ and $\neg p$. *Contraries*, on the other hand, are propositions where there is opposition in the sense of mutual incompatibility but where these options don't exhaust the pool of possibilities: I don't think that *p*, but I may not think that *not p* either – I just don't know, don't care, or don't watch the show at all. *Neg*-raising takes place because human psychology has a tendency towards simple contrasts: if something is not good, it is bad; if a person is not happy, they are unhappy. Paired with the advantage of being less direct and as such more polite, the form is often the socially preferred one in discourse. It is less direct because the higher-clause negation is more general than the lower-clause negation (and the specific entails the general). For this reason, it is also considered to be a case of pragmatic *strengthening* rather than *ambiguity* – analogous to the pragmatic strengthening of other connectives discussed earlier. On the other hand, since there are good

---

[29] On *Neg*-raising, see Horn 2020a. For evidence that *Neg*-raising is not a syntactic process but is sensitive to the meaning of the sentence, see Jacobson 2018. For an introduction to Aristotelian oppositions and negation, see e.g. Horn 2020b and his classic *A Natural History of Negation* (Horn 1989). For a comprehensive introduction to different aspects of negation, see Horn and Wansing 2020.

[30] See Horn 2020a for references and a discussion.

## 4.5 Negation

arguments for syntactic, as well as semantic and pragmatic, explanations of the phenomenon, Horn points out that a satisfactory explanation still lies in the future.[31] Be that as it may, as we will see in the discussion of Gricean pragmatics in Stage 7, such strengthening obeys general rules (heuristics) of conversational behaviour: put informally, it would not be rational to say more if it suffices to say less.

Next, intonation can affect the meaning of negation, as the comparison of (4.52a) and (4.52b) demonstrates.

(4.52a)   *Fido* didn't eat your cake.

(4.52b)   Fido didn't eat your *cake*.

While they could both be translated as 'It is not the case that Fido ate your cake', and thus as ¬p, they invite different *alternatives*: *Rex* might have eaten the cake instead in (4.52a), while Fido might have eaten the addressee's *sandwich* in (4.52b).[32]

### 4.5.2 Objecting to 'The Way of Putting It'

Negation in English can perform other functions than negating a proposition or a constituent of a proposition. In (4.53), it signals objecting to the speaker's use of slang.

(4.53)   The story is not 'cool', it's 'interesting'.

In the somewhat clichéd (4.54), it is used to convey an optimistic view of a situation.

(4.54)   The glass isn't half empty – it's half full.

In (4.55), it is used to correct the grammar.

(4.55)   They are not 'alumnuses' of the university; they are 'alumni'.[33]

We can also negate a *presupposition* of the sentence, as in (4.56).

(4.56)   Anna didn't *quit* smoking; she has never smoked.

A little detour is needed at this point in order to explain the term *presupposition*. The concept is discussed in more detail, and from different angles, in Section 6.3.3, but on the most common understanding, presupposition is a relation between two sentences where if sentence $S_1$ presupposes sentence $S_2$, the truth of $S_2$ follows from $S_1$. No matter whether $S_1$ is true or false, $S_2$ is true. But if $S_2$ is false, then $S_1$ has no truth value. This is summarized in Table 4.6. '⊘' stands for a 'truth-value gap'.

So, both (4.57a) and (4.57b) presuppose (4.58).

(4.57a)   Anna quit smoking.

(4.57b)   Anna didn't quit smoking.

(4.58)   Anna used to smoke.

---

[31] See Horn 2020a, p. 215.
[32] The effect of focus on meaning is pursued in the theory of alternative semantics by Mats Rooth (Rooth 1996). See also contributions to Bosch and van der Sandt 1999 and Section 6.3 below.
[33] For more examples see Horn 1985, pp. 132–133.

**Table 4.6** Truth table for the relation of presupposition

| $S_1$ | | $S_2$ |
|---|---|---|
| t | → | t |
| ∅ | ← | f |
| f | → | t |

At this point more has to be said about presupposing the existence of the referent, also called *existential presupposition*. This is a widely discussed phenomenon in semantics and pragmatics due to its importance for the use of definite descriptions and the way it interacts with negation. We will return to it in Section 6.3.3, as well as, briefly, in Section 4.5.3, so for now we can confine ourselves to one pair of examples with negation. In (4.59), the existence of the person who is the PM of the United Kingdom seems to be presupposed and it is asserted that they are not a slim person.

(4.59)   The British Prime Minister is not slim.

On the other hand, (4.60) appears confusing and potentially ambiguous: to a reader not familiar with the fact that Poland is not a monarchy, the presupposition that there is a king of Poland tends to be part of the salient, default reading. But to readers who know that Poland is a republic, the only sensible way to interpret the negation would be as in (4.61).

(4.60)   The king of Poland is not slim.

(4.61)   The king of Poland is *not* slim; Poland doesn't have a king.

And it is precisely the additional clarification in (4.61), *negating the existential presupposition*, that one would expect from a rational speaker who avoids misleading in using negation.[34]

Let us return to the truth-value gap in Table 4.6 because it pertains to an important landmark in presupposition research that is relevant here. In his reaction to Russell's seminal 'On referring', an Oxford philosopher, Peter Strawson, suggested that it is statements, not sentences, that are true or false.[35] This is so because sentence (4.60), for example, is neither true nor false but it can be *used* to make true or false *statements*. If used in 1386, it would have had a truth value: it would have been false about the king of Poland Władysław Jagiełło (if we trust existing portraits). This put the semantics and pragmatics of presupposition on the right track: something has to be added to a 'raw' sentence before it can be assessed for truth.

Presupposition may appear to be a similar relation to entailment that we encountered earlier but it differs from it in the following way. Entailment is a relation between sentences where the truth of $S_2$ necessarily follows from the truth of $S_1$, as in Table 4.7.

---

[34] This is my variation on the much overused example involving the alleged present king of France. For references and more discussion, see Section 6.3.3 below.
[35] See Russell 1996 [1905] and Strawson 1997 [1950].

## 4.5 Negation

**Table 4.7** Truth table for the relation of entailment

| S₁ | | S₂ |
|---|---|---|
| t | → | t |
| f | ← | f |
| f | → | t ∨ f |

To compare, entailment is a 'weaker' relation, so to speak, than presupposition in that the falsity of S₁ does not guarantee the truth of S₂. For example, (4.62) entails (4.63) but the falsity of (4.62) does not guarantee (4.63): it does not guarantee that Anna bought any flowers at all.

(4.62)   Anna bought some tulips.

(4.63)   Anna bought some flowers.

Note that entailment is not only a relation between propositions. We have also encountered it in Section 2.2 in the lexical relation of hyponymy or inclusion: TULIP entails (or is a hyponym of) FLOWER.

Finally, meanings that addressees could potentially *infer* from utterances can be negated. In Section 7.1, we will discuss those as potential implicatures – inferences that go beyond the semantic content of the sentence.[36] Sentence (4.64) is an example of negating a potential implicature whereby the inference from 'not warm' to 'cold' or 'lukewarm' is cancelled or altogether prevented.

(4.64)   The water isn't warm, it's hot.

When negation is used to object to the style, grammar, presupposition, or implicature, it does not function as truth-functional negation – or at least not as truth-functional negation of the semantic content of the sentence. It is a means for objecting to someone's utterance on some different grounds, including the way it was pronounced. It is not the proposition that is denied but its assertability, the plausibility of asserting it. Faced with these examples, Laurence Horn suggested in his seminal 'Metalinguistic negation and pragmatic ambiguity' in the 1980s that there is a *duality of use* of negation in English.[37] Apart from the standard *descriptive* negation, there is also *metalinguistic negation* which is not analysable as 'It is not true that *p*'. In metalinguistic negation, style, presupposition, or implicature are negated. But the existence of these two types of negation does not mean that negation is semantically ambiguous. Instead, there is a 'built-in duality of use' (Horn 1985: 132), or pragmatic ambiguity. Context helps decide whether negation is descriptive or metalinguistic.

---

[36] The topic I repeatedly return to is how much of the inferred information contributes to truth conditions and how much constitutes a true implicature. A detailed discussion has to wait until Sections 7.2–7.3.

[37] See Horn 1985. See there also for the tests of morphological incorporation and negative polarity discussed in examples (4.65) and (4.66)–(4.67) respectively.

Metalinguistic negation can be submitted to a number of tests. For example, it has been observed that morphologically incorporated negation does not work for the metalinguistic use, as (4.65) demonstrates.

(4.65)   * Bill is *un*intelligent – he is a genius.

But what does it exactly mean to say that there is a duality of use? What does it mean that the ambiguity between descriptive and metalinguistic negation is a *pragmatic* ambiguity? If it is not semantic, then wouldn't we have to concede that on the level of semantic content, the meaning is that of truth-functional, propositional negation? After all, propositional negation appears to be there when we attempt to translate the sentence into the metalanguage of propositional logic. Or perhaps, it is pragmatic because the assertability of a proposition is itself the very *content* on which such unary (non-ambiguous) logical negation operates? This point has been discussed at length in the literature in that it is also plausible to think of negation as such a simple, non-ambiguous operator whose scope can vary between the proposition, as in Horn's descriptive negation, and some form of assertability of the proposition, as in Horn's metalinguistic negation.

Alternatively, negation can be deemed to operate on a proposition that is 'put in quotes', so to speak ($\neg$ 'p') or, more generally, as Robyn Carston puts it, to operate on the 'echoic use'.[38] The idea is that we 'echo' someone's earlier utterance, or perhaps someone's insinuated thought, and object to some aspect of it but not to the proposition itself, as in other examples above – say, in (4.64), when calling water in the shower 'warm' sounds like an understatement. This solution also denies the ambiguity of negation and allows for its translation as a truth-functional negation of propositional logic but it adds the proposal that negation operates on an enriched proposition. This standpoint, also represented by Ruth Kempson and Deirdre Wilson among others (called by Horn (1989: 432) 'the London School of Parsimony'), considers negation to be a simple propositional connective ($\neg p$) but it allows pragmatic processes that contribute to the propositional form. Substitution of positive for negative polarity items provides an argument for such an analysis. Negative polarity items are expressions the use of which is restricted to negative contexts and some other contexts semantically related to negative contexts, such as questions and conditional sentences. *Ever* is an example of a negative polarity item. In (4.67), the use of *sometimes* (normally also emphasized through intonation), rather than the ordinary negative polarity item *ever* as in (4.66), is said to signal that the expression is 'put in quotes', so to speak. Negation then operates on the result of this process of putting in quotes.

(4.66)   She isn't ever late; she's always punctual.

(4.67)   She isn't *sometimes* late; she's always late.

(adapted from Carston 1996: 321–322)

---

[38] The literature on the topic is vast. See e.g. Carston 1996.

The proposal focuses on addressing the question as to whether negation is a single phenomenon that can be handled by means of its truth-functional logical equivalent. As such, it addresses an intra-theoretic question and its appeal may not be immediately obvious. Negation is truth-functional on one hand, but on the other the content it operates on can be quite freely modified by just about any means: intonation, register, grammar, non-linguistic communication, and so on. But this also shows that the difference between metalinguistic negation and truth-functional negation operating on enriched propositions is not as significant as it appears to be. In a way, both solutions admit a duality of use, they just attach different emphasis to this fact: one assigns it to the *negation operator*, making it pragmatically ambiguous, and the other distinguishes between (a) enriched and (b) simple sentential *negated content*. Perhaps it is better to think of 'metalinguistic' as a *function* of negation rather than its form, as suggested by James McCawley.[39] After all, as we have seen, negation can convey an objection to the proposition on any grounds whatsoever. In this spirit, Bart Geurts[40] suggests an amendment to Carston's and Horn's proposals whereby negation is neither echoic nor metalinguistic but rather is aimed both at 'linguistic objects' and 'objects in the world'. As such, it is not ambiguous. Food for thought.

Before we move on, it is necessary to pause in this journey through meaning and ask how, in their reasoning, semanticists got to the point where pragmatic ambiguity of negation was put on the agenda in the first place. In order to do so, we have to start with Aristotle, Russell, and others for whom ambiguity was simple: if there is duality of meaning, there is by definition semantic ambiguity. The next section shows that such enviable simplicity is now only wishful thinking.

## 4.5.3 Negation vis-à-vis the Semantic Ambiguity/Underspecification Debate

The term 'ambiguity' appeared in the preceding stages of this journey when we contrasted lexical and structural ambiguity, or semantic ambiguity with semantic underdeterminacy. It has also appeared in the discussion of other sentential connectives where we pointed to Grice's pragmatic principle of economy (Modified Occam's Razor) as a good reason for avoiding postulating ambiguities. At this point, the question looms large in that *pragmatic* ambiguity has also been thrown in. So, we have to address briefly the crucial question: when should we talk about semantic ambiguity and when about underdetermination, underspecification, generality of sense, and so forth? Sometimes it is not possible to discuss meaning without a dose of history, and this is one such moment. It takes us back to the highlights of the debate in the 1970s. In their seminal paper on ambiguity tests, Arnold Zwicky and Jerrold Sadock[41] define ambiguity as having several underlying semantic/logical representations. Generality, on the other hand, is the case when the sentence has one single representation corresponding to different states of affairs. According to the so-called *identity test*, deemed to be the most reliable of the ambiguity tests, conjunction

---

[39] See McCawley 1993, p. 204.   [40] See Geurts 1998a, p. 293, fn 17.
[41] See their 'Ambiguity tests and how to fail them' (Zwicky and Sadock 1975).

reduction should be possible only when the conjoined constituents have matching understandings. Crossed understandings, i.e. readings where the senses of the conjuncts are incompatible, do not arise for such ambiguous sentences. Such readings are impossible for (4.70): it can only mean seeing the action of ducking and swallowing or seeing two birds: a duck and a swallow. That is, only matching understandings of (4.68) and (4.69) can be conjoined.

(4.68)   They saw her duck.   (bird or physical action)

(4.69)   They saw her swallow   (bird or eating)

(4.70)   They saw her duck and (her) swallow.
(from Zwicky and Sadock 1975: 18)

This test closely resembles George Lakoff's[42] test that uses the reduction ' ... and so did Bill', ' ... and the same goes for Bill', ' ... but Bill wouldn't do so', as, for example, in (4.71). A crossed reading where Tom saw, say, Anna perform an action of ducking and Bill saw a duck in Anna's garden are clearly ruled out.

(4.71)   Tom saw her duck and so did Bill.

Crossed readings are not semantically well-formed, unless they are used humorously, for punning effect, on which more in a moment.

Zwicky and Sadock also assess other ambiguity tests. *Semantic difference* requires that for a sentence to be regarded as ambiguous, the readings have very little in common. Next, *contradiction* is the possibility of both asserting and denying the truth of the resulting proposition – for example, *dog* is ambiguous because it is both true and false when predicated about a bitch. This is so because *dog* as a term for the subspecies *canis familiaris* stands in *privative opposition* to *dog* as a male representative of this subspecies. For privative opposites, one understanding includes a specification which the other lacks. Another test for ambiguity is *inconstancy under substitution* of semantically related terms. There are also syntactic tests such as an argument from having two syntactic structures, or disambiguation by a syntactic operation, such as passivization of (4.68) in (4.72).

(4.72)   Her duck was seen by them.

Although the identity test is deemed to be the most reliable of them all, none of the tests is perfect. Identity tests are too strict for some constructions, for example some types of privative opposition, some adverbials, metaphors, and certainly for irony, jokes, or exaggeration. Also, a crossed understanding may be impossible even though there is no ambiguity involved when pragmatic, situation- and context-driven meaning so dictates.

The word punning effect (*zeugma*) in conjunction reduction, as in (4.73), has also been considered as a test but found too weak.

---

[42] See Lakoff 1970, esp. p. 357.

## 4.5 Negation

(4.73)   Mr. Pickwick took his hat and his leave.
(from Lascarides, Copestake, and Briscoe 1996: 43, after Dickens, *Pickwick Papers*)

Juxtapositions of two senses sometimes work well and at other times do not, which suggests that there is no ambiguity involved. The punning effect may be caused by syntactic or pragmatic factors as well as by lexical-semantic ones. So, Lascarides, Copestake, and Briscoe[43] suggest that the phenomenon is better conceptualized as pragmatic ambiguity instead, in the sense of the underdetermination of coherence, or what they call an uncertainty of the rhetorical connection.

A battery of tests and theories has been tried on various alleged ambiguities, including negation, conjunction, disjunction, conditional, definite and indefinite noun phrases, numerals, or propositional attitude reports. So, we will be returning to the question 'ambiguity or underspecification?' throughout this journey in relation to different constructions, and will also discuss it more theoretically in Stage 7 when we move to the proposed boundaries between semantics and pragmatics.

Let us now return to negation. Can negation be considered semantically ambiguous? Lakoff's test has been applied to assess the potential ambiguity of negation but it produced mixed results in terms of acceptability judgements. (4.74) is deemed to be acceptable by some but ill-formed by others.

(4.74)   The king of France is not bald, and the same (thing) goes for the Queen of the United Kingdom.
(adapted from Atlas 1977: 326 – so, written during the second Elizabethan era)

The culprit here is the status of the existential presupposition: can we juxtapose negating (i) that it is the case that the king of France is bald OR that there is no such person (a 'wide-scope negation') with negating that (ii) the (existing) Queen of the UK is bald? Jay Atlas, one of the key figures in the semantic ambiguity debates, claims that (4.74) is not anomalous; it allows for a crossed understanding, where the presupposition of existence is negated in the first but not in the other conjunct. This would suggest that there is no semantic ambiguity here. But ambiguity tests on their own are not entirely reliable – they can produce different results in different consultants. So, Atlas and other key players in the ambiguity debates had to come up with a good theoretical argument against semantic ambiguity. And they did.

The argument is this. Let us take the classic example in (4.75) and try to assess whether the sentence is semantically ambiguous.

(4.75)   The king of France is not bald.

On one reading, there is a king of France who doesn't have a property of being bald. Using the metalanguage of propositional logic introduced in Stage 3, we obtain the logical form in (4.76). The need for the use of both the existential and the universal quantifier will be attended to in Section 6.2.3 but the gist is this. To say that 'there is someone who is a king of

---
[43] See here Lascarides et al. 1996.

France' will not suffice to translate the definiteness signalled by the definite article 'the'. We also need a phrase that says that 'for all $y$s who have the property of being king of France, this $y$ will have to equal $x$'. In other words, there is only one, unique, *the* king of France. Negation operates here only on the property of being bald predicated of the king of France.

(4.76)   $\exists x \, (\text{KoF}(x) \wedge \forall y (\text{KoF}(y) \rightarrow y = x) \wedge \neg \text{Bald}\,(x))$

On the other reading, we negate the presupposition of existence: it is not true that the king of France is not bald – there is no such person. The relevant logical form in (4.77) shows how negation takes a wide scope – a scope over the existential quantifier.

(4.77)   $\neg \exists x \, (\text{KoF}(x) \wedge \forall y (\text{KoF}(y) \rightarrow y = x) \wedge \text{Bald}\,(x))$

Now, it might appear natural to assume that because negation can result in these two different logical forms, then negation is semantically ambiguous. After all, it can take either narrow or wide scope with respect to the existential operator. Indeed, this solution was advocated by Bertrand Russell[44] and many others at the beginning of the twentieth century. It has its respectable roots in Aristotle. But it is not the dominant position nowadays for the following reason. Notice that the meanings conveyed by the two logical forms are connected in a very special way in that (4.76) *entails* the more general (4.77). This is important because it shows that the latter is more general. 'It is not the case that', that is the wide-scope negation, is compatible with both readings; it may 'not be the case' because the king is not bald or because he does not exist. As such, we have a logical form (4.77) that can, so to speak, cover both senses: the negation of the existential presupposition but also the more specific reading on which the existence of the king is presupposed. So, (4.76) is not logically independent from (4.77): (4.76) merely adds a precisification to the more general (4.77).

Looked at in this way, an interesting option appears: we can deem the representation with the wide-scope negation (as in (4.77)) to be the correct semantic representation for both readings and then deem the precisification to the existential reading and narrow-scope negation (4.76) to be added pragmatically. In this way, the intuition that negation is not ambiguous in English can be preserved and the price to pay is to accept that the semantic representation is underspecified – it does not tell us all that we need to know about the meaning of (4.75): it does not tell us which of the two readings we are dealing with. To sum up, this will amount to saying that the processing of the lexicon and the structure of (4.75) renders an underspecified semantic representation, while the exact reading is obtained through pragmatic enrichment performed by the addressee in the particular discourse context. And it is this view of semantic underdetermination, also dubbed semantic underspecification or sense-generality, that opened the floodgates for ambiguity debates. We owe the theoretical proposal of semantic underdetermination of negation to Jay Atlas's and independently Ruth Kempson's seminal work in the mid 1970s and 1980s. The idea is now known as the Atlas-Kempson thesis.[45] The idea that

---

[44] See e.g. Russell 1996 [1905] and Russell 1997 [1919].
[45] The literature from that period is vast but the seminal works are the following: Atlas 1977, 1979, 1989, 2005; Kempson 1975, 1979, 1986.

semantics takes us part-way, while pragmatic 'overlay' completes the recovery of utterance meaning also became known as *radical pragmatics*.[46]

In short, while in the case of a lexically or syntactically ambiguous sentence there are two *independent* logical forms pertaining to its two readings, in the case of semantic underdetermination there is one underspecified logical form that can be subjected to further determinations of meaning. These take place through pragmatic inference or through some other pragmatic process such as accepting salient, default interpretations. Looked at in this way, underdetermination and inference are closely intertwined aspects of utterance interpretation. Atlas captures this very well in his apt pastiche of German philosopher Immanuel Kant (referred to in Section 2.2 while discussing concepts and sensations): 'Pragmatic inference without sense-generality is blind, but sense-generality without pragmatic inference is empty' (Atlas 1989: 124). So, the currently dominant view is that of a unitary semantics of negation where the negation operator is underspecified as to its scope. In the process, semantic presupposition has been successfully reanalysed as pragmatic presupposition or as entailment in assertions but an implicature (that is, cancellable inference) in the corresponding negative statements.[47]

Semantic underdetermination was a ground-breaking idea for the theory of meaning. For this reason, this historical detour is important. Underdetermination was a reaction to a trend in the 1960s and early 1970s to search for syntactic explanations to all kinds of linguistic phenomena, even those that, in hindsight, are better pursued within semantics or pragmatics. The fall of this temporary 'oversyntacticization' of linguistics can be attributed to the influence of Oxford philosophers such as John Austin, Paul Grice, Peter Strawson, as well as Ludwig Wittgenstein in Cambridge in the later phase of his philosophy. It was then continued by Gerald Gazdar, Bruce Fraser, Jerry Morgan, Jay Atlas, Ruth Kempson, Deirdre Wilson, and many other linguists whom we will meet again in Sections 7.2–7.3 in discussing the semantics/pragmatics boundary disputes that followed suit and are still continuing. Jay Atlas recollects those days as follows in his 'A personal history of linguistic pragmatics 1969–2000', a paper delivered at the University of Cambridge in 2006:

I read the first, introductory paragraph to Sadock and Zwicky's paper, and I thought to myself, 'That's it. If 'not' is not ambiguous, it's semantically non-specific. Let's try the tests.' Ten minutes later I had satisfied myself that 'not' in definite description sentences failed Sadock's ambiguity tests. ... The solution had to be in the utterance-meanings, in one of two ways. Either the utterance-meanings were produced by a Griceanish inference, not from classical logical forms as Grice thought, e.g. sentential exclusion negation, but from a non-specific, semantical representation of a sentence-type whose meaning was not that of either a choice or an exclusion negation proposition, or the utterance-meanings were produced by a classical Gricean inference from the sentential exclusion negation logical form, which on classical Gricean grounds one would have to 'posit' as the semantic content of 'what is said' in the asserted sentence – Grice's version of the 'minimal proposition'. (Atlas 2006: 4)

---

[46] See Cole 1981. For pertinent terminology, see also Zwicky and Sadock 1975, p. 2; Green 1996, p. 1; Jaszczolt 1999, Chapter 1 and Jaszczolt 2005, Chapter 1.

[47] See also the discussion in Horn 1989, esp. p. 362 and Horn 1996.

In short, the semantic representation of (4.75) is either the formula with wide-scope negation (that is, (4.77)) or it is genuinely left underspecified in the sense that we can't write it down as a complete, truth-evaluable formula in our metalanguage of predicate logic. But the difference between these two ways of conceptualizing it is not significant.

Perhaps the most interesting legacy of this fascinating movement was opening up the debate as to whether these pragmatic 'specifications' are part of the semantic, truth-conditional content – as we called it in Section 1.3, or part of the contextualist, functionalist proposition. But this topic, again, will have to wait for the 'boundary wars' in Stage 7 of this journey.

Note at this point that the common-sense claim accepted in cognitive linguistics that negation is a *cognitive universal* may prove to be correct. We can conclude that if there is any ambiguity of negation there, it is merely an ambiguity between negating the 'simple' and negating the 'complicated' proposition. And this is an observation that has only an intra-theoretic, and as such limited, value. The alternative would be to admit graded, progressive context dependence of the functional proposition and nothing would be lost. Food for thought.

## 4.6 Linguistic Diversity: Snakes and Ladders, Cluedo, and Monopoly

We alternated between presenting the utility of the connectives of propositional logic for providing the semantics of English sentential connectives and observing the differences between the metalanguage and the object language. The assessment of the utility of a formal approach of this kind in face of so many departures from the property of truth-functionality is a task for every linguist's own journey through meaning, so it is left for the reader. Suffice it to say that throughout this journey we are uncovering more and more ways of supplementing the 'skeleton' that a truth-conditional account provides us with. In the process, it was also argued that instead of postulating semantic ambiguities in the case of negation, implication, and conjunction, it is more adequate and parsimonious to adhere to a uniform analysis where information from the sentence is 'precisified' as situations and contexts require.

Differences between natural-language connectives and their logical equivalents become even more evident when we realize that natural languages themselves display a considerable diversity in this respect. For example, Wari', a Chapacura-Wanham language of the Amazon, and Tzeltal, a Mayan language spoken in Mexico, have no lexical equivalent of *or*. In Wari', disjunction is communicated as epistemic possibility as in (4.78).

(4.78)  'am       'e'      ca       'am       mi'      pin        ca
        **Perhaps** live   *3SgM*   **perhaps** give   complete   *3SgM*
        'Either he will live or he will die.' (lit. 'Perhaps he will live, perhaps he will die.')
                                            (adapted from Mauri and van der Auwera 2012: 391)

Upriver Halkomelen, a Salish language spoken in British Columbia, uses the same connective (*qə*) to express conjunction and disjunction (albeit it tends to be translated as 'and' in assertions and as 'or' in questions).[48] We would call it underspecified, where precisification is added by inference from the situation and context. Next, Maricopa, a Yuman language, spoken by Native American Maricopa people in Arizona, has no equivalent of *and*. Potential ambiguities are prevented in different ways, such as using a switch-reference marker on the verb in $S_1$ to signal that $S_2$ has a different subject.[49] Guugu Yimithirr, an Australian Aboriginal language from Queensland, has no equivalent of *if*. In Tamil, a Dravidian language spoken in Southern India and Sri Lanka, the negative can be marked by replacing a tense morpheme from the equivalent positive with a negative morpheme.[50]

These are only a few examples from the rich and fascinating field of cross-linguistic variation studies. The question is how this variation can be accounted for by the tools introduced here. The key is to acknowledge that the linguistic diversity displayed by sentential connectives does not necessarily undermine the universality of the underlying concepts. Expressing the concepts of conjoining propositions, or the existence of alternatives, a causal link, or negation are important in human reasoning. Even if there is no lexical item in a language that translates as *or* or *if*, there may be an underlying concept. It is reasonable to assume that the composition of meaning on the level of conceptual structures follows universal principles and the sources of this universality are the structure and operations of the human brain, aided by the fact that humans use language for broadly the same range of purposes and in broadly the same physical and social environments. Arguably, it would not be justifiable to ascribe this universality to natural-language syntax in that cross-linguistic variation appears to be greater than a universal generative theory of grammar can cater for. Not all languages have recursion (as in, for example, *Anna said that Bill thinks that Cesar suspects that* ...), and even the constituent structure of some free-order languages is hard to explain without 'tricks' that purport to fit a language into an allegedly universal syntactic mould. Nicholas Evans and Stephen Levinson's seminal paper 'The myth of language universals: Language diversity and its importance for cognitive science'[51] caused a major stir, especially in Chomskyan generative syntactic circles, by its argumentation and empirical evidence against language universals and in favour of proposing universals on the level of conceptual structures.[52] They conclude that

although recursion may not be found in the syntax of languages, it is always found in the conceptual structure, that is, the semantics or pragmatics – in the sense that it is always possible in any language to express complex propositions. (Evans and Levinson 2009: 444)

This means that generative power is seen as a property of conceptual structures. And conceptual structures draw on information conveyed by different means – syntactic, lexical, as well as pragmatic – or on 'the lexicon/grammar/pragmatics trade-offs'

---

[48] Mauri and van der Auwera 2012, p. 381, after Ohori.
[49] For discussion and an example see Mauri and van der Auwera 2012, p. 385.
[50] See Evans and Levinson 2009.
[51] See Evans and Levinson 2009 and the open peer commentary in the same issue.
[52] See also Pinker and Jackendoff 2009 on conceptual universals and Müller 2009 for a neurobiological account.

referred to in Stage 2.[53] So, if there are no lexical means to convey a concept, there may be syntactic ways, as in some of the above examples, or pragmatic ones. The latter was exemplified in our discussion of cross-sentential conjunction in Section 4.2 where a juxtaposition of sentences carried different meanings depending on whether they conveyed states or events and depending on how context informs our interpretation. Kai von Fintel and Lisa Matthewson[54] propose here adopting universal semantic principles of meaning composition or universal principles of utterance interpretation. The latter have been briefly invoked while mentioning Gricean pragmatics and are discussed in more detail in Section 7.1. To anticipate, they spell out principles of rational conversational cooperation based on informativeness, economy, contextual relevance, and the manner of expression.

All in all, one way of looking at the utility of the tools from propositional logic is this. A precise, formal metalanguage offers a translation into syntactic operators that are semantically clear and regular, in that their meaning is truth-functional, and as such does not change from sentence to sentence. This, arguably, gives us a useful 'ladder' which we can climb in searching for the meaning of English sentential connectives. But the ladder is too short: it does not take us all the way to their semantics and pragmatics. Sometimes, we even have to 'slide down', like in the game of Snakes and Ladders – for example when an *if*-clause does not function as an antecedent expressing dependence but is a marker of politeness, or when *and* means 'if ... then' and we have to go down and climb another ladder instead. In the process, we have to employ a great deal of pragmatic inference from context, the situation, the common ground, or world knowledge – such as knowledge of standard scenarios, encyclopedic information, knowledge of, say, how substances and organisms function (scientific knowledge), knowledge of how individuals, societies, and cultures function (psychology, sociology, and anthropology), and so forth. To continue with the board games metaphor, we are collecting clues – who, where, and how, a little like in Cluedo. My final metaphor in the title was Monopoly in that we exchange the assets for a construction of a theory of meaning that we have accumulated through employing logical rules, rules pertaining to regularities of human conversational cooperation, or through empirical research into cross-linguistic variation – somewhat like building houses and hotels, and in the end the entire city (when one wins), using currency, exchange of goods, logical reasoning, probabilistic reasoning, and a bit of luck. But all within the mutually agreed paradigm – or 'rules of the game'.

**Suggested Further Reading**

Many introductions to natural-language semantics contain sections on connectives in propositional logic. For a comprehensive, reader-friendly account, see for example Kearns' (2011) *Semantics*, Section 2.2 or de Swart's (1998) classic *Introduction to Natural Language Semantics*, Chapter 3. Connectives in the context of the semantics/

---

[53] The idea is further developed in the theory of Default Semantics that spells out how different sources of information contribute to conceptual structure. See Section 7.2.3 below and Jaszczolt 2005, 2010, and for full bibliographical references, including applications to different languages, Jaszczolt 2021b.
[54] See von Fintel and Matthewson 2008.

pragmatics boundary and ambiguity/underspecification debates are also a well-trodden area; see for example Carston's (2002) *Thoughts and Utterances*, Chapter 3 on *and*-conjunction and Chapter 4 on negation; Horn's (1985) seminal 'Metalinguistic negation and pragmatic ambiguity', or for an overview of negation in semantics and pragmatics, Atlas's (2012) 'Negation'. On conditionals in reasoning see Williamson's (2020) *Suppose and Tell: The Semantics and Heuristics of Conditionals*. On presupposition, the literature is vast but for comprehensive introductions try Szabó and Thomason's (2019) *Philosophy of Language*, Chapter 8 and the classics: Beaver's (1997) 'Presupposition' and Levinson's (1983) *Pragmatics*, Chapter 4. For connectives vis-à-vis the ambiguity/underspecification and inference/defaultness debates see also Jaszczolt's (1999) *Discourse, Beliefs and Intentions: Semantic Defaults and Propositional Attitude Ascription*, Chapters 1 and 2. Cross-linguistic variation is excellently discussed in Mauri and van der Auwera's (2012) 'Connectives'.

Detailed, including advanced, reading suggestions regarding particular connectives, problems, and ideas were given in the footnotes as we moved along, as set out in the 'two-tier' template for this journey through meaning.

# Stage 5  Inside the Sentence

## 5.1  Limitations of the Metalanguage

The operations on sentences discussed in the previous stage of the journey proved to be more complicated in natural language than in the formal metalanguage of propositional logic. We concluded that we could bend and twist the metalanguage and 'kick it up', so to speak, from being a tool to represent *sentences* to being a tool for representing *conceptual structures*. We can then represent all those fine-grained aspects of meaning that were unaccounted for on the level of English sentences. After all, it is precisely those intended and conveyed meanings that drive communication and cognition, so it is only appropriate that the theory of meaning should represent those. And it is only fair that we try to use the best available tools to do so.

In comparison with the intricacies of meanings found in a sentence, analysing sentential connectives is almost a trifle. First, like in the case of sentential connectives, we have to put up with the fact that the translation is rarely isomorphic; that is, it often does not preserve the form of the natural-language sentence. One example is a structure that requires quantifiers and variables. The existential and universal quantifiers are by no means ideal devices to translate the structure of English sentences. For example, (5.1) has to be translated as (5.2) that amounts to 'there is an entity that has a property of being a dog and a property of barking' – no isomorphism whatsoever.

(5.1)   A dog barks.

(5.2)   $\exists x \, (Dog \, (x) \land Bark \, (x))$

So, compositionality is somewhat compromised: we can arrive at a representation that is quite faithful to the meaning of (5.1) but we cannot arrive at it by following its compositional structure – and all this even before we begin to think about how to deal with the grammatical tense (on which there will be more in Section 5.3).

It gets worse. Unlike connectives without equivalents in propositional logic, such as *but* – which, arguably, can be catered for by combining logical conjunction with a periphrastic way of translating contrast as we did in Section 4.1 – simple sentences come with various kinds of structures for which entirely new tools are needed. We have just seen that some natural-language quantifying expressions belong to this category. While in predicate logic there are two standard quantifiers, the existential and the universal, English has many more. Only some of them bear a close resemblance to the quantifiers in predicate logic and can be translated as in (5.2). However, like in the case of connectives, there are ways of accommodating what is 'lost in translation'. For example, when little Billy uses the expression *everybody* or *all* in conversation, as in (5.3), he does not mean that 'all people', or 'everybody in the world' has a mobile phone. Rather, he is likely to mean that all his friends, all the children in his class, or all the people he knows have a mobile phone (and, as we will discuss in Section 7.1, he is likely to strongly convey something different still – say, that he wants his parents to buy him a phone).

(5.3)   Everybody has a mobile phone.

When using these quantifying expressions people are normally talking about certain restricted groups of individuals. In other words, quantification is normally *restricted* to a certain *range*. We can represent this restriction as in (5.4).

(5.4)   $\exists x$ Has-a-mobile-phone $(x)$
        $x \in G$   (G = range)

Sentence (5.5) exemplifies this particularly well. It also shows that the domain of quantification may vary within one sentence: 'everyone$_1$' is interpreted with respect to the domain of people inside the building, looking out of the window, while 'everyone$_2$' with respect to the domain of people who are outside and are within the visual field of the members of the first group.

(5.5)   When we looked out of the window, everyone$_1$ saw everyone$_2$ putting up their umbrellas.
        (adapted from Stanley and Williamson 1995: 294)

There are various proposals in semantics and pragmatics (and even syntax) for how to *restrict the domain of quantification*.[1] Whether we consider this restriction to be semantic or pragmatic will depend on our initial goals and assumptions – that is, what *kind of meaning* we want the semantic theory to be about (the question that we have also been asking while analysing English sentential connectives). If the semantics is to be a semantics of natural-language sentences, then we can accept that, semantically, (5.1) is unrestricted. But if, like in our current journey through meaning, we impose a stricter requirement on the semantics, wanting the truth conditions to be intuitive truth conditions, and *a fortiori* the semantics to be a cognitively real semantics, then the restriction has to be semantic. We have to build it into the semantic representation somehow or other. Jason Stanley and Zoltán Gendler Szabó built it into the logical form.[2] They proposed that 'each common noun (e.g. 'bottle' and 'cat') co-habits a node with a contextual variable' (Stanley and Szabó 2000: 251). For example, in the syntactic representation of their sentence (5.6), the 'N' node in the syntactic structure is filled by <man, f(i)>, where 'f' stands for a mapping (function) that is applied to object ('i'), where both are provided by the context and together, as 'f(i)', provide a restriction to 'man'.

(5.6)   Every man runs.

---

[1] See e.g. Westerståhl 1985; Recanati 1996; Stanley and Szabó 2000; Bach 2000.
[2] See Stanley and Szabó 2000. For a postscript to this solution see Stanley 2007.

There are good arguments from sentence processing in support of this view – arguments that Jason Stanley also pursues in his subsequent more general proposal in a paper 'Making it articulated',[3] in which different kinds of expressions that enter the logical form come with the enrichment, restriction, mode of presentation, or some other embellishment that makes them fit the contextual requirements. As constituents of the logical form, they are all 'visible' or *articulated*, in contrast with the proposal on which such pragmatic precisifications are *unarticulated constituents of the logical form* – something added 'top-down', so to speak, that is not 'visible' in the logical form obtained through syntactic processing of the sentence (that is, not arrived at 'bottom-up'). As he says, 'I want to argue in favor of the view that all the constituents of the propositions hearers would intuitively believe to be expressed by utterances are the result of assigning values to the elements of the sentence uttered, and combining them in accord with its structure' (Stanley 2002: 150–151). In Section 7.3.3, we will refer to this view as *semantic indexicalism*. In contrast, the pragmatic, 'top-down' solution is advocated among others by François Recanati, who defends unarticulated constituents using his own theory of Truth-Conditional Pragmatics. This is discussed in the 'pragmaticky' phase of this journey in Section 7.2.2.[4]

Be that as it may, this restriction is not simply projected from the syntactic form of the sentence. If we want to introduce it into the truth-conditional representation, we have to either postulate domain variables in the logical form or add the domain restriction to the semantic representation independently of the syntactic processing. As to whether this truth-conditional representation is then best regarded as a truth-conditional *semantic* or truth-conditional *pragmatic* representation, views vary – Recanati opts for the latter, while, as is clear by now, in this journey we veer towards the first: formal, truth-conditional, semantic, and at the same time conceptual, 'pragmatics-rich' representation. The debate is by no means only terminological. We will address this question again in Stage 7 of this journey as part of the minimalism–contextualism debate, in that minimalists about meaning prefer to reserve the term 'semantics' for the kind of meaning that is 'uncontaminated', so to speak, by pragmatic influences such as inferences from context, from conventions and standards of behaviour, general knowledge, and so forth. While it may be of little interest to some linguists whether the truth-conditional representation ought to be called 'semantic' or 'pragmatic', it is definitely of considerable interest when we ask what 'kind of' meaning a theory of meaning ought to pursue: the minimal, syntax-driven sentence meaning, or the cognitively real, intuitive, contextually embedded meaning – or perhaps both, depending on the objectives, as we have briefly indicated in observing the difference in goals between the philosophical semantics of human communication and the semantics in computational linguistics that is to serve the purpose of training machines to communicate. But to continue would be to digress too far.

---

[3] Stanley 2002. See also Stanley 2000.

[4] See e.g. Recanati 2002a for a direct response to Stanley. For the introduction to Truth-Conditional Pragmatics, see Recanati 2010. See also Bach (2000: 271) who argues that 'quantifier domain restriction is not constitutively determined by context; it is epistemically determined by the audience in the context, and that is a *pragmatic matter*'.

Now, in addition to the problem of the lack of isomorphism that we can just about tolerate, and the problem of the restricted domain of natural-language quantifiers that is solvable in one way or another, there is also a problem that requires additional tools. This is the problem of the paucity of quantifiers we encountered before: there are quantifiers in natural languages that do not correspond to the two found in standard predicate logic, such as English *three, several, most, many, few*, and others. Small numerals might possibly be catered for, albeit with difficulty: *two*, for example, can be represented by spelling out in the logical form that '$\exists x \, \exists y$ where $y \neq x$' and adding that '$\neg \exists z$ such that $z = x$ or such that $z = y$'. We can also use the existential quantifier only with difficulty to represent uniqueness – the fact that there is only one object with a certain property, as we have done for the definite noun phrase *the king of France* in examples (4.75)–(4.77) in Section 4.5.3. But for the remaining examples of English quantifiers we would be stuck. This is where we need an entirely new concept of a *quantifier as a relation between sets*. But before we introduce it, we have to attend to one other limitation of first-order logic.

We have seen that first-order logic predicates things about *individuals* and quantifies over *individuals*: individual constants and individual variables (hence its name: 'first-order'). This is rather restrictive because we cannot predicate anything about properties – say, that Anna *sings* beautifully or that *smoking* is dangerous. We cannot quantify over properties either – say, to represent the meaning that Bill has some properties that Anna has. Neither can we represent quantifying over properties of properties – say, that being cautious and being experienced have something in common. Higher-order logic allows us to do precisely that. (5.7) is an example of predicating something about the *property*: the property of Anna's singing. It can be represented as in (5.8) in second-order logic.

(5.7)    Anna sings beautifully.

(5.8)    Sing ($a$) ∧ Beautiful (Sing)

Likewise, in (5.10), we quantify over a *property* – Anna's property that has a property of being special, as in (5.9). '$P$' is a property variable.

(5.9)    Anna has a special property.

(5.10)   $\exists P \, (P(a) \wedge \text{Special} \, (P))$

On the next level up, we predicate something of, or quantify over, *properties of properties*, as in (5.11) represented in (5.12), where 'being related' is a way of saying that these two properties have some common characteristics (or properties).

(5.11)   Being cautious is related to being experienced.

(5.12)   $\exists P \, (P(\text{Cautious}) \wedge P(\text{Experienced}))$

Going higher up to third-order logic is useful, for example, in representing modifiers of modifiers, such as in adding an intensifier *particularly* to qualify the modifier *beautifully*, as in (5.13).

(5.13)   Anna sings particularly beautifully.

In first-order logic we could represent the meaning that Anna has the property of singing. Now we can represent the meaning that singing has the property of being beautiful, as well as the meaning that beautiful is in fact particularly, very, specially, etc. beautiful. We can also represent the meaning of relative adjectives such as *big* in (5.14).

(5.14)   There is a big spider in the bath.

The representation has to account for the fact that there is something that has properties of being a spider, being big, and being in the bath. But this will not suffice yet: *big*, unlike, say, *dead*, is relative: the $x$ is *big as spiders go*, not, say, as grizzly bears or crocodiles go. So, the size has to be predicated not of the individual variable $x$ but of the property of being a spider. The intensifier 'very' further adds to the fun of translation. This shows that even a simple English sentence may require the resources of second- or third-order logic.

We would also be stuck if we tried to represent tense or modality. Like in the case of recalcitrant natural-language quantifiers, we will need some additional tools to represent and explain the meaning of, say, past-tense constructions or epistemic *must*. But let us turn to quantification first.

## 5.2   Quantification

### 5.2.1   Quantifiers as Relations between Sets

Not to be able to represent quantifying expressions such as *most* or *few* in the metalanguage would be restrictive indeed. First, it is important to understand why they can't simply be added using the standard devices of predicate logic. Let us attempt a translation of (5.15) as in (5.16) where $\mathcal{M}$ stands for a proposed quantifier *most*.

(5.15)   Most dogs are cute.

(5.16)   $\mathcal{M} \, x \, (\text{Dog}(x) \, ? \, \text{Cute}(x))$

We can't go very far with such a quantifier without encountering a problem, in that we lack a suitable connective: conjunction won't do because the proposed formula would mean that most things in the universe of discourse have the properties of being a dog *and* being cute. Implication won't do either because it would mean that for most things in the universe of discourse if they are dogs, they are cute. If most individuals in the universe of discourse are not dogs (and it would be an unusual restriction indeed if they were), then the implication will come out true, no matter how many dogs are cute.

## 5.2 Quantification

We have seen that if the antecedent is false, the implication always comes out as true (see Table 4.3 in Section 4.4). The other connectives can be discarded in an analogous way.

So, there is no way of representing the meaning that a *proportion* of the set of dogs has a property of being cute. To do so, we need to go beyond first-order logic and adopt the concept of a *generalized quantifier*. Like above, we go to the second order and the concept of the set of sets – adopted in the semantics of English by Richard Montague in his seminal 'The proper treatment of quantification in ordinary English' in the 1970s and developed into a theory of general quantifiers for English in 'General quantifiers in natural language' by Jon Barwise and Robin Cooper several years later.[5] Think of (5.17) as a set that consists of those individuals that belong to the subset of cute things such that they are also members of the set of dogs (they are not, say, cute cats, hamsters, or ideas).

(5.17)  Dogs are cute.

Likewise, proper treatment of quantification in general requires a comparison of objects satisfying two formulae. So, the way of looking at *most* is now this: (5.15) means that the intersection (that is, the common part) of the set of dogs with the set of cute individuals contains more than half of the dogs in it. Other quantifiers can be conceptualized analogously, as relations between sets. The concept was introduced to logic by Andrzej Mostowski in the 1950s and developed for natural-language semantics by Montague and Barwise and Cooper already mentioned, as well as by Dag Westerståhl, Hans Kamp and Uwe Reyle, and many others.[6]

One of the intuitively appealing ways to represent quantifiers is to use a theory that will be more extensively discussed in Section 6.1.2.1, called Discourse Representation Theory (DRT) developed by Hans Kamp.[7] All we need at the moment is to know what the boxes and formulae inside the boxes represent. The boxes stand for mental representations of fragments of discourse, so-called Discourse Representation Structures (DRSs). A DRS allows for representing ongoing discourse as it develops incrementally, and as such it lets us represent the dynamic development of meaning going beyond the unit of the sentence. The letters in the top row stand for discourse referents. The formulae below them are the so-called DRS-conditions and they closely resemble the logical forms in predicate logic that we have encountered before. The sentence in (5.18) can be represented as in Figure 5.1. The DRS is dubbed 'partial' because it does not represent aspects of meaning that are not relevant in the current discussion, such as temporal reference.

(5.18)  Few dogs like cats.

---

[5] See Montague 2002 [1973] and Barwise and Cooper 1981.
[6] Recommendations for accessible introductions to generalized quantifiers are given at the end of this stage. For more in-depth and challenging but *ab initio* introductions, see Westerståhl 2019 and Peters and Westerståhl 2006. See also Westerståhl 1985 and other articles in van Benthem and ter Meulen 1985. For a broadly cross-linguistic investigation into quantification using generalized quantifiers, see Szabolcsi 2010.
[7] On generalized quantifiers and the treatment of plurals in DRT, see Kamp and Reyle 1993, Chapter 4.

## 5 Inside the Sentence

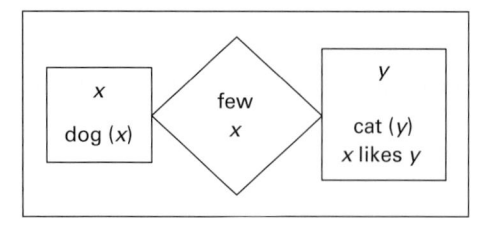

**Figure 5.1** Partial DRS for (5.18) ('Few dogs like cats.')

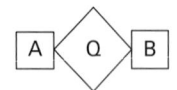

**Figure 5.2** Duplex condition

The DRS-condition with a diamond-shaped box in it is called a *duplex condition*. It consists of three units: a *restrictor* on the left (A in Figure 5.2), a *quantifier* in the middle, and a *scope* on the right (B in Figure 5.2).

Standard universal and existential quantifiers can also be represented as relations between two sets, which means that employing generalized quantifiers provides a uniform treatment for all quantifying expressions.

It goes without saying that this way of conceptualizing quantifiers is very different from that in standard predicate logic. Relations between sets better appeal to common sense and allow for a more accurate representation of the structure of the sentence. The concept of relations between sets is summarized as in (5.19a)–(5.19d). The vertical lines stand for the *cardinality* of the sets, that is for the number of elements in a set. '∩' stands for the *intersection* (common part) of the two sets. The 'minus' symbol stands for the *difference* between the sets. In set theory, the difference between set A and set B consists of the set of those elements that are members of set A but are not members of set B.

(5.19a) [every $x$] ($P_Ax$: $P_Bx$) iff $|A-B| = 0$
(5.19b) [some $x$] ($P_Ax$: $P_Bx$) iff $|A \cap B| \geq 1$
(5.19c) [most $x$] ($P_Ax$: $P_Bx$) iff $|A \cap B| > |A-B|$
(5.19d) [no $x$] ($P_Ax$: $P_Bx$) iff $|A \cap B| = 0$

In words, (5.19a) says that 'every $x$ that has the property $A$ has the property $B$' is true if and only if the *difference* between set A and set B is zero. (5.19c) says that 'most $x$s that have the property $A$ have the property $B$' is true if and only if the intersection of the sets A and B is greater than the difference between the sets A and B.

There are two standard ways of representing quantifiers as relations between sets. Above we introduced the concept of the so-called *binary quantifier*, where a quantifier (or a *determiner*) combines with a pair of predicates. In other words, the determiner, such as *most*, represented as 'most $x$', combines with two properties, such as 'dog $x$' and 'cute $x$', as in (5.20).

(5.20)  [most $x$] (dog $x$: cute $x$)

The duplex condition in Figure 5.2 is how such binary quantifiers are represented in DRT. Another standard approach is that of the restricted quantifier, where the quantifier, for example *most*, first combines with predicate $A$, for example 'dog', to form a (restricted) quantifier 'most dogs', written as [most $x$: dog $x$]. This restricted quantifier then combines with the predicate $B$, for example 'cute', as in (5.21).

(5.21)  [most $x$: dog $x$] (cute $x$)

On this version, generalized quantifiers are noun phrases ('most dogs') rather than merely determiners ('most'). The difference between the two ways of relating sets is not very significant, though. Most of the time, binary quantification gives the same result as restricted quantification. This is so because the duplex condition has the property that the set on the right is a subset of the set on the left: B is an additional description of a situation described in A. So, joining A and B amounts to the same as joining A and the intersection of A and B. This property of natural-language quantifiers is called *conservativity*. It can be represented formally as in (5.22).

(5.22)  Q(A, B) iff Q(A, A ∩ B)

So, (5.15), repeated below, means the same as (5.23).

(5.15)  Most dogs are cute.

(5.23)  Most dogs are dogs that are cute.

But, as usual, there are exceptions. For example, some contextually salient interpretations of *many* don't conform to this pattern. (5.24) is not likely to mean the same as (5.25); it more likely means (5.26).

(5.24)  Many Brits are international leaders in the music industry.

(5.25)  Many Brits are Brits who are international leaders in the music industry.

(5.26)  Many individuals who are international leaders in the music industry are Brits who are international leaders in music industry.

Next, since quantifiers are relations between sets, we can classify them according to the property of inference to subsets or supersets, called *monotonicity*. In other words, we can classify them with respect to the entailment relations they exhibit. This is important in that these relations depict some patterns of valid reasoning. Monotonicity is the relation with the following property: when a sentence with a quantifier licenses an inference to a more general sentence – that is, to a larger set in a way specified in (5.27), the quantifier is *monotone increasing* (standardly symbolized as 'mon$_\uparrow$'). '$\subseteq$' means inclusion ('is a subset of'), Q stands for a quantifier, and A, B, and C for sets.

(5.27)   Q(A, B) and B $\subseteq$ C implies Q(A, C)

*All* and *most* are examples of monotone increasing quantifiers. The relevance for capturing patterns of reasoning is made clear in (5.28a) that implies (5.28b) and (5.29a) that implies (5.29b).

(5.28a)   All guests arrived early.

(5.28b)   All guests arrived.

(5.29a)   Most guests arrived late.

(5.29b)   Most guests arrived.

In contrast, when a sentence with a quantifier licenses an inference to a more specific sentence – that is, to a smaller set in a way specified in (5.30), the quantifier is *monotone decreasing* ('mon$_\downarrow$').

(5.30)   Q(A, B) and C $\subseteq$ B implies Q(A, C)

For example, *no* and *not all* are monotone decreasing, as demonstrated in (5.31a)–(5.31b) and (5.32a)–(5.32b) respectively. (Nuances of meaning will have to wait until later in the journey.)

(5.31a)   No guests arrived.

(5.31b)   No guests arrived early.

(5.32a)   Not all guests arrived.

(5.32b)   Not all guests arrived early.

The above definitions of monotonicity are formed with respect to the verb phrase and the B set. But we can also define monotonicity with respect to the noun phrase and the A set in order to account for the relation between such pairs of statements as (5.33a) and (5.33b).

(5.33a)   Every guest arrived.

(5.33b)   Every invited guest arrived.

With respect to the set A, *every* is monotone decreasing. Some quantifiers, such as *exactly*, are non-monotonic: the relation does not hold either way.

Upward and downward monotonicity capture patterns of reasoning, but they also do more than that. Monotonicity helps explain various puzzling phenomena in semantics, among them the negative polarity items introduced in Section 4.5.2 and defined as expressions that occur only in sentences with overtly or covertly marked negative contexts, such as *ever* in (5.34) and *anywhere* in (5.35).

(5.34)   I don't think Bill has *ever* been abroad.

(5.35)   Bill seldom goes *anywhere*.

'Covertly marked' negative contexts, such as those marked by *seldom, few*, or *at most*, are much more precisely delimited when we refer to the property of downward monotonicity instead: as a rule, they occur in monotone-decreasing contexts.

Other properties of quantifiers also serve explanatory roles in semantics. For example, some quantifiers are acceptable in what can be broadly called existential constructions, while others are normally not: (5.36)–(5.38) are grammatical, while (5.39)–(5.41) are normally not. ('Normally' in that there is a rather special reading of *there* that makes sentences with these quantifiers grammatical – think of, say, (5.39) uttered as a reminder.[8])

(5.36)   There is a dog in the garden.

(5.37)   There are some dogs in the garden.

(5.38)   There are many dogs in the garden.

(5.39)   *There is the dog in the garden.

(5.40)   *There is every dog in the garden.

(5.41)   *There are most dogs in the garden.

Distinguishing the classes of quantifiers acceptable in these contexts on the basis of definiteness alone would be rather vague: it works well for (5.36) and (5.39) but not so well for other quantifying expressions. Instead, we can use the distinction into the so-called *strong* and *weak* quantifiers, or strong and weak noun phrases. Weak quantifiers in English (or, weak determiners, if we go along with the terminology of binary quantifiers) are those that can follow 'there is / there are'. Noun phrases can now be classified according to their acceptability in existential sentences. Quantifiers such as *a*, number terms, most ordinary uses of *some* and *many*, are weak by this criterion, while, for example, *the, all, every* are not. In this way we can replace the rather vague definite/indefinite distinction with a more adequate categorization by appealing to this property of quantifiers. We owe this to the work of Gary L. Milsark.[9] Intuitively, following Milsark's generalization, a quantifier is strong when it is an expression of quantification and weak when it is an expression of cardinality. It is strong when it induces existential presuppositions, that is it comes with a domain of quantification. But there is a complication: weak quantifiers, apart from their standard, weak, cardinal reading, can have strong, presuppositional, specific readings. For example, in *some of the* and *most of the* constructions, *some* and *most* are strong: they come with the domain of quantification. Further, when *many* or *some* are in a position of sentence topic, they can acquire strong interpretation.[10]

---

[8] I owe this observation to Keith Allan, p.c. For more examples and a discussion of the meaning of *there* in existential sentences, see Allan 1971.
[9] See Milsark 1977, esp. p. 22.   [10] See also Büring 1999.

Alternative ways of classifying quantifiers for existential contexts have also been developed, for example based on tautology and contradiction or on the property of *symmetry*.[11] A quantifier is symmetrical when it fulfils the relation in (5.42).

(5.42)   Q(A, B) → Q(B, A)

*Some, no, at least n, at most n* are symmetrical, while *every* and *most* are not.

## 5.2.2 Quantifiers and Quirks of Interpretation

Quantifier expressions are subject to various quirks of interpretation and cross-linguistic differences. We have seen that *some* often means 'some but not all', but it can also mean 'some and perhaps all', 'some but I am not sure if all', or even, arguably, 'some but I want to be modest and won't say all', and so forth. (4.35), repeated below, is an example where the strengthening to 'not all' is likely to take place, unless, say, we have grounds to believe that the speaker is a very accomplished pianist who is trying to be modest.

(4.35)   I can play some nocturnes by Chopin. (≫ I can't play them all.)

In other words, we can stipulate that *some* is semantically (i) *bilaterally bounded*, that is, bounded from both ends: meaning not 'at least some', not 'at most some', but 'exactly some', so to speak, or that it is (ii) *unilaterally bounded*, that is, only *lower-bounded*, producing a, so to speak, 'at least some', 'some or more' interpretation. Or the semantics could be (iii) underspecified, especially in view of the fact that context can also occasionally warrant a 'some or less' interpretation, as in (5.43a), analogous to the interpretation of number terms as exemplified in (5.43b) and discussed in the next section.

(5.43a)   Anna can spend some money without going into overdraft.

(5.43b)   Anna can spend £100 without going into overdraft.

But notice that examples such as (5.43a)–(5.43b) appear to convey some sense of negation or restriction: she *mustn't* spend more, she is *allowed* to spend a certain amount but not more, she *can* spend a certain amount but not more. Terms such as *mustn't, allow,* and *can* may be responsible for the behaviour of the quantifier. If so, then the suitable contexts are independently constrained.

One well-entrenched proposal is to adopt the lower-bounded semantics ('some and possibly all') and ascribe the precisification to 'some but not all' to rules of rational communication, such as the Gricean or post-Gricean principles briefly referred to

---

[11] See also Barwise and Cooper 1981. For example, *Not all dogs are dogs* (contradiction) and *All dogs are dogs* (tautology). For a more extensive discussion of the tests, see e.g. de Swart 1998, pp. 181–183. On symmetry, see Keenan, e.g. 1996.

during Stage 4 and discussed at length in Section 7.1. The gist of the explanation is that it is normally assumed by interlocutors that it would have been rational to use a stronger alternative such as *all* if the speaker had sufficient information to utter it truthfully. In the Gricean tradition further developed by Laurence Horn in the 1980s,[12] expressions that allow for such weaker and stronger alternatives are called *scalar* in that they allow for weaker and stronger items ordered on a scale. The assertion of a weaker expression is said to conversationally imply that none of the stronger ones on the scale apply. As was already anticipated, Gricean pragmatics is discussed in more depth in Stage 7 but suffice it to say that the topic has generated extensive theoretical debates, as well as a plethora (or even overabundance) of experimentation, especially in the 1990s and early 2010s.[13] With hindsight, arguably, it is fair to say that the bulk of contributions that amount to this excessive attention underplayed the obvious fact that the bilaterally bounded ('some but not all') interpretation is neither the general, default interpretation (what we will later call, after Grice, the *generalized conversational implicature*), nor a context-driven (*particularized*) one. As is often the case, the truth is somewhere in between: both interpretations pertain to conventions, or salient interpretations for particular contexts. For example, in (5.44), *some* is used with a clear intention to minimize criticism and as such is not upper-bounded. And this is so, arguably, in virtue of social, cultural, and partly linguistic conventions (insofar as the construction itself evolved to play this role).[14]

(5.44)    Some people say that you are too assertive.

Likewise, the use of the quantifier *most* in discourse does not quite conform to the said/implicated distinction that is often readily imposed. Using an analogous explanation to that offered for *some*, it may seem that *most* ought to semantically encode the 'more than half' meaning, while pragmatically implying the (cancellable) 'upper-boundary' meaning 'not all'. However, empirical evidence suggests that this mould does not quite fit the data. As Mira Ariel (2004: 700) points out, 'the circumbounded meaning has a privileged status, which the lower-bounded-only meaning does not enjoy'. Interestingly, this meaning does not conform to the 'more than fifty per cent' interpretation that is often assumed but rather depends on standards that are normally set for a given scenario. So, perhaps it is some default situated meaning that ought to be taken as the semantic-lexical content of *most*, with the compatibility with the 'possibly all' interpretation being carefully controlled by context. She does not go that far in that this privileged meaning can be cancelled in some contexts, but it is certainly a possibility that semantic content is rich and 'reducible' rather than underspecified and able to be 'enriched'. It is even more plausible that semantic content is *just right for*

---

[12] See Horn, e.g. 1984, 1988.
[13] The literature is vast. See e.g. Noveck 2018; Cummins and Katsos 2019; and for early work, contributions to Noveck and Sperber 2004.
[14] See also van Tiel, Noveck, and Kissine 2018, who demonstrate experimentally that *some* behaves differently in different scenarios and 'subtle features of the [experimental] display influence the frequency of embedded upper-bounded construals' (p. 757).

*the context* – the desideratum to which we keep returning in this journey through meaning.

Needless to say, the usefulness of generalized quantifiers for such ambiguities of interpretation is at present very limited. Similarly, semantic ambiguities posed by the distributive/collective reading distinction discussed in Section 4.2, exemplified in (5.45), can only be represented but not resolved.

(5.45)   Few children got a dessert they wanted.

Although the reading on which they got different desserts each (the distributive reading) is, arguably, more intuitive, it is also possible to envisage a context in which only one type of dessert was served at a party and it happened to be one that not so many children liked (the collective reading). Representations such as DRSs can distinguish between the two readings, but the theory only allows us to *list* such readings rather than *choose* which one to represent. The selection of the interpretation that was intended, meant by the speaker, and/or recovered by the addressee is a matter for a different theory: a pragmatic theory of discourse interpretation. For us here, however, it is part of *the same* story about meaning, by whatever name one wants to think of it.

DRT has already made tremendous inroads into such a unified theory. First, DRSs are conceived of as mental representations. Next, the strength of DRT, as will be more evident in Section 6.1.2.1, is to represent discourses rather than merely separate sentences. Finally, the theory allows for incorporation of pragmatic information – information derived from context and from the surrounding text (*co-text*). But it is a theory in the computational linguistics tradition, so its strength lies in accounting for various possible interpretations rather than eliminating all but one, like we do in inquiring into human cognitive processes in discourse. We also want to know how one particular interpretation materializes as the correct one in a given context. Important advances towards such extensions of the theory that formalize rules of how discourse combines information from a variety of sources have already been made. We have already mentioned, for example, SDRT and Default Semantics and will attend to such options in Stages 6 and 7. But, as has been emphasized throughout this journey, the issue as to what kind of meaning a semantic theory should investigate has to be addressed pre-semantically, in philosophical semantics (or metasemantics).[15] It is on this meta-level of analysis that decisions are made concerning the goals and scope of inquiry, as well as the choices of theories and method to pursue it. Hence we stipulated it as one of our desiderata from the start.

## 5.2.3   Number Terms and Counting

As was briefly indicated above, generalized quantifiers cater not only for expressions such as *some*, *few*, or *most* but, importantly, can also be useful for counting. *Numerals*, sometimes dubbed *numericals*, are expressions that convey numbers and are used for

---

[15] See Jaszczolt 2022.

this purpose. But the way numerals work in natural languages can be quite quirky. First, although in what follows we will adhere to the view that they ought to be treated as determiners, their behaviour also makes them akin to adjectives and they are sometimes analysed formally as such. For example, they do not necessarily occur in the determiner position, as exemplified by the well-formedness of such phrases as *the three dogs* or *every three dogs*.[16] Next, numerals are obvious candidates for semantic ambiguity. In English, like in many other languages, and like in the case of other quantifiers discussed in the previous sections, there is often no overt indicator as to whether the number term is meant collectively, as in (5.46), or distributively, as in (5.47).

(5.46)    Three boys sang a Christmas carol (together).

(5.47)    Three boys passed the exam (individually).

While in these examples the sentence itself provides fairly disambiguating context, it is not always the case. In (5.48), the boys could have shared a pizza or ordered one each.

(5.48)    Three boys ordered a pizza.

Representations such as DRSs can distinguish between the two readings, treating the distributive one as a quantifier that calls for a duplex condition and the collective as, simply, a plural subject, as in Figs. 5.3 and 5.4 respectively. Upper-case letters stand for plural (non-atomic) referents.[17]

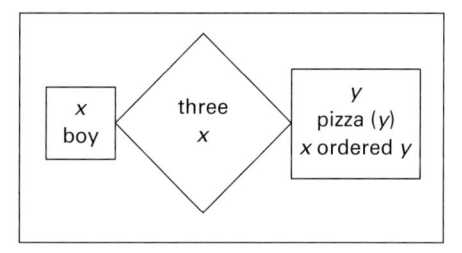

```
┌─────────┐   ◇        ┌──────────┐
│   x     │  three     │    y     │
│  boy    │    x       │ pizza (y)│
│         │            │x ordered y│
└─────────┘            └──────────┘
```

**Figure 5.3**  Partial DRS for the distributive reading of (5.48) ('Three boys ordered a pizza.')

---

[16] See e.g. Rothstein 2017, esp. Chapter 2. On her analysis, cardinal numerals are property expressions that can stand for adjectives or nominals. So, *three* denotes the property of 'being three in number' as in (i).

(i)    $\lambda x \, [|x| = 3]$

See also Szabó 2018 on what counts as a quantifier.

[17] This is only one possible way of representing the distributive reading. Another is to introduce the plural discourse referent $X$ and the associated conditions into the main DRS, then the singular referent $x$ and the condition $x \in X$ to the restrictor, and quantify over 'every $x$' from this set. This option would facilitate a switch from a distributive to a collective reading in subsequent sentences, as in (5.47) followed by *They celebrated* (together). See Kamp and Reyle 1993, Sections 4.1.5 and 4.4.1 for a detailed discussion of semantic ambiguities of sentences with numerals. The meaning of 'non-atomic' is explained there in terms of divisibility in Section 4.3.1. Examples (5.48)–(5.49) are loosely modelled on those Kamp and Reyle employ for their explanation of the phenomenon.

$$\boxed{\begin{array}{c} Xy \\ \\ \text{boy}(X) \\ |X| = 3 \\ \text{pizza}(y) \\ X \text{ ordered } y \end{array}}$$

**Figure 5.4** Partial DRS for the collective reading of (5.48) ('Three boys ordered a pizza.')

In Figure 5.3, there is no need to distinguish between different pizzas they ordered (*y*s) because the scope of the duplex condition (the box on the right) already does it for us. DRT opts to start with the intuitive plural referent and then add the 'distribution over pizzas' later.

So, DRSs provide a way of representing the possible meanings of a natural-language construction (that is, a sentence or a string of sentences) that can potentially have different readings. But they can also do more than that. As I indicated earlier, since DRT is a theory of *discourse* meaning, it also aims to represent multi-sentence discourses. It does so in order to account for the structure of information that is dynamically revealed through consecutive sentences. Representing numerals as in Figures 5.3–5.4 will also allow us to represent the plural anaphoric pronoun *they* in the second sentence of (5.49).

(5.49)    Three boys ordered a pizza. They were hungry.

The DRS can now be easily constructed by adding a discourse referent standing for *they* and making it anaphoric on *three boys*. Figure 5.5 represents this two-sentence discourse on the collective reading (and fn 17 addresses the distributive reading).

The theory also allows for the incorporation of some aspects of pragmatically conveyed meanings such as, for example, presuppositions. And since it is a theory in progress and with various offshoots, and its DRSs aspire to the status of cognitively real representations, it should in principle allow us to home in on the cognitively real meaning instead of merely listing the possible interpretations. Its offshoots such as SDRT and Default Semantics referred to before incorporate, in very different ways, such generalizations over contexts. But the theory itself can be employed in the service of different objectives. To reiterate, computational linguists normally find it more relevant to *list possible interpretations* and provide their semantic analyses because doing so gives them an important explanatory step in training machines. And they can list them using DRT. Stemming from the computational tradition, this was what the theory was first designed to do. But, as was mentioned in the previous section, 'kicking the DRS up', so to speak, to the level of contextually salient interpretations is also a possible way of employing it. This has been done in Default Semantics, where representations stand for the main intended meanings, irrespectively of how they were conveyed: by saying it overtly, contextually implying, or appealing to conventions. For example, anticipating somewhat, (5.47) can mean in a specific context that,

```
┌─────────────────┐
│     X y Z       │
├─────────────────┤
│    boy (X)      │
│    |X| = 3      │
│    pizza (y)    │
│   X ordered y   │
│     X = Z       │
│    hungry (Z)   │
└─────────────────┘
```

**Figure 5.5** Partial DRS for the collective reading of (5.49) ('Three boys ordered a pizza. They were hungry.')

say, *only* three boys passed the exam and communicate the main message that the exam was much too difficult or that the rest of the class were not well prepared.

Ambiguities and vagaries of interpretation posed by numerals do not end there. First, there is the problem of the relative scope of numerals that was discussed in Section 3.2 in example (3.43) repeated below.

(3.43)  Three boys sent five Christmas presents to four friends.

Calculating the ways in which this sentence can be ambiguous is a treat for semantics enthusiasts. But even if a sentence contains only one numeral, such as (5.50), the context can endow it with different interpretations. (5.50a) and (5.50b) demonstrate how this can occur – especially with a dedicated intonation pattern in (5.50b).

(5.50)  Bill has three dogs.

(5.50a)  Bill has three dogs – in fact, he has four if you count the one that lives in his workshop.

(5.50b)  Bill doesn't have *three* dogs – he has *four*.

There doesn't appear to be a sense of contradiction in (5.50a) or in (5.50b). To make the argument more persuasive, let us think of the same situation, Bill's having four dogs, and imagine they are working dogs, used as sniffer dogs. The conversation proceeds as in (5.51).

(5.51)  A   I need to borrow three sniffer dogs. Do you know who can help?
        B   Bill has three sniffer dogs.

Because it is relevant in this context that Bill has (at least) three sniffer dogs, this is what was volunteered in the response (the fourth dog can stay at home and have a rest).

Similarly, in (5.43b), repeated below, the speaker is not claiming that Anna can spend exactly £100. Just as in (5.51) the context induces the 'at least $n$' interpretation, in (5.43b) it induces the 'at most $n$' one.

(5.43b)  Anna can spend £100 without going into overdraft.

Another possible reading is 'approximately', 'more or less', often preferred in the case of round numbers. The most natural reading of (5.52) is that Bill earns roughly £30,000 a year.

(5.52)   Bill earns £30,000 a year.

The meaning of number terms is a fascinating topic in semantics and pragmatics and it has led to many interesting proposals.[18] It has been suggested that sense-generality (or underdetermination, discussed in Section 4.5.3) may account for the diversity of readings: the semantics of numerals is underspecified and the missing aspects of meaning are filled in by pragmatic processing of the utterance. Or, assuming that we can ignore cases of the 'at most' interpretation in that they can be explained by their syntactic environment as was discussed in the previous section, we could suggest that numerals have the 'at least $n$' semantics, analogous to the lower-bound as opposed to the bilaterally-bound quantifier *some* just discussed. The precisification to 'exactly $n$' can then be ascribed to rules of rational communication, such as the Gricean or post-Gricean principles already referred to. The gist of this explanation is that it is assumed by interlocutors that the speaker has chosen the most relevant and informative statement for the given situation. After all, the readings vary. Some distributive readings may carry upward entailments as their standard interpretations (contextual defaults), as in (5.53). Cheating four or more times is also likely to result in a fine.

(5.53)   If Bill cheats three times, he will be fined.

On the other hand, there are good arguments in favour of punctual ('exactly $n$') semantics. It is more parsimonious in that it does not suggest an extra layer of utterance processing. Moreover, collective readings of sentences such as (5.46) fare most happily with punctual semantics, in that downward entailments (two boys, one boy) do not arise. Since 'exactly three' is normally more informative than 'at least three' or 'at least, at most, approximately, or exactly three', it makes sense to adopt it as the semantic content – not to be adopted in special contexts such as (5.43), (5.51), or (5.52). It is more informative because the set of numbers that make 'exactly $n$' true is a subset of the sets of numbers that make the other interpretations true. As Jean-Pierre Koenig emphasizes in his insightful study of numerals, '[i]f the truth set of a sentence A is a proper subset of the truth set of a sentence B, A is more informative than B' (Koenig 1993: 147). Arguably, if *three* didn't mean 'exactly three', the speaker would have said, according to this pragmatic principle, 'exactly three' instead. This, however, is not normally the case. Hence, assuming the correctness of the principle of informativeness, numerals have punctual ('exactly') semantics. Examples with multiple numerals such as (3.43) also point to punctual semantics. Furthermore, experimental evidence appears to suggest that the 'exactly $n$' interpretation is much more psychologically salient.[19]

---

[18] For a diversified selection, see Koenig 1993; Geurts 1998c; Carston 1998a; Horn 1992, 2006; Bultinck 2005; Cummins 2015; Rothstein 2017.

[19] See e.g. Musolino 2004.

In fact, it has been suggested that the semantics of expressions, including quantifiers, should be decided on an individual basis, allowing for some generalizations concerning the most basic meaning. Bart Geurts proposes that for some expressions the 'exactly' sense may be basic, while for others it is the 'at least' sense.[20] Numerals belong to the first category, while adjectives such as *warm* or *bad* are in the other. In other words, whatever is described as warm may also be hot, while when I have £20, I don't at the same time have £100, unless the context strongly suggests that admitting only to the ownership of £20 is required. This seems to be a common-sense proposal, and broadly in the spirit of the more recent developments in lexical semantics discussed in Stage 2.

Be that as it may, numerals are definitely fascinating and their quirkiness does not end here. There are also considerable cross-linguistic differences. Some languages foreground counting, that is have numerals in everyday parlance that correspond to numbers as abstract objects in arithmetic, while others lexicalize more vague distinctions, such as 'one', 'two', and 'many'. Daniel Everett, who spent several years living among the Pirahã people, a hunter-gatherer tribe in the Amazon region of Brazil, reports that the Pirahã language lacks numbers. Instead of saying that one has one, or eight, children, a mother would say she has a 'small' or 'large' quantity – in fact, the word that would be most likely to mean 'one' means 'small'. This is not an isolated case; in many Australian Aboriginal languages words for numerals are later borrowings from other languages. While this state of affairs could arguably be explained by the lexicon/grammar/pragmatics trade-off (referred to in Section 4.6) in that speakers of these languages are capable of *acquiring* concepts for counting, it suggests that the difference is deeper than that. If the culture does not require precise counting, if there is no need for it in everyday life, there are no means whatsoever, trade-offs including, to convey numbers. But when there is a need to, say, understand prices for trading purposes, the concepts are brought to the fore, and so are corresponding words.[21]

On the other hand, there also appear to be semantic universals in the domain of numerals. Numerals are standardly used for counting as well as for measuring: we say *three apples* but also *three metres of string* or *three litres of wine*. Sometimes a phrase can be ambiguous between counting and measuring: *three bottles of wine* can mean a physical three glass bottles filled with wine or the content amounting to three bottles of wine – that is, standardly $3 \times 0.75 \, l = 2.25 \, l$ in whatever kind and number of containers. As Susan Rothstein shows in her recent book *Semantics for Counting and Measuring*,[22] counting and measuring are syntactically and semantically two very different operations, even in spite of the fact that sometimes the same construction can be used for both, as in her examples (5.54)–(5.56) to which we are just moving. But the counting/measuring distinction displays a striking syntactic entrenchment cross-linguistically. In other words, various typologically diverse languages she investigated appear to display this syntactic difference between counting and measuring. It can be

---

[20] See Geurts 1998a, p. 296.
[21] For discussions see e.g. Everett 2006, 2012. For counting across cultures see also Rothstein 2017.
[22] See Rothstein 2017.

found even in languages in which numerals cannot directly modify nouns but instead require classifiers. In Mandarin Chinese, the classifier *píng* ('bottle') in the phrase meaning 'three bottles of wine' can stand for measuring, as in (5.54), or for counting, as in (5.55). However, since it is possible to obtain an unambiguous measure reading by inserting *de*, there is evidence that the semantics of (5.54) and (5.55) is different. This can be tested by attempting to insert *de* in a sentence with the unambiguously counting reading such as (5.55), as in (5.56).

(5.54)  wǒ    de    jiǔliàng              shì    sān     píng             jiǔ.
        my    de    drinking-ability     be     three   $Class_{bottle}$ wine
        'My drinking ability is three bottles of wine.'

(5.55)  tā    kāi    le      sān     píng              jiǔ.
        he    open   Perf    three   $Class_{bottle}$  wine
        'He opened three bottles of wine.'

(5.56)  ?tā   kāi    le      sān     píng              de    jiǔ.
        he    open   Perf    three   $Class_{bottle}$  de    wine

(adapted from Rothstein 2017: 79)[23]

The measure interpretation in (5.54) is [[sān píng] jiǔ], that is, [[Numerical Classifier] NP]. The counting interpretation in (5.55) is [sān [píng jiǔ]], that is, [Numerical [Classifier NP]]. After adding *de* to (5.55), as in (5.56), the relevant part of the structure 'tries to become' [[[sān píng] de] jiǔ], analogous to [[sān píng] jiǔ], the measure reading (adapted from Rothstein 2017: 73, 93). In short, the explanation is that in the measuring structure, Numerical Classifier and NP combine to form a measure predicate. Quantifying is a fascinating topic indeed, in its own right.

## 5.3 Representing Time

The temporal location of the situations to which sentences (and utterances of them) refer also requires a metalanguage that goes beyond the standard devices of predicate logic. At the very least, it requires an extension to the metalanguage, such as that offered by *tense logic*. But before discussing how to represent time in semantics, it is important to attend to the object that such temporal reference is about, namely situations.

### 5.3.1 Eventualities and Their Types

Most sentences that speakers of English produce come with an indication of the time of the situation referred to by the sentence. In other words, they come with an expression of *temporality*. Temporality is conveyed mainly through tense, indicated by verb forms

---

[23] Rothstein also provides an interesting formal semantic analysis there. On the mass/count distinction, see also e.g. Allan 1980; Bunt 2006; or Laycock 2006.

or by temporal adverbials such as *now, yesterday, a year ago*, or by both. Since temporality marks the time of the situation presented by the sentence, we have to start by discussing the properties of situations.

Situations are characterized by their type, tense, and aspect. There are various typologies available on the market.[24] According to one, type involves the distinction between *states*, that is situations that do not involve an action, and *dynamic situations* – the ones that do. The latter are divided into *events* and *processes*. Processes emphasize the action of 'doing something' rather than the effect of the action. As such, processes focus on the internal structure of the situation, while in events the situation is presented 'as a whole', so to speak. Following Emmon Bach, semanticists often refer to the category comprising states, events and processes as *eventualities*.[25] (5–57)-(5.59) exemplify these three types of situations.

(5.57) Bill likes Lady Gaga. (state)

(5.58) Anna built a house. (event)

(5.59) I am writing a book. (process)

Unlike events, processes and states often subdivide into parts that are processes and states (respectively) of the same kind.

Although more-fine-grained classifications will not concern us very much in the journey through meaning we are pursuing here, some are worth mentioning in that they are often referred to in the relevant literature. First, there are subdivisions within processes, where there are, for example, *inchoatives*, pertaining to a change of state, as in (5.60), and *resultatives*, processes with completion, as in (5.61).

(5.60) Water evaporated.

(5.61) Tom baked a cake.

It is important to remember that the distinction between events, states, and processes is a matter of degree rather than exactness. A sentence can be classified as representing a resultative process or an event, as (5.61) demonstrates.

Linguists interested in the classification of verbs come up with related typologies but, as will become clear shortly, we should not confuse classifying situations with classifying verbs that help represent them. First, there are *stative verbs* such as *have, know, believe*, or *be*. These verbs rarely take progressive or imperative forms and when they do take a progressive form, they do so to mark an impermanent, transient state as in (5.62).

(5.62) Anna is being silly.

Next, there are *dynamic verbs*, that can be *durative*, describing a process that lasts for a period of time, as in (5.63), or *punctual*, describing instantaneous (*semelfactive*)

---

[24] For a discussion of different classifications, see e.g. Rothstein 2004.
[25] See Bach 1981, p. 69 and for an introduction, Kamp and Reyle 1993, Chapter 5.

events, as in (5.64). Punctual verbs can also have an *iterative* (i.e. repetitive) interpretation, as in (5.65)

(5.63)   Bill walked.

(5.64)   Bill coughed.

(5.65)   Bill coughed all the time.

Dynamic verbs can also be *telic*, that is have a completion, like *build*, or *atelic*, that is have no natural end, like *sleep*. The difference is quite significant. For example, if the process in (5.66) is interrupted, (5.67) is true. But the same relation does not hold of (5.68) and (5.58) repeated below. So, telic verbs correspond to resultative processes/events.

(5.66)   Anna was sleeping.

(5.67)   Anna slept.

(5.68)   Anna was building a house.

(5.58)   Anna built a house.

But it has to be remembered that the classification of verbs is not the same enterprise as classifying situations. We can learn very little about the situation type by looking at the verb alone. For example, the atelic verb *run* can be used in a resultative (telic) construction in (5.69).

(5.69)   Bill was running in the school charity event.

Distinctions between verb types only help with classifying situations to a certain degree.[26]

For the purpose of our search for an adequate metalanguage, detailed subdivisions are of little use. Although they are conceptually important, they do not translate well

---

[26] Zeno Vendler's (1967) typology is of some historical interest here. He classified situation types into activities, accomplishments, achievements, and states. The problem with his classification is that Vendler assumes the unit of time to be an *instant* (moment) rather than, more adequately, an *interval* (stretch of time). His attempted definitions are presented below and clearly demonstrate the shortcomings of an instant-based account. *Activities* are processes exemplified by (i) where the time instant $t$ belongs to a time stretch throughout which Bill was running.
   (i) Bill was running (at $t$).
      *Accomplishments* are *protracted events* and concern unique and definite time periods. In (ii), the time instant $t$ is on the time stretch in which Bill built the shed.
   (ii) Bill built a shed (at $t$).
      Next, *achievements* are *instantaneous events* and as such pertain to unique and definite time instants. In (iii), the time instant at which Bill won the race is between some instants $t_1$ and $t_2$.
   (iii) Bill won a race (between $t_1$ and $t_2$).
      Finally, *states* are said to be about indefinite and non-unique time instants. For example, (iv) means that at any instant between instants $t_1$ and $t_2$, John loved this person.
   (iv) John loved somebody (from $t_1$ to $t_2$).
      Next, Dowty 1979 is credited with proposing a taxonomy of the classes of verbs where the basic unit of time is an *interval* rather than an *instant*. See esp. Dowty 1979, p. 184. See also Dowty 1986 on the temporal relation between sentences in discourse and the role of pragmatics.

into a formal representation. Instead, formal semanticists often adopt a binary distinction into (i) events, understood as eventualities that involve a change, and (ii) states, understood as eventualities that involve a continuation of some condition. This binary distinction is employed, for example, in DRT and will figure in the DRSs later on in this journey. The preference for the binary distinction is dictated by the fact that formal semantics has drawn on the distinctions in formal languages of logic rather than on the morphology and grammar of natural language. To reiterate, it has done so for a range of very good reasons revolving around the need for a clear, unambiguous, formal metalanguage with which the often fuzzy, vague, and ambiguous constructions can be tackled. Just as it worked for sentence structure in predicate-argument constructions and for connecting sentences, so, as we will see, does it work for representing time. But, as can be anticipated, it only works up to a point.

### 5.3.2 Tense and Aspect

Eventualities happen in time. But time is itself a complex notion. There is time that is *external* to the situation, such as location in the present, the past, or the future, normally expressed by tense in English, and time *internal* to the situation, where situations are presented as extended in time or instantaneous, complete or incomplete, iterated or non-iterated. Such distinctions are expressed by aspect. The distinctions just discussed, such as punctual/durative, telic/atelic, are aspectual distinctions.

Aspectual distinctions are often subjective and hence do not necessarily result in differences in truth conditions (but they can be truth-conditionally relevant). On the crudest of definitions, the *perfective/imperfective* distinction is a distinction between a completed situation and a situation in which we refer to its internal, temporal structure. Next, within imperfective, we have the *habitual/continuous* distinction. Habitual pertains to a situation characteristic of a longer period, frequently rendered by the '*used to* + *verb*' construction, as in (5.70).

(5.70)   Anna used to play the violin.

Continuous means durative and is subdivided into *progressive* and *non-progressive*, where progressive pertains to a situation in progress, standardly rendered by the '*be* + V-*ing*' form, as in (5.71).[27]

(5.71)   Bill is playing the piano.

We are interested here in aspect from the point of view of its meaning, that is aspect as a semantic category. It has to be remembered that aspectual distinctions can be expressed through grammar or the lexicon and there is no clear boundary between the two. They can also be left to pragmatics – to inference from the context or to default interpretations, for example relying on invoking conventional scenarios and scripts. In some languages, for example Polish or Russian, aspect belongs largely to word formation. In others, like English, it is a grammatical phenomenon. In Polish, the perfective/

---

[27] For a diagram of standard aspectual oppositions, see Comrie 1976, p. 25.

imperfective distinction is often marked on the verb by prefixes, such as *na-* and *prze-* in (5.72) and (5.73).

(5.72)  pisać                napisać
        'write' *Imperf*     'write' *Perf*

(5.73)  czytać               przeczytać
        'read' *Imperf*      'read' *Perf*

Different prefixes can be added to the stem and they can also affect the basic lexical meaning of the verb. For example, adding prefix *prze-* to *pisać* results in *przepisać* that means 'to copy'; adding *za-* results in *zapisać* ('to fill completely with writing'). The number of such perfective prefixes is considerably large. In English, progressive normally renders the meaning of imperfective. In (5.74), it is opposed to the 'default perfective', so to speak, that stems from the very essence of the verb *to build*.

(5.74)  Bill was building a house./ Bill built a house.

Some languages, for example Mandarin Chinese, Malay, or Classical Hebrew, grammaticalize aspectual distinctions, having no grammaticalized tense. Some other languages have both, tense and aspect combined, like English. There are also languages where grammatical markings of both time and aspect are optional, like Thai.

In what follows, we will focus on temporality, both external and internal, as a semantic category. That is, we will focus on ways to express concepts to do with location in time, duration, the passing of time, and any other related notions. The fact that time can be conveyed by the lexicon, grammar, or pragmatics, does, however, have to be borne in mind as different formal theories of meaning go to different lengths to represent what is not overtly expressed. As such, they will have different renderings of situations where there is a tense–time mismatch, as in (5.75).

(5.75)  This is what happened to me yesterday. I go to the office, I sit at my desk, and this guy comes and says ...

This is a case of the 'vivid present', or the 'past of narration'. Since the adverb *yesterday* is there, the temporal location in the past is transparent. But whether we should choose to represent the grammatical present-tense form and tweak the mismatch later on in pragmatics, or rather include in the formal representation what is actually intended, is a matter for debate – and, of course, a matter of the initial desiderata. I return to such mismatches after dealing with the preliminary essentials.

Tense allows the speaker to describe a situation as happening prior to, concurrent with, or following the act of speaking. But it is also perspectival: it is a *deictic* category, in that the point of reference (*deictic centre*) need not be the act of speaking; it can be located in the past or in the future, as in (5.76) and (5.77). We assume that both sentences were produced at the time of writing this, that is 2021.

(5.76)  Tom had written half of the novel by 2010.

(5.77)  Tom will have written half of the novel by 2030.

Deixis is the topic of Section 6.2.4 but for now the deictic category can be conceptualized as follows. Time can be represented (among other ways) as a straight line with past events to the left and future to the right of the point representing the present moment, as in Figure 5.6.

Tense can now be viewed as a 'grammaticalized expression of location in time' (Comrie 1985: 9). Absolute tense is a tense which takes the present moment as its point of reference, as in Figure 5.6. Relative tense shifts the deictic centre to the past or to the future.

Within absolute tense, there is the conceptual distinction into the past, the present, and the future. However, many languages follow two-way grammatical distinctions, into (i) past and non-past or (ii) future and non-future. English has no morphological future tense and the category of future tense is itself contentious. Future in English and some other languages is commonly rendered by what diachronically is a modal expression (such as *will* or *shall*). According to one view, this gives it a different conceptual status that is best represented as in Figure 5.7, where instead of representing the future as a straight continuation of the past as in Figure 5.6, we conceptualize it as open – as a bundle of possibilities. As such, it is conceptually a kind of modality – a category to which I return in Section 5.4.

## 5.3.3 Tense Logic?

First, let us see how far we would be able to get without formalizing situation types. Let us see how useful it would be to use simple tense logic – an extension to our metalanguage of predicate logic that adds only tense operators. We will consider for this purpose tense logic developed by logician and philosopher Arthur Prior in the 1960s. Priorean tense logic, which was an important landmark at the time, is a standard predicate logic to which two tense operators are added: P and F. P and F are one-place sentential connectives, analogous to the negation operator. We can prefix them to

**Figure 5.6** A possible representation of time flow

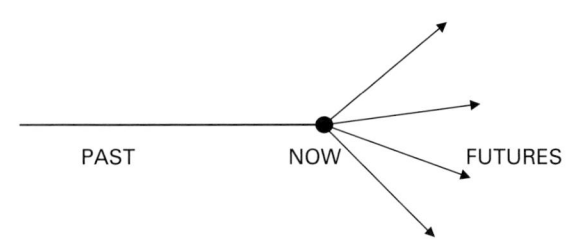

**Figure 5.7** A possible representation of branching future

formulae, that is to any sentences in our metalanguage: P$\varphi$, F$\varphi$. Symbols '$\varphi$' and '$\phi$' stand here for *metalinguistic sentential variables*, or *metavariables*, that is for sentences of a formal language such as propositional logic *when it is used in the role of a metalanguage*. They stand for any sentences, not merely simple ones such as *p* or *q* but also for complex ones such as *p* → *q*. This allows us to analyse any, simple or complex, sentences of natural language in this way. P$\varphi$ means 'it was the case that $\varphi$' and F$\varphi$ means 'it will be the case that $\varphi$'. We can make 'P' stand for Simple Past in English and 'F' for Simple Future. To reiterate, Priorean tense logic does not represent states or events, so (5.78) can be represented as in (5.79).

(5.78) Anna bought a house.

(5.79) $\exists x$ (House $(x) \land$ P Buy $(a, x)$)

The extension of a predicate is now relativized to time; it is a function of time, by the same token making the truth value of the sentence dependent on time. So, an adequate model should specify the extensions of all the predicates in the language *at a given time*. In Priorean logic, times are understood as indivisible instants, ordered by the earlier–later relation, represented symbolically as e.g. '$t_1 < t_2$'. Taking this relativization to time into account, a model *M* can now be defined as a pair consisting of (i) a *time structure* which consists of a set of temporal instants and the earlier–later relation and (ii) a function that assigns to each time *t* a corresponding model $M_t$. The truth conditions for P$\varphi$ and F$\varphi$ are as in (5.80) and (5.81).

(5.80) P$\varphi$ is true in *M* at *t* iff $\exists t'$ ($t' < t \land \varphi$ is true in *M* at $t'$)

(5.81) F$\varphi$ is true in *M* at *t* iff $\exists t'$ ($t' > t \land \varphi$ is true in *M* at $t'$)

(adapted from Kamp and Reyle 1993: 486–487)[28]

To linguists who want to use Priorean logic as a metalanguage for sentences in natural language, this system may already begin to look somewhat inadequate. Likewise, it may look somewhat restrictive to subsequent generations of readers like us who are equipped with the arguments (even if only from concepts familiar from traditional grammar such as grammatical aspect) in favour of incorporating situation types into semantics. First, there are problems with expressing, for example, the sense of Present Perfect Continuous as in (5.82), in that we have to represent the fact that the process of reading began in the past but continues up to the present and will perhaps continue into the future.

(5.82) Bill has been reading *The Handmaid's Tale* since breakfast.

But there are also different tense logics. One of them has operators that can be loosely translated as 'since' (S) and 'until' (U), where S stands for 'it has been the case

---

[28] For a more detailed introduction and formalization, see Kamp and Reyle 1993, p. 486. For advanced readers, original texts by Prior may be of interest, such as Prior 1957, 1967, 1968a, 1968b.

that $\phi$ since it was the case that $\varphi$' and temporal variations on it ('it had/will have been ...') and U for 'it was the case that $\phi$ until it was the case that $\varphi$' and temporal variations ('it will be/had been ...'). These would help to account for (5.82). The truth conditions for S ($\varphi, \phi$) and U ($\varphi,\phi$) can now be intuitively worked out: for S ($\varphi, \phi$) to be true there has to be a time $t'$ earlier than some deictic $t$ ($t' < t$) at which $\varphi$ is true and for all times $t''$ such that they fall in the interval between $t$ and $t'$ ($t' < t''$ and $t'' < t$), $\phi$ has to be true. But, as Kamp and Reyle explain in considerable detail, even this improvement does not take us far enough: the definitions of S and U are not a perfect match with what we want to use them for in that, in tense logic, by definition $q$ need not be true at time $t$. (As Kamp and Reyle say, S($\varphi, \phi$) $\wedge \phi$ would be the correct match of the English use of *since*.)[29] In addition, natural language can express many more nuances of temporal meanings. It can do so, for example, by cross-sentential temporal anaphora, as in (5.83), where the Simple Past verb form interacts with the order of the sentences $S_1$ and $S_2$ and the situation type (both are events) to produce the effect of a narration, where the temporal reference of $S_2$ follows that of $S_1$.

(5.83)   Bill found a hedgehog. He took it to an animal rescue centre.

Temporal anaphora as a link between sentences is very important in DRT in that, to reiterate, one of the core objectives of the theory is to build representations of entire discourses.

Looked at from the historical perspective, the idea of the anaphoric dimension of tenses is due to Hans Reichenbach who, in his seminal *Elements of Symbolic Logic* published in the 1940s, defined tenses by two relations: (i) the relation between reference time and speech time and (ii) the relation between eventuality and reference time. For instance, Simple Past has reference time preceding speech time and the eventuality is located at the reference time. Reference time is provided by the context. Following Reichenbach, we can represent tenses as in Figure 5.8. S is the speech point, the time of utterance; R is the reference point, the time talked about; and E is the event point. The arrow indicates the flow of time.

Past Perfect
E   R   S
'I had written a book.'

Simple Past
R,E   S
'I wrote a book.'

Present Perfect
E   S,R
'I have written a book.'

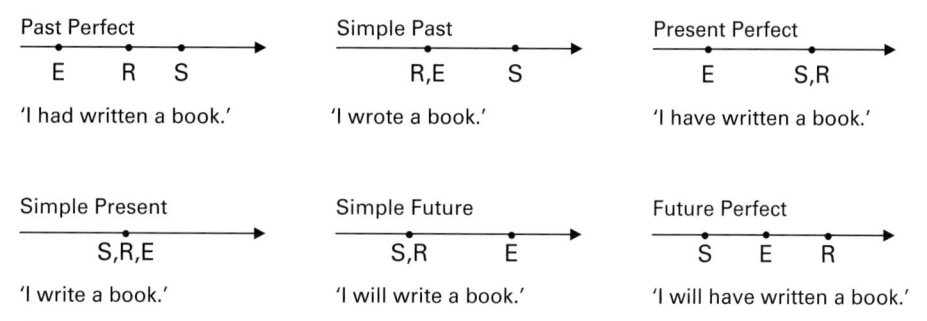

Simple Present
S,R,E
'I write a book.'

Simple Future
S,R   E
'I will write a book.'

Future Perfect
S   E   R
'I will have written a book.'

**Figure 5.8** Representation of tenses using S, R, E (adapted from Reichenbach 1948: 290)

---

[29] See Kamp and Reyle 1993, p. 492, fn 3. For a detailed discussion of problems with tense logics see Sections 5.1.1–5.1.2 there.

Present Continuous

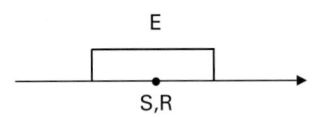

```
              E
         ┌────────┐
─────────┤        ├──────▶
         •
        S,R
```

'I am writing a book.'

**Figure 5.9** Representation of progressive aspect/extended event (adapted from Reichenbach 1948: 290)

Other tenses, also combined with aspects, can be represented analogously. For example, Figure 5.9 represents Present Progressive.[30]

All in all, tense is anaphoric and it is also a deictic category and as such relies on context for its interpretation. In other words, tense is *indexical*. And indexicality is a property that tense logics just introduced cannot capture. The simplest way to think about it is that we have to fill in the temporal location using information from context, common ground, surrounding text (co-text), or other available sources of information, such as social and cultural conventions and conventional scenarios and scripts. Suffice it to say that Barbara Partee in her seminal paper 'Some structural analogies between tenses and pronouns in English'[31] provides a compelling argument that tenses are structurally analogous to pronouns – a point briefly discussed in the analysis of temporal conjunction in Section 4.2. Just as pronouns pick out their referents through deixis or anaphoric links, so tenses can be linked with the time (temporal reference) through deixis and anaphora. Partee represents grammatical tenses not as operators but as variables, in this way anchoring the temporal reference to the speaker and to the situation. When I exclaim in horror 'I didn't turn off the stove' (Partee 2004 [1973]: 51), I don't think that there is a certain time $t$ at which it is not the case that I turned off the stove but I likely think of a situation that has current relevance for me. That is, I think about an interval for which not turning off the stove might result in adverse consequences. It is this observation that triggered the suggestion that there are uses of tenses that make them analogous to pronouns in their properties of context dependence, and in particular deixis and anaphora, and that temporal sequence should be reflected as such in the syntactic representation by the so-called $t$-variable. The question as to whether we want to trace it back to syntax in this way is not crucial to this journey through meaning, but we will return to the topic of anaphora once again in Section 6.1.2.1 when we discuss the semantics of multi-sentential discourses. We will also return to the concept of indexicality while discussing reference in Section 6.2.4.

Next, conceptualizing time in terms of temporal instants rather than intervals is also a great weakness of tense logic. The earlier discussion of situation types and aspect revolved around the fact that eventualities are normally extended in time. Sleeping, for example, is a state that can be subdivided into shorter intervals with the same property

---

[30] See also Steedman 1997, pp. 905, 910.   [31] See Partee 2004 [1973].

(sleeping). Speech time, reference time, and event time from Reichenbach's system are also naturally intervals.

All in all, the four sentential operators P, F, S, and U are too limited to handle all this richness of temporal meaning. But there are semantic theories of natural language that build on the notions of events and states plus temporal relation and go quite a long way towards a successful explanation. There is a semantics of eventualities that we can equip ourselves with and replace predicating truth and falsity of instances with predicating it of intervals – that is, of situations extended in time.

### 5.3.4 Logical Form and Events

We have established that in order to represent time, we have to represent eventualities. The relation of verbs to events has been discussed in the history of philosophy at least since Plato, and more recently in Port Royal logic in the seventeenth century and in the twentieth century by Frank Ramsey and Hans Reichenbach.[32] But we owe the introduction of events to formal semantics to Donald Davidson and his seminal papers from the 1960s, and most notably 'The logical form of action sentences'.[33] Davidson proposes that action sentences contain reference to events, where the event is placed in the argument position of the verbal predicate. The event itself becomes an argument in manner, place, and time adverbials which are represented as predicates added to the logical form by means of conjunction. So, the logical form of his famous sentence in (5.84) can be represented as in (5.85), where $e$ stands for an event. By introducing events he could represent the intuition that it was the action of buttering, rather than the agent (Jones), that had these attributes.

(5.84)　　Jones buttered the toast slowly, deliberately, in the bathroom, with a knife, at midnight.
(from Davidson 1980a: 106)

(5.85)　　$\exists e$ (Butter (Jones, toast, $e$) $\wedge$ Slowly ($e$) $\wedge$ Deliberately ($e$) $\wedge$ In ($e$, bathroom) $\wedge$ With ($e$, knife) $\wedge$ At ($e$, midnight))

Later on, amendments were suggested, some of which have proved useful in different formal semantic frameworks. In the so-called *neo-Davidsonian* analysis, due mostly to Terence Parsons,[34] the action verb is regarded as a one-place predicate, with the argument for the subject and the object removed and represented separately as predicates, as in (5.86).

(5.86)　　$\exists e$ (Butter ($e$) $\wedge$ Subject (Jones, $e$) $\wedge$ Object (toast, $e$) $\wedge$ Slowly ($e$) ... etc.).

Parsons calls this analysis a *subatomic semantics* in that it descends to the relations found 'underneath the sentence', so to speak: '[s]ince no such quantification is

---

[32] See e.g. Parsons 1990, pp. 4–5.　　[33] Davidson 1980a [1967]. See also Davidson 1980b [1969].
[34] See Parsons 1990.

explicitly indicated in the sentence ..., I call it an "underlying" quantification' (Parsons 1990: 3). So, (5.87) will be represented as (5.88).

(5.87)   Caesar died.

(5.88)   $\exists e$ (Dying ($e$) $\wedge$ Object ($e$, Caesar) $\wedge$ Culminate ($e$, before now))

(adapted from Parsons 1990: 6)

The predicate 'Culminate' is an example of such an important addition to the semantics, whose utility we will return to while representing time using DRSs.

Let us see what it would mean to incorporate temporality into truth-conditional semantics. On a Davidsonian analysis, sentence (5.89) is true if and only if there was a past time $t$ at which an event of entering the hall by Bill took place and at which Bill was in a state of being happy.

(5.89)   Bill entered the hall happy.

What we need from our metalanguage is a combination of Davidson's logical form that incorporates events and an account of temporal relations founded on tense logic that would account for nuances conveyed by the English tenses and aspects. However, we also need a sufficiently firm grasp of the concept of an event to incorporate it into truth-conditional semantics. We must remember that in addition to events that Davidson focused on, there are also other situation types to represent. Following DRT, we will limit the inventory of situation types to states and events because of their specific interaction with temporal location. While states can extend *beyond* the reference time, events are located *within* the time of reference, as the comparison between (5.90) and (5.91) shows.

(5.90)   Anna gave a lecture on Monday.   (event)

(5.91)   Bill was ill on Monday.   (state)

While the state of being ill may have extended into the preceding and following days, giving the lecture is temporally located within Monday. So, although processes are dynamic situations and as such classifiable with events, by this criterion they will be classified as a kind of a state, so to speak: preparing a lecture in (5.92) may have extended into the previous and following days as well. Also, it has to be remembered that while events entail that some change of situation has taken place, states (with processes now subsumed under them) do not: (5.92) does not suggest that the preparation has ever been completed.

(5.92)   Anna was preparing a lecture on Thursday.

This is how DRT represents time, using the concepts of events and states. To reiterate, events ($e$) are *included* in a certain time, where time $t$ is a discourse referent, while states ($s$) *overlap* with it. They are all treated as discourse referents, just as individuals in the DRSs discussed earlier. Referring to an eventuality captures the fact that the truth value of the sentence may vary depending on the time of the utterance, the identity of the speaker, and the audience. For example, sentence (5.90) above has the DRS as in

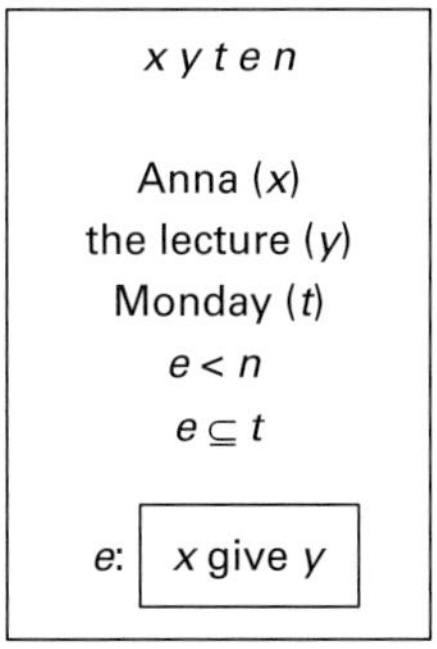

## 5.3 Representing Time

```
┌─────────────────────┐
│      x y t e n      │
│                     │
│      Anna (x)       │
│   the lecture (y)   │
│     Monday (t)      │
│       e < n         │
│       e ⊆ t         │
│                     │
│  ┌───┬───────────┐  │
│  │ e:│  x give y │  │
│  └───┴───────────┘  │
└─────────────────────┘
```

**Figure 5.10** DRS for (5.90) ('Anna gave a lecture on Monday.')

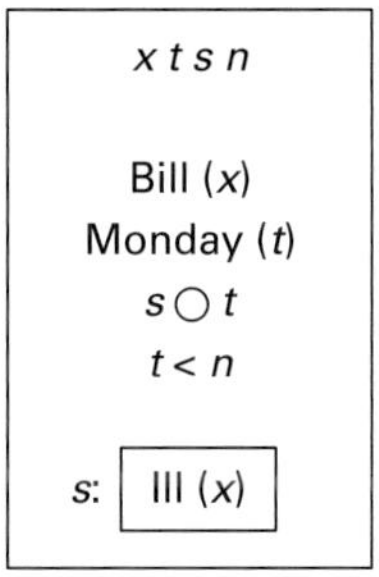

```
┌─────────────────┐
│    x t s n      │
│                 │
│    Bill (x)     │
│   Monday (t)    │
│     s ○ t       │
│     t < n       │
│                 │
│ ┌──┬─────────┐  │
│ │s:│  Ill (x)│  │
│ └──┴─────────┘  │
└─────────────────┘
```

**Figure 5.11** DRS for (5.91) ('Bill was ill on Monday.')

Figure 5.10, where $n$ is a discourse referent referring to the utterance time and $e \subseteq t$ means that $e$ is temporally included within $t$.

A state in sentence (5.91) can be represented as in Figure 5.11, where $s \bigcirc t$ indicates that Bill's being ill took place on Monday but was not necessarily restricted to that day alone (that is, was not necessarily temporally included in $t$).

The ability of DRT to represent stretches of discourse longer than a sentence is of particular advantage for the analysis of temporality in that we can capture the anaphoric dimension. If, say, a past-tense form occurs in a sentence that is not initial in the discourse and no overt specification of time is given, as in (5.83) repeated below, we can easily relate the eventuality to the previous discourse by representing the relative temporal order ($e_1 < e_2$). I return to representing longer discourses while discussing dynamic semantics in Section 6.1.2.1.

(5.83)    Bill found a hedgehog. He took it to an animal rescue centre.

Aspect can also be represented in DRT. For example, the perfective of activity verbs as in (5.93) is represented as a state that is the result of an event: $s$ starts at the very moment $e$ ends, represented as $e \supset \subset s$ in Figure 5.12.

(5.93)    Anna has given a lecture.

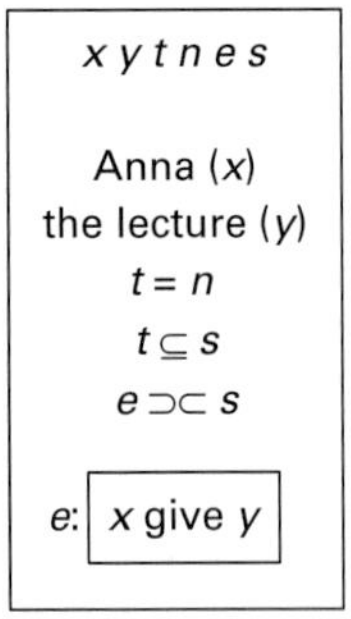

```
┌─────────────────────┐
│  x y t n e s        │
│                     │
│   Anna (x)          │
│  the lecture (y)    │
│     t = n           │
│     t ⊆ s           │
│     e ⊃⊂ s          │
│  ┌──────────────┐   │
│  e: │ x give y  │   │
│  └──────────────┘   │
└─────────────────────┘
```

**Figure 5.12** DRS for (5.93) ('Anna has given a lecture.')

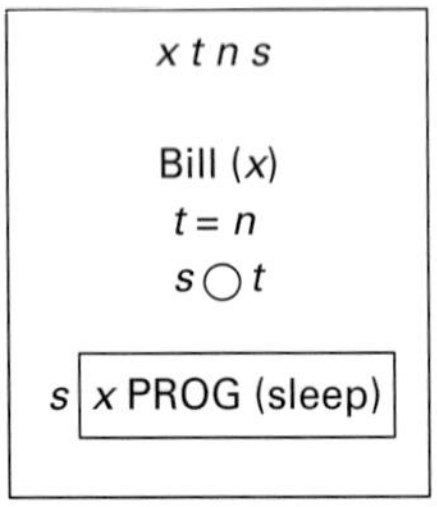

```
┌─────────────────────┐
│   x t n s           │
│                     │
│    Bill (x)         │
│    t = n            │
│    s ◯ t            │
│  ┌────────────────┐ │
│  s│ x PROG (sleep)│ │
│  └────────────────┘ │
└─────────────────────┘
```

**Figure 5.13** DRS for (5.94) ('Bill is sleeping.')

The progressive is represented by adding a progressive operator PROG to the predicate, as in Figure 5.13 that represents sentence (5.94).

(5.94)  Bill is sleeping.

In general, the representation of temporality, including relative time in multi-sentence discourse, as well as aspect, makes use of the manipulation of concepts such as state ($s$), event ($e$), their temporal locations ($t$), and the deictic point ($n$).[35]

## 5.3.5  Time: Semantics, Pragmatics, and Metaphysics

The construct of events and states employed here comes with the property that eventualities themselves are neither past, present, nor future. One way of making them temporal is to assume that what is now seen as future will be seen as present and then as past. In the philosophy of time, this is called A-theory, after John M. E. McTaggart and his seminal paper 'The unreality of time' published at the beginning of the twentieth century.[36] According to the alternative and better scientifically grounded view, called B-theory, there is a sequence of unchanging events, lined up

---

[35] For a more extensive introduction, see Chapter 5 of Kamp and Reyle 1993 and Kamp 2019.
[36] See McTaggart 1934 [1908]. For an A-theoretic tense logic, see Prior 1967, 1968a, 1968b.

## 5.3 Representing Time

as earlier-than/later-than. That gives a choice of an 'A-series' and a 'B-series' of positions in time:

> I shall speak of the series of positions running from the far past through the near past to the present, and then from the present to the near future and the far future, as the A series. The series of positions which runs from earlier to later I shall call the B series. The contents of a position in time are called events. (McTaggart 1934 [1908]: 111)

McTaggart concludes that neither series gives an adequate account of time: time has to involve change, so the B-series does not suffice. On the other hand, in order to talk about events 'sliding along the scale', so to speak, from the future through the present and into the past, one has to presuppose time in order to define it. In current philosophy of time arguments still mount on both sides, with interesting subdivisions within each camp. For example, some A-theorists propose that only the present is real (the so-called *presentism*), some that only the present and the future (the *growing block* view), and others award reality to all three (the *moving spotlight* view).[37] When we add to this leading scientific theories of the 'micro-level' universe of the laws of physics, we could say that neither theory is correct in that the universe is symmetrical: not only does time not flow but there is no objective past or future either – all depends on the direction from which we look, so to speak. This is what McTaggart referred to as a C-series: an ordering of events but without an 'arrow of time'.[38] We have to leave it at that in this journey through meaning in that the metaphysics of time would take us too far from the semantics of temporal reference, remembering, however, that the two are intimately connected, each discipline providing arguments for the other. Prior's tense logic assumed A-theory, while DRT uses timeless eventualities in the essentially B-theoretic time, focusing on the relative order of events ($e_1 < e_2$), but also evades 'big metaphysical questions' by incorporating the discourse referent $t$ for time itself and the deictic centre $n$ to capture the indexicality of time. It can also represent the anaphoric dimension of tenses. So, it gives us a metalanguage and the ideas for representing time in semantics, but addressing the metaphysics behind it would give us a better overall picture of the human concept of time. The conceptual representations of Default Semantics (discussed in Section 7.2.3) bring us a little closer to this goal of combining insights from semantics and metaphysics.[39] The semantics of time assumes there is a symmetrical universe of modern physics, where, to reiterate, time does not flow and does not have a direction. Then, the question arises of how this 'real time' can be reconciled with the ways speakers of different languages refer to the past, the present, and the future. Tenseless languages, for example, can foreground the attitude to an event, the degree of certainty, or source of information, and leave the location in the past, present, or future entirely unspecified. We will attend to these cross-linguistic differences in a moment. But suffice it to say that the indexicality to the self, to the speaker, appears to be the core property of

---

[37] The literature is vast. For an introduction, see e.g. Parts I and II of Callender 2011.
[38] Sadly, there is no room to expand on the ontology and metaphysics of real time here, but there are many extremely interesting discussions of the symmetrical universe, 'universe without time as we know it', in the literature. Try Rovelli 2018 for an excellent popular introduction or, for a more philosophical take on the micro-level of the world and how the human world emerges from it, Ismael 2016.
[39] See e.g. Jaszczolt 2009a, 2018a, 2020 and in press.

human time. The concept of time is a complex concept and can vary among cultures, but on the level of the 'conceptual atoms', the basic concepts, it is the same: it is all about the commitment to the eventualities that the speaker's utterance is about. On the level of these basic concepts, human time does not flow – like in a symmetrical universe. In other words, time is *epistemic modality*. So, we will have an occasion to return to this fascinating connection between semantics, pragmatics, and metaphysics when we discuss modality in Section 5.4.

All in all, by combining various extensions to our metalanguage it appears to be possible to get a fair grasp on the concept of time as it is represented in natural-language sentences. But there is a sense of something lacking. There are big questions left unanswered, not only concerning the relation between semantics and metaphysics, but also the relation between semantics and pragmatics. For example, tense–time mismatches, such as (5.75), repeated below, or (5.95).

(5.75)   This is what happened to me yesterday. I go to the office, I sit at my desk, and this guy comes and says . . .

(5.95)   A: Let's go to London next Thursday.
B: I can't. I am giving a lecture.

The discourse in (5.75) is clearly about the past (yesterday), but uses the Simple Present – the so-called 'vivid present' of narration or, as formal linguists prefer to call it, 'tenseless future'. (5.95) is clearly uttered to mean 'I will be giving a lecture next Thursday'. Faithful to our quest for a psychologically real semantics, or semantics of conceptual representations, we would want our theory to cater for such mismatches. We would also like it to apply to languages in which tense and aspect are optional and as such don't have to be overtly marked in the sentence. In Thai, sentence (5.96) can have any of the meanings (a)–(i).[40]

(5.96)   $m_3ae{:}r_3i{:}^I$           $kh_2ian$           $n_3iy_3ai{:}$
Mary           write           novel
a. Mary wrote a novel.
b. Mary was writing a novel.
c. Mary started writing a novel (but did not finish it).
d. Mary has written a novel.
e. Mary has been writing a novel (but has not finished it).
f. Mary writes novels. / Mary is a novelist.
g. Mary is writing a novel.
h. Mary will write a novel.
i. Mary will be writing a novel.

(adapted from Srioutai 2006: 45)

---

[40] Srioutai uses the transliteration system based on Diller (1996). In brief, (i) vowel phonemes are transliterated as (high) i, u', u, (mid) e, oe, o, and (low) ae, a, o'; (ii) colon stands for long vowels; (iii) diphthongs are transliterated as ia, u'a, and ua; (iv) Arabic numerals 1, 2, 3 in the subscript stand for the tone class of the syllable-initial consonant; and (v) Roman numerals I and II in the superscript stand for tone markers.

Likewise, we would like it to apply to languages in which tense and/or aspect are not grammatically marked and neither do they have to be overtly specified by lexical items such as temporal adverbials. For example, Paraguayan Guaraní is considered to be an inherently tenseless language – 'inherently' in that it even defies the theory that tenseless languages have an unarticulated, 'covert' tense morpheme that ought to be captured by the syntactic representation of a sentence.[41] In (5.97), *Prosp* stands for prospective aspect or modal form but not for tense in the sense of temporal location.

(5.97)     A-     karú-     ta
             *1Sg-*     eat-     *Prosp*
             'I am going to eat.'

(adapted from Tonhauser 2011: 263)

We would also like the semantics to be flexible enough to represent temporal distinctions that are specific to only some languages and not found in others. For example, Northern Paiute, a Uto-Aztecan language spoken in the western United States, has relative tenses. Where English uses subordination with *after* or *while*, Northern Paiute uses coordination between clauses, combined with relative tense, marked for example with a sequential suffix *-si* for temporal precedence or *-na* for simultaneity.[42] An example is given in (5.98). *Nom* stands for nominative; *Perf* for perfective; *Seq* for sequential suffix; *Poss-Refl-Pron* for possessive reflexive pronoun, and '=' marks a clitic boundary.

(5.98)     Su=naatsi'i     tɨbuni-hu-**si**,     tɨ=pa'mogo     yaa-hu.
             *Nom*=boy     wake.up-*Perf*-***Seq***     *Refl*=frog     miss-*Perf*
             'After the boy woke up, he missed his frog (i.e. the frog escaped while he was asleep).'

(adapted from Toosarvandani 2016: 867)

Similarly, Swahili uses the marker *-ka-* to signal a sequence of events, be it in the past or in the future.[43] To compare, in English a sequence of events can be marked by the sequence of tenses or it can be left to pragmatic inference. The latter can be explained, for example, by the rhetorical structure rule of *Narration* discussed in Section 4.2 or by pragmatic inference from the rationality of human communication (in that events are likely to be reported in the order in which they happen), to be discussed at length in Section 7.1 on Gricean pragmatics.

In order to be able to account for temporality across languages, as well as do justice to various features and facets of temporal reference in any individual natural language, we can draw on the resources just presented. But the formal semantic representation will have to be sensitive to a variety of sources of information, not merely the lexicon and grammar. The representation will have to incorporate information from inferences from context, cultural and social assumptions, default scripts, or previously

---

[41] For the proposal and some evidence that certain overtly tenseless languages can be analysed that way, see Matthewson 2006. As she says (p. 705), 'In a linguistic theory which accepts the existence of phonologically null elements, there is in principle nothing which could *prevent* tense morphology from being covert.'
[42] See Toosarvandani 2016.     [43] Sometimes called *consecutive* tense. See Givón 2005, p. 154.

encountered scenarios. As part of this exercise, one may want, for example, to give time metaphors a closer look in order to establish how much evidence there is that humans conceptualize time in terms of space (metaphor is discussed in Section 8.2).[44] We have good foundations for how to build such representations. But *how exactly* to 'kick them up', so to speak, from the level of English sentences to the level of conceptual structures is what we will continue figuring out through the more 'pragmaticky' part of this journey through meaning. It is 'pragmaticky', but as part of semantics understood as a theory of psychologically real meaning. In particular, we will return briefly to tense–time mismatches in Section 7.2.3.

## 5.4 Modality

### 5.4.1 Types of Modality and Modal Logic

Other types of constructions that require additional resources beyond standard predicate logic are expressions of necessity and possibility – for example, *it is necessary that* p, *it is possible that* p, *it is probable that* p, *it is likely that* p, as well as sentences with modal verbs such as *must, might, may, can*, or *could*. In order to represent the meaning of sentences containing these expressions, we could try to employ an extension to propositional logic in the form of *modal logic*, using the (already familiar) concept of possible worlds. In particular, we need the concept of necessity as truth in all possible worlds, and possibility as truth in some possible worlds. Necessity and possibility are modal operators. Like tense operators in Prior's logic, they are sentential operators. They are normally represented by the symbols in (5.99).

(5.99)    $\Box \varphi$    It is necessary that $\varphi$
          $\Diamond \varphi$    It is possible that $\varphi$

So, for example, sentences with *must* have to be evaluated for truth with respect to possible worlds different from the actual world: for (5.100) to be true, in all possible worlds it must be the case that the temperature is below 0°C for water to freeze.

(5.100)    For water to freeze, the temperature must be below 0°C.

In other words, *must* comes with universal modal force. More formally, 'It is necessary that $\varphi$' or 'must $\varphi$' is true in model $M$ and world $w$ if and only if for all possible worlds accessible from the world $w$, $\varphi$ is true. In (5.101), R($w$) stands for the worlds accessible from $w$.

(5.101)    $[\Box \varphi]^{M,w} = 1$ iff for all $w' \in R(w)$, $[\varphi]^{M,w'} = 1$

By analogy, *may* comes with existential modal force. (5.102) is true if and only if in some possible world it snows tomorrow – as per (5.103) that says, in words, 'It is possible that $\varphi$' (or 'may/might $\varphi$') is true in model $M$ and world $w$ if and only if for

---

[44] See e.g. Casasanto and Boroditsky 2008 or Vallesi, Binns, and Shallice 2008.

some possible world (that is, at least one possible world) accessible from the world $w$, $\varphi$ is true.

(5.102)   It may snow tomorrow.

(5.103)   $[\![ \Diamond \varphi ]\!]^{M,w} = 1$ iff for at least one $w' \in R(w)$, $[\![ \varphi ]\!]^{M,w'} = 1$

This is the kind of modality that captures people's knowledge and belief and it is called epistemic modality. There are different classifications of modality available, some more fine-grained than others. Logicians often distinguish epistemic modality from *alethic modality* that is concerned with truth per se, such as logical necessity, rather than with *knowing* truth. But it is a big philosophical (if not also scientific!) question as to whether humans can distinguish truth in itself from people's judgements about truth, or whether there is 'truth in itself' in the first place. There is also *metaphysical modality* – to do with metaphysical possibilities and necessities, such as in (5.100). Again, it can be difficult to distinguish from epistemic modality, as for example in (5.102). It is epistemic modality that is, for obvious reasons, more commonly discussed in linguistics.

Epistemic modal sentences can express a degree of commitment to a proposition, as in the patterns in (5.104)–(5.106). Expressions in (5.104) contain an adjective of modality in a higher clause, those in (5.105) contain a verb of propositional attitude in a higher clause,[45] and those in (5.106) contain modal verbs.

(5.104)   It is possible/necessary/certain/probable/likely that $p$.

(5.105)   I know/believe/think/doubt that $p$.

(5.106)   She must/might/could/needn't/couldn't have + *past participle*.

A strict assignment of modal constructions to types of modality is difficult, as many of them can express different types of modality. Standardly, (5.104)–(5.106) are examples of epistemic modality, describing degrees of certainty, commitment to some eventuality. We conceptualize such statements by using possible worlds – 'ways the world might have been'. For example, (5.107) expresses a prediction of a strong match between the hypothetical situation and reality.

(5.107)   Lidia must have arrived by now.

This is somewhat analogous to the conditionals discussed in Section 4.4, which also set up hypothetical worlds, as exemplified in (5.108).

(5.108)   If I were a physicist, I would be searching for a theory of everything.

Next, obligation and permission, exemplified in (5.109), belong to *deontic modality*. They generally follow the patterns in (5.110).

---

[45] For an example of a formal semantic approach to modality that can be applied to attitude reports see Hegarty 2016.

(5.109)   You must be quiet in the library.

(5.110)   She can/may/could/might/must/should/ought to + *verb*

But accounting for the meaning of the English modals is not an easy task. First, there is potential ambiguity; *can* can be either epistemic (or alethic or metaphysical, if we wish to distinguish them for natural languages) or deontic, meaning either 'it is possible for her to ... ' or 'she has permission to ... '.[46] Similarly, *must* can be epistemic (or alethic or metaphysical) or deontic. On this distinction, (5.111) is an example of epistemic modality, while (5.112) is deontic.

(5.111)   You may find this difficult.

(5.112)   You may have a dessert now.

There are also various other classifications on the market. For example, *can* expressing ability or willingness can be classified as *dynamic* modality, *must* expressing a wish is *bouletic*, and *must* expressing someone's disposition to do certain things or behave in a certain way is *dispositional*.[47]

In modal logic, deontic modality can be handled by operators similar to those used for alethic modality. Such operators rely on the notion of morally and legally ideal worlds. The devices are there in the metalanguage but, as examples in this section demonstrate, natural-language expressions call for more than that. Confusingly, modal verbs such as *may* or *must* cover them all. Moreover, as was the case with other constructions such as sentential connectives, the inventories differ considerably from language to language and what is conveyed by the lexicon in one language can be conveyed by grammar or pragmatic inference from context in the other. But the concepts are there and conceptual semantics ought to capture them.

## 5.4.2  Modals as Relational Expressions

Since English modal verbs can serve so many different modal functions, it behoves semantic theory to introduce conceptual distinctions that will distinguish between such roles. Angelika Kratzer, in her ground-breaking paper 'What *must* and *can* must and can mean',[48] proposes to conceptualize modals in a very different way: modals are for her *relational* expressions. On her analysis, *must* means 'must in view of' and as such takes two arguments: (i) a free relative, for example 'what is known', 'what is good', and so on, that functions as a *restriction*, and (ii) a sentence, that functions as a *scope*. Restriction is often left unsaid in that it can usually be inferred from context or assumed on the basis of sociocultural conventions or standard situations and salient scripts. In her 'The notional category of modality',[49] Kratzer also uses the concept of a *conversational background*: some modals have a background that comes from evidence, information content, or stereotypes, others have a deontic background defined as follows:

---

[46] See here Austin 1979 [1961].   [47] See also Portner's 2009.   [48] See Kratzer 2012b [1977].
[49] See Kratzer 2012c [1981].

A deontic conversational background is a function *f* such that for any world *w*, *f*(*w*) represents the content of a body of laws or regulations in *w*. (Kratzer 2012c [1981]: 37)

On this account, English modals can be described as having specified *quantificational force*; that is, there is an overt distinction between universal (e.g. *must*) and existential force (e.g. *can*). But their conversational background (such as deontic or epistemic) is not overtly specified, which explains the ambiguities.

This account also allows for grading modality, using the notion of grading how close given possible worlds come to some relevant standard or norm. Conversational backgrounds can then function as so-called *ordering sources* used for this grading (ordering) – an idea inherited from David Lewis.[50] Such ordered worlds are centred: each world is more similar to itself than any other world. By this reasoning, 'a proposition is a necessity just in case it is true in all accessible worlds that come closest to the ideal determined by the ordering source' (Kratzer 2012c [1981]: 40). The question of graded modality and what areas of language it affects has also been recently comprehensively explored by Daniel Lassiter.[51]

## 5.4.3 Modality and Mood

When modality is encoded in the grammar, it is called *mood*. The distinction between indicative and subjunctive found in many languages is such a distinction of mood. The subjunctive in French is exemplified in (5.113). As always, grammatical information that is not relevant for the current discussion is omitted.

(5.113)  Il      vaut    mieux   qu'   elle  le   sache.
         It      worth   better  that  she   it   know *Subj Pres 3Sg*
         'It's better that she *know* it.'

Generally, the subjunctive expresses non-factuality. Examples (5.114) and (5.115) from Polish demonstrate the difference of the degree of doubt rendered by a difference of mood, subjunctive as opposed to indicative, in *that*-clauses. The complementizer *żeby* in (5.114) is composed of *że* ('that') and the subjunctive mood marker *by*. Subjunctive conveys greater detachment – greater doubt.

(5.114)  Nie   wierzę,              żeby          on   był              szpiegiem.
         Not   believe *Ind Pres 1Sg*   that + *Subj*   he   be *Subj 3Sg*   spy
         'I don't believe that he could be a spy.'

(5.115)  Nie   wierzę,              że     on   jest             szpiegiem.
         Not   believe *Ind Pres 1Sg*   that   he   be *Ind Pres 3Sg*   spy
         'I don't believe that he is a spy.'

So, mood expresses an opinion or attitude of mind of the speaker towards the proposition. It is a grammatical category, like tense, whereas modality is a semantic category, like temporality. Mood is usually marked on the verb and is

---

[50] See Lewis 1973.   [51] See Lassiter 2017.

sometimes called a morphosyntactic category of the verb, to distinguish it from modality in general.

To complicate matters somewhat, the distinction between declarative, interrogative, and imperative is also sometimes called a distinction of mood. For example, Paul Portner in his recent book *Mood* applies the term both to the verb form and the role the sentence plays as a speech act:

> Mood is an aspect of linguistic form which indicates how a proposition is used in the expression of modal meaning. (Portner 2018: 4)

There are good reasons for this definition because 'indicating' modality can be performed by means of verb forms, 'purpose-made' modals, or sentence types, among other devices. On the other hand, just as we distinguished *tense* from *temporality*, so may we wish to distinguish between *mood* and *modality* using the criterion of levels of linguistic analysis. In order to maintain clarity about what level of units we are talking about: utterances (basic, sentence-type driven speech-act types[52]), sentence types, or morphosyntactic devices within sentences, we could restrict the label 'mood' to the latter category, while for the first two follow the well-established distinctions in (5.116). Not much depends on the choice: since a sentence is a syntactic category, one may wish to go along with Portner's choice. But this little exercise is useful in demonstrating that classifications always have to follow carefully selected and justified principles of ordering.

(5.116)  Sentence types:
 declaratives interrogatives imperatives
 Utterance types:
 statements questions commands[53]

Different languages grammaticalize different modal distinctions into mood. For example, as was indicated in the discussion of (5.113)–(5.115), the subjunctive is used for expressing a claim whose status is different from a statement of certainty, where the latter is expressed through the indicative mood. Although English does not have a specific form for the subjunctive, it can be marked by using a bare verb form as in (5.117).

(5.117)  I suggest that you *be* on time.

To add to these examples of cross-linguistic differences, an optative is used in Ancient Greek for wishes: *She come-OPT* is then a form for *I wish she would come*. We need not go further into cross-linguistic differences here. Suffice it to say that sentence types and mood are probably better kept apart.

---

[52] In Speech Act Theory, classifications of speech acts are based on functional criteria in order to account for, for example, requests, orders, complaints, and so forth. See Section 8.3.

[53] See also Portner 2018 for definitions. Lyons (1977: 748) proposes that the term *imperative* be used only for mood. For sentence type, he suggests the term *jussive*. In common linguistic parlance, however, the label 'jussive' is rarely used.

## 5.4.4 Modality and Temporality

Now, tense is sometimes regarded as a type of modality, although more often by philosophers and logicians than by linguists. This is partly justified by the fact that philosophers apply the term 'tensed' more broadly. For philosophers, being 'tensed' can be predicated of reality: if time is real, then reality is tensed; if time is unreal, if past/present/future is a distinction imposed by our mind, something to the effect of memory/current experience/anticipation, then reality is not tensed. For linguists, tense is a grammatical category: sentences are tensed. But the concepts are not so very different. There is a compelling case for associating futurity with modality in that the future is more speculative than the present.

Let us briefly consider the English *will*. Some linguists consider it to be a morpheme ambiguous between tense and modal, others class it entirely with modals.[54] It can express epistemic necessity, as in (5.118), or dispositional necessity – a tendency to act in a certain way – as in (5.119).

(5.118) Bill will be in London by now.

(5.119) Bill will sometimes drink whisky to shock his parents.

On the other hand, regular future *will* in (5.120) refers to future time in our real world, without referring to other worlds like modals do, and hence is not modal.

(5.120) Bill will go to London tomorrow.

However, as was argued by Mürvet Enç, reference to only one world need not preclude modality. (5.121) is modal and refers to one possible world.

(5.121) It is certain that Bill went to London yesterday.

Further, we may argue that *will* involves prediction which is itself a type of modality. It involves the future, but so do other modalities, such as *must* in (5.122).

(5.122) You must come to see me on Sunday.

Historical linguistic considerations also testify to the close link between modality and time.[55]

Moreover, the modal flavour is not associated merely with expressions of futurity. Even the present and the past have a flavour of degrees of modality: in unreal conditionals, the past-tense form suitably functions as a marker of *irrealis*, as in (5.123).

(5.123) If you *helped* me, we would finish on time.

Arguably, all three temporal categories exhibit a gradation of modal commitment to the eventuality expressed by the sentence. Lists of examples in (5.124a)–(5.124f), (5.125a)–(5.125e) and (5.126a)–(5.126g) demonstrate it for the past, the present, and the future

---

[54] See Enç 1996, p. 347 for detailed references and various arguments in support of temporality as modality.
[55] The literature is vast. See e.g. Bybee, Perkins, and Pagliuca 1994 and for a brief survey Jaszczolt 2009a, Chapter 2.

respectively, putting the earlier discussion of (5.114)–(5.115) in a broader context. The constructions exemplify the categories of temporal expression given in brackets.

(5.124a)  a. Lidia went to a concert yesterday.
(*regular past*)

(5.124b)  This is what happened yesterday. Lidia goes to a concert, meets her school friend and tells her ...
(*past of narration*)

(5.124c)  Lidia would have gone to a concert (then).
(*epistemic necessity past*)

(5.124d)  Lidia must have gone to a concert (yesterday).
(*epistemic necessity past*)

(5.124e)  Lidia may have gone to a concert (yesterday).
(*epistemic possibility past*)

(5.124f)  Lidia might have gone to a concert (yesterday).
(*epistemic possibility past*)

(5.125a)  Lidia is at a concert now.
(*regular present*)

(5.125b)  Lidia will be at a concert now.
(*epistemic necessity present*)

(5.125c)  Lidia must be at a concert now.
(*epistemic necessity present*)

(5.125d)  Lidia may be at a concert now.
(*epistemic possibility present*)

(5.125e)  Lidia might be at a concert now.
(*epistemic possibility present*)

(5.126a)  Lidia goes to a concert tomorrow evening.
(*'tenseless' future*)

(5.126b)  Lidia is going to a concert tomorrow evening.
(*futurate progressive*)

(5.126c)  Lidia is going to go to a concert tomorrow evening.
(*periphrastic future*)

(5.126d)  Lidia will go to a concert tomorrow evening.
(*regular future*)

(5.126e)  Lidia must be going to a concert tomorrow evening.
(*epistemic necessity future*)

(5.126f)  Lidia may go to a concert tomorrow evening.
(*epistemic possibility future*)

(5.126g)  Lidia might go to a concert tomorrow evening.
(*epistemic possibility future*)

Arguably, the fact that there is a choice of forms with which we can express thoughts about the past, the present, and the future suggests that the concept of time may be founded on the concept of epistemic modality. Philosophers might say here that it is *supervenient* on modality, which roughly means that it is

## 5.4 Modality

dependent on it in terms of its constitutive characteristics.[56] I argued in *Representing Time: An Essay on Temporality as Modality* that these categories represent degrees of epistemic commitment to the situation expressed by the sentence, and as such represent degrees of epistemic modality.[57] As was mentioned in the preceding section, linguistic diversity in expressing temporal reference also testifies to the modal nature of human time. I return briefly to this topic in Section 7.2.3 in that by then we will come to the part of our journey in which formal representations become more and more cognitively real.

This was a philosophical–semantic discussion of the relation between the semantic category of temporality and the semantic category of modality. But let us now continue with the grammatical and lexical tools themselves. Modality is also closely related to the concept of *evidentiality*. Van der Auwera and Plungian (1998: 85) define evidentiality as follows:

Evidentiality concerns the indication of the source or kind of evidence speakers have for their statements. The evidence is marked as, e.g., direct or non-direct, first-hand or second-hand, based on visual or auditory evidence, on hearsay or on reasoning.

According to this definition, evidentiality and modality are clearly related. But evidentiality, like some other concepts just discussed, is entangled in definitional controversies. On Alexandra Aikhenvald's definition, evidentiality means 'the grammatical means of expressing information source' (Aikhenvald 2004: xi); the source of information has to be grammaticalized as the core meaning. In other words, '[t]o be considered as an evidential, a morpheme has to have "source of information" as its core meaning; that is, the unmarked, or default interpretation' (p. 3). So defined, '[e]videntiality is a category in its own right, and not a subcategory of any modality' (p. 7). On the other hand, just as we distinguished tense from temporality and mood from modality, it is useful to distinguish the semantic qua conceptual category of evidentiality and the more specific grammatical evidentials, especially in view of the clear affinity of evidentiality so-conceived with modality. This affinity can be easily noticed. For example, epistemic necessity in (5.124d) above can also be classified as *inferential evidentiality*: the sentence conveys an expression of conviction that borders on *certainty*, but it also conveys that the speaker must have had *evidence* for making this statement. The construction suggests that the speaker is making an inference on the basis of some other facts or judgements.[58] All in all, it is useful to reserve 'evidentiality' for this conceptual notion when we are aiming, as we are in this journey through meaning, at combining cognitive, semantic, and pragmatic considerations.[59]

---

[56] For an excellent introduction to the concept of supervenience, see McLaughlin and Bennet 2018.
[57] See Jaszczolt 2009a. Evidence from a wide range of languages from different language families, as well as philosophical arguments for the modal nature of time, are also provided there.
[58] See van der Auwera and Plungian 1998, p. 86.
[59] On Palmer's (2001, p. 8) classification, epistemic modality and evidentiality both belong to the category of the so-called *propositional modality*. The latter is contrasted with *event modality*. Propositional modality refers to the speaker's judgement about the expressed eventuality, while event modality refers to an attitude the speaker expresses towards a possible future eventuality. Epistemic modality and evidentiality can both be further subdivided – languages vary in how elaborate they are. For example,

Modality is a fascinating topic not only for linguists, philosophers, and logicians but also for psychologists in that they strive to understand the cognitive underpinnings of reasoning in terms of the graded alternatives that it offers, and the types of ordering of these alternatives. States of affairs can be more, or less, certain in virtue of physical laws; more, or less, certain as measured by what we know; more, or less, desirable; more, or less, possible in virtue of the agent's capabilities and opportunities, to name a few such orderings.[60]

## 5.5 Propositional Attitude Reports

From the earlier discussions of intensional contexts, and now of modality, we can conjecture that representing propositional attitude reports, such as those briefly discussed in Section 1.4, will also require additional tools. (5.127) is another relevant example.

(5.127)   Anna believes that George Eliot wrote *Middlemarch*.

First, the tools are needed because we have to represent complement clauses (*that*-clauses) embedded in an '*a* believes that *p*'-type construction. Next, we have to represent the propositional attitude, an attitude such as belief or doubt, towards the proposition expressed in that *that*-clause, with all the nuances of meaning that make a difference – say, a difference between (5.127) and (5.128), where George Eliot is a pen name of Mary Ann Evans. In other words, the belief can be reported using two different but coreferential names.

(5.128)   Anna believes that Mary Ann Evans wrote *Middlemarch*.

We have to account for the individual way of thinking about the referent, or at least some social, shareable approximation to it that serves the role of Frege's sense introduced in Section 1.4. As was pointed out there, in propositional attitude reports, substitution of coreferential terms is not always truth-preserving.

In other words again, the principle of substitutivity *salva veritate* does not hold for them: substitution of coreferential referring terms is not always truth-preserving. For now, by 'referring terms' we mean descriptions as well as proper names, although it will become important in Section 6.2 that they have somewhat different referring properties. And if substitution is not *always* truth-preserving, then, for many semanticists and philosophers, it means that it is *not* truth-preserving *tout court*: if truth-preserving substitutivity cannot be guaranteed, then for the purpose of semantic theory that aims at predictive power, there is no substitutivity in such constructions, full stop. But since this is a philosophical journey through semantics and pragmatics, and since not only predictability, but also cognitive plausibility are among our top desiderata, this principle deserves closer attention.

---

within epistemic modality, he distinguishes the categories of *speculative* (*John may be in London now*), *deductive* (*John must be in London now*, asserted on the basis of evidence), and *assumptive* (*John will be in London now*, asserted on the basis of knowledge from experience. See Palmer 2001, pp. 24–25.

[60] One recent example of research on reasoning with modality is Johnson-Laird and Ragni 2019.

The problem with belief constructions has traditionally been approached in the literature through the non-applicability of Leibniz's Law that states that two things (here: two expressions) are identical if they are substitutable preserving the truth. This is based on the more general principle known as the *identity of indiscernibles*: if things have all properties in common, then they are identical (they are one thing). It follows that if all that can be said of one thing can be said of another, then it is said about *one* thing under two guises. But there is also another principle that has, through historical vicissitudes, been conflated with Leibniz's Law and which is in fact due to W. V. O. Quine. It states that *if* things are identical (i.e. *if* they are one thing), then they have all properties in common. This law is dubbed the *indiscernibility of identicals*. It follows that if we take one object described using two different expressions, all that can be said of the object using one expression can also be said of it using the other. And it is the latter principle that has made a career in philosophy of language, albeit under a wrong guise (!) – mistakenly taken to be Leibniz's Law.

Now, as was discussed earlier, extensional semantics does not account for propositional attitude reports such as (5.127)–(5.128). We wouldn't get correct truth conditions. If we tried to translate (5.127) as in (5.129) (assuming we add a sentential operator for '*a* believes that' to the metalanguage), we would not manage to account for the importance of the way of thinking about the author: the individual constant always stands for the individual, not for the name or description. In other words, it stands for the author of *Middlemarch* as if, so to speak, the person herself were in that logical form. 'Bel$_a$' stands for such a sentential belief operator, '*a*' for Anna, '*c*' for *Middlemarch*, and '*b*' for the person who wrote it.

(5.129)    Bel$_a$ (Write ($b, c$))

Remember that just as in the case of *The Morning Star* and *The Evening Star* discussed in Section 1.4, so here the problem is that the speaker may consent to one version of the report, such as (5.127), but dissent from the other, such as (5.128).

Moreover, if the names were semantically identical, then (5.130) and (5.131) would be identical. They clearly are not, even in extensional contexts like these, simply because (5.131) is a tautology and, as such, is not informative.

(5.130)    George Eliot is Mary Ann Evans.

(5.131)    George Eliot is George Eliot.

We have seen that this difference in informativeness between $a = a$ and coreferential $a = b$ is precisely what prompted Frege to introduce sense as an explanans for such intensional contexts.[61] In short, identity of reference is not sufficient to represent correctly beliefs in belief reports.

That much we already know from earlier discussions. But additional tools let us go further. First, it is necessary to remember that not all propositional attitudes are alike. 'Believing that *p*' generates more puzzles than, say, 'knowing that *p*'. This is so

---

[61] In Frege 1997a [1892]. See the discussion in Section 1.4.

because knowing is a *factive attitude* and believing *non-factive*. Analogously, *know* is a factive verb and *believe* non-factive. Factives are verbs that generate a proposition the truth of which entails that the proposition embedded in the *that*-clause is itself true. So, '*a* knows that *p*' entails that *p* is true. Non-factives do not require that the embedded proposition be true. Moreover, verbs such as *wish* or *imagine* are sometimes classified as belonging to a third category of so-called *counterfactives* (or *contrafactives*) in that they entail the falsity of the embedded proposition: you wish for or imagine things that in reality are not there. Needless to say, non-factive attitudes, such as belief, have been the most widely studied category in that they pose most puzzles: there is no commitment on the part of the believer and the reporter of the belief to the truth of the proposition.

Let us track the ways of thinking that philosophers of language followed in order to tame such constructions. Propositional attitude reports have traditionally been regarded as ambiguous between the *transparent* and the *opaque* reading. On the opaque reading, substitutivity *salva veritate* does not hold. When it does, the reading is transparent. Sentence (5.132) has two representations that correspond to the wide and narrow scope of the existential quantifier, as in (5.133) and (5.134). Notice that these are semi-formal representations, fit only to clarify the issue of the relative difference of scope of the belief vis-à-vis the existence of the king of France: the transparent reading in (5.133) carries an existential presupposition, while the opaque one in (5.134) does not. 'Bel$_m$' stands for 'Max believes that ... ' and 'KoF' for 'the king of France'. The need for $\forall y$ (KoF $(y) \rightarrow y = x$) was explained in Section 4.5.3 while discussing examples (4.75)–(4.77).

(5.132)   Max believes that the king of France is bald.

(5.133)   $\exists x$ (KoF$(x)$ & $\forall y$ (KoF$(y) \rightarrow y = x$) & Bel$_m$ Bald$(x)$)

(5.134)   Bel$_m \exists x$(KoF$(x)$ & $\forall y$ (KoF$(y) \rightarrow y = x$) & Bald$(x)$)

Simplifying somewhat, in (5.133) the reporter ascribes to Max a belief about a particular, known individual (called also a belief *de re* – about a *res*, Latin for 'thing'). In (5.134), the reporter states that Max believes a certain proposition (holds a belief *de dicto* – about a *dictum*, Latin for 'proposition', 'something said').

But now imagine that Max is referentially mistaken (as he, obviously, is, since France is not a monarchy). If the reporter realizes this, they may substitute the correct description or name for the object of the belief – say, 'the king of Sweden'. The logical representation will then be as in (5.135). 'KoS' stands for 'the king of Sweden'.

(5.135)   $\exists x$ (KoS$(x)$ & $\forall y$ (KoS$(y) \rightarrow y = x$) & Bel$_m$ Bald$(x)$)

So, here we have to distinguish between *de re and de dicto beliefs* and *de re and de dicto reports on beliefs*. Now, arguably, we have to distinguish two sub-types of *de dicto* reports: *de dicto* about whoever undergoes the name or description, and *de dicto* involving a referential mistake. The latter is a confusing albeit necessary category in that it corresponds to a *belief* about a particular individual (belief *de re*) but it is not itself a *de re report* because it creates an opaque context, a context in which substitutivity does not hold. This third case is not often distinguished in the philosophical literature but if the semantics is to aspire to cognitive reality, it has to account for such cases of referential mistakes.[62] To reiterate, there are some important differences between the ways definite descriptions such as *the king of Sweden* and proper names such as *George Eliot* refer and they will be attended to in Section 6.2. But for now, it is important to flag that the unreliable substitutions of coreferential terms affect both categories of expressions if we want the representation of meaning to be cognitively accurate.

The determination of the exact reading of such constructions requires pragmatic considerations. Context is essential in order to determine whether the report, and the belief, are *de re* or *de dicto*. The semantics of these expressions need not require postulating a semantic ambiguity, though. Recall that other seemingly semantic ambiguities, such as the ambiguity of negation discussed in Section 4.5, turned out to be distinctions of *use* that could be accommodated in underdetermined semantics. On this view, semantics can 'consult', so to speak, a theory of use (pragmatics) and fill in what is missing in the representation. Likewise, the *de re/de dicto* distinction may be a matter of such pragmatic interpretations.

The *de re/de dicto* distinction has frequently been understood, rather unfortunately, as a distinction between cases where substitution of coreferential terms (Leibniz's Law) holds and those where it does not. This happened due to the widespread interest in the mid twentieth century in the problem of 'quantifying into' intensional contexts.[63] *De re* beliefs began to be identified with relations between believers and real objects, and hence as relations that could be captured by the logical form of the report in which quantifying into the belief context is possible, as in (5.133) above. So, Max believes something *about* the king of France. In contrast, on the *de dicto* reading in (5.134), Max believes something about somebody whom he calls 'the king of France' in his 'belief world'. But equating the *de re/de dicto* distinction with the difference of scope poses problems when we want to incorporate it into a conceptual semantics. It cannot account for referential mistakes such as (5.135). Neither does it capture the distinction in the 'strength' of referring: when the belief is *de re*, held about a person or other entity, perhaps it is better to represent the entity by means of an individual constant rather than a quantifier expression, even when a definite description rather than a proper name is used. Examples are (5.136) and (5.137), where *f* and *s* stand for 'the king of France' and 'the king of Sweden' respectively. After all, it is the thought, not the linguistic expression, that is

---

[62] The tripartite distinction was introduced in Jaszczolt 1997. See also Jaszczolt 1999 and 2005. For an introduction to *de re/de dicto*, and to attitude reports in general, see e.g. Nelson 2019.

[63] The seminal source here is Quine 1972 [1956] and his distinction of relational and notional beliefs. Quine postulated *degrees of intensions* for quantifying into such contexts.

represented when semantic representations are conceptual structures. The strength of referring will be one of the main topics of Section 6.2.

(5.136)   $Bel_m$ Bald $(f)$

(5.137)   $Bel_m$ Bald $(s)$

Attempts to capture the meaning of attitude reports abound – to the extent, as we saw earlier, that the semantics of propositional attitude reports has often been considered as a criterion of adequacy of semantic theories. We can only mention some interesting tasters in these debates. Belief is an epistemic attitude, and just as we can make use of modal logic to represent modality (including, by the way, the similar concept of epistemic modality), so can we make some use of *epistemic logic* to represent knowledge and belief. Formal representation of propositional attitude sentences will use the devices of epistemic logic such as operators $B_a\varphi$ and $K_a\varphi$ for '*a* believes that $\varphi$' and '*a* knows that $\varphi$', where *a* stands for the holder of the epistemic attitude of believing or knowing, respectively. Then, following the celebrated proposal by Jaakko Hintikka,[64] '*a* knows that $\varphi$' is true in a possible world *w* if and only if in all possible worlds *w'* compatible with what *a* knows at *w*, it is true that $\varphi$. R(*w*) stands for the worlds compatible with what *a* knows at *w*. Believing can now be defined by analogy to knowing, as represented in (5.138) and (5.139).

(5.138)   $[\![ K_a\varphi ]\!]^{M,w} = 1$ iff for all w' $\in$ R(w), $[\![ \varphi ]\!]^{M,w'} = 1$

(5.139)   $[\![ B_a\varphi ]\!]^{M,w} = 1$ iff for at least one w' $\in$ R(w), $[\![ \varphi ]\!]^{M,w'} = 1$

Operators B and K can be reiterated. For example, $K\varphi \rightarrow KK\varphi$ is a famous *KK thesis* introduced by Jaakko Hintikka (although the idea of infallibility of knowledge itself can be traced back to Plato). It says that if you know that *p*, you also *know that you know* that *p*.[65]

However, like in the case of modal operators, a sentential operator alone will not yet cater for the meaning. We need a metalanguage that would allow us to 'look inside' the structure of the *that*-clause, for all the reasons we have just discussed. And we need a semantics of natural language that is able to incorporate the insights from the logic of belief. They are intensional contexts, so we can apply the intensional semantics discussed in Stage 3. Montague's own treatment of belief reports essentially amounted to the formalization of Frege's view: a belief report is an attitude to a proposition but it is the attitude to the *intension* of a sentence. The *that*-clause is represented by an intensional type <*s, t*>. So, substitutivity is truth-preserving in the extensional context *t* but blocked in the intensional counterpart <*s, t*>. His intensional semantics is powerful enough to represent quantifying into intensional contexts and to block substitutivity.

---

[64] See Hintikka 1962.
[65] Note that the thesis only holds when one knows one's self-identity – that is, if one knows that one is the person referred to by *a*.

Remember that this is the standard view, saying that there is something special to intensional contexts such as belief reports; they are intensional rather than extensional, and as such they are difficult for semantic theory to deal with. But recall also that by now we are more comfortable with a common-sense view that any simple sentence can be an intensional context, as long as the way of referring to the object or the person matters for the meaning: I may know a person as, say, Lady Gaga but not as Stefani Joanne Angelina Germanotta. So, while the research on propositional attitude reports is important in that *that*-clauses embedded in them are indeed special because they contain reporting which is second-hand information, so to speak, it has to be remembered that the problem with substitution is more widespread. As such, it may need a more general solution in the form of a conceptual semantics for *any type of construction*. Food for thought (or cause for frustration).

To spell this frustration in words, formally representing belief reports and formalizing Frege's intensions to obtain more plausible truth conditions is not the end of the task. We need to get closer to their meaning: to the conditions under which substitutivity goes through and to what it is exactly that makes belief reports compositional – on the assumption that they simply have to be compositional, on some level or other, as was concluded in Section 3.4. Here DRT goes some way towards capturing the importance of the *psychological* mode of presentation – the way the holder of the belief thinks about the individual. Hans Kamp[66] distinguishes between the *de re* and *de dicto* readings by using so-called internal and external anchors for discourse referents. An external anchor 'anchors' the referent to an object in the world, so to speak. Such anchors are required because the sentence (and its representation, the DRS) can only have truth conditions if the discourse referent is connected with an entity in the domain to which the conversation pertains. An internal anchor anchors the discourse referent to a *concept*, or a *mental file*, to information about the referent that is available to the holder of the belief.[67] On this approach, an internal anchor alone does not suffice for the representation to have truth conditions, and so it does not suffice to make it meaningful. Let us consider sentence (5.132) again, repeated below.

(5.132)   Max believes that the king of France is bald.

The representation is given in Figure 5.14. '<[ANCH, $y'$], DRS>' stands for an internal anchor for the discourse referent $y'$. Next, a predicate '*Att*' (for 'attitude') is added to the vocabulary of the DRT language. Attitudes are states represented as '$s$: Att ($x$, DRS, external anchor)', where the external anchor is '$\{<y', y>\}$'.

In Figure 5.14, $y$ is internally and externally anchored. It represents a reading on which 'the king of France' is used referentially (the *de re* reading) – or the wide-scope reading in (5.133) above.

---

[66] After Kamp 1990, and specifically 2003.
[67] For a discussion of the role of mental files in DRT, see Meier 2016.

```
                    x y s

                  Max (x)
               King of France (y)

                        y'
   <[ANCH, y'],  ┌──────────────────┐  >,
                 │  King of France (y') │
                 └──────────────────┘

                        s'
   s:  Att (x, <BEL,  ┌──────────────┐  >, {<y', y>})
                      │ s': y' is bald │
                      └──────────────┘
```

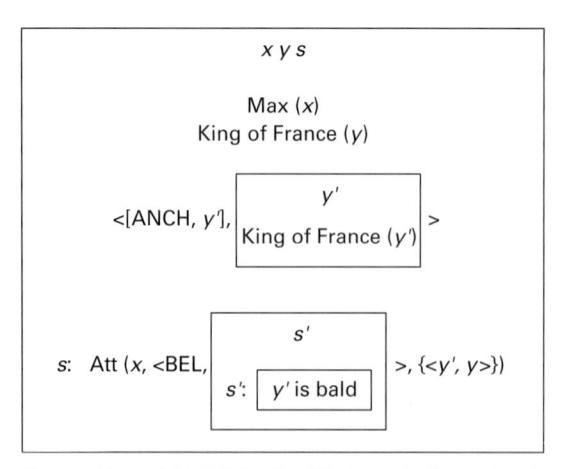

**Figure 5.14** Partial DRS for (5.132) ('Max believes that the king of France is bald.')

But we have to remember that if an internally anchored discourse referent is not also externally anchored, then the DRS does not express any proposition. This is not what a semantics of conceptual structures would be satisfied with. We want to include attributive as well as mistaken referential uses of referring terms, just as we represent other contextual information, without at the same time giving up the powerful tool of truth conditions. Let us continue the journey through semantics and philosophy of language to get a bit closer to pragmatics of communication.

As we have seen, at the most radical end of the spectrum, some philosophers suggest that compositionality as a property of natural languages should be abandoned: perhaps such intensional contexts demonstrate that natural languages are not compositional (*pace* the attempts of Montague semantics to incorporate senses into formal theory). Or we could preserve compositionality but predicate it of conceptual structures that draw on linguistic as well as non-linguistic information. Or else, we could assume the supervenience (the concept introduced in Section 5.4) of natural language on the composition of thought, or even the composition of reality. If our thoughts are composed out of smaller parts, or if situations in the world are logically composed of smaller parts, then language has meaning because it supervenes on such compositional reality – mental reality (thoughts) or physical reality (situations). But for that, we need a different concept of a proposition – a kind of Fregean proposition that accounts for the differences that matter, such as differences in the guises under which we think and refer to objects.

Now, in the neo-Fregean tradition, there have been proposals to include the mode of presentation, as a so-called *hidden*, or *unarticulated*, constituent, in the logical form – as in the case of the *hidden-indexical theory* advocated, among others, by Mark Crimmins, John Perry, and, tentatively, Stephen Schiffer.[68] The way to think about the theory is as if the structure were '*a so-believes* that ... ' or '*a* believes that *b*,

---

[68] The seminal works include Schiffer 1987, 1992, 1996; Crimmins and Perry 1989; Crimmins 1992.

*so-labelled*, VP', where VP stands for a verb phrase and 'so-believes' and 'so-labelled' allude to the way of thinking.[69] Let us now look at Schiffer's tentative proposal. (The word 'tentative' will prove important in a moment, as may be anticipated from our earlier discussions in Sections 1.3 and 3.4.) Believing is a three-place relation among the holder of the belief, the proposition, and the mode of presentation under which the person believes this proposition. The mode of presentation of the proposition is determined by the modes of presentation of the objects and properties (corresponding to arguments and predicates of the logical form) and their position in the structure of the sentence. So, (5.140) has the logical form something to the effect of (5.141). $\Phi^*m$ is a type of mode of presentation, i.e. a property of modes of presentation, determined by the context.

(5.140)   Ralph believes that Fido is a dog.

(5.141)   $\exists m\, (\Phi^*m\ \&\ \text{Bel}\, (\text{Ralph}, [\![\text{Fido, doghood}]\!], m))$

(adapted from Schiffer 1992: 503)

But inserting a construct called 'types of modes of presentation' is only the tip of the iceberg. Recall that we still don't know what information falls under $\Phi^*m$, or what types of contextual information $\Phi^*m$ can draw on. So, we don't know how to determine $m$ on particular occasions. If $m$ is to be a constituent of the logical form and as such 'save' a compositional account of meaning of attitude reports, we would have to know what it is. Inserting a mysterious constituent does not by itself fix compositionality. And it is mostly for this reason that Schiffer's proposal ends with a twist: he rejects it in the end, remains sceptical about whether natural languages have compositional semantics, and opts for unstructured propositions instead. He proposes a kind of proposition that captures the *thought* with a suitable fineness of grain but the pay-off is that it does not capture the structure of natural-language *that*-clauses:

> According to the hypothesis being entertained, the propositions that these *that*-clauses refer to are not structured entities individuated by their constituents

and

> Propositions ... are not ... to be identified and individuated by the propositional building blocks that construct them. Although abstract and language independent, propositions are really conceptual products of the conceptual and linguistic practices governing our use of that-clauses.
> (Schiffer 1994: 313, 315–316)

Since his more recent book *The Things We Mean*, Schiffer's propositions have been known as pleonastic propositions. They were briefly introduced in Section 1.3, where I pointed out that they had some affinities with our functional proposition.[70]

Now, while the truth-conditional representation of belief reports is often in need of context-dependent resolution, it will rarely need the totality of information that a 'way of thinking' about the entity contains. Modes of presentation are too rich, too fine grained for semantic purposes; we need only those aspects of them that make the

---

[69] For a discussion of these solutions, see Forbes 1990, 1997; Recanati 2000.
[70] On pleonastic propositions, see Schiffer 2003 and a discussion in Jaszczolt 2021a, where the functional proposition is proposed. For an introduction to propositions, see Section 1.3 above.

difference. Arguably, sometimes we may not need modes of presentation at all, when the substitution happens to be truth-preserving – say, in our earlier example, when the holder of the belief knows that the real name of George Eliot was Mary Ann Evans. Conceptual semantics should be sufficiently fine grained to cater for a variety of cases: (a) where a lot of information about the mode of presentation is required; (b) where only, say, 'so-labelled' is required; and (c) where the context is entirely transparent. Defaulting to the most problematic (first) scenario makes for a bad theory: it captures all the eventualities but it complicates the explanation in order to do so. Instead, it would be better to 'write it into the theory' that different aspects and degrees of such pragmatic contribution are required on different occasions to account for cognitively real propositions. It is a 'pragmaticky' complication of semantics but done for a good reason.[71]

Such solutions stand in opposition to the so-called neo-Russellian approaches, represented, among others, by Nathan Salmon and Scott Soames,[72] that deny the contribution of the mode of presentation to the logical form and as such to the semantics of attitude reports. (NB: we can see now why Soames' more recent idea of a cognitive proposition discussed in Section 1.3 does not suit our purpose: it is neo-Russellian in the sense of being coarsely grained, not allowing for the ways of thinking to contribute to the semantic representation.) Next, Mark Richard[73] suggests that the verb *believe* is itself context-sensitive – that is, it is similar to standard indexical expressions. (Indexicality is discussed at length in Section 6.2.4.) Next come proposals of various versions of indexicality, where logical forms are annotated with relevant information that is not overt in the sentence. Richard Larson and Peter Ludlow[74] propose so-called *interpreted logical forms* that are the combinations of linguistic forms and extralinguistic objects and in this way they account for the difference between using, say, *George Eliot* and *Mary Ann Evans* in an attitude report.

The semantics of proper names is still a matter of controversy. There will be more on proper names in Section 6.2.2 but what is interesting in the context of propositional attitude reports is that they pose problems without even invoking substitutivity. Here Saul Kripke presents the following puzzle.[75] Pierre, a speaker of French who lives in France, holds a belief about some distant city called Londres, expressed in (5.142). This belief can be reported by an English sentence (5.143).

(5.142)   Londres est jolie.

(5.143)   Pierre believes that London is pretty.

---

[71] Aspects of such an account have been developed in Recanati 1993, where he distinguishes psychological and linguistic mode of presentation, and mainly in Recanati 2002a, where he proposes a *variadic function* that increases the number of arguments taken by predicates such as *eat* or *rain* when we move from constructions such as *John eats* (*Whenever May cooks, John eats*) to *John eats mushrooms* or *It is raining* to *It is raining in Cambridge*. Then a variadic function was applied to propositional attitude reports in Jaszczolt 2005, Chapter 5 and in more detail in Jaszczolt 2007.

[72] See e.g. Salmon 1986; Soames 1997 [1987].     [73] See e.g. Richard 1990.

[74] See Larson and Ludlow 1997 [1993] and Ludlow 2000.     [75] See Kripke 1996 [1979], pp. 392–393.

There are two principles that make this report adequate. The first one is the *disquotational principle* which says that if a speaker assents to 'p', then they believe that *p*. The second one is the *principle of translation*. It says that if a sentence in a particular language is true, then any of its translations into any other language is also true. The story continues as follows. Pierre moves from France to England, lives in London and acquires a belief that London is not pretty. He happily assents to (5.144), while still holding the belief expressed in (5.142), unaware of the identity of London and Londres.

(5.144)    London is not pretty.

The beliefs in (5.142) and (5.144) are clearly contradictory. The belief in (5.144) can be reported on by (5.145) which is contradictory to (5.143).

(5.145)    Pierre believes that London is not pretty.

So, just as coreferentiality of names does not suffice for substitution, so translation is unreliable. The puzzle also further corroborates that proper names, like definite descriptions and other expressions that are used to refer, convey modes of presentation that exhibit a varying degree of contribution to meaning. Kripke does not offer a solution to the puzzle. For our purpose, we can only observe that since the representation under which Pierre holds his beliefs concerning London's pulchritude makes such a difference, cognitively sensitive semantics would have to make the representations count – not only in the context of a report but also in (5.142) and (5.144). Proper names are not free from referential puzzles across a wide range of contexts.

Finally, we ought to mention the so-called *semantic innocence* view, although it invoked debates mostly in philosophy rather than linguistics. On Donald Davidson's proposal, *that* is a demonstrative referring to the whole embedded sentence that follows.[76] A report is to be understood as a juxtaposition '*a* said that. *b* VP'. (He extends the analysis to verbs of saying.) For this reason, it is also called a *paratactic account*. The gist of Davidson's view of propositional attitude reports is that *p* embedded in an attitude report contributes exactly what it does in ordinary, extensional environments.

Looked at from the perspective of more recent discussions, it is interesting to notice that the denial that attitude reports are 'special' in any way has been catching on. Just as the truth value of (5.127) can be sensitive to the way of thinking about the author, so can the ordinary, extensional (5.130), as was already discussed in Section 3.4. In many ways, this observation appears to have 'demystified' attitude reports and stripped them of the important status they had enjoyed, that is the status of the criterion by which semantic theories are assessed. But while attitude reports no longer have this status, such traditionally defined intensional contexts still occupy an important place in semantic theory, even though the overall focus of semantics has shifted. First, interests have shifted to addressing the question as to whether semantics ought to be

[76] See Davidson 1997 [1968–69].

minimalistic and cater only for the meaning of the sentence (where propositional attitudes are indeed a thorny subject), or, rather, contextualist and cater for cognitively real meaning (where they can be more easily accommodated). As a result of this shift, the label 'criterion of adequacy' would now only make sense, at most, for the minimalist approaches. For contextualist views, resorting to context, intentions, conventional meanings grasped intuitively, and so forth is absolutely no problem, as long as we are prepared to go far enough with rethinking compositionality of meaning. As before, we delay a full discussion until Stage 7. Second, interests are also shifting in the direction of 'practically engaged' topics to do with speaker commitment and accountability, often in connection with the semantics and pragmatics of lying or use of offensive language. These are flagged in Section 8.4. But one has to remember that without having the tools that researchers on meaning have developed, tackling such sociopragmatic and ethical issues with the purpose of meaning representation would be difficult.

## 5.6 Interim Conclusions: Semantic Tools for Formal Cognitive Representations?

Representing meaning in natural language can be rewarding and fun when we appreciate the existing tools to analyse and represent meaning, but also adapt, revise them, use them in novel ways, searching for ways to represent recalcitrant phenomena and constructions. This includes using them for what *we* want to call 'meaning' – to reiterate, we may want a semantics that is sensitive to meaning in the mind that utterances of sentences convey. We have done it here for a handful of issues that crop up when we try to represent what is 'inside the sentence'. We have looked at quantifiers, temporal reference, modality, and propositional attitude constructions. During Stage 3, we tackled some problems with representing non-declaratives, specifically questions (Section 3.2). During Stage 4, we looked at connecting sentences. The interim conclusion is, arguably, that if we want a theory of meaning that enjoys a normative status and, as such, predictability – that is, that can be applied to novel constructions making accurate predictions – we may want to take the ill-fitting tools in the form of standard predicate logic and its extensions, adapt its vocabulary and syntax, combine them with other tools, and go as far as we can.

A large part of the remainder of this journey will be centred around the objective of striving for the cognitive plausibility of meaning representations. This is a goal that we have been repeatedly keeping in mind throughout this journey, adopting precisely this premise that the truth-conditional method is a scrutable, rigorous way to analyse meaning and that it is applicable to representations of what information, attitudes, feelings, and the like, utterances actually convey. Recent progress in semantics and pragmatics (that will be easier to appreciate when we complete Stage 8) suggests that focusing on the thinking agents and the users of natural language in discourse is a more promising option than a search for the Holy Grail of elusive Sentence Meaning. We learn from the tools that the great forefathers devised for this elusive Holy Grail but we employ them to Meaning that is constructed, conveyed, recovered, and often also jointly constructed, in discourse.

The philosophy of this journey continues to be that while we can lay out and discuss these tools, and demonstrate how they *might* be reused, answers to what meaning is and how to represent it have to be one's own: *learning* semantics and pragmatics cannot be separated from *doing* semantics and pragmatics one's own way. This is what thinking about meaning like a linguist and a philosopher is, and this is why they can't be separated.

**Suggested Further Reading**
This part of the journey through meaning is rather broad in scope as the overall idea was to show the connections between issues that are often split apart in introductions to meaning. My teaching experience tells me that classifying information sometimes under theories, sometimes under tools, and at other times under phenomena in the same book can be quite confusing. So, I have used here a conceptual 'glue'. This stage, 'Inside the sentence', has as its main thread asking about the available tools, moving through types of constructions and phenomena for which additional tools are needed. Then, the book guides us through what are arguably the best proposals on the market to choose from and work on (and with) to fix the problems with these phenomena and constructions. This makes a more uniform structure and a more progressive, goal-oriented journey.

With this caveat in mind, see e.g. Kearns' (2011) *Semantics*, Chapters 3 and 6 for classical and generalized quantifiers; Chapters 9 and 11 for temporality and events; Chapter 5 for modality; and Chapter 7 for propositional attitude reports. Also, see de Swart's (1998) classic *Introduction to Natural Language Semantics*, Chapter 7 on the limitations of first-order logic; Chapter 4 on predicate-argument structure and classical quantifiers; Chapter 8 for an accessible introduction to generalized quantifiers; and Chapter 9 on time and modality. Allan's (2001) *Natural Language Semantics* has an accessible introduction to quantifiers in English (Chapter 13) and to modality (Chapter 11). Cann et al.'s (2009) *Semantics: An Introduction to Meaning in Language* has Chapter 4 on quantification and Chapter 6 on time and events, from a more formal than philosophical perspective. Szabó and Thomason's (2019) *Philosophy of Language* has philosophical introductions to quantification (Section 3.3) and time and modality (Chapter 4). Portner's (2005) *What Is Meaning?* offers introductions to quantifiers (Chapter 6) and propositional attitudes (Chapter 9). Kamp and Reyle's (1993) *From Discourse to Logic* is also a good place to start on generalized quantifiers (Chapter 4) and time and events (Chapter 5), with the proviso that the introductions seamlessly merge with the treatment of these phenomena in DRT. Rothstein's (2004) *Structuring Events* is a comprehensive discussion of lexical aspect. On events see also the contributions to *The Oxford Handbook of Event Structure* (Truswell 2019). Chapter 4 of Altshuler, Parsons, and Schwarzschild's (2019) *A Course in Semantics* offers an interesting introduction to event semantics within generative grammar – the paradigm not followed in this journey but worth checking as 'food for thought'. Nelson's (2019)

'Propositional attitude reports' is a philosophical introduction to the problem in the title, including a discussion of seminal solutions. It also provides a detailed, well-selected and up-to-date list of references for this profusely researched topic.

More detailed, including advanced, reading suggestions on the topics covered here are given in the footnotes throughout, in accordance with the 'two-tier' design of this guide through meaning.

# Stage 6  Conveying Information

## 6.1 From Sentences to Discourses: Dynamic Semantics for Dynamic Meaning

So far, we have discussed meaning as if it was a static, given property of sentences or at least of their utterances in context. In fact, meaning 'grows'. It grows in two senses. First, in the psycholinguistic sense, it grows because discourse interpretation is incremental: it proceeds chunk by chunk, where previous chunks create updates to the context in which the following chunks are interpreted. Next, quite analogously, it grows in the semantic sense because the linguistic expressions (words, phrases, as well as sentences) provide information for how to assign meaning to what follows them. For example, pronouns are used not only deictically, that is, to point to a situationally salient individual (sometimes accompanied by an act of demonstration), but they can also be used anaphorically – to refer to an entity that was introduced with a more informative name or description earlier in the sentence or even through cross-sentential anaphora. Such dependencies do not obey sentence boundaries: when discourse grows, information grows and becomes the new background for upcoming information.

What seems to be required, then, is incorporating context, as well as changes in that context, into semantics. Conversational common ground changes with the moves and actions of the participants, so the interpretation of an utterance has to make use of the most up-to-date information available. This change has been captured in dynamic approaches to meaning, such as Discourse Representation Theory (DRT),[1] to which we have already referred throughout this journey and about which more has to be said, specifically to explain the benefits of capturing the dynamic nature of meaning.

This ability to account for changing context is the essential property of dynamic semantics in general. Dynamic semantics is an umbrella term for a group of approaches that conceptualize this dynamicity somewhat differently. Irene Heim's File Change Semantics, developed simultaneously but independently from DRT in the 1980s,[2] makes use of the metaphor of files: the hearer constructs a file, so to speak, and regularly updates it with information revealed by the speaker and obtained from context. Meaning is conceptualized there as *context change potential*. For example, for indefinite descriptions, the hearer starts a new file card. Similarly, in DRT, the hearer introduces a new discourse referent.[3] For a definite description, an existing file

---

[1] Kamp and Reyle 1993.   [2] See Heim 1988.   [3] On discourse referents see Karttunen 1976.

card is updated according to the conditions specified in the theory. Files, as interpretative devices that mediate between the language and the world, perform the role of a monitor that records the changes of the situation, including both linguistic and non-linguistic information such as that from perception and background knowledge. Changes in the situation cannot be recorded *after* the representation has been constructed because they may affect the truth-conditional content. So, Kamp's and Heim's proposals capture this dynamic nature of situations by introducing a level on which utterances and other sources of information 'write down' anything that is required for the assignment of meaning. *Context* is given there a formal definition. It can be conceptualized as a set of possible worlds or a pair consisting of a set of variables and a set of assignment functions, where assignment functions are functions from sets of variables to sets of individuals, as was discussed in Stage 3.

Another influential approach is Dynamic Predicate Logic (DPL) developed by Jeroen Groenendijk and Martin Stokhof in the late 1980s.[4] The syntax of DPL is the same as that of ordinary predicate logic but the semantics is dynamic. For example, existential quantifiers can bind variables that are outside their ordinary scope – or, so to speak, 'beyond the bracket' that marks their scope, as introduced in Section 3.2. DPL is an alternative to DRT in that it achieves compositionality without invoking mental representations. Instead, by altering the *language* of predicate logic (that is, making its semantic dynamic) it achieves the desired result of representing cohesive discourses – such as those discussed in Sections 6.1.1 and 6.1.2, that is variable binding in so-called donkey sentences and cross-sentential anaphora.

## 6.1.1 Donkey Sentences

The primary motivation for a dynamic theory of representation of discourse was to attempt to solve a problem with the so-called *donkey anaphora*, named after the seminal example, first discussed by Peter Geach,[5] amended here slightly (in order to respect animal rights) as (6.1).

(6.1)   Every farmer who owns a donkey is fond of it.

The problem is this. The sentence contains an anaphoric pronoun *it* whose antecedent is the phrase *a donkey*. But *a donkey* is not a referring expression: it is an indefinite noun phrase and it is intuitively bound by the quantifier *every farmer* in (6.1), and as such can refer to different donkeys owned by different farmers. The pronoun *it* would then have to remain a free variable in the logical form and the anaphoric relation is difficult to capture.

In terms of generative syntax, the problem is this. The antecedent of the pronoun (*a donkey*) is a variable bound by a quantified expression (*every farmer*), and the antecedent and the pronoun are not joined by binding in the syntactic sense. There is no *c-commanding* relation between *a donkey* and *it*, where c-commanding is a relation between nodes in a tree diagram. A node A c-commands another node B if both are

---

[4] See Groenendijk and Stokhof 1991.   [5] See Geach 1962, p. 128.

offshoots of the same node C located higher up the tree and C is the lowest branching node that dominates A.

Now, the standard metalanguage of predicate logic introduced in Stage 3 allows us to represent such sentences, but neither of the available representations ((6.2a) or (6.2b)) is satisfactory. On the one hand, we can derive the meaning compositionally but the formula does not give the required interpretation. Notice that the sentence means that if a farmer owns a donkey, they are fond of it, hence the conditional in (6.2a). But the final occurrences of the variables $x$ and $y$ are not in the scope of the quantifiers, so the anaphoric relation is lost.

(6.2a)   $\exists x \exists y$ (Farmer $(x)$ ∧ Donkey $(y)$ ∧ Owns $(x,y)$) → Fond-of $(x,y)$

On the other hand, the formula in (6.2b) has the required interpretation but cannot be derived compositionally: *a donkey* is an indefinite noun phrase and as such there is no obvious reason why it ought to be translated as a universal quantifier. We have to reconceptualize the English sentence, so to speak.

(6.2b)   $\forall x \forall y$ ((Farmer $(x)$ ∧ Donkey $(y)$ ∧ Owns $(x,y)$) → Fond-of $(x,y)$)

So, we end up with an attempted translation that is not a sentence of predicate logic (it is an open formula) and as such suggests that the English sentence ought to be ungrammatical, or with a translation that gives us the correct meaning and truth conditions but no principled way of arriving at this translation compositionally.

Solutions abound. One of them, proposed by Gareth Evans, is the *E-type anaphora*.[6] According to the E-type analysis, since there is no binding relation between the indefinite noun phrase and the pronoun, the indefinite noun phrase must be given a different explanation and a different semantics. Evans suggests that it does not translate as an existential quantifier in such contexts but that it is a disguised description – something to the effect of 'for every case we examine, the farmer who owns a donkey' or 'for every case we examine, the donkey owned by a farmer'. The proposal concerns anaphoric pronouns that lie outside of the scope of the binding operator, so this type of anaphora also includes instances where the antecedent can be found in the previous sentence, as in (6.3) where *he* is a disguised description 'the farmer who came into the pub'.

(6.3)   A farmer came into the pub. He said he was fond of his donkey.

However, the link between the antecedent and the anaphor is more 'syntacticky' than it appears. In (6.4), the pronoun *it* cannot be bound in the same way as in (6.1). Neither can it in the attempted cross-sentential anaphora in (6.5) if *it* is to refer to a donkey rather than the state of being a donkey-owner.

(6.4)   *Every donkey-owning farmer is fond of it.

(6.5)   Farmer Bill is a donkey-owner. He is fond of *it.

---

[6] See Evans 1985a [1977]; 1985b [1980].

To complicate things further, (6.1) has multiple readings. Imagine a farmer who owns a hundred donkeys. What does *it* stand for? Imagine that the farmer owns a hundred donkeys but is fond of only ten of them. Is (6.1) true? That depends on whether we think of it in terms of 'farmer–donkey' pairs, where every donkey's fate contributes to the truth conditions, or in terms of farmers, quantifying over donkey-owning farmers. The problem is well exemplified in conjunction with adverbials in that indefinites pose a scope problem with respect to adverbials in sentences such as (6.6).

(6.6)   If *a farmer* owns a donkey, *he* is usually rich.

(from Heim 1990: 150)

There is no indication in this sentence as to how to interpret the relative scope of the indefinite descriptions *a farmer* and *a donkey*. The adverb can quantify over the farmer–donkey pairs, over instances of the first indefinite, or over instances of the second indefinite. When we take ninety-nine poor farmers who own one donkey each and one farmer with two hundred donkeys, the difference becomes obvious: *usually* can be attached to farmer–donkey pairs and the sentence is true, or to donkey-owning farmers and the sentence is false. It can also be attached to farmer-owned donkeys. This is called *the proportion problem*.

Now, one of these readings, namely the second, is intuitively more plausible and the semantic theory that aims at cognitive plausibility (like the one we are in pursuit of here), should be able to arrive at it. Heim suggests that the topic–focus distinction helps with the choice of the correct interpretation, and so can the situation of discourse. If so, then the task of a cognitively real truth-conditional semantics does not end with listing the readings that depend on what *usually* quantifies over. It pursues the interpretation on the level where information structure contributes to the representation. This is the kind of semantics we are striving for in this journey, adopting all these fantastic tools and solutions but pushing them a little further. Information structure is the topic of Section 6.3.

In DRT, indefinite noun phrases are not translated as existential quantifiers but as variables. Combined with the understanding of binding as the so-called *unselective binding* represented in Figure 6.1, donkey sentences obtain a correct semantics. On unselective binding, both $x$ and $y$ are bound, resulting in the reading of (6.1), repeated below, as (6.7).

(6.1)   Every farmer who owns a donkey is fond of it.

(6.7)   For every farmer $x$ and for every donkey $y$ that $x$ owns, $x$ is fond of $y$.

Figure 6.1 is a DRS for example (6.1).

Notice that discourse referents are introduced in the embedded left-hand-side DRS and as such, by rule, are available ('visible') for the right-hand-side DRS. Then we add a condition $u = y$, like we did in Section 5.2.3, to account for the anaphoric nature of the pronoun *it*. The trick of the unselective binding now lies in the meaning of the connective '⇒': it allows for binding of all the discourse referents from the left-hand-side DRS. This process was not available in standard

## 6.1 From Sentences to Discourses

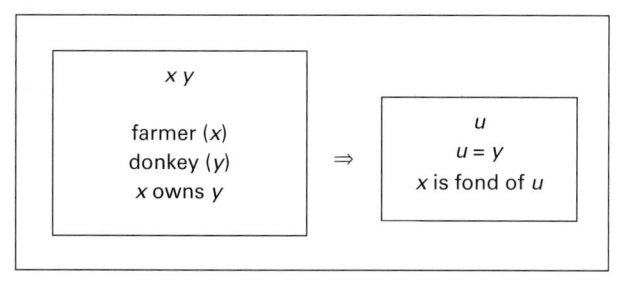

```
┌─────────────────────────────────────────────┐
│    ┌──────────────┐                         │
│    │    x y       │         ┌─────────────┐ │
│    │              │         │     u       │ │
│    │  farmer (x)  │   ⇒     │   u = y     │ │
│    │  donkey (y)  │         │ x is fond of u│
│    │  x owns y    │         │             │ │
│    └──────────────┘         └─────────────┘ │
└─────────────────────────────────────────────┘
```

**Figure 6.1** Partial DRS for (6.1) ('Every farmer who owns a donkey is fond of it.')

predicate logic, where universal and existential quantifiers bind only the variable that follows: $\forall x$ or $\exists x$.[7]

The solution to donkey anaphora in DPL is not dramatically different in that it relies on the dynamic notion of context, where information accrues incrementally. But, to reiterate, here 'tweaking' the metalanguage alone can account for the meaning (although, by now, the differences between DPL and DRT have been considerably minimized). Let us consider (6.1) again. Like in DRT, we consider the conceptually conditional structure of the sentence whereby (6.1) means that 'if a farmer owns a donkey, they are fond of it'. Making semantics dynamic allows us now to bind the final occurrences of $x$ and $y$ in 'Fond-of $(x,y)$' in (6.8).

(6.8)    $\exists x$ (Farmer $(x) \wedge \exists y$ (Donkey $(y) \wedge$ Own $(x,y))) \rightarrow$ Fond-of $(x,y)$

The DPL rules that allow for this 'dynamic binding' are rules for dynamic existential quantifier and dynamic implication. Dynamic existential quantifier works as follows. The dynamic interpretation of $\exists x\ P(x)$ has an input $g$ and output $h$ if and only if $h$ differs from $g$ at most in the value of $x$, and the value assigned to $x$ at any assignment $h$ has to belong to the interpretation function for the predicate $P$, as in (6.9). '{... | ...}' means that the variables on the left (the ordered pair) satisfy the properties on the right.

(6.9)    $[\![\exists x\ P(x))]\!] = \{<g,h> | h[x]g \wedge h(x) \in f(P)\}$

(after de Swart 1998: 142)

In other words, there will be a possible progression from the initial context to the incrementally 'increased' context in which $x$ will obtain the same reference, in that the dynamic existential quantifier can pass referents from left to right in the formula beyond the traditional scope of $\exists$, as summarized in (6.10). As we will see in Section 6.1.2, it can pass them on also across the sentence boundary.

(6.10)   $\exists x(P(x) \wedge Q(x))$ equals $\exists x P(x) \wedge Q(x)$

Dynamic implication can now be devised using the same principle but now all possible assignments (indicated in (6.11) as $\forall k$) will constitute acceptable input to the consequent ($\phi$).

---

[7] For a comparative discussion of treatments of donkey anaphora in description-based views and in dynamic semantics, see Elbourne 2005.

(6.11) $\llbracket \varphi \to \phi \rrbracket = \{<g,h> \mid h = g \wedge \forall k{:}<h,k> \in \llbracket \varphi \rrbracket \Rightarrow \exists j{:}<k,j> \in \llbracket \phi \rrbracket \}$

(after de Swart 1998: 144)

The symbol '$\Rightarrow$' stands for implication in the sense of consequence, or inferential link, which is here worth distinguishing from material implication (or 'logical implication') as a logical connective in that, in (6.11), it is the material implication that we revise to make semantics dynamic. In words, the dynamic interpretation of $\varphi \to \phi$ has an input $g$ and output $h$ if and only if (i) $h$ equals $g$ and (ii) for all assignments $k$, if the input–output pair $<h,k>$ belongs to the interpretation of $\varphi$, then there is an assignment $j$ such that $<k,j>$ belongs to $\phi$. Put simply, all assignments in the interpretation of $\varphi$ are fine, which is the essence of the dynamic nature of implication. The dynamic properties of existential quantifier and implication are not exactly the same, which will become important when we move to multi-sentence discourses and cross-sentential anaphora.

As was explained in Section 5.3.3, '$\phi$' and '$\varphi$' stand here for propositional variables, or metavariables, in that they are used in the metalanguage, the language of description. Note that we adhered to sentential variables $p$, $q$, etc. while introducing propositional logic as a *language* earlier on, merely *considering it as a possible metalanguage* for natural-language semantics. Here we can either relate sentential metavariables to such sentential variables but note that we also have some freedom as to what we want to capture by these variables and metavariables: we can operate on a level where a symbolically represented proposition is merely equivalent to what was physically uttered, or, instead, we can operate on the assumption that the meaning we capture by these symbols is more 'pragmaticky': 'infused' with aspects of meaning given in the context. The formalization will work equally well both for these pure, minimal, sentence-based propositions and for the cognitively real, contextually appropriate ones. But I anticipate – more about it in Stage 7.

### 6.1.2 Multi-Sentence Discourses

Pronouns dependent on quantificational expressions have a tricky semantics. Notice that anaphoric relations between pronouns and quantificational antecedents can end at the sentence boundary. (6.12) is well-formed, while (6.13) is not. The subscript stands for the attempted coreference.

(6.12) Every donkey$_1$ thought it$_1$ was the luckiest.

(6.13) *Every donkey$_1$ was well fed. It$_1$ was lucky.

The simplified[8] representation of (6.13) in (6.14) shows that the variable for *it* will indeed have to remain unbound – that is, outside the scope of the quantifier and as such

---

[8] This is, of course, a partial representation in that it does not represent temporal reference provided by the past tense and neither does it represent the structure of the predicate *well fed* that, if broken down, would require second-order resources (to predicate something *about the predicate fed* by the qualifier *well*). Higher-order logics were introduced in Section 5.1. On partial representations, see the discussion of Figure 5.1 in Section 5.2.1.

standing for an uninterpreted 'dummy' rather than for a referent with the properties of being a donkey and well fed.

(6.14)     $\forall x$ (Donkey $(x)$ → Well-Fed $(x)$) $\wedge$ Lucky $(x)$

On the other hand, (6.15) is well-formed but it gives rise to a problem with binding that is analogous to that in the donkey sentence (6.1) in that although (6.1) is well-formed in English, the anaphoric link (in this case, cross-sentential) cannot be represented in standard, sentence-based static formal semantics. Standard translation gives us (6.16a)–(6.16b) or at best (6.16c), where $x$ is unbound. In other words, it predicts that (6.15) should be ill-formed: it leaves the pronoun *it* outside the scope of the quantifier.

(6.15)     A donkey brayed. It was hungry.

(6.16a)    $\exists x$ (Donkey (x) $\wedge$ Brayed $(x)$)

(6.16b)    Hungry $(x)$

(6.16c)    $\exists x$ (Donkey (x) $\wedge$ Brayed $(x)$) $\wedge$ Hungry $(x)$

We have seen that the DRT account, with its treatment of indefinites as giving rise to variables rather than quantifiers, provides a solution. And so does DPL, with its 'trick' to keep the syntax of first-order predicate logic but make its semantics dynamics.

### 6.1.2.1 Multi-Sentence Discourses in DRT

From these initial motivations to account for variable-bound and cross-sentential anaphora, DRT progressed to providing a theory of representation of discourses, focusing on the incremental nature of interpretation as it is performed by the addressee. Since we are moving beyond representing single-sentence structures to representing multi-sentence discourses and their cohesiveness, it is time now to discuss in more depth the devices that DRSs make use of to do so. DRSs are a result of the application of rules, called DRS Construction Rules. We have already seen that these rules can appeal to information from previously constructed DRSs, reflecting the fact that interpretation of discourse is incremental and that discourse is cohesive. An interpretation is obtained for the first sentence, and then this interpretation serves as context for the interpretation of the next sentence. In more formal terms, *merging DRSs* proceeds in the order of producing the sentences: the initial DRS is interpreted in the initial context (assignment) $s$ and brings about context $s''$, which is an initial context for interpreting DRS$'$, as in (6.17). ';' stands for a sequencing operator for merging *proto-DRSs*.

(6.17)     $_s[\![DRS;DRS']\!]_{s'}^{M}$ iff there is a $s''$ such that $_s[\![DRS]\!]_{s''}^{M}$ and $_{s''}[\![DRS']\!]_{s'}^{M}$

(adapted from van Eijck and Kamp 1997: 199)

The theory distinguishes three major stages of interpretation: (i) some form of generative syntax (that is supposed to stand for our 'mental grammar'); (ii) rules that derive representations from syntactic constructions; and (iii) mappings from representations to a

```
┌─────────────┐
│    x y      │
│             │
│   Bill (x)  │
│  donkey (y) │
│   x owns y  │
└─────────────┘
```

**Figure 6.2** Partial DRS for (6.18) ('Bill owns a donkey.')

```
              (S)
             /   \
          (NP)   (VP)
           |    /    \
          (PN) (V)   (NP)
           |    |    /   \
           |    |  (DET) (N)
           |    |   |     |
          Bill owns a   donkey
```

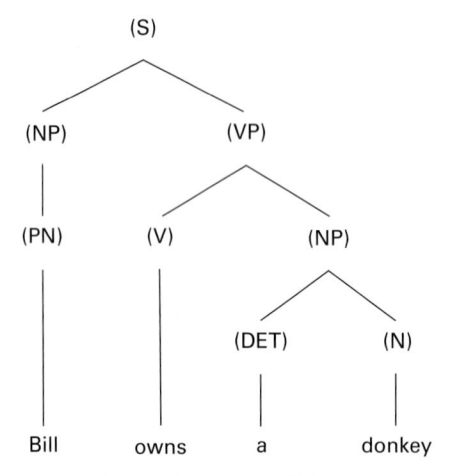

**Figure 6.3** Mental structure of (6.18) ('Bill owns a donkey.')

model. To reiterate, a DRS consists of two components: a set of discourse referents that function as 'formal representatives' of individuals, which we now call the *universe* of the DRS, and a set of DRS-conditions. Let us now take a closer look at these conditions in a simple example that involves a proper name and an indefinite description, such as (6.18) and the corresponding DRS in Figure 6.2.

(6.18)    Bill owns a donkey.

The operation of inserting the discourse referent $x$ for Bill is governed by the Construction Rule for Proper Names. But first, we have to imagine starting with mental syntax: the structure of the sentence whose semantics we want to represent. This is the 'origin' of our DRS. We can roughly represent (6.18) as in Figure 6.3.

We are not committing ourselves to a particular theory of syntax, and the authors Kamp and Reyle only tentatively do so. They select Generalized Phrase Structure Grammar (GPSG) only because, as they say, it fits the explanatory purposes. As such, their structural representations also contain, for example, relevant features such as gender to mark grammatical gender agreement.[9] We won't be addressing the question as to what syntactic theory best fits the requirement of mental grammar. As was evident from the discussions in Stage 2, this would also involve making assumptions about

---
[9] See Kamp and Reyle 1993.

what the language of thought is: a natural language we speak or some kind of Mentalese. So, we assume, after Fodor and other authors discussed there, that whatever the language of thought is, its structure would have to resemble pretty closely the structure of natural languages. Moreover, in view of the discussion of the suitability of categorial grammars for representing mental structures without the burden of non-basic categories, the standard category labels are encased in brackets in Figure 6.3, which means they are there merely for presentation purposes to explain the steps in DRT construction rules.

We are now ready to start. We introduce a new discourse referent (say, $x$ for Bill) into the universe of discourse (i.e. into the main DRS). Next, the rule stipulates two so-called *triggering configurations* in which the proper name can occur, as in Figure 6.4.

Sentence (6.18) exemplifies the first triggering configuration in that the proper name is in the subject position. We introduce a condition which consists of this triggering configuration, in which we insert a condition 'Bill $(x)$' below the PN node. We also introduce a condition 'Gen = male'. Next, we replace the entire NP node with $x$ in the triggering configuration and delete the entire syntactic structure in Figure 6.3 from the DRS.

Triggering configurations for indefinite descriptions (here: *a donkey*) are postulated in an analogous way, as in Figure 6.5.

The main difference is that a construction rule for indefinite noun phrases stipulates that the discourse referent is normally introduced into the current, rather than the main,

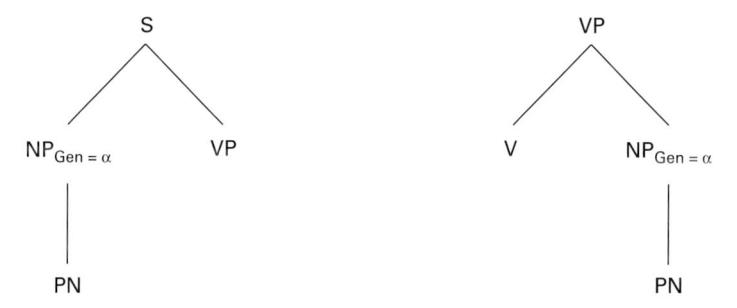

**Figure 6.4** Triggering configurations for proper name (adapted from Kamp and Reyle 1993: 65)

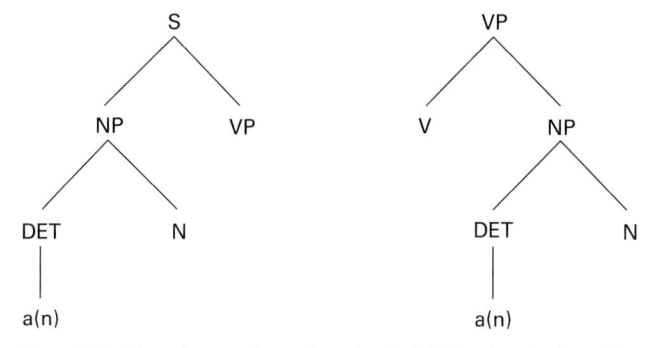

**Figure 6.5** Triggering configurations for indefinite description (adapted from Kamp and Reyle 1993: 75)

```
┌─────────────────┐
│   x y u v       │
│                 │
│   Bill (x)      │
│   donkey (y)    │
│   x owns y      │
│   u = x         │
│   v = y         │
│   u is fond of v│
└─────────────────┘
```

**Figure 6.6** Partial DRS for (6.19) ('Bill owns a donkey. He is fond of it.')

DRS. By 'current' we mean the DRS that contains the relevant discourse condition. This can be the main DRS, as in Figure 6.6, or a subordinate DRS (an embedded box). In the case of (6.18), where there are no subordinate DRSs, there is no obvious difference. But we will see shortly in example (6.20) why this is important.

Cross-sentential anaphora can now be regarded as a relation between pronouns and those discourse referents that have already been introduced for the antecedents in the representation of previous sentences. (Remember that the strength of dynamic semantics is to represent multi-sentence discourses.) So, for the mini-discourse in (6.19), we can now apply a construction rule for pronouns, as we did for donkey anaphora in Figure 6.1, and complete the DRS as in Figure 6.6. Conditions '$u = x$' and '$v = y$' link an anaphoric pronoun to its antecedent.

(6.19)   Bill owns a donkey. He is fond of it.

Let us now return to the question of subordinate DRSs. In (6.20), the discourse referent for *a horse* is introduced in the subordinate DRS (inner box), as in Figure 6.7, following the rule for indefinite descriptions.

(6.20)   Bill doesn't own a horse$_i$. He is fond of *it$_i$.

This allows us to represent correctly the lack of anaphoric relation between 'a horse' and 'it' (co-indexed in (6.20) for clarity) in that discourse referents in subordinate DRSs are not 'visible' from the main DRS – *it* remains unbound. *It* could at best stand for the state of not being an owner of a horse, in which case it would have to be bound to the state. (States and events in DRT were introduced in the discussion of temporal reference in Section 5.3.4.) In short, the rule is that a discourse referent introduced in the main DRS is accessible in the subordinate DRSs but a discourse referent introduced in the subordinate DRS is not accessible for anaphoric binding later on in the discourse. Representing the problematic two-sentence discourse in (6.13) can now be left as an exercise for the reader in that it follows the principles just laid out.

Figure 6.7 is a DRS for the standard reading of (6.20), that is, narrow-scope negation that does not have scope over the subject. Metalinguistic negation, discussed in Section 4.5.2, would have the power to introduce the discourse referent for the proper name 'Bill' in the embedded DRS, in that it would amount to saying that 'It is not the case that Bill owns a horse because there is no such person as Bill' (in the universe of discourse).

```
      x u

      Bill (x)

         ┌─────────┐
         │    y    │
      ¬  │ horse(y)│
         │ x owns y│
         └─────────┘

      u = x
      u is fond of *it
```

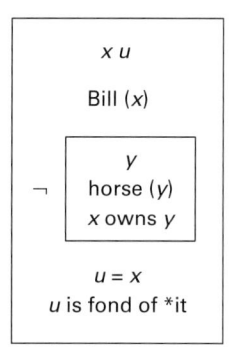

**Figure 6.7** Partial DRS for (6.20) ('Bill doesn't own a horse$_i$. He is fond of *it$_i$.')

Analogously, a discourse referent for an indefinite description can sometimes be introduced in the main DRS. This is the case when it represents a specific reading of the noun phrase – that is, when it stands for a particular individual the speaker has in mind, similar to proper names and definite descriptions. While this may appear somewhat ad hoc at the moment, we will see in Section 6.2 that there are robust semantic regularities that account for this variation.

Accounting for longer stretches of text has the general advantage of capturing the cohesive nature of discourses and the incremental nature of discourse interpretation. It has to be remembered that this is still model-theoretic truth-conditional semantics and that DRSs are representations that have truth conditions. They are true if and only if all discourse referents correspond to individuals in the universe of discourse and those individuals satisfy the discourse conditions stated in the DRS.

Having discussed the motivations for, and the meaning of, dynamicity in semantics, as well as the principles by which DRT can handle multi-sentence discourses, we can now represent more sophisticated constructions and longer discourses using these devices. We can also see how the devices for representing quantification and temporality introduced in Stage 5 fit into this theory. We have seen how quantification often necessitates going beyond sentence boundaries. Equally, or even more so, 'it is not very useful to study tense and aspect at the sentence level, as generative approaches to linguistics maintain; tense and aspect really come into their own only at the discourse level' (Hamm, Kamp, and van Lambalgen 2006: 9–10).

We have seen in Section 5.3 how important the deictic dimension is to representing temporality. But this is not a 'hands-on' coursebook on DRT, so we will not continue with the details. What is important for our journey through meaning is that DRSs represent the incremental process of interpreting discourse, in that this takes us a big step closer to representing the cognitive reality of discourse interaction. Whereas traditional formal semantics represents language as an abstract system, DRT attempts to capture meaning as a psychological phenomenon – an externalization of human thought. Language users interpret discourses, and that includes of course multi-sentence discourses, by constructing abstract conceptual-semantic structures which DRT attempts to capture in the DRSs.

The theory is still quite a long way away from achieving this aim, in that DRSs remain strongly grammar-driven. Recall, for example, the problem with representing tense–time mismatches discussed in Section 5.3 (examples (5.75) and (5.95)). The theory is not 'pragmaticky' enough to account for the functional proposition – the main meaning conveyed by the speaker who uses a variety of available means and resources, including indirectness, conventions, situational context, and so forth. But neither is it likely that DRT itself will go that far in that it grew out of the tradition in computational linguistics where the emphasis on *structures* is necessary for applications to machine learning. The aspiration to mental structures comes from the assumption that DRSs are results of processing of sentences performed in a 'mental grammar' – a generative grammar of some kind or other.

At the same time, DRT has been a springboard to various offshoots and extensions. We refer to two of them. One is Segmented Discourse Representation Theory (SDRT), whose rhetorical structure rules were introduced in Section 4.2 to show how SDRT represents meaningful relations between sentences, such as *Narration*, *Explanation*, or *Background*. Maximization of coherence of discourse is one of the important facets of the rationality of human communication that is emphasized and theoretically exploited in many approaches to discourse meaning. SDRT adopts it as the underlying principle behind rhetorical structure rules, where, as we have seen, these rules pertain to the meaningful links between adjacent sentences. In SDRT, this meaning originates on a level between syntax and pragmatics, in so-called glue logic that shows how the content of particular sentences is 'packaged' together, or how it is conveyed in discourse by ordering sentences.[10]

The other offshoot we will discuss, Default Semantics, veers in a very different direction in that it moves the analysis of discourse entirely from sentences (and strings of sentences) to the level of conceptual structures, using an amended language of DRT and the principle of dynamically composed intended and recovered meaning. The theory is introduced in the more 'pragmaticky' part of this journey in Section 7.2.3.

### 6.1.2.2 Multi-Sentence Discourses in DPL

Like DRT, DPL also has a solution to cross-sentential binding as it embraces the dynamic nature of discourse. Like in DRT, the meaning of (6.15), repeated below, is conceptualized as the way the sentence changes the information state of the addressee. So, meaning is a relation between information states.

(6.15)   A donkey brayed. It was hungry.

The dynamic existential quantifier that we introduced in Section 6.1.1 can pass referents from left to right in the formula. It can do so not only within a sentence, like in the case of donkey anaphora, but also across a sentence boundary. In other words, it is *internally and externally dynamic*. This means that in (6.10), repeated below, where $P(x)$ and $Q(x)$ now stand for the structures of two separate sentences,

---

[10] See Asher and Lascarides, e.g. 2003.

we can insert the conjunction on the assumption that discourse is cohesive and the anaphoric pronoun in the second sentence can acquire the antecedent from the first.

(6.10)   $\exists x(P(x) \land Q(x))$ equals $\exists x\, P(x) \land Q(x)$

Now, in order to represent the cross-sentential anaphora in (6.15), we need a dynamic quantifier and a dynamic conjunction. Dynamic conjunction works as follows. The interpretation of $\varphi \land \phi$ with information state $s$ brings about information state $s'$ if and only if there is some input $s''$ such that interpreting $\varphi$ in $s$ results in $s''$ and interpreting $\phi$ in $s''$ leads to $s'$ – or, in short, (6.21a).

(6.21a)   $_s[\![\varphi \land \phi]\!]_{s'}$ iff there is a $s''$ such that $_s[\![\varphi]\!]_{s''} \land\ _{s''}[\![\phi]\!]_{s'}$

The formulation in (6.21a) shows that this is essentially the same mechanism as merging DRSs in (6.17), but while DRT invokes mental representations, DPL 'tweaks the semantics' of predicate logic to make it dynamic. For enthusiasts of symbolic representations: by analogy with our previous definitions in DPL, we can also formulate it as (6.21b).

(6.21b)   $[\![\varphi \land \phi]\!] = \{<g, h> \mid \exists k: <g, k> \in [\![\varphi]\!] \land <k, h> \in [\![\phi]\!]\}$

(after de Swart 1998: 143)

Conjunction is internally dynamic as well as externally dynamic: it passes referents from left to right, and also to conjuncts yet to come in the following sentences in discourse. The interpretation of $\phi$ can only proceed in contexts which make $\varphi$ true. This also means that conjunction is asymmetric, as in (6.22).

(6.22)   $\varphi \land \phi \neq \phi \land \varphi$

This accounts for the cohesion of (6.15) and the problem with interpreting (6.23) – at least in standard discourse. In literary texts analogous examples are more natural and to be expected: we can often assimilate them as cases *cataphora* – a reverse-order binding, where, as in (6.24), the informative expression (the cataphor) follows its attenuated uptake (the pronoun).

(6.23)   $^?$It was hungry. A donkey brayed.

(6.24)   Ever since he remembered, he always wanted to work with horses. Peter was determined to become a stud manager.

On the other hand, implication is only internally dynamic; it passes referents from left to right within the sentence but stops at the sentence boundary. Negation is also only internally dynamic, which is another way of explaining (6.20) above, and so is the universal quantifier, as demonstrated in (6.25).

(6.25)   Every farmer owns a donkey. $^{*/?}$He is fond of it.

This brief introduction to two seminal dynamic semantic approaches, DRT and DPL, demonstrates how they conceptualize the dynamic nature of meaning, that is, its incremental growth in discourse, accounting for such phenomena as problematic anaphoric links – the bound-variable anaphora, as in donkey sentences, cross-sentential anaphora, and also the presupposed antecedent to which we will turn in Section 6.3. There is plenty of scope for extending this approach to incorporate more information, such as discourse coherence in SDRT, or presupposed content just mentioned, or even 'kicking the entire representation up', so to speak, to the level of conceptual structure to account for those elements of communicated content that remain covert, implicated, or presumed as common ground. These will be discussed in Stage 7. But the conceptual foundations are already there and they can be used as one sees fit: either for representing the meaning of syntactic structures or, for the purpose of this journey, they can be adapted to represent cognitive structures and as such, also what is not expressed but 'lurks under the surface'.

## 6.2 Referring and Its Tools

### 6.2.1 Types and Hierarchies of Referring

Discourse referents in donkey anaphora and cross-sentential anaphora receive a very insightful treatment in dynamic approaches to meaning but there are some pertinent questions left to address, to do with the properties of expressions that are used to refer, for instance *Bill*, *donkey*, or *it*. DRT provides answers to such questions as to whether to treat them as constants or variables (quantifying expressions) and how to assign referents to them. But in a philosophical journey through meaning, we need to delve deeper and ask what properties these different classes of expressions have that make them function well in one context but not so well in another.

Referring has been the subject of controversy in one way or another probably ever since philosophy began. In the context of the theory of meaning, the main confusions and disagreements lie around the question as to *who*, or *what*, does the referring: do expressions refer or do their users refer? Perhaps expressions at most *denote* – or not even that, since context may be needed? Peter Strawson's celebrated response to Bertrand Russell's 'On denoting', aptly entitled 'On referring',[11] conveys the gist: the sentence 'The king of France is bald' has no meaning because it is statements, that is, the uses of sentences, not sentences themselves, that refer. (We have referred to this view in Stage 5 and will return to it again shortly in Section 6.3 while discussing presupposition.) So, some philosophers of language claim that referring is a function that an expression performs and as such is not a part of semantics at all: it belongs to pragmatics understood as a separate enterprise.[12] But since we are following the path of a cognitively real theory of meaning, this answer won't do: for such an approach, one needs the context and goals of the interlocutors to get any meaning at all. The semantics/pragmatics boundary, if there is any, has to be looked for elsewhere. (Hence the title of Section 7.3.4: 'Semantics or Pragmatics? Or, Who Cares?'.) We can start

---

[11] Russell 1996 [1905] and Strawson 1997 [1950].  [12] See e.g. Bach 1987, p. 61.

with analysing expressions and sentences but very quickly we will have to resort to information about the agents who do the referring and to the circumstances.

Let us begin with analysing expressions that are used to refer and see how far the discussion takes us. We have already seen how an answer to the question *What is meaning?* is deeply reliant on the property of meaning composition. In particular, we have seen how the structure of the sentence, built from predicates and their arguments, allows us to apply conditions (truth conditions) to formal representations of sentences. We have seen that predicates can take individual constants as their arguments, and these are normally proper names in natural language, like our *Anna* or *Bill*. Or they can take individual variables when these are bound by quantifiers, and these are normally definite or indefinite descriptions. As we have seen, definites require a somewhat convoluted way of stating the uniqueness of the referent, as in the logical form for the 'king of France' example discussed in Section 4.5.3, adapted here (since we are not discussing negation now) as (6.26)–(6.27).

(6.26) The king of France is bald.

(6.27) $\exists x\, (\text{KoF}(x) \wedge \forall y\, (\text{KoF}(y) \to y = x) \wedge \text{Bald}\,(x))$

Since the definite article *the* signals uniqueness, we have to specify that for all *y*s who have the property of being king of France, this *y* has to be the same individual as *x*.

We now have to systematize the properties of proper names, definites, and indefinites, as well as the category that we have neglected so far, namely indexicals, that is pronouns and other heavily context-dependent expressions used for referring. In the process, we will encounter questions such as (i) *how* and *why* referring terms sometimes end up as constants and at other times as variables; (ii) why different philosophers and semanticists have different views on what category these expressions belong to; or (iii) how, in virtue of what aspect of their meaning, they can be associated with particular referents. The latter question will be even trickier to answer in the case of indexicals, as we have seen in the previous section. Co-indexing '$u = x$' or '$v = y$' (see e.g. Figure 6.6) to make a proper name or an indefinite description co-refer with a pronoun (*Bill* and *he*, and *a donkey* and *it*, respectively) relies on clearly worked-out dynamic semantic mechanisms. (Remember that sentence-based syntactic explanations, such as c-commanding, could not cater for them.) Why they are all variables rather than quantifiers in DRT and why DPL tweaks the semantics of quantifiers and conjunction in predicate logic to account for them are questions for metasemantics: questions of what it is exactly to be a proper name or a description. But, arguably, metasemantics is inseparable from semantics. So, off we go.

A word of warning: after the initial clarity of the classification, we have to be prepared for ending up with a mess, in that category distinctions are not as clear as a formalist would ideally like them to be; living language does not conform to moulds. But this is fine. At the beginning of this journey we put forward a desideratum that a semantic theory shouldn't stop at explaining basic sentence meaning as it is obtained through the system of a lexicon and syntax of a particular language, but rather venture further to the level of cognitively plausible meanings that these sentences convey. So, what looks like an indefinite description may end up in the cognitively real representation as something else altogether. As has been demonstrated throughout this journey, and will be brought to culmination in Section 7.1, separating semantics from pragmatics is a non-starter for any theory of meaning. Even enthusiasts of minimalist semantics admit a need for some pragmatic input (we will return to this shortly in Section 6.2.4.3 and more properly in Sections 7.2–7.3), and those for whom 'meaning' should stand for that content that is conveyed in discourse go the whole hog. While this journey has been veering towards the latter stance, what we are about to say about reference is equally relevant for both camps.

There is no consensus concerning the membership of the category *referring expressions* in the literature in that it depends on the theoretical assumptions one adopts, unless one opts to go for a very broad, functional definition according to which any expression that is put to use in order to refer to an entity can be dubbed so. In what follows, we will do a bit of both. We will consider expressions that are commonly used to refer to individuals (objects, animals, people) in discourse, discuss some theoretical motivations for classifying them, as well as remark on the fluid nature of such categories in that form and function can sometimes part ways.

In order to avoid a terminological commitment from the start, I will call such terms *expressions that are used to refer*. Referring can be performed by using proper nouns (*Anna*), personal pronouns (*she*), demonstrative pronouns (*this, that*), demonstrative phrases (*that woman*), and definite descriptions (*the woman in a red jumper*). But, as we could glean from the way constants and variables are used for referring in the metalanguage of predicate logic, the property of referring is not simple. Proper nouns refer to individuals in a, so to speak, more direct, straightforward way than definite noun phrases. Pronouns and demonstrative phrases refer in yet another way in that they have very little inherent semantic content.

One standard way to categorize them is to distinguish *directly referential* expressions and expressions whose referring function is assigned to them by the context of the utterance. Directly referential expressions, also called *type-referential*, are said to contribute an object, rather than the descriptive meaning, to the proposition. This class includes proper names, some pronouns, including demonstratives, and demonstrative phrases. Somewhat confusingly, direct reference is often identified with *rigidity* that can be defined as follows. An expression referring to an individual is a *rigid designator* if and only if, in every counterfactual situation, the truth conditions of a sentence that includes this expression involve this individual. In other words, an expression is rigid if and only if it stands for the same individual in all possible worlds. The problem is that some definite descriptions, such as *the sum of two and two*, are also rigid on this criterion.[13] However, the majority of definite descriptions are contextually referential rather than directly referential. In other words, they are *token-referential* rather than

---

[13] On rigidity and direct reference, see Kripke 1980 [1972]; Kaplan 1989a, and e.g. Recanati 1981, 1988, 1993. For a comprehensive introduction to rigid designators, see LaPorte 2016.

type-referential.[14] On the other hand, some names refer by tokens rather than types in that a name can be applicable to many individuals. So, the boundary between proper names and definite descriptions appears to be rather fuzzy in natural languages and a strict binary distinction into directly referential and contextually referential expressions is difficult to justify. Both categories are used to refer to entities in discourse and both exhibit referring properties, albeit to various degrees and in different ways.[15]

Needless to say, the situations in which they can be used also overlap. It may be worth remembering that in many Indo-European languages the definite article and third-person pronouns derive diachronically from the same source (demonstrative pronouns). Similarly, what counts as a proper name may have had an origin in a description. Most common examples are place names such as *The Old Vicarage* or *Devil's Dyke*. So, as far as natural languages are concerned, it is more accurate to talk about degrees of informativeness than about a strict binary distinction.

But an overlap does not mean arbitrary use: speakers don't choose arbitrarily whether to use *the cat that we saw in the garden yesterday* or *it*. There are regularities. Various linguists have demonstrated in data-based research that noun phrases present a *continuum of referentiality*, from a lack of referring to full, salient referring. Talmy Givón (1993: 224) calls it 'a continuum of referential intent'. He proposes a scale based on the correlation between the predictability of the topic and the type of a referring expression used (to be discussed in more detail in Section 6.3.1). Depending on the language we analyse, we start with no marker or an unstressed pronoun when the predictability is high, proceeding up the scale towards a suitably informative description.[16]

Gundel, Hedberg, and Zacharski go further.[17] Their scale is founded on the tenet that there is a fairly reliable correlation between the *form* of the referring expression and its *cognitive status*, by which they mean 'information about location in memory and attention state' (Gundel 1996: 145). In other words,

> It is widely recognized that the form of referring expressions, like such other aspects of language as word order and sentence intonation, depends on the assumed cognitive status of the referent, i.e. on assumptions that a coöperative speaker can reasonably make regarding the addressee's knowledge and attention state in the particular context in which the expression is used. (Gundel, Hedberg, and Zacharski 1993: 275)

They propose six cognitive statuses, given in Table 6.1, that correspond to the forms of referring expressions in English, and, *mutatis mutandis*, can also be associated with appropriate forms in other natural languages.

The category of proper name is conspicuously absent from this cline but Mulkern subsequently suggested incorporating it as follows: full names refer to entities which

---

[14] For a comprehensive introduction and philosophical discussion of properties of expressions used to refer, focusing on definite descriptions, see Neale 1990.
[15] For discussions see also Larson and Segal 1995; Salmon 1986; Bach 1987; Jaszczolt 1997, 1999.
[16] See Givón 1983a, p. 359. For a discussion, see other contributions to Givón 1983c and Givón 1993.
[17] See Gundel et al. 1993; see also Gundel 1998.

**Table 6.1** Givenness Hierarchy (adapted from Gundel et al. 1993: 275)

| in focus | > | activated | > | familiar | > | uniquely identifiable | > | referential | > | type identifiable |
|---|---|---|---|---|---|---|---|---|---|---|
| it |   | that  this  this N |   | that N |   | the N |   | indefinite this N |   | a N |

are at least 'uniquely identifiable', and single names to entities which are at least 'familiar'.[18]

Gundel et al. point out that each status entails all lower statuses. So, when the referent, say, a dog, is, for example, uniquely identifiable in the situation of discourse, the speaker will normally say *the dog* but it would not be confusing to say *this dog* (using an indefinite *this* as in *There is this dog that . . .* etc.) or *a dog*. But the choice of the type of expression (so, here, *the dog*) is independently explained by the pragmatic principle of informativeness, according to which speakers say neither too much nor too little for the current purpose of the discourse. We return to the principle of informativeness in the next stage of this journey.

Now, while it is a universal fact that the forms which correspond to the referent being in focus of attention need contain the least semantic (and even phonetic) content, the authors found that the correlations between the cognitive status and the actual linguistic category show considerable cross-linguistic differences. There are cross-linguistic differences in the status of proximal, medial (if any), and distal demonstratives. Chinese, for example, allows for a distal demonstrative determiner in contexts where the referent is only uniquely identifiable but not familiar.

The Givenness Hierarchy essentially demonstrates that referring expressions come with different degrees of information, adjusted to allow the hearer to pick out the referent. The degree of informativeness may also differ *within* a particular referring expression on different occasions of its use. So, only some of the 'thresholds' of informativeness are lexicalized. Such a coarse-grained correlation between cognitive statuses and linguistic expressions is intuitively plausible and partially confirmed by data, but the flexibility of this correlation has to be borne in mind. The statuses reflect the natural fuzzy boundaries to be found both in natural languages and in the levels of cognitive processing, for example due to assumptions made by the speaker about the addressee's knowledge and interest.

Scales are also pertinent to referent accessibility in anaphora resolution. Mira Ariel[19] argued that in processing anaphoric expressions, the accessibility of noun phrase antecedents is affected by such factors as the distance between the antecedent and the anaphor, the number of competitors for the role of the antecedent, topicality, and frames (scenarios). Anaphors are said to conform to a scale of accessibility, arranged from high

---

[18] See Mulkern 1996.  [19] See e.g. Ariel 1990.

to low. For example, reflexive pronouns are placed towards the high accessibility end, while long, informative definite descriptions and full proper names towards the low accessibility end. We will say more about referring in the context of cognitive status while discussing information structure in Section 6.3. For now, suffice it to say that the properties of proper names, descriptions, and indexicals to which we now turn have to be thought of in the context of the flexibility of choice and fluidity of category boundaries that natural languages, unlike predicate logic, are famous for.

Before we proceed, a terminological remark is due. We shall continue using the label 'proper name' for the semantic category essentially corresponding to proper nouns. When a discussed definition departs from this use, this will be flagged. The label 'definite description' will continue to be used for the semantic category normally corresponding to definite noun phrases. But it has to be borne in mind that not all definite noun phrases are definite descriptions: to reiterate, they can be used to refer to genres or kinds (generically) rather than individuals. More on this in Section 6.2.3.

## 6.2.2 Proper Names

Proper names are rather unusual in that there is no unique convention associated with their use. The speaker need not know anything about the individual referred to except for the name. In other words, one can use the name *Leonard Cohen* even when one knows nothing about the person, whereas one cannot use the word *singer* without knowing what singers are and do. The speaker has to have a concept associated with a singer in order to use the word meaningfully. So, despite the gradation of referring properties just discussed, proper nouns are also rather different from other expressions in language. Their *sense* is often said to be the bearer of the name.

John Stuart Mill argued in his *System of Logic*[20] that the function of a proper noun is exhausted in denoting an individual. They are only 'marks', slot holders in discourse. They belong to the category of *non-connotative* expressions, together with expressions that imply an attribute; *London*, *virtue*, or *whiteness* belong to this category. Connotative expressions, on the other hand, both denote an object and imply an attribute; *man*, *blue*, and *long* belong to this category. This tradition is now continued in the *direct reference* view of proper names popularized in semantics by David Kaplan.[21]

But it is not necessary to uphold the view that proper names are devoid of any other aspects of meaning. Kripke continues Mill's tradition but also claims that although referring to Socrates means referring to a man called 'Socrates', which is circular and uninformative, if we include in the semantics the social custom of calling, or 'initial baptism', then circularity disappears. In his seminal *Naming and Necessity*,[22] a series of lectures delivered in 1970, Kripke proposes what is known as a *causal* (or *causal-historical*) *theory of reference*, whereby names refer because an initial act of naming established a unique link between a name and a referent for the community of speakers. For Kripke, names are directly referential, they are rigid designators, but the historical

---

[20] Mill 1959 [1843].   [21] See Kaplan 1989a, 1989b.
[22] See his seminal *Naming and Necessity* (Kripke 1980 [1972]. See also Kripke 1997 [1977].

chain of referring *is part of their semantics* rather than merely a 'metasemantic foundation of meaning'.[23]

The direct reference view stands in opposition to the descriptivism about names defended (albeit in different ways) by Frege and Russell. Descriptivism, the *descriptivist theory of names*, states that there is a set of descriptions that delimits the reference of a name. Let us focus on Frege first. Frege challenged Mill's view by pointing out problems that, from our twenty-first-century perspective on philosophy, appear rather obvious and difficult to ignore. First, the Millian view has a problem with explaining the properties of empty proper names, that is proper names that do not have an individual associated with them, such as 'Zeus' or 'Santa Claus' (the film *Miracle on 34th Street*, where the jury gives a verdict that Santa Claus exists, notwithstanding ☺).

Next comes the oft-debated 'Frege's puzzle' of coreferential names that we have been mentioning throughout this book. A direct referentialist finds it difficult to explain the semantic significance of a name when one object has more than one name associated with it, such as the already mentioned *Mary Ann Evans* and *George Eliot*, or *Superman* and *Clark Kent*, or *Snowdon* and *Yr Wyddfa*, and so forth. Here Frege remarked on the difference in meaning between (6.28) and (6.29), more clearly 'proper name-ish' equivalents of *The Morning Star* and *The Evening Star* introduced in Section 1.4.

(6.28)   Hesperus is Hesperus.

(6.29)   Hesperus is Phosphorus.

The first is a tautology, whereas the second is informative. And Frege was not happy with identifying coreference with identity of meaning, as we know from his proposal of sense, introduced in Section 1.4: sense differentiates between them. For Frege, definite descriptions and proper names were quite alike: the difference between such coreferential expressions lies in their sense, the intersubjective way of thinking about the object. One is the celestial body that appears in the evening in some parts of the year, while the other is a celestial body that appears in the morning in others. After all, $a = a$ differs from $a = b$.

We have seen in Stage 5 that coreferential names can have different distributions not only in specific constructions such as propositional attitude reports but across a variety of what are traditionally called extensional and intensional contexts. So, any cognitively plausible semantics would struggle with direct referentialism in that coreferential proper names have different meanings for different speakers, and even by convention: the properties picked up by the name *Superman* are certainly not picked up by the name *Clark Kent*, and the contexts of use hardly overlap either.

According to descriptivists, proper names *describe* a particular individual. They predicate something of that individual, and hence are called *descriptive names*. On Russell's version, proper names are disguised descriptions. For example, an entity is Zeus if and only if it is an Ancient Greek supreme god and, in order to capture

---

[23] For a discussion of foundations of meaning vs. theory of meaning (metasemantics vs. semantics), see a comprehensive introduction in Jaszczolt 2022 and further references there.

uniqueness like we did, for example, in (6.27), whatever is an Ancient Greek supreme god is this particular entity, as in (6.30).

(6.30)   Zeus $(x)$ iff Ancient-Greek-supreme-god $(x) \land \forall y$ (Ancient-Greek-supreme-god $(y) \rightarrow y = x$)

This view was put forward by Russell in his seminal 'On denoting' referred to before.[24] His theory of descriptions is mainly developed for definite noun phrases but it assimilates names to descriptions as well. (6.30) suggests that descriptive names resemble descriptions in that their meaning is given in a definition and is independent from any objects that satisfy it. In other words, according to the description theory, proper nouns would have their meaning derived from their definitions rather than from an existing or non-existing object. As a result, coreferential and empty names pose no problem for this theory.

So, there may be more to the meaning of proper names than their reference. And if so, this ought to have its reflection in any semantic theory that aspires to cognitive reality. Contemporary formal semantic theories such as DRT see the latter as their goal, and, as before, so do we throughout this journey.[25]

Descriptive theories appear to face fewer challenges than direct referential ones, but they still face some. Perhaps most importantly, there is one characteristic property of proper names that has been ignored. Let us consider (6.31) and (6.32).

(6.31)   Margaret Atwood is a captivating novelist.

(6.32)   The author of *The Handmaid's Tale* is a captivating novelist.

But imagine that it is discovered that, say, Gloria Steinem wrote *The Handmaid's Tale*. Then, (6.31) would still refer to Margaret Atwood, while (6.32) could happily be taken to refer to Gloria Steinem: it would be *about Gloria Steinem* in a way in which (6.31) cannot be.

The reason for this difference is obvious to sympathizers of the direct reference view. Proper names refer directly, while definite descriptions can refer 'contextually'; they can refer to different people, depending on the actual state of affairs. Semantic properties of proper names and definite descriptions simply are different. Proper names are rigid designators, their meaning depends on the object they name. Imagining different possible ways the world might have been does not make any difference to their meaning. Descriptions are non-rigid: their meaning can remain unchanged while the person or object they refer to differs with scenarios. To make the descriptive theory of proper names work, we would have to add a qualifier such as 'actual' to make the description rigid: *the actual author of* The Handmaid's Tale. Or *the actual Ancient Greek supreme god*, which brings back the initial problem.

Problems with the description theory of proper names do not end here. The exact content of the description would have to be established. If names are descriptive, then

---

[24] Russell 1996 [1905]. See also Russell 1956 [1918–19].
[25] On the lack of opposition between cognitive and formal semantics, and on DRT as a (potentially) cognitive formal semantic theory, see e.g. Hamm et al. 2006 referred to in the previous section.

there should be one particular description (ideally, also in each speaker's mind!) that corresponds to that name. This is an implausible demand. Speakers are not guided by any such unique description. Neither does the language system offer any for proper names. Speakers may even use a name successfully without being in a position to provide any identifying description. Or they can use a name while they have an incorrect associated description (or incorrect 'mental dossier'), as we have seen in (6.31): even if the speaker intends to refer to, say, the author of *My Life on the Road* (that is, in reality, Gloria Steinem), the name *Margaret Atwood* will stubbornly refer to Margaret Atwood, *tout court*.[26] In other words, while a description does not attach itself, so to speak, permanently to an object, a proper name does.

Be that as it may, on the one hand it is rather counterintuitive to say, as direct referentialists do, that to associate an expression with an individual exhausts the function of proper names. On the other, the entrenchment of proper names, their 'sticking to the individual', so to speak, requires an explanation. Granted, tokens of names such as *Anna* or even *William Shakespeare* have many bearers. But direct referentialists, David Kaplan included, have an explanation of this in social practices and customs of naming. Once the pre-semantic sociopragmatic explanation is in place and we can move to semantics proper, a name becomes uniquely, and directly, referential. After all, language users normally agree on the reference of proper names and normally resorting to descriptions or 'ways of thinking' is not necessary. We wheel them in when things get tricky: when beliefs and reports on beliefs don't match with respect to who or what they are thought to be about, or when we want to stress that Superman *is* Clark Kent; clearly, as far as information content goes, this is *a = b*, not a tautologous *a = a*.

The solution may lie in combining the minimalism of direct referentialism with the contextualism of cognitively oriented truth-conditional semantics. First, to reiterate, the direct reference view holds that proper names are rigid: they have the same referent across possible worlds. Then, for sentences such as (6.33) and (6.34), the bunch of possible worlds in which the sentence has a referent and in which it is true that the individual went to the concert or is angry, respectively, gives the sentence its meaning (intension).

(6.33)   Anna went to a concert.

(6.34)   Zeus is angry.

Concerning (6.33), the first step in the semantics makes the name rigid: it makes it 'be about' a unique individual across situations (worlds). As to (6.34), empty proper names do not have an 'actual' referent but they certainly have meaning. Sentence (6.34) has meaning, although its truth value will have to depend on the narratives rather than the actual world since being angry is not predicated of anybody or anything in existence. But possible worlds will do the trick.

---

[26] Discussions of these properties can be found in Larson and Segal 1995, Chapter 5 and Neale 1990, Chapter 2.

We continue as follows. In cognitively plausible semantics, we want to preserve simplicity when it is the best way to handle the meaning in a particular context, but we do not shun adding levels of psychological overlay when meaning representation requires it. Direct referentialists cannot make this move because it would contradict their minimalist view of truth-conditional content. They make some modest inroads, such as Soames' proposal of a cognitive proposition discussed in Section 1.3,[27] but they cannot make such a proposition have a bearing on the semantic content. But we can go further. Since, as we have seen, ways of thinking, and names we use for referring, matter in all kinds of contexts, both intensional and those traditionally called extensional, we can 'pragmaticize' the theory of proper names. The theory could preserve, so to speak, direct reference for cases where more information about the individual would make no difference to the meaning, while for other cases it would 'go Fregean', so to speak, and include senses – and sometimes even 'go cognitive' and include individual, psychological modes of presentation (speaker's mental dossiers) – in the semantic representation. Cognitively inspired semantics must not complicate representations beyond necessity, but it must be allowed to 'tailor-make' them, as long as independent criteria are provided as to when to use which 'tailor's pattern'. The journey through meaning continues with this 'tailor-made' semantics on the table. More on this in Section 7.2.3.

## 6.2.3 Definite and Indefinite Descriptions

The semantics of definite descriptions has been a matter of controversy in the philosophy of language for a long time, with the interest intensifying in the early and mid twentieth century, around the work of Russell, Strawson, Donnellan, and many others. We have to remember that by definite descriptions we mean those uses of definite noun phrases that refer to a particular entity or concept, such as *the cat* or *Anna's cat* or, in the realm of abstract referents, *the conferment of degrees* or *Bill's dream*. The primary function of definite noun phrases is to act as such descriptions of entities. To reiterate, they can also have other functions, such as referring to genres or kinds, as in (6.35).

(6.35)  The lion is a dangerous predator.

This is the generic use. Generics are statements that express generalizations, but they are not quantifiers. They can also be expressed using bare plural forms or indefinite noun phrases as in (6.36) and (6.37).

(6.36)  Lions are dangerous.

(6.37)  A female lion is pregnant for approximately four months.

Generics are best analysed in the context of default reasoning (cf. *Lions are* normally *dangerous*) and we shall not discuss them here, but suffice it to say that the semantics of generics is not an easy subject, in that none of the above forms are well suited for expressing generic generalizations.[28]

---

[27] For references see Section 1.3, fn 11.
[28] For introductions see e.g. Carlson 2011; Leslie and Lerner 2016; Pelletier and Asher 1997.

We have established in the previous section that the way definite descriptions refer is different from the way proper names refer and that there is either (i) a categorial difference whereby the first category is contextually referential while the latter is directly referential, or (ii) a difference in the degree to which they 'stick' to an individual referred to. Put simply, descriptions normally refer *in virtue of the meaning of the description* and as such their referent can vary with different states of affairs. Since they have been appearing in this journey through meaning in the context of various other topics, let us now begin by summarizing what has already been discussed.

First, to distil the essence, definite descriptions are commonly represented, after Russell,[29] as quantified expressions with the uniqueness condition built in, as in (6.26)–(6.27) repeated below.

(6.26)   The king of France is bald.

(6.27)   $\exists x \, (\text{KoF}(x) \wedge \forall y \, (\text{KoF}(y) \rightarrow y = x) \wedge \text{Bald}(x))$

We have seen in Section 2.5 that definite descriptions can refer to a particular, known individual or be used to predicate something about whoever fulfils the description. The relevant example, where the context was that a speaker points at the church La Sagrada Família in Barcelona, is (2.5), repeated here.

(2.5)   The architect of this church was mad.

The phrase *the architect of this church* can be used referentially, to refer to Antoni Gaudí, or attributively, about whoever is responsible for the extraordinary design of La Sagrada Família.

Next, we have seen in Section 4.5.3 how they interact with the scope of negation. Example (4.75) and its analyses as (4.76) and (4.77) are repeated below.

(4.75)   The king of France is not bald.

(4.76)   $\exists x \, (\text{KoF}(x) \wedge \forall y \, (\text{KoF}(y) \rightarrow y = x) \wedge \neg \text{Bald}(x))$

(4.77)   $\neg \exists x \, (\text{KoF}(x) \wedge \forall y \, (\text{KoF}(y) \rightarrow y = x) \wedge \text{Bald}(x))$

We have also seen in Section 5.5 that in propositional attitude reports they can sometimes be best represented as directly referring expressions (that is, as individual constants in the logical form), to best capture the *de re* reading. Example (5.132) and its various representations discussed there are repeated below, where the belief about a particular individual (*de re*), say, Henry IV, can arguably be represented as in (5.136) rather than as a wide-scope existential quantifier in (5.133). (5.134) represents belief report *de dicto*.

(5.132)   Max believes that the king of France is bald.

(5.133)   $\exists x \, (\text{KoF}(x) \, \& \, \forall y \, (\text{KoF}(y) \rightarrow y = x) \, \& \, \text{Bel}_m \text{Bald}(x))$

---

[29] See Section 4.5.3 and references in fn 44 there.

(5.134)    $Bel_m \exists x \, (KoF(x) \, \& \, \forall y \, (KoF(y) \rightarrow y = x \, ) \, \& \, Bald(x))$

(5.136)    $Bel_m Bald(f)$

To summarize, the logical form for a sentence predicating a property of a description is this: 'The A is B' is true if and only if at least one thing is A (has the property A, that is $P_A$), and at most one thing is A, and whatever is A is B. In terms of generalized quantifiers, it means that it is true when the difference between set A and set B is 0 and when set A contains only one element, as in (6.38).

(6.38)    '[the $x$: $P_A x$] ($P_B x$)' is true iff $|A–B| = 0$ and $|A| = 1$

In other words, all As are Bs and there is only one A. The meaning of a definite description is conceptualized as a set that fulfils the specified conditions, while the individual is its denotation. This is important in that in this way we can also conceptualize the essential difference between descriptions and names, in that the meaning of a definite description is kept independent from its referent (denotation), while the meaning of a proper name depends on the referent: it 'sticks', like *Margaret Atwood* in example (6.31) in the previous section. This means that the truth conditions of a sentence with a proper name are object-dependent – the sentence is about the individual so named. On the other hand, the truth conditions of a sentence with a definite description state only that there is some entity or other that has a certain property. The truth conditions are object-independent and this is the reason that those who represent definite descriptions as quantifying expressions do not classify them as belonging to the category of referring expressions. They are conceptualized as different from the class that contains proper names, pronouns, and demonstratives. But the debate continues.

Now, representing descriptions in this way poses a problem for *incomplete descriptions*. The phrase *the table* clearly does not mean that there is only one, unique table that can be so called. We need some restrictions. The speaker can often safely utter (6.39) even though there may be more than one table in the situation of discourse – say, in a restaurant – or even in the perceptual field.

(6.39)    The table is set for two.

Although Russell's requirement of uniqueness 'there is exactly one A ... ' is not fulfilled, the sentence can successfully communicate the message when one table is *salient* in the discourse. So, various adjustments to the representation have been offered. First, one can argue that although (6.39) is, arguably, literally false (in that the uniqueness requirement is not fulfilled), it can convey something true thanks to pragmatic embellishment. But a theory that allows for saying something false while communicating something true does not appear enticing. Another explanation holds that (6.39) is elliptical for, for example, (6.40).

(6.40)    The restaurant table at which we will eat is set for two.

The problem with this explanation is reminiscent of that with the descriptive theory of proper names: there can be countless such possible qualifications. The speaker may not have any particular expanded description in mind and so no particular expansion will have to be recovered by the hearer. The third solution relies on restricting the domain of quantification that we have already encountered in Section 5.1.

Next, we have to attend to the fact that descriptions can be ambiguous. This has to be put in the context of the two conceptions of descriptions: while according to Russell and neo-Russellians, they are quantifying expressions, according to Frege and neo-Fregeans, they are referring expressions. The third view, argued for most famously by Keith Donnellan in his seminal 'Reference and definite descriptions' in the 1960s,[30] holds that they are ambiguous between the referential interpretation, which makes them akin to proper names, and the attributive interpretation, which makes them akin to quantifying expressions. We have attended to this ambiguity in example (2.5) in Section 2.5, repeated below, pointing out that the description 'the architect (of this church)' can have an attributive or a referential interpretation.

(2.5)    The architect of this church was mad.

The referential use takes care of the incompleteness problem discussed in example (6.39) above that does not have a satisfactory explanation on the quantificational account. It also accords with intuitions: we intuitively know that the speaker may have said something true in that the description is used referentially here and as such it refers directly to a certain, contextually salient entity. The referential use also accounts for the cases of mistaken descriptions such as that on Donnellan's oft-quoted (1996 [1966]: 234) scenario:

Suppose one is at a party and, seeing an interesting-looking person holding a martini glass, one asks, 'Who is the man drinking a martini?' If it should turn out that there is only water in the glass, one has nevertheless asked a question about a particular person, a question that it is possible for someone to answer.

By using the description referentially, the speaker may say something true (in virtue of succeeding in referring) even though the description does not fit the individual. On this use, the truth conditions are object-dependent; the description behaves akin to demonstratives such as *this* or *that*. Used attributively, the description would not fit anybody and the utterance would not be successful. The truth conditions of a declarative sentence that incorporates this description would be object-independent and the sentence would be about whoever fulfils the description (so, no one in this context). The scenario also shows that, *mutatis mutandis*, the distinction works not only for assertions but also for questions (and, as Donnellan also shows, it works for commands too).

---

[30] See Donnellan 1996 [1966].

Needless to say, the ambiguity is normally resolved in the context, or it can be left without being noticed or without an uptake when resolving it is not important for the purpose of the conversation. For instance, if I say, while talking about Oscars and old Hollywood movies, that the director of *Casablanca* won an Oscar for it, it may not be important to the addressee whether I know (or at least want to communicate, or communicate that I know) the identity of the director, and as such whether I'm using the description referentially or attributively. More about these nuances later in this section.

An analogous distinction can now be made between so-called *singular* and *general* propositions. If a proposition is about a particular individual to whom the speaker is ascribing a certain property, the proposition is singular (and so is the corresponding thought). But when a proposition is about whoever (uniquely) satisfies the description, it is general (and so is the corresponding thought). For the purpose of truth-conditional analysis, the first proposition 'has the individual as its constituent', so to speak: it has an individual constant in its logical form. The latter does not: it is represented as a quantified expression.

Now, on the above scenario, it appears that, say, (6.41) would be true when used referentially.

(6.41) The man drinking a martini looks interesting.

But it also appears that we have landed in a semantics/pragmatics muddle. First, for Russell, (6.41) is false when no one fits the description. As we already know, Peter Strawson[31] assesses it as lacking truth value in that statements, not sentences, have truth values. If the presupposition of existence of the individual is not fulfilled, we get a truth-value gap. But then, as Donnellan argues, neither Russell nor Strawson offer a satisfactory account of descriptions: we have both readings to consider. But does it mean that (6.41) is false on one reading and true on the other? Or does it merely mean that we can *use* the sentence successfully in two different ways but there is no semantic ambiguity? This is precisely the semantics/pragmatics tug of war. Donnellan does not fully commit himself but remarks that it is a matter of the speaker's intentions how the description was used on a particular occasion. He continues by maintaining that postulating a syntactic or lexical (semantic) ambiguity does not appear plausible and tentatively opts for a pragmatic ambiguity: a difference between speaker intentions.[32]

On the other hand, Saul Kripke[33] is much more committed to qualifying this distinction as merely a difference in use, upholding the Russellian analysis. The argument is that if *the* is ambiguous, then so are other quantifiers, such as *exactly*

---

[31] See Strawson 1997 [1950].
[32] See also Searle 1979a, who argues that the referential/attributive distinction is not a steadfast binary distinction but rather signals that the degree of referring may vary. It varies even more conspicuously in the case of reporting on someone's referent: in a propositional attitude report, the reporter may be committed to various degrees to the mode of presentation (or, in Searle's terminology, aspect) under which reference was made.
[33] See Kripke 1997 [1977].

*one* in (6.42). And insisting that (6.42) is semantically ambiguous would be a rather odd thing to do.

(6.42)   Exactly one man is drinking martini and he looks interesting.

But these were the 1970s. Half a century on, things have moved on. As we have seen in the discussion of quantifiers in Section 5.1, there are ways of fixing the uniqueness problem. We have also seen that this does not have to mean that the Russellian analysis has to stay. After all, adopting it would mean that (6.41) is false and that the speaker made a successful statement by using a false sentence. And that, we argued, won't do. Hence semantic determination and pragmatic enrichment of semantic representations began their long career. While discussing different meanings of sentential connectives, we assessed arguments against postulating semantic or even pragmatic ambiguities where more parsimonious solutions are possible. We appealed there (Section 4.2) to Grice's principle of not postulating multiple meanings when this can be avoided (Modified Occam's Razor). We will say more on that topic in the next stage of this journey but suffice it to point out that when we opt for semantic representations that the syntactic structure leaves underspecified, then we allow for some contribution of speakers' intentions to the semantic representation itself, in that they act as pointers to one or the other reading. So, a solution is to make semantics itself context-dependent, like in contextualist, cognitively plausible theories, at the same time avoiding semantic ambiguity of the description itself.

But such a proposal is not yet entirely satisfactory. One can argue that it would be what Recanati (1993: 280) called a 'Subjective Reference View', where reference depends on intentions. In order to make the theory more normative and as such endow it with more predictive power, it would seem prudent to ask if there is a standard, salient, or default use. Perhaps, unless context suggests otherwise, the referential use ought to be regarded as the salient, and even automatically retrieved one. As I have argued elsewhere, this option can be traced to the principle of the strongest informativeness, and as such the strongest referentiality, that speakers normally associate with classes of expressions – as an example of the overall rationality of human communication. One can also trace this strength of informativeness to the strength of *intentionality* (not to be confused with 'intensionality' in possible-world semantics!) of the underlying mental states – intentionality, or, in other words, 'being about' something, as a property of beliefs and other mental attitudes. It explains the rational priority of the referential over attributive, and, in the case of propositional attitudes discussed in Section 5.5, *de re* over *de dicto* interpretations.[34] We will come back to intentionality while discussing speech acts in Section 8.3.

Next, there is also a third use of definite descriptions that we can define using the apparatus summarized in (6.43). Ludlow and Neale applied it to indefinite descriptions (to which we will move in a moment) but the categories are equally relevant for definites.

---

[34] For a detailed discussion, see e.g. Jaszczolt 1999, Chapters 3–4; Jaszczolt 2005, Chapter 5, or Jaszczolt 2012b.

(6.43)  (i)  proposition expressed (PE): What the speaker literally says
        (ii) proposition meant (PM): What the speaker intends to convey
        (iii) speaker's grounds (SG): Speaker's beliefs that lead to the statement.
                                              (after Ludlow and Neale 1997 [1991])

If PE, PM, and SG are all the same and are all general, that is, the representation is quantificational with the condition of uniqueness, as on Russell's analysis, the use of the description is attributive. If PE is general but PM and SG are singular (about the concrete individual: compare here the definitions of singular and general propositions above), the use is referential. But when PE and PM are general, but SG are singular, about the specific individual, then we have a *specific* use. For instance, let us assume that in (6.44) the speaker knows that Joe Biden (I am writing this in 2021) is the president of the United States but they also know that the hearer, let us say a small child, does not know it and need not know it. Let us also assume that the conversation is about the actual person, the current president, rather than about 'the president' as a role. All the speaker wants to convey is a proposition about the residence of that person – the name of the individual has no relevance for the discourse. So, PE and PM are as in the attributive case, but SG are as in the referential case.

(6.44)  The president of the United States lives in the White House.

The specific use is more common in the case of indefinite descriptions when they are used about a specifically intended individual but, clearly, it also applies to definites. For indefinites, it applies to phrases with the indefinite *a(n)* but also with indefinite *this*, as in (6.45). It applies when the speaker knows the identity of the person but does not intend to reveal it (most commonly, finds revealing it irrelevant for the conversation).

(6.45)  There is a/this guy in my year group who speaks ten languages.

Let us move to indefinites. Indefinite descriptions are normally represented as quantifying expressions without the uniqueness phrase: this is their purely *quantificational* use. For Russell, like in predicate logic, '*a* has the property *P*' does not differ from 'Some *as* have the property *P* '. Normally, two uses of indefinites are distinguished: the standard non-specific and the marked, specific. But influenced by post-Russellian developments, and notably by Strawson's emphasis on the existential presupposition (there will be more about presuppositions in Section 6.3.3), Ludlow and Neale go further. In addition to the quantificational use where PE, PM, and SG are all general, that is, quantificational and without the condition of uniqueness, they also distinguish the following uses for situations where uniqueness, and sometimes also identity, of the referent make a difference. When PE is general but SG and PM are singular, the use is referential. An example of this use is (6.46) when the speaker knows that the sentence is about Bill, in the context where the addressee knows (for example, can see) that it is about Bill.

(6.46)  A friend is at your front door.

Next, when PE and PM are general and SG are singular, the use is specific. So, their analysis is analogous to that of definites, apart from the *form* of PE: when the PE is general, this will now mean 'general for indefinites'. In PE, *a(n)* does not carry the condition of uniqueness attributed before to *the*. (6.45) above is a good example of this use. Finally, a slightly more complicated case: when PE is general, as above, and PM and SG are general, quantificational, but also include the concept of uniqueness, like in the case of definites, then the use is definite. This use captures cases such as (6.47) where the speaker, looking at the clean windows of their house, utters it meaning that some window cleaner or other must have just cleaned the windows (as they do, leaving the bill in the letter box).

(6.47)  A window cleaner has been.

To sum up, we have looked at different possibilities of the semantics for definites, trying to take it far enough to account for their different uses. We have also looked at different uses of indefinites to which the question as to which aspects of meaning belong to semantics and which to pragmatics also applies. We continue assuming that the cognitive reality of a theory of meaning is important: we don't want to find ourselves in the situation where we would have to claim that the speaker *says something true* by using *a sentence that is false* or *a sentence that in itself does not have meaning*. But the desideratum of cognitive plausibility is not the only route to meaning. The issue is still unresolved, and perhaps will remain so, because how different linguists and philosophers choose to use the label 'semantics' can vary depending on what they are using semantic theory *for*. As was said, computational linguistics often thrives on searching for ambiguities because it means identifying different possible meanings in big data, and as such listing meanings that machines have to learn. A psychologically plausible theory of human communication, on the other hand, often exorcises ambiguity because it can help itself to those aspects of meaning that make intentions unambiguous through the interaction of bits of information communicated through different channels, such as speech with its prosody, body movements, situational placement, social and cultural conventions, scientific knowledge, or theoretical assumptions about how the human brain functions, and so forth. What I have said here about referring feeds equally well into those various journeys through meaning. The 'philosophical overlay' of the desiderata just mentioned can be adopted, adapted, or rejected through argumentation on the metasemantic level (about which more in Stage 9).

Rather unfortunately, debates around referring have predominantly focused on the English language, and in particular on the distinction between proper names and definite descriptions. This historical fact in western, mostly analytic, philosophy of language creates a distortion. There are many languages that do not have overt markers for definiteness. They leave this feature completely unmarked, or, when necessary for clarity, use a demonstrative pronoun to specify the concrete referent. We shall not go here into the historical origins of markers of definiteness but suffice it to say that the discussion of indefinite descriptions brings us closer to the conceptual take on the matter of reference: expressions can be used with different degrees of 'sticking' to the individual about which/whom they are used. And we can go further: just like *the man drinking a martini* in (6.41), proper names can also be used incorrectly: by saying

*Jones* I can actually mean 'Johansson' if I have poor memory for names. So, perhaps, proper nouns are not straightforwardly directly referential? Perhaps they can be used as complex demonstratives, such as 'that Jones', where the demonstrative makes it directly referential but referring to Johansson? Or perhaps there is an attributive use as well? Be that as it may, it would be going too far to postulate a semantic ambiguity or underspecification of proper names when it is an ambiguity between an individual incorrectly meant by the speaker and whoever correctly fits the name. Such mismatches can be captured on the level of conceptual representations to which we will move in Stage 7.

When kicked up to the level of conceptual distinctions, the meanings of expressions that are used to refer become more universal: no matter whether a language overtly marks definiteness, we can still use the extant resources of the particular language to express various kinds and degrees of reference. And, we concluded, how much of this information about the kind of use we put in the semantic theory will depend on what it is the semantics *of* – sentences or contextualized propositions – and what this semantic theory is *for* – representing conveyed thoughts or listing possible, empirically attested, meanings of expressions.

But the story about referring is far from complete: the closer we come to contemporary theories of meaning, the more they have to say about context dependence. Deictic (indexical) expressions such as personal pronouns, traditionally considered somewhat inferior or even 'faulty' in that they create a problem for translation into the formal metalanguage, come to the forefront as the most fascinating devices human languages have for referring. They also give a fuller picture of the degrees of referring. So, we move to them next.

## 6.2.4 Indexical Expressions

### 6.2.4.1 Indexicality or Deixis?

Pronouns – personal and demonstrative – and demonstrative noun phrases are also prominent examples of referring expressions, so they have to be subjected to closer scrutiny. For direct referentialists, they stand for the individual and exhaust their semantic role by doing so. In other words, like proper names, they refer directly. But unlike the referring terms we discussed earlier, pronouns (including demonstrative) and demonstrative noun phrases have little semantic content of their own; they rely heavily on context in their interpretation. Sentence (6.48) cannot be subjected to truth-conditional semantic analysis until the context, often including the co-text, that is, adjacent utterances, help supply the referents to the pronouns.

(6.48)   She said it to me.

So far we have been calling such context-bound expressions *indexicals*. This is the term standardly used in formal semantics and philosophy of language in that it emphasizes the role of such expressions as indices – slots to be filled with content. In pragmatics and sociolinguistics, as well as in traditional linguistics, they are called *deictics*. Since the traditions of deixis and indexicality foreground somewhat different characteristics of these expressions, and as a result the various proposed classifications of indexicals and deictic terms stretch them in somewhat different directions (or, as we will see, even very substantially different on some accounts), it will be useful to have a quick look at both.

But before we continue with discussing indexicals (no matter how labelled) as if they were a separate category of referring expressions, we have to ask: are they really that different? After all, in order to associate *the man in a blue jumper* or *Bill* with a referent, we also need context. So, indexicality has to be approached with an open mind: what is it about their meaning that makes indexicals so special? Is it that they are more context-dependent than other kinds of expressions that we use to refer? Is it a matter of degree? They have some semantic content: *she* tells us that the referent is a unique female individual, by default at least animate if not human. *That book* has even more semantic content in virtue of containing a content word – a common noun. The question that we have to leave dangling throughout the discussion is whether there is a need for a clear categorial difference between indexical and non-indexical expressions. And if there is, on what grounds do we make this distinction? On the grounds of the grammatical category such as a personal pronoun vs. a definite noun phrase, or perhaps on the grounds of the function the expression has in the particular context? For now, suffice it to say that we might find ourselves in need of the concept of an indexical that is functionally defined.

### 6.2.4.2 Deixis and Traditional-Descriptive Classifications

The term 'deixis' derives from Ancient Greek δείκνῡμι, meaning 'show', 'point out'. Accordingly, deixis is a phenomenon of encoding contextual information by means of lexical items or grammatical distinctions that provide this information only when 'filled in' by this context. In other words, it means lexicalizing or grammaticalizing contextual information, i.e. making it into obligatory grammatical or lexical distinctions. Pronouns are one example of such terms, tense is another, as was discussed in Section 5.3. In (6.49), the past-tense form of the verb is an example of grammaticalized deixis, while pronouns *she*, *it*, *me* and the temporal adverb *then* are examples of lexicalization.

(6.49)   She said it to me then.

*Person deixis* encodes the role of participants in the speech event, such as speaker, addressee, or others, as in pronouns: *I* for the speaker, *you* for the addressee(s), or *they* for others. Pronoun systems differ from language to language and they can include various types of information, such as dual number, gender, social status, and social distance. Grammaticalizing social status, that is, expressing variations of social distance and power between the interlocutors, as in the *tu/vous* distinction in French, is sometimes called *social deixis*. However, as will be evident shortly, the label arguably belongs to a somewhat different classification. Languages differ with respect to the amount of social deixis they encode. Japanese and Korean are much richer in it than English, due to their elaborate systems of *honorifics*, that is expressions used to express respect, such as special, socially appropriate pronouns or forms of verbs and nouns.

Kinship terms can also encode deixis. For example, in some Australian Aboriginal languages, there is a term used for someone who is the speaker's father and the addressee's grandfather. The speaker's father who is not the addressee's grandfather would be denoted by a different term.

*Place deixis* encodes spatial locations relative to the interlocutors. Here we have *proximal* and *distal* demonstratives in English (*this, these* vs. *that, those*) and adverbs of place (*here* vs. *there*). Place deixis normally uses the speaker's location as the deictic centre: the distinctions rely on the proximity to the speaker, although the boundary between proximal and distal expressions is flexible, context-dependent. Various languages divide the space around the speaker differently. For example, Spanish has a three-way distinction between *esto* ('this'), *eso* ('that') and *aquello* ('that over there'). There are languages that distinguish demonstratives on some other grounds, such as directions or visibility to the speaker; some have very elaborate, complex systems of such demonstrative pronouns.[35] The context dependence of such place terms is twofold: not only does the location depend on the current act of speaking but the size of the location can differ. *Here* can mean the town, the room, or the exact point. In the case of demonstrative pronouns *this* and *that*, the choice can also be dictated by considerations of emotional closeness (empathy). In this case we sometimes talk about *empathetic deixis*. Moreover, Charles Fillmore distinguished gestural from symbolic deixis. On that distinction, *here* in (6.50) is symbolic when it refers to some identifiable group.

(6.50)   We don't celebrate Easter here.

There are also deictic verbs: *come* involves motion towards the speaker. Spatial deixis is often extended to the temporal domain: *here* and *there* can mean 'at this/that point of discourse'; *this year* or *that week* can qualify time.

*Time deixis* encodes temporal units relative to the time of the utterance. Here we distinguish *coding time* (time of utterance), and *receiving time* (time of the recovery of the information by the hearer). Tense markers and adverbs of time such as *now, tomorrow,* or *next year* belong to this category. The deictic centre can be projected on the addressee, as in (6.51): *now* refers to the time at which the addressee learns the truth.

(6.51)   Thank you for taking the time to read this letter. You know the whole truth *now*.

Another interesting point to notice is that expressions such as *today* or *yesterday* refer either to the whole day or to a moment or interval within them, as in (6.52) and (6.53) respectively.

(6.52)   Yesterday was Sunday.

(6.53)   I fell off my bike yesterday.

The number of such deictically named days also differs from language to language.

---

[35] There is extensive work on categorization of space in different cultures by Stephen Levinson and his Max Planck group – see e.g. Levinson 2003; Pederson et al. 1998.

In tensed languages such as English, it is tense that makes most sentences deictic. But as was discussed in Section 5.3, grammatical tenses have to be distinguished from temporal reference. For example, generic sentences such as (6.54) are non-deictic and atemporal, although they have tense in the grammatical sense. On the other hand, the second sentence of (5.75), repeated below, is temporal but is an example of a tense–time mismatch.

(6.54)   A whale is a mammal.

(5.75)   This is what happened to me yesterday. I go to the office, I sit at my desk, and this guy comes and says ...

Again, as we discussed at some length in Section 5.3, temporal deixis reflects culture-dependent distinctions and culture-specific foregrounding of some aspects of temporality over others.

In addition to these three basic linguistic categories of deixis, it may be useful to distinguish *discourse deixis* that encodes reference to portions of discourse, as in (6.55).

(6.55)   'Love me tender, love me sweet' – *that*'s what a song says.

By means of this device we can refer to portions of discourse as in *in the last paragraph*, *this story*, sentence-initial *therefore*, *in conclusion*, *anyway*, or *all in all*, where reference is relative to the current discourse. There are also cases of the *discourse-deictic use* of pronouns as in (6.56), where *it* is the so-called *pronoun of laziness*; it stands in a sloppy relation to the antecedent in that there is no real identity there between the two referents: Bill keeps *his* money in shares. It is also sometimes called, after John Robert 'Haj' Ross, *identity of sense anaphora*.[36]

(6.56)   Anna keeps her money in a savings account but Bill keeps it in shares.

This 'lazy use' of a pronoun belongs to the category of discourse deixis as it refers to a chunk of discourse – the noun phrase that would otherwise have to be repeated with the necessary qualifications (*his money*). Finally, in some languages, topic markers, such as Japanese -*wa*, or to some extent word order, as in English, have a discourse-deictic function in that they relate the topic to the previous discourse.

Now, the question arises, how categories such as social and empathetic deixis briefly mentioned above fit into this classification. While person, space, time, and discourse deixis mark 'slots' that have to be filled in the formal representation in order to represent a sentence for the purpose of truth-conditional analysis, these two are clearly more subjective: they capture the sociolinguistic 'overlay', so to speak, rather than the language-world relation that formal semantic representations standardly capture. On the other hand, since we are consistently aiming at cognitively plausible truth-conditional semantics, perhaps semantics so-conceived should capture even this type of distinction?

---

[36] See Ross 1967. Many thanks to Keith Allan for telling me about the origin of the term. See also Lyons 1999, p. 28.

Next, both discourse and social deixis could be argued to be the odd ones out in that although they encode distinctions relative to context, they do not necessarily need context for interpreting them. Some linguists consider person, space, time, discourse, and social deixis to be types of the same phenomenon,[37] but as we can see, the ways to classify deixis vary, and so do the principles on which the particular categories are founded.

As usual, natural languages present us with interesting complications in that it is not always easy to decide whether the use of an expression is deictic or non-deictic. For example, in (6.57), the cat can be hidden from view by the car (a deictic use of *behind*) or simply be at the back of the car, say, sitting behind a back wheel (non-deictic use). In the latter case, the cat could be, say, to the right or left of the car from the perspective of the speaker.

(6.57)  The cat is behind the car.

Similarly, in (6.58), Anna can be seen by the speaker as positioned to the left of Bill (deictic use) or stand to Bill's left, that is, on the side of Bill's left arm (non-deictic use).

(6.58)  Anna is standing to the left of Bill.

Many expressions that appear to be typical examples of deixis also have such non-deictic uses, as exemplified in (6.59)–(6.61).

(6.59)  There is *this* man I met.

(6.60)  *There you* are.

(6.61)  He does a bit of *this*, a bit of *that* for a living.

Pronouns are also used non-deictically when they are anaphors. But, unlike in the examples just discussed, the difference between anaphoric and deictic use does not often lead to ambiguities. In (6.62), the referent is to be found in the previous text (co-text) rather than in the situational context. Hence, *the cat* is the antecedent for the anaphor *it*.

(6.62)  *The cat* wandered off and was lost for a week but *it* was eventually found in a shed.

It would take some contortions of context and intonational contour to make *it* refer deictically rather than anaphorically in this sentence. Moreover, theories of anaphora resolution, some of which we discuss in Section 6.3, identify regularities in binding and accommodation of referents.

Next, we have bound-variable use, as in (6.63), where the antecedent is a quantified expression. We also have donkey sentences such as (6.1) repeated below, solutions to which were discussed at length in Section 6.1.1.

(6.63)  *Every child* thinks *he/she* should have a dog.

(6.1)   Every farmer who owns *a donkey* is fond of *it*.

---

[37] See Levinson 1983, Chapter 2.

The classifications summarized in this section don't take us very far. When we aim to translate these strongly context-dependent expressions into formal representations, and subsequently provide their truth conditions, the problems with such a descriptive approach don't take long to surface. We need a semantic theory of such expressions and we also need distinctions that foreground not so much the parameters of context such as person, space, or time but rather the different kinds of semantic behaviour of such terms. For example, *I* tends to 'stick' more to the referent than *he* does: it is pretty difficult, at least in English, to use it about someone other than oneself unless we shift the context by putting it in the scope of quotation. As such, it belongs with 'here' and 'now'. Those kinds of formal-semantics-oriented classifications have been developed, largely within philosophy of language rather than descriptive linguistics, under the label of indexicality. So, this is the concept to which we now turn, remembering that this concept is not an identical twin.

### 6.2.4.3 Indexicality: Two-Dimensional Semantics and the Roles of Context

The terms 'indexical' or 'indexical expression' are used more, or less, broadly, depending on the adopted definition. Some philosophers, after David Kaplan's seminal 'Demonstratives' and 'Afterthoughts', distinguish between 'pure' and 'demonstrative' indexicals.[38] Pure indexicals include expressions such as *I* and *you*, adverbs *here*, *now*, *today*, and *tomorrow*, or adjectives such as *present* and *actual*. They are deemed to be different from the rest in that their role in the sentence is claimed to be *constant*: only the speaker or writer of the current message can call themselves *I* and only the time of the current utterance can be labelled as *now*, save for deictic shift and quotation. The philosophical questions surrounding this alleged lack of shift of reference are very much in vogue and we will return to them in a moment. The remaining indexicals are demonstrative – note that these need not be accompanied by an act of demonstration and that the category is so broad because the same analysis is said to apply to them in demonstrative and anaphoric use (more about that in what follows). But before continuing with Kaplan's view, let us see whether Frege's versatile concept of sense could be useful.

First, we could attempt to accommodate indexicals within Frege's proposal of sense and reference. We would have to establish what would count as the sense of, say, *today* or *I*. But this is tricky with indexicals because although the *role* of, say, *I* is always the same, the corresponding *thought* differs with occasions of use.[39] According to Perry (1997 [1977]: 704),

> [i]n the case of proper names, Frege supposes that different persons attach different senses to the same proper name. ... Perhaps, with demonstratives too, Frege supposes that speakers and listeners, in grasping the thought, provide the demonstrative with an appropriate sense. To understand a demonstrative, is to be able to supply a sense for it on each occasion, which determines as reference the value the demonstrative has on that occasion.

---

[38] See Kaplan 1989a, 1989b.
[39] See Frege 1956 [1918–19]. 'Role' is the term used by John Perry (1997 [1977]) and is equivalent to Kaplan's (1989a) 'character' discussed later in this section.

But, Perry points out, this is not yet good enough. While proper names could just about be argued to have associated descriptions as their senses (although even this claim was found problematic), in the case of indexicals, the variability of referents (which, we can argue, is their raison d'être in a language), would mean postulating an infinite number of descriptions per expression. And this is on top of an infinite number of possible descriptions of a particular referent in the particular context. Moreover, Frege suggests that people associate private, primitive, and incommunicable senses with the indexical *I*. But this proposal still does not explain how this private sense leads to the identification of the referent: how does *I* refer to me? As Perry says, '[w]hat is needed is a primitive aspect of me, which is not simply one that only I am aware of myself as having, but that I alone have' (p. 708). And there is no independent reason or evidence to assume such a primitive sense – neither would one be able to identify it as such if there were one.

If we now try to encompass 'non-pure' indexicals as well, the problem we had earlier with proper names as descriptions escalates to the level of an explosion. If we explain the fact that the same situation is referenced as *today* (pure indexical) today but tomorrow will be talked about as having taken place *yesterday* ('non-pure' indexical), we could perhaps, after Gareth Evans,[40] resuscitate Frege's concept of an objective, shareable thought and accompany it with an explanation of tracking time. But do we then need a separate account for 'non-pure' indexicals, that is indexicals with non-fixed roles that don't come with such a history of tracking the referent down?

Next, if speakers don't even have to use *he* about, say, William Shakespeare with a particular description in mind, how can we attach descriptions to *he* at large if no referents 'stick' to *he*? Senses have to 'stick' to referents but the link between referents and indexical terms remains problematic. By now we are getting a clear sense of getting deeper and deeper into muddy waters.

On the other hand, like descriptions used attributively and referentially, pronominals allow for different kinds of referring and for referential mistakes. For example, in (6.64), the remark by speaker A, who observed the scene, can be responded to as in $B_1$ or $B_2$.

(6.64)  [*Scenario: Bill was given a lift to work by his sister Ann.*]
  A:   His mother gave him a lift.
  $B_1$:  No, *she* didn't. The woman you saw was his sister.
  $B_2$:  *She* did but she isn't his mother – she is his sister.

Let us return to Kaplan's account and see if it fares any better. According to Kaplan, both pure and demonstrative indexicals are directly referential, but while the referent of a pure indexical depends on the context, the referent of a demonstrative indexical is provided by the act of demonstration or, as he later adds, by the speaker's intention, which he calls a *directing intention*.[41] The labels 'demonstratives' and 'demonstrative expressions' introduced some terminological confusions in the literature in that,

---

[40] See Evans 1985c.   [41] See Kaplan 1989b; Perry 2009.

intuitively, the term 'demonstrative' is used for expressions whose meaning has to be completed by an actual *act of demonstration*, such as in the case of *that* or *that man* accompanied by pointing. However, since, according to some philosophers, including Kaplan, their uses with and without demonstration can be explained by the same theory, expressions such as *I*, *here*, or *now* began to be subsumed under the category. Here John Perry's distinction between *automatic* and *discretionary* indexicals closely resembles Kaplan's.[42] He adds to it another classification – that into *narrow* and *wide* indexicals, defined as those terms whose reference can be provided by the so-called narrow and wide context, where the narrow context includes only the parameters of speaker, time, and location. Wide indexicals, on the other hand, can rely on speakers' intentions or conversational assumptions for their reference assignment. Well – they can and they cannot: the matter is still unresolved and largely depends on what one chooses to mean by semantics. Christopher Gauker,[43] for example, argued recently against a speaker-intention theory of demonstratives, defending the view that the meaning of an utterance need not be equated with what the speaker intended: sometimes these two get 'unstuck'. As he claims, it is better to glean the *intentions from meaning*, rather than *meaning from intentions*. In a more conciliatory spirit, Emanuel Viebahn points out that intentionalism about demonstratives (which he strongly defends) would have to answer many questions, such as what makes speaker intention work as a *semantic* intention: is it its accessibility to the addressee, say, due to common background information?[44] The latter has been defended recently by Jeffrey King (2014: 225):

> [A]n object o is the value of an occurrence of a demonstrative in context just in case the speaker intends o to be the value and the speaker successfully reveals her intention. I'll call this account of how demonstratives acquire values the *coordination account*.

Another terminological confusion to be borne in mind is that philosophers also sometimes refer to 'pronouns and demonstratives', meaning by pronouns only personal pronouns.[45] In linguistics, demonstratives are defined by lexical or phrasal category membership: there are demonstrative pronouns and demonstrative noun phrases, the latter normally including a common noun (*that dog*). These differences have to be borne in mind while approaching linguistic and philosophical literature on the subject, especially since the divisions between categories are not just terminological vagaries; they demonstrate (no pun intended!) important commitments to different principles on which distinctions are drawn.

All in all, indexicality is a conceptual category founded on the property of shifting reference from context to context. Many different categories of expressions can shift reference, but in the case of indexicals, this is their raison d'être: very little semantic content has to be expressed because information is readily available elsewhere in the situation of discourse. So defined, their category membership can be conceived of very

---

[42] See e.g. Perry 2001.   [43] See Gauker 2019.   [44] See Viebahn 2020a and King 2014.
[45] See e.g. Larson and Segal 1995, p. 197.

differently indeed. What is now known as 'Kaplan's list' contains the examples in (6.65) – among others.

(6.65)  *I*, *my*, *you*, *he*, *his*, *she*, *it*, the demonstrative pronouns *that*, *this*, the adverbs *here*, *now*, *tomorrow*, *yesterday*, the adjectives *actual*, *present*
(adapted from Kaplan 1989a: 489)

Many go further and include at least some of the categories in (6.66). These are indexical expressions in the wide sense. (The anglocentrism of this analysis is something we will turn to in a moment.)

(6.66)  verbs *come*, *go*; words and morphemes indicating tense; modal expressions *necessarily*, *possibly*; adjectives/adverbs *left*, *right*; conditional connectives (*if* ... *then*); propositional attitude verbs (*believe*, *know* – because the truth value differs from context to context), or even common nouns (because the domain of quantification has to be restricted: *the table* ≫ 'the table we are looking at', as discussed in Section 5.1); vague expressions (*bald*); gradable adjectives (*tall*); and quantifiers.

For Kaplan, indexicals are directly referential expressions and rigid designators. As devices of direct reference, they contribute only the referent, rather than any descriptive content, to the semantic representation. (These concepts were introduced at the beginning of Section 6.2.) So, since proper names and the first-person indexical are both devices of direct reference, (6.67) and (6.68) end up having the same semantic contribution – as in (6.69). The referent exhausts the semantic role. The abstraction operator λ stands here for 'the property of being the speaker'.

(6.67)  I am the author of this book.

(6.68)  Kasia Jaszczolt is the author of this book.

(6.69)  $\lambda x$ [speaker $(x)$] (kasia jaszczolt)

Now, as rigid designators, indexicals by definition designate the same referent in all possible worlds. And this gives us a lever for their semantics. Kaplan distinguishes two kinds of meaning: the linguistic meaning, called *character*, and the meaning that is obtained through filling in the reference, called *content*. For example, the character of *I* is 'speaker or writer', while the content varies: in (6.67), it is the individual Kasia Jaszczolt. Reference assignment proceeds as follows: we fix the referent for the character in the context, which allows us to proceed to the evaluation of the sentence in possible-world semantics (the content becomes fixed). Or, as Kaplan (1989a: 506) says,

Indexicals have a *context-sensitive* character. It is characteristic of an indexical that its content varies with context. Nonindexicals have a *fixed* character. The same content is invoked in all contexts. This content will typically be sensitive to circumstances, that is, the non-indexicals are typically not rigid designators but will vary in extension from circumstance to circumstance.

So, on this account, we make use of context twice, so to speak. First, context takes us from linguistic meaning (character) to content (intension). Then, once we have assigned the referent to the indexical term, we use context to evaluate the sentence in possible worlds – to 'check' its truth value, thinking in abstract terms, and identify the worlds (for Kaplan: circumstances) in which the sentence is true.

In more formal terms, the meaning of a sentence is conceived of as a mapping (function) from context to propositions. Context (now called *index*) is conceptualized as a set of parameters. These include agent, time, location, and world, but further parameters can be added when required. As Kaplan (1989b: 591) says, 'context provides whatever parameters are needed'.[46] So, *the meaning of a sentence is a function from sets of parameters (=context) to propositions*. Next, we remember that propositions are functions from possible worlds to truth values. So, putting it together, the proposition expressed by a sentence in a context is a function from possible worlds and this particular context to truth values.

This is the gist of Kaplan's *two-dimensional semantics*. But it has to be noted that the concept of two-dimensional semantics has been used in somewhat different ways by different authors. Stalnaker's account, developed in his seminal paper 'Assertion', construes the two dimensions giving more credit to discourse participants' meaning, as opposed to purely linguistic meaning.[47] For Stalnaker, an assertion is an act whose purpose is to change the common ground – or the set of presuppositions of the participants (more on presupposition shortly, in Section 6.3). He focuses on two facts: that an indexical expression can be filled in differently by different interlocutors, and, independently, the utterance so resolved can be regarded as true or as false by different interlocutors. Using a variation on Stalnaker's original (pre-Harry-Potter) story, let us say that Hermione, assessing the ongoing plot at Hogwarts, sincerely utters (6.70) to Harry, with Ron present at the scene.

(6.70) You are in danger.

And let us say that Harry understood *you* as referring to himself (Harry), while Ron mistakenly took it to refer to Ron. At the same time, neither Harry nor Ron think they personally are in danger: they think the sentence (resolved differently by each of them) is false. But Ron agrees with Hermione that Harry is in danger. Put simply, both Harry and Ron think (6.70) is false, but while Harry understood what was intended but disagrees with Hermione's assessment of the situation, Ron agrees with Hermione's assessment of the situation but misunderstood what was intended.

This gives us two dimensions: (i) what is said, as resolved by different participants (reference assignment), and (ii) what the participants believe the facts to be (possible worlds). The resulting matrix of possibilities Stalnaker calls a *propositional concept*. It captures, so to speak, *whatever is, according to different participants, said by the speaker, evaluated in the contexts of participants' different beliefs*.[48]

---

[46] One of them is a *point of evaluation*: the purpose or perspective from which a sentence is to be taken as true or false, discussed in Section 3.1 in example (3.4). See Travis 2008a [1997] and a discussion in Predelli 2005a, b: Russet leaves of a maple tree, when painted green, are green to a photographer looking for a green background but are still russet to a botanist interested in their real colour. For a discussion of an index, see Kaplan 1989b. I come back to this topic briefly in Section 8.1.

[47] See Stalnaker 1999c [1978]. See also other papers in Stalnaker 1999a and Stalnaker 2014 on context.

[48] See Stalnaker 1999c, p. 81 for the matrix these options produce and for the associated concept of a diagonal proposition.

To sum up, the main varieties of two-dimensional semantics useful for our journey are Kaplan's with its character and content and Stalnaker's with its propositional concept. Two-dimensional semantics is a powerful theory that has also been used to answer a variety of philosophical questions, including questions about access to self-knowledge. These go beyond the scope of this journey but it is important to flag that the two kinds of use of context distinguished there open up interesting possibilities.[49] This can be gleaned from Chalmers' (2006: 59) apt summary,

> The core idea of two-dimensional semantics is that there are two different ways in which the extension of an expression depends on possible states of the world. First, the actual extension of an expression depends on the character of the actual world in which an expression is uttered. Second, the counterfactual extension of an expression depends on the character of the counterfactual world in which the expression is evaluated. Corresponding to these two sorts of dependence, expressions correspondingly have two sorts of intensions, associating possible states of the world with extensions in different ways. On the two-dimensional framework, these two intensions can be seen as capturing two dimensions of meaning.

All in all, it is evident that indexicals, as pursued by philosophers and formal semanticists, have led to classifications that foreground the *roles* played by context in their referential resolution rather than the particular *parameters* of context, such as person, place, and time, as is the case with descriptive linguistic classifications of deixis. In other words, what matters is whether the semantic role is taken as stable, like in the case of *I*, or variable, like in the case of *he*, or whether they have to rely on the act of demonstration or intention recovery.

Linguistic approaches are also different in foregrounding the difference between deictic and anaphoric uses of the same expressions, and as such foregrounding the aspects of context and co-text where the referent is to be sought. We also have to remember the intuitive use of the label 'demonstrative' in linguistic categorizations. For philosophers, parameters of context affect the analysis but do not dictate the categorization. But they have good reasons for it: *I* behaves more like *now* than like *he*, although one would have been classified as person, and the other as time deixis. This is important for truth-conditional semantics. At least equally important is the fact that the category of indexicals is so flexible, understood more, or less, broadly, as the lists in (6.65) and (6.66) demonstrate. This opens up a question as to whether the distinction between indexical and non-indexical expressions ought to be blurred even further. And here support comes both from philosophical argumentation and linguistic evidence and theory. We will now try to make use both of linguistic and philosophical wisdom that have so unfortunately been kept apart. But before we answer that question, we have to look at Kaplan's famous 'monster contexts'.

---

[49] For introductions to two-dimensional semantics, see e.g. García-Carpintero and Macià 2006 (Introduction); Chalmers 2006; or Schroeter 2017. On the notion of context in two-dimensional semantics, see e.g. contributions to Almog and Leonardi 2009; Perry 2001; Predelli 2005a, b.

### 6.2.4.4 From Monster Contexts to Indexicals as Functions of Expressions

Kaplan's well-known proclamation that uttering 'I' and pointing at someone else is 'irrelevance or madness or what?' (Kaplan 1989a: 491) has triggered an avalanche of responses, mostly pointing to the different uses of the first-person indexical (be it pronoun or something else) across different languages. According to Kaplan, pure indexicals such as *I*, *here*, or *now* acquire a referent only from the context of the current speech act. *I* has to refer to the speaker or writer, and any operator that attempts to overcome it he calls a *monster*. In other words, 'monster' is Kaplan's term[50] for putative operators that would attempt to shift the *context of evaluation* of such indexical expressions. Since, as he says, the reference of a pure indexical is fixed by the context of utterance, monster operators are impossible.

All one can do is encase an indexical in quotation marks to make it refer to someone other than a current speaker, as in (6.71).

(6.71)    Hermione said 'I am in danger'.[51]

But it seems that his claim is in need of a strong qualification. First, is Kaplan's theory supposed to apply to *concepts* such as the self, the time, and place of utterance, or to *English indexical terms* only? In other languages, there appear to be such monster operators. In Amharic, as pointed out by Schlenker in the early 2000s,[52] the belief operator 'shifts' the reference of *I* from the speaker to the subject of the main clause as in (6.72). The subscript stands for co-indexing.

(6.72)    John$_i$ believes that I$_i$ am late.

This observation triggered a hunt for languages that allow for such 'monster contexts'.[53] But let us have a closer look at the situation with Amharic *I* to evaluate this acclaimed counterexample. In Amharic free indirect speech, the first-person marker can take a referent either from the context of the current speech or from the reported context. Context shifts can take place even *within* a sentence, as in (6.73).

(6.73)    wänəmme      käne gar       albälamm              alä
          my-brother   'with-**me**   I-will-not-eat',      he-said
          'My brother refused to eat with me.'

(from Leslau 1995: 778)

---

[50] See Kaplan 1989a, p. 511. For an analysis of Kaplan's 'monsters', see Predelli 2014.
[51] Even quotation is not as straightforward as it seems when pure indexicals are concerned. For varied behaviour of the first-person indexical in mixed quotation, see Jaszczolt and Huang 2017.
[52] See Schlenker 2003.
[53] See e.g. Shklovsky and Sudo 2014 and Roberts 2014 for examples of languages and further references to sources. For example, in Zazaki, many pure indexicals can shift but only in the context of a certain verb; in Slave, only first-person and sometimes second-person indexicals shift, with few restrictions. Some shifts are obligatory, others optional. Other languages that in various ways testify against Kaplan's generalization include Navajo, Nez Perze, Uyghur, Matses, Turkish, and Japanese. For a discussion see also Jaszczolt 2016, Chapter 5.

What is important is that this is *not a quotation*; the brother need not have uttered anything like 'I will not eat with you' – he would merely have had to make his intention clear in some way or other. But what is particularly striking, and often unnoticed in the discussions of monsters, is that inanimate objects can also be referred to using the first-person indexical, as in (6.74).

(6.74)  mäskotu          aləkkäffät                    alä
        the-window       'I-will-not-be opened'        it-said
        'The window wouldn't open.'

(from Leslau 1995: 782)

A little insight into the ways of thinking that lead to such conceptualization seems to reveal that this may not be a case of a 'shift' at all: it is considered as a shift of context only when looked at from the anglocentric, and particularly, Kaplanesque, perspective. First, to native speakers, the construction appears to have a 'quotative feeling' to it in some sense.[54] But this is so only in the sense of self-quoting by the reporter, or 'quoting' one's own thoughts about how the subject thought about the matter. In other words, the utterance reflects the subject's thought processes in progress – or thought processes of a personified object. This is further supported by the fact that inanimate objects can enter such constructions only when they 'behave' contrary to the speaker's will or expectation – as if, the window *refuses* to open; it *acts against* the speaker. All in all, on this interpretation, we obtain something to the effect of 'The reporter thinks that the window 'says'(≫ acts against the human in such a way) that '*I*' (window) will not open [for *me* (reporter)]'). So, it appears that the first-personhood is conceptually there in the action reflected in the sentence: there is an actor, with assigned volition, and as such there is an *I*. As always, a little recourse to the cognitive reality of underlying thoughts solves what for anglocentric semanticists appeared to be a matter of idiosyncratic behaviour that is in need of such semantic measures as monsters.

But hold on: perhaps Kaplan's theory of indexicals could be claimed to work for English – or at least for Kaplan's list. Well, even this is debatable: uttering 'I' and pointing at different 'temporal slices' of oneself, as in (6.75), is not uncommon in English – and it does not seem to create a monster context.

(6.75)  [*Scenario: The speaker and the addressee watch a video recording from a holiday in which the speaker is in a nature reserve information centre.*]

Look, here a goat is about to attack me but I don't realize it is me because I think all the time that this is a window, not a mirror. So, I'm trying to get outside to warn her until . . .

(adapted from Jaszczolt 2016: 168)

Context shifts on written messages or old-style automated telephone messages, as in (6.76) are even more persuasive as counterexamples.

(6.76)  [*Scenario: A shop assistant fixes a note to the entrance door.*]

I am not here now to assist you. The shop will reopen at 2pm.

---

[54] Yoseph Mengistu, p.c. I discuss this at length in Jaszczolt 2016, Chapter 5.

One can, of course, consider such messages to be exceptions: Eros Corazza explains them as conventional settings. One can also, like Stefano Predelli, appeal to speakers' intentions, just as Kaplan's account of demonstrative indexicals allows you to do.[55] Be that as it may, these are cases where a pure indexical takes a referent from a context other than the speaker's speech act. So – monsters galore, even in English.

This growing interest in Kaplan's monster context has had one other important effect, namely that the various uses of indexicals have begun to be seen less as exceptions from the norm and more as a norm itself: indexicals can have very different functions indeed, some of which were discussed in Section 6.2.4.2. As we saw earlier, they can be bound by variables as in (6.63); they can also give rise to unselective binding, as in donkey sentences, or be bound across the sentence boundary – both of which sparked the evolution of dynamic semantics discussed in Section 6.1. But what is more striking is that even pure indexicals such as *I* can have a bound-variable use, as in (6.77) and (6.78a). (Italics don't stand for intonational focus here but mark the relevant indexical.)

(6.77)   I'm the only one around here who can take care of *my* children.
                              (from Kratzer 2009: 188, adapted from Partee)

(6.78a)   Only I admitted what *I* did wrong.[56]
                                                        (modelled on Kratzer)

Kratzer calls such uses a 'fake indexical', in that *my* in (6.77) and the second occurrence of *I* in (6.78a) are semantically unspecified. And although fake indexicality does not generalize well to other languages, in that another way of expressing variable binding is to use a reflexive pronoun (meaning: 'one's own'), as in the Polish version of (6.78a) in (6.78b), it is a good example of the variability of the use of pure indexicals.

(6.78b)   Tylko    ja    jedna   przyznałam      się   do   (swojego)
          Only     I     soleF   admit*I*SgPastF  Refl  to   ReflPronSgMGen
          błędu.
          mistake*SgMGen*

                                                                (my translation)

We can go further. Just as pronouns can be used in a non-indexical role, so common nouns can be used as indexicals. In (6.79), said by a child's mother, *mummy* contributes the speaker to the content, just as *I* does.

(6.79)   Mummy will be with you in a moment.

One could argue that this is the specificity of child-directed speech, just as using one's name instead of the first-person indexical as in (6.80) is specific to child speech at a certain level of language development.

---

[55] See e.g. Corazza 2004 and Predelli 2011.
[56] See also Schlenker 2003, pp. 89–90 on the role of *only* that is similar to that of a syntactic binder. Cf. also an argument from ellipsis for the bound-variable use: *Not only I admitted what I did wrong; Peter did too.*

(6.80)   Katie wants a biscuit.

But the phenomenon easily extends to standard discourse, as in (6.81).

(6.81)   [*Scenario: A conversation between a faculty member and Peter, who is the faculty dean.*]
         Peter: You will get a pay rise. You have the dean's word for it.
                                                        (adapted from Jaszczolt and Witek 2018: 201)

One can argue that *mummy* or *the dean* are not directly referential in that they also contribute some descriptive semantic content to do with the relevant role. But then, so do indexicals: *she*, for example, contributes information about the gender and number. And so do proper names for that matter, in spite of being regarded as a paradigmatic case of direct referentiality, on a par with indexicals. *Yours truly* or a more informal British self-deprecating *muggins* in (6.82), as recorded by Elizabeth Manning, also fall in this category.

(6.82)   The first drive was to be done from Redditch to Knebworth with no support vehicle and muggins was to drive it.[57]

The indexical/non-indexical distinction also suffers from other problems. Demonstrative noun phrases, also called *complex demonstratives*, appear to be more than pointers to the referent; they contain substantial semantic content, as in (6.83).

(6.83)   That student knows a lot about indexicals.

If 'that student' is an indexical expression, then it should be directly referential and as such function as a 'slot holder' for a referent, nothing more. But the demonstrative phrase clearly contributes more meaning than that: it contains the common noun 'student'. On the other hand, suppose I point to a person who has just asked a very insightful question in my lecture on indexicals and utter (6.83), wondering who that student was. Unbeknownst to me, this was not a student but a young visiting professor. Did I say something true? If we answer 'yes', then demonstrative indexicals are merely devices of direct reference: being mistaken about the description is not relevant for reference assignment and as such, arguably, for the meaning – or at least it is not relevant for the main informative content, that is, what is *at-issue* (more on 'at-issue' in the following section). If we answer 'no', then complex demonstratives appear to be quantificational expressions, like descriptions.[58] The issue is still debatable and thought-provoking for those sensitive to quirks of linguistic meanings.

---

[57] See her blog on www.macmillandictionaryblog.com/muggins [accessed 16 March 2021]. She also records the uses of *muggins here* or *the muggins* that are more common in English (Keith Allan, p.c.), as in (i)–(ii), and even a non-self-referring use in (iii), but this does not discredit the expression as a functional first-person indexical in (6.82).
  (i) One of the sight screens fell over and muggins here went to try and fix it.
  (ii) I'm the muggins who has to arrange everything.
  (iii) Let's find some other muggins to do it.

[58] For such accounts see e.g. King 2001; Lepore and Ludwig 2000.

Somewhat analogously, if demonstratives are merely slot holders, then we will need a separate explanation for the contribution of grammatical gender. For example, if the speaker utters (6.84), pointing to the name *George Eliot* on the cover of the book, did the speaker say something true about the author – a woman writing under a pen name?

(6.84)    He also wrote *Middlemarch*.

On one hand, gender information is not the topic at-issue in this context, so perhaps the mistake is not semantically relevant? And yet, even if it is not at-issue, it does contribute to the meaning of the sentence. The example is particularly pertinent in the times of a multi-gender society and it demonstrates how philosophy of language, semantics, and ethics are interrelated. After all, getting the pronoun wrong may cause distress or offence. More about this in Section 8.4.1 when we discuss accountability.

A further argument for a 'soft' boundary between indexicals and non-indexicals comes from languages with honorifics. Languages such as Japanese, Thai, Burmese, Javanese, Khmer, Korean, Malay, or Vietnamese have first-person markers that have the characteristics of both a pronoun and a noun. Like nouns, they do not form a closed class and can form the plural by adding a plural morpheme. Such first-person referential terms typically contain self-denigration and originate from nouns meaning 'slave', 'servant', 'royal slave', or 'lord's servant'. Thai is reported to have twenty-seven such forms for first person (including 'mouse' for female speakers), and Japanese as many as fifty-one (when we include archaic forms)[59]. Languages also employ spatial deixis for self-reference, for example Thai 'one male this' or Vietnamese 'here', or reflexives.

Now, in formal semantics, the *value* of a pronoun is conceptualized in an abstract way. It is given by indexing it with a number and then defining it with reference to a *sequence* – an abstract concept of a string of individuals that we have to think of as one of an infinite number of such possible strings. Individuals can occur several times, or not at all, in any given sequence. The way to conceptualize this formalism is as follows. An individual indexed, for example, '3' is a *semantic value of the pronoun with respect to a particular sequence* if and only if the individual is in the third place in the sequence. So, 'She$_3$ is happy' is true with respect to any sequence if and only if the third member of the sequence is happy. How does it help in the search for meaning? Invoking sequences may not be intuitively appealing but this is an important move in formal semantics because it is an attempt at a formalization of something that is so tricky to formalize, namely the context dependence that is so crucial for these items. Using the concept of infinite sequences is a way of assimilating indexical expressions to other lexical devices natural languages have, in order to handle them in the same framework of truth-conditional semantics. But since ours is a philosophical journey through meaning that aims at conceptualizing meaning representation rather than giving a 'hands-on' guide to formal methods, we will leave it at that, just as we left formal devices in Stage 3 once their benefits for conceptualizing meaning had been discussed.[60] Suffice it to say that the method of indexing runs into problems with pure

---

[59] See Siewierska 2004 and Tanaka 2012, respectively.
[60] For an introduction to sequences see e.g. Larson and Segal 1995, p. 203.

indexicals in that we would have to capture the fact that they normally have constant roles: *I* as the utterer; *here* as the place of the utterance; *now* as the time of the utterance, and so forth. Even though, as we have just seen, pure indexicals are not in fact so very 'pure', the fact that they *as a norm* obtain reference in the context of the speech act in which they occur is hardly disputable. So, they ought to be given *constant indices*. And since the number of pure indexicals is considerable, they are hardly an exception. We could perhaps stipulate that the first, say, eight positions in every sequence be reserved for pure indexicals *I, you, here, now, today, yesterday, tomorrow, present*, and *actual*. But, surely, there are more such expressions. So, how many positions do we reserve for indexicals with pretty much constant roles? And what happens when the role shifts as, say, from the time of coding to the time of receiving the message in (6.76) above? Also, how do we account for the fact that languages differ quite dramatically in the meaning conveyed by indexicals, as the examples of first-person honorifics in East Asian languages demonstrate?

Perhaps the simplest solution would be to ditch pure indexicality and assume that all indexicals are essentially context-dependent with variable roles, just some roles 'stick' more than others. But most philosophers would protest: this would open up a plethora of problems with important philosophical questions around, say, personal identity, including self-awareness. Compare the self-reference in (6.85) with (6.86), imagining that I utter (6.86) being an amnesiac.

(6.85)    I am the author of that book.

(6.86)    Kasia Jaszczolt is the author of that book.

Or compare the deictic time reference in (6.87) with (6.88), imagining that it is 9am at the time of the utterance but I am not aware it is already that time. Examples are easy to construe or encounter.

(6.87)    The meeting starts now.

(6.88)    The meeting starts at 9am.

Similarly, sometimes first-person perspective comes with a privileged point of view. When I think that I have a headache, I cannot be mistaken as to whose headache it is: it must be mine. But if I think that I am wearing a blue jumper and think I am looking at myself in a mirror, while in fact I am looking through a window pane at somebody who from a distance looks just like me, I may be wrong. So, the first kind of belief about myself (belief *de se*) comes with so-called *immunity to error through misidentification* (often referred to as IEM), while the other doesn't. These are fascinating and widely researched questions but they would take us too far into philosophy of mind for this journey.[61]

All in all, we have ended up in another muddle. But muddles are a good thing: they allow us to rethink old dogmas, and even to throw off the shackles and move forward to

---

[61] The literature on self-awareness is vast. Start with the classics, Perry 1979 and Lewis 1979, in that they best set out the questions for discussion. On IEM, see e.g. articles in Prosser and Recanati 2012.

better ideas. Direct referentiality has some benefits in explaining standard uses of indexicals, but, as we have seen, we also need some version of descriptive meaning – perhaps psychologically real *ways of thinking* about the referent rather than Frege's objective sense. Muddles are also a good thing because seeing the benefits and drawbacks allows us to fly off with big ideas to see where they take us. In this journey, we postulated (i) that a theory of meaning has to be formal but at the same time cognitively real and (ii) that attending to the *functions* that expressions have in discourse is more important than attending to rigid, conventional semantic or grammatical categories of expressions. In Section 1.3, these desiderata took us to the concept of a *functional proposition*. In the case of indexicals, they can take us to a *functional indexical*: a conceptual category that plays the role of an indexical expression, no matter what clothing it wears. In other words, we can entertain the view that indexicals are not types of expressions, like, say, those on Kaplan's list, but at most functions of expressions: just as common nouns or proper names can be used with an indexical role, so personal pronouns such as *I* can be used with a non-indexical role.

Another argument against a strict indexical/non-indexical distinction comes from related phenomena discussed under the heading of *relativism about truth*. As John MacFarlane (2005: 305) says,

[t]o be a relativist about truth is to allow that a sentence or proposition might be assessment-sensitive: that is, its truth value might vary with the *context of assessment* as well as the context of use.

Relativism about truth is, naturally, intrinsically connected with relativism about meaning as long as truth is the explanans for meaning, as it is in truth-conditional semantics.

Various relativist semantic accounts have been developed to tackle recalcitrant phenomena, the celebrity among them being so-called *predicates of personal taste*. When I utter (6.89), you may disagree if you absolutely hate the (thrilling for me!) sensation of swallowing them.

(6.89)   Oysters are tasty.

So, while the sentence is true for the speaker, it may be false for the addressee. However, there is no real disagreement. Semanticists call it instead a *faultless disagreement* in that the perspective from which it is evaluated explains any divergences. This is a little like assigning different referents to indexicals, but not quite:

sentences like these do not express different contents relative to different individuals. Yet ... they do vary in truth value from person to person. This means that the relativization is not like what we get with ordinary indexicals, and calls for a different semantic technique. (Lasersohn 2009: 360)

On the one hand, it is like indexicality. On the other, the variable that matters here is that of a judge: 'tasty for whom?'. This gets further complicated when we substitute *this cat food* for *oysters*! Who is the judge? The discussion on the correct, satisfactory semantics continues and gathers in strength.[62]

---

[62] See e.g. McFarlane 2005, 2011, 2014; Lasersohn 2005, 2009, 2017, and Pearson 2013.

Returning to indexicals proper, it appears that, when we consider the variety of use in one single language, as well as cross-linguistic variation, the indexical/non-indexical distinction is best seen not as a dichotomy but as a variety of referring roles that language expressions can perform. And even if on your own journey through meaning you may find the idea of indexicality as a functional category too radical for semantic theory, the fact is that flexible referring properties better reflect the reality of natural-language discourse. This opens up new possibilities for a theory of meaning.[63]

## 6.3 Organizing Information in Discourse

### 6.3.1 Topic and Coherence

Putting together the discussion of multi-sentential discourses in Section 6.1 and the properties of expressions that can be used to refer in Section 6.2, we can now further explore the fact that speakers' use of different categories of expressions largely depends on the salience of the referent in discourse. Dynamic semantics provided tools for representing cross-sentential reference dependencies; the Givenness Hierarchy explored the role of such cognitive salience, from 'type-identifiable' to 'in focus of attention'; and an exploration of the properties of such expressions gave us an insight into how exactly they (or, rather, speakers using them) refer. In short, we have established that successful approaches to meaning must (i) be based on *discourse* as a unit and (ii) account for the contribution of context to the meaning as conversation proceeds, that is, in a dynamic way. Next, an important element of the organization of discourse is its information structure. *Topic* is the core concept of information structure in that it substantially contributes to coherence and relevance in discourse. I will briefly introduce several views on topic as there is no consensus in the literature on what the term means.

The notion of topic cannot be easily formalized but it is intuitively known as *that which makes a section of a discourse about something*.[64] Before we settle on the definition that would be most useful for our formal/cognitive journey through meaning, it is only fair to start with the old masters who attempted to define topic in terms of the structure of the sentence. They proposed distinctions such as that between *theme*, which is traditionally regarded as the element that comes first in the sentence, and *rheme*, saying something about the theme, as in (6.90).

(6.90)   Working with animals |   is what Bill has always wanted to do.
         THEME                    RHEME

In Japanese, for example, the theme is announced by a particle, postposition *-wa*. Whatever immediately precedes *-wa* is thematic. English has no formal marking of a theme except for the standard position in the clause: normally, theme precedes rheme. The distinction originated in the Prague school linguistics tradition, dating from the

---
[63] This question is discussed at length in Jaszczolt 2013a, 2016, and 2018b.
[64] See e.g. Brown and Yule 1983 for a discussion.

1930s, that proposed a functional view of the sentence, subsequently espoused, among others, by Michael Halliday.[65]

A related distinction, that between *topic* and *comment* (or *focus*), takes us away from sentence structure: topic is *being about* something, while comment (focus) *says something about the topic*. This distinction was developed largely by Charles Hockett, followed by Talmy Givón. On this view, it is easier to accommodate the fact that sentence topic is independent of its position in the sentence, or even that there are *degrees* of topichood.[66] The degrees are explained as follows. It is often difficult to pinpoint the topic of a piece of discourse in that the discourse may have more than one topic – aboutness is an inherently vague notion. There are degrees to which elements of sentences qualify as topics. Referring expressions are good candidates for topics so understood. In Section 6.2.1 I introduced scales of referring expressions and we have seen that there is a fairly reliable correlation between the form of the referring expression and availability of the referent from memory: for example, if the referent is in the focus of attention, it can be rendered as *it*. And, according to Givón's scale based on the correlation between the expression type and the degree of topichood, the more familiar the referent, the more likely it is to be a topic.

In other words again, information content is structured into *given* information, already provided by the context or by the previous discourse, and *new* information, believed by the speaker to be new to the addressee. This is what Michael Halliday calls *information structure*: the structure of a unit of information communicated to an addressee.[67] Information structure relates structures and meanings to how information is represented in the mind. In English, it can be indicated by (i) particular constructions that bring an expression into the focus of attention, as in (6.91); (ii) intonational contours, using focal stress, as in (6.92); or (iii) left to be inferred from the general *discourse topic* – a different notion altogether, to which we will turn shortly.

(6.91)   It is Bill who spilled the beans.

(6.92)   BILL spilled the beans.

All in all, it is clear that there are problems with defining topic in relation to parts of the sentence. But the common-sense importance of the notion of topic for the analysis of meaning in discourse is obvious, even if the history of the term is far from satisfactory. For the purpose of our journey, it will be more useful to adhere to a more informal definition, whereby topic (or *discourse topic*) is treated more intuitively: not as part of a sentence but as *what the speaker talks about*. Seen in this way, topic is not, for example, a noun phrase, but an idea, a proposition communicated by the speaker.

In order to recover the topic, the addressee needs some background information, such as the purpose of the speaker's contribution, the significance of the timing and

---

[65] See e.g. Halliday 1994 [1985].

[66] See e.g. Lambrecht 1994 and Givón 1983a, b; 1993. As Lambrecht (1994, p. 119) suggests, this multiplicity of topics is the reason for the absence of clear formal marking of the topic in many languages and the limited usefulness of this marking in others.

[67] See Halliday 1967.

location, and so forth. This can be gleaned from the physical context and the co-text. Relevant context, co-text and general, shared information constitute the so-called *topic framework*, also called the *presupposition pool*. Most speakers conform to the topic framework, that is 'speak topically'; they conform to the pragmatic principle of cooperation by being informative, truthful, clear, and relevant – a principle best captured by Paul Grice, referred to occasionally in the previous sections and attended to in more detail in Section 7.1. Speaking topically is a common characteristic of everyday conversation. A more formal, organized exchange is characterized by *speaking on a topic* – for example, climate change, social gender, misogyny, and so forth. So, *speaking topically* differs from *speaking on a topic*.

Nevertheless, interlocutors often have their own perspectives on such a discourse topic, so we also have to distinguish *speaker's topic*. For example, interlocutors can have their own topics caused by their personal culinary experiences of exotic food, such as Mexican or Russian cuisine. These topics then fit into the shared discourse topic. And, needless to say, topics develop dynamically in that new topics become introduced (through topic shifts) and take over. Topic shifts may correlate with structural units of discourse (sometimes called paratones, on analogy with paragraphs), marked by intonation patterns, such as raised pitch for the beginning of a paratone, or lexical markers such as *moreover, another question is,* among others.

Adhering to the topic is one of the factors that make discourse coherent. We have already encountered the concept of coherence while discussing rhetorical structure rules of SDRT such as *Narration* in Sections 4.2 and 6.1.2.1 in that coherence becomes an important concept once the theory of meaning operates on larger units, as is the case in dynamic semantics. Coherence is an important aspect of the organization of discourse and it permeates many approaches mentioned so far. The Givenness Hierarchy[68] just mentioned, for example, that maps referring expressions onto cognitive statuses, is best viewed in the context of the so-called *centering theory*. The theory models the relationship between (i) attentional state, (i.e. the availability, degree of activation of discourse referents at a given point in discourse); (ii) the form of a referring expression; and (iii) the coherence of an utterance assessed within a certain fragment of discourse. In other words, in centering theory we model the interlocutors' centre of attention by considering the degree of activation of the referent, the complexity of the required processing, and the form of the referring expression. Utterances are said to activate so-called *forward-looking centres* and a *backward-looking centre*, that is, the discourse topic. Forward-looking centres represent discourse entities evoked by the given utterance. A set of such forward-looking centres is created and they are ranked according to their salience. These centres connect the utterances with previous discourse. The relations between elements are subject to certain constraints; for example, pronominalization of a lower-ranked element requires that the higher-ranked one is also realized as a pronoun. Through capturing attention states associated with referents in the processing of discourse (degrees of topichood), the theory

---

[68] The model by Gundel et al. 1993 (see Table 6.1).

accounts quite well for some regularities in discourse anaphora. The theory was developed, among others, by Barbara Grosz, Aravind Joshi, and Scott Weinstein.[69]

The regularities that govern cross-sentential anaphora are still a matter of controversy. Lepore and Stone, for example, in their well-aired (because rather controversial) book *Imagination and Convention: Distinguishing Grammar and Inference in Language* (2015) that we referred to in Chapter 4, follow attention theory, and in particular the so-called *grammatical role hierarchy*[70] and claim that the rule for reference assignment in examples such as (6.93) and (6.94) is present in natural-language grammar. In particular, when both the subject and the object of the first sentence are viable candidates for a referent, there is a preference for binding the pronoun to the referent in the subject position. So, in (6.93), *he* stands for the president, while in (6.94) it stands for Jones.

(6.93)   The president nominated Jones. He expected a quick confirmation.

(6.94)   Jones was nominated by the president. He expected a quick confirmation.

(from Lepore and Stone 2015: 91)

Salience is considered to be strongly dependent on the structure of the sentence. As a result, attention and coherence in discourse are presented as dependent on linguistic rules, where the latter are stretched to account for the context. For example, they argue that linguistic rules account for the values of pronouns in that the rules also account for context.[71] In general, sources of linguistic conventions receive a lot of attention in theories of discourse coherence that refer to various semantic and pragmatic factors.[72] They appeal to, among other things, subjecthood, or semantic (or *thematic*) roles such as Agent or Patient, and, like Lepore and Stone, to parallelism between the function and the grammatical role. But it is important to note that the approaches to information structure here mentioned are not in direct opposition to each other: some are more grammar-driven, while others are more inference-driven, focusing on speakers' expectations of coherence. As such, language-driven regularities can be given a more prominent or a more modest place. The rhetorical structure rules of SDRT such as *Narration*, *Background*, or *Result* can be placed towards the pragmatics-end of the spectrum in that they find regularities in such expectations. This leads to typologies of coherence relations.[73] Coherence theorists point out that since new information (comment, semantic focus) often correlates with the object position in the sentence, objects are strong candidates for antecedents. Centering theorists point out that since the subject is often a discourse topic, in virtue of being the *psychological focus*, or

---

[69] See Grosz et al. 1995; Grosz and Sidner 1998; Walker et al. 1998.    [70] See e.g. Grosz et al. 1995.

[71] See e.g. Stojnić, Stone, and Lepore 2017, 2020. For grammar as a set of linguistic conventions, see also Ariel 2010.

[72] See e.g. Hobbs 1979, 1990; Kehler 2002; Kehler et al. 2008; Kehler and Rohde 2013; Asher and Lascarides 2003.

[73] See here Kehler's (2002, p. 143) discussion of Kameyama's empirical evidence concerning the prominence of the subject vs. the object position; Kehler et al. 2008, and the discussion below on the convergences in the discussed approaches.

'backward-looking focus' in discourse, it is also a good source for referents of pronouns. Both observations are correct and a battle would be futile.[74]

All in all, the question is: what sort of account of information structure offers a useful, adequate explanation? As we have seen, this varies with where we stand. A pragmatics of human communication that appeals to speakers' intentions and addressees' inferences, such as the Gricean and post-Gricean pragmatics discussed in Stage 7, aims at cognitively plausible explanations: we focus on discourses that follow the principles of rational communicative behaviour. Computational linguistics, on the other hand, aims at regularities that can feed algorithms for machine learning, and as such is less satisfied with the 'processing mess' presented by the human mind with its capacity to extract information from so many different sources. As we have seen throughout these six stages of the journey, formalization of the output of such complex processing is a gargantuan task – but a task well worth the effort, as the two remaining, more 'pragmaticky' stages of our journey will show. Moreover, although at first the phenomenon may appear to be in need of an empirical resolution, so far experiments have shown to be of limited use in that the number of factors that would have to be controlled for is likely to make the experiment inconclusive or even circular. Whether one searches for an explanation in the vagaries of the human brain or in big data, the fact is that it is difficult to answer even basic questions, such as what counts as contextual influence and what as a non-biasing context.[75] The well-quoted pair of sentences in (6.95) and (6.96) provides a clear example. Co-indexing shows how the reference of *they* is normally resolved.

(6.95)  The city councilmen$_i$ refused the demonstrators a permit because they$_i$ feared violence.

(6.96)  The city councilmen denied the demonstrators$_i$ a permit because they$_i$ advocated revolution.

(adapted from Winograd 1972: 33)

Here it goes without saying that the context has an upper hand: the city council wants to avoid demonstrations, while the protesters, as the term suggest, plan it. But the earlier (6.93) is much less clear. Moreover, if there is a gradation of candidates, detecting clear rules becomes difficult. Here knowing what people construe as a probable, default scenario on an occasion is not likely to benefit from data-based quantitative studies. So, neither is machine learning, unless we identify a wide range of parameters and ways these parameters influence each other. This brings us back to the starting point of a 'processing mess' and the observation that the methods of research in philosophy of language and computational linguistics should meet. We shall leave these debates here, remembering that every journey through meaning has different desiderata and assumptions but also that this doesn't mean that they shouldn't communicate and exchange wisdom.

---

[74] See the discussion in Gundel 1999. See also Kehler and Rohde 2013 for an argument for a reconciliation of coherence-based and centering-based approaches to the reference of pronouns.
[75] See here Sileo and Jaszczolt 2021 for some case studies and a discussion of relevant factors.

## 6.3.2 Focus and Truth Conditions

Focus is another theoretical concept that, in spite of being intuitively clear, has led to a medley of different uses. In addition to functioning in the topic–focus dichotomy just discussed, it can mean prominence in various, sometimes incompatible, senses. Most intuitively, focus means prominence in speech that can be brought about by speech melody – mostly changes in pitch. In the context of information structure, focus can refer to the part of an utterance that bears informational stress, which is in itself often marked by intonation pattern. This definition is supported by phonology-oriented approaches. So, informational focus and intonational focus often coincide. But informational focus is not necessarily intonational focus: it refers to the new, informationally more relevant part of an utterance, contrasted with topic, which in turn stands for the material that is backgrounded. As such, it also includes syntactic prominence, achieved, for example, by cleft and pseudo-cleft constructions, as in (6.97) and (6.98) as opposed to (6.99), as well as the so-called *deaccented focus* appealed to in formal semantics, with no marking of focus on the focal element.[76]

(6.97)   It is a cup of strong coffee that she needs.

(6.98)   What she needs is a cup of strong coffee.

(6.99)   She needs a cup of strong coffee.

A cognitively plausible semantic theory has to make use of informational focus in all these guises, in that focus, including intonational focus, can affect the truth conditions of the sentence through affecting its presuppositions. But incorporating thematic structure is not an easy task. The relation between focus, anaphora, and presupposition is very much at the forefront of research in formal semantics and we will discuss it in the next section. For now, let us have a look at some examples of the truth-conditional relevance of focus.

Here negation is a good example. Kuboň,[77] following Kratzer,[78] analyses negation as a tripartite quantifier and represents it in DRT with the topic in the restrictor and focus in the nuclear scope, as in Figure 6.8 for sentence (6.100). (See the explanation of quantified expressions as duplex conditions in Section 5.2.1.)

(6.100)   Paula isn't registered in PARIS.

This sentence presupposes that Paula is registered somewhere: that there is some place $x$ at which she is registered. What is denied is that $x$ is Paris. Focus is very important for representing negation – compare, for example, versions of (6.100) with intonational focus on *Paula* or on *registered*.

One influential theory goes as follows. According to Mats Rooth (1996: 271), focus means 'prosodic prominences serving pragmatic and semantic functions' and as such can have truth-conditional effects and introduce presuppositions and implicatures. On his theory, called *alternative semantics*, the semantics of focus depends on evoking so-called *alternatives* to the focused element. In order to interpret a sentence with a

---

[76] See e.g. Partee 1999.   [77] See Kuboň 2004.   [78] See Kratzer 1989.

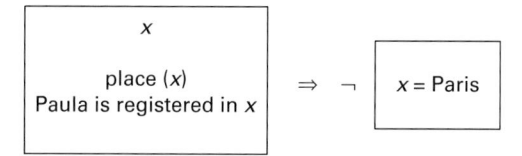

**Figure 6.8** Restrictor and scope for (6.100) ('Paula isn't registered in PARIS.') (adapted from Kuboň 2004: 211)

focused element, we have to relate the meaning of this sentence, when unfocused, to a set of alternatives. These alternatives are the interpretation of this sentence when the denotation of the focused constituent is replaced by other denotations. For example, focus on *Paris* in (6.100) evokes a set of alternative locations at which Paula could be registered. Focusing on *Paula* or on *registered* comes with different sets of alternatives – a set of people who could be registered in Paris and a set of different associations that Paula could have with Paris: living there, being born there, and so forth. Such alternatives are constrained by context, as well as by focusing constructions in a particular language.[79]

Examples (6.101a) and (6.101b) well demonstrate the truth-conditional relevance of focus.

(6.101a) The largest demonstrations took place in PRAGUE in November (in) 1989.

(6.101b) The largest demonstrations took place in Prague in NOVEMBER (in) 1989.

(from Gundel 1999: 301, after Partee)

(6.101a) would be false if the largest demonstrations in November 1989 took place in a different city, while (6.101b) could still be true. The reason is that in (6.101b) *in Prague* belongs to the topic and as such restricts the discussion to demonstrations only in Prague.

Let us now look at the role of focus in the interpretation of quantified sentences. If the information in the scope of the quantifier is not in focus (that is, it is backgrounded, or presupposed), it is interpreted as if it came from the restrictor of the duplex condition. Focused material remains interpreted as part of nuclear scope.[80] This general tendency to interpret presuppositions as part of the restrictor is largely triggered by focus. So, in sentences such as (6.102), focus determines both the restrictor and the scope.

(6.102) Many POETS frequented this café in the 1920s.

Note that *many* does not behave here as it should, so to speak: it does not behave like a conservative quantifier in that the sentence does not mean that many poets were poets who came to this café but, intuitively, means that many people who came to this café were poets. Assuming a scenario of Paris Rive Gauche in Montparnasse in the Années

---

[79] See Rooth 1996 and for a discussion, e.g. Blok and Eberle 1999; Büring 1999.
[80] See e.g. Eckardt 1999.

folles (1920s), *poets* could evoke a set of alternatives as in (6.103) in Rooth's alternative semantics. 'R' stands for the restrictor and 'S' for scope.

(6.103)  R = {x | x is a poet or a painter or a novelist or a playwright or a theatre critic or . . . who frequented this café in the 1920s}

S = {x | x is a poet who frequented this café in the 1920s}

The sentence says that the ratio |S| : |R| is big for the selected context, that is the context in which we are talking not about the qualities of poets in general but about the professions of people who were frequenting a certain venue. Hence, information about being a customer of this café is present in the restrictor. Only weak quantifiers such as *many* clearly interact with focus; strong quantifiers, such as *all*, don't always exhibit this property.

Focus also helps with the interpretation of number terms. Number terms were discussed in Section 5.2.3, where I pointed out that they can have different readings: 'exactly *n*' 'at least *n*', 'at most *n*', or 'approximately *n*'. When a number term is in a focus position, it usually has the 'exactly *n*' interpretation. So, let us look at an earlier example (5.50a) again (repeated below), now as part of (6.104) and (6.105). The element in the focus position is marked by a subscript $f$.

(5.50a)  Bill has three dogs – in fact, he has four if you count the one that lives in his workshop.

(6.104)  A:  Who has three dogs?
         B:  Bill$_f$ has three dogs – in fact, he has four if you count the one that lives in his workshop.

(6.105)  A:  How many dogs does Bill have?
         B:  Bill has three$_f$ dogs – in fact, he has four if you count the one that lives in his workshop.

(modelled on van Kuppevelt 1996: 411)[81]

When the number term is in the topic position, the 'at least *n*' interpretation is plausible, as in (6.104). But when it is in the focus position, 'exactly *n*' is the standard interpretation. The only way B's response in (6.105) could be considered well-formed is when the explanation that he has four dogs acts as a *self-correction* by means of which the speaker withdraws the earlier claim that the number of dogs is three.

Next, adverbial quantifiers such as *always* are sensitive to focus and quantify over the topic part. In (6.106), the time adverbial *after drinking red wine* is in the topic position and as such is interpreted as belonging to the restrictor of the quantified expression. The resulting meaning is that all instances of Anne's drinking red wine have an instance of Anne's having a headache following them.

(6.106)  After drinking red wine, [Anne always has a headache]$_f$.

But when the time adverbial is not preposed (that is, when it does not precede the rest of the sentence), the sentence is ambiguous, unless we add some indication of what

---

[81] See also Krifka 1999.

counts as focus: two readings are possible, depending on which element is in focus, as in (6.107a) and (6.107b).

(6.107a)   [Anne always has a headache]$_f$ after drinking red wine.

(6.107b)   Anne always has a headache [after drinking red wine]$_f$.

(modelled on de Swart 1998: 345)

The reading of (6.107a) is the same as that of (6.106): all instances of Anne's drinking red wine have an instance of Anne's having a headache following them. But (6.107b), where the adverb *always* quantifies over instances of Anne's having a headache, means that all instances of Anne's having a headache have an instance of Anne's drinking red wine preceding them. So, focus matters a lot: there is only one cause of Anne's headaches in (6.107b), while there can be more causes, leading to more headaches, in (6.107a). (If you can think of an example where this ambiguity is more striking, or even humorous, please let me know!)

Such examples of the truth-conditional relevance of focus demonstrate how important information structure is for representing meaning. Formal theories such as DRT can account for it, as is exemplified in Figure 6.8 and throughout this discussion, by juggling what information goes into the restrictor and what into the scope of the duplex condition.

At the same time, like with the term 'topic', one has to be careful: material in focus in information structure is not the same thing as material that is, for example, 'in focus of attention' in the hierarchy that associates cognitive statuses with types of referring expressions discussed in Section 6.2.1 (see Table 6.1). It is a semantically attenuated expression precisely because the referent is already activated, and as such, likely to be the topic. So, being in focus$_1$ of attention marks the topic of which something new can be predicated, and this new information will then have the status of focus$_2$ (or comment) in information structure. This is yet another terminological muddle. Perhaps the best way to think about it is that *topic* is what is *already in focus of attention*. We shall now move to what is presupposed in information structure and next, to recent influential research on 'at-issue' and 'not-at-issue' content and the properties of information that this distinction reveals.

## 6.3.3 Presupposition and Projective Content

Continuing the discussion of representing foregrounded and backgrounded information, we now turn to the concept of presupposition and, more generally, to the concept of projective content. Presupposition was introduced in Section 4.5.2 during the discussion of negation. We said that presupposition is that part of the content of the sentence that has to be true for the sentence to be either true or false (see Table 4.6 there). So, to reiterate, both (4.57a) and (4.57b) presuppose (4.58).

(4.57a)   Anna quit smoking.

(4.57b)   Anna didn't quit smoking.

(4.58)    Anna used to smoke.

Current discussions of presupposition can be traced back to the late nineteenth century and Gottlob Frege, followed by landmarks by Bertrand Russell in the early twentieth century and Peter Strawson half a century later, whose views I introduced in Section 6.2.1 while discussing definite descriptions. It was pointed out there that Russell, in his theory of descriptions,[82] claimed that a sentence with a definite description such as (6.26) asserts the existence of the described individual, and its semantic representation (logical form) is as in (6.27) – both repeated below.

(6.26)   The king of France is bald.

(6.27)   $\exists x\,(\text{KoF}(x) \wedge \forall y\,(\text{KoF}(y) \to y = x) \wedge \text{Bald}(x))$

For Russell, when the requirement of existence is not fulfilled, the sentence is false. But this, as we saw, complicates the meaning of negation. Next, according to Peter Strawson,[83] sentences in themselves don't have truth values; it is statements made with them that are either true or false, in that a sentence can be used at different times and in different contexts, only in some of which the existential presupposition ('There is a present king of France') is fulfilled. On this view, negating (6.26) amounts to narrow-scope negation: the existence of the king of France is still presupposed.

Strawson's notion of presupposition gave rise to the notion of semantic presupposition, whereby, on one conception of logical presupposition (there are others), sentence $S_1$ semantically presupposes sentence $S_2$ if and only if sentence $S_1$ entails sentence $S_2$ and the negation of sentence $S_1$ also entails $S_2$ (for properties of entailment, see Table 4.7 in Section 4.5.2 above). If $S_2$, for example (4.58) above, is false, then $S_1$, for example (4.57a) or (4.57b), has no truth value. Famous as it is, problems with this account are ample. Firstly, we have already encountered the concept of metalinguistic negation and know that such negation takes a wide scope and as such can negate both the proposition at-issue and the presupposition. (We are moving to 'at-issue content' in the next section.) This is exemplified in (6.108), which can be plausibly regarded as true rather than truth-valueless. Stressing NOT strengthens the intuitions of correctness.

(6.108)   The present king of France is NOT bald. There isn't any king of France!

So, while Russell was wrong in saying that presupposition failure leads to falsehood, Strawson appears to be wrong in saying that it leads to a truth-value gap, unless we opt for a very complicated semantic representation of the first sentence in (6.108).

Presuppositions appear to be much more 'pragmaticky' than that. Attaching them to sentences, or even statements, won't do, because speakers can make negative statements without intending to presuppose existence. So, it looks like they have to be tied to us: speakers or addressees. As in the previous discussions of various aspects of meaning, so here it is all down to us, language users, and to various parameters of discourse with its aims, topics, foci, and so forth, to explain what is going on – also

---

[82] See Russell 1996 [1905] and 1997 [1912].   [83] See Strawson 1997 [1950].

with presupposed content. A speaker-focused concept of presupposition states that sentence $S_1$ presupposes sentence $S_2$ *when in uttering $S_1$ the speaker presupposes $S_2$.*[84] Here presuppositions are beliefs of the speaker of $S_1$ which have to be held *together with the belief that corresponds to $S_1$.*

To sum up, presuppositions can be tied to a sentence, a statement, or to a speaker.

One way to exorcise semantic presuppositions is to reconceptualize them as entailment and implicature. This was an important landmark in presupposition research in the 1970s.[85] For example, (6.26) entails the existence of the person, while its negation in (4.75) (repeated below) merely implicates it – 'merely', in that, as we know from the discussion of metalinguistic negation in Section 4.5.2 and from (6.108) above, the presumption of existence can easily be cancelled.

(4.75)   The king of France is not bald.

Theories of presupposition are ample in the literature but what will interest us in this philosophico-linguistic journey is not the details but rather the concept of presupposing and its properties that make it useful for analysing meaning. We have seen that presupposition displays the property of constancy under negation, as in (4.57b) and the property of defeasibility, that is the possibility of cancelling it under certain conditions (as in 6.108). Sometimes, it doesn't even arise, as in (6.109), contrasted here with (6.110) which, on the contrary, carries a strong sense of presupposing (6.111) (if you can think of a less gruesome example, please let me know!).

(6.109)   Anne died before her wisdom tooth extraction.

(6.110)   Anne worried before her wisdom tooth extraction.

(6.111)   Anne had a wisdom tooth extraction.

This is explained by the sensitivity of presuppositions to context, including background knowledge, such as that people don't normally have their wisdom teeth extracted posthumously. We will look at some more properties of pragmatic presupposition in the next section when we move to the property of projection.

To recap at this point, it seems most prudent to conclude that presupposition is a pragmatic phenomenon and should be viewed as what is presupposed by an utterance in a context. According to one influential approach, presuppositions are beliefs of the speaker that are entailed by the context: they *update* the context, where the latter is understood as common ground. This is called the theory of *contextual satisfaction* and is represented, among others, by Karttunen, Stalnaker, and Heim.[86] On the other hand, DRT supports the binding theory. Rob van der Sandt's[87] proposal of presupposition as anaphora formalizes information from context and the surrounding texts. Since in our

---

[84] On pragmatic presupposition, see e.g. Stalnaker 1973, 1999d [1974]; Gazdar 1979; van der Sandt 1988; García-Carpintero 2020.

[85] See e.g. the discussions in Atlas 1977, 1979; Kempson 1975, 1979; Boër and Lycan 1976; Wilson 1975; Carston 1998b.

[86] See e.g. Geurts 1999, Chapter 3 for a more detailed discussion.

[87] See van der Sandt 1992, 2012. On presupposition in dynamic semantics see Beaver 2001 or 1997.

journey through meaning DRT has so far played an important role, let us look at this proposal in a little more detail.

Van der Sandt suggests that expressions that presuppose the existence of some referent should not be regarded as referring expressions, as the standard Fregean view has it. This is because although sentences such as (6.112)–(6.114) should have no truth value when the second component of the complex sentence suffers from presupposition failure, in fact, they are not truth-valueless. (6.112) may appear an 'odd one out' here but it is included in that 'Anna has a dog' is *said*, not presupposed, and this will become relevant shortly.

(6.112)   Anna has a dog and *her dog* is black.

(6.113)   If Anna has a dog, *her dog* is black.

(6.114)   Either Anna doesn't have a dog, or *her dog* is black.

Next, we cannot define presupposition in terms of entailment because presupposition can disappear with the growth of information, as it does in the extension to (6.115) in (6.116). In other words, presupposition is a *non-monotonic* relation.

(6.115)   It is possible that Anna's dog is in a kennel.

(6.116)   It is possible that Anna doesn't have a dog, but it is also possible that it is in a kennel.

(modelled on van der Sandt 1992: 334–335)

Although presuppositions are non-monotonic, and hence cancellable (defeasible), there are some regularities worth capturing. Van der Sandt does it with DRT in mind, suggesting a way of incorporating presupposed information in DRSs. Presupposition is neither strictly semantic, nor strictly pragmatic. Instead, on that view, presuppositional expressions are anaphoric expressions, similar to pronouns and other anaphors. As such, they have the capacity to *bind to an antecedent* or to *accommodate in the relevant context*. This proposal benefits from a dynamic approach to semantics in that, as was discussed in Section 6.1, in dynamic semantics utterance interpretation is represented as growing incrementally, bit by bit. The dynamic theory mirrors this incremental process by collecting relevant information in a DRS as discourse progresses. Now, since presuppositional expressions are anaphors, they can be analysed in the way that pronominal and other anaphors are analysed. And this is where a dynamic approach fits in: it can represent anaphoric relations not only within a sentence but also across sentences in discourse. So, we can bind presuppositions to antecedents in earlier discourse.

Unlike anaphors such as pronouns *it* or *he*, presuppositional expressions such as *her dog* have a fair amount of descriptive content. So, they can also function successfully when the antecedent *cannot* be found. In such cases, they are accommodated. Accommodation, a concept first introduced by David Lewis,[88] should be understood as a process of 'repairing' conversation. In (6.117), the presuppositional expression *his children* does not have a proper antecedent.

(6.117)   If John has grandchildren, his children will be happy.

[88] See Lewis 1991 [1979].

Since it cannot be bound, it is accommodated. Here van der Sandt suggests that 'global' accommodation is preferred to 'local' accommodation: the presupposition that John has children becomes the presupposition of the entire sentence. Now (6.117) has a presupposing reading, which allows for a continuation as in (6.118), where *they* is anaphoric on *his* (John's) *children*.

(6.118)  If John has grandchildren, his children will be happy. They wanted to have offspring long ago.

On the other hand, local accommodation would mean accommodating the presupposition in the antecedent of the conditional, producing a non-presupposing interpretation. So, accommodation is essentially a common-sense mechanism of making context-driven assumptions when the antecedent cannot be found in the preceding discourse.

Nonetheless, sometimes global accommodation is not plausible. In the case of (6.119), presupposition (6.120), resulting from the factive verb *regret*, would not be plausible as a presupposition of the entire sentence; it is subordinate to the antecedent of the conditional (*If John has children*) and does not project out.

(6.119)  If John has children, he will regret that all of his children are bald.

(6.120)  *All of John's children are bald.

(examples from van der Sandt 1992: 351–353)

The relevant rule is that if an embedded anaphor is already bound to an antecedent, we cannot accommodate it anywhere higher up in the representation. In DRT it would mean 'taking the presupposition out', so to speak, of the embedded DRS and placing it in the parent DRS, that is, adding it to the representation of that discourse as part of the common ground.

Generally, binding and accommodation are systematically ordered in that accommodation takes place when binding cannot work. For example, (6.121) has the interpretation in (6.122) rather than, say, (6.123) because of the priority of binding over accommodation. This is so even though binding is problematic in this example in that it is a case of binding to a quantified noun phrase rather than to a referring expression.

(6.121)  Every farmer likes his horse.

(6.122)  Every farmer who has a horse likes it.

(6.123)  Every farmer likes Bill's horse.[89]

To reiterate, accommodation generally occurs at the highest level rather than in subordinate clauses – that is, there is preference for global over local accommodation, as in (6.118) above. On the other hand, binding takes place at the nearest accessible site from the anaphor. The intuitive explanation of this rule is that in search for a binding element we may go all the way up the *projection line* (tracking antecedents that are 'visible' in the DRS) and not find a suitable antecedent. Then, at the top of the

---

[89] See van der Sandt 1992, pp. 363–367 for a detailed analysis of an analogous example in terms of DRSs.

projection line, that is 'globally', attempts to accommodate begin and various kinds of contextual and shared pragmatic information are used at this stage. If global accommodation is not possible or suitable, we start moving back in the projection line to a more local one.

The qualifier 'generally' is important. A potential antecedent may be discarded even though it agrees with the anaphor grammatically (say, in number and gender) and seems intuitively appropriate for the context. This is because anaphors can be ambiguous and it may be a matter of inferring the speaker's intended meaning to choose between them. There can be more than one suitable antecedent or there may be a choice between binding and accommodation. Sometimes, the antecedent and an anaphor constitute a partial match, as in (6.124), where *the protesters* can be (i) coreferential with *the students*, or (ii) a subset (or some other overlapping set) of them, or (iii) a different group of dissatisfied people.[90]

(6.124)   If the police fine the protesters, the students will stage more protests.

As was discussed in the previous section with the help of example (6.102), focus is an element of information given in an utterance of a sentence, so as part of the context it can induce presuppositions. The systematic nature of this association was well argued for by Bart Geurts and Rob van der Sandt.[91] The semantic role of focus is well accounted for by Rooth's alternative semantics, also introduced earlier. So, focus can now be regarded as a contextual clue for accommodation. Theories of presupposition and theories of information based on the topic/comment or topic/focus distinction have a lot in common. For example, strong quantifiers but also accented weak quantifiers induce an existence presupposition.[92] Accenting can also disambiguate sentences where there is an ambiguity between potential anaphors, as in (6.124) just discussed (try it with accented 'students'). So, partial matches do not seem to exhibit a genuine ambiguity: there are default rules that tie topic (unstressed anaphor) with binding on the one hand, and focus (stressed anaphor) with accommodation on the other.

All in all, presupposition is anaphora, but, equally, as van der Sandt argues, anaphors are just short, attenuated, devoid of content, presuppositional expressions. An anaphoric pronoun such as *he* or *it* is an instruction to the hearer to search for a referent. On this view, *anaphora can be subsumed under the overarching concept of presupposition*. Binding theory is then the *binding theory of presupposition*.

One obvious criticism of this approach is that not all presuppositions are anaphors because if there is no element of discourse to which we could bind the presuppositional expression, the expression does not function anaphorically but rather has to be accommodated.[93] But then, one can reconceptualize anaphora, extending the use of the term even beyond binding to antecedents present in the preceding discourse and

---

[90] On partial matches see Krahmer and van Deemter 1998. For a proposal of a principle of binding preferences in partial matches, see Jaszczolt 2002a.

[91] See Geurts and van der Sandt 1999 and 2004. See also A. Cohen 1999 for a different view: that Rooth's alternatives that arise in the focusing of a phrase are induced by presuppositions.

[92] See van Deemter 1998; Asher and Lascarides 1998; Jäger 1999.

[93] See Geurts 1998b and 1999 for a discussion.

## 6.3 Organizing Information in Discourse

allowing for *binding to extralinguistic context*, thereby dispensing with the concept of accommodation altogether.[94] The rules governing the choice of anaphors can be spelled out in different ways. One of them is van der Sandt's preference order, where discourse principles and non-linguistic knowledge remain somewhat elusive territories as relevant parameters, but binding and accommodation are carefully worked out. Another is Asher and Lascarides' rhetorical relations, where accommodation can be dispensed of in favour of the overarching relation of binding presuppositions to the context through rhetorical links – the pay-off being the multitude of discourse rules, like those we encountered earlier in this journey. Note that the latter move also reconceptualizes binding in that binding is a technical concept in generative syntax whereby a *theory of binding* sets out the rules for finding an antecedent within a sentence. There are three such rules, called Principles A, B, and C, that specify the site of an antecedent for reflexive pronouns and personal pronouns, as well as the unbound status of full, referential noun phrases.[95] But from the perspective of our cognitively aspired journey through meaning, such a rethinking of binding is a good thing: conceptually, binding becomes synonymous with having an antecedent, be it in the same sentence, or in preceding (and sometimes following) discourse, or even in the common ground. We are moving from natural-language syntax (which, as we have seen in Stages 3–5, does not give us a compositional theory of meaning), to the domain of mental representations of meaning, but retaining the formal tools such as dynamic semantics and useful explanantia such as truth conditions.

Next, there are various diagnostics for testing the presuppositional status of information. For example, it is normally the foregrounded (focused, or *at-issue*), rather than presupposed, content that generates direct assent or dissent, as in (6.125). This is so because presupposition normally, albeit not always, pertains to the common ground.

(6.125)   A:   Anna quit smoking.
          B:   That's not true.

It would be difficult to make B's response mean that it is not true that Anna used to smoke, unless the speaker makes it clear that it is a case of metalinguistic negation – for example by continuing as in (6.126).

(6.126)   It's not true that Anna quit smoking – she has never smoked in her life.

And even then, it can be argued that B is still objecting to A's statement but on the grounds that the presupposition is not fulfilled. We either follow Strawson and say that B's negative statement has no truth value or opt for a wide-scope negation, or, best, like we do throughout this journey, take the scope of negation to be dependent on the context and intentions, and thereby take presupposition to be a pragmatic phenomenon.

Now, if it is a pragmatic phenomenon, then an interesting question arises: can one lie through presuppositions? Is A lying in (6.125)? Emanuel Viebahn gives an affirmative

---

[94] See Asher and Lascarides 1998.    [95] See e.g. Haegeman 1991, pp. 187–230.

answer and calls it a *presuppositional lie*,[96] thereby claiming that speakers are committed not only to what they explicitly say (which may be taken as neither true nor false) but also to what they presuppose. This analysis is interesting not only from the point of view of ethics but also for information structure: it shows that presupposition can sometimes hide new information, 'camouflage' it, so to speak, as part of the background that had already been shared. (6.127) may deliberately convey untrue information that John owns a Mercedes – for example in order to make the addressee believe that John can afford an expensive car.

(6.127) Did you know that John owns a Mercedes?

(from Viebahn 2020b: 735)

Whether we still want to call them 'presuppositions' or some other type of content is the question we will come back to during the discussion of projection in the next section.

The presupposing status of information can be diagnosed by the so-called 'Hey, wait a minute!' (HWAM) test, as in (6.128). The test was first used by Benny Shanon[97] (strictly speaking, in the 'one moment, ... ' form) in order to distinguish between logical and pragmatic presuppositions, but is now widely used for various types of backgrounded information.

(6.128) A: Anna quit smoking.
B: Hey, wait a minute – I didn't know Anna used to smoke.

But since the test picks up on shared, backgrounded information, it will only work for standard presuppositions that contain information presumed to be shared, rather than 'camouflaged' or 'smuggled' new information just mentioned. More about this in the next section.

Now, presuppositions are a kind of *projective content*. In general, projective content stands for information that is triggered by certain words or constructions and as such has potential to 'project out', 'percolate', or 'escape' the operators that 'ought to destroy it', so to speak, such as negation (see (4.57b) at the beginning of this section) and some others that we will encounter in a moment. As we have seen, definite descriptions such as *the king of France* trigger existential presuppositions; 'quit' triggers the presupposition that the quit eventuality used to be the case, and so forth. These presuppositions survive under negation, so we say that they project – they are not stopped by the negation operator like entailments are. Neither are they stopped in questions, as in (6.129), antecedents of a conditional (6.130) or modal operators (6.131).

(6.129) Did Anna quit smoking?

(6.130) If Anna quit smoking, Bill will be pleased.

(6.131) It is possible that Anna quit smoking.

---

[96] See Viebahn 2020b, p. 733.   [97] See Shanon 1976.

We will return to projective content at large and information structure in Section 6.3.4 but first let us continue with presuppositions. Sometimes, but not always, presuppositions of an embedded sentence can be inherited by the whole sentence. As such, they give rise to the *projection problem* – a problem that was at the forefront of research in the 1970s and has returned, in a somewhat different form, in the 2000s. The problem is to determine the conditions under which this projection takes place. For example, let us compare (6.132) and (6.135). *Know* is a factive verb and factive verbs quite legitimately allow for presuppositions to 'percolate up' in that they require that the embedded sentence be true. So, (6.132) presupposes not only (6.133), but also (6.134).

(6.132)   Anne knows that Bill's dog is called Zeus.

(6.133)   Anne knows that Bill has a dog.

(6.134)   Bill has a dog.

On the other hand, *believe* is a non-factive verb, and non-factives, by definition, do not 'guarantee', so to speak, that the embedded sentence is true. So, they should not license such a projection. And yet they do. (6.135) should presuppose (6.136), whereas, intuitively, it presupposes (6.137).

(6.135)   Bill believes that Anne stopped smoking.

(6.136)   Bill believes that Anne used to smoke.

(6.137)   Anne used to smoke.

Discussions of projection out of non-factive attitude contexts are ample. Different approaches give rise to different theories of presupposition projection.[98] In early research in the 1970s, a classification of predicates, based on their semantic properties, was proposed so as to distinguish between those predicates that block off the projection, those that allow it, and those that display a mixed behaviour. These were Karttunen's *plugs*, *holes*, and *filters*, respectively.[99] But by such criteria, non-factives ought to belong to the first group, while they appear to belong to the second. So, it appears that judgements concerning presupposition projection have more to do with rules of discourse and speakers' assessment of the common ground, of what can *plausibly be assumed*. In other words, presuppositions are better thought of as background beliefs of the speaker's that are taken for granted by the addressee when there is no misunderstanding as to what constitutes their shared background knowledge or common ground.[100] They can also be taken to be commitments of the speaker's. Conceptualized as such background beliefs, they are attached to utterances rather than to sentences and appear when context allows them to appear.

---

[98] See e.g. Heim 1992 and Geurts 1998b.     [99] See Karttunen 1973.
[100] On projective content, see e.g. Simons et al. 2010 and the discussion later on in this section. On representing projective content in DRT, see Venhuizen et al. 2018.

## 6.3.4 At-Issue Content vis-à-vis Projective Content

It is not only presupposed content that projects – projection is also a property of other kinds of information. For example, information in non-restrictive relative clauses, as well as in appositives, projects out of its local environment, although it is not presupposed, as in (6.138).[101]

(6.138)   Malfoy believes that Hermione, (who is) Harry's friend, told him about the plot.

The projection properties of what is sometimes called *expressive content* (discussed at length in Section 8.4.2.2) are more complicated. Following David Kaplan, *damn* in (6.139) is said to contribute to such expressive, as opposed to main descriptive, content.

(6.139)   That damn window won't open.

(modelled on Kaplan 2008)

The complicated projection properties of expressives are well captured in (6.140)–(6.141). In (6.140) the term *bastard* appears to convey the speaker's derogatory attitude, while *fucking* in (6.141) more likely conveys Bill's attitude, and as such is to be interpreted *in situ*.[102]

(6.140)   Would you believe it that Anna is fond of Nigel? She thinks the bastard is a hero.

(6.141)   The parrot will be sold. Bill says he hates the fucking bird.

So, it is not the case that expressive content always projects. As a rule, it can project when it is not in the focus/at-issue position, as in (6.140) and (6.141). Notice how differently such terms behave in a predicative position that makes them in focus/at-issue, as in (6.142).

(6.142)   Bill believes that Nigel is a bastard.

As was said, we will return to expressives while discussing pejoratives at the end of the journey where we will attend to this question more carefully. But suffice it to say for now that the boundaries of projective content are not clear. Before we continue, it is worth observing that projection properties may also affect *semantic* representation, as on a contextualist cognitively motivated approach. So, the question arises when and how expressive content contributes to such representation on such a construal. Perhaps expressive content could be considered part of the semantic representation *tout court*, whatever the status of information it is associated with? On the one hand, expressive content is different from descriptive content: paraphrasing an expressive/swear/taboo word is not easy. On the other, complete dissociation from the main truth-conditional content does not work either if we strive for cognitively plausible semantics. In short, neither a minimal semantic representation nor a contextualist-semantic representation does it justice. (6.143) and (6.144) give examples of respective paraphrases.

---

[101] See Chierchia and McConnell-Ginet 2000 [1990]; Potts 2005, 2012.
[102] For a discussion see Potts 2012.

(6.143) Nigel is a contemptible person.

(6.144) Nigel is a contemptible person and the speaker has strong negative feelings about him.

Be that as it may, it is debatable whether we can draw a clear distinction between descriptive and expressive content.

But let us continue with projective content in general. It has now been well acknowledged, and well supported empirically in cross-linguistic analyses, that *various kinds of contents project when they don't have the status of being at-issue*. The concept of being at-issue was introduced in the 1990s by the group of researchers who make use of it to bring such typologies and properties of projective content to the fore of pragmatics. These include Mandy Simons, Craige Roberts, Judith Tonhauser, David Beaver, and Chris Potts, among others.[103] At-issueness is defined on this account using the concept of question under discussion (QUD). QUD is a concept that is easy to grasp intuitively in that it corresponds to the discourse topic. Simons et al.'s definition goes as follows:

a. A proposition $p$ is at-issue iff the speaker intends to address the QUD via ?$p$.
b. An intention to address the QUD via ?$p$ is *felicitous* only if:
   i. ?$p$ is relevant to the QUD, and
   ii. the speaker can reasonably expect the addressee to recognize this intention.

(Simons et al. 2010: 323)

So, at-issueness is a matter of the speaker's intending, and communicating, a certain discourse topic (QUD) to which their utterance contributes. And as such it helps decide whether certain content is projective – that is, whether it can escape from, or survive, the embedding under negation, question, conditional (with the material in question in the antecedent), and epistemic modal operators. In (6.145), QUD is conveyed directly by A, so it is easy to determine what content is at-issue: that B didn't come to the party because B's brother was ill.

(6.145) A: Why didn't you come to the party?
        B: My brother was ill.

On the other hand, the content that B has a brother is not at-issue; neither is the content that B was expected at the party. Content projects when it is not at-issue. The at-issue/not-at-issue status of information can also be diagnosed by the tests we used for pragmatic presupposition in the previous section, namely direct assent/dissent or HWAM. But in what follows, we will focus on QUD as it appears to run into fewer problems than the other tests.[104]

It is important to understand that QUD is not a sentence or a proposition but a discourse topic – simply, the topic talked about. As such, it can be expressed in various ways, some of them more direct than others:

---

[103] See e.g. Simons et al. 2010 (and very useful references there); Tonhauser et al. 2013; Potts 2005, 2012; Tonhauser, Beaver, and Degen 2018.
[104] For a discussion see Potts 2012.

An assertion is relevant to QUD iff it contextually entails a partial or complete answer to the QUD.

and

A question is relevant to QUD iff it has an answer which contextually entails a partial or complete answer to the QUD. (Simons et al. 2010: 316)

As such, at-issue content addresses QUD, and, as focused information, determines a set of alternatives, such as those used in the alternative semantics discussed above.

So, projection is a matter of discourse structure rather than a property of presuppositions alone. But the hunt for 'what projects' gets messy on various fronts and is still in its early stages. First, what kind of objects we are hunting for depends on how we classify them. Some of them are *types of structures*, such as appositive clauses, or non-restrictive relative clauses (that, conceptually, are also 'in apposition' to the main content), parenthetical expressions such as *as you know*, or speech-act modifiers such as *to be honest*. Others are categories of meaning. Expressives are distinguished as a category, but then, the word *damn* can also be a part of an appositive construction. Adding honorifics (e.g. French singular *vous*) to the mix, as well as the criss-crossing categories of epithets, slurs, swear words, and so forth, only contributes to the conclusion that projection is a property that can be investigated with respect to different objects of study: phenomena or constructions. Sometimes what we stress is the structure, at other times it is the assertability of an expression, its function in social interaction or emotional load. Christopher Potts,[105] for example, attempted to group non-presupposing projective content under conventional implicature, only to notice that the behaviour of different categories is not the same: slurs, for example, have very strong projection properties. Tonhauser, Beaver, and Degen have recently tested nineteen expressions from American English and reported their projection variability. Their experiments also suggest that projection depends on the extent to which the content is not at-issue – an association that they call the Gradient Projection Principle.[106]

All in all, it appears that 'hunting for what projects', that is identifying types of expressions that project, is not the right thing to do. It is likely that in future pragmatics research, projection will be regarded as a gradable property. It seems to crop up, to a greater or lesser degree, and with different restrictions, in sociolinguistic phenomena such as politeness and impoliteness, or psycholinguistic phenomena such as emotions in discourse, or structural phenomena such as apposition. As Simons et al. (2010: 325) rightly observe,

projection is not a matter of elements of content 'escaping' the scope of an operator, but rather of elements being 'ignored' by operators. Speakers use operators to target content which is central to their conversational goals.

So, while the structure of information is crucial, so are the speakers who convey it.

---

[105] See Potts 2005, 2012.    [106] See Tonhauser et al. 2018.

**Suggested Further Reading**

*Dynamic Semantics*
For more detailed introductions, try Asher's (2016) 'Discourse semantics' or Dekker's (2012) *Dynamic Semantics*. On DRT, it is best to start with Kamp and Reyle's (1993) detailed and well-paced *From Discourse to Logic*. Comprehensive, although faster-progressing towards advanced, summaries are Geurts, Beaver, and Maier's (2020) 'Discourse Representation Theory'; Kamp and Reyle's (2011) 'Discourse Representation Theory'; van Eijck's (2006) 'Discourse Representation Theory' and van Eijck and Kamp's (1997) 'Representing discourse in context'.

*Referring*
To begin, try introductions such as Abbott's (2010) *Reference*; Michaelson and Reimer's (2019) 'Reference'; Cappelen and Dever's (2018) *Puzzles of Reference*; Neale's (1990) *Descriptions*, Chapters 1–2; Ludlow's (2018) 'Descriptions'; Cumming's (2019) 'Names'; Levinson's (1983) *Pragmatics*, Chapter 2; Braun's (2015) 'Indexicals', before moving to seminal papers referred to in Section 6.2.

*Information Structure and Presupposition*
Start with Gundel's (1999) 'On different kinds of focus' and perhaps Rooth's (1996) 'Focus' and Geurts and van der Sandt's (2004) 'Interpreting focus' on the relation between focus and presupposition. For a detailed survey of research on focus and givenness, with emphasis on intonation, see Büring's (2016) *Intonation and Meaning*. On pragmatic presupposition, read the classic: Stalnaker's (1999d [1974]) 'Pragmatic presuppositions'. On pragmatic presupposition you may also be interested in García-Carpintero's (2020) 'On the nature of presupposition: a normative speech act account' – or read it after reading Section 8.3 on speech acts. On presupposition and projective content, start with Potts' (2015) 'Presupposition and implicature' (Section 2, or the entire chapter after reading Section 7.1 below on implicature). Simons et al. (2010) 'What projects and why' gives a very clear exposition of the utility of the at-issue/not-at-issue distinction and the concept of QUD for determining projection, as well as a survey of approaches to projection.

Suggestions for more detailed and advanced reading are given, as always, in the footnotes throughout. Since 'going beyond the boundaries of the sentence' is a rather broad theme, with different approaches discussed, those suggestions may be particularly worth consulting.

# Stage 7  Utterance Meaning, or What Lurks under the Surface

## 7.1  Saying, Implicating, and Inferring

We have now travelled through different units of meaning, beginning with words and associated concepts, through sentences and the meaning associated with their compositional structure, to multi-sentence discourses and meaning that can be gleaned from cross-sentential relations. But in the process we have also left a lot of topics and questions dangling. It is time to return to them and explore the more practical side of the 'What is meaning?' question, namely how meanings get communicated in discourse. From the speaker's perspective, they are communicated through saying, implying, and relying on what is assumed to be known. From the addressee's perspective, they are communicated through understanding speech, inferring what is not said, and identifying what was assumed as mutually known. It is now time to go deeper into such meanings that, so to speak, have always 'lurked under the surface', that is meanings that are neither word meanings nor sentence meanings *tout court*, and meanings for which we have no overt indication in the sentence that they are to be recovered. And yet, these are meanings that kept popping up at every stage of our journey: meanings as context- or situation-dependent, or even as conventional, default interpretations. Although they are weaker, in a sense, in that they are 'only inferred' and as such can be denied by the speaker (although more on this later), we have always had a sense of their importance and even perhaps their right to be included in a semantic representation if that representation is to be a cognitively real representation. But even if we wished to keep them separate from semantics and relegate them to a separate type of inquiry – pragmatics (more on this interface in Sections 7.2–7.3), they still deserve close attention. So, keeping an open mind on these options of either (i) subsuming them within one cognitively real truth-conditional theory of meaning or (ii) investigating them as pragmatic 'what is implicitly conveyed' and keeping semantics 'uncontaminated', let us now look properly at what lurks under the surface of uttered (or written) units: that is, under sentences, sentence fragments, or strings of sentences.

### 7.1.1  Beginning with Grice: From Intentions to Utterance Meaning

One of the questions left dangling was how exactly, if at all, we can capture in truth-conditional representations those meanings that are not straightforwardly translated

## 7.1 Saying, Implicating, and Inferring

into the metalanguage of predicate logic and its extensions. For example, as we have seen, sentential connectives or definite descriptions are used in English in ways that are not adequately captured by such translations in that they contain some specific aspects of meaning that would have to be left out. These are, for example, the temporal meaning of conjunction or the referential meaning of descriptions. There are two routes we could follow. First, we could look for a separate, pragmatic explanation of these facts and be reconciled with the situation that truth-conditional representations fall short of representing psychologically real, 'practical' meanings. But even then we would have to acknowledge, as Paul Grice already did in the 1970s, that some pragmatic contributions to semantic representations cannot be avoided.[1] Indexicals are context-driven through and through and their reference has to be resolved before truth conditions can be gleaned. Similarly, ambiguous expressions, at least those that are non-controversially, lexically or syntactically, ambiguous, need to be brought down to one of their meanings, unless we simply want to list the readings and associate with them their respective truth conditions. The other option is the one we have been journeying towards, but not quite reaching, throughout this book. To sum up, we set the principal desideratum as follows: 'What is meaning?' is to be understood as cognitively real meaning, meaning that emerges in between the interlocutors, not only through what the expressions overtly convey but also through various additional channels or modalities. This includes leaving it to 'lurk under the surface', as something meant but not said, because it can be assumed to be retrievable from context or from conventions (on which more later). This direction necessitates being 'positively eclectic' and mixing and matching directions, theories, and tools from different journeys through meaning, as long as they are recalibrated to jointly do the job we want done. And this is how we ended up with the best there is on offer: (i) formal tools of truth-conditional semantics that offer precision and predictive power and (ii) insights of psychologism that allow us to reach the meanings co-constructed by the speaker and the addressee (again, more on this later), where (i) is put in the service of (ii).

But formal tools will only help accomplish the task if we supplement them with equally theoretically precise principles of human rational communication that allow the communicators to rely on what 'lurks under the surface'. When we combine information conveyed by natural-language structures (multi-sentential strings, or free-standing sentences, or sentence fragments, or words) with information conveyed but not physically said or written that such principles help retrieve, then the formal tools can operate on the *total output*. As was said, on a different journey through meaning, the tools can be applied to the object that is construed differently. At one end, it could be (a) only information conveyed by linguistic structures. Next, it could be (b) the linguistic structures and Gricean minimal pragmatic additions just mentioned. Moving further on the scale, it could be (c) some other 'in-between meanings', such as the precisification of the domain of the quantifier 'everybody', for example. Finally, we can 'go the whole hog' to (d) the main, primary message, as it was intended, recovered, and often also

---

[1] See Grice 1989c [1978].

co-constructed by the interactants. We are beginning here with Grice – and hence with (b), supplemented with his pragmatic account of what lurks under the surface.

Grice focused on the rationality principles that govern conversational inference. In (7.1), one of Grice's celebrated examples, speaker B clearly communicates more than just the content of the sentence. It is implied that Smith may have a girlfriend in New York.

(7.1)   A:  Smith doesn't seem to have a girlfriend these days.
        B:  He has been paying a lot of visits to New York lately.

(from Grice 1989b [1975]: 32)

One of the principles of rational communication is that speakers are normally relevant: what they say is relevant to the topic of discourse. So, unless A has a reason to think that B is not a rational communicator, A will assign the most contextually relevant interpretation. This is likely to be something to the effect that, on the contrary, Smith may have a girlfriend in New York, since this is a likely explanation of his frequent visits there.

So, with the benefit of hindsight, we can say that Grice didn't 'go beyond' option (b) in his view of semantics. He called this main communicated content a *conversational implicature* and distinguished it from *what is said*, where only the latter is to be analysed using the formal methods of truth-conditional semantics. They both contribute to what is communicated, where what is communicated consists of what is said and what is implicated in various ways (on which more shortly). In his seminal paper 'Meaning', he called this amalgam *non-natural meaning* (*meaning$_{NN}$*), to differentiate it from *natural meaning* where 'A meant that $p$' entails $p$.[2] For example, in (7.2), the entailment from having the type of spots to having measles is fixed; we cannot meaningfully say (7.3).

(7.2)   Those spots meant measles.

(7.3)   ?Those spots meant measles, but he hadn't got measles.

(from Grice 1989a [1957]: 213)

Natural meaning is of little interest to pragmatics. In contrast, non-natural meaning, as in (7.4), is very interesting: it is what the utterance communicates – correctly or incorrectly, as (7.5) makes clear.

(7.4)   Those three rings on the bell (of the bus) mean that the bus is full.

(7.5)   But it isn't in fact full – the conductor has made a mistake.

(from Grice 1989a [1957]: 214)

It is interesting precisely because the entailment is not there. The distinction is akin to that between natural and conventional signs: spots that unequivocally mean measles on the one hand, and on the other, bell rings that *merely normally should* mean that the bus is full.

---

[2] See Grice 1989a [1957].

One word of warning before we proceed: Grice was a philosopher and for him the same account of 'what lurks beneath the surface' applied to linguistic and non-linguistic communication. So, in his papers, he often uses examples of non-linguistic actions, such as, say, putting money on a shop counter, showing someone a photo, or, like here, a bus conductor ringing the bell on the bus (remember this was 1957 – don't we just love old, quaint examples as long as they are politically correct!). For him, they are all *utterances* – linguistic or non-linguistic, but utterances. So, meaning$_{NN}$ is an amalgam. Grice defines it as follows. For the speaker to mean something by $x$, the speaker must intend to induce by $x$ a belief in the hearer. Moreover, the speaker must intend their utterance to be recognized as so intended:

'$A$ meant$_{NN}$ something by $x$' is roughly equivalent to '$A$ uttered $x$ with the intention of inducing a belief by means of the recognition of this intention.' (Grice 1989a [1957]: 219)

Intentions act here as an explanans, while speaker meaning acts as an explanandum (labels introduced in Section 1.4). Intending means acting out of one's beliefs and desires. In the paper 'Utterer's meaning and intentions', he further develops the intention-based account as follows:

'$U$ meant something by uttering $x$' is true iff, for some audience $A$, $U$ uttered $x$ intending:

(1) $A$ to produce a particular response $r$
(2) $A$ to think (recognize) that U intends (1)
(3) $A$ to fulfill (1) on the basis of his fulfillment of (2).

(Grice 1989e [1969]: 92)

Again, the response in (1) has to be cognitive or physical, but 'physical' does not necessarily have to be linguistic, in accord with his use of the term 'utterance' just discussed. This proposal works well for most cases of speakers' 'meaning something' by an utterance. But in some situations it appears to be necessary to add more levels of sub-intentions – like, for example, in circumstances where the intention to convey a certain meaning is supposed to be recognized but *the addressee is supposed to think that the utterer did not intend to reveal this intention*. Grice exemplifies this sophisticated case with a situation (attributed to Stampe) where in a game of bridge an employee wants his boss to win and wants the boss to know that he wants him to win, without at the same time blatantly disclosing this intention. So, the employee smiles in a way that suggests that it is a simulated smile rather than a genuine 'I have a good hand' smile. Grice argues that in this example the employee can't be said to have *meant* anything by his smile. And yet the conditions in the above definition are fulfilled: 'the boss is intended to think that the employee wants him to think that the hand is a good one'. On the other hand, 'he is *not* intended to think that he is *intended* to think that the employee wants him to think that the hand is a good one' (Grice 1989e [1969]: 95). This example, discussed in the literature by a number of philosophers (Grice, Strawson, Schiffer), arguably shows that we may have to add another level of sub-intentions, specifying that the utterer U uttered $x$ *not only* with the intention$_2$ that A should think that U intends$_1$ to elicit a response from A. What is needed is a restriction that U intends$_3$ that A recognizes that U has that intention$_2$.[3] Indexing levels of intentions should help with those mind-boggling scenarios dreamt up by philosophers of language. Some philosophers find them exciting, other more practically minded meaning hunters do not.

These were the 1960s. In the intervening decades, many aspects of Grice's approach to communicated meaning have been questioned. And still many remain to be questioned. In the intention-based definition, it is disputable whether we need to go to the $n$th level of sub-intentions; it is even debatable whether, in the above example, the employee *didn't mean anything*. So, the very definition of meaning qua what is intended to be communicated is open to debate. It is also debatable whether the best way to talk about meaning is to adopt the speaker's perspective, rather than focus on the addressee's recovered meaning, meaning co-constructed by the interactants, or even some model interlocutors' meaning in which conventions and predictions from context can be subsumed under better generalizations. More about these post-Gricean developments later but let us first conclude our business with the original account.

All in all, for Grice, communication is about intentions and inferences; the recognition of an intention may lead directly to the fulfilment of this intention in that the speaker's intention to inform the addressee about something is *fulfilled by being recognized b*y the addressee. Bach and Harnish refer to it as *illocutionary-informative intention*[4] and say that it is guaranteed by the so-called *communicative presumption* that whenever the speaker says something to the addressee, it is taken to be communicated with some intention. Sperber and Wilson[5] phrase it as a distinction between the *communicative* intention and the *informative* intention embedded in it, whereby the communicative intention signals to the addressee that the speaker has an intention to inform them about something. We will say more about this while discussing their theory in Section 7.2.2. To anticipate again, some post-Griceans found it important to focus on *referential intention* which, according to Bach, is part of the communicative intention: 'what is said, to the extent that it is not fixed by linguistic meaning, is determined by speaker intention, which itself can include the intention to refer to what one is demonstrating' (Bach 1992: 140). Communication is successful not when the addressee recognizes the linguistic meaning of the utterance but when they infer the speaker's meaning from it. The mechanism according to which interlocutors recognize the intentions of the speaker is worked out in Grice's elaborate theory of meaning$_{NN}$ that is founded on the idea of cooperation and the principles of cooperative behaviour to which we now pass.

## 7.1.2 The Cooperative Principle and Maxims of Conversation

The key to the analysis of examples such as (7.1) (repeated below) is the notion of implicature that I have just intuitively described but will now attend to more closely.

(7.1)  A:  Smith doesn't seem to have a girlfriend these days.
       B:  He has been paying a lot of visits to New York lately.

---

[3] See Grice 1989e [1969], p. 95, after Strawson.    [4] See Bach and Harnish 1979.
[5] See Sperber and Wilson 1995 [1986].

Implicatures are meanings that are suggested by the speaker but not expressed in utterances. Inferences that are drawn from an utterance by the addressee, such as that Smith is likely to have a girlfriend in New York, are normally meanings *implicated* by the speaker. Grice originally distinguished between two different terms derived from the verb 'to implicate': *implicature* as *the act of implicating*, and *implicatum* as the *content of what is implicated*.[6] Useful as it may have been, the distinction is no longer observed and we will refer to the implicated propositions as implicatures.

In this task of the recovery of implicated information the hearer is guided by a principle of rational communicative behaviour that Grice called the Cooperative Principle. The principle covers the observation that the speaker's contributions to a conversation are, and are assumed to be, 'communicatively correct', so to speak: they are what is required at the particular step in conversation, on the assumptions that the interactants agreed on the 'purpose or direction of the talk exchange in which [they] are engaged' (Grice 1989b [1975]: 26).

The principle breaks down into maxims and sub-maxims that summarize particular assumptions about conversation: the maxim of (i) *Quantity* accounts for the shared tacit assumption that contributions to discourse come with the required amount of information (not too much, not too little); (ii) *Quality* stands for the shared tacit understanding that speakers are truthful and have evidence for their claims; (iii) *Relation* (or what would better be called 'Relevance') covers being relevant as one of the aspects of rational behaviour; and (iv) *Manner* summarizes such aspects of rationality as not normally using obscure or ambiguous expressions, being appropriately brief and giving accounts in an appropriate order. In addition to these conversational maxims, he admits that there are also social, aesthetic, and other principles that explain, for example, polite behaviour.

It is important that the content of the maxims is supposed to be tacitly presumed by interlocutors. As a result, in (7.1), B's answer is taken to be informative, true, relevant, and as clear as it is possible for the speaker to be, bearing all situational considerations in mind. It is this 'unsaid' meaning based on the presumption of cooperation that Grice calls *conversational implicature*. In other words, the maxims produce inferences in the addressee that go beyond the meaning of the sentences uttered (Grice's *what is said*).

We do not follow here Grice's original formulation of such regularities of behaviour for one very good reason: his use of the imperative mood made them sound like rules to be obeyed, or even to be acquired or learned, which is contrary to the spirit of the whole Gricean enterprise. They are simply theoretical generalizations over what speakers normally do: they are neither prescribed rules of behaviour, nor norms, nor even exact principles that we tacitly keep in our minds. This has often been misunderstood by Grice's critics but it is important to remember that Grice was neither a linguist nor a psychologist: he was a philosopher who tried to crack the logic of human communication.

---

[6] See Grice 1989b [1975], p. 24. For a critical study of the concept of implicature in Grice's and selected post-Gricean approaches, see also Zufferey, Moeschler, and Reboul 2019.

In the interests of historical accuracy, it has to be noted that Grice was not the first to observe that we can mean more than we say. In the following extract, John Stuart Mill (1872: 517) discusses the standard inference that is reminiscent of the maxim of Quantity, in that it draws on the fact that we assume our interlocutors to be appropriately informative:

> If I say to any one, 'I saw some of your children to-day', he might be justified in inferring that I did not see them all, not because the words mean it, but because, if I had seen them all, it is most likely that I should have said so: though even this cannot be presumed unless it is presupposed that I must have known whether the children I saw were all or not. But to carry this colloquial mode of interpreting a statement into Logic, is something novel.

To give an example of Grice's contemporary, Oswald Ducrot in *Dire et ne pas dire* (1972: 134) talks about the 'law of exhaustiveness' (*loi d'exhaustivité*) according to which the speaker provides the strongest information that can be of interest to the interlocutor. Above all, these examples give evidence of the intuitive plausibility of that aspect of the maxim of Quantity that addresses providing *sufficient* information.

Next, in the interests of cross-cultural accuracy, it is increasingly frequently pointed out that this fixed set of maxims suffers from anglocentrism, or even Western-centrism. The maxim of Manner does not, for example, apply to African cultures in which, as Ameka and Terkourafi (2019: 76) summarize it, being cooperative can subsume being 'opaque', 'obscure' (using 'veiled speech'), 'ambiguous', 'long-winded', and 'circuitous'. These are the exact opposites of Grice's sub-maxims of Manner: being 'perspicuous', avoiding 'obscurity of expression' and 'ambiguity', being 'brief' (avoiding 'unnecessary prolixity'), and being 'orderly'.[7] Wierzbicka (2014: 11) aptly says that employing standard English language as a metalanguage for discussing principles of conversation, or, for that matter, any other issues in humanities, carries with it the load of being stuck in a 'conceptual prison'. As she says, 'much of contemporary research in the social sciences needs to liberate itself from an excessive conceptual dependence on English' (p. 197). This is how analysis is still predominantly conducted, although more in philosophy of language than in the linguistic pragmatics that has developed a robust cross-cultural strand. So, let us move on, bearing in mind the importance of sociocultural considerations.

Now, implicatures can arise out of the observance, non-observance, or blatant breaching (flouting) of the maxims. In (7.1), the assumption of cooperative behaviour and in particular the maxim of Relation makes B's addressee (that is, A) search for a relevant interpretation of what may seem like an irrelevant piece of information. In (7.6), B violates the maxim of Quantity by providing less information than is required.

(7.6)      A: Where does C live?
           B: Somewhere in the South of France.

(from Grice 1989b [1975]: 32)

---

[7] See Ameka and Terkourafi 2019. For general criticism of anglocentrism in theory of meaning, see Wierzbicka 2003 [1991], 2014.

## 7.1 Saying, Implicating, and Inferring

The violation can be explained by a clash with the maxim of Quality if B cannot truthfully provide more detailed information. Note that, in some contexts, the answer can be taken as carrying an implicature that the speaker does not, for some reason or other, want to reveal C's precise location – an interpretation that has led to some substantial rethinking of the understanding of truthfulness vis-à-vis literalness in communication (on which there will be more in Sections 7.1.4 and 8.1).[8]

If a maxim is ostentatiously flouted, the hearer infers that the speaker must have had a reason for not observing it, and this, according to Grice, means that something has been implicated, left 'unsaid'. For example, (7.7) is a tautology and as such a superficially blatantly uninformative sentence, flouting the maxim of Quantity.

(7.7)  A deadline is a deadline.

This leads to implicatures, such as that deadlines are to be taken as strict and non-negotiable or, perhaps, that the addressee should treat the deadline more seriously. We will turn to the degree of context dependence of implicatures in a moment.

While Grice's concept of a principled 'going beyond what is said' may seem fairly uncontroversial, with hindsight it has been generally accepted that there are flaws. For Grice, metaphor and irony are standard examples of flouting of the maxim of Quality. So, it is the obvious literal falsity of (7.8) that leads to implicatures such as (7.9).

(7.8)  Bill has two left hands.

(7.9)  Bill is clumsy.

For Grice, implicatures arise out of the understanding of what is said in the utterance. But he constructs what is said with psychological strings attached to it, namely as *entailing that the speaker means it*. At the same time, Grice admits that in the case of metaphors, the speaker does not 'say' what the expression literally says but rather conveys it 'as if to say'. So, the metaphor arises not out of what is said but, strictly speaking, out of what is made 'as if to say' – the inconsistency later put right by Grice's followers, notably Deirdre Wilson and Dan Sperber, followed by Robyn Carston.[9]

This pattern of conversational inferences works only on the assumption that the interlocutors share some common ground (also called common background knowledge, or mutual assumptions) that allows the speaker to produce utterances with the appropriate level of informativeness and clarity, and the hearer to infer what was intended by the speaker. In other words, the speaker is assumed to tailor the utterances to the addressee's needs and inferential ability so as to ensure that the implicated sense can in fact be recovered. But the distinction between invited implicatures and implicatures arising unintentionally can be very difficult to draw. The speaker does not necessarily have a full picture of what baggage of facts, assumptions, and contextual clues the addressee brings to the situation of discourse and may not target the message

---

[8] See here Wilson and Sperber 2012a [2002].
[9] For their views on literalness, see e.g. Sperber and Wilson 1995 [1986], Chapter 4 (especially the discussion of the diagram in Fig. 3); Wilson and Sperber 2012a [2002] again; and Carston 2002, Chapter 5. Or do so after reading Section 7.1.4 below.

sufficiently precisely. On the other hand, the addressee has no direct access to the speaker's intentions and hence can only *make assumptions* as to what meaning was intended. Many frustrating instances of miscommunication originate from such a misconstrual of speaker intentions and from the attribution of alleged implicatures that the speaker did not intend to communicate. In fact, the concept of 'implicating' is rather counterintuitive in many respects, one of which is its relation to the common concept of *implying something*. So, although, as eminent post-Gricean Laurence Horn reminds us, implicating is what speakers do, while inferring is what addressees do, the delimitation is not a simple matter:

> [T]he assimilation of implicature to inference has been deplored as an instance of the *imply/infer* confusion. But just as the latter turns out to be more complex than meets the eye, so too the subsumption of conversational implicature within the category of speaker meaning is not entirely straightforward. ... we can unintentionally *imply* propositions, whether or not we can unintentionally *implicate* them.[10] (Horn 2012: 86)

We can of course distinguish between implicatures and *putative* or *potential* implicatures, or emphasize the role of intentions in *speaker's implicature* and conventions in *sentence implicature*.[11] But such distinctions in turn affect the unity of the concept of implicature itself.

Another problem with implicature is its demarcation from what is said. This is a question that has permeated pretty much every discussion in this journey so far – it turns up whenever we debate how much content and what kind of content a cognitively real (and at the same time truth-conditional) semantic representation ought to represent. We will return to this question, full steam ahead this time, later in Sections 7.2 and 7.3.

Implicated meanings are weaker than deductive inference such as the inference to the truth of $q$ in (7.10) discussed in Stage 3.

(7.10)  $((p \rightarrow q) \land p) \rightarrow q$

The addressee's inference that leads to an implicature is *cancellable*, as (7.11b) demonstrates.

(7.11a)  Bill finished the essay and went swimming.
 ≫ First, Bill finished the essay and then he went swimming.

(7.11b)  Bill finished the essay and went swimming. But not in this order – I'm just trying to recall everything he did on Friday.

But although potential implicatures are weaker than semantic content and in principle cancellable, they can be entrenched to a variable degree. For example, the implicature in (7.12a) is rather difficult, albeit not impossible, to cancel, as shown in (7.12b).

(7.12a)  The pianist sat down at the instrument and hit the keys in a way resembling Chopin's Nocturne in C minor.
 ≫ The pianist was not particularly accomplished.

---

[10] My emphasis.   [11] See Grice 1989c [1978]; Gazdar 1979; and Davis 1998 respectively.

(7.12b)   After a few bars, I realized it *was* Chopin's Nocturne in C minor, played with unprecedented insight and feeling.

(adapted from Jaszczolt 2019a: 373)

We will return to problems with the criterion of cancellability in Section 7.2.4.

Implicatures also have some other properties. *Calculability* means inferability from the presumption of the rational nature of conversation captured in the Cooperative Principle and its maxims. *Non-conventionality* means that implicated content is *not* part of the meaning that comes from lexical or grammatical conventions such as the meaning of *cat* or *The cat is happy* – meaning that is arbitrary and unpredictable. Next, implicatures arising out of *content maxims* (Quality, Quantity, and Relation) are non-detachable. *Non-detachability* means that the implicatures are equally inferable from synonymous sentences, understood here as linguistic structures that translate into the same logical forms. The reason for the restriction to the above three maxims is easily deducible when one thinks how differently the maxim of Manner operates: synonyms, such as *buy* and *purchase*, can carry nuances of meaning that lead to inferences.[12] Note also that for Grice, the notion of a 'synonym' was dictated by his dedication to truth-conditional semantics: for him, *and* and *but* are synonymous in that they are translated by the same logical connective (conjunction). (More about this idea, which with hindsight clearly looks like a bad idea, in a moment.) On a positive note, what this shows is that we often have to know the semantic representation in order to compute pragmatic inferences.

One important utility of implicatures is that they are a common-sense alternative to pragmatic ambiguity. As was discussed in Section 4.2 in the example of sentential connectives, we don't have to proliferate senses of *and* to account for the temporal and causal meaning (*and then* and *and therefore*). Neither do we have to see inclusive and exclusive readings of *or* as evidence of its lexical-semantic ambiguity. Grice's principle of Modified Occam's Razor discussed there captures the desideratum not to multiply senses unnecessarily; a more adequate explanation of the differences in meanings that these connectives can communicate is a pragmatic explanation. This methodological principle is the foundation stone of many current approaches to discourse meaning where semantic ambiguity is shunned, while the variations in communicated meaning are attributed to modifications of one, *informationally underdetermined* and also, according to some, *semantically underspecified* logical form. But let us not get ahead of ourselves – more on this shortly.

Next, Grice found it important to emphasize the following distinction. Some implicatures arise only in particular contexts and in virtue of these contexts; these are what he called *particularized conversational implicatures* (PCIs). Those that allegedly arise independently of the context of utterance he dubbed *generalized conversational implicatures* (GCIs). For example, the implicature in (7.13) is said to be generalized and to arise in virtue of the general 'mental scale' <*and, or*>.

---

[12] See Grice 1989b [1975], p. 39.

(7.13) You can have chocolate mousse or a piece of fruit.
≫ You can have chocolate mousse or a piece of fruit *but not both*.
(= You can't have chocolate mousse *and* a piece of fruit.)

Another example of a scalar implicature is that arising from the uttered quantifier *some* to the implicated 'not all', as discussed in Section 5.2.2. To reiterate, on this view, scalar predicates are inherently (semantically) lower-bounded (as in 'at least some'), whilst the upper bound ('not all') is implicated and as such cancellable. Such examples show how generalized implicature allows for a classification of utterances according to their strength: when the speaker uses a weaker item on the scale, they allegedly pragmatically imply that the stronger item or items, that is, the items to its left on the scale, do not hold.[13] Number terms also used to be analysed in terms of scales, whereby the 'at least *n*' meaning was considered to be the semantic boundary, while the precisification to 'exactly *n*' was provided by the scale. But, as was extensively argued in Section 5.2.3, there is an increasing consensus (and very good reasons) that the semantics of number terms is in fact precise and punctual, albeit other interpretations, such as 'at least *n*', 'at most *n*', or 'approximately *n*', are available in relevant contexts.[14]

The utility of scales notwithstanding, decades later we have ample evidence against automatic, generalized implicatures. There are contexts in which they appear not only to be automatically cancelled by the addressee but where it is simply not plausible to suggest that they arise in the first place, as (7.14) attempts to demonstrate.

(7.14) Some people say that you are too self-confident.
≫ You have an opinion of being too self-confident.
≫ ?Some but not all people say that you are too self-confident.

A strong version of GCI, proposed by Grice's close follower Stephen Levinson, has been subjected to multiple experimental tests and found wanting. According to Levinson (2000: 1), such implicatures, called by him *presumptive meanings*, 'are carried by the structure of utterances, given the structure of the language, and not by virtue of the particular contexts of utterance'. But we have experimental evidence against their automatic appearance, founded on measurements of the speed of processing, eye tracking, and truth-value judgements.[15,16]

It has to be remembered that scales can also be construed ad hoc, using purpose-selected criteria, such as the degree of seniority, desirability, social status, or some other ranking. For example, in (7.15), speaker B implies that they haven't met the most senior British royal (by saying that they have met one ranked not far off on the seniority list).[17]

---

[13] For discussions of scalars see also Geurts 1998c, 2009, 2010.
[14] See also e. g. Koenig 1993; Geurts 1998a; Bultinck 2005; Jaszczolt 2005; Horn 1992, 2006.
[15] For some examples, see contributions to Noveck and Sperber 2004. See also Noveck 2018 and Cummins and Katsos 2019.
[16] See also Spector and Sudo 2017 on the interaction of scalars with prosody and presuppositions.
[17] For principles of creating *ad hoc* scales see Hirschberg 1991.

(7.15)   A: Have you met the King?
          B: I have met the Prince of Wales.

But such scales are clearly context-driven and as such are a very different, and less contentious, phenomenon.

We should now mention what is perhaps Grice's greatest blunder, namely the concept of a *conventional implicature*. Grice was a dedicated defender of predicate logic as a tool for analysing meaning in natural language. But it could not escape his notice that translation of English sentences into such a metalanguage does not always do them justice. There are words whose lexical content does not appear to be easy to include in the logical form and which does not seem to contribute to the main proposition conveyed by such sentences. Grice's examples are connectives *but* and *therefore* and the verb *manage*. On his proposal, *but* and *therefore* translate as the logical conjunction (so, are 'synonymous' with *and*), while the sense of contrast and causation respectively are only implicated. Likewise, *managing to finish the essay* translates as *finishing the essay*, with the entailed difficulty conveyed via a conventional implicature.

These are not conversational implicatures. They are permanently associated with certain expressions and as such are *non-cancellable, detachable*, and *not calculable* from the maxims. (Notice that they have to be detachable: if *and* and *but* are taken to be both translatable as logical conjunction, then if these implicatures were not detachable, the meaning of contrast would have to arise out of both of them.) Grice called such implicatures 'conventional' in that their meaning is conventional meaning, just like any other meaning derived from lexical and grammatical conventions of a language. But he argued that by using *therefore* the speaker is not committing themselves to the causal link; the link is merely conventionally implicated.[18]

An obvious question arises, if it is lexical meaning, a kind of meaning that is akin to the meaning of, say, *cat* or *sleep*, then why call it a conventional implicature rather than simply lexical meaning? This is precisely because in this way (i) predicate logic can be saved as a tool, and (ii) truth conditions can be saved as a tool for what is considered to be the main communicated content. This resembles the tail wagging the dog: what does not fit is deemed not to be *said*. Quite rightly, conventional implicature pretty much disappeared from the post-Gricean picture, until it was revived in the 2000s by Chris Potts, who approached it with an emphasis on its not-at-issueness or secondary dimension of meaning (introduced in Section 6.3.4). For example, (7.16)–(7.18) are said to have the at-issue content and implicatures stated below.

(7.16)   Alfie is a baby but he is quiet.
          *at-issue content:* Alfie is a baby and he is quiet.
          *conventional implicature to the effect of:* Babies are not usually quiet.

(7.17)   Isak is still swimming.
          *at-issue content:* Isak is swimming.
          *conventional implicature to the effect of:* Isak was swimming earlier.

---

[18] See Grice 1989b [1975], pp. 25–26.

(7.18)   Even Bart passed the test.
*at-issue content:* Bart passed the test.
*conventional implicature to the effect of:* Bart was among the least likely to pass.

By this criterion, coming from information structure, appositives, as in (7.19), are regarded as an example of such conventional implicatures.

(7.19)   Charlie, an infamous axe murderer, is at the door!
*at-issue content:* Charlie is at the door.
*conventional implicature:* Charlie is an infamous axe murderer.

Moreover, as we discussed in Section 6.3.4, what Potts calls expressives, that is words such as *damn* or *bastard*, used as in (7.20), are said by him to behave in a similar manner when they have a secondary, not-at-issue status, in that they are said to contribute only the expressive, as contrasted with the descriptive, component of meaning.

(7.20)   The damn dog is on the couch.
*at-issue content:* The dog is on the couch.

(all examples adapted from Potts 2012: 2516–2517)

However, we will not attempt to separate and identify the expressive content, in agreement with our overall stance in this journey according to which 'all words are words', so to speak. We will assume for now that they always contribute content of some sort, sometimes more, and sometimes less, crucial to the main communicated message. Arguments and a detailed discussion will have to wait for the time in our journey when we tackle pejoratives in more detail, that is until Section 8.4.2.2.

Now, if there is no need to make expressives special, then by analogy there is no need to waste time pondering over the uniqueness of *but*, *therefore*, *still*, or *manage*: they are words like any other and they have descriptive content. On the other hand, one can try to defend the concept of conventional implicature by demonstrating that generalized quantity implicatures and conventional implicatures have a lot in common in spite of their superficially opposite characteristics, in that they both exhibit degrees of conventionality of meaning. As Davis (1998: 157) says,

[t]he difference between 'conventional' and 'conversational' implicatures at the level of sentences lies in the *nature* of the conventions involved. Both are semantic conventions, but only the former are first-order conventions. The contrastive implication is part of the meaning of *but*. The nonuniversal implication is no part of the meaning of *some*.

On this reasoning, conventional implicatures as well as generalized conversational implicatures are both conventional meanings. This outlook is part of a broader criticism that Davis launches against Grice's theory of implicature, arguing that 'the conversational principles have insufficient power to enable rigorous derivation of specific implicatures' and 'any principle-based theory like Grice's understates both the intentionality of speaker implicature and the conventionality of sentence implicature' (p. 2). As he adds later, conventions and situation-driven inferences are not very distinct in that

> [c]onversational implicatures are rarely if ever calculable. Speakers can properly make their implicatures available by following established practices, whether they be general conventions or personal habits. (Davis 2007: 1671)

All in all, there is a case for redrawing the boundary to foreground the distinction between (i) what springs out of the sentence and various associated conventions and (ii) what lurks under the surface and waits for the speaker's intentions to be recognized to bring it to the surface.

The term 'convention' subsumes many things, from lexical meaning at one end, to mere precedents on the other, as explained in the next section. So, to pursue this argument further, we may as well 'go the whole hog' and subsume all conventional content under one label. In fact, the claim that generalized quantity implicatures are part of the semantics of scalar words is well supported. Allan (2000: 212) suggests the following move:

> semantic specification in the lexicon should incorporate defeasible default (probable) meaning of a lexicon item together with the logically necessary components of lexical meaning. The defeasible default meaning is a conversational implicature.... Despite the fact that conversational implicatures are pragmatic entities, generalised quantity implicatures ... are readily included in a lexicon entry.

But bearing in mind the arguments against the existence of any such context-free, automatic implicatures, as a separate category from particularized ones, this inclusion in the semantics would, arguably, have to stretch to the entire category of conversational implicatures. After all, as the next section makes clear, conventionality comes in various types and strengths and it is difficult to pinpoint a non-arbitrary boundary. Such a stretch is indeed possible, but only when we adopt a fluid concept of word meaning – the question discussed at the beginning of our journey in Stage 2.

## 7.1.3 Intentions and Conventions

For Grice, all acts of communicating meaning can be accounted for by the same theory, mostly appealing to intentions as an explanans. Conventions are not afforded a prominent place. But they are at least equally important. First, conventionalized utterances, such as bidding in a game of bridge (say, *three no trump*), give the players a 'shortcut', so to speak, in that a process of intention recognition needn't take place. The only intentions that have to be recognized are those pertaining to how the bridge partner is supposed to react – and even those are conventionalized to a certain degree in that the bid tends to be understood as a hint about how to follow up. So, conventions alone may automatically secure the uptake of the intention.[19]

---

[19] On intentions and conventions, especially with reference to Speech Act Theory discussed in Section 8.3, see Strawson 1964. On conventions in non-Gricean approaches, see e.g. Lewis 2002 [1969], 1991 [1979]; Lepore and Stone 2015; Geurts 2018.

Conventions tend to be relied upon to a much greater degree in non-Gricean theories, such as those in computational linguistics that focus on predictability for the purpose of machine learning. For example, SDRT,[20] discussed in Section 6.1.2.1, and theories of information structure discussed in Section 6.3.1, appeal to conventional rules of discourse coherence. In David Lewis's game theory[21] and its offshoots, for example Prashant Parikh's Equilibrium Semantics,[22] conversational interaction is conceptualized as a language game in which the players attempt to reach an equilibrium, accommodating each other's moves wherever the common ground requires recalibration of previous assumptions. As Lewis (1991: 420) puts it, 'conversational score does tend to evolve in such a way as is required in order to make whatever occurs count as correct play'. But the correct balance between intention- and convention-based explanations has not been achieved in either camp: while Gricean and post-Gricean accounts fall short of scrutinizing the types and roles of conventions, alternative, non-Gricean accounts often overplay conventions. The search for rules for cross-sentential pronominal anaphora resolution in theories of information structure discussed in Section 6.3.1 serves as a good example.

We have regularly appealed to conventions in this journey, mostly sociocultural but also linguistic. But it is important to note that conventions are not merely 'shortcuts through intentions' as an intentionalist stance would prefer to conceptualize them. They are much more. First, there are different types of them. As Geurts (2018: 115) states in the summary of his paper 'Convention and common ground',

[c]onventions are regularities in social behaviour of the past that enable us to coordinate our actions. Some conventions are lawlike: they are expected to be observed always or nearly always. However, in order to coordinate our actions, it may suffice that a precedent has occurred often enough, and sometimes even a single precedent will do. So, in general, conventions merely enable us to solve our coordination problems; lawlike conventions are a special case. Grammatical conventions are often lawlike; sense conventions are typically enabling.

So, 'three no trump' exploits a lawlike convention – both in virtue of the meaning of the words and in virtue of what they stand for in the game of bridge. But how to act on this bid is at most an enabling convention: a beginner at bridge can play (albeit to the frustration of the other players) without invoking such enabling conventions. These conventions are not shortcuts; they are the foundation of mutual understanding in communication, and as such the foundation of meaning.[23] As Geurts continues (*ibid.*),

In order to resolve the indeterminacies that sense conventions give rise to, interlocutors must rely on the common ground. In this and other ways, common ground is a prerequisite for convention-based communication.

The downplaying of conventions in Grice's account of meaning$_{NN}$ has important repercussions for the scope of applicability of Grice's intentional stance, in that non-

---

[20] See e.g. Asher and Lascarides 2003.  [21] See e.g. Lewis 1991.  [22] See Parikh 2010.
[23] See also Bach 1995 on standardization vs. conventionalization.

cooperative conversation is not easy to accommodate. And yet such conversations are not uncommon, to mention only bartering for the price of goods or a defendant's evasive answers in a courtroom trial. The latter is exemplified in (7.21).

(7.21)  Prosecutor: Do you have any bank accounts in Swiss banks, Mr. Bronston?
Bronston: No, sir.
Prosecutor: Have you ever?
Bronston: The company had an account there for about six months, in Zurich.
(adapted from Asher and Lascarides 2013: 2, after Solan and Tiersma)

Even though Bronston's responses are both true, the latter one is clearly aimed at avoiding a direct answer. As such, it is misleading in that the defendant neither admits guilt nor denies it. Whether the assumption of cooperation is applicable there is a moot point: on one hand, one can argue that the defendant produces such an answer because he hopes for the Cooperative Principle to kick in and produce an implicature that, if said, would definitely be a lie (namely, 'I have not.'). On the other, one can argue, like Asher and Lascarides do, that public and private commitments have to be kept apart in a theory of communication: when there is no actual cooperation, that is, no private commitment to cooperation, the theory of communication must flag it. That is why they introduce a notion of *rhetorical cooperativity*:

Rhetorical cooperativity makes a speaker appear to be Gricean cooperative although he may not actually be so. This is a frequent feature of strategic conversations, in which agents' interests do not align. (Asher and Lascarides 2013: 3)

Non-cooperative contexts give ammunition to game theorists and coherence-based accounts (and the overlap thereof) in that they can spread their wings much more widely over different types of human communicative behaviour. But they also give ammunition to post-Gricean accounts such as Relevance Theory to rethink truthfulness but retain intentions as explanantia. More on this in what follows.

## 7.1.4 Post-Gricean Principles and Heuristics

The perspective of decades of post-Gricean developments makes it easy to be critical. It has been pointed out that the maxims display a substantial overlap and, as such, redundancy. They were devised by a philosopher of language in order to generalize over patterns of rational behaviour, so they are of limited utility to those who seek an insight into the psychology of human communication and cognition. Further, the maxims are naturally prone to further extensions to include more sociopragmatic aspects of rational interaction, such as principles of politeness, tact, or witty, humorous behaviour.[24] Next, Grice's account of meaning was focused on the speaker and on intentions rather than on the addressee's inferences (that is, the *recovery* of intentions)

---

[24] Leech 1983 offers an early attempt to supplement Grice's maxims with maxims of politeness; see also Brown and Levinson 1987 for a Gricean model of politeness as a strategy and an implicature. I attend to these sociopragmatic aspects of communication in Section 8.4.2.1.

and as such it engendered strong criticism in that it does not cater for misunderstandings of intentions or for cases where meaning does not go through at all. The problem is that Grice's theory concerns not intersubjective meaning but rather what the speaker meant – a speaker understood as a model speaker whose rational communicative behaviour can be captured by the principle of cooperation. Alternative options would be (i) to take on board the addressee's recovered meaning, as in Sperber and Wilson's Relevance Theory discussed in Section 7.2.2,[25] or perhaps (ii) to foreground the assumption that interlocutors have collective, or conjoint, intentions and they co-construct meaning collectively. The latter is offered in various proposals, including game theory, Arundale's Conjoint Co-constituting Model of Communication that emphasizes the interactive construction of implicatures,[26] or Elder and Haugh's model of meaning as an interactional achievement – all discussed in Section 8.4.1.[27] Another option is (iii) to turn non-Gricean and invoke the game theory just discussed. The important question 'Whose meaning?' is by no means settled – perhaps it will always be left up for grabs, depending on what a theory of discourse meaning aims to achieve: to theorize about intended content, jointly constructed content, or the content that the utterances lead to in the addressees' or hearers' minds.[28] This calls for an observation that the spirit of the ground-breaking orientation of dynamic semantics discussed in Section 6.1 now reappears in various effectively *dynamic pragmatic* solutions!

It also calls for an observation that what counts as *communication* is still far from settled: if the addressee 'recovers' some content that is not intended by the speaker, has this content been 'communicated'? And, if it happens to be unintentionally offensive, is the speaker to be accountable? In the current journey we focus on meanings that are intended and recovered, and we define communication as such a transfer of meaning that is recovered – through conventional means or through the recovery of speaker intentions – at least to a degree that is required to keep conversation on track and free of misunderstandings. But in current pragmatic research, the questions of commitment to certain content, accountability, liability, and the normative expectations that assertions give rise to are increasingly brought to the fore, spanning pragmatics (and within it sociopragmatics), semantics, philosophy of language, and ethics. These questions require ways of journeying through meaning that are somewhat different in their goals and even desiderata from the ones we have encountered so far. They raise some important concerns, for language, communication, and society. I give a nod in their direction in Section 8.4.

Now, there are two main directions in post-Gricean debates. One concerns the adequate number and scope of maxims of conversation, subsequently reconceptualized

---

[25] See Sperber and Wilson 1995 [1986].
[26] See e.g. Arundale 1999, 2010. For implementations see also Haugh 2007, 2008, 2009; Haugh and Jaszczolt 2012.
[27] See Elder and Haugh 2018. See also Geurts' (2019) proposal of communication as sharing and negotiating commitments. For a comparison of inference-based, commitment-based and interactional accounts see Elder 2021.
[28] See e.g. the discussions in Jaszczolt 2016 and 2021a.

as principles or heuristics. This is what we will attend to in this section. The other direction concerns the boundary between truth-conditional and non-truth-conditional content, and, relatedly, also between semantics and pragmatics. This is what we called, after Laurence Horn, 'the border wars'.[29] (As we will see, these two debates can come apart.) This other direction will be attended to in Sections 7.2–7.3.

There is no doubt that Grice's maxims – or 'super-maxims' when we account for the way they were analysed in terms of more detailed 'sub-maxims' – suffer from redundancy and overlap. It is often difficult to tell whether to attribute an implicature to, say, the sub-maxim of Quality, according to which speakers do not reveal superfluous information without reason, or the maxim of Relation that concerns being relevant as an aspect of rational communicative behaviour. As a result, they have limited predictive power. The assumption is that the set of maxims ought to ensure implicature calculability, as explicitly demanded in the property of calculability of conversational implicatures. In fact, Wayne Davis, whose criticism of Grice's approach we discussed in the previous section, goes as far as saying that 'the theory generates erroneous predictions as readily as it generates correct ones' (Davis 1998: 2) and that '[c]onversational implicatures are rarely if ever calculable. Speakers can properly make their implicatures available by following established practices, whether they be general conventions or personal habits' (Davis 2007: 1671). Food for thought.

But let us discuss improvements. Some stay close to the Gricean spirit. In the 1980s, Laurence Horn reduced the maxims to two principles: maximization of informational content (Q-principle) and minimization of form (R-principle)[30]. The Q- and R-principles work in tandem, acting as their mutual constraints: 'Make your contribution sufficient; say as much as you can (given $R$)' and 'Make your contribution necessary; say no more than you must (given $Q$)'. (Remember that the imperative mood does not signal a prescriptive rule here.) Horn also carefully works out the mapping onto Grice's original sub-maxims. The principle of truthfulness (Quality) is assumed as well, but does not operate on the same level; it is an overarching, higher-order characteristic of rational communication.

Next, Stephen Levinson's proposal reworks the maxims into heuristics and fixes the overlap in a rather similar way. Again, Quality is assumed, while other components of conversational rationality are captured by three heuristics: 'What isn't said isn't' (Q-heuristic); 'What is expressed simply is stereotypically exemplified' (I-heuristic); and 'What's said in an abnormal way isn't normal' (M-heuristic).[31] Levinson justifies the need for the latter heuristic by the need to distinguish between the *minimization of content* and the *minimization of form*: it is one thing not to provide too much information, and another to use appropriately simple, short, and widely familiar expressions rather than long and obscure ones.

The proposal also includes the order of preference in which the heuristics are implemented in the process of utterance interpretation, inspired by Gerald Gazdar's[32] broader picture of the order in which information is added to the content

---

[29] See Horn 2006. [30] See Horn 1984, p. 13; also Horn 1988, p. 132 and Horn 2004.
[31] See Levinson 2000, pp. 35–38; also Levinson 1987, 1995. [32] See Gazdar 1979, pp. 132–135.

of the sentence. First come background assumptions from general knowledge; next, semantic entailments, followed by what Gazdar calls potential conversational implicatures (clausal first, such as that in (7.22), and scalar next); and finally, potential presuppositions – 'potential' in that while the utterance suggests such an inference, they may disappear in this overall picture of adding pragmatic information.

(7.22)   Bill *believes* that Arsenal won the League.
   ≫ Bill doesn't *know* that (= is not certain whether) Arsenal won the League.

Every added piece of information has to be consistent with those already incremented. Levinson expands on this proposal with respect to potential implicatures and proposes that they are added in the following order: potential Q-implicatures, first clausal, then scalar; potential M-implicatures; and potential I-implicatures. This ordering of adding information explains why some potential implicatures or presuppositions do not arise: when added to what has already been incremented, they would render an inconsistent piece of information.

So, the order of preference explains what happens when there is a clash between potentially employing more than one heuristic, as in example (7.23).

(7.23)   Bill caused his hamster to die.

In agreement with the preference order Q > M > I, here the M-heuristic overrides the I-heuristic: while we might infer from the I-heuristic that the speaker simply did not need to be more specific, the M-heuristic leads to the inference that the unusual way of expression ('cause to die' instead of 'kill') results in the implicature that Bill did not directly or intentionally kill his pet hamster but, perhaps, neglected it in some way that led to its death, such as forgetting to feed it.

Levinson employs his heuristics in what he calls a theory of GCI in that the heuristics supposedly give rise to default interpretations. These are, to reiterate, presumptive meanings, that is meanings that are strongly associated with certain words and complex expressions but that can be cancelled when the context so dictates. Scalar implicatures from *some* to 'not all' are captured by the Q-heuristic, while an implicature in (7.24) by the I-heuristic.

(7.24)   William and Kate celebrated Charlotte's sixth birthday.
   ≫ William and Kate celebrated Charlotte's sixth birthday *together*.

This rekindled the discussions concerning the justification for such generalized, context-free implicatures that we mentioned in Section 7.1.2, with overwhelming evidence and argumentation against such strong and readily cancellable defaults – albeit not against *context-dependent but automatic* rather than effortful, conscious inference-driven interpretations. (It is important to stress this difference before we move to context-driven default interpretations in Section 7.2.3.) It rekindled the debate between Levinson-type *defaultism* and its opposite, namely the proposal, now very well experimentally supported, that meaning arises in a contextually grounded, 'one-off' process of interpretation (sometimes referred to in the discussions of scalar implicature as *noncism*).

It is also rather difficult to see in his proposal how semantics and pragmatics are kept apart: 'semantic and pragmatic processes can interleave, in ways that are probably controlled by the constructional types in the semantic representation' (Levinson 2000: 168). Demonstrating that this is indeed so is not possible when we talk about the entire category of GCIs triggered by his Q-, I-, and M-heuristics discussed in Section 7.1.4, in that so much is attributed to these heuristics in discourse interpretation. And yet, Levinson's proposal contains an attempt to keep semantics and pragmatics clearly distinguished. He considers his GCIs to be strongly entrenched – almost as strongly as encoded meanings, save for their cancellability when context so dictates. To reiterate,

Utterance-type meanings are matters of preferred interpretations ... which are carried by the structure of utterances, *given* the structure of the language, and not by virtue of the particular contexts of utterance. (Levinson 2000: 1)

They constitute a *middle level* between semantics and pragmatics:

This third layer is a level of systematic pragmatic inference based *not* on direct computations about speaker-intentions, but rather on *general expectations about how language is normally used*. These expectations give rise to presumptions, default inferences, about both content and force; and it is at this level (if at all) that we can sensibly talk about *speech acts, presuppositions, felicity conditions, conversational pre-sequences, preference organisation* and, of especial concern to us, *generalised conversational implicatures*. (Levinson 1995: 93)

At the same time, as he says, GCIs feel more 'semanticky' than 'pragmaticky' – grouped with such strong, language-system-driven meanings:

it is the default nature of GCIs that causes them to be deeply entangled in grammar and semantics – they are both hard to distinguish from encoded content, and they exert functional pressure on syntax, lexicon, and semantics. (Levinson 2000: 169)[33]

As such, GCIs contribute to the truth-conditional content – as was said earlier, they contribute 'locally' and can be cancelled at any future point of utterance or discourse interpretation. But as we mentioned above, there is ample evidence by now that cancellability does not quite work that way. Moreover, consideration of the economy of processing alone suggests that it is less advantageous to propose strong, system-based presumptions that have to be cancelled than to propose that modifications of meaning take place when they ought to (and don't take place when they are not needed). Then, 'cancellation' only takes place when it is like a *repair strategy* that smooths things over when the interlocutors' assumptions or common ground are misaligned and there is a risk of miscommunication. But repair is not a cancellation of a GCI. We return to cancellation in Section 7.2.4, and to more fully fledged accounts of the semantics/pragmatics boundary in Sections 7.2 and 7.3.

Looked at from the historical perspective, Grice's foregrounding of context-free implicatures and paying relatively little attention to PCIs rekindled an interest in conventions. Presumptive meanings are only one example but there are many others. Delving into the maxim of Manner and orderliness of discourse,

---

[33] See there for examples of 'functional pressure'.

Horn[34] discloses various conventional patterns in coordination. Default Semantics (discussed in Section 7.2.3) appeals to sociocultural conventions that trigger automatic interpretations. We will be returning to intention recognition vis-à-vis automatic interpretation shortly.

There is another debate that Levinson's theory helped rekindle, namely a debate between those who, like Grice, view implicature as calculated on the basis of the entire sentence, that is *post-propositionally* (this view is also called *globalism*), and those who, like Levinson, propose that implicatures arise 'locally', as the incremental processing of the utterance progresses. Empirical evidence and theoretical arguments have been wheeled in on both sides and the debate continues.[35] It is likely that the question might be impossible to settle without extensive experimental evidence about processing, in that the unit on which inference is based varies from context to context: sometimes an entire phrase or clause is understood as a primitive unit, while at other times its components may give rise to implicatures on their own. *Somewhere over the rainbow* (≫ 'Far away, in an imaginary land') is unlikely to be processed in the same way as *Seeds have germinated in some places* (≫ 'some but not other places'). This flexibility of inferential bases gives rise to what I called elsewhere *fluid characters*: Kaplanian characters, that is linguistic meanings, that pertain to larger, or smaller, units, as the particular circumstances of discourse dictate.[36] *Somewhere over the rainbow* is likely to be just one, single, character – fluid because if the addressee is not familiar with the song, they have to resort to a compositional analysis in terms of word-based characters.

Now, post-Gricean accounts differ in the degree to which they adhere to Grice's original four-maxim (or nine-maxim if we include the sub-maxims) proposal. But that does not make their adequacy directly comparable; this is so because they also differ in the degree to which they strive for psychological reality. While the so-called *neo-Gricean* approaches, namely those by Horn and Levinson just discussed, remain close to Grice's original set-up, but at the same time remain close to the original desideratum of capturing rationality of communication, Dan Sperber and Deirdre Wilson, in their Relevance Theory, go much further into the psychology of processing. They propose one principle of relevance that appeals to the balance between what they call *cognitive effects* and *processing effort* in production and recovery of meaning.[37] The effort invested by the addressee in the processing of an utterance is offset by the revisions of, and additions to, the addressee's information state. Relevance is approached from the perspective of communication as well as cognition. The communicative principle of relevance says that '[e]very act of ostensive communication communicates a presumption of its own optimal relevance' (Sperber and Wilson 1995 [1986]: 158), where 'ostensive communication' means intentional communicative behaviour that 'makes manifest an intention to make something manifest' to the addressee (p. 49). In a later edition, this communicative principle is supplemented with its cognitive

---

[34] See Horn 2019.   [35] See e.g. Geurts 2009, 2010.   [36] See Jaszczolt 2012c.
[37] See Sperber and Wilson 1995 [1986] and e.g. articles in Wilson and Sperber 2012b. For an in-depth introduction to the theory see Clark 2013.

counterpart, which states that '[h]uman cognition tends to be geared to the maximisation of relevance' (Sperber and Wilson 1995 [1986]: 260). The principles operate without exceptions, in the sense that they are general presumptions about human ostensive communication and cognition. This amounts to purporting that the addressee stops interpreting the utterance once an interpretation has been reached that is tacitly assumed to fulfil the criteria stated in these principles. In short, by focusing on the *process* of utterance interpretation, Relevance Theory focuses on the psychology of human communication and cognition. Relevance-driven utterance interpretation is presented as a human evolutionary adaptation and a sub-module of mindreading.[38]

As a result, a comparison between neo-Gricean approaches and Relevance Theory is not straightforward in that they differ somewhat in their respective objectives, emphases, and motivations. As we will see in the next section, they also differ in how faithful they are to Grice's original delimitation of the concept of an implicature, which has repercussions for the stances they take on the semantics/pragmatics boundary. Discussions that overplay these differences tend even to reserve the term 'post-Gricean' for Relevance Theory in order to contrast it with the more 'faithful' 'neo-Gricean' approaches by Horn and Levinson. But this non-standard use of the label 'post-Gricean' is problematic, in that there are many theorists of meaning who consider themselves to be post-Griceans and for whom the term defines the broad orientation that the meaning of the prefix 'post-' suggests: those who adopt the Gricean general assumptions that intentions and inferences ought to be employed as explanantia for meaning in communication. Neo-Griceans, Relevance Theory, as well as Truth-Conditional Pragmatics and Default Semantics discussed in the next section are all post-Gricean in these essential respects. This is not the place to go into a metatheoretic discussion on what counts as criteria for belonging to the 'Gricean camp', so these essential characteristics will suffice for now.[39]

A comparison is also difficult because of different stances on the 'Whose meaning?' question that we have been returning to throughout this part of the journey. While Grice's adopted perspective was that of speaker meaning, Relevance theorists focus on the interpretation of utterances, i.e. on the meaning recovered by the addressee, or, generally, a hearer. So, the explanatory role of intentions is somewhat different on these two accounts. They stress the importance of appealing to speakers' intentions, categorizing them as communicative intentions, and, embedded in them, informative intentions,[40] but in their theory they discuss them from the perspective of their recovery by the addressee. It is the addressee who recovers what is communicated by making informed assumptions about the speaker's intentions. This perspective on the 'Whose meaning?' question is one of the aspects that contributes to the differences in the stance on psychological reality between Grice, neo-Griceans, and Relevance theorists. And, sadly, also to talking at cross-purposes![41]

---

[38] On mindreading, see especially Sperber and Wilson 2012 [2002].
[39] For a discussion of 'being Gricean' in the twenty-first century, see Jaszczolt 2019b.
[40] See Sperber and Wilson 1995 [1986], Sections 1.9–1.12.
[41] On the Gricean programme vis-à-vis Relevance theory, see especially Saul 2002.

It is important to stress that what neo-Griceans lose in proposing distinct principles that are unlikely to find equivalents in the architecture and processes of the human brain, they gain in predictive power and formalizability. Neo-Griceans' modelling rational conversational behaviour produced concrete principles that powered computational modelling of discourse. A good example here is Optimality Theory Pragmatics developed, among others, by Reinhard Blutner and Henk Zeevat, with constraints on interpretation that are modelled on Levinson's heuristics.[42]

To sum up, these differences come with different drawbacks. While neo-Gricean principles and heuristics remain the theoretician's generalization, they are more easily implemented as constraints in computational linguistics and make for a more precise (and as such, falsifiable) theory. On the other hand, while the two principles of relevance answer many questions posed by cognitive scientists and psycholinguists, they do not amount to an equally rigid, falsifiable, and formalizable theory that would generate precise predictions and feed algorithms. Here we appeal to the well-acknowledged proposal from the methodology of science according to which a good theory is not a theory that is proven right, or *verified*, but a theory about which it is clear what it would take to show that it is wrong, or to *falsify* it.[43]

But the falsifiability of the principles of relevance is a different issue from the falsifiability of the predictions these principles make. On the latter, the theory of Relevance has the upper hand in that, to reiterate, the analysed meaning is the meaning recovered by the hearer, and as such it 'must be correct', so to speak: the principle of relevance has to apply. So, arguably, falsifiability either does not apply to such principles at all, or it would have to apply to what is 'hidden underneath' – some putative algorithms that guide communication and cognition, if such could be found in principle. In this journey we hope they will be found, perhaps somewhere at the crossroads of philosophical semantics and pragmatics with neurolinguistics and computational linguistics. But now we speculate. And also anticipate; there will be more about such regularities and predictions when we move to other approaches later in this section. Suffice it to say that ample empirical evidence has been accumulated against cancellable defaults associated with words and structures – that is, against Levinson's presumptive meanings. The latter are also easy to question through theoretical argumentation in that the onus of proof is always on those who assume costly processing, such as cancellations of previous interpretations, when a simpler and equally explanatory model of processing is available.

Another take-home message from this comparison is that there may sometimes be good reasons why psychologism is not a welcome characteristic of a theory of meaning. Just as we saw in the previous stages of this journey that striving for cognitive reality hasn't traditionally been an objective of formal theories of meaning, so do we see it in Grice and in neo-Griceans. In formal semantics, this was so because semanticists attempted to give a precise, formal account of how the language system works in producing sentence meanings rather than an account of how the human mind works in composing them. Here the reasons are analogous, but kicked up to the level of

---

[42] See Blutner and Zeevat 2004. [43] See Popper 1959 [1934].

communication: a search for principles, regularities that would capture the rationality of communication but with different views on how psychologically real such principles ought to be. Grice's and neo-Gricean principles are not aiming at cognitive reality: no one claims that they are woven into the architecture of the brain in this exact form or that we use them consciously. But they provide foundations for formal modelling of discourse. On the other hand, Relevance Theory is driven by the desideratum to deliver a cognitively real account.

Psychologism requires a bit more attention as the term still often comes with negative connotations in some, especially formal, linguistic circles.[44] These date back to the late nineteenth century and are the legacy of Gottlob Frege,[45] who advocated banning subjective thoughts from logic and mathematics. The function/argument analysis, where reference of a predicate is a function from objects to truth values, familiar from the introduction to formal semantics in Stages 3–5, was inherited by linguists from Frege's new, subjectivism-free conception of logic. As Frege says, '[t]here must be a sharp separation of the psychological from the logical, the subjective from the objective' (Frege 1997c [1884]: 90). He points out that '*being true* is quite different from *being held as true*' and as such refers to a 'corrupting intrusion' of psychology into logic (Frege 1997d [1893]: 202). So, a ban on psychologism has a long tradition and its repeated revivals are the result of fluctuating objectives: conceptualizing a theory of meaning more like the natural sciences that study objects in themselves, rather than people's views or experiences of them, or more like social and cognitive sciences with human social and cognitive behaviour at their centre.

To sum up, we have to distinguish theories that aim at formal representations of utterance meaning and maximizing the predictive power from those that focus on discourse interactants and utterance processing. For example, discussions about the order in which said and implicated components of meaning are processed,[46] or the extent to which communication relies on inference,[47] or the local vis-à-vis global (post-propositional) processing of implicatures just discussed, properly belong with the latter. But at the same time, all post-Griceans study cooperative language use, making use of intentions and inferences, and as such cannot avoid some dose of psychologism, no matter where the precise emphasis of the theory lies.[48]

Differences aside, all post-Gricean revisions are deep down conceptually alike in that they stress the balancing forces of sufficient informativeness on the one hand, and optimal formulation of the message on the other, where what can be relied on as inferable can be left unsaid. As such, comparing and contrasting the views looks relatively unexciting. But the views are important in their own right in that, arguably, they improve on Grice's programme, taking it in two different directions. Comparisons, so common in the post-Gricean literature, only reveal the mistake of

---

[44] See Travis 2006 for a discussion. [45] See e.g. Frege 1997b [1879]. [46] See e.g. Carston 2007.
[47] See e.g. Recanati 2016.
[48] For a defence of psychologism in natural-language semantics and pragmatics, see also Jaszczolt 2008.

## 7.2 Truth-Conditional vs. Non-Truth-Conditional, Semantic vs. Pragmatic: What to Include and What to Leave Out

### 7.2.1 The Point of Departure

Post-Gricean debates concerning the scope of truth-conditional vis-à-vis non-truth-conditional content and, often relatedly, the scope of semantic vis-à-vis pragmatic content will evidence some fundamentally different views not only on which components are decoded, or more broadly automatically retrieved, and which inferred, but also on the relative scopes of what is said and what is implicated. The semantics/pragmatics boundary will not preoccupy us very much in virtue of the overall direction adopted on this journey that the truth-conditional, and as such for us *semantic* as well as *cognitively accurate* representation, has to pertain to the main intended and recovered message. This message pertains to what we called a functional proposition (introduced in Section 1.3). But semantics/pragmatics boundary disputes deserve attention in their own right. The starting point for this part of the journey will have to be a clear understanding of Grice's stance on meaning$_{NN}$, that is what is meant and communicated. To sum up, for Grice, the total communicated message is composed of what is said and what is implicated – a distinction that has since undergone many different transformations. What is implicated, in turn, subsumes what is implicated conventionally and what is implicated non-conventionally. Next, non-conventional implicatures can be conversational or non-conversational, where the latter are not attributable to the maxims of conversation. (We won't have much to say on the latter in this journey.) Finally, Grice's conversational implicatures can be generalized and particularized – again, a distinction that has suffered very strong blows. This classification is summarized in Figure 7.1.

In spite of Grice's attempted separation of the truth-conditional and non-truth-conditional content evident in the diagram, it doesn't take long to notice that such a

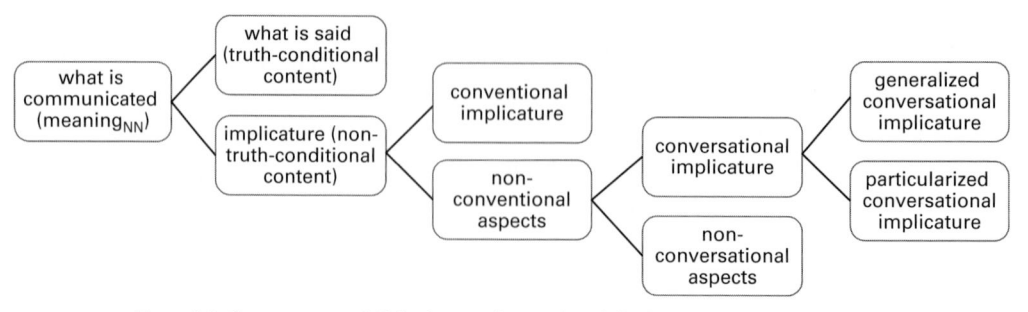

**Figure 7.1** Components of Grice's meaning$_{NN}$ (modelled on Horn 1988: 121)

strict demarcation is problematic. After all, his conventional implicatures are word meanings and his generalized conversational implicatures are context-free meanings, so there is no independent reason (that is, no extra-theoretic reason, a reason that is not to do with goals such as saving the metalanguage of predicate logic) to subsume all such aspects of meaning under non-truth-conditional content, leaving what is said undifferentiated. Here we can follow the post-Griceans instead and adopt some other specific theoretical assumptions as to how much of what is not easily translated into the adopted formal metalanguage, and how much of what is not explicitly uttered but 'lurking beneath', we want to include in the category of truth-conditional content. We can thereby make 'what is said' more inclusive, to allow for cases where what is not *uttered* is nevertheless still *said* and as such carries with it the speaker's commitment and accountability. If we were to pinpoint which categories in this classification belong to semantics and which to pragmatics, we would end up with some problematic ones and a fuzzy boundary. We would have to adopt a theoretic stance somewhere on the spectrum from semantic minimalism at one end and radical contextualism at the other. But even this choice is not a simple unidimensional spectrum: the principles on which the selection is made come with different dimensions which sometimes necessitate substantial departures from Grice's distinctions, if not abandoning them altogether. The plot thickens.

We can now return to the discussion of the scope of truth-conditional content that we encountered in Section 4.5.3 when presenting the properties of English negation vis-à-vis the question of semantic ambiguity vs. underspecification. It was said there that research on negation and presupposition in the 1970s resulted in the proposal of the semantic underdetermination of negation. It was also called *sense-generality* or *radical pragmatics* among other labels,[49] and was developed by Jay Atlas and Ruth Kempson – hence the so-called Atlas-Kempson thesis.[50] The idea is this. Due to an ambiguity where one logical form is more general, and as such is entailed by the other, the semantic representation of negation is deemed to be underdetermined. Further precisification is obtained through processing of the sentence in context, like in the oft-quoted 'king of France' example (4.75) repeated below, where the logical form with the wide-scope negation (standing for the non-presupposing reading) is entailed in that with narrow-scope negation (the more specific one, standing for the presupposing reading).

(4.75) The king of France is not bald.

Semantic ambiguity was already proscribed by Grice's Modified Occam's Razor (discussed in Section 7.1.2). Grice remarked on the need for pragmatic 'finishing touches' to the semantic representation before truth conditions can be assigned – this is necessary in the case of indexical expressions and lexical and syntactic ambiguity. But negation proved to be another example of this need for the 'interference' of pragmatics

---

[49] See Zwicky and Sadock 1975; Jaszczolt 2019a [2012], 2023. For radical pragmatics, see Cole 1981.
[50] See Atlas 1977, 1979, 1989, 2005, 2006, 2012; Kempson 1975, 1979, 1986; Wilson 1975 – and the discussion of negation in Section 4.5.3.

and it opened the floodgates to other cases of semantic underdetermination. In other words, semantics takes us part of the way, and pragmatics completes the representation. Underdetermined 'what is said' invites inferences to what 'lurks under the surface'. Or, recalling once again Atlas's pastiche of Kant, 'Pragmatic inference without sense-generality is blind, but sense-generality without pragmatic inference is empty' (Atlas 1989: 124). In what follows we will follow the custom of using the term 'underdetermination' to describe the property of semantic content, and 'underspecification' as a property of the logical form arrived at through the translation of the sentence into the metalanguage of predicate logic (although there is no consistency of use of the terms in the literature).

It is worth remembering that semantic underdetermination was a reaction to the tendency in the 1960s and 1970s to explain pragmatic phenomena by subsuming them under syntax, most notably in the orientation called generative semantics. But new trends successfully turned the tide towards pragmatic explanations of what is, incontrovertibly, pragmatic. Here we have to mention, on the one hand, ordinary language philosophy, with philosophers such as John L. Austin, Peter F. Strawson, and Ludwig Wittgenstein in his later phase (discussed in Section 8.3), and on the other, the already discussed H. Paul Grice, followed by Gerald Gazdar, Jay Atlas, Ruth Kempson, and Deirdre Wilson, among others. Attempts to explicate pragmatic information by means of syntactic theory do resurface from time to time in generative syntax but with relatively little impact or little independent justification. What matters more is what users do with language, not what the language system can be construed as capable of if we tweak the explanation of it and endow it with supernatural powers. On the other hand, for its critics, radical pragmatics does the opposite, endowing *pragmatics* with too much explanatory power in that 'the radical pragmatist would be like an anatomist who, realizing that birds fly, loses all interest in the structure of their wings' (Sadock 1984: 142). Food for thought.

## 7.2.2 Making Truth Conditions Intuitive: Relevance Theory and Truth-Conditional Pragmatics

Semantic underdetermination was an important landmark in the analysis of meaning. It is also a step that takes us closer to the cognitively real, truth-conditional theory of meaning we are journeying towards in this book. Truth conditions can now be predicated of *utterances* (or even *thoughts*) rather than of *sentences*. The boundary between semantics and pragmatics has shifted in the direction of the pragmatic end of what we have already conceptualized as a spectrum of possibilities. If pragmatic contributions to the truth-conditional content need not be syntactically triggered, then we are free to identify various kinds of phenomena and circumstances that give rise to them, as long as we know at what point addressees (and other hearers) put a stop to such inferencing. In processing, the stop can be provided by the principle of relevance. This is what was proposed by Sperber and Wilson and subsequently developed by Robyn Carston.[51] For

---

[51] See e.g. Carston 1988, 1998c, 2002.

example, the temporal reading of the connective *and*, as in (7.25), is such a pragmatic addition to the semantic content.

(7.25)   Bill opened the door and saw that the room was full of people.

Other sentential connectives, notably disjunction *or*, implication *if ... then*, as well as the already mentioned negation, give rise to similar pragmatic embellishment, as was discussed in Stage 4. Relevance theorists call such developments of the logical form *explicatures*, drawing on the concept of explicit content, reserving the term 'implicature' only for those of Grice's implicatures that do not contribute to the logical form of the sentence, but rather, as Carston says, pertain to separate thoughts, with their own truth conditions. More about this boundary in a moment.

An enrichment proposition is a useful concept in that the intended meaning is often likely to be more elaborate than what is uttered, as in (7.26).

(7.26)   It will take us some time to get there.
         ≫ It will take us longer than you anticipate to get there.
                                                    (adapted from Carston 1988: 164)

The utterance intuitively requires an extra specification of the amount of time, on the assumption that the speaker was cooperative and as such relevant qua being appropriately informative and appropriately economical with the formulation of the message.

When a sentence appears to convey an obvious, and as such uninformative, truth as in (7.27a), or a blatant falsehood as in (7.28), pragmatic modifications such as those below are so obviously necessary that they seem to provide a strong argument for such a concept of explicit content or explicature.

(7.27a)  Tom has eaten.
         ≫ e.g. Tom has already eaten dinner on that day.

(7.28)   Everybody passed the test.
         ≫ e.g. Every student in the class passed the test.

The enrichment is also useful when the sentence itself does not correspond to a complete proposition, as in (7.29).

(7.29)   Bill is not good enough.
         ≫ e.g. Bill is not good enough to play first violin in the orchestra.

Carston points to a test that demonstrates the truth-conditional relevance of some pragmatic enrichments, namely *falling within the scope of logical operators* such as negation, disjunction, and conditional. (7.30) is an example.

(7.30)   If the old king died of a heart attack and a republic was declared Sam will be happy, but if a republic was declared and the old king died of a heart attack Sam will be unhappy.
                                                    (from Carston 1988: 172, after Cohen 1971)

An attempt to contrast the 'bare', unenriched logical forms in (7.31) makes it clearer: while the order in which $p$ and $q$ are conjoined should not make a difference to truth conditions (in that it does not in propositional logic), it clearly does in English. While one implies $r$, the other implies its negation.

(7.31)     $(p \wedge q) \rightarrow r$
            but
            $(q \wedge p) \rightarrow \neg r$

This is known as the *scope principle*. Cohen used this principle to make a strong claim, namely that enriched meanings, such as 'and then' of conjunction *and*, are part of the lexical content of sentential connectives, as was discussed in Section 4.2. Carston points to it to argue that there is a need for a separate concept (explicature) of such pragmatic enrichments which, for her, are dictated and delimited by the principle of relevance.

In Relevance Theory, explicatures are normally the outcome of the same kind of pragmatic processes as implicatures. This engendered a discussion with another prominent contributor to the debate, François Recanati, who proposed that the first are different in being automatic and effortless. Recanati claims that such an enriched proposition, called by him *what is said*,[52] is in fact the smallest proposition that is consciously available. This is so because it is arrived at through a process that is not available to consciousness but rather is sub-personal, automatic, and as such non-inferential. As he says, 'communication is as direct as perception' (Recanati 2002b: 109), and '[t]he determination of what is said takes place at a sub-personal level, like the determination of what we see' (Recanati 2004: 39). So, unlike Relevance theorists, he distinguishes such processes, calling them *primary pragmatic processes*, from those that produce implicatures (*secondary processes*). Various counterexamples wheeled into this debate have demonstrated that the boundary is not so clear-cut, and neither can the understanding of the term 'inferential process' be easily calibrated to facilitate debates: is inference necessarily conscious? If not, then perhaps at least the label 'non-inferential' ought to be rethought?[53] Later in this journey we will adopt a middle-of-the-road stance, allowing for both automatic and conscious-inferential contributions to the main message. But we will upturn the roots of the logical form, in the spirit of learning about meaning 'hands-on', treating this journey as an example of adopting, adapting, and implementing what we encounter on the way.

Next, suggesting that the modifications to the logical form stop when optimal relevance is reached called for more precisification. Here Carston proposes the following criterion. While the explicature is a development of the logical form of the sentence, implicatures have to have their own, separate, logical forms. In other words, implicatures are *functionally independent* from the explicature – they function as independent premises in the process of reasoning. For example, in (7.27) above, there is likely to be an implicature that Tom is not hungry.

---

[52] See Recanati 1991 [1989].
[53] See especially a discussion between Carston (2007) and Recanati (2007); also Recanati 2004, 2010.

But even this criterion is not precise enough when we reformulate it as an entailment. First, if the logical forms are to be independent, then the implicature ought not entail the explicature – if an enriched form does so, then it is not an implicature but rather an explicature. This works for most examples: in (7.27), the enriched proposition entails the (more general) uttered one, and we can postulate that it is only the enriched one that the interlocutors use as a premise in reasoning. The implicature that Bill is not hungry does not exhibit such an entailment – and as such, if present, it functions as a separate premise. But then, independence works in two directions. So, arguably, an explicature ought not to entail an implicature either. And in this direction independence is more often violated, as exemplified in (7.32).

(7.32)  A: Did Tom buy flowers for Anna's birthday?
        B: He bought a dozen red roses.
           ≫ (*explicature:*) Tom bought a dozen red roses for Anna's birthday.
           ≫ (*implicature:*) Tom bought some flowers for Anna's birthday.

Here B's answer entails, but, arguably, at the same time implicates, that Tom bought some flowers. So, it has to be remembered that Carston's principle of independence is to be thought of more as functional, cognitive independence than as a strict, formal criterion[54] – as is evidenced by how the theory has since developed, on which we will have more to say in Section 8.2 when we move to the literal/non-literal distinction.

In his response, Recanati proposes his own criteria for delimiting *what is said* – ones that could inform a formal truth-conditional analysis. First, psychological reality is attended to in that *what is said* has to correspond to our 'pre-theoretic intuitions' – a proposal that he dubs the Availability Principle.[55] But this is not yet progress with respect to precision, so he strengthens it by reviving the scope principle exemplified in (7.30) above. In (7.30), the temporal reading of *and* ('and then') is part of *what is said* because the precisification is needed in the scope of implication (*if . . . then*) if the statement is to make sense. It is worth reiterating here that by this time in the development of pragmatics, the scope principle had been used to support two very different arguments: one for the lexical-semantic provenance of 'rich' content of words such as *and* (by Cohen) and one for its pragmatic, inferential origin within what is said (by Recanati). Food for thought – both about meaning and about methodology.

This rich notion of *what is said* is more intuitively plausible than traditional semantic content with only syntactically licensed pragmatic additions. But it appears that intuitive *what is said* does not *always* correspond to such a freely enriched, or modulated, proposition. On some occasions, it can intuitively be taken to be the bare uttered, proposition, on others, a freely enriched one, and yet on others it appears to be what is implicated.[56] For example, it is not difficult to imagine that in a scenario where a friend suggests going for a meal with Tom, (7.27a) above can communicate (or, perhaps, even 'say') (7.27b).

(7.27b)  Tom wouldn't like to go for a meal.

---

[54] See Recanati 1991 [1989] and Carston 1998c for a response; also e.g. Carston 2001.
[55] See Recanati 1991, p. 106.  [56] See Nicolle and Clark 1999, in response to Gibbs and Moise 1997.

So, perhaps what is said ought to be extended then to subsume implicatures in the cases when they communicate what is felt to be *really said* by the speaker, that is when they communicate the main message? It appears that, although we have just journeyed through an immense landmark in making truth-conditional content intuitive, there is still some way to go. We will travel a bit further in the following section.

First, we should pause and do two things: *ask how exactly* to modify the formal representation, and also *remind ourselves why* we would want to do so. This is important in that post-Griceans have different opinions on where those various aspects of pragmatic additions belong: within, or outside, the truth-conditional representation, and (which is not the same thing) within, or outside, semantics. The approach we have just discussed classifies the development of the logical form as part of truth-conditional, as well as part of semantic, content. But this is only one logically possible way of cutting the pie, and also only one of several actually proposed. Perhaps all those pragmatically implied aspects of meaning, be they developments of the sentence-based representation or separate thoughts, should be grouped together? And if so, perhaps they ought to be left outside the truth-conditional representation, and also out of semantics, as in traditional formal semantics? Or perhaps they should be included in the truth-conditional representation but left out of semantic theory? After all, not everyone agrees that semantic theory has to use truth conditions as a tool (more about this in Section 7.3.1). At the other end of the spectrum, perhaps pragmatic aspects ought to be included both in truth-conditional representation and in semantic theory? And if they ought to be placed in the same boat and *all included*, then perhaps we should include not only developments of the logical form but also implicatures proper? To recall example (7.27b), it is the implicature that dictates what the logical form is to be when the speaker chooses to communicate the main content indirectly. A list of logically possible combinations is fun to draw, and looking at which options have in fact been proposed and developed is even more fun. If, as in this journey, one wants to harness truth conditions in pursuit of a theory of meaning that is cognitively real, then one goes for the latter end of the spectrum of possibilities.

At the same time, we continue with a disclaimer that it is not necessary to subscribe to my desiderata to follow this journey. They enable one possible 'hands-on' application of the proposals we are journeying through. The discussion of the available choices for 'what is said' is meant as an encouraging example of how to adopt and adapt, but also sometimes reject, what is on offer, and how to use what one subscribes to – use it in one's own journey towards meaning, in full awareness of the reasons for the choices made. Too many university courses train students in one selected semantic theory. This is not right: it deprives the recipient of the opportunity to make informed choices. On this note, let's move on with thinking about meaning *like a linguist and a philosopher*.

Criteria for delimiting explicit content, or *what is said*, vis-à-vis implicatures became a widely debated question in post-Gricean research in the late 1980s. We will now look at a view that emphasizes the freedom with which modification to the logical form, and as such delimiting the more intuitively correct truth-conditional content, can be achieved, but at the same time does not compromise the formal character of semantics and its rules of meaning composition. Recanati agrees with Relevance theorists that the explicit content, or his *what is said* (which, of course, is 'richer' than Grice's understanding of the term in Figure 7.1) is assessed in a context. He popularized this as a version of contextualism that we briefly encountered before in opposition to minimalist semantics. As Recanati (2004: 4) says,

> According to Contextualism, the contrast between what the speaker means and what she literally says is illusory, and the notion of 'what the sentence says' incoherent. What is said (the truth-conditional content of the utterance) is nothing but an aspect of speaker's meaning. That is not to deny that there *is* a legitimate contrast to be drawn between what the speaker says and what he or she (*sic*) merely implies. Both, however, belong to the realm of 'speaker's meaning' and are pragmatic through and through.[57]

Now, pragmatic processes can work 'bottom-up' or 'top-down'. Indexical expressions serve as indicators, or 'slots', 'indices' in the logical form to which a referent has to be assigned. So, this is a 'bottom-up' process of *saturation* of such slots. On the other hand, (7.26)–(7.28) above exemplify a free, 'top-down' process of sense *modulation* (that subsumes what we earlier called *strengthening*).[58] Modulation is a 'top-down' process in that it does not rely on any indicators, or 'prompts' from the logical form that the representation needs modifying (although the 'very top', the proposition, has a special status, as will be explained in a moment).

Not that postulating some 'made-up' or 'unarticulated' slots *in the logical form* is not theoretically possible – it is a view I will shortly present as 'fixing'.[59] Pragmatic operations are seen there as having syntactic provenance and amounting to filling in slots in the logical form. But, Recanati points out, this theoretical option encounters a problem of circularity: in order to know what slots to make up, one already has to know *what is said*. In other words, one has to mentally enrich the proposition 'top-down' before one can theoretically postulate what slots are needed in order to be able to do it 'bottom-up'! No doubt, enthusiasts of Chomskyan syntax that abounds in functional categories can find a way of explaining away this potential circularity. But the onus of proof seems to be on those who insist on such slots – those who are not happy with a straightforward explanation that in a conversation we simply interpret what is uttered using the assumption of rationality of human communication, founded on informativeness vis-à-vis economy of processing.

To reiterate, for Recanati, the contextualist stance means that pragmatic modification (modulation) is always present: 'there is no level of meaning which is both (i) propositional (truth-evaluable) and (ii) minimalist, that is, unaffected by top-down factors' (Recanati 2004: 90). Truth-conditional content becomes then a product of various sources of information. Let us take example (7.33).

---

[57] See also Recanati 2005, 2012a. Note that *contextualism about meaning* should not be confused with other uses of the term, such as *contextualism about knowledge attributions* where 'knowing that $p$' can, or cannot, be attributed, depending, so to speak, on 'how much is at stake'. 'I know the office will be open on Saturday' may be fine if not more is at stake than a needless trip to town, but more hesitance is required when, say, the office being closed on that particular Saturday would result in missing the last opportunity to finalize a lucrative transaction. These are called in the literature 'low-stake' and 'high-stake' scenarios (see e.g. DeRose 1992, 2009).

[58] See e.g. Recanati 2004, 2005, 2010, 2012a, 2012b.

[59] I also discuss 'minimalists', 'maximalists', and 'fixers' about meaning in Jaszczolt 2016, Section 1.3.

(7.33)    There is a lion in the middle of the piazza.

(from Recanati 2010: 5)

It is likely that the speaker meant here a stone statue of a lion. So, the lexical item *lion* undergoes an operation of modulation (and in particular a kind of it called *sense extension*) – a 'top-down' process, since there is nothing inherent in the lexeme, nor, arguably, in the sentence structure, that could trigger it and set off a 'bottom-up' process. The *free enrichment* that we encountered before, for example in the temporal interpretation of conjunction *and*, or *predicate transfer*, as in the case of using a contextually relevant feature as a label for a referent, also belong here. An example of the latter is (7.34): imagine it is a comment about members of an orchestra. 'Cellos' will then refer to cello players rather than to musical instruments.

(7.34)    The cellos are complaining about their work load.

Semantic composition now operates on such modulated senses. In other words, 'pragmatic modulation is allowed to enter into the determination of semantic content' (Recanati 2010: 10). Such processes of modulation are pre-propositional, that is, operate locally, before the composition of meaning takes place. They are also primary, in the sense discussed above, namely that they are automatic and operate below the level of consciousness. It is also important to understand that these processes do not just introduce unarticulated constituents, or what we have referred to as 'slots'. (We introduced the term 'unarticulated constituent' in Section 5.1.) In brief, the unarticulated constituents view amounts to explaining various pragmatic additions to the semantic structure as unarticulated elements of the syntactic structure. Unarticulated constituents have engendered interesting discussions in the literature in connection with sentences such as (7.35).[60]

(7.35)    It is raining.

It has been debated whether a truth-conditional analysis requires ('bottom-up') saturation, or ('top-down') modulation, that provides an implicit argument – a location. Does *to rain* always mean 'to rain-at-a-location'? Intuitions may differ somewhat with respect to (7.36).

(7.36)    Whenever Anna goes hill walking, it rains.

Recanati's view is rather intricate here, not to say perhaps overly complicated. First, he proposes that there are no unarticulated constituents pertaining to elements of the sentence – so, *lion* in (7.33) is perfectly 'articulated', and so are all the other elements, including *rain* in (7.35) and (7.36), before they enter semantic composition. Originally, Recanati proposed a device of the variadic function (introduced in Stage 5, fn 71) that would account for the fact that an implicit argument of location may have to be present in some cases while not in others – just as in the case of the arguably variable adicity (that is, the number of arguments) of *eat* evidenced by (7.27a), repeated below.

---

[60] See e.g. Recanati 2002a, 2010; Korta and Perry 2011, Chapter 9.

(7.27a)  Tom has eaten.

First, imagine a situation where Bill wants to invite Tom for dinner. The utterance is likely to convey something to the effect of (7.37). That is, *eat* acts as a predicate with two arguments: 'Tom' (the subject) and 'dinner' (the object).

(7.37)   Tom has just eaten dinner.

On a different scenario, imagine that Tom is recuperating from an operation and his family are anxiously waiting for him to start eating without the support of a tube. In this case, the adicity of *eat* is, arguably, different: now *eat* seems to be a unary (one-place) predicate, corresponding to an intransitive verb, in that it is the very activity of eating, rather than eating *something*, that is relevant.

This analysis has evolved to a more intricate account that also shows how the predicate *rain* is both similar and different. On Recanati's proposal, modulation can take place at every step of meaning composition (that is, is available for lexemes as well as phrases) but *it is not available at the top level*. So, it is available for *lion*, to arrive at the non-literal sense of the word. It is also available for *eat*, where the conventions of use will assign the correct number of arguments, as was just discussed. Now, weather predicates such as *rain* in (7.35), are both similar and different. On this new analysis, just as in the case of the other two predicates, nothing is missing *in the proposition*: there is no need for unarticulated constituents. The composition produces a so-called *lekton* – a proposition that is subjected to a truth-conditional analysis. But in the case of the predicate *rain* in (7.35), there is no scope for modulation. Since modulation cannot occur at the top level of the composition process, in the case of 'It is raining', we already have a complete lekton: there is no way to fit in the location, so to speak (think what the logical form looks like). This move may look like an unnecessary restriction but it is needed to keep 'Recanati-style semantics' compositional: items in a sentence can 'elbow each other', so to speak, and push each other around, start adjusting their meaning a bit, but the total product cannot wobble any further. So, what do we trace the *location of the rainy weather* to? If Anna and Bill walk in Hyde Park in London and Anna utters (7.35), surely she is referring to the weather in the park where they are walking rather than, say, Central Park in New York. Here is the twist: unarticulated constituents re-enter the picture but as part of the *situation of evaluation* rather than part of the *compositional content*. Put simply, the uttered sentence is evaluated in the situation that makes it *about Hyde Park*.

There are intricate arguments in favour of such local (free) modulation vis-à-vis saturation of slots (indexicals) on one end of the spectrum and putting things in the situation of evaluation on the other. But, one may argue, a simpler, unified analysis would be an improvement. Perhaps every word, including *lion*, *eat*, and *rain*, is like an indexical and has to be worked on 'bottom-up' to get the meaning right? And in the process of composition the indices on lexical items carry on to indices on phrases? Or perhaps every word needs to be modulated, worked on 'top-down', and this need for modulation carries on through the process of composition? In other words, perhaps we should treat *all* lexical items *either* like indexicals *or* like non-indexicals, like content words, rejecting the distinction between 'top-down' and 'bottom-up' enrichment?

Adopting 'indexicality galore' would mean saying that just as *he* or *yesterday* require fixing in context, so do *lion* and *eat*. Here theorists have been remarking on the difference between those sentences that can be assigned truth conditions and those for which assigning them almost leads to absurd generality in that so many situations would make them true. Compare, for example, (7.38) with (7.39).

(7.38) The world is smiling at Bill.

(7.39) She said it to him then.

*She*, *it*, *him*, and *then* provide slots to fill – we are free to search in the context for adequate referents, only slightly nudged in the process by the word itself in that the referent has to observe the constraints such as number, gender, or animacy. On the other hand, we are quite limited with *the world* and *smile* – quite limited with conventional metaphors and somewhat more free with novel ones. But then, arguably, perhaps there is no clear boundary between cases such as (7.38) and (7.39)? Food for thought again, and a foretaste of Stage 8 to come.

Going in the opposite direction of 'modulation galore', we would also encounter problems in that this time it is indexicals rather than content words that pose a problem. An index is just a slot, decorated slightly with gender, number, or other morphosyntactic features; there is little to 'modulate' there: a slot has to be assigned a referent, respecting the slot's constraints (that is, its linguistic meaning, or what we called after Kaplan 'character'). Such reference assignment is hardly a case of modulation. But then, what is it exactly that we modulate in the case of *smile*? Is there a core meaning that ought to be shifted? How is such a context-free meaning identified in the first place? While discussing concepts at the beginning of this journey, we looked at a proposal according to which concepts don't have any 'hard core', so to speak, but rather are like a 'grab bag': they are constructed by the agent out of past experiences, memories, some encyclopedic knowledge, and so forth. Adopting the grab-bag view would mean that we deny the existence of such a core. So, perhaps modulation makes some assumptions about context-free meanings that are rather untenable? Perhaps a swing in the direction of a rich but messy, 'grab-bag'-style lexical semantics would enable a return to the formal, traditional truth-conditional semantics that had so much going for it? After all, word meanings were not well attended to in the 1960 and 70s when formal sentence semantics flourished?[61] Perhaps bringing them together would fulfil both of our desiderata? Again, food for thought.

Next, we can consider option (iii) where all, or almost all, pragmatic precisification is classified as belonging to the post-semantic, post-propositional level. We would have to work with a concept of a literal interpretation, say, of (7.38). These (minimalist) approaches will be discussed in the next section, providing even more food for thought.

---

[61] This is argued for in Del Pinal 2018. See also the discussions in Stage 2.

Let us look at the modulation process a bit more closely, though. What is appealing in it is the idea of the lateral (or sideways) adjustment of meanings: elements of the sentence act on each other and adjust to each other. But how do we know what exactly adjusts in (7.38)? Does *the world* adjust to *smile* or the other way round? Or do they both adjust to each other and if so, how? For example, does the sentence mean that Bill's life is full of positive and ambient experiences ('smiles') or that all of the people whom Bill encounters ('the world') smile at him? How adjustments work in practice will have to be left to post-Gricean principles of utterance interpretation – probably best the psychology-driven ones of Relevance Theory. What is important in the modulation approach is how it solves the problem of compositionality. Recanati (2012c: 189) says that 'the interpretation (content) of a complex expression α ∗ β is a function of the modulated meanings of its parts and the way they are put together (and nothing else)' – as stated formally in (7.40) (from *ibid.*), where $I$ stands for interpretation, *mod* for modulation, $f$ for function, $c^1$ and $c^2$ for the relevant parts of the context, and finally $g_1$ and $g_2$ for *functions of pragmatic modulation enabled by the context*.

(7.40)  $I(α ∗ β)_c = f(mod(α, c^1)(I(α)_c^1), mod(β, c^2)(I(β)_c^2)) = f(g_1(I(α)_c^1), g_2(I(β)_c^2))$

Note that if the interpretation of α ∗ β were a straightforward function of the interpretations of unmodulated α and β, the formula would simply be $I(α ∗ β)_c = f(I(α)_c, I(β)_c)$.

Rules of composition operate just as they do in traditional semantics but the units that they operate on are different: they are meanings that are modulated through primary pragmatic processes. So, semantics is supposed to remain a formal composition process but what it combines are units that come into being by elements of the sentence 'elbowing each other' to get to the most comfortable position that suits them all – as in the case of the world smiling at Bill.

Remember that modulation does not work on the top, propositional level. To reiterate, here Recanati proposes the concept of a lekton, that is a proposition undergoing truth-conditional analysis where information about, say, time and location is obtained from the situation of evaluation. Why are such aspects of information not included in a proposition? Surely, if we want a cognitively real proposition, or our functional proposition, we put all information from all modalities and channels of communication in it and in its representation. But remember that Recanati's objectives are different from those of this journey: he wants a unit that would preserve compositional semantics on the level of the *pragmatically modulated sentence*. So, elements elbowing each other inside the sentence is allowed, but only within the limits of a crate from which semantics can't escape. Food for thought again.

Recanati calls this view Truth-Conditional Pragmatics, precisely because he models semantics and pragmatics as intertwined but not diminishing in their precision, as (7.40) illustrates. But in what sense exactly is it truth-conditional *pragmatics*? Is it 'pragmatics' because the units are pragmatically modulated and it is a theory of how such truth-conditionally relevant pragmatic aspects operate? Note that conceptually this is also truth-conditional *semantics* – a contextualist one that, like Relevance Theory and other radical proposals of the Atlas-Kempson orientation, has shed the shackles of tradition and modernized the understanding of the term 'meaning', freeing it from the prison of an abstract concept of a language *system* and letting it fly quite a long way with those who *make* the meaning – us. Or, perhaps, who cares what we call it, as long as it gets such cognitively real and conversationally real meaning right, applying formal and precise tools of truth conditions that happened to be tested on wrong units in the past? But remember the previous paragraphs – we fly, but within the constraints of the structure, the logical form of the sentence. Perhaps the crate can be opened too? Perhaps truth-conditional semanticists could make better friends with the cognitive semanticists who opened the crate back in the 1970s but, sadly, have given up on formal tools? After all, language is both objective and subjective, as we will no doubt conclude by the end of this journey, and perhaps there is no need to take sides? Lots of food for thought!

Now, it is worth pointing out that such pragmatics-infused compositionality is increasingly more widely accepted among formal semanticists. In addition to the Default Semantics theory discussed in the next section, it is also proposed in the formal Montagovian tradition. Peter Lasersohn[62] points out that it is in fact perfectly compatible with Montague's original thoughts on the matter in that

> [t]here is no inconsistency ... between saying that the grammar does not change from context to context and saying that we use different semantic operations in different contexts. The grammar must provide some systematic, context-invariant way of saying what those operations are, but this does not mean that the operations themselves are context invariant. (Lasersohn 2012: 185)

In other words, the grammar stays the same, but, for example, quantifier domain restriction, or the sense of a definite description when embedded in a propositional attitude construction, can be resolved differently in different contexts, without harm to compositionality. As he says, grammar leads to the assignment of content compositionally, but pragmatic contributions are not only possible but even welcome: they save compositionality from counterexamples rather than threatening it. Montague had worked out language-system-dependent meaning, using Frege's senses as necessary concepts in intensional semantics of a fragment of English; Lasersohn, Recanati, and others proceed to discussions about the units from which meaning composes in general. Yet others rethink grammar and move its operations entirely to the conceptual domain. On that note, it is time to move on.

### 7.2.3 Making Truth Conditions Functional: Default Semantics

The next question to address in our journey through meaning is the following: Since contextualists have succeeded in making intuitive, pragmatically enriched meanings the object of study, is this the end of the road? Or can we go further to fulfil the desideratum of cognitive reality? In other words, is it always the (enriched or not) sentence's logical form that ought to be the object of study? What about cases where the main meaning is

---

[62] See here Lasersohn's (2012) 'Contextualism and compositionality' for more advanced reading.

conveyed indirectly, through a strong implicature? Let us consider (7.27a) and (7.29) again, but this time embedding them in scenarios as in (7.41) and (7.42), where the main, strongest, communicated message is conveyed via an implicature.

(7.41)  A: Shall we ask Tom if he wants to go out for dinner?
        B: Tom has eaten.
        ≫ We shouldn't ask Tom to go out for dinner.

(7.42)  A: Will Bill get a job with the London Symphony?
        B: Bill is not good enough.
        ≫ Bill will not get a job with the London Symphony Orchestra.

Such implicit communication is a natural and very common occurrence in discourse. This is so for various reasons, the main ones being considerations of politeness, adhering to tacitly adopted principles of social interaction, being tactful – and sometimes also trying to avoid full responsibility for the message. (We will address these issues in Stage 8.) So, if the implicature is the main message, shouldn't a theory of meaning that adopts the desiderata of cognitive reality and formal analysis do just that: analyse such *primary* (now in the sense of main, intended and communicated) meanings using truth conditions as a tool?

Yes and no. On the one hand (the 'no'), the question of compositionality of meaning would have to depart substantially from the issue of compositionality of the uttered sentence. On the other (the 'yes'), we would be addressing the composition of a proposition that matters the most. In adopting such a stance, Default Semantics does precisely that. Relying on the immense transformation of pragmatics achieved by its predecessors, most notably Relevance Theory and Truth-Conditional Pragmatics, it takes this extra step in contextualist analysis in that the primary meanings that are its object of study don't have to bear any structural resemblance to the logical form of the uttered sentence. The representation may, but need not, be a development of the logical form of the sentence. In other words, it need not obey the *syntactic constraint*. What a representation *has* to be is a representation of the functional proposition that we introduced in Section 1.3. The theory represents the main meaning intended by the speaker and recovered by the addressee, using truth-conditional, formal, representations of it.[63] It was developed in the late 1990s and has since been applied to different types of constructions and phenomena in different languages.[64] Since semantic representations are conceptual representations of the main intended and recovered meaning, they cut across the explicit/implicit divide: sometimes they pertain to the minimal, sentence meaning, at other times to the pragmatically enriched/modulated meanings, and at yet others (and quite often in fact) to the strongest implicature. 'Intended and recovered' meaning is indicative here of the stance on the 'Whose meaning?' question we addressed earlier. To reiterate, Grice focused on the intended, 'model speaker', meaning, while Relevance Theory focuses on the 'model addressee' meaning – 'model' in that they both propose universal principles of cooperative communication.

---

[63] See Jaszczolt 2005, 2010, 2021b.
[64] For an extensive bibliography on the theory and applications to phenomena and languages, see the entry in *Oxford Bibliographies in Linguistics*: Jaszczolt 2021b.

Default Semantics models cognitively plausible main messages as intended by a model speaker and recovered by a model addressee. It recognizes the fact that we can't always be certain about the speaker's actual intentions and, as a corollary, we can't be certain whether miscommunication hasn't occurred. It also recognizes the pitfalls of taking perspectives. But since the objective is to model meanings that follow pragmatic universals such as the post-Gricean principles, focusing on communication that *doesn't* go wrong seems the right thing to do.

Semantic representation can combine information drawn from five sources: word meaning and sentence structure (WS); situation of discourse (SD); properties of the human inferential system (IS); stereotypes and presumptions about society and culture (SC); and world knowledge (WK). All sources of information are treated on an equal footing, which means that the output of any of them can override the output of another. As a result, the representation can be (i) a 'bare' logical form of the sentence; (ii) a saturated logical form where indexicals are resolved; (iii) a freely modified (modulated) logical form; or (iv) a logical form that is independent of the logical form of the sentence. The above sources of information can be mapped onto types of processes that interact in producing the representation: processing of word meaning and sentence structure (WS); conscious pragmatic inference (CPI); cognitive defaults (CD); and social, cultural, or world-knowledge defaults (SCWD).

It is important to point out that defaults are *not* understood there as strong, language-system-based meanings that arise pretty much 'no matter what' and can later be cancelled, like Levinson's presumptive meanings discussed earlier. They couldn't be further from that. 'Default' stands for the *automatic, and as such not consciously inferential, interpretation* that arises in a given context and for the given model-speaker–model-addressee pair, given the common ground, with its shared and negotiated assumptions and information. As such, defaults are, by definition, *not cancellable*. They also cut across the noncism-defaultism controversies discussed earlier in relation to Levinson's theory of GCIs vis-à-vis Relevance Theory, in that they arise in a given context and as such are pretty entrenched and rarely in need of denying. As was said in Section 7.1.4, if they *are* denied, this is not cancellation but rather a repair strategy, signalling that something went wrong in the calibration of mutual knowledge and assumptions or with the ongoing co-construction of the common ground. (We return to Grice's criterion of cancellability very shortly, in Section 7.2.4.)

More specifically, CDs stand for the automatic processing (at both ends of the communication channel) of meaning that comes with strong informativeness or strong intentionality of the underlying mental states, as in the case of the default referential, as opposed to attributive, reading of definite descriptions, exemplified in (2.5) and adapted as (7.43).

(7.43) [Scenario: *The interlocutors are standing in front of the church La Sagrada Família in Barcelona.*]

    The architect of this church was mad.
    ≫ Antoni Gaudí was an eccentric.

## 7.2 What to Include and What to Leave Out

Next, SCWDs capture the automatic nature of relevant sociocultural conventions and encyclopedic knowledge ('world knowledge'), including scientific laws, empirical data, and other factual information, as exemplified in (7.44).

(7.44) A Botticelli was stolen from the Uffizi last week.
≫ A painting by Botticelli was stolen from the Uffizi Gallery in Florence last week.
(from Jaszczolt 2010: 198)

There are regular, albeit not bi-unique (one-to-one) mappings between sources and processes, where CD is processed via IS, SCWD by SC or WK, while inference (CPI) relies on IS, WK, or SC.

Post-Gricean developments are highly illuminating – and fun to follow, in that they provide an excellent example to trace how a thought can inspire further thoughts to the point where one has to stop and ask oneself: how did we get here? How much of these developments of Grice's view on meaning is really *improvement* on the Gricean programme and how much amounts to *taking different perspectives or adopting different objectives*? One example is the difference in objectives and perspectives between Grice's meaning$_{NN}$ and Relevance-theoretic recovered meaning already discussed. Different understandings of default interpretations on Levinson's theory of GCI (as presumptive meanings) and in Default Semantics is another example. Remember that presumptive meanings are fairly context-free assignments of interpretations that stem out of the language system, while the defaults of Default Semantics are automatic meanings obtained through processes SCWD and CD in a particular context (all, annoyingly, discussed in the literature as 'defaults' and sometimes confused). Default Semantics takes its name from the latter understanding: developed in the times when post-Gricean accounts paid little attention to automatic retrieval of information, be it information that can be attributed to the workings and architecture of the human brain (here: CD) or to employing sociocultural conventions (here: SCWD), it began as a voice in that debate. It also began as a voice in the debate on how far semantics can go in pursuit of contextualism, and as such of representing the meaning that really matters.

Returning to the main discussion, a semantic representation combines information from the sources just listed, arrived at through the combination of the above processes. Such a representation is called a *merger representation* (or Σ, for summation of information). It is a representation of the primary content, or of what we earlier called a functional proposition. Like in Truth-Conditional Pragmatics, such a representation is compositional. But unlike in Truth-Conditional Pragmatics, Σ need not be a composition of the modulated senses of the components of the sentence. Modification can also take place at the global level, as in (7.41) and (7.42) above, where the primary meaning is the implicit meaning and as such is the meaning represented by Σ. Compositionality is in this theory a *methodological and ontological assumption*. Methodological assumption means that a theory of meaning has to be compositional to fulfil its raison d'être, even if the natural language is not (recall problems with the compositionality of intensional constructions such as propositional attitude reports from Section 5.5). To achieve this, an ontological assumption kicks in, saying that human languages are compositional when they are analysed on the appropriate level. The level of conceptual structures such as Σs is where both assumptions can be satisfied. Figure 7.2 is an example of a possible merger representation for (7.42) and Figure 7.3 for (7.43).

Merger representations use a revised and extended language of DRT. The language is amended in order to represent 'pragmaticky', contextualist meaning, that is the meaning intended and recovered in discourse. It is not necessary to go into the details of the representations here, but the gist of how it works is important in our journey through meaning. The subscripts after the square brackets indicate the type of processes involved. So, for example, in (7.43), 'the architect of this church' can be automatically processed as 'Antoni Gaudí' by an addressee who makes use of (i) SCWD, in that they have this information about the identity of the architect of La Sagrada Família, as well as (ii) CD, in that the human inferential system tends to home in on the most informative interpretation and the strongest intentionality of the underlying mental state.

One element of the representation that we have to focus on is $ACC_\Delta^{rp} \vdash \Sigma'$. This is so because temporal reference is a topic we left dangling in our earlier discussion of representing time in Section 5.3. Default Semantics models time as epistemic modality, and in particular as degrees of epistemic commitment to the represented eventuality.[65] For example, while both (7.45) and (7.46) convey temporal location in the past, (7.45) comes with a stronger degree of commitment than (7.46).

(7.45)    Bill went to Scotland last summer.

(7.46)    Bill may have gone to Scotland last summer.

In Figure 7.3, '$ACC_\Delta^{rp} \vdash \Sigma'$' stands for 'it is acceptable to the degree pertaining to regular past that it is the case that $\Sigma'$'. Analogously for regular future (rf) in Figure 7.2.

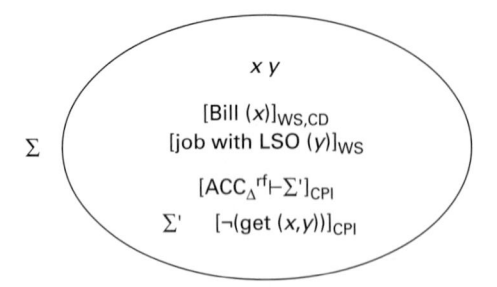

**Figure 7.2** Merger representation for a possible primary meaning of (7.42) ('Bill will not get a job with the London Symphony Orchestra.')

---

[65] See e.g. Jaszczolt 2009a, 2013b, 2018a.

## 7.2 What to Include and What to Leave Out

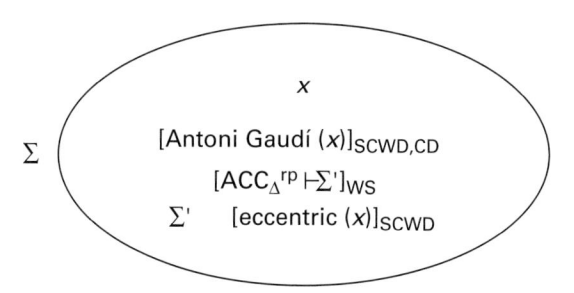

$\Sigma$ [ oval containing:
$x$
$[\text{Antoni Gaudí }(x)]_{\text{SCWD,CD}}$
$[\text{ACC}_\Delta{}^{rp} \vdash \Sigma']_{\text{WS}}$
$\Sigma'$ $[\text{eccentric }(x)]_{\text{SCWD}}$ ]

**Figure 7.3** Merger representation for a possible primary meaning of (7.43) ('Antoni Gaudí was an eccentric.')

In (7.46), the degree is within the range representing epistemic possibility past (epp). What is important is that now we come much closer to being able to represent tense–time mismatches, such as those discussed in Section 5.3.5. When there is a mismatch between the grammatical tense and the intended temporal reference, for example when future-time reference is conveyed using Simple Present, as in (5.95) repeated below, then the grammatically conveyed reference need not figure in merger representation because information from WS is overridden by that obtained through CPI.

(5.95) A: Let's go to London next Thursday.
B: I can't. I am giving a lecture.

We represent it as $[\text{ACC}_\Delta{}^{rn} \vdash \Sigma']_{\text{CPI}}$ (with 'rn' for 'regular *now*'). Representing tense–time mismatches takes us much closer to fulfilling the desideratum of cognitively real semantic representations. At the same time, it is important not to endow Σs with too much overlay about how cognition works in the mind as there are still many unknowns in that domain. Most importantly, does a merger representation signal that there is some kind of 'central processor' in the mind, or what Daniel Dennett calls 'Central Meaner', where all information comes together?[66] In his dismantling of the standard view of consciousness, Dennett would argue against it. Default Semantics remains neutral – just as it remains neutral on the question as to whether language processing requires a specialized module or modules à la Jerry Fodor, or follows general patterns of parallel distributed processing à la connectionists, both discussed in Section 2.3. In many aspects, it is still a theory in progress.

This theory is conceptually close to the end of the spectrum of contextualist proposals in that, to reiterate, the pragmatic influence on the semantic representation crosses the explicit/implicit boundary and allows for implicitly communicated content to be modelled as the primary message that is intended and conveyed. In this, it agrees with Mira Ariel's foregrounding of the main speaker's contribution that she captures under the notion of *privileged interactional interpretation*,[67] although it does not share its commitment to the level of explicature. It is argued in Default Semantics that once the main message is acknowledged as crossing the said/implicated boundary, all we

---

[66] See Dennett 1993. [67] See Ariel 2002a, 2016, 2019; Sternau et al. 2015.

need is a distinction between what is physically uttered (WS source) and the communicated message, be it communicated directly, directly with enrichment, or indirectly. It also agrees with Speech Act Theory discussed in Section 8.3 in emphasizing the importance of indirect speech acts, but disagrees with it in advocating the need for a formal account of such meanings (for reasons to be discussed there). Needless to say, it is not the end of the road for contextualism yet. For example, there are interesting proposals on the semantics of gestures appearing on the market that may allow for more emphasis on non-linguistic aspects of communication.[68] The last word on the speaker's and the addressee's joint construction of meaning has not been said either. Moreover, the sources and processes proposed in Default Semantics are merely a sketch – there is nothing to suggest that if these were to be empirically identified, the categorization wouldn't be somewhat different. But making compositionality apply to the main message, and harnessing truth conditions to represent and explicate such primary conveyed messages is a start when one accepts our initial desiderata. Future journeys through meaning can continue in this direction, or, alternatively, they can take a U-turn and make semantic content less psychologically real but at the same time more concrete – tied to what is audible or visible. It is to those that we turn next in Section 7.3, after revisiting Grice's criterion of cancellability.

We can conclude by noting that there are different ways in which contextualism can be a *radical* view. First, lexical items may not have fixed, coded meanings; they may merely be pointers to the contextually determined senses, or have only *semantic potential*. This is the stance of *being radical about word meaning* (let us call it 'radical$_w$').[69] Truth-Conditional Pragmatics takes this stance in building a theory of meaning composition around the lateral influences that expressions exert on one another in a sentence. (Remember that these are not entirely 'top-down' influences but rather sub-propositional ones, of the 'elbowing' kind.) Relevance Theory has also developed in this direction in order to better account for the lack of the literal–non-literal distinction.[70] But a view can also be 'radical' on the scope of the pragmatic contribution it allows to the truth-conditional content. Default Semantics is radical in the latter sense, in that, as was explained earlier, it represents the primary, main message intended by the speaker without obeying the syntactic constraint: the truth-conditional representation of the main, primary meaning may bear no resemblance to the logical form of the sentence when that meaning is conveyed indirectly. The contextualism of Truth-Conditional Pragmatics, Relevance Theory, and Default Semantics is 'radical' in the sense that truth conditions are applied to the conceptual representation that is a merger of information coming from a variety of sources and through a variety of interacting processes. Lexicon and structure are not privileged here (let us call it 'radical$_c$' for radical composition). On this radical$_c$ axis, Default Semantics goes the furthest in that its primary meanings can unreservedly cross the explicit/implicit boundary, while the other views make such 'promotion of the implicit

---

[68] See e.g. Lascarides and Stone 2009 and Schlenker 2019.
[69] See e.g. Travis 2008a; Recanati 2004; Carston 2012a.
[70] See e.g. Carston 2002, 2012a, b.

to the status of primary' more constrained – albeit not without good reasons that were discussed in the earlier section in relation to contextualism vis-à-vis compositionality.

The question now arises whether Default Semantics is also radical in the first sense. Here the tentative answer is yes – but 'tentative' because the adequacy of talking about 'core meaning' is still a topic in progress for all contextualist accounts. It may appear that the best solution is to invoke degrees of indexicality and deny that, say, *he* and *dog* are qualitatively different as an indexical vs. non-indexical expression. Rather, albeit contrary to received wisdom, they are both on a cline of the *degree of contextual contribution* they require for the utterance in which they are used to have meaning. This is one of the possible avenues for a future journey through meaning – theoretical, philosophical, as well as empirical, possibly to be pursued with the help of the fast-developing areas of neurosemantics and neuropragmatics.

### 7.2.4 Cancellability Revisited

Grice's criterion of cancellability[71] says that a potential, or what he calls 'putative', conversational implicature can be cancelled either *explicitly* or *contextually*. Explicit cancellation can take place when an utterance that implicates *p* is followed by something to the effect of 'but not *p*' or 'I don't mean to imply that *p*'. This can take place when either (i) the addressee infers something the speaker did not intend to implicate and it is subsequently cancelled by the added clarification, or (ii) the potential implicature does not arise at all because a cancellation phrase pre-empted it. It is this explicit cancellation that many post-Gricean pragmaticists adopt. Contextual cancellation is something different altogether, although, curiously, Grice lumped the two under the same criterion of cancellability. The latter means that there are potential situations in which this putative implicature would not arise. From the post-Gricean perspective, we can best interpret them in the following way. Contextual cancellation concerns implicatures that are *potential for the sentence (or its parts)*, whilst explicit cancellation concerns implicatures that can be *potential for the current discourse situation* and arise when the common ground is misjudged.[72] As was said earlier, the latter can act as conversational repair – putting the conversation back on track.

First, a terminological remark is in order. So far we have been following the rule that *implicating* is what speakers do, while *inferring* is what addressees and other hearers do. But in the context of cancellation as a criterion, potential or 'putative' implicature gets stuck somewhere in between. Putative implicatures are, by this terminology, also 'putative inferences'. Analogous reasoning should also apply to what Grice quite needlessly distinguished as GCIs: if I say 'some people' and *correct* myself saying 'all people', this is a simple act of conversational repair because I realize that in that context an unwanted inference may arise. There is no need to postulate context-free implicatures just to fit the meaning of *all* under the universal quantifier and the

---

[71] See Grice 1989c [1978], p. 44.   [72] For potential implicatures see Gazdar 1979.

meaning of *some* under the existential one of an imperfect metalanguage. It is like cutting the cloth according to the tools we have for sewing it rather than according to what garment we want to make.

Now, the criterion of cancellability has been put to a variety of tests. It has been argued that not all potential conversational implicatures are explicitly cancellable – in the case of irony, an attempted cancellation may even strengthen the effect rather than take it away. But then, how useful is such a specific phenomenon as irony for building one's argumentation on?[73] The criterion was also revisited in another way, inspired by the attempts to redraw the boundary between what is said and what is implicated in post-Gricean approaches, and most notably in Relevance Theory and in Default Semantics. First, in Relevance Theory, it was observed that the freely modulated *what is said*/explicit is quite entrenched. Explicatures are, arguably, not cancellable by definition in that they are defined from the perspective of the recovered meaning: what the addressee inferred is what the utterance means.[74] When they have to be withdrawn, they signal a rather different phenomenon of miscommunication that can come to the surface in a dynamic discourse, as that discourse progresses.

Next, let us consider cancellability with respect to two distinctions. First, the *what is said vs. what is implicit* distinction, where the demarcation is understood as in Truth-Conditional Pragmatics, and similar to the Relevance-theoretic explicit/implicit distinction. Second, the *primary meaning/secondary meaning* distinction as it is understood in Default Semantics. Remember that these two distinctions (let us call them A and B) are orthogonal: in the latter theory, primary meanings can be explicit or implicit. It has been exemplified and suggested through theoretical arguments that what is said (as in distinction A) can be fairly entrenched. But potential primary meanings from distinction B seem to be considerably more entrenched – they have to be, since by definition they also cover cases of communicating the main content through an implicature. When such a potential primary meaning goes through, then potential secondary meanings are also more entrenched than in cases where it does not. To reiterate, such secondary meanings can be explicit or implicit – they are explicit when the primary meaning is communicated indirectly (is implicit). It is interesting to notice that when a potential secondary meaning corresponds to the explicit content of the uttered sentence, then it can be cancelled analogously to potential implicit secondary meanings.

Such discussions always benefit from a consideration of the logically possible options: for A, what happens to the implicature when the potential explicit content goes through, and what when it does not? For B, we distinguish cases where the primary meaning is implicit or explicit, and then ask what happens to the secondary meaning when such a primary meaning goes through and what when it does not. All in all, for A, there are some easily cancellable potential explicit meanings, as well as easily cancellable potential implicit meanings. But primary meanings of

---

[73] See Weiner 2006 for an example and Blome-Tillmann 2008 and Jaszczolt 2009b for discussions.
[74] See here Capone 2006, 2009.

B appear to be more strongly entrenched. Secondary meanings, both explicit and implicit, are cancellable but they are more entrenched when the primary meaning goes through. This much is predictable: explicit and corresponding implicit stick together, be it in A or B playing field. Now, the principal reason for the entrenchment of primary meanings can easily be stipulated when we think how communication works: it is not the *manner* of communication that matters but the *status* of the message. There is no reason why a strong implicature that is the principal raison d'être of the particular utterance should not be as entrenched as the equivalent of this message that is conveyed explicitly. Well, *arguably* none: here opinions differ, with arguments on each side. We will discuss this further when we come to lying, misleading, and accountability for one's conveyed message in Section 8.4.1.[75] Now we make a U-turn and attend to those who want to keep semantics simple and 'uncontaminated'.

## 7.3 Keeping Semantics and Pragmatics Apart

Maintaining a clear boundary between semantics and pragmatics can take different forms. Let us start with the logically possible options. First, one could try to (i) keep semantics 'absolutely minimal' and not allow even for disambiguation or resolution of indexicals. This would entail not being able to use truth conditions as a tool in that there is no constructive way of employing them for such vague matrices of propositions. Next, one can (ii) allow only 'bottom-up' enrichment. This can come in two flavours: (ii.a) the standard resolution of indexicals, such as those on Kaplan's list discussed earlier (see (6.65)), or, one can (ii.b) postulate that other lexical items, such as common nouns, also come with indices and the resolution of their meaning takes place in a given context (where this resolution is, by definition, traceable to the logical form of the sentence). Notice that the polar options (i) and (ii.b) also, in a sense, carry a strong flavour of contextualism in spite of keeping semantics and pragmatics apart, in that the truth-conditional content can in principle be very rich: *truth-conditional but not semantic* (when truth conditions are employed for pragmatic content but left out of semantics) in (i) and *truth-conditional, rich, and semantic* in (iib). On the other hand, (ii.a) advocates both minimal semantics and minimal truth-conditional content. More on these reflections in what follows. Let us first turn to questioning the need for truth conditions in semantics.

### 7.3.1 Minimalism without Propositions

The views we analysed in Section 7.2 advocate the notions of *explicature*, *what is said*, or *primary content* (*functional proposition*) that conceptually link those aspects of meaning that are physically uttered or written with those that are not but are felt to be there. They assign intuitively plausible truth conditions, albeit where they draw the

---

[75] For arguments and ample examples see Jaszczolt 2009b.

boundary between truth-conditional and non-truth-conditional content varies between accounts. As such, they are all contextualist accounts. On the other hand, Kent Bach[76] distinguishes not only what is said and what is implicated but also those parts of the content that are *implicit in what is said* without being implicatures proper. His argument is that people often speak imprecisely in one way or another because it is more efficient to do so since the addressee can recover missing bits of information. For example, a mother who hears her child cry about a cut finger may say (7.47), using it non-literally.

(7.47)   You are not going to die, Peter.

(from Bach 1994a: 267)

On Bach's analysis, the content of the sentence (the *minimal proposition*) is that Peter is going to live forever. But *what is implicit in what is said* produces (7.48) instead – or something to that effect.

(7.48)   You are not going to die from this cut, Peter.

Why didn't the mother add '... from this cut'? Because it was obvious that this is what she meant. But for Bach these missing aspects are not free enrichments: they are not proper constituents of what is said. His *what is said* differs from *what is meant*; what is said remains minimal and faithful to what was physically uttered. The mother was not speaking literally, although she did not use any figures of speech: no *part* of the sentence was used non-literally. This non-literality results in an *expansion* of such a minimal proposition, that is *what is meant*.

Speakers also utter sentences that do not correspond to any complete proposition. (7.29), repeated below, is semantically incomplete and as such cannot be associated with any truth conditions. The sentence is semantically underdetermined, or underspecified.

(7.29)   Bill is not good enough.
         ≫ Bill is not good enough to play first violin in the orchestra.

One could argue that (7.29) *could* be associated with some very general truth conditions to the effect that 'it is not the case that Bill is good enough for something or other' but this is not what Bach chooses to do. He says that such sentences express a *propositional radical* that has to be pragmatically completed to become a proposition and to stand for the intended meaning, like the one suggested in the above example. Propositional radicals do not have slots to fill in their syntactic representation. They only have 'conceptual slots', so to speak, in their conceptual logical form: 'incomplete logical forms can be generated by complete syntactic forms' (Bach 1994a: 283).

In short, he distinguishes two cases where what is said triggers a search for implicit components: that of (a) *sentence non-literality*, where the minimal proposition requires expansion – or, as he calls it, 'fleshing out', and (b) *semantic underdetermination*, where the propositional radical requires completion – or 'filling in'.[77] Expansions and

---

[76] See e.g. Bach 1994a, 1994b, 2001, 2006.    [77] See Bach 1994a, p. 269.

completions belong neither to what is said nor to what is implicated but rather constitute a 'middle ground'. A proposition that has been subjected to such expansion or completion is then called an *impliciture* – for 'implicit in what is said', as contrasted with implicature – what is implicated. As Bach (1994a: 270) says, 'there is no *line* to be drawn between what is said and what is implicated. Instead, there is considerable middle ground between them'. But here is the crux of the proposal: the 'middle level' of impliciture does not muddy the boundary between semantics and pragmatics in that implicitures do not contribute to the semantic representation. This is his solution to keeping semantics and pragmatics apart: by clearly distinguishing between the content of sentences and the intended content of utterances. Semantics means sentence meaning, nothing else:

I am not disputing the idea that . . . there are pragmatic aspects to what is said as well as to what is implicated . . ., but in my view these aspects are properly regarded as pertaining to what is implicit in what is said. (Bach 1994a: 280)

At the same time, implicitures *do* contribute to truth-conditional content. Notice that for Relevance Theory and for Truth-Conditional Pragmatics, pragmatic contributions to the truth-conditional content mean that semantic analysis operates on such pragmatics-enriched units. In contrast, here semantics remains pure and minimal. The only way to achieve this split between what is semantic and what is truth-conditional is for Bach to say that semantic theory does not need to be truth-conditional; truth conditions remain on the other side of the fence, in pragmatics. Altogether, we have a position here labelled *radical semantic minimalism*: no implicit intrusions and no need for truth conditions on the semantic side of the fence. The proposal is close to Grice's original ideas in many respects and appeals to Grice's close followers. Horn, for example, adopts this semantics/pragmatics distinction, as well as Bach's concept of an impliciture.[78]

Now, unlike the contextualists just mentioned, Bach argues that we ought to distinguish this middle level in order to distinguish between saying and stating, as well as between sentence meaning and speaker meaning. But let us imagine that by uttering (7.49) the speaker intends the following meaning.

(7.49)   Anna has been vaccinated.
     ≫ Anna has been vaccinated against something or other (that is, she had the experience of being vaccinated some time in her life).

At the time of writing this, the likely interpretation of (7.49) would be that Anna has been vaccinated against COVID-19 within a time span that still gives her protection against infection. But it is not impossible to think of a scenario where a minimal interpretation, such as that suggested in (7.49), is intended. Then, the 'middle level' not only collapses to the level of minimal semantic content but it can be construed as expressing *less* than the ordinary what is said when we try to apply the contextualist, common-sense analysis. This is how a contextualist would argue that this weakens the case for Bach's clear semantics/pragmatics boundary but preserves common sense:

---

[78] See Horn 2006, p. 24.

what is meant cannot stay on the wrong side of semantics. What is meant could be minimal as in (7.49), but when it is not, there is little extra-theoretic reason to invoke such a middle level of meaning.

Moreover, both underdetermination and non-literality are rather fuzzy categories. While this is precisely what made Bach assign them to pragmatics, it also leads to some questions. (7.50) and (7.51) do not intuitively appear to be underdetermined.

(7.50)   That lamp is old.        [+ relative to what?]

(7.51)   John wants a taxi.       [+ to do what with?]

(adapted from Bach 1994a: 286)

Underdetermination is a very diversified category; unlike ellipsis or indexical resolution, it requires no 'prompt' from the structure as to what needs resolving. Likewise, non-literality is also a large and diversified category. It includes, among numerous other categories, implicit qualification as in (7.52) and approximation as in (7.53).

(7.52)   Jack and Jill are married.
         ≫ Jack and Jill are married *to each other*.

(7.53)   France is hexagonal.
         ≫ France is hexagonal, *roughly speaking*.

(adapted from Bach 1994a: 287)

Like underdetermination, non-literality looks like an assortment, not to say a jumble, of different phenomena, grouped together in search of all possible pragmatic contaminations of pure and minimal semantics. The problem is that this 'contamination' may prove to be not a contamination but rather an essence – it certainly has, on this particular journey through meaning, where what is truth-conditional and what is semantic do not fall apart so easily. But every journey has its own desiderata and assumptions, and Bach's is to identify the properties of the language system and the properties of what the system can be used for – a lot like other minimalists who, however, unlike Bach, keep truth conditions on the side of such minimal semantics. It's time to turn to these views.

## 7.3.2 'Minimal' and 'Insensitive' Semantics

We are now coming progressively closer to questioning the research agenda that has been in fashion for several decades, namely semantics/pragmatics boundary disputes. This is so because of the mismatch of desiderata and objectives. It is easy to see that every journey through meaning has its merits and demerits. While contextualists search for a functional semantic theory that has as its object intuitive meanings, minimalists search for system-driven, 'uncontaminated' purity. In the process, they either sacrifice truth conditions, like Bach, or make use of them but only so as to analyse the meaning of a sentence thrown up by the language system, with pragmatic additions restricted to filling in 'slots' already marked in the syntactic structure. The latter is a variant of the traditional stance, reminiscent of the standard truth-conditional

## 7.3 Keeping Semantics and Pragmatics Apart

semantics discussed in the earlier stages of this journey, with a provision for indexicals modelled on Kaplan's two-dimensional semantics discussed in Section 6.2.4.3 and taking 'Kaplan's list' of indexicals (in (6.65) there) as a starting point.

In Emma Borg's *Minimal Semantics*,[79] pragmatic inference is only allowed if it is constrained by the grammar. Semantic theory is a theory of *literal linguistic meaning*. The main justification for keeping semantics and pragmatics apart in this way is the assumed modularity whereby processing of sentence meaning relies on deductive inference and as such is separate from the processing of speaker intentions and from any other non-deductive inference. Truth conditions are employed in the service of explicating such minimal meaning. This is not considered to be a downside, though, in that truth conditions are not supposed to be the same thing as *conditions of verification* of the sentence: (7.29) or (7.49) are perfectly fine as they are for this particular semantic agenda. As she says in discussion with those advocating unarticulated constituents,

[T]he proposition the addressee is capable of recovering on the basis of their linguistic knowledge alone is the one where the identifying conditions themselves act as reference-fixers rather than as genuine elements of the propositional content. (Borg 2004: 192)

This is important in that even if the addressee is not in a position to identify the missing aspects, a proposition *is* recovered. In practice,

[f]aced with an utterance 'That is red', the competent language user needs to recognize that 'that' is a singular term, and that it thereby introduces a singular concept into the truth-conditions of the utterance, a singular concept the content of which is exhausted by whichever object is referred to by the speaker in this context. (p. 196)

The extent to which truth conditions can be 'liberal' on this form of minimalism (that is, satisfied by a range of situations that are more specific than what the sentence says), is considerable:

even sentences like 'She can't continue' are truth-evaluable, though we need to be clear about exactly what information is syntactically represented in a sentence like this. (p. 220)[80]

Such liberal truth conditions will be something to the effect of: 'If $u$ is an utterance of "Jane can't continue" in a context $c$ then $u$ is true iff Jane can't continue something in $c$.' (p. 230).

Next, in their *Insensitive Semantics: A Defense of Semantic Minimalism and Speech Act Pluralism*, Herman Cappelen and Ernie Lepore[81] offer a similar proposal, whereby the *content of a speech act* should be kept apart from the content of a sentence. A sentence, when uttered, can produce a whole array of speech acts – hence the 'speech act pluralism' in the title. This amounts to keeping semantics and pragmatics clearly distinguished. Indexicals are filled in. Like Kaplan before, they compile their own set of indexical expressions, understood as the only expressions that are allowed contextual resolution. The view is not as well developed in that Cappelen and Lepore

---

[79] See Borg 2004, 2012.   [80] The latter is pursued in her next book – see Borg 2012.
[81] See Cappelen and Lepore 2005.

subsequently moved in different directions: to semantic relativism (and as such, a view with a contextualist flavour) in the case of the first author, and a convention-infused grammar in the other (discussed in Section 6.3.1).[82] Relativism, a view that we briefly mentioned in the discussion of predicates of personal taste in Section 6.2.4.4, reopens important metasemantic or foundational questions that have been permeating this journey from the beginning and that we will force to a conclusion before we finish. Nevertheless, minimalism lives on, mainly tapping into the intuitive distinction between mental and non-mental phenomena. As Stotts (2020: 185) argues, this may be going against the tide but at the same time is based on solid foundations: 'semantic facts arise from context-independent meaning, compositional rules, and non-mental elements of context, whereas pragmatic facts are a matter of speakers' mental states and hearers' inferences about them'. Needless to say, problems with 'non-mental' core meanings reappear with full force but this does not necessarily mean that the enterprise is flawed: abstractions over meanings have their value, even if they are not psychologically real – that is, even if they are intermingled with modulation.[83] Finally, recently rekindled discussions over liability for what one asserts open up the possibility that we need both minimal content and the enriched content – perhaps, as Borg (2019: 517) suggests, distinguishing 'different notions of "what is said" depending on the kind of sociolinguistic role appealed to'. The journey continues.

## 7.3.3 Semantic 'Indexicalisms'

As was remarked earlier, minimalism comes in different versions. The final one we will consider is the view that truth-conditional content is more richly infiltrated by the results of pragmatic inference but this inference is constrained by the logical form: the syntactic representation is quite generously peppered with slots that are to be filled in. The more slots we postulate, the closer sentence meaning can be kept to utterance meaning. The main representatives of this view are Jason Stanley and Zoltán Gendler Szabó. This view was discussed earlier in Section 5.1 (see the discussion of example (5.6) there) when we considered different ways of restricting the domain of quantification. To reiterate, the proposal is that in the structure of the sentence, each common noun comes with an indicator in the N node that contextual qualification is required. It contains information that the domain of quantification is to be restricted. For the common noun *dog*, this information is captured in the following way: <dog, $f(i)$>, where $f$ is a function that maps objects onto quantifier domains, and $i$ is an object given by the context. In this way, enrichment is conceptualized as being triggered by the *semantic qualification* of the noun in the quantifier phrase of the structure. In other terms again, the noun and an index for this qualification 'co-habit' a node in the structure of the sentence, in that '[m]uch syntactic structure is unpronounced, but no less real for being unpronounced' (Stanley 2002: 152).[84]

---

[82] See Cappelen and Hawthorne 2009 and Lepore and Stone 2015 respectively.
[83] On abstraction that merges with modulation, see Recanati 2005, esp. Fig. 7.2 there.
[84] See also Stanley and Szabó 2000 and King and Stanley 2005.

We are now in a position to compare and contrast this proposal with other attempts to keep semantics 'uncontaminated' from 'top-down' influences. Probably the conceptually simplest generalization is this: Borg's and Cappelen and Lepore's semantic minimalism can be called the *standard minimalist views* in that both semantics and truth-conditional content are kept on the 'minimal-meaning side'. On the other hand, Bach's and Stanley and Szabó's views flank the centre. Bach's radical semantic minimalism view keeps semantics so minimal that truth conditions end up on the pragmatics side, while Stanley and Szabó's proposal does keep both semantics and truth conditions on the same side, but at the expense of imagining (and, to be fair, partly justifying) indices that allow for a lot of pragmatic information to sneak in. That is why this view is sometimes called *semantic indexicalism*: postulating indices to do the trick. In principle, one could go even further and postulate indices for all syntactic categories until, as we discussed earlier, the distinction between indexical and non-indexical expressions evaporates. I sometimes refer to proponents of such views as 'fixers'.[85] When what we want from semantics and what we get from the sentence do not match, fix the representation of the sentence! On the other hand, what one loses in intuitive plausibility one gains in clarity of representation. All the journeys through meaning discussed here are important landmarks and have their strong and weak points – especially considering that 'strong' and 'weak' are often relative to the particular objectives and desiderata.

A different attempt to trace to the logical form some of the meanings that contextualists freely added 'top-down' is Gennaro Chierchia's account of scalar implicatures.[86] As he suggests, 'some of the Grice-inspired pragmatics is probably part of the computational system of grammar' (Chierchia 2004: 59). He argues that grammar, which for Chierchia comprises syntax and semantics, gives two kinds of values to expressions, in that it offers two interpretive procedures. There is a plain value, such as 'some' for *some*, and a strengthened, 'scalar' (and as such defeasible) value, such as 'some but not all', as in (7.54a). It is the stronger value that is normally selected by the system. There are also strict conditions that dictate when implicatures do not arise, such as reversing monotonicity (discussed in Section 5.2.1): embedding (7.54a) under negation in (7.54b) removes the original scalar implicature, as the attempted chains of inference marked as # indicate. In general, embedding *p* in a downward-entailing context, such as, for example, negation or an 'A doubts that ...' construction, removes any scalar implicatures of *p* (an observation already made by Larry Horn, whose views were discussed when we introduced negation in Section 4.5).[87] But it adds new ones that conform to the rule that *implicatures must lead to strengthening*. So, the <*all, some*> scale becomes inverted, as in (7.54c) and (7.55).

(7.54a)  Some breeds of dogs are intelligent.
　　　　≫ Some but not all breeds of dogs are intelligent.

(7.54b)  It is not true that some breeds of dogs are intelligent.
　　　　# It is not true that some but not all breeds of dogs are intelligent.
　　　　# All breeds of dogs are intelligent.

---

[85] See Jaszczolt 2016.   [86] See Chierchia 2004.   [87] See Horn 1989.

(7.54c)  It is not true that all breeds of dogs are intelligent.
  ≫ Some breeds of dogs are intelligent.

(7.55)  Bill doubts that all breeds of dogs are intelligent.
  ≫ Bill believes that some breeds of dogs are intelligent.

To test it, you can try the same pattern with, say, the <*and, or*> scale. Notice that this discussion can also be used as an argument for the local (vs. global, post-propositional) origin of implicatures in that the structure of the sentence is responsible for their arising or non-arising.

We are now in a position to remark on other meanings of the terms 'contextualism' and 'radical'. I classified the two versions of semantic indexicalism presented here as accounts that aim at keeping semantics and pragmatics apart, at the same time putting in the semantics, and in the logical form of the sentence, some types of the 'enrichments' that contextualists consider to be purely pragmatic and 'top-down'. As such, they combine elements of minimalism, trying to keep semantics 'uncontaminated' by anything 'pragmaticky' that cannot be traced to the structure, and contextualism, in that they allow for a fair amount of information from context to enter this structure. We can therefore discern another sense of 'radical', applied to the semantic structure, as in Stanley and Szabó (let us call it 'radical$_s$'), and to grammar, as in Chierchia (let us call it 'radical$_g$'). But realizing that no labelling and classifying is ever unquestionable is often a harbinger of progress. It is now time for 'Who cares?'

## 7.3.4  Semantics or Pragmatics? Or, Who Cares?

Semantic/pragmatic boundary disputes have been a hot topic since the origins of radical pragmatics in the 1970s but there is now an overwhelming sense that the enthusiasm is running out. If semantics can be one thing or another, depending on what one wants to achieve, then, frankly, who cares? Perhaps one merely has to clarify the terminology to distinguish between minimalist semantics and contextualist (or 'maximalist') semantics, but there shouldn't be any semantics/pragmatics 'border wars'!

Or should there be? Remember that for contextualists the only level on which a theory of meaning can be pursued is one where meanings are freely modified. Or, as we quoted earlier, '[a]ccording to Contextualism, the contrast between what the speaker means and what she literally says is illusory, and the notion of "what the sentence says" incoherent' (Recanati 2004: 4). So, the crux of the matter is whether we adhere to the tenet that has accompanied us until now, that is that one can be, so to speak, a minimalist in the morning and contextualist in the afternoon, depending on what questions one addresses. If so, then truth conditions can be used for each of these pursuits – like a knife and fork that we use to eat a small ('minimalist') meal or a large ('maximalist') meal – or a meal in *nouvelle cuisine* or a meal in *cuisine classique* respectively (although what counts as 'nouvelle' and what as 'classique' has to be reversed in this simile: 'nouvelle' is indeed small but not new ☺). If, however, one denies the possibility of a 'minimalist meal' altogether, then there is nothing to be eaten – and that is the stance captured in the above quotation.

But even this way of thinking gets us into a muddle. Linguists researching the psychology of utterance interpretation, such as Rachel Giora and her group, distinguish between *default interpretations* that correspond to the intuitive, 'contextualist' content, and *salient meanings* that are 'stored or coded in the mental lexicon' (Giora 2003: 15). The latter can be activated to some degree even in contexts where they are not intended or appropriate. They are activated in that '[w]hile context may be predictive of certain meanings, it is deemed ineffective in obstructing initial access of salient information' (p. 24). As Giora's empirically supported *graded salience hypothesis* predicts, such salient meanings can be activated automatically, even if the context is biased against them.[88]

Either way, the semantics/pragmatics distinction ceases to take centre stage. Either (i) pursuing minimal meaning shouldn't stop you from also pursuing intuitive meaning if you so wish, using the same tools, or (ii) pursuing intuitive meaning pre-empts any need to pursue anything else because there is nothing else to pursue. There is (ii.a) contextualism galore or (ii.b) contextualism weakened by graded salience. Either way, 'border wars' blow over. The realization of this fact is spreading fast through the literature:

My own experience was that, over time, I simply lost my confidence in my ability to see [the] semantics–pragmatics line, or even to know quite what it was I was looking for. The result, as is often the way with childhood faiths, was not so much a *renunciation* but a simple *falling away*, in the sense of ceasing to be able to see why the question mattered so much. (Dever 2013: 105)

And yet, incontrovertibly, the 'wars' *used to* matter. The contextualist stance didn't appear out of nowhere. Contextualism has a considerable history. It is an orientation in the philosophy of language according to which a sentence expresses fully determined content only in the context of a speech act (more on the latter in Section 8.3). This was a stance held in the 1950s by ordinary language philosophers. Ordinary language philosophers (mentioned earlier in this journey and to be attended to when we move to speech acts in Section 8.3) take contextualism to its limits in denying any context-independent meaning 'core' – a view sometimes referred to, somewhat misleadingly, as 'meaning eliminativism'.[89] But together with accepting a speech act as the unit of analysis, those early contextualists rejected formal methods. In contrast, the contextualists we discussed here in Stage 7 retain the principle that the only way to do semantics is to investigate such contextually grounded utterances, while at the same time applying formal methods that stem out of the 'opposition' to this early contextualism. They revive the methods applied by those who attempted to fit natural languages into the mould of formal languages of logic, as discussed earlier in this journey. They foreground the importance of a compositional, truth-conditional analysis. So, while contextualism is a reaction to the traditional view that sentences themselves can be ascribed truth conditions, it can vary in what it does with formal methods: throw them away or reuse them for a new kind of meal. Either way, the reaction to the 'small meal' introduced some ground-breaking ideas to the theory of meaning.

The question remains, how big can this meal be that we eat with the knife and fork of truth conditions? For example, what do we do with metaphors such as this one?

[88] See Giora 2003 and e.g. 2012; Peleg and Giora 2011; Giora, Givoni, and Fein 2015.
[89] See Recanati 2005. On meaning contextualism in philosophy, see also other essays in that volume.

How does irony fit in? What about speech acts other than assertions or questions? (Remember that the formal semantics of questions has been fairly extensively worked out, as was discussed in Section 3.2.) And which 'sociopragmaticky' elements of speech acts do we retain and which do we peel off and discard before eating the meal? What about meaning that is not just intended and recovered but rather *negotiated* or *jointly constructed* by the speaker and addressee? Some of these questions, and others, will be given a start in the next, final, stage, intended as a springboard to propagate new journeys where this one ends.

**Suggested Further Reading**

Grice's and post-Gricean pragmatics are best approached by tackling directly the position papers written by their core representatives. It is the best way to appreciate the strength and the nuances of the arguments, thinking about such crucial issues as the role of intention in determining what meaning is and 'whose meaning' pragmatic theory ought to take on board. The semantics/pragmatics boundary disputes have also developed around such foundational questions and are best appreciated first-hand. The literature is vast. As has been the case throughout this journey, suggestions for specialist, detailed and more advanced reading have been given in the footnotes as we moved along. But to begin, it is best to start with Grice's seminal paper 'Meaning' (Grice 1989a [1957]), perhaps followed by 'Utterer's meaning and intention' (Grice 1989e [1969]), to see the merits and demerits of the intention-driven definition first-hand. For the truth-conditional vis-à-vis implicated meaning, begin with 'Logic and conversation' (Grice 1989b [1975]), perhaps followed by 'Further notes on logic and conversation' (Grice 1989c [1978]), where the pragmatic rescue of a truth-conditional semantics is skilfully laid out. ('Skilfully' in that there is so much in meaning$_{NN}$ that, in hindsight, goes against it!) Unfair as it may be on Grice, for the purpose of making one's own journey through meaning, it is best to think about his ideas from the perspective of *what we now know and think*, with the benefit of hindsight. For post-Griceans, try Sperber and Wilson's (1995 [1986]) *Relevance: Communication and Cognition*, Chapter 3 and the 'Postface' to the 1995 edition, Horn's (2004) 'Implicature', and Levinson's (2000) *Presumptive Meanings*, Chapters 1–2. On the semantics/pragmatics distinction and the minimalism/contextualism debates, follow the suggestions in the footnotes in that there are many important landmarks on the way and singling out any of the aspects of these debates would do injustice to others. I also recommend thinking about the merits and demerits of the indexicalist solution – the best text to start with is, arguably, Stanley and Szabó's (2000) 'On quantifier domain restriction'. (Don't forget here Stanley's (2007) conciliatory 'Postscript'.) But the section yields itself to picking and choosing what grips one as right and as wrong, so, follow the footnotes – and, as a rule, search for the latest developments and specific avenues of research not covered in my recommendations, remembering that an objective and unbiased journey through meaning is neither possible nor wished for! On that note, for what it means to be Gricean now (well, in 2019) see my 'Rethinking being Gricean: New challenges for metapragmatics' (Jaszczolt 2019b).

# Stage 8 Meaning in Service of Its Makers

## 8.1 Who Needs Literal Meanings?

Meaning is incredibly flexible. We have encountered theories according to which there is no core meaning to be discerned but merely fluid, adjustable concepts – in line with what, back in the 1950s, Ludwig Wittgenstein called family resemblance: words are related to each other but do not exhibit core characteristics. Not all games are competitive and not all games are physical; defining what counts as a 'game' is not that easy (see Section 2.2). This is what we referred to earlier as radical$_w$ contextualism – 'radical' with respect to the meaning of words: there is no core to be abstracted from words, there are only ongoing processes of context-driven precisification as discourse progresses. We have also seen that this view fits well with meaning adjustment, or what in Truth-Conditional Pragmatics was called modulation, that takes place in tandem with what the addressee happened to abstract from past uses of the word.[1]

If words are so incredibly flexible, then where does this leave the traditional distinction between literal and non-literal meaning? We have encountered some instances of speaking non-literally in Stage 7 but did not attend there to the core phenomenon, namely metaphor. We shall now begin with the question as to what 'literal' can, cannot, should, and should not mean in state-of-the-art approaches to meaning, before moving to the concept of metaphor.

There is no doubt that on some occasions, the best fit between the thought to be communicated and the expression is achieved through communicating it metaphorically. But if it is the best fit, then, arguably, it captures the speaker's thought *literally*, in the common-sense meaning of the term. There is only an apparent paradox here: when metaphor provides the most suitable concept, then it is this concept that, for this context, becomes 'literal'. This line of thinking about metaphorical concepts comes from Relevance-theoretic research where concepts can be constructed ad hoc, to fit the context.[2] Carston (2002: 340) calls it an 'apparent paradox' in that 'metaphorical (and other loose) uses are no less *literal* interpretations of speakers' thoughts than standard literal uses are'. Literalness (or literality) becomes then a property of thoughts

---

[1] See Section 7.3.2, fn 83.  [2] See e.g. Carston 2002, Chapter 5.

rather than a property of words and sentences. And this is the right move to make if one wants a conceptual, cognitively real theory of meaning.

'Literal' means many things. One contextualist account complicates literalness to a mind-boggling degree – at least at first sight. Recanati's *Literal Meaning* reaches a rather surreal peak in its attempt to clarify the concept, only to show that it cannot be clarified because it is inherently many-ways ambiguous.[3] Recanati devises the following taxonomy. First, there is t[ype]-literalness – the meaning of an expression type, where 'type' is contrasted with a particular 'token' or 'occurrence' of this expression in context. Departures from t-literalness can be of two kinds. When the use of an expression involves only 'bottom-up' processes, it is still m[inimally]-literal. Meaning is m-literal when it can be recovered through the conventions of the language. By this criterion, the meaning of a sentence with an indexical term such as (8.1) is m-literal because the referent of *I* can be recovered through a convention of the English language. So, the meaning 'Kasia' for *I* constitutes only a minimal departure. But it is t-non-literal because this operation involves context: there is no type-literalness.

(8.1)    I live in Cambridge.

Departures that involve 'top-down' processing are classified as m-non-literal. It is at this point that the term 'literalness' is beginning to resemble the ordinary use of the word (but not quite). Within m-non-literal uses, we have uses that are still 'literal' in another sense of the term: they are p[rimary]-literal in that they are 'primary' in Recanati's sense and akin to the Relevance-theoretic explicature. That is, they are not what they call an implicature (a separate, independent proposition). So, (8.2) is an example of a p-literal (but m-non-literal) meaning.

(8.2)    I will tell you a secret *if* ($\gg$ *if and only if*) you promise to be discreet.

Metaphorical expressions are also p-literal: their main, primary meaning is the metaphorical meaning. It follows that p-non-literal meanings are implicit meanings – implicatures, such as those used in indirect speech acts. When I make a request by hinting, I use the sentence p-non-literally.

Now, as primary meanings, metaphorical meanings are p-literal. Recanati describes them as ranging from simple enrichments, sense elaborations, as in the case of unnoticeable metaphors (*win an argument, waste time*), through more noticeable sense extensions, to sense extensions that are above the level of conscious awareness and as such can properly be called 'figurative'. (And 'figurative' is precisely what 'literal' customarily means.) In other words, although metaphorical meanings are p-literal, not all of them are conscious, deliberate, or noticeable. So, not all metaphors are examples of figurative meaning – something we will return to shortly while discussing cognitive approaches to metaphor. Figure 8.1 summarizes the distinctions.

---

[3] See Recanati 2004, Chapter 5.

## 8.1 Who Needs Literal Meanings? 293

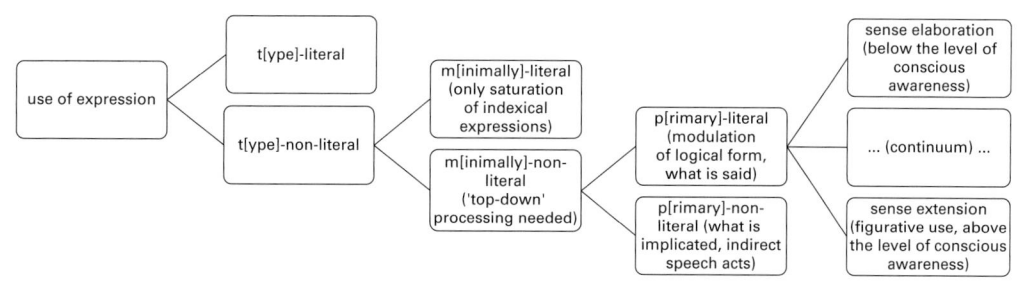

**Figure 8.1** Typology of literalness modelled on Recanati (2004: 68–78 and Fig. 5.1)

It is indeed the case that literalness is a vague term and can be appropriated in these, and also some other, ways. So, does this classification justify literalness as a theoretical term? I have discussed this elsewhere[4] as follows:

> Clearly, something has gone awry if one feels compelled to split the intuitively simple concept of literalness into such a mind-boggling taxonomy, and, to make things worse, also subsume 'customary non-literal' [i.e. 'figurative'] under a sub-type of 'literal' [i.e. p-literal]. Surely, the search for the cognitive reality of the unit of the truth-conditional analysis which is the leading directive for contextualists cannot require such conceptual contortions and sacrifices of common sense. Where the reasoning that leads to the distinctions in the typology is faultless while the resulting theoretical labels end up out of kilter, one has to address the issue of the source of the trouble. (Jaszczolt 2016: 41)

At the same time, Recanati's taxonomy simply makes use of widely accepted contextualist concepts such as saturation and modulation, or automatic and conscious processing. It also demonstrates what options we have to consider before we use the term 'literal' at all, leading to the predictable conclusions, first, that there is a colossal terminological muddle in the literature, and, second, that we should probably consider making do without the term altogether. So, the taxonomy clearly reveals that the problem is with the concept of literalness itself. We could perhaps abandon it, or, alternatively, just use it like speakers commonly do, as in (8.3).

(8.3)   Anna is a computer, literally. She can process numbers in a flash.

But literal meaning won't go without a fight. Take, for example, the argument from meaning activation. There is experimental evidence showing that when lexical meaning is not relevant for the context, it can still be activated. Rachel Giora and her group, for example, obtained such evidence in support of her graded salience hypothesis discussed in Section 7.3.4. The hypothesis appears to offer some degree of vindication in that salient meanings are often the literal ones and they can be activated to some degree even when they are not relevant for the context.[5] But 'often' is not 'always': as Giora (2003: 33) says, 'literality is not a component of salience'; salience is related to accessibility in memory and is caused by experience, and most notably the frequency of use. Her empirical evidence shows that 'familiar instances of metaphor and irony

---

[4] See Jaszczolt 2016.   [5] See Giora 2003, p. 33, 2012; Peleg and Giora 2011.

activated their salient (*figurative and literal*) meanings initially, regardless of contextual information' Giora (2003: 140, my emphasis).

Now, since experimental evidence accumulated by Giora and her lab strongly suggests that the concept of salience overlaps to a great degree with that of literalness, at the same time letting in cases of salient non-literalness, it may be that focusing on literalness is indeed superfluous. Or, perhaps, we could redefine 'literal' in terms of 'salient' – in agreement with common usage exemplified in (8.3). In other words, a speaker means something 'literally' *not* because this particular meaning is fixed by the lexicon and grammar of the language – there may not even be such a thing, as progressing contextualism purports to show. Instead, the meaning is literal because it is salient qua automatically activated – at the same time allowing that it can be activated to a greater or lesser degree, in accordance with Giora's graded salience hypothesis. This is where the common usage and the theoretical arguments seem to converge on what 'literal' means – 'really', 'in fact', as a human conceptualization of *natural* meaning.

On the other hand, tampering with the concept 'literal' may not be the best way to go. Conceptual engineering is risky: legitimizing the new sense that is still seen as sloppy may not catch on. Perhaps what we have been looking for is a concept that does agree with the common usage of 'literal' but focuses on the characteristics such as salient, automatic, primary, or even default – if we understand the latter as *default for the type of situation*, rather than default for the expression in a void, as discussed in Stage 7.

All in all, it appears that, somewhat surprisingly, literalness is best taken to mean the common-sense, obvious meaning for the given context. If this is literalness, then we should probably reject semantic minimalism in that the units in a syntactic composition are themselves context-dependent. Also, what counts as a compositional unit is carved *in*, and *by*, *the context* – these are sometimes words, and at other times longer constructions. That is why in Section 7.1.4. we made Kaplan's concept of a character more discourse-dependent as a flexible, *fluid character* – to capture the fact that interlocutors are relatively free to delimit it. Interpretation progresses incrementally and addressees identify units of varying lengths as primitive, not further decomposable, for the purpose at hand. For example, arguably, 'some-people-say' in (8.4), when used in a context in a conventionalized way, is a candidate for such a primitive character and as such does not enrich to 'some but not all'.

(8.4)   Some people say John is a miser.

Note that this means that all characters are, unlike for Kaplan (discussed in Section 6.2.4.3), dictated by their *purpose* – contextualist, flexible characters for contextualist, functional propositions. Metaphors that rely on conventional collocations such as, say, *to feel down* could be analysed in an analogous way.

Is there really no room for the minimalist sense of 'literal'? Kaplan's concept of a character is supposed to delimit the 'pure', 'use-free', 'language-only' dimension of meaning. And we do have intuitive understanding of such minimal meanings – many standard jokes rely on misusing them in context. So, why exorcise them as nonexisting? In the United Kingdom, jokes found on pieces of paper in Christmas crackers make use mostly of such meanings and the homonyms and puns they come with. While we try to locate 'contextualist, common-sense literalness' in fluid characters, standard 'minimalist literalness' is located in ordinary Kaplan's characters. Food for thought.

On the other hand, what exactly is this minimalist literalness? There are circumstances in which the situational context is not sufficient to provide the right kind of content. Recall the 'painted leaves' scenarios discussed in Section 3.1 (also discussed briefly in Section 6.2.4.3). Utterance (3.4), repeated below, can be true or false on the same occasion of its use, depending on the purpose of its uttering – or, in other words, on the circumstances under which it is evaluated. Leaves of a russet Japanese maple, when sprayed with green paint, will count as green for the purpose of finding a green background but not for a botanist who is looking for specimens of green-leaved plants.

(3.4)   The leaves are green.

So, it looks like pragmatics seeps in whatever we try to do. Stefano Predelli[6] proposes here special functions that he calls *applications* that make truth evaluation sensitive not only to the context but also to such reasons for evaluation. But then, can we extend this to the case of irony, for example, where a sentence ought to be evaluated as its opposite (or just different, in that irony does not always reverse the meaning[7])? Any solution that works for reasons for evaluation in (3.4) ought to work for ironic statements; after all, in saying (8.5) ironically the speaker is not only conveying that the addressee is not well-mannered but also that he was expected to have better manners than he turns out to have, which in some circumstances of evaluation is the core sense.

(8.5)   You are so well-mannered, Nigel ☺

Next, shouldn't we expect a solution to (3.4) to extend to metaphorical expressions, in particular to novel ones, in that they are often deliberately left vague to make room for such different goals of evaluation? But to make the circumstances of evaluation so fine grained would amount to admitting that salient uses of language are entirely purpose-of-evaluation dependent and as such not literal in the standard sense – not traceable to the lexicon of the language system but malleable, squidgy, more like snorts, grunts, squeaks, and squeals. Can words and structures adapt like chameleons to what their users want them to do? It goes without saying that no language as a means of communication can make use of such 'gooey' signs.

Predelli (2005a: 366) also adds a formal definition that appears to offer some restriction on how the evaluation of the utterance meaning is to proceed – unlike the 'ad-hocness' of Wittgenstein's 'meaning eliminativism' discussed in Section 7.3.4.

given a representation of $z$ by means of the clause-index pair $<s, i>$ and the application $a$, $z$ is true with respect to worldly conditions $w$ iff $j(a(w)) = $ truth, where $j$ is the intension associated by [an interpretive system] S with $<s,i>$.

---

[6] See Predelli 2005a, b.   [7] See Kapogianni 2022. For an introduction to irony see Garmendia 2018.

But it would become only a patina of rigour if we tried to extend Predelli's proposal in the way suggested above. It looks like the path may become circular: applications are sensitive to anything that might be relevant for specifying what makes an utterance true or false across a range of goal-dependent (as in 3.4), ironic, metaphorical, humorous, or polite uses (a word of warning: these concepts can intersect). In other words, we have a theoretical construct that allows us to put whatever we need in the conditions of truth evaluation in order to get whatever we need to get. Is this a dead end, then? Or perhaps only a realization that 'literal' meaning is precisely such meaning that is salient for the context, and therefore that *all meaning is 'literal'*? And a realization that context dependence, purpose-of-evaluation dependence and non-literalness are not cases of divergence from some straight, literal path?

What follows is that the concept 'literal' becomes void: there is only meaning, or there is only jointly constructed meaning, constructed out of how words are used in the structures in which they are involved. Perhaps this meaning is what a post-Kaplanian character, qua linguistic meaning, ought to capture? After all, there are regularities to be found on the level of human mental and social activities. The next step is then to try to capture the concept of a metaphor: if it is not a departure from literalness, then there is a chance that the concept of a *metaphor as a uniform phenomenon* should also be given the axe.

## 8.2 What Makes a Metaphor

### 8.2.1 Objectivism and Subjectivism Revisited

'Metaphor' is a kind of semi-technical term that is almost as mischievous as 'proposition' or 'truth value' when left unqualified. Is (8.6) metaphorical?

(8.6)   The debate was quite even but the Labour Party won in the end.

If this sentence weren't placed here as an example of a potential metaphor, would it strike you as metaphorical? If not, then how important is this *awareness* that an expression is metaphorical that was discussed in relation to Figure 8.1? How about (8.7)?

(8.7)   The end of term is approaching fast.

But even if these sentences *are metaphorical*, does it mean that they contain *metaphors*? Perhaps metaphors are thoughts rather than expressions? One thing is certain: just as we couldn't find a clear minimalism/contextualism distinction, semantics/pragmatics distinction, speaker meaning/addressee meaning distinction, literal/non-literal distinction (we could continue!), so the metaphorical/non-metaphorical distinction will be lined with different demarcations, all of them problematic in one way or another. We could stop here and point out that we ended the last section by subsuming 'metaphorical' under 'literal', so the point was made already. It would be a great load off our shoulders in this journey if it were so. But, literal or not, 'load off the shoulders' evokes a lot of meanings that, for example, 'relief' or 'help' do not – and this has to be explained. The fact is that metaphor remains one of the most researched topics in the study of meaning. Syntacticians have largely managed to bypass it, subscribing to a popular philosophical stance that metaphor is a phenomenon of invoking just about *any* meaning by using just about *any* expression (more about this later, without trivialization), and as such does not merit much attention. But what to formal syntacticians may look like a deterrent may look like an exciting challenge to semanticists and pragmaticists. Hence the topic thrives. So, let us journey through some selected attempts to harness the phenomenon.

For twenty-first-century linguists, metaphors are not what they used to be: for many, they pertain to ways of thinking about reality rather than to ways of describing it. Linguistic behaviour is governed by general cognitive abilities and it is there that we can find regularities about our concepts. Needless to say, this outlook is categorially different from the proposal of specialized linguistic modules in the mind defended by Fodor, discussed in Section 2.3. In cognitive linguistics, studying syntax, phonology, or semantics in isolation would go against this defence of general cognitive mechanisms; they are not separate modules or faculties in the brain. By analogous reasoning, 'literal' and 'metaphorical' use of language are not categorially different either: they merely reflect ways of conceptualizing the world – ways that are equally well suited for the purpose at hand. Next, metaphorical meanings can be conventionalized and even become part of the lexicon of the language: '*foot* of the mountain' is not considered to be a metaphorical expression any longer. Cognitive linguists explain such historical changes of lexicalization as results of general cognitive mechanisms.

This view comes with all-pervasive subjectivism. George Lakoff[8] is an iconic figure in the rejection of the objectivism of truth-conditional semantics. He claims that since objective reality is inaccessible, natural languages do not come with objective meanings of words or sentences. Instead, like for Immanuel Kant long before, meaning depends on conceptualization: the mind imposes categories on the world, in the process 'chopping it into meaningful pieces', so to speak. What we call 'meaning' arises when such conceptualizations are conventionalized, shared by people, becoming common, interpersonal categorizations of reality. This leads cognitive linguists of this orientation, arguably quite unnecessarily, to the rejection of truth conditions. But at this point in our journey we can venture the proposal that, perhaps, instead of concluding that truth conditions are of no use, it is better to see them as a versatile tool that doesn't lose its enormous merits when we 'kick the analysis up' to the level of cognitive structures.

Subjectivism is not difficult to notice in that speakers can conceptualize situations differently not only across different languages but also within them. Even within one language, we can think of a situation in terms of different schemas, prioritising different aspects of it, as in the well-quoted *spray/load* pairs of examples in (8.8a)–(8.8b) and (8.9a)–(8.9b).

---

[8] See e.g. Lakoff 1987.

(8.8a) He loaded the dry hay onto the truck.

(8.8b) He loaded the truck with the dry hay.

(8.9a) She sprayed the leftover paint onto the wall.//
(8.9b) She sprayed the wall with the leftover paint.

(after Kay 1996: 105)

So, what Sapir and Whorf memorialized as linguistic relativity (discussed briefly in Section 2.2[9]) is in fact cognitive reality that is not only more pronounced across languages but is also present within a single language. Moreover, as we have discussed throughout different parts of this journey, the conceptual 'building blocks' from which such lexical and sentential concepts are built are very likely to be universal.[10] There is one step from there to making the subjectivist and objectivist outlooks on meaning compatible: when we look at the blocks we can play with, it is likely to be the same set. After all, human mental architecture and mental operations are universal.[11] But when we look at what we create out of these blocks when we speak, the differences can be glaring. So, perhaps objectivists and subjectivists about meaning and truth are both partly right? And perhaps formal methods of truth-conditional semantics are not necessarily invalidated by the observation that conceptualization is subjective and that truth conditions will have to be sensitive to that? This is what we have been asking throughout this journey, discussing different views and trying to find a unified picture rather than divisions and debates. And this is what we will try to do looking at approaches to metaphor.

It is no exaggeration to say that cognitive linguistics revolves around metaphor. Lakoff and Johnson, in their seminal *Metaphors We Live By*,[12] stirred up the international semantic community by proposing that when people impose their concepts on the world to understand it and act in it, they do so largely through metaphors. For them, metaphors belong not only to the domain of linguistic expressions (these are merely *metaphorical expressions*) but also to the domain of thought: metaphors are *conceptual metaphors*. As such, they are reflected in different modalities: in language, but also in gestures and visual, including artistic, representations. Hence the label Conceptual Metaphor Theory (CMT). They track many metaphors to abstract structures that arise prior to concepts and pertain to recurring patterns that are acquired through experiencing aspects of the world, such as moving bodies, relations between objects, force exerted by objects on other objects, and so forth.[13] It is therefore clear why they renounce the boundary between literal and figurative use of language. To compare, contextualists of the post-Gricean orientation attempt to accommodate metaphor in their view on meaning as truth-conditional content supplemented with implicatures, merely pointing out a gradual distinction between the literal and the metaphorical. On the other hand,

---

[9] See Section 2.2, fn 11 for references to the universalism/relativity debate and in particular the neo-Whorfian stance.

[10] One of the most influential proposals of universal semantic primitive concepts (and 'cognitive building blocks') is Wierzbicka's Natural Semantic Metalanguage. See e.g. Wierzbicka 1996.

[11] The debate is still ongoing: see e.g. Levinson et al.'s (2003) findings on spatial adpositions (IN, ON, UNDER, ...) in different languages and the lack of their mutual translatability.

[12] See Lakoff and Johnson 1980.    [13] See e.g. Johnson 1987, Chapter 2; Lakoff and Johnson 1999.

cognitivists of the Lakoff-Johnson orientation go the whole hog, making metaphors the centre of conceptualization and concluding that truth conditions have to go. In this way they deprive themselves of the powerful tools that give us a formal grip on meaning and on understanding by looking at natural language from the outside, so to speak. But perhaps we can take the tools and adjust them. After all, formalists are increasingly sensitive to the cognitive reality of meaning, as was surveyed in the preceding stage of this journey. We will discuss metaphor in post-Gricean pragmatics and in CMT in a moment but first we begin with the traditional views of *comparison* and *semantic interaction*.

### 8.2.2 Metaphor: Comparison and Interaction

Comparison theories say that metaphorical utterances involve similarity, resemblance, or a comparison between *objects*. As such, they are also called *referentialist views* and have been traced back to Aristotle, Cicero, and Quintilian.[14] This is probably the most commonly shared understanding of the term 'metaphor', coming from Greek *meta-* ('after', 'beyond', cf. *trans-*) and *phérō-* ('carry'). On the other hand, according to the interaction view, attributed to I. A. Richards and Max Black,[15] an explanation is to be found in the interaction, or opposition, between the content of the expression used metaphorically and the literal context (co-text). This view is also called a *descriptivist view* in that the interpretation is determined by the descriptive content.

These views provide important foundations for metaphor research but many aspects of them have been contested. Crucially, comparison theories do not explain how an utterance ends up obtaining the intuitive truth conditions of the metaphor. At the same time, arguably, these are the only truth conditions that can be sensibly assigned to it, not the 'official', literal ones. No theory of meaning that aspires to cognitive reality should have to claim that (8.10) ought to have the truth conditions pertaining to the literal interpretation.

(8.10)   My physics teacher is an angel.

We will see in the next section that Grice attempted to rescue the truth-conditional analysis of metaphor and its literal truth conditions by calling the literal meaning not 'what is said' (which it clearly is not, since *saying* something for him entailed *meaning* it) but what is 'made as if to say'. But this was merely a move to save truth-conditional semantics rather than a pursuit of intuitive truth conditions. There was no such rescue at the time: there was the literal, truth-conditional content and its metaphorical overlay.

Another problem with the comparison view is that similarity need not be the case for metaphors to be successful. Moreover, 'similar' is such a vague predicate that, when pressed or, say, trying to make a joke, one can find similarities between any two objects

---

[14] Introductions are ample. For a critical discussion of these views, see e.g. Searle 1993 [1979] or Leezenberg 2001. Some suggestions, as usual, are listed at the end of this stage.
[15] See Richards 1936 and Black 1962, 1993 [1977].

or concepts, and along many different dimensions too. In (8.10), the teacher is likely to be a human being and as such have no wings – not to mention that, arguably, angels don't even exist. The teacher can be *like an angel* in a metaphorical, not literal, sense, so the concept of metaphor still remains unexplained. As Searle observes in his critical assessment, similarity between the referents may help in comprehension of metaphors but it is not part of their meaning.[16]

Neither does comparison theory explain the *open-endedness* of metaphors – the fact that what they bring to mind can be endless and that their meaning may be left to the hearer or reader to supply. (8.11) may convey and suggest many different attributes of Romeo's lover.

(8.11)   Juliet is the sun.

At the same time, we need a theory that would sift through the interpretations to distinguish between the plausible and the implausible ones and exclude, for example, (8.12) and (8.13).

(8.12)   Juliet is for the most part gaseous.

(8.13)   Juliet is 90 million miles from the earth.

(from Searle 1993: 96)

This has since been accomplished by an Oxford philosopher, Jonathan Cohen,[17] who suggests that the meaning of sentences such as (8.14) can be explained through *cancellation of some essential features of objects*.

(8.14)   The clouds are made of pure gold.

(from Cohen 1993 [1979]: 64)

In (8.14), *gold* is used metaphorically; the feature 'metallic' has been cancelled. So, cancellation affects word meaning. As such, this proposal fits with the semantic interaction view. Cohen then asks if there is a rule to this cancellation – in other words, whether cancellation is systematic. He points out that for this account to work, semantic features have to be ordered on a scale of importance: for example 'metallic' is more of a core feature than 'yellow'. He also observes that in terms of information content (discussed in Section 6.3), metaphorical meaning often occurs in the comment rather than the topic position in the sentence. So, the theory goes, cancellation of features is imposed by the topic (old information) on the comment (new information). In (8.14), cancellation proceeds from *clouds* (in the topic position) to *gold* (in the comment position). It is true that no such fixed ordering of features is available, and neither is it likely to be found, apart from some general common-sense indicators and clues from what is definitional, essential, and what only accidental. However, what is important is that Cohen's overall conviction that an explanation of metaphor is to be found in the domain of semantics rather than pragmatics has withstood the test of time:

---

[16] See Searle 1993 [1979], p. 92.    [17] See Cohen 1993 [1979].

more satisfactory semantic approaches continue coming to the fore, especially when semantics is understood as resting on contextualist foundations.

Interactionism is by no means dead. Elisabeth Camp and, following her, Chris Genovesi,[18] for example, have recently pushed it in the direction of commitments: is the speaker committed to the content of a metaphorical expression – or, at least, is this commitment as strong as it is while speaking literally? This question arises because a metaphor can communicate a whole range of different propositions. So, is metaphor 'said' or only 'meant'? Adopting a version of the interactionist view allows researchers to delve deeper into where metaphorical expression ought to be placed on the route between meaning and saying. I return to this question when discussing commitment and accountability in Section 8.4.1.

All in all, just like comparison theories, interaction theories have also been found wanting – not only from the methodological point of view, as in the case of Cohen's ordered features, but also as an approach in general. First, their disregard of the speaker's intended meaning (and the addressee's recovered meaning for that matter) makes them too restricted. Next, it is not clear what the grounds for an interaction/opposition would be: how do we distinguish the 'right candidates' for such an interaction? Is there anything in the expression itself that signals 'I am a metaphorical expression, so search for my meaning by consulting the rest of the sentence'? Moreover, interaction need not play a part in the understanding of an expression. Substituting a contextually salient metaphor for *my teacher* in (8.10), as in (8.15), is a case in point.

(8.15)  Our local Einstein is an angel.

There is no opposition there between the literal and the non-literal part of the sentence, and so there is no interaction: both the subject and the predicate are expressed metaphorically and don't seem to 'interact' in any revealing way.

### 8.2.3  Towards a Contextualist-Semantic/Pragmatic Account

It is frequently assumed that metaphor is based on a shift of properties from one concept (*source domain*) to another (*target domain*). This can be explained either (i) on the level of the sentence and its semantics or (ii) from the perspective of discourse interactants, in pragmatics.

Traditionally, following Aristotle, metaphor was regarded as an additional layer of meaning, 'on top of' the literal. And here is where pragmatic approaches fit in. In the case of metaphor, like in the case of irony, indirect requests, and other indirect speech, what the speaker means differs from what the sentence means: sentence meaning is literal meaning (remember that 'literal' was still simple back then) and speaker meaning is metaphorical meaning. The pragmatic stance can be summarized in the claim that metaphorical meaning gets across because the addressee makes assumptions about the possible intentions of the speaker. According to Searle, metaphorical

---

[18] See Camp 2006 and Genovesi 2020.

meaning is always the speaker's utterance meaning. Metaphors allow the speaker to mean more than, or something different from, what is literally said. Interlocutors then rely on background information and background assumptions in arriving at the meaning. For example, (8.16) can be used literally, metaphorically, or literally but ironically, or as an indirect request. Background assumptions and contextual clues facilitate arriving at the relevant interpretation.

(8.16)   It's chilly in the room.

But this line of reasoning opens up the possibility that, since the general knowledge and assumptions affect both literal and figurative use of language alike, there is no boundary between the two. Needless to say, pragmatic approaches facilitated this demise of the literal/non-literal distinction we have just travelled through in Section 8.1.

On the other hand, intuitively, metaphors *are* different. They have a richness to them that is often lacking from speaking literally; poetic, novel metaphors especially, can convey a sense of open-endedness. Moreover, conventionalization of some metaphors, such as (8.17), provides compelling evidence that they are needed when existing lexical devices fail.

(8.17)   You are my sunshine.

Metaphors become conventional because they are needed – they fill in some semantic gap. As Searle (1993 [1979]: 89) puts it,

[t]he basic principle on which all metaphor works is that the utterance of an expression with its literal meaning and corresponding truth conditions can, in various ways that are specific to metaphor, call to mind another meaning and corresponding set of truth conditions.

The meaning that is 'called to mind' has to be restricted to, say, some patterns of making analogies, and systematic; it has to be shared between interlocutors. And it is precisely this 'calling to mind' that requires a theory of how it happens. Searle provides some suggestions here. For example, the pattern *S is P* results in the interpretation *S is R* when *P*s are by definition *R*s, as in (8.18).

(8.18)   Sam is a giant. ≫ Sam is big.

Next, metaphorical meaning arises when *P* and *R* are similar in meaning but *P* is restricted in application and does not literally apply to *S*, as in (8.19).

(8.19)   His brain is addled. ≫ His brain is muddled.

(adapted from Searle 1993 [1979]: 104, 106)

These mechanisms exploit world knowledge and the ability to think analogically. For example, (8.19) displays such a general pattern of associations: the mental with the physical, where mental decay is physical decay. We also associate emotional coldness with physical coldness along this schema, understanding with seeing, and so forth – a systematization that was developed into a ground-breaking cognitive theory of metaphor to which we return in the next section.

At the same time, pragmatic approaches push the literal/metaphorical distinction further and deeper into the muddy waters of the semantics/pragmatics boundary debates. For Grice,[19] sentences have only their literal meaning and the corresponding truth-conditional content. Metaphorical meaning belongs to utterances in virtue of being implicated: in uttering, say, (8.17), the speaker flouts the maxim of Quality, which facilitates inferring the implicated meaning. And this is where Grice's ambivalence on the concept of saying opened the floodgates for quick progress in the pragmatics of metaphor. To reiterate, Grice's definition of *what is said*, discussed in Section 7.1.1, requires that saying something entails meaning it. So, the speaker who utters (8.17) has not really *said* it – at best, the speaker 'has made as if to say' (Grice 1989b [1975]), just as is the case with irony and other sentence non-literality. Metaphorical meaning then becomes relegated to the status of metaphor, but not a well-behaved metaphor that arises from what is said, but instead a rather odd case of a metaphor that arises out of what was 'made as if to say'.

Dan Sperber and Deirdre Wilson's discussion of this ambiguity in Grice's notion of saying and the exposed flaw in his Quality-based account of metaphor is what opened these floodgates. In their 'Truthfulness and relevance', they point out this possible equivocation that subsequently acted as an eye-opener for many post-Gricean researchers (me included):

If the speaker of metaphor or irony merely 'makes as if to say' something, then the stronger notion of saying must be in force; on the other hand, if the speaker of a trope merely 'makes as if' to say something, then surely the maxim of truthfulness is not violated. But if the maxim of truthfulness is not violated, how does Grice's analysis of metaphor and irony go through at all? (Wilson and Sperber 2012a [2002]: 53)

Wilson and Sperber are charitable to Grice: they do not accuse him of a lack of conceptual rigour. Instead, they credit him with the awareness that the notion of *saying* is itself problematic in that it cannot at the same time account for the vagueness, underdetermination, and multi-functionality of natural-language structures and be sufficiently precise for the kind of truth-conditional theory of meaning that he wants to defend. But if, like Sperber, Wilson, Carston, and other Relevance theorists have done, we loosen the distinction between literal and non-literal, or even contemplate abandoning it altogether, then a much more satisfactory account clicks into place. As they say,

[f]rom the standpoint of relevance theory, there is no reason to think that the optimally relevant interpretive expression of a thought is always the most literal one. The speaker is presumed to aim at optimal relevance, not at literal truth. The optimal interpretive expression of a thought should give the hearer information about that thought which is relevant enough to be worth processing, and should require as little processing effort as possible. (Sperber and Wilson 1995 [1986]: 233)

Metaphor is, so to speak, a link that connects a mental representation with the propositional form of the utterance in that 'metaphor involves an interpretive relation

---

[19] See e.g. Grice 1989b [1975].

between the propositional form of an utterance and the thought it represents' (Sperber and Wilson 1995 [1986]: 231). As such, it is on a par with any other device that interactants make use of while putting their message into words in a form that obeys the tacitly followed principle of human rational behaviour.[20]

Metaphorical meanings are not implicated but are better conceived of as part of the truth-conditional content (their 'explicature'). The process of arriving at these meanings in discourse ought to be explicable via a theory that advocates ad hoc concept construction – construction *in situ*, for the purpose at hand and based on assumptions and information relevant for the current purpose that facilitate the adjustment. This is the gist of the proposal developed by Robyn Carston. As was discussed in Section 7.2.3, the next step is to see concepts as being constructed entirely *in situ*, rather than see them as a result of contextual shift (whether conscious or not). Research continues, and it continues clearly in the direction of strongly situated meanings.[21]

Relevance-theoretic research exerts an important influence on the journey we are pursuing here. Within the context of the post-Gricean underdetermined-semantics movement, it has reconceptualized truth-conditional content to make it pertain to the level of thoughts – conceptual units, rather than physical utterances, let alone sentences. It has also retained the powerful tool of truth conditions, so the assumptions that we take as our desiderata are already present there. But we have to go a little further. What we would like in this journey is to represent not what is explicit and implicit, but what is *main* and *secondary* according to both parties in discourse – a desideratum to which Relevance Theory comes close, for example in incorporating metaphorical meaning in the truth-conditional representation, but not close enough. After all, the metaphorical meaning of the uttered sentence can still be its secondary meaning; by saying that Sam is a giant the speaker may be giving an answer to the question as to whether Sam would fit into size XS clothes. And it is this main meaning, the functional proposition qua conceptually plausible main proposition, that we want to model on this journey. Default Semantics discussed in Stage 7 has taken us a little further but a formal theory of composition of such meanings is still work in collective progress among many different orientations within meaning contextualism.

Next, let us see what can be achieved within semantic approaches. In agreement with the contextualist stance to incorporate contextual information into semantic interpretation, the accounts by Stern and Leezenberg stand out as particularly notable.[22] Stern makes use of Kaplan's distinction between character and content originally used to explain indexicals (see Section 6.2.4.3). Like any other expressions, metaphorical expressions have character and content. So, '[a]s with the character of any expression, the character of an expression interpreted metaphorically is a function, or rule, that determines, for each context, its content in that context'

---

[20] See here the diagram in Sperber and Wilson 1995 [1986], p. 232.
[21] The literature is ample: see e.g. Sperber and Wilson 1995 [1986], Section 4.8; Carston 2002, Chapter 5; Carston 2012a, b; articles in Wilson and Sperber 2012b.
[22] See Stern 2000 and Leezenberg 2001.

(Stern 2000: 105). A pronoun *she*, for example, comes with linguistic meaning to the effect of '3rd person singular, female', and as such 'a female other than the speaker or addressee', and acquires different content in different contexts. And so does metaphor. In other words,

> The 'interpretations' of a metaphor (type) are the *contents* its tokens express in their respective contexts. Since there is an unlimited, or not antecedently fixed, number of different possible contexts in which those tokens can occur, there is an unlimited number of different possible contents those tokens can express metaphorically. (Stern 2000: 105)

But there are also constraints, or rules, on what the content of an expression (type) can be, just as there are constraints in discourse on who the referent of *she* can be. And this is what a character of a metaphorical expression is:

> These facts suggest that a speaker has a more abstract kind of knowledge apart from his knowledge of the particular content of each metaphorical token in its respective context. This more abstract piece of knowledge is the *character* of the metaphor. (Stern 2000: 105)

It is the character that determines different contents for different contexts – character that stands for linguistic meaning that triggers particular content.

In a somewhat similar spirit, Leezenberg focuses on the context dependence of metaphorical interpretations in his revival of the descriptivist semantic approach. Metaphorical meaning is carried there by sentence tokens – units that are somewhere between sentence types and utterances. This is so because metaphorical interpretations are fairly entrenched: they don't disappear under embedding, indirect quotation, negation, or other operations that serve as standard tests. Metaphorical meaning is not assigned by speakers' intentions: interpretation is a semantic process but a process that is 'crucially and systematically context-dependent':

> a metaphor like *John is a wolf* expresses the assertion that John belongs to the extension of the predicate *wolf* within a specific thematic dimension of the context; in other words, it ascribes a contextually determined property to John. (Leezenberg 2001: 251)

Here the extension of 'wolf' is the metaphorical extension: it has people in it rather than wolves. After this extension shift, formal semantic analysis applies. So, this is yet another way of pursuing contextualist truth-conditional semantics.

Can we now conclude that there is nothing special to metaphor? Yes and no. Indeed, there is no need for a separate semantic/pragmatic theory dedicated specifically to metaphor; it appears that one can handle metaphor by appealing to standard pragmatic mechanisms of discourse. But there is still a nagging feeling that metaphorical expressions are often artistic, aesthetically pleasing, open to endless interpretations, and, in fact, often deliberately used, not only for aesthetic reasons but also for the purpose of explanation or persuasion. So, our contextualist-semantic *journey* is revealing multiple *paths* that appear quite *rocky* (!).

Now, while arguments are still mounting on both sides as to whether metaphorical meaning yields itself to a truth-conditional analysis, Donald Davidson's[23] view stands

---

[23] See Davidson 1984b [1978].

out as particularly radical on this score. Davidson denies metaphors are non-literal. Metaphors simply *mean what the words literally mean*. They may invoke certain interpretations in the addressee but metaphorical expressions do not *mean* any of these things. As he says, 'there is no limit to what a metaphor calls to our attention, and much of what we are caused to notice is not propositional in character' (Davidson 1984b [1978]: 263). Remember that Davidson is one of the fathers of truth-conditional semantics for natural languages in that he adapted Tarski's theory of truth to explain natural-language meaning. What is not truth-conditional naturally falls outside of the domain of inquiry: what is not propositional and not finite is not meaning at all. But does 'propositional' have to mean 'sentential'?[24] A few decades on, we have well-developed contextualist accounts of propositions, such as the Relevance-theoretic account of explicature. We also have functional propositions and Default Semantics. To digress, we can also question whether images or non-linguistic sounds can be construed as propositional if they are created out of, or invoke, conceptual representations. But these fall outside an inquiry into language. We only invoke them here as part of situational context. Still, lots of food for thought.

Next, even if we go along with the feeling that metaphors are somehow special, is there a single phenomenon that we can legitimately call 'metaphor'? Is it a uniform category?

We normally think metaphors are live, indeterminate, and open to new interpretations that don't appear to be governed by any strict rules – the less systematicity the better for the openness of invoked meanings and for the aesthetic value. Conventional metaphors, however, lack this openness and, as was discussed in connection with Figure 8.1, often operate below the level of conscious awareness. We also have expressions such as *the mouth of the river* that are, arguably, not metaphors any longer. There appears to be a spectrum of inferred meanings, from context-dependent, then becoming conventionalized if successful, that are still 'felt' as metaphorical before full lexicalization takes place. This is what Traugott[25] describes as a semantic process of *metaphorical extension* of meaning whereby metaphorical expressions that become entrenched follow the path from context-dependent implicatures (or, using her Gricean labels, PCIs), through conventionalized ones (or GCIs), to semantic meaning (SM), as in (8.20). The arrow means 'may become'.

(8.20)    PCI → GCI → SM

Or, from the perspective of the addressee, we can conceptualize this as a historical path from particularized through generalized invited inferences (PIIN, GIIN) to SM, as in (8.21).

(8.21)    PIIN → GIIN → SM

(adapted from Traugott 2004: 547, 552)[26]

---

[24] For a discussion see Moran 1997, p. 256.    [25] See Traugott, e.g. 2004.
[26] For pragmatics in semantic change, see also Traugott 2012.

Such metaphors have 'made it' through conventionalization to semantic, in the sense of minimalist-semantic, meaning: to the lexicon and grammar of a natural language. So, we can leave them out from a synchronic inquiry into metaphor. Next, let us consider metaphorical expressions that show a striking conceptual similarity to analogous expressions in other languages, suggesting that they rely on some universal patterns. Many of these are not felt as metaphorical. They rely on metaphorical thoughts that drive our cognition.

Some cognitive scientists think that most of language use relies on such metaphorical interpretations. We have already seen that within post-Gricean contextualism we can locate metaphor on the level of thoughts rather than expressions and question the literal/non-literal distinction. The cognitive approaches to which we now turn take a more radical step away from the 'literal' through adopting the idea of embodiment of human cognition. Again, as we will see, the difference in objectives makes the orientations difficult to compare fairly. But first things first.

### 8.2.4 Metaphor in Cognition

Cognitive linguists go the whole hog as far as the literal/metaphorical distinction is concerned: people don't arrive at metaphors through reinterpretation of the literal but through having access to mechanisms of conceptualization, as well as to preconceptual experience. That is why they emphasize the predictability of metaphors: they are interested in the systematicity of metaphors in human conceptualization and in the systematicity of metaphorical expressions that are their results. Lakoff and Johnson, in their *Philosophy in the Flesh*,[27] stress that metaphor is omnipresent in language use and that searching for a literal/figurative distinction is addressing the wrong question. As was said in the discussion of concepts in Section 2.2, the mind is embodied: we perceive reality and exist in it thanks to the sensorimotor apparatus and the structure of the brain that have evolved with humans. The sensorimotor apparatus is sensitive to individual experience; there are no objective categories that would endow meaning on the world. Instead,

> the qualities of things as we can experience and comprehend them depend crucially on our neural makeup, our bodily interactions with them, and our purposes and interests. For real human beings, the only realism is an embodied realism. (Lakoff and Johnson 1999: 26)

There is no objective–subjective interaction. Metaphors are abstract concepts we make use of in comprehending the world – that is, in imposing our own categorization upon the world. As was briefly discussed in Sections 2.2 and 8.2.1, philosophers trace this view to the noble tradition of embodied cognition that includes Immanuel Kant; linguists tend to begin with the empirical findings of cognitive science that point in precisely this direction.

Now, in virtue of being embodied, human experience does not entirely rely on concept formation. The widely adopted *experiential hypothesis* has it that children also

---

[27] See Lakoff and Johnson 1999, p. 17. For a discussion, see e.g. articles in Hampe 2017.

have *pre-conceptual experiences*, such as body movements or ability to move objects and perceive them as entities. They also have *image-schemas* (or *schemata*), such as containers, paths, part and whole, up and down, front and back. Pre-conceptual physical experiences then give rise to abstract concepts by metaphorical projection as in (8.22)–(8.24).[28]

(8.22)   Inflation is *rising*.

(8.23)   He's feeling *down*.

(8.24)   How do I *get out of* this difficulty?

According to experientialism, truth is relative to the conceptual system that is founded on some universal principles. Then,

> [i]mage schemata and metaphorical projections are *experiential* structures of meaning that are essential to most of our abstract understanding and reasoning. The metaphorical projections are not arbitrary but rather are highly constrained by other aspects of our bodily functioning and experience. 'Experience', then, is to be understood in a very rich, broad sense as including basic perceptual, motor-program, emotional, historical, social, and linguistic dimensions. (Johnson 1987: xvi)

Although, for cognitivists, there is no literal/figurative distinction, there is metaphorical mapping: metaphor is defined as a *cognitive process* of conceptualization that depends on mappings between two domains, or mental models. It is a *mapping from source models to target models*. For example, in (8.25), BODY is the source and MIND is the target, producing a *conceptual metaphor* that gives rise to *metaphorical expressions* such as (8.26)–(8.27).

(8.25)   MIND IS BODY.

(8.26)   I can *see* the problem.

(8.27)   This idea can be difficult to *grasp*.

Examples (8.28)–(8.30) contain other commonly discussed mappings and their instantiations.

(8.28)   LIFE IS A JOURNEY.
         (e.g. There are always obstacles on a *road to success*.)

(8.29)   TIME IS MONEY.
         (e.g. Let's drive there, to *save* time.)

(8.30)   UP IS GOOD, DOWN IS BAD.
         (e.g. I'm feeling *down*.)

Such mappings are *asymmetrical*: metaphors are usually created by transferring features of a more concrete object (the source) to a more abstract one (the target): from BODY to MIND, from JOURNEY to LIFE, from MONEY to TIME, and so on.

---

[28] See e.g. Lakoff and Johnson 1980, p. 226; Johnson 1987, p. xvi.

Sometimes the mapping between the source model and the target model is not straightforward and can lead to the construction of so-called *blends*. To use an example by Gilles Fauconnier, *to dig one's own grave*, meaning doing something to one's disadvantage, is not a simple mapping. On a closer look, there is no straightforward projection from the domain of burial to the domain of trouble in that the causal relationship is inverted: foolish actions cause one's own trouble but grave-digging does *not* cause death. Moreover, the structure of the event is peculiar in that, normally, people do not dig their own graves. And yet, somewhat paradoxically, this mismatch produces a highly successful metaphor. Fauconnier (1997: 169–170) explains the mechanism of the blend in terms of mental spaces as follows. It shows that the interaction between the source and the target can be very intricate.

This paradox dissolves when we consider, in addition to the source and target input spaces, the construction of the blended space. The blend inherits the concrete structure of graves, digging, and burial from the input source; but it inherits causal, intentional, and internal event structure from the input target. They are not simply juxtaposed. Rather, *emergent* structure specific to the blend is created. In the blend, all the curious properties ... actually hold. The existence of a satisfactory grave causes death and is a necessary precondition for it. It follows straightforwardly that the deeper the grave, the closer it is to completion and the greater the chance for the grave's intended occupant to die. It follows that in the blend (as opposed to the source), digging one's grave is a grave mistake, as it makes dying more probable. In the blend, it becomes *possible* to be unaware of one's very concrete actions. This is projected from the target input, where it is indeed fully possible, and frequent, to be unaware of the significance of one's actions. But in the blend, it remains *highly foolish* to be unaware of such concrete actions; this is projected from the source input. And it will project back to the target input to produce suitable inferences (i.e., highlight the foolishness and misperception of an individual's behavior).

According to some cognitive approaches,[29] blending is an even more fundamental cognitive mechanism than cognitive metaphor itself.

It is important to understand why research in cognitive semantics revolves around metaphors. They are the underlying mechanisms of our thinking – the *Metaphors We Live By* from the title of the ground-breaking book by Lakoff and Johnson.[30] To reiterate, metaphors are not expressions – they are metaphorical concepts. The language constructions that they produce are not additions to literal language; they are not embellishments. Metaphors so-conceived are *systematic* in that a whole range of metaphorical expressions can be traced to a single metaphor. (8.29), for instance (TIME IS MONEY), is said to produce a wide range of expressions such as *to spend time*, *to save time*, *to waste time*, and so forth. (8.25) (MIND IS BODY) accounts for an even broader range of expressions in that it subsumes narrower schemas such as UNDERSTANDING IS SEEING, OBEYING IS HEARING, or CHOOSING IS TASTING. But this hierarchical structure of the schemas poses a problem for cognitivists in that it is impossible to decide without empirical proof (say, from neuroimaging) which exact

---

[29] See Kövecses 2020, Section 6.3.
[30] See Lakoff and Johnson 1980, 1999. The literature is vast; for some seminal work, see Lakoff 1987, 1996; Johnson 1987; Lakoff and Turner 1989.

schema is responsible for the metaphorical expression and how far up we ought to go in generalizing – perhaps even to ABSTRACT IS CONCRETE? An interim improvement is a proposal of multiple levels by Zoltán Kövecses[31] – 'interim' because the question of empirical corroboration still remains. Recent advances in neurosemantics and neuropragmatics have made some progress but criticism aptly levelled by opponents still stands. Most importantly, it stands because mappings between schemas are heavily determined by context, so without systematizing context dependence there is little explanatory power the theory can offer.[32]

Again, Kövecses' proposal goes some way towards ameliorating this weakness. The problem is this. For example, the mental model of an ARGUMENT can make use of several schemas, as in (8.31a)–(8.31d). Examples of expressions are easy to find: we *reach a resolution to an argument*, we *win the argument*, and so forth.

(8.31a)  AN ARGUMENT IS A JOURNEY.

(8.31b)  ARGUMENT IS WAR.

(8.31c)  AN ARGUMENT IS A CONTAINER.

(8.31d)  AN ARGUMENT IS A BUILDING.[33]

As Kövecses says in his proposal for an extended conceptual metaphor theory (*extended CMT*), conceptual metaphors appear to be not just conceptual but also 'contextual': 'in many cases we find novel metaphors (both conceptual and linguistic) that require us to take into consideration a variety of contextual factors, and not just universal body-based metaphors or universal cognitive processes' (Kövecses 2020: 20). And, since metaphorical expressions can not only reveal subdoxastic (i.e. below the level of thought) mappings but also, in some cases, be deliberately constructed, for the purpose of explanation, persuasion/manipulation, or aesthetic value, '[i]t may be that conceptual metaphor is simultaneously an offline and online phenomenon (i.e., it is not only offline)' (p. xii).

CMT hypothesizes that there is a neural basis for metaphorical mappings in that they correspond to neural circuits between groups of neurons (nodes). These mappings connect sensorimotor experience with abstract experience. Decisive evidence to this effect will be of crucial importance for understanding metaphor:

> If the neural theory of metaphor is correct, it leads to an important conclusion concerning our functioning in the world: we do not only *understand* (or conceptualize or think) about target domains *in terms of* source domains, but we *experience* target domains *as* source domains. (Kövecses 2020: 10)

This is reminiscent of our earlier question as to whether concepts are entirely constructed in and for the situation, without involving any kind of shift. As was briefly discussed in Section 2.2, neurosemantics/neuropragmatics has made some

---

[31] See Kövecses 2020.   [32] See e.g. a critical discussion in Stern 2000, pp. 176–187.
[33] See Lakoff and Johnson 1980, p. 4; Ungerer and Schmid 1996, p. 122.

progress in uncovering the neural basis for some metaphorical links whereby neural activation in processing an expression pertaining to a *mental* phenomenon corresponds to that of processing it when used about a *physical* phenomenon. It is not part of our journey to assess current evidence in favour of the neural underpinnings of CMT, but suffice it to say that the theory is still in need of more empirical support. Likewise, until contextual triggers are integrated into the theory, perhaps along the lines recently proposed in the extended CMT, there will remain ample questions. But it has to be observed that this attention to context ties well with what happened to semantics generally in its continuing move to contextualism.

Following this focus on conceptualization, some attention has also been given to metaphors that are used in politics and in science. If, say, (8.32) can be traced back to (8.33), then the conceptualization reveals the grounding and motivation for the surrounding narrative.

(8.32)   Unemployment is a contagious disease.

(8.33)   THE COUNTRY IS A PERSON THAT IS ILL.

(adapted from Ungerer and Schmid 1996: 150)

Such metaphors can either be used deliberately to influence the audience, or function entirely subdoxastically as parts of the speaker's inherent conceptualization. Deliberately used expressions can rely on a schema, just as the automatic ones do. But in either case, their power lies mostly in being unnoticed.[34] In his *Moral Politics*, Lakoff analysed relationships between the ideologies and forms of discourse of conservatives and liberals in the United States. He proposed that the 'Strict Father' morality of conservatives and the 'Nurturant Parent' morality of liberals can underlie very similar sets of expressions used by both parties:

using analytic techniques from cognitive linguistics, I could describe the moral systems of both conservatives and liberals in considerable detail, and could list the metaphors for morality that conservatives and liberals seemed to prefer. What was particularly interesting was that they seemed to use virtually the same metaphors for morality but with different – almost opposite – priorities. This seemed to explain why liberals and conservatives could seem to be talking about the same thing and yet reach opposite conclusions – and why they could seem to be talking past each other with little understanding much of the time.

... Deeply embedded in conservative and liberal politics are different models of the family. Conservatism ... is based on a Strict Father model, while liberalism is centered around a Nurturant Parent model. These two models of the family give rise to different moral systems and different discourse forms, that is, different choices of words and different modes of reasoning. (Lakoff 1996: 11–12)

The jury is still out. If we had found only *different* sets of expressions for *different* conceptualizations, evidence would be pretty strong. But when we proceed from

---

[34] On the deliberate use of metaphorical expressions in extended CMT, where different levels of conceptual patterns are distinguished, see Kövecses 2020, Chapter 4.

expressions to stipulating underlying concepts, the usual criticism of speculative reasoning and even circularity take force. Be that as it may, metaphorical expressions are used persuasively and this function has been of increasing interest to theorists of various orientations.[35]

## 8.2.5 The Demise of 'Metaphor'?

It appears that it is possible to imagine a successful approach to metaphor that would combine what is best in post-Gricean pragmatic accounts and contextualist-semantic accounts, also adding the cognitive underpinnings provided by CMT, that is the foundation that people 'think and behave metaphorically'. In the search for a contextualist, cognitively real, but also formal theory of meaning we can calibrate ideas from all these big orientations. While textbooks normally portray cognitive 'subjectivist' approaches as diametrically different from formal 'objectivist' ones, in fact it is not as rebellious as it may seem to suggest a conciliatory approach. Points of convergence between what appear to be fundamentally different approaches to metaphor have been discussed before[36] and the 'metaphor wars' from the title of Gibbs' book may be coming to an end:

> The paradox of metaphor is that it can be creative, novel, and culturally sensitive, allowing us to transcend the mundane, while also being rooted in bodily experiences and unconscious thought patterns common to all people. Metaphor wars are the result of our continued struggle with this paradox. Yet in the metaphor wars, it may be ultimately wiser to accept the multiple functions that metaphors have in human life than to proclaim victory for one side, and defeat for the other. (Gibbs 2017: 16)

But is the subjectivism/objectivism opposition also open to such levelling out? After all, CMT begins with the assumption that the human mind imposes subjective categories on the world and denies the possibility of objective truth. Isn't that an insurmountable impediment for unifying different strands of metaphor research?

Let us have a closer look. Lakoff and Johnson (1980: 159) say the following:

> We do not believe that there is such a thing as *objective* (absolute and unconditional) *truth*, though it has been a long-standing theme in Western culture that there is. We do believe there are *truths* but think that the idea of truth need not be tied to the objectivist view. ... [T]ruth is always relative to a conceptual system that is defined in large part by metaphor.

In other words, truth is grounded in human cognition, human understanding of the world, and these make use of metaphor as a 'vehicle'. But metaphors can be true or false in this sense: if we conceptualize reality in terms of a metaphor, say, LIFE IS A JOURNEY, then we judge it as true. And, as we have done so far, we can then utilize the

---

[35] See e.g. Macagno 2020 on strong and weak inferences in metaphorically constructed acts of persuasion. See also Wilson and Carston 2019 on the importance of weak effects of creative metaphors.

[36] On differences and possible convergence between Relevance-theoretic view and CMT see e.g. Carston 2012b. See also Carston 2002, pp. 354–355 on the possible explanation of her *ad hoc* concept construction using conceptual schemas of CMT. Points of convergence and a possible conciliatory approach are also discussed in Jaszczolt 2002b, Section 17.7.

versatile tool of truth conditions precisely for the purpose of representing formally such human conceptualizations – as we do in the radically contextualist semantics discussed in Section 7.2. After all, to continue with our metaphor, truth conditions are the utensils while expressed thoughts are the meal!

A very different argument in support of the compatibility of cognitive and truth-conditional semantics comes from *mereology*, the theory of parts, wholes, and boundaries. In lexical semantics, *meronymy* is a part–whole relation (for example, between *finger* and *hand*) – a lexical relation alongside synonymy, antonymy, and hyponymy.[37] On the other hand, *mereology* belongs with philosophy. It is the study of parts and wholes of objects and boundaries of objects, spanning metaphysics and epistemology and formalized in logic.[38] Now, entities that are extended in (real or imaginary) space are of two types: (i) those that exist independently of our cognition, like, for example, the planet Earth, and (ii) those that exist by virtue of our cognition, like, for example, the city of London. The same goes for their boundaries. This can help us with a unified theory in that although it has been traditionally assumed that the meaning of a sentence is explicable using truth as correspondence with reality, this 'correspondence' can be further deconstructed. The relation between sentences and the corresponding portions of reality is not straightforward, in that in the case of type (ii) entities, there are no such independent 'portions of reality'. Created boundaries (called *fiat* boundaries) and created objects (called *fiat* objects) can be transient. For example, they can be created by the constraints of the visual field during the act of perception, as in the case of a horizon while looking around. They are also constructed by the use of language. So, the way to look at the relation between language and reality is this: language imposes boundaries on entities, creating states of affairs that Barry Smith calls *judgement fields*.[39] Just as there are visual fields that are parts of reality with artificially created boundaries, so there are judgement fields that contain all the entities that are relevant for the truth of a judgement. These judgement fields are language-dependent. The influence of language proceeds through what Talmy[40] calls the *windowing of attention*. For example, (8.34a) and (8.34b) correspond to the same set of objects and processes.

(8.34a)   Blood flowed from his nose.

(8.34b)   He was bleeding from the nose.

(from Smith 1999: 326)

Just as there are created, *fiat* boundaries of objects, so there are *fiat* boundaries of states of affairs.

Such subjective conceptualizations are not far off what cognitivists propose. But now we can see that we don't have to choose between the subjective and the objective: we need both. That leads to the possibility that the cognitive perspective on reality can fit with the truth-conditional methods. We are adding here an extra dimension to cognitive semantics, namely we are *going beyond conceptual*

---

[37] See also Section 2.2, fn 19.   [38] See e.g. Smith 1999.   [39] See Smith 1999.   [40] See Talmy 1996.

*reality to objective reality*. The processes of constructing judgement fields create, so to speak, this subjective, conceptual reality out of the objective (although 'judgement' is not the best label if it is to include subconscious conceptualizations). On this construal, meaning is still tied, albeit indirectly, to truth conditions and to truth as correspondence with reality. But now the objects of this correspondence are *linguistic constructions* at one end, and *reality with both type (i) and type (ii) entities in it, and also with freedom of conceptualization as in* (8.34a)–(8.34b). So, the correspondence with reality, so important for formal, truth-conditional semantics, becomes a possibility – just as it was for contextualist post-Gricean accounts:

> The theory of language-induced fiat boundaries can ... allow us to treat judgment itself as a way to draw fiat boundaries around entities in reality of the appropriate (truth-making) sort. In this fashion it yields a way of putting the world back into semantics, or of anchoring true judgment to a reality of exactly the sort required by the correspondence theory. (Smith 1999: 328)

For CMT-theorists, cognitive metaphors, present in conceptualization, guide the cognitive mechanisms that produce linguistic expressions. But we can now refine the notion of subjective reality thanks to the account of *how to get from objective reality to this conceptual reality*. The inklings of such a synthesis are already present in Smith's account:

> [C]ognitive linguistics can replace its confused notion of conceptual reality with the geographer's notion of reality as subject to fiat articulations. It will then be in a position to exploit its remarkably sophisticated resources for the analysis of the grammatical structures at work in natural language in order to produce a truly adequate account of truth for natural language in correspondence-theoretic terms. (Smith 1999: 329)

Putting it together, we have there the beginnings of an approach which connects (a) objective and (b) subjective reality through patterns of conceptualization that then result in (c) using language to express them. Cognitive linguistics has tried to replace (a) with (b), but such reductionism will not do: we need them both in that the brain that does the representing of external reality appears to make use of both, as the discussion of 'concepts in the mind vs. concepts in the world' debates in Stage 2 concluded. Our conceptualization of reality is tied to this reality. On the other hand, it is also tied to the way the human brain works, so there is nothing to stop us from assuming that if aliens landed on Earth they might have a very different set of concepts for our objects and situations – but concepts that are grounded in these objects and situations nevertheless.

It is at level (c) that the metaphorical/literal distinction disappears: we conceptualize the world in the most appropriate way arrived at through evolution, life experience, and context-sensitivity. Needless to say, the demise of the literal/metaphorical distinction makes it much easier to adopt the tool of truth conditions for representing this mind- and context-dependent way of saying things.

It is also likely that even the source–target mappings proposed by CMT may be superfluous to explain our cognition and communication. If neural activation in the case of *winning a war* and *winning an argument*, or *going up the mountain* and *prices going up* show strong similarities, then perhaps all there is, is one kind of experiencing and one set of linguistic tools to talk about it. Time will tell.

Does this mean that the notion 'metaphor' becomes redundant? Kövecses considers a complementary question as to whether the notion of 'literal meaning' is redundant. He replies that without it, CMT would be 'incoherent'. As he puts it, in CMT, 'abstract experiences are comprehended and created via concrete ones that are expressed by apparently literal language' (Kövecses 2020: 27). Instead, he proposes to make the figurative fundamental and the literal a special case where, put simply, the conceptualization of concrete reality no longer appears figurative – that is, where the *ontological* aspects of the concept dominate over the subjective *cognitive* aspects. CMT is a theory in progress, and so is, to a much greater extent, a unified approach. Evidence from neuronal activation can bring the domains of sources and targets together, just as in linguistic semantics we have now departed from the 'shift' from the literal to the metaphorical. Instead, we conceive the literal and the metaphorical as gradable properties on a scale of influence that the lexicon and grammar of a language system have on what we actually say – gradation that is either below the level of conscious thought or above it, when we wish to exploit it for a purpose.

Likewise, when Relevance theorists adopt context-driven online concept construction, they tap into the questions of the offline vs. online status of conceptual metaphors, as well as the context dependence of conceptual metaphors. So does Mira Ariel when she replaces the 'literal' with different senses of *minimal meaning*, where one sense of 'minimal' is the main interpretation for a given context – similar to the primary meaning of Default Semantics, as was discussed in Section 7.2.3.[41] By extension, the concept of metaphor may retain its utility as long as we subscribe to the hypothesis that there is a need for positing source domains and target domains. But, to reiterate, if it is empirically demonstrated that conceptualization in abstract and physical domains is not categorically different – and that not only do we 'experience' target domains in terms of source domains but that the distinction is superfluous – metaphor disappears, like spells cast by witches disappeared as explanations of the causes of diseases when scientific facts became known. This is, of course, speculation, but blue-sky speculation about future directions is always a very important part of scientific and philosophical inquiry.

The next step is to lay a uniform foundation before integrating these good ideas, stripping them from their current attachments to different theoretical assumptions. This journey is only preparing the ground, showing that it *might* be possible. Zoltán Kövecses moves in a similar direction, building on what is best, but he does so specifically in the domain of metaphor research, whereas our desiderata cover linguistic meaning at large, as was evident from the previous stages of this journey. We are not just learning about formal semantics of sentences on the one hand and of cognitively

---

[41] See Ariel 2002b.

real discourse meanings on the other, but building, 'hands-on', a unified picture of meaning, with the help of the views we discuss here. Perhaps paradigm clashes and theoretical choices in meaning research will come to an end one day – after all, groundbreaking landmarks in formal semantics, pragmatics, and cognitive semantics are there, and dialogue is in the air.

The end of this journey is in sight. But there are several paths left that need to be flagged. For example, we may want to know whether, when we speak non-literally (on the standard use of the term), we commit ourselves to the content equally strongly as when we speak literally.[42] After all, while speaking non-literally, different propositions can be recovered from the sentence we produce. Who is responsible for non-literal meaning and accountable for it? On what occasions may speaking non-literally be more appropriate? Some of these questions belong to the paths we still need to flag.

## 8.3 Speech and Action

### 8.3.1 Speech Acts and Mental States

Meaning has many faces and one of them is the actions performed by issuing utterances, such as thanking, praising, complimenting, requesting, complaining, and so forth. We are now turning to such practical aspects of using language and to the ways to talk about them. We have touched upon these topics throughout this journey while discussing, for example, intentions, primary meanings, implicatures, or co-constructed meanings, but also, in formal semantics, ways to formalize the semantics of non-declaratives. We will now discuss the view that considers the *use* of language to be the only justifiable way of approaching meaning. This is the approach of *ordinary language philosophers* according to whom, as Ludwig Wittgenstein argued in his *Philosophical Investigations*, meaning *is* use.[43] This reaction against formal methods in studying meaning dates back to the 1930s, and its main representatives are John L. Austin, the central figure of the Oxford school of ordinary language philosophy and Ludwig Wittgenstein in Cambridge, in the later phase of his work. An *act of speech*, rather than a sentence, utterance, or proposition, became the object of inquiry. The programme of this orientation is best laid out in Austin's *How to Do Things with Words*[44] and was further developed in the United States by his student John Searle into what we now know as Speech Act Theory (SAT).

SAT is often, and too eagerly, regarded as an innovative twentieth-century reaction to formal, truth-conditional semantics. In fact, 'meaning as use' is a kind of U-turn in traditional ways of thinking about language that had also motivated various scholars in the past. Inquiring into what we can *do* with words has a long history in philosophy, to mention only the stoics in Ancient Greece. To give a few more recent

---

[42] See here e.g. Camp 2006 and Genovesi 2020 on metaphor and what is said.
[43] See Wittgenstein 1958 [1953], §43, p. 20ᵉ.   [44] See Austin 1975 [1962].

examples, Thomas Reid,[45] an eighteenth-century Scottish philosopher, emphasized the importance of acts such as promising, asking, giving commands, refusing, or threatening. He called them *social operations* of the human mind, distinguishing them from *solitary operations* such as judging, intending, deliberating, or desiring, focusing on the essential role of language in both. He discussed the conditions of a promise, concentrating on obligation, in a spirit not very different from the discussion in SAT two centuries later. His discussion was directed mainly against the philosopher David Hume, who maintained that speech acts such as promising are only a form of mental acts such as intending. Such 'linguistic social acts' were also studied in some depth in the philosophical tradition of phenomenology in the late nineteenth and early twentieth century, led by Franz Brentano and Edmund Husserl.[46] Husserl focused on the distinction between a *proposition* and an *attitude towards the proposition*: for him, a social act had a truth-conditional content and a mental attitude associated with it. For example, a question is a statement about a mental attitude; a wish expresses a state of desiring, and so forth. Decomposed in this way, (8.35a) means (8.35b).

(8.35a)   *Bill to Anna:* Help me!

(8.35b)   Anna's helping Bill is Bill's current request.

In Husserl's phenomenology, meaning is bestowed on expressions by internal experience in intentional mental acts, that is acts aimed at an object (discussed in Section 6.2.3), called there *objectifying acts*.[47] The tradition was then continued by Munich phenomenologists:[48] Reinach gave a systematic account of promising, questioning, requesting, commanding, accusing, and so forth, called by him *social acts*. Pfänder discussed, among others, questions, assertions, reports, thankings, recommendings, requests, warnings, allowings, promisings, invitings, summonings, incitements, prescribings, orders, decrees, prohibitions, commands, and laws, which share propositional content with judgements.[49] Daubert further discussed the relationship between a linguistic act of, for example, questioning or wishing and the corresponding mental act, distinguishing a variety of 'meaning-giving acts'. Another phenomenologist who contributed to this discussion is a student of Brentano, Anton Marty, whose ideas were later taken up by Karl Bühler. They took the investigation even further away from the concept of a proposition and argued that we should look instead at the way questions, commands, and other acts exert influence on the addressee.

This often forgotten history is very important in that it shows that thinking about meaning in terms of acts performed by using speech is not a sudden, mid-twentieth-century reaction to formal methods, as it is often portrayed, but rather a revival of old inquiry into the use of language in social interaction. Coming after the period of

---

[45] See Reid 1788, Essay 5: *Of Morals*, Chapter 6: 'Of the nature and obligation of a contract', pp. 369–493, and esp. p. 447.
[46] See Brentano 1973 [1874] and Husserl 1970 [1900–1901].
[47] See Husserl 1970 [1900–1901]; see also Jaszczolt 1996 and 1999 for a discussion.
[48] For a detailed account and references, see Smith 1990, 1984 and Mulligan 1987.
[49] See Smith 1990, p. 33.

preoccupation with formal semantics, however, it gave its advocates a sense of novelty and breadth. Handling non-declaratives, expressions such as *Thank you*, *How are you?*, or *Watch out!*, as well as the purpose with which an utterance was made, such as making a request, issuing a complaint, and so forth, was no longer a problem. We also gained a cross-disciplinary perspective: discussing socially acceptable, moral, or lawful behaviour in sociology, ethics, or law lends itself easily to adopting speech acts as units. But, as we will see in what follows, SAT on its own is not sufficient to explain meaning in language with the necessary rigour and attention to systematicity.

A speech act is not correlated with a particular form of expression (more on this shortly) but rather depends on the intentions of the speaker – and often also the addressee who is responsible for its uptake. In this, a speech act is a little like a physical act (hitting a tennis ball) and a little like a mental act (imagining hitting a tennis ball), but mostly it is a social act – an act to convey information, ask for information, give orders or warnings, make requests, threats, promises, and so forth, consistent with the view that language is a public, social phenomenon. To start with, in Austin's seminal William James Lectures delivered at Harvard,[50] speech acts were divided into those that assert or state a fact (called *constative utterances*) and those that 'do something' (*performative utterances*). Performatives in turn can be *explicit* or *implicit* (or *explicit* and *primary*, as Austin preferred to call them[51]), where the explicit ones contain a performative verb, such as 'ask' in (8.36).

(8.36)   I ask you to leave the room.

But the performative/constative dichotomy proved to be untenable. The view evolved throughout his lectures. Details aside, constatives, which were supposed to have truth values, proved not to be distinguishable from performatives. For example, (8.37) is supposedly a constative and yet its truth value clearly depends on the actual act of stating and the expectations in the context: for the purpose of drawing a rough sketch, it will be true; for the purpose of a traveller walking along the coastline, it will not.

(8.37)   France is hexagonal.

On the other hand, (8.38) is a statement, and hence supposedly a constative, and yet is a performative at the same time: it is true because the very act of *stating* is being performed through uttering it. As such, it is different from the supposed constative in (8.39), which can be true or false.

(8.38)   I state I am guilty.

(8.39)   I am guilty.

But then, (8.39) *does* something: it is an admission of guilt. So, Austin was left with speech acts as acts of doing things after all. This led him to distinguish three aspects of an act: *locutionary*, the act of uttering a linguistic expression; *illocutionary*, the act of

---

[50] See Austin 1975 [1962]).   [51] See Austin 1979 (1961), p. 244; Austin 1975 (1962), p. 69.

stating, requesting, and so forth; and *perlocutionary*, exerting an influence on the addressee, such as convincing or persuading them to do something.[52] The term 'act' is somewhat unfortunate: they are, in fact, aspects of the same speech act. Austin talks about locutions having the force of a question, a request, and so forth and about their effects, and it is more intuitive to think in terms of *illocutionary forces* and *perlocutionary effects*.

Speech acts so-conceived are not true or false; they are *felicitous* or *infelicitous*. They have to conform to certain conditions, called *felicity conditions*, in order to perform the act they are supposed to perform. A speech act is infelicitous ('unhappy') when such conditions are not met. For example, felicity conditions for questioning are as follows: (i) the speaker does not know the truth about the state of affairs; (ii) the speaker wants to know the truth about the state of affairs; (iii) the speaker believes that the hearer may be able to supply information about the state of affairs. Searle distinguishes here *propositional content, preparatory, sincerity, and essential conditions*.[53] These conditions belong to the characteristics of the illocutionary force about which we will see more in the next section. To give a different example, in the case of a promise, there has to be a sentence used with the content of the promise (propositional content condition); the promise must be about an event beneficial to the addressee (otherwise it would be a warning or threat, as in *I promise I will hit you*) and about an event that is not going to happen anyway (*preparatory conditions*); and the promiser must have the corresponding intentions (*sincerity condition*), as well as an awareness of undertaking an obligation to perform the action (*essential condition*). Then, an act of promising needs the addressee's uptake in order to be a promise.

The term 'infelicitous', however, has been criticized as too coarsely grained. First, there are speech acts that are unsuccessful outright. For example, if I, a university professor, assumed the authority of a football referee, my act would be *unsuccessful*. But there are also acts that are conveyed successfully in spite of being insincere or in spite of their presuppositions not being satisfied for some reason or other. An academic who knows a lot about football could in fact succeed in pretending to be a referee in a football match. In such cases, Searle and Vanderveken say, the act is successful but *defective*. As they say,

Austin's distinction between 'felicitous' and 'infelicitous' speech acts fails to distinguish between those speech acts which are successful but defective and those which are not even successful.... In the ideal case a speech act is both successful and nondefective, and for each illocutionary force the components of that illocutionary force [discussed in Section 8.3.2] serve to determine under what conditions that type of speech act is both *successful* and *nondefective*, at least as far as its illocutionary force is concerned. (Searle and Vanderveken 1985: 13, after Searle 1969)

With the wisdom of hindsight, it is fair to say that the question of sincerity in particular proved important in the subsequent discussions of accountability and other sociopragmatic and ethical issues in which the category of speech act made its career.

---

[52] See Austin 1975 [1962], esp. pp. 101–102, 147.   [53] See Searle 1996a [1965]; 1969.

**Defining Speech Acts: Intentionality or Social Interaction? (a Digression)**
Speech acts are social acts and 'doing things with words' impacts the interactants in a discourse. But people have mental states associated with them that are equally crucial to their understanding: a promise would not be a promise not only if the content were not achieving something particular in the relation between the speaker and the addressee, but also if the speech act were not issued with an intention of a promise. Intentions to do something and to represent something reside in mental states, and ultimately in their aboutness, or intentionality – or what Husserl called intentional mental acts discussed a little earlier in this section. As was said already, this opened up the possibility in the phenomenological tradition of analysing the meaning of speech acts in terms of the meaning of underlying beliefs, desires, and so forth.

Intentionality has always been an important aspect of discussions about acts of speech but Searle offered his own independent theory of it that, on closer inspection, introduces some unnecessary complications.[54] He proposes that the mind *imposes* Intentionality (that is, 'Searle-Intentionality', intentionality as understood by him) on linguistic expressions. An agent who produces a speech act has an intention to communicate and also an intention to represent something. This intention to represent characterizes the speaker's meaning which, in turn, reflects the Intentionality of the corresponding belief or other mental state. This parallel between intentions and his Intentionality allows Searle to propose that mental states have *intrinsic* Intentionality, while utterances have *derived* Intentionality:[55]

> The mind imposes Intentionality on entities that are not intrinsically Intentional by intentionally conferring the conditions of satisfaction of the expressed psychological state upon the external physical entity. The double level of Intentionality in the speech act can be described by saying that by intentionally uttering something with a certain set of conditions of satisfaction, those that are specified by the essential condition for that speech act, I have made the utterance Intentional, and thus necessarily expressed the corresponding psychological state. . . . So, I impose Intentionality on my utterances by intentionally conferring on them certain conditions of satisfaction which are the conditions of satisfaction of certain psychological states. (Searle 1983: 27–28)

But this 'double level of intentionality' is debatable: why double, if language is one of the modalities, and perhaps the most common one, in which these mental states are formed? Or, at least, language is what makes beliefs etc., intersubjectively recognizable as such mental states. And if so, then there is nothing to 'confer' or 'transfer' between levels. Moreover, what does it mean to 'confer conditions of satisfaction'? If one could intentionally confer them, then, as Harnish aptly points out, how can it be that one can never *fail* to do so?[56]

Next, there is no good, independent reason for deriving properties of language from the properties of an act of uttering linguistic expressions if, as we have observed,

---

[54] See Searle 1983.    [55] See Searle 1983, pp. 27–28 and Searle 1991, p. 84.    [56] See Harnish 1990, p. 189.

it is not only the mental state but also the social impact that defines them. Several decades before, phenomenologists had argued that linguistic meaning was social, and as such 'in the world' rather than 'in the mind' – or, as Reinach proposed, intentions and mental states are 'read off the world' (Smith 1990: 54), and as such also off the *use of language in the world*. So, the intentionality of a speech act, and the conditions of satisfaction, depend primarily on the devices of a language system as a social phenomenon and on the situation in which they are used.

The qualifier 'primarily' is debatable as well. What is certain is that speech acts are defined *both* by the properties of the associated mental states and by their social impact. What needs to be taken with caution, then, in SAT is the underplaying of the social aspects and the rather free-handed take on what intentionality of mental states is.

Instead, Searle talks about social conventions that are separate from language. He says that a promise and the obligation inherent in the promise are established by arbitrary conventions of social life and by the conventional use of language in society. But the very concept of a promise is not established by such conventions alone. It is established by the properties of the mental states and aspects of social reality together, ultimately by intentions and conventions, with language as a vehicle, a modality, in both. If we want to know what meaning in language is, then this is important: 'conferring properties on language' does not take us any closer, while slowly biting through how language behaves with respect to mental *and* social life does.[57] Some food for philosophical thoughts.

## 8.3.2 Harnessing Illocutionary Force

SAT opens up new doors that are separate from our journey and from the 'What is meaning?' inquiry. Speech acts are extremely useful for discussing practical questions to do with social, moral, or legal aspects of illocutions and perlocutions. But for the purpose of a theory of meaning, a speech act is an elusive concept. To begin with, (i) there are as many types of illocutions as we choose to distinguish, depending on how detailed we want to be in proposing distinctions. Relatedly, (ii) there is no one-to-one correspondence between illocutions and performative verbs, or types of linguistic constructions, or any other clearly identifiable linguistic object. To reiterate, while *I promise* typically comes with the force of the promise, it may also be a warning; *to advise* can mean recommending something or, in formal communication, also informing about something, as in (8.40) and (8.41).

(8.40)　The teacher advised us to do a mock exam.

(8.41)　The teacher advised us that we have passed the exam.

---

[57] For a more in-depth discussion see Jaszczolt 1999, Section 3.6.

Syntactic indicators of illocutionary force cannot be relied on either: an interrogative sentence form may correspond to a question, a request, or even a complaint. Imperatives and indicatives are no more reliable: there is no such *literal force*, as it is often called, that language exerts on action.[58] Next, (iii) what is a perlocution in one language (or culture, or even situation) can be an illocution in another – or the distinction can be fuzzy. A's question in (8.42) carries some force of a question in Polish, where it is not as strongly conventionalized as a request as its equivalent is in English (we will discuss this further in the context of indirect speech acts). B's response, which includes an answer to the direct speech act of a question, is the norm.

(8.42)    A:   Możesz podać mi tę książkę?
               *Can you pass me that book?*

           B:   Tak. Proszę.
               *Yes (I can). Here you are.*

Finally, (iv) perlocutions are even more difficult to systematize: they are indefinite in number and difficult to determine precisely. After all, a speech act is a definitional mongrel of mental state and a social act, all dumped on language, as seen in the digression!

Attempts to formalize SAT inherit these problems. Although it is normally intuitively easy to identify the illocutionary force, or 'doing' something, and dissociate it from the proposition that it concerns, there are no reliable principles for delimiting it from the utterance alone. We could perhaps consider larger discourse chunks but formalization is even harder then.

Nevertheless, it has been attempted. First, remember that Husserl distinguished between a proposition and an attitude to a proposition, analysing, say, (8.35a) above as (8.35b). In a broadly similar spirit, Searle and Vanderveken[59] proposed a formalization called *illocutionary logic*, addressing questions such as 'Can the set of all illocutionary forces be defined recursively from a few primitives, and if so, how?' and 'What is the relation between illocutionary force and the meaning of sentences?' or, crucially, 'What is the logical form of performative sentences?' (Searle and Vanderveken 1985: ix). They attempted to provide a formal apparatus of illocutionary logic and use it to analyse over a hundred English illocutionary verbs. It was a formidable task, remembering that there is no one-to-one correspondence between illocutionary verbs and forces and that '[i]llocutionary forces are realized in the syntax of actual natural languages in a variety of ways, e.g. mood, punctuation, word-order, intonation contour, and stress' (p. 1). Moreover, illocutionary force may have no overt indicator whatsoever, or several non-synonymous verbs can correspond to one illocutionary force.

In principle, constructing logical forms is easy. If $F$ stands for illocutionary force and $p$ for propositional content, then we obtain $F(p)$. For example, (8.43) and (8.44) share the propositional content $p$ but vary in the force $F$.

---

[58] For the literal force hypothesis, see Levinson 1983, Section 5.5 and references to Gerald Gazdar there. On the relation between imperative mood and directive force, see especially Jary and Kissine 2014.

[59] See Searle and Vanderveken 1985.

(8.43)  Slow down!
$F_1(p)$ = Request (The addressee will slow down.)

(8.44)  You will slow down.
$F_2(p)$ = Prediction (The addressee will slow down.)

So, an illocutionary act has a logical form and it is easy to see from these examples how this form determines its conditions of success. Then, $F$ and $p$ can interact with logical operators to handle some important meaning distinctions. For example, (8.45) and (8.46) show how negating $F$ differs from negating $p$.

(8.45)  I don't promise to slow down.
$\neg F(p)$

(8.46)  I promise not to slow down.
$F(\neg p)$

Negating the illocutionary force as in (8.45) results in what is called *illocutionary denegation* and is clearly different in semantic and pragmatic import from illocutionary acts with a negated propositional content, as in (8.46). In the authors' words, 'an act of illocutionary denegation is one whose aim is to make it explicit that the speaker does not perform a certain illocutionary act' (p. 4). What is interesting is that there are also explicit performative verbs of denegation: *forbid* is a denegation of *allow* (and so is *prohibit*); *refuse* is a denegation of *accept*; and *disclaim* can be interpreted as a denegation of *claim*.

But all this is only a patina of successful formalization. Just as there are no reliable ways of mapping utterances onto $F(p)$-type forms, so there are no reliable ways of using operators such as negation on $F$s. Neither is there a reliable regularity whereby denying a proposition could be mapped onto accepting a denegation of its assertion. The pair of examples just discussed shows beyond doubt that (8.47) is true.

(8.47)  $\neg F(p) \neq F(\neg p)$

Vanderveken[60] developed this formalization further as an extension of Montague semantics (discussed in Stages 3 and 5), attempting to capture the 'success value' of an act, in addition to the truth value of a proposition. After all, it is, ultimately, the felicity conditions that matter because they represent what is in the speaker's mind. The gist of it is this: The success value is determined by the conditions of satisfaction, just as the truth value is determined by the truth conditions. These conditions of satisfaction depend on the truth conditions of the proposition $p$ embedded in $F(p)$, where $p$ is related to the world through the *direction of fit* – one of the properties of $F$ about which more in a moment.

Arguably, time has shown that this is not the way to formalize speech acts. Not only would we fail in formulating adequate logical forms, but we would, in addition, have to substitute truth conditions with elusive conditions of satisfaction for $F(p)$. At present

---

[60] See Vanderveken 1990a, esp. pp. 35, 81–85; 1990b, esp. p. 207; 1991; 1994.

the construct of a 'speech act' is used mainly by philosophers of language and sociopragmaticists who focus on practical issues such as the power of speech acts to offend, manipulate, form ideologies, promote gender or race inequality, and so forth. But in order to research these applied topics from the domains bordering on sociology, politics, ethics, or psychology, one needs to deconstruct speech act as a theoretical concept. At the same time, formalizing speech acts is not a dead end: it will simply have to proceed with the spirit of the times and be attempted very differently. This is what is currently pursued in some areas of computational linguistics and what we are attempting to do in this journey from a metalinguistic, philosophical perspective. Illocutionary forces won't go away: we *do* 'do things with words' and this fact has to be embraced in any successful theory of meaning. So, perhaps, the way to go about it is to adhere to our desiderata of a successful formal method and the cognitive reality of the theory and see what can be borrowed from SAT that would bring us closer to where we want to be in this journey?

To better represent speech acts, we might use the radical contextualist view of content. This will ensure that the meaning we are modelling is the kind of meaning we *want* to model: what is intended, recovered, and partly co-constructed in the course of discourse interaction (such as a contextualist, modulated, or functional proposition from Section 7.2). Then, we can assume that $F(p)$ is an intuitively recovered structure. Now the fact that there is no overt, or no reliable linguistic counterpart of $F$ ceases to be a problem: in contextualism, we draw on information obtained through different modalities, just as interactants do in a situation of discourse. Neither is it a problem when there is no complete sentence from which $p$ is to be constructed – for exactly the same reason. So, (8.48) becomes sufficient and unproblematic for constructing a logical form, as explained step-by-step below.

(8.48)   [Scenario: *A and B are discussing plans for dinner for the next day.*]
   A:   Restaurant tomorrow?
   ≫ Do you want to go to dinner tomorrow evening?
   $F$ = Suggestion
   $p$ = A and B will go out to a restaurant for dinner the following evening.
   $F(p)$
   Suggestion (A and B will go out to a restaurant for dinner the following evening.)

There will be different ways of unpacking such utterances with an incomplete $p$ and incomplete $F$ (in that the interrogative form does not uniquely signal a suggestion). We already have contextualist theories of unpacking $p$ at our disposal, such as Relevance Theory, Truth-Conditional Pragmatics, or Default Semantics discussed in Section 7.2 (NB: Default Semantics will seamlessly handle indirect speech acts in that it allows for substituting the implicated proposition for $p$). Concerning $F$, contextualist principles apply here too: it can be automatically or inferentially recovered from the situation.

Let us now consider what illocutionary force exactly means in SAT. Searle and Vanderveken distinguish seven components of illocutionary force: (i) the illocutionary point, which is the purpose of the illocution – for example, the point of a promise is to commit the speaker to $p$; (ii) the degree of strength of the illocutionary point, which allows the comparison of, for example, requesting and ordering; (iii) the mode of achievement, for example the authority that makes an act a request rather than an order or a command; (iv) the propositional content conditions; (v) the preparatory conditions; (vi) the sincerity conditions, all defined above; and (vii) the degree of strength of the sincerity conditions. For example, begging expresses a *stronger* desire than a request. The illocutionary point is the most important feature and it provided the foundations for an attempted classification of speech acts to which we will pass shortly.

It is clear that we need contextualist principles to identify some of these categories – think of how to assess (i), for example, or even the gradable (ii). But then, do we always have to identify them? Relevance theorists point out that, often, a speech act need not be identified as being of a specific type in order to function successfully. For example, (8.49) need not be identified as a prediction – it simply functions as a successful act of conveying an assumption about a future state of affairs, no matter what category label we attach to $F$.

(8.49)   The weather will be warmer tomorrow.

(from Sperber and Wilson 1995 [1986]: 245)

Other examples include asserting, hypothesizing, suggesting, claiming, denying, warning, or threatening. As they say, for many speech acts, the recognition of their category membership is not necessary in communication and cognition. But there is also a group of speech acts called by Sperber and Wilson *institutional speech acts* which have to be identified in order to be performed: succeeding in declaring war requires the knowledge of the 'institution' that makes it work as a declaration of war. The same goes for bidding in bridge, promising, or thanking.[61] Identifying these acts stems from knowing customs, rules, or societal conventions, not from knowing the linguistic content. They also allow a third category that includes saying, asking, and telling in that these generally follow the grammatical criteria of sentence types: declarative, interrogative, and imperative. But even there, as we have seen in (8.49), there are no reliable one-to-one mappings. Also, how exactly do we pinpoint the boundary between institutional and non-institutional acts?

These are not arguments against $F$; they are only arguments against a fully specified, clearly delimited $F$. If we accept that every act has a force of 'doing something', by definition, then all is well: we conceptualize them on the level of cognitive/contextualist representations where, say, (8.49) has an $F$ and a $p$, and $F$ happens to be, on this occasion quite fuzzy, while $p$ is pretty well spelled out.

What in SAT *cannot* be rescued is the classification of speech acts. Austin (1975 [1962]: 163, my emphasis) originally proposed the following intuitively distinguished classes:

we may say that the *verdictive* is an exercise of judgement, the *exercitive* is an assertion of influence or exercising of power, the *commissive* is an assuming of an obligation or declaring of

---

[61] See Sperber and Wilson 1995 [1986], Section 4.10.

an intention, the *behabitive* is the adopting of an attitude, and the *expositive* is the clarifying of reasons, arguments, and communications.

Allocating acts to particular types is rife with overlap and a lack of precision. Searle's subsequent attempt[62] doesn't fare much better, although he attempted a cross-linguistically applicable typology based on some universal principles.[63] Decades of attempted implementations have shown that identifying a speech act as well as the type to which it belongs is quite arbitrary. So, as was said earlier, while speech act remains a useful concept for cross-cultural and multidisciplinary research on 'doing things with words', the category labels are best thought of as up for grabs – after all, even what counts as an assertion is still a buoyant topic of research in epistemology and ethics. (We will turn to some fascinating questions about assertion shortly.) SAT can only pick up the pieces and adopt what has been achieved there.

One characteristic that helps with classification is the *direction of fit*. A speech act can *correspond* to what the world is like, so to speak (the *words-to-world* direction) or it can *affect* the ways the world is (the *world-to-words* direction). For example, when the speaker describes a state of affairs, the words describe the world, or 'adjust to the way the world is'. The direction of fit is words-to-world. On the other hand, by requesting something, the speaker affects the way the world is: the world 'adjusts itself to the words'. This distinction offers an independent principle for classification but not a sufficient one. The group of acts that broadly *assert* something (to follow for a moment Searle's proposed classes) have the words-to-world direction of fit, so we might accept assertives as a category (although even there differences are rife). But those that *direct* someone to do something (like a request) and the ones that *commit* the speaker to doing something (like a promise) all have the world-to-words direction, in spite of being very different. Next, *expressing* gratitude, for example, like in thanking, or expressing praise or condolences, have no direction of fit, while *declaring* something, like, for example, in appointing someone to a job can have either world-to-words or words-to-world directions of fit, in spite of being intuitively (and by Searle) put in the same class.[64] Next, all classifications partly rely on the linguistic criteria whereby the indicative mood renders assertives, imperative mood renders directives, and interrogative renders questions, with full knowledge that these are only very coarse correlations. Remembering that the lexicon and sentence structure are not the sole sources of information about meaning, and that what they throw up can be overridden by the output of other sources (as discussed at length in Section 7.2.3), adding this correlation won't produce reliable principles for classification either. It is probably fair to say that classifying speech acts is a futile exercise, both because they are too slippery to formalize in this way and because putting them into classes doesn't serve any theoretical or practical purpose. After all, according to this vision of meaning, *meaning is use*.

---

[62] See Searle 1979b [1975].
[63] On speech acts in a cross-cultural perspective see e.g. Wierzbicka 1991, Chapter 2 and, for applications, essays in Jaszczolt and Turner 2003, section 'Cross-cultural pragmatics and speech acts'.
[64] See also Searle 1979b [1975]; Searle and Vanderveken 1985.

## 8.3.3  Indirect Speech Acts?

We have been tentatively suggesting how one might espouse the insights of SAT, half a century later, in modern radical contextualism about meaning. But if we want to do so, we have to say more about those speech acts that are astoundingly common in discourse across various languages and cultures and yet are most thorny for SAT, namely *indirect speech acts* (ISAs).

Speaking indirectly has many social benefits. We often engage in indirect communication of observations, opinions, requests, expressions of gratitude or complaint, to name a few. We do so more often in some languages and cultures than in others (there will be more on this in Section 8.4.2.1 on politeness) but it is considered to be a universal human trait, or a pragmatic universal, to implicate meanings and infer them according to some intersubjectively recognizable principles. The latter are often identified with Gricean or post-Gricean principles of rational cooperation.[65] There can be little doubt that the main act performed by B in (8.50) is a refusal. But at the same time, the effect exerted on A is likely to differ from that of a direct *No, I don't*.

(8.50)    A:    Do you want to go out tonight?
           B:    I am not feeling great.

On the surface, B's response is a statement of fact rather than a refusal. So, it is an ISA. But what exactly is an ISA? In (8.50) we have an instance of communication by an implicature. On the other hand, some indirect speech acts are conventionalized in that their 'literal' content no longer plays a part in the conveyed message. Or they are *standardized*, or on the way to conventionalization, where the 'literal' content is still retrievable in the online process of interpretation, but not sufficiently to either understand this act as a direct one (say, A's as a question) or to consciously extract the intended indirect act (say, A's as an invitation or suggestion).[66] But how do we tell whether a construction is fully conventionalized? Compare *can you* in (8.51) with Polish (8.42). Is (8.51) conventionalized? Would experimental evidence help? Or is the possibility of jokingly replying *Yes, I can*, followed by no action, sufficient to answer this question?

(8.51)    Can you close the door?

It is true that one can concoct a scenario where *can* will mean 'do you have the ability/opportunity to ... ' in (8.51), but only at a push. And, when the construction is fully conventionalized, such as *would you like/mind*, is the speech act still an ISA? If it is, then what is its counterpart, the complementary category of direct speech act? Remember that we couldn't define it using any linguistic principles.

Searle (1996b [1975]: 168) says that in the case of an ISA, 'a sentence that contains the illocutionary force indicators for one kind of illocutionary act can be uttered to

---

[65] On pragmatic (and semantic) universals see e.g. von Fintel and Matthewson 2006.
[66] For conventionalization and speech act see e.g. Reimer 1995 and the difference between standardization and conventionalization Bach 1995.

perform, in addition, another type of illocutionary act.' This conception of ISAs as having two illocutionary forces, indirect (or 'primary') and direct (or 'secondary') has often been disputed.[67] Searle claims that in uttering an ISA the speaker 'means what he says, but also means something more' (p. 168) – this 'something more' is then reached via inference. But as we have pointed out during the discussion of implicature in post-Gricean pragmatics in Section 7.1, speakers don't normally 'mean both' – arguably, we may be better off representing just one, intended, cognitively real meaning, rather than focusing on the interaction of two potential illocutionary forces. The problem is further aggravated in the case of conventionalized expressions as in (8.51), even though there are some discernible regularities there in that the meaning of an ISA is, after all, constrained by the conditions of satisfaction of the literal, directly uttered act:

> the reason I can ask you to pass the salt by saying 'Can you pass the salt?' but not by saying 'Salt is made of sodium chloride' or 'Salt is mined in the Tatra mountains' is that your ability to pass the salt is a preparatory condition for requesting you to pass the salt in a way that the other sentences are not related to requesting you to pass the salt. (Searle 1996b [1975]: 176)

There are still questions to be answered. Do the addressees actually grasp the request in virtue of grasping the question about abilities as an indirect request? Or, perhaps, it doesn't matter if they don't and this is just a theoretical correlation? Why should we assign an illocutionary force of a question to the request in (8.51) just on the basis of its interrogative sentence form? We know that there is no reliable correlation between sentence types and forces. And what about utterances without any clear indicators such as (8.52)?

(8.52)   The dog wants to go out.

It is true that (8.52) works better as a request to take the dog out than, say, *The dog is a golden retriever*, but is it a request, or perhaps an order or a reproof? Or none of these? Or perhaps several speech acts are performed all at once? Or, like Relevance theorists say, it doesn't matter what it is as long as it does its job in communication?

There may be some indicators, such as intonation, tone of voice, the presence of *please*, *let's*, or clues from power relationships and situational context, but none of them are decisive in saving ISA as a category. Illocutionary force indicators can be very diversified and as such they don't offer a precise definition of indirectness. Essentially, the category of an ISA inherits all the problems with its delimitation from the category of a speech act itself, and via the somewhat vaguely delimited illocutionary force itself. What follows is that there are no reliable principles for distinguishing direct and indirect speech acts: there are no reliable criteria for judging directness. Perhaps the direct/indirect speech act is another distinction that, like semantics/pragmatics or literal/non-literal, is best left behind? Be that as it may, ISAs are another slippery category of SAT – but not any less popular for this in sociolinguistics, ethics, politics, or jurisprudence, to name a few. Food for thought.

---

[67] See e.g. Bertolet 1994 and Meibauer 2019a.

Another practical application is the pragmatics of cross-cultural communication, where intuitively conceived categories (complaining, requesting, complimenting, to name some popular ones), as well as intuitive indirectness, often suffice to delimit objects of inquiry. Speech acts are issued differently in different cultures – or different speech acts can be issued in analogous situations in different cultures. For example, a compliment normally calls for an expression of thanks in English but quite often for an expression of self-denigration in Polish, even though cross-cultural pragmatic borrowing and other mechanisms of language change often even this out. We can observe these facts and conduct empirical investigations, remembering that matching morphosyntactic categories with illocutionary forces, sometimes attempted, has particularly adverse effects on cross-cultural studies of speech acts. As Jary and Kissine (2014: 292) aptly point out, '[c]utting the tie between mood and force enables a much more flexible relationship between sentence types and speech acts' not only within a language but also cross-linguistically, in that, as they say, there are, for example, languages with no imperative sentences, so imperative mood and directive force cannot be closely related.[68] But it is important to remember that the grammar–pragmatics interface still has a lot to offer: there may be 'prototypical effects', some of which have been traced by Meibauer, that take us part-way, providing some insight into generalizations. As he says (Meibauer 2019a: 79), '[i]f this term [ISA] has any theoretical use, this use has to do with the grammar–pragmatics interface'. This is a conditional statement and it is unlikely that the 'theoretical use' can be defended when one means by it a clearly determinable term, but there is certainly an intuitive sense in which we speak indirectly, issue a speech act in a way that is not a standard, typical one. A lot of food for thought again.[69]

What is then the principal appeal of the concept of a speech act in the 2020s? The cross-cultural communication just discussed is one such area. Another is philosophy: ethics, epistemology, and law. But there an elusive concept of a speech act is not a tool but an object of study: it is pursued on the higher (*meta-*) level, such as metaethics (on which more in Section 8.4.1.1). One asks what counts as an assertion, insult, harassment, slur, and so forth. Debates revolve around the concept itself, sometimes also around conceptual engineering. To give one example: philosopher of language Sanford Goldberg has been investigating the properties of the speech act of assertion, asking questions such as what constitutes an assertion, and what norm – norm to do with knowledge on which the assertion is based – assertion should satisfy. As he says, assertions are 'speech acts in which a given proposition is *presented as true*, where this presentation has certain *force* (what we might call *assertoric force*)' (Goldberg 2015: 5). He proposes that '[i]t is mutually manifest to participants in a speech exchange that assertion has a robustly epistemic norm; that is, that one must: assert that p, only if E(one, [p])' (p. 96), where 'E' stands here for a description of a certain mutually manifest epistemic standard. This is how it works:

---

[68] See also Kissine's (2013) much broader cognitive-pragmatic inquiry into the assignment of illocutionary forces to utterances in which he reaches similar conclusions.

[69] Attempts to 'syntacticize' speech acts, that is to demonstrate that 'things we do with words' are syntactically encoded, permeate their history. For early attempts, see Stenius 1967; Ross 1970; or Lewis 1970. For a recent theory, see Wiltschko 2021.

take a speaker *S* who testifies that *p*. Such a speaker knows – or, at any rate, is in a position to know, and should know – that she has performed a speech act whose propriety *qua* assertion depends (perhaps among other things) on the satisfaction of an epistemic norm. (Goldberg 2011: 179)

This 'mutually manifest epistemic norm of assertion' then opens up various questions such as what counts as asserted content, also for social, legal, and ethical purposes.[70] We return to some of these in the following section when we address the speaker's commitment, accountability, and liability for what they are saying.[71] This also shows how speech-act theorists oscillate between speaker-centred and audience-centred views. While early accounts tended to focus on the speaker, for example on the importance of sincerity conditions and as such on speakers' beliefs and intentions, more recent accounts focus on commitment, where the question 'whose meaning' that permeates all parts of our journey is addressed from different perspectives: the linguistic one, such as the linguistically encoded commitments,[72] as well as practical ones, such as accountability, responsibility, or legal liability. This brings us to a crossroads with such practical – social, moral, legal, and other – debates.

## 8.4 At a Crossroads with Ethical and Social Debates

In a journey through meaning there are many junctions with several branching paths. But there are also end points where, if we want to continue, we'd better call it the beginning of a different journey, with its own goals and assumptions, and with paths that branch off according to different interests. We are now at such a point, where an inquiry into what meaning is and how best to represent it, albeit by no means complete, is beginning to branch out. We can, in principle, branch out into methods that we briefly touched upon, such as corpus studies (including computational), experimental data elicitation, neuroimaging, and so forth. But this would be a journey through methodology in the study of meaning. We could also venture into anthropological linguistics and the question of culture- or language-relativity vs. universality of meaning, or into applications of theories of meaning in various disciplinary and situational discourses. These are just examples, to show the vast scope and interconnectivity. However, making choices galore is not what theorists and philosophers of meaning would proudly do: human inquiry into meaning has to follow a path with clearly set assumptions and objectives, without answering at every single step why a different path hadn't been taken instead at a certain crossroads. Otherwise, we would never take a step forward.

---

[70] For more examples of such work on speech acts, see e.g. the essays in Fogal, Harris, and Moss 2018. For speech acts and various facets of intersubjectivity, see Moran 2018.

[71] For another example of recent work on speech acts in philosophy of language, see Caponetto 2020 – on 'undoing things with words', that is on annulment, retraction, and amendment of a previously issued speech act.

[72] For an example of such an analysis, see Faller's (2019) work on discourse commitments in illocutionary reportatives in Cuzco Quechua.

This is one such journey, where we described what we want from a theory of meaning, what we want meaning to mean, justified such choices, but then pushed ahead. We arrived at a *meaning in discourse*: dynamic, intended, recovered, and partly co-constructed meaning that is conveyed not only by an utterance of a linguistic expression but also by other modalities available in the situation of discourse. As such, we have aimed at a representation of meaning that has the status of cognitive representation and whose composition is not a mystery, in spite of being so much more elusive than the structure of the sentence, but rather something that can be tackled with the tools that various theories of various kinds of meaning have to offer and that we have picked up on the way.

As was said before, these tools need adjusting of course: we know that truth is not simple, it can depend on context, purpose of assessment, and the assessors themselves. We know that possible worlds are theoretical constructs, but we also know that some ways the world might be or might have been are 'more possible' than others. We also know that there is no (clear) literal/non-literal, explicit/implicit, or direct/indirect distinction, but these are obstacles only when we approach meaning through its one medium: a linguistic structure. Here we tried to avoid that.

In this final section I flag some ways of branching off, selecting a few paths that particularly feed on big questions about meaning in language, such as accountability for one's utterances, lying, conveying politeness, or causing offence. These are just selected highlights, among possible others, and some suggested food for thought.

## 8.4.1 Commitment and Accountability

### 8.4.1.1 Negotiation of Meaning and Taking Responsibility

The discussion of the normativity of assertion at the end of the previous section is an example of how meaning theories interact with issues to do with ethics – normative, applied, but also metaethics, where the latter includes the study of presuppositions and commitments (including semantic ones) of moral thought and action, including linguistic action.[73] In the most general terms, ethics, or moral philosophy, focuses on the concepts of right and wrong. So, moral theories can focus on personalities, actions, or consequences of linguistic actions. All these are interwoven with what our linguistic actions mean, but also with what should count as meaning – especially meaning for which the speaker is held accountable.

We have already established that what counts as meaning is best construed neither merely as what is intended by the speaker nor what is merely recovered by the addressee or other audience – it is what is both intended, successfully recovered as such, but also co-constructed in the dynamic process of discourse. In this way we exclude significant misunderstandings, where being accountable for what one was *taken to mean* would require a very different discussion. We also eliminate misfires,

---

[73] For an introduction to metaethics, see Sayre-McCord 2012.

where intentions do not go through. What we foreground is joint commitments, dynamically arrived at, often through negotiation in a dialogue. As such, we can, however, include moderate misunderstandings where meaning can be adjusted in the process of negotiation.[74] In fact, the analysis of how meaning is negotiated brings to our attention the fact that there is no clear boundary between communication and miscommunication. Meanings are dynamically adjusted as conversation progresses not only when the speaker's meaning is indeterminate and in need of precisification, or when the discrepancies in understanding are acceptable to both interactants; it can also be adjusted when the speaker's intended meaning is initially misconstrued but there is room for flexibility. This demonstrates that communication is often imperfect and the recovery of intentions is a gradable and dynamic concept.

All in all, negotiation is an important aspect of meaning construction. Arguably it is best thought of against the background of what we know about conventions, intentions, and common ground, although, as will be evident, the extent to which these concepts play a role in different dynamic frameworks varies extensively. Only with such background firmly decided on can we branch out into questions of accountability for one's linguistic actions, questions of the use and misuse of authority and power, as well as issues of the normative expectations that the speaker faces – the latter addressed for example by Goldberg discussed in the previous section. This branching out also demonstrates that understanding what it means to *mean* something is not merely a theoretical – philosophical or linguistic – issue. It is the foundation stone on which we can build applications to ethics, law, sociology, anthropology, or even economics and theology, among other disciplines in human and social sciences. Understanding, and deciding on, the concept of meaning enables metadiscursive understanding of the effects of situated discourse.

Joint construction of meaning is not a new topic – we have encountered it throughout this journey. One example is game-theoretic approaches (see Section 7.1.3) where interlocutors aim at maintaining an equilibrium while they 'gain' or 'lose' in a speech-act game.[75] Next, Searle emphasized the importance of collective intentions that do not amount to the sum of individual intentions. Clark approaches language use as an example of *joint action*.[76] Joint utterances have also been studied with the focus on conversational structure, formal modelling of discourse, and the semantics of subsentential speech.[77] Then, there are pragmatic interactionist models, such as Arundale's Conjoint Co-constituting Model of Communication or Elder and Haugh's model of 'emergent meanings' briefly introduced in Section 7.1.4.[78]

Arundale applies his model to account for the dynamic conversational face (discussed in Section 8.4.2.1) which, just like meanings, can also evolve. His approach largely follows the assumptions of Conversation Analysis (CA)[79] that focuses on

---

[74] Geurts 2019 is a good introduction to this topic.
[75] See e.g. Lewis 1979; Parikh 2010; Asher and Lascarides 2013.  [76] See Searle 1990 and Clark 1996.
[77] See, respectively, e.g. (i) Sacks, Schegloff, and Jefferson 1974 or an introduction in Levinson 1983, Chapter 6; (ii) Gregoromichelaki and Kempson 2016 and Stainton 2006.
[78] See Arundale 1999, 2010, 2020 and Elder and Haugh 2018 respectively. See also Haugh 2007, 2008.
[79] See (i) in fn 76. See also Arundale 2013 on the pragmatics of linguistic interaction.

conversational structure across turns and on gleaning information from turn organization, following the method that *interactants themselves use* to make sense of the conversation, without imposing the 'burden' of theoretical concepts such as intentions or beliefs – a method that after Harold Garfinkel is called *ethnomethodology*.[80] This perspective foregrounds the fact that the addressee (unlike an analyst) can't predict the forthcoming turns and has to resort to so-called *provisional interpreting*, to be corroborated or modified in the upcoming turns. This interpreting then becomes *operative interpreting*, that is meaning that is settled on and as such often not identical with, and sometimes not even consistent with, the addressee's provisional interpretation. This meaning may not even be consistent with what the speaker originally meant. The dialogue in (8.53) provides an apt example where the meaning settled on is what is called, after Clark, an 'accepted misconstrual'.

(8.53)    W:   And what would you like to drink?
           C:   Hot tea, please. Uh, English Breakfast.
           W:   That was Earl Grey?
           C:   Right.

(from Elder 2019: 121, after H. Clark)

The example shows that the meaning that is settled on can depart from the one intended when it does not significantly matter for the situation at hand to be precise (that is, that it was the exact brand of English Breakfast tea that had been meant). In general, co-constructed meaning is found to depend on various parameters, including the type of conversation. In doctor–patient talk, for example, co-construction will progress along different parameters in order to reflect the specificity of goals.[81]

The fact that speakers hold (and make) themselves accountable for the truth of what they say has often been explored in the history of philosophy, for example by Augustine, Hobbes, Hume, Husserl, or Reid, to name a few. But the joint construction of the meaning the interlocutors settle on adds a new light to the old 'whose meaning?' debate: perhaps we are responsible not just for what we intended to communicate, or what we inadvertently communicate (but, say, should have known better if we stuck to the common ground), but for this dynamically, interactively achieved construct? This dynamic perspective on meaning has an important impact on issues of commitment and accountability. Food for thought – especially in view of important ethical and legal implications. Suffice it to say that the journeys through accountability that would be compatible with our current path are the ones in interactional pragmatics.

In this vein, Haugh (2013: 53) regards speaker meaning as a *deontic concept*, in that

[f]irst, what a speaker is held accountable for goes beyond the veracity of information to include other moral concerns, such as social rights, obligations, responsibilities and the like. Second, to be held *interactionally* accountable differs from inferring commitment. The former is tied to an understanding of speaker meaning as arising through incremental, sequentially grounded discourse processing ..., while the latter is tied to a punctuated view of speaker meaning that arises at the level of utterance processing.

---

[80] See Garfinkel 1967 and Heritage 1984.
[81] See here e.g. Peräkylä 1997 and for an overview Jaszczolt and Berthon, in press.

And this gives the foundation for a new journey through meaning along one of the branches we have come to at our crossroads:

while a deontological notion of speaker meaning may seem of limited value to those focusing on speaker meaning at the level of utterance processing ..., participants do evidently orient to the deontological aspects of speaker meaning through holding speakers accountable to the moral order for such meanings in interaction. *To dismiss such concerns is to ignore the very real-world consequentiality of what we are taken to mean.* (Haugh 2013: 53, my emphasis)[82]

*Deontology*, or *deontological ethics*, is an important concept. Derived from the Greek for 'duty' (*deon*) (cf. 'deontic modality' discussed in Section 5.4) and learning (*logos*), it addresses questions in moral philosophy concerning norms for what we ought and ought not to do – that is, which actions are permitted and which are not.[83]

As Haugh says, making speaker meaning deontological points the study in the direction of practical applications: moral norms of behaviour and their consequences (NB: not to be confused with *consequentialism* in ethics which argues from consequences, states of affairs, to behaviours[84]). But it also dovetails with the metasemantic concern to delimit meaning, such as the minimalism/contextualism debates, which, in turn, helps address the question as to what speakers are accountable for: the minimal, sentence meaning (as minimalists tend to argue) or some form of the contextually enhanced content – the kinds of content that occupied us throughout Stage 7. This topic is well researched in recent philosophical debates.[85] Emma Borg, for example, distinguishes two kinds of liability: strict liability, for the minimal proposition uttered, followed by degrees of conversational liability for potential interpretations. Fabrizio Macagno, on the other hand, stresses the importance of interpretations that are *default for the context*, exposing the dangers of attributing to the speaker decontextualized meaning – or what is called a strategy of ignoring qualifications in order to manipulate meaning, discussed since Aristotle as *secundum quid et simpliciter*. Macagno gives the following example:

Everyone has a right to his or her own property. Therefore, even though Jones has been declared insane, you had no right to take away his weapon. (Macagno 2022: 1, after S. M. Engel)

Note here the benefits of the radically contextualist accounts of meaning discussed in Section 7.2, such as Default Semantics, for capturing the 'right', contextualized kind of meaning. We return to the topic of content vis-à-vis accountability later on in this section and in Section 8.4.1.2.

Now, Elder and Haugh develop deontological meaning into a model of operative meaning. They emphasize again that 'speaker meaning is not simply a theoretical construct grounded in (a presumed) cognitive reality, but a deontological one with real-world consequences for speakers' (Elder and Haugh 2018: 594). Like for Arundale, for

---

[82] Haugh 2013 is a good source of references to other advocates of such co-constructed meanings in linguistics. For a very different philosophical discussion of accountability, see e.g. Moran 2018, and also Goldberg 2011, 2015, discussed in the previous section – among many others.
[83] For a comprehensive introduction to deontological ethics, see Alexander and Moore 2020.
[84] On consequentialism, see also Alexander and Moore 2020.
[85] See e.g. Saul 2012; Borg 2019; Borg and Connolly 2022.

them, operative meaning rests on the idea that the addressee's response makes the speaker accountable for the meaning that emerges at the given point in conversation. They propose to focus on '*the most salient propositional meaning* that is ostensively made operative between interlocutors' (p. 595), such as Jaszczolt's primary meaning of Default Semantics or Ariel's privileged interactional interpretation (see Section 7.2.3), in order to get away from the unhelpful traditional distinctions between what is 'said' and what is 'implicated'. (Remember that either of these can pertain to the most salient message.) This allows them to offer a model of communication that purports to explain operative meaning – meaning that is dynamic, in the sense that the addressee's response makes the speaker accountable for the meaning that emerged, to be settled on through *reflexive accountability* in the original speaker's response. Like in CA, following Garfinkel and Heritage, what they mean by this is that the meaning for which the speaker is accountable is settled over a number of turns – or in what is often called a conceptual 'third turn' – some later turn (not necessarily numerically third) in which the differences are resolved.[86] They adopt here the distinction between (i) *private inferences*, that is inferences that the addressee can be assumed to draw, that in turn lead to (ii) inferences that are *publicly available* when the addressee reveals their understanding of the speaker's utterance in their own turn. In their words, 'speakers make inferences about individual utterances ... until they converge on a meaning that is sufficient for the purposes of the discourse' (Elder and Haugh 2018: 608). Compare here the earlier discussion of provisional interpreting.

It is worth noting at this point that the early programmatic opposition to the explanatory role of intentions and beliefs in CA can be relaxed without the risk of incompatibility: ethnomethodology provides an invaluable insight into the dynamicity of meaning in interaction but need not necessarily serve as an alternative to more cognitively oriented, such as post-Gricean, insights. Elder and Haugh's model testifies to the possibility of positive eclecticism, at the same time pushing forward post-Gricean pragmatics towards a dynamic concept of meaning. For example, Jaszczolt and Berthon (in press) point out that such a dynamic unit of meaning may be multi-propositional, or what they call a *dynamic functional propositional construal*.

All in all, as food for thought, we can now consider the idea that the concept of meaning is best construed as a dynamic one: meaning that evolves, partly through negotiation. It is precisely this kind of meaning – meaning that is settled for – for which we need the concepts of joint (reflexive) accountability and joint commitment. This leads us to the observation that, just as meaning, commitments can also be negotiated and co-constructed. In the process, commitments can be rejected, denied, or retracted later in a conversation – commitments understood here not as beliefs, but as functions of acts of uttering something, that is making the meaning public.[87] To quote Geurts' (2019: 1) influential paper, 'human communication is first and foremost a matter of negotiating commitments, rather than one of conveying intentions, beliefs, and other mental states'. For Geurts, commitment is a three-place relation where speaker A is committed to speaker B to act on a certain proposition. Commitment applies to a wide

---

[86] See fn 79.    [87] See Hamblin 1971; Brandom 1994.

category of speech acts, including assertion, as discussed earlier, in that the speaker is committed to the truth of the asserted (and on some accounts, also implied) proposition. A good example is a promise – standardly classified as a *commissive* speech act – in that the speaker undertakes a commitment to bringing about a certain state of affairs (or, on an alternative definition, to making a certain proposition true). Another good example is a request, whereby the speaker undertakes a commitment that the addressee achieves a certain goal (or, on an alternative definition, makes a certain proposition true). As Geurts puts it, such mutual commitments bring about the common ground. Then negotiation of commitments works as follows: in the example of a promise, the speaker is committed to it if the addressee understands that the speaker is committed to it and both the speaker and the addressee share this commitment. In other words, the proposed commitment is accepted and becomes a mutual, shared commitment. This brings us back to the concept of interactional commitment foregrounded in the conversational-analytic studies discussed earlier – an example of how rather different frameworks can converge on a rather similar idea of dynamic, interactive meaning.

Note that the labels 'commitment' and 'accountability' don't have a standardized use – different linguistic and philosophical approaches use them differently along several dimensions. First, being held accountable, or being considered committed, need not mean the same as being *aware* of making oneself answerable. Second, it can, but need not, be a dyadic concept – that is, a commitment *to someone*. Third, commitment can be to situations, or propositions, or to some other constructs.[88] CA research adopted the term 'accountability', while some other approaches referred to here (such as Geurts', following Hamblin and Brandom), adopt 'commitment'. We are using the terms largely interchangeably, following the original theories' preferences, in that the way they are used normally sheds light on the meaning they come with and on the assumptions made in the respective theory on the above three dimensions. For example, *holding oneself* accountable, or *being aware of having committed oneself*, are closely related concepts. In other words, the terms are still largely used in the intra-theoretic sense.

We have flagged here that questions of commitment, accountability, or liability, which are not normally included in linguistic debates on meaning and are only beginning to get to the forefront of mainstream philosophy of language, ought not to be the subject of separate investigations in ethics or epistemology. Instead, these issues are best thought of in conjunction with discussions about meaning in semantics and pragmatics, as well as in the metasemantics and metapragmatics that provide the philosophical foundations for them. Just as Goldberg's discussion of accepted epistemological standards, interpersonal ethical standards, and so forth discussed in the previous section can be taken further by venturing into interactional pragmatics, so the discussions of accountability (and liability) for what one says (and implies) and the perception of authority best sit on top of linguistic pragmatic investigations.

---

[88] See also Elder 2021.

Negotiating meaning inevitably touches upon such ethical and social aspects of what a speaker says and/or implies and what a speaker is taken to say and/or imply. Discussions of commitment, accountability, or liability are a clear case of this mutual relevance. As such, it also touches upon the question of normativity. In his philosophical essay on assertoric speech and testimony, Moran (2018: 51), for example, points out that 'the speaker, in presenting her utterance as *assertion*, one with the force of *telling* the audience something, presents herself as *accountable* for the truth of what she says, and in doing so offers a kind of guarantee for this truth'. But this guarantee can be misunderstood, when intentions are misunderstood or not fully clear, or it can be deliberately manipulated when intentions are perceived as insincere. We have also seen that epistemic norms for assertion discussed in the previous section have to be sensitive to the situation; what counts as true (or 'true enough') in one situation may not do at all in another. There are 'low-stakes' and 'high-stakes' scenarios that we invoked throughout Stage 7. There are also salient contextual interpretations, and, as we have seen throughout this journey, accounting for these wreaks havoc on any attempts to make meaning neat and simple. The dynamic pragmatic perspective becomes crucial. Although this topic is largely pursued in accountability ethics (a branch of normative, applied ethics), it is clear how a pragmatic theory with its account of dynamic meaning provides invaluable background to delimit the object of analysis.

Normativity does not come cheap. As Goldberg points out in his *Conversational Pressure: Normativity in Speech Exchanges*,[89] interaction in discourse leads to pressures that can be caused by epistemic, ethical, or social norms. In other words, we are bound by various kinds of expectations: that one tells the truth, that one holds oneself accountable for the content of what one is saying, or that one conforms to the conventions of conversation – its structure as well as acceptable content. (Note here that what philosophers classify as types of normativity, linguists elaborate with a different focus, invoking Gricean maxims or post-Gricean principles and heuristics, accounts of politeness (discussed in Section 8.4.2) and conversational structure (such as in CA just discussed) – food for thought on the benefits and perils of interdisciplinarity!) As Goldberg says, being addressed by someone can itself put the addressee under conversational-normative pressure in that we are expected to react and respond. So, it is not only meanings that may have to be negotiated; negotiation of norms is also an important issue – something that in Jaszczolt and Berthon (in press) is called *metanegotiation of meaning*.

Neither does normativity come without social abuses or struggles. To give an example, socially situated epistemic practices – that is, how we approach acquiring knowledge in social situations, can reveal abuse of shared ethical standards when a speaker's assertion is doubted or rejected due to prejudice. An assertion may also fall on deaf ears when society lacks the crucial concept. Such 'epistemic injustice', to use the term from the title of her book, Fricker (2007: 1) insightfully analyses as 'testimonial injustice' and 'hermeneutical injustice' respectively:

---

[89] Goldberg 2020.

Testimonial injustice occurs when prejudice causes a hearer to give a deflated level of credibility to a speaker's word; hermeneutical injustice occurs at a prior stage, when a gap in collective interpretive resources puts someone at an unfair disadvantage when it comes to making sense of their social experiences. An example of the first might be that the police do not believe you because you are black; an example of the second might be that you suffer sexual harassment in a culture that still lacks that critical concept.

The topic of negotiation of norms is best left to experts on the interface between ethics and epistemology as it is a rich and extensive field of research in its own right. But it gives us some food for thought at this point in the journey, and a glimpse of a road to a very different, albeit not unrelated, domain of inquiry.

Let us return to our journey. To reiterate before we move on: as far as practical applications are concerned, such as those to normative ethics or jurisprudence, it is a matter of dispute as to whether a normative approach ought to consider a speaker accountable only for what they explicitly say, or for conventional or salient interpretations thereof, or perhaps even for interpretations easily inferable in a given situation. If the latter, do they have to be intended? This takes us to the question of insincerity, and in particular the concepts of lying and misleading.

### 8.4.1.2 Lying, Misleading, and Liability

Lying, misleading, and other forms of linguistic insincerity interact with questions about meaning in obvious ways. Insincerity is an important factor to consider in theories of meaning and communication, suffice it to mention Grice's maxim of Quality, the sincerity condition of SAT, or the proposal of the common ground and pragmatic presupposition such as that by Stalnaker. Lying and deception have also been widely discussed by philosophers at least since Augustine's treatises in the fourth century CE. Lying was already an object of some attention in the philosophy of Ancient Greece, although the focus was then on the morality of lying rather than on its definition and delimitation.[90] Questions are ample, and answers to them are still largely up for grabs. Let us skim over a few. First, what exactly counts as lying? We normally say that lying is saying something that the speaker believes to be false. But is intention to deceive part of it? Are bald-faced lies really lies when there is a mutual understanding that there is no deception? And what about *bullshitting* – by now a technical term for uttering something when one is unconcerned whether it is true or false? Also, if lying is 'saying something', then how should we define 'saying' – in terms of minimalism or as contextually embellished 'saying'? And, does it have to be 'saying' in the first place? That is, can't we lie by producing strong implicatures? Aren't they de facto lies if they clearly pertain to the question under discussion (QUD discussed in Section 6.3.4)? And what about lying through false presuppositions such as (8.54b) for (8.54a)?

(8.54a)  John didn't stop sleepwalking.

(8.54b)  John used to sleepwalk.

---

[90] See Stokke 2018 and Mahon 2019.

## 8.4 At a Crossroads with Ethical and Social Debates

This is just a selection of questions – the field is rife with them and with exciting proposals by linguists, philosophers of language and mind, moral philosophers, epistemologists, and others.

Let us begin with insincerity. For Andreas Stokke, a lie is a form of insincerity but it has to be an insincere *assertion*. Lies need not involve an intention to deceive; they do, however, have to be insincere assertions. On this account, accidentally saying something true (when believed to be false) is also a lie, and so is bullshitting. Otherwise it is some form of deception or misleading, such as conveying false implicatures.

So, on this account, non-declaratives cannot be lies in that they are not assertions. But, rather contentiously, bald-faced lies *are* lies, even though they are not aimed at deceiving; they are lies because they are assertions. A typical example of a bald-faced lie he quotes is (8.55).

(8.55) [Scenario: *A student accused of cheating on an exam is called to the Dean's office. The student knows that the Dean knows that she did in fact cheat. But as it is also well known that the Dean will not punish someone unless they explicitly admit their guilt, the student says,*]

'I didn't cheat.'

(adapted from Stokke 2018: 18, after Carson 2010)

But are bald-faced lies assertions? Not everyone agrees. Jörg Meibauer[91] argues quite convincingly that utterances such as that in (8.55) are not assertions – neither are they lies, precisely because they don't involve an intention to deceive. When we make the intention to deceive a definitional requirement of lying but drop the assertion requirement, the landscape changes: neither bald-faced lies not self-deception are lies, but falsely implicating something and falsely presupposing results is a lie. As he says,

a comprehensive notion of lying should include lying by deliberately using false implicatures and false presuppositions. Implicatures and presuppositions are additional propositions that are derived from an utterance in an interactional context. (Meibauer 2014: 234)

He focuses on the linguistic aspects of lying and demonstrates how the question of what should count as lying dovetails with theoretical concerns such as the grammar–pragmatics and semantics–pragmatics interfaces. He also includes linguistic analysis of structures that speakers use for lying. The importance of this linguistic sensitivity will surface again when we discuss linguistic politeness in Section 8.4.2.1.

Accounts are not easily comparable in that they adopt very different concepts of lying and address different (linguistic, moral, legal, and other) questions. But a philosophical proposal veering towards minimalist meaning should be mentioned here. For Jennifer Saul, in her celebrated *Lying, Misleading, and What Is Said*,[92] lying is saying what one believes to be false in a context where sincerity is expected – that is, in a warranting situation. She admits a degree of context dependence in that

---

[91] See Meibauer 2014. See also a helpful and thoughtful review in Dynel 2015.   [92] See Saul 2012.

saying something underdetermined where all relevant completions are believed to be false is also a lie. So, one can lie with propositions that are not as minimal as Borg's or Cappelen and Lepore's but not as freely adapted as those of contextualists: she allows only for completions, that is structure-driven enrichments, and only for a strict subset of those. Other forms of insincerity count as misleading. From the perspective of ethical considerations, however, Saul argues that lying is not necessarily morally worse than misleading.

From the perspective of our journey, what we have here is a practical application of such concepts as saying, implicating, or primary message, in that lying by implicit content is a vital part of the debates. The question also touches upon the role of context in truth-value judgements discussed throughout Stage 7, for example DeRose's high- and low-stakes scenarios: what counts as true when stakes are low may count as false when stakes are high.[93] What counts as knowing that $p$ can depend on how much one has to lose if one is wrong.[94]

It is worth pointing out here that in analysing lying one can use different research methods: philosophical arguments, linguistic analysis of constructions, as well as empirical testing of people's judgements. Concerning the latter, Weissman and Terkourafi,[95] for example, tested whether one can lie through implicatures. Their results showed that speakers consider only some types of implicatures to be lies. This in turn opens up the question as to whether these are instances of an implicature in the first place or rather parts of semantic content. Or, perhaps, speakers count as lying whatever functions as a functional proposition, or the main, primary meaning in the sense of Default Semantics, and as such addresses QUD à la Stokke? Food for thought.

We won't branch out much further in this journey, although one could easily do so. On the linguistic side, there is a carefully developed, albeit not uncontroversial, framework for discussing untruthfulness in discourse, focusing on the breadth of what should count as untruthful conversational behaviour and on the role of situated context in judging untruthfulness and assigning responsibility for it. This is Chris Heffer's TRUST – or Trust-Related Untruthfulness in Situated Text. As he says,

we need to extend the *scope* of untruthfulness both from utterance insincerity (lying and misleading) to discursive insincerity (withholding), and from intentional insincerity to epistemic irresponsibility. (Heffer 2020: 6)

He addresses the main two dimensions discussed here: (i) intentional vs. non-intentional and (ii) 'strictly uttering' vs. other ways of being insincere. He also steers in the direction of co-constructed meaning in focusing on relations of trust between speakers and how they establish the ethical value of untruthfulness. Grice's Cooperative Principle is, in the process, extended to cater not only for 'saying' but also for 'non-saying': withholding information is a breach of trust and of the rational assumption of cooperative behaviour. Venturing even further, Thomas Carson, in his *Lying and*

---

[93] See DeRose 1992, 2009. See also Dinges 2018 on the role of implicatures in such truth-value judgements.
[94] See Section 7.2.2, fn 57.
[95] See Weissman and Terkourafi 2019. For a defence of the role of speakers' judgements in semantic theory see Michaelson 2016. See also contributions to Meibauer 2019b.

*Deception*,[96] analyses all these forms of insincerity in different private and public settings, focusing on questions of ethics. This, of course, brings us back to the question as to what consequences of their utterances speakers are (or ought to be) held responsible for, and as such takes us further into language and law.[97]

To sum up, our 'branching off' turns out to reveal mutual benefits for philosophy of language, semantics, and pragmatics on the one hand, and moral theory, legal theory, sociology, and other human and social sciences on the other. Crucially, it brings to the fore the inquiry into *the self* in its various facets: the self in discourse interaction, the self and its moral values, or the self and its social responsibilities. We now continue on the social self in flagging the topic of linguistic politeness.

## 8.4.2 Social Persona

### 8.4.2.1 Being Polite and Being Proper

Is being insincere always wrong – morally reprehensible, socially unacceptable? People sometimes say baldly what is not true, or mislead, or withhold information, for good reasons, such as to be polite or to spare someone grief. On the other hand, is being sincere always socially and morally uncontroversial? Why do we sometimes tone it down with disclaimers, expressions of uneasiness or even embarrassment? The way we say things, and what we implicate by it, can have enormous consequences for social interaction. Here the most relevant areas of research are linguistic politeness and linguistic offence or use of 'bad language'. Let us begin with politeness.

Knowing what we know about semantics and pragmatics so far, how is the phenomenon of linguistic politeness best approached? Neither Gricean or post-Gricean maxims or principles, nor SAT, nor game theory, or any other approach to meaning in discourse will suffice on its own. And yet the phenomenon cannot be ignored in that it affects not only how things are said but also what is said and why. Grice originally suggested that other maxims might also be needed, among them a maxim of politeness, but that they were tangential to his inquiry:

> There are, of course, all sorts of other maxims (aesthetic, social, or moral in character), such as 'Be polite', that are also normally observed by participants in talk exchanges, and these may also generate nonconventional implicatures. The conversational maxims, however, and the conversational implicatures connected with them, are specially connected (I hope) with the particular purposes that talk (and so, talk exchange) is adapted to serve and is primarily employed to serve. I have stated my maxims as if this purpose were a maximally effective exchange of information. (Grice 1989b [1975]: 28)

It is not unassailable that such social or moral maxims can be left out. On the other hand, it is also debatable as to whether harnessing polite linguistic behaviour by putting it into maxims is the right way to go about it. What effect does

---

[96] See Carson 2010.
[97] The literature here is vast again. On language and law, start with contributions to Tiersma and Solan 2012. For pragmatics and law, see e.g. contributions to Poggi and Capone 2017.

polite behaviour achieve? Does it generate implicatures? Or, perhaps, it often goes unnoticed, and it is only *impoliteness* that immediately strikes us in conversation? Or, perhaps, a bit of both: politeness is sometimes just tacit propriety, and at other times an overt display of a social attitude? But then, doesn't too much of such a display have an opposite effect when it is improper for the circumstances? There is a lot of food for thought, and quite a few approaches to choose from too, in that studies of linguistic politeness now have quite a rich history. They have focused on such questions as politeness and implicature, politeness and the state of social harmony, impoliteness, the search for universal principles of politeness, politeness and conventions, form–function correlations, or cross-cultural differences in politeness strategies, to name a few.

Predictably, Grice's suggestion triggered attempts to formulate such maxims. Robin Lakoff[98] makes 'Be polite' interact with 'Be clear', where the latter consists of Grice's maxims. 'Be polite' is further spelled out in terms of such sub-maxims as (i) 'Don't impose', (ii) 'Give options', (iii) 'Make the addressee feel good – be friendly'. But it doesn't take long to notice that the attempt is quite anglocentric. In many cultures, imposition can be polite. For example, the degree of insistence with which the host encourages guests to help themselves to food differs rather dramatically from culture to culture. Likewise, 'giving options' and making one 'feel good' sound dubious: in more hierarchical cultures it is often pre-empting the need to choose, not troubling the addressee with making choices, or, in general, 'not making the addressee feel bad' that are foregrounded. Universal tendencies are difficult to find if one goes about it in this way. Lakoff's attempt to give relativized preferences to (i)–(iii) for different cultures won't do the trick either.

Next, an improved attempt at universality is Geoffrey Leech's[99] proposal to supplement Grice's Cooperative Principle with a Politeness Principle that consists of at least six maxims: those of Tact, Generosity, Approbation, Modesty, Agreement, and Sympathy, and perhaps some others, such as Phatic ('Keep talking'). As he adds later, there seems to be a 'General Strategy of Politeness' that underlies them:

In order to be polite, S expresses or implies meanings that associate a favorable value with what pertains to O[ther] or associates an unfavourable value with what pertains to S[elf]. (Leech 2014: 90)

For example, 'Minimize praise of self', working in tandem with 'Maximize dispraise of self' as the maxim of Modesty accounts for the asymmetries in (8.56a)–(8.56b). At the same time, these examples demonstrate the working of the maxim of Approbation – 'Minimize dispraise of other/ Maximize praise of other.' The marked, pragmatically awkward alternatives, if uttered, tend to have the default ironic sense.

(8.56a)   How clever of you!/$^?$How clever of me!

(8.56b)   How stupid of me!/$^?$How stupid of you!

(adapted from Leech 1983: 136)

---

[98] See Lakoff 1973.    [99] See Leech 1983.

## 8.4 At a Crossroads with Ethical and Social Debates

Next, Leech embeds these maxims in the overall model that he calls *Interpersonal Rhetoric*, where in addition to Grice's maxims and his six maxims of politeness he also includes general principles that account for other aspects of composing utterance meaning. He does so, first, to account for irony and banter that operate on the output of the previous two kinds of maxims, altering, and often reversing, the meaning. Then, he adds general strategies that account for attempts to be interesting/unpredictable, to the extent of exaggeration, and for appearing optimistic. However, again, even adjusting the weights of the components for different cultures did not quite account for cross-cultural variation; the proposed categories were overlapping, or sometimes redundant or insufficient. Where I come from, 'Being optimistic' is certainly not what people expect when they open up to you with their woes. Nor do they expect gentle agreement when they have just confided in you with their views – say, political convictions – and expect you to do the same as a display of trust. It is not only the values of the categories that may need to be calibrated, but the category labels themselves – if, indeed, labels are the way to go. Judging from the fate of Grice's maxims, they probably are not.[100]

A less ethnocentric model developed in the late 1970s focused on the concept of *face*. Face, a term adopted from sociology, means 'the positive social value' (Goffman 1967: 5) that is associated with the person in the process of social interaction. In other words, it means honour, self-esteem, or public self-image. It is omnipresent in conversation and deemed to be universal (present in conversation in all cultures): speakers are assumed to be rational (the model assumes Grice's Cooperative Principle) and to have face. The model was proposed by Brown and Levinson,[101] who began with the assumption that in conversational interaction people are governed by two desires: to be unimpeded in actions (called *negative face*) and to be approved of (*positive face*). The terms are not intended to imply evaluation; they simply stand for two kinds of desires constituting face.

This notion of face is central to the theory. The negative face includes the basic rights to privacy, non-distraction, freedom of action, and freedom from imposition. The positive face includes the desire that the person's self-image is approved of and appreciated. When interacting in conversation, interlocutors can affect both their own and each other's face – for example threaten the addressee's face by criticizing or making requests, or threaten one's own by expressing indebtedness or guilt. Orthogonally, each of these can involve positive and negative face. In hindsight, however, the four-way distinction proved to be difficult to maintain. This is because, first, matching negative and positive face with linguistic *strategies* was not as easy as Brown and Levinson had anticipated. This is part of the problem with allocating speech acts to forms of expression discussed in Section 8.3. Second, the categories of 'positive' and 'negative' do not adequately ascribe the conversational facework of many cultures. And, finally: politeness cannot be measured by single sentences and

---

[100] Subsequent developments of Leech's view will not interest us here in that we are flagging it as an early landmark. But see Leech 2014.
[101] See Brown and Levinson 1987.

single propositions and their correspondence with strategies. This latter criticism applies to many non-dynamic pragmatic approaches, with post-Griceans still in the lead.

Relevant acts of communication are called there *face-threatening acts* (FTAs). But then, since most of what we say does affect one or another aspect of face (or both) of one or the other interlocutor (or both), then aren't all speech acts potential FTAs? Moreover, why should we treat face threat as something special, different from other kinds of effects that speech acts can have? Food for thought. Nevertheless, with these reservations in mind, it is still, arguably, the best formally worked-out model to date and still resonates in a lot of empirical cross-cultural research, as well as in theoretical critical studies. So, it is worth a bit more attention.

FTAs can be performed *on record* (directly) or *off record* (indirectly). The category *on record* allows for two sub-types: (i) *without redressive action*, as in (8.57), and *with redressive action*, the latter being either of (ii) *positive* or of (iii) *negative* politeness type, as in (8.58) and (8.59) respectively.

(8.57)   Sit down!

(8.58)   Oh, how nice to see you – sit down!

(8.59)   Would you like to sit down, please?

Going (iv) off record means communicating implicitly, as in (8.60).

(8.60)   It would be easier to talk if you sat down for a while.

Going on record gives the speaker credit for honesty, in that the speaker is seen as trustworthy: the intention is communicated clearly. Going off record makes the speaker appear tactful as, arguably, more than one intention can be attributed to the utterance and the commitment to the content is unspecified (as discussed in the previous two sections). Next, it is presumed that rational agents use the same type of strategy under the same conditions. The strategies are then spelled out as sets of sub-strategies corresponding to the types of (mostly) linguistic behaviour by which they can be realized. This linguistic behaviour then produces an *implicature of politeness*.

Let us consider the strategies in a little more detail. Type (i), bald on record, means speaking in conformity with Grice's maxims because there is no face threat to moderate. Welcomings, farewells, offers can also be expressed in this way. Type (ii), on record with positive politeness, renders familiar, joking behaviour. One of the sub-strategies is 'Claim common ground', exemplified in (8.61), where the speaker uses the address form *mate* as an in-group identity marker.

(8.61)   Well done, mate.

Type (iii) makes use of negative politeness. An example is 'Don't coerce the hearer: be pessimistic, give deference, minimize the imposition', as in constructions such as *I am sorry to disturb you but* ... or *I don't suppose you could* ... . Next, type (iv), performing the FTA off record, relies on the fact that the intention is obfuscated – the addressee must perform some inference in order to recover what was intended.

## 8.4 At a Crossroads with Ethical and Social Debates

Here the reliance on Grice's maxims is most visible in that the strategy is defined as violating them. An example of a sub-strategy is 'Give hints', as in (8.62), meant as a request for help.

(8.62)  The box is too heavy for me to carry.

We now come to the question of the intended universality of the model. It is easy to see that (i)–(iv) are arranged by increasing potential of face threat: where one can't say (8.57), one might be able to say one of (8.58)–(8.60). If not, then there is also strategy (v): not to do the FTA. The strength of face threat, or *weightiness* of the FTA, is supposed to be a universal notion, calculable as the sum of (a) the social distance between the interlocutors, (b) the relative power of the hearer over the speaker, and (c) the degree to which the FTA is ranked as an imposition in that culture. In other words, weightiness is the reason why the speaker chooses among the five sets of politeness strategies.

To digress a little, it is interesting to observe that speakers can also produce evasive answers to avoid threats to the speaker's or addressee's face. Evasive answers are defined by Marsh (2018: 59) as answers that '1) are not relevant to the question under discussion [that is, are not even partial answers to it; see Section 6.3.4 for QUD]; 2) do not deny the presupposition contained in the question under discussion; and 3) do not assert that the question under discussion is unanswerable'. So, for example, B's answer in (8.63) is an evasive answer by these criteria, while in (8.64) it is not.

(8.63)  A: What kind of seafood will John eat?
        B: John eats some seafood.

(8.64)  A: What kind of seafood will John eat?
        B: John doesn't eat seafood.

(from Marsh 2018: 59)

Coming back to the model, Brown and Levinson also gave a formula for calculating the value of weightiness but it has never got off the ground in that the components (a)–(c) were left hopelessly underdetermined, and, moreover, are supposed to be estimated by the interlocutors *in situ*. But, unlike the formula, the concept of weightiness itself is crucial for the model in that it is supposed to allow its universal application. The norms and conventions that underlie (a)–(c) are all understood as being prone to cultural differences, and making weightiness depend on them is supposed to account for its cultural variability. For instance, in one culture hierarchical relationships may be the norm, while in another relationships are egalitarian (although these are relative rather than absolute labels). Or the individualism of one culture can be juxtaposed with the social harmony of another. Should the model work for all cultures, then this would show that interaction is based on such universal principles. This universality is one of the main characteristics that Brown and Levinson set out to demonstrate by comparing strategies in three genetically very different languages. Their conclusion was that cultural diversity could be accounted for by placing different cultures, so to speak, in different places on the cline from strategy (i) to strategy (v) in the following way. Some cultures have high values of weightiness and use small FTAs. These are *negative-politeness cultures*, but, as was said earlier, only relatively so: for example the British in the eyes of the Americans, or the Japanese in the eyes of the British. On the other hand, *positive-politeness cultures* have a low level of weightiness: impositions, social distance, and relative power are small there. Crucially, universal application of the model is supposed to come from the hypothesis that no society will use, say, (i) or (ii) for big FTAs and (iii) or (iv) for small ones. Cultures can be placed on different points (more likely, sections) of the (i)–(v) cline, in that what requires on-record strategy with redress may require off-record strategy in another culture, but the relation between weightiness and the strategy has to be directly proportional and cannot be inverted. Inverting it would amount to falsifying the model.

So, is indirectness indeed always used for greater face threat than being on record? For many cultures, Polish included, this does not seem to be the case.[102] Moreover, a lot depends on the situation at hand. Indirectness can also be a mark of power, and as such can be used where the speaker's power over the addressee is great. Tannen gives here an example of a Greek father indirectly giving orders to his daughter – a scenario that, in fact, extends to many cultures to some degree where a parent indicates that an adolescent child is supposed to grasp the hints rather than be told overtly what to do (doesn't that sound familiar? ☺).[103]

Decades later, the model is still an important landmark in politeness research but not so much because of its form–function, or linguistic-strategy–weight-of-imposition correlation but because it ricocheted in the field, giving rise to sparkling observations and criticism, including

(a) that the degree of face threat and the order of strategies are not always correlated,

as was just discussed, but also

(b) that face is not a universal concept, and neither is the positive/negative distinction,[104]
(c) that linguistic strategies cannot be compartmentalized under politeness strategies or sub-strategies,
(d) that politeness doesn't seem to be a strategy, not even an unconsciously employed one,

and, perhaps most importantly,

(e) that politeness does not seem to be what speakers implicate.

Instead, politeness is what takes place between interlocutors as a norm – something we normally don't even think about unless the utterance is out of sync with the situation.

---

[102] See here Blum-Kulka 1987 for Israeli culture and Wierzbicka 1985 for Polish. For a discussion see e.g. Kádár and Haugh 2013.
[103] See e.g. Tannen 1994, pp. 175–194.
[104] See e.g. Mao 1994. For different understandings of what universality of politeness means, see Leech 2014, Chapter 4.

## 8.4 At a Crossroads with Ethical and Social Debates 347

So, perhaps,

(f) politeness is not a *strategy* and it is not *communicated* either?

Or,

(g) politeness is many things? It is sometimes implicated and noticed as such by the participants and sometimes just taken for granted and only discussed on the meta-level by researchers?

More about that soon. But

(h) when it *is* an implicature, what exactly is its content? Is it propositional content, like that of any other implicature? Perhaps 'I am trying to be polite' fits the bill? And if so, is it cancellable? Perhaps it is, when it is recovered as an implicature of politeness, but upon further consideration the utterance can be understood as ironic, as discussed in our journey through cancellability in Section 7.2.4?

Food for thought again, with reference to the ideas on implicature and cancellability from Section 7.2.4.

Here the evolution of views progressed in line with the evolution of post-Gricean pragmatics. While in the early days, communication was conceived of along the lines of speakers' implicating and hearers' inferring the implicatures, subsequently the view of jointly constructed meaning came to the fore, making meaning more dynamic and obliterating many divisions between Griceans on one hand and, say, game theorists on the other. (Co-constructed meaning was discussed in Section 8.4.1.1.) Likewise, Haugh (2007: 85) proposes that politeness implicatures arise from such collaborative interaction: they arise 'not as a result of inferences made about the intentions of individual speakers by addressees, but rather as the interactional achievements of speaker-hearer dyads'. As such, they are explicable by such models as Arundale's Conjoint Co-constituting Model of Communication (which, note, Arundale used to propose the co-construction of face[105]) or Elder and Haugh's model discussed earlier.

As Haugh says, politeness is anticipated because the situation as a whole suggests such an interpretation. Perhaps, as he suggests, there is more to meaning than what is said and what is implicated, and politeness is one such thing? After all, to reiterate, politeness does not seem to have a clear communicated content: 'I am being polite' or 'I am trying to be polite' is not exactly what speakers do, or even try to, get across. Arguably, politeness is also what characterizes conversation in the absence of noticeable impolite behaviour.

What emerges from these inquiries is that politeness is not to be discussed in a void: an indirect request is not 'more polite' in absolute terms than a direct one – this is not the case either within one culture or across cultures.[106] The way we communicate fits

---

[105] See Arundale 2010.
[106] For some early work on cross-cultural variation, see e.g. Pavlidou 1994; Koike 1994; Wierzbicka 1991; Fukushima 1996. On politeness and gender, see e.g. Holmes 1995.

the social variables that characterize the relations between the interlocutors and the cultural norms and expectations of what is to be conveyed and how. That is why Bruce Fraser conceptualizes politeness as acting within the conditions of a *conversational contract*: a set of rights and obligations brought into a conversation by the participants and renegotiated, if necessary, as conversation proceeds:

> Politeness is a state that one expects to exist in every conversation; participants note not that someone is being polite – this is the norm – but rather that the speaker is violating the C[onversational] C[ontract]. Being polite does not involve making the hearer 'feel good' à la Lakoff or Leech, nor ... making the hearer not 'feel bad', à la B[rown] and L[evinson]. It simply involves getting on with the task at hand in light of the terms and conditions of the CC.' (Fraser 1990b: 233)[107]

Perhaps politeness can be either: sometimes it is *overt* (or, as Relevance theorist say, *mutually manifest* to the speaker and the hearer), and at other times it is not. Next, throwing in Brown and Levinson's category of *strategic but subconscious* politeness, it can also be strategic, that is intentional, but *covert*. At the same time, 'when interactional mistakes occur, or actors try to manipulate others, they may very well emerge into awareness' (Brown and Levinson 1987: 85). It appears that politeness can be many things – because it can be achieved intentionally and deliberately or simply through subconscious adhering to norms, conventions, and internalized codes of practice. It can also be many things in that it means one thing to those involved in a linguistic interaction and another to analysts, with further categories of, so to speak, 'whose politeness' mounting in the literature that focuses on metadiscursive awareness.[108] It is immersed in social practices, it is co-constructed, but either as a non-salient emergent property of behaviour (or what Watts[109] calls *politic behaviour*), or as salient linguistic behaviour that becomes noticed as polite or impolite – as Watts suggests, behaviour that goes beyond what is expected in either direction, using different linguistic means. The latter, impolite behaviour, has also acquired its specialist studies. Jonathan Culpeper looks into different aspects of situated behaviours that 'conflict with how one expects them to be, how one wants them to be and/or how one thinks they ought to be' (Culpeper 2011: 254). The degree of offence is viewed in terms of mental attitudes and linguistic factors, as well as contextual (including sociological) aspects to do with, for example, cultural conventions or violation of social power.[110]

Every reliable journey through meaning is an opinionated journey – opinionated in a positive sense of providing good reasons for agreement or disagreement. So, let us try the following to conclude. In spite of the overwhelming popularity of politeness

---

[107] See also Escandell-Vidal 1996 on politeness as social adequacy. For discussions of these issues see Jary 1998 and Escandell-Vidal 1998. For politeness and awareness see also Terkourafi 2012 or Kádár and Haugh 2013.

[108] See here Watts 2003 for what came to be known as politeness$_1$ (first-level) and politeness$_2$ (second-level) and Kádár and Haugh 2013, Chapter 5 for an example of such a multi-layer classification.

[109] See Watts 2003.

[110] On perceived impoliteness discussed in terms of expectations, see also Locher and Watts 2008.

research, the topic is still burdened by a lack of clarity as to what exactly is being researched and by the lack of precise methods of approaching it – whatever the 'it' means for the particular participants in these debates. As such, it is probably best discussed in terms of the effects, causes, facets, aspects, and so forth of linguistic interaction rather than as a phenomenon in its own right that is ready to undergo attempts to put it into linguistic strategies or other ways of mapping function with form. There has as yet been no agreement on such a phenomenon. There are myriad interesting questions but no systematicity to how to answer them, no precise tools, and effectively no clear object of study. At the same time, politeness permeates accountability, liability for causing offence, and other areas at a crossroads of disciplines. So, perhaps, what one should do is use the precise tools we have for analysing intentions, conventions, co-constructed meaning, the extent to which the lexicon and grammar of a sentence can be modulated in context, and other core topics of our journey so far but without delimiting politeness as a separate object of study? Food for thought – and for many, a cat among the pigeons!

### 8.4.2.2 'Forbidden Words' and 'Bad Language': Semantics, Pragmatics, or Neither?

While approaches to politeness and impoliteness discuss socially appropriate and inappropriate linguistic behaviour in general, there are aspects of them that overlap with multidisciplinary studies of 'bad language' or 'forbidden words', to use the titles from two books on the subject.[111] The topic has been differently labelled and subdivided in different ways into pejoratives, taboo expressions, swear words, expressives, expletives, slurs, to name a few criss-crossing categories. The studies have been part of lexical semantics, sociolinguistics, and ethics for some time but truth-conditional semantics and philosophy of language have now also woken up to them. They woke up with a big splash: debates about the meaning of slurs are mushrooming at what appears to be an exponential rate, to the extent that in their recent introduction to *Bad Language*, Cappelen and Dever say the following:

> [W]e might need a sharp change from the picture of language that has dominated ... philosophy of language since its origin at the beginning of the twentieth century [*sic*]. In much of that work, the emphasis has been on the *content* conveyed by language: what is said, what is implicated, and what is communicated. That is to say, the emphasis has been on information – something that can be true or false. ... This emphasis on content, information and truth has had the result that philosophical studies of language have ignored feelings, emotions, associations, and other non-cognitive effects of language. (Cappelen and Dever 2019: 11–12)

The 'sharp change' may be an overstatement, but what is happening seems to be a debate whether to incorporate the social and psychological effects of what and how we say into formal truth-conditional accounts of meaning. Or even treat them as part of lexical content. Or, perhaps, think of them as presuppositions – or, at the other end of the spectrum, as aspects of speech that evoke emotions and

---

[111] Cappelen and Dever 2019 and Allan and Burridge 2006 respectively, both discussed below.

feelings, and are caused by emotions and feelings, to be treated as what Potts[112] calls the *expressive dimension* of meaning.

Is it possible to have a unified account of all such terms and their functions? Is it feasible to assume that one size might fit all? Isn't an attempt to account for, say, the bad language in (8.65)–(8.69) doomed from the start?

(8.65) That damn/fucking dog is barking again.

(8.66) That bastard John won the trophy.

(8.67) We don't want [racial slur] in this neighbourhood.

(8.68) Anna is a [sexist slur].

(8.69) Bill won't do it – he's not an arse-licker.

To this we have to add expletives such as *Shit!* (analogous to *Ouch!* and *Oops!* that have made a career in semantics thanks to David Kaplan's lecture widely available on YouTube[113]).

First of all, some such expressions are more socially acceptable than others. On the other hand, some are so powerful and offensive or degrading that they have to be left out even when they are to be *mentioned* rather than *used*. Next, some are in an attributive and others in a predicative position – in fact, 'bad words' can fulfil many different syntactic functions. In short, one could try to classify them on the basis of (i) the semantic-conceptual category they are best fitted under or (ii) the syntactic position they occupy. Some have neutral meanings as well as pejorative ones (*bitch*). Some have neutral counterparts (*shit/faeces*). Some are complex, sometimes newly coined derogatory descriptions, utilizing, for example, terms for ethnic cuisine or social customs as ethnic slurs. We can also ask about (iii) their truth-conditional significance and whether it is the same for them all. (Compare here *John is a bastard* with *Fuck!*). In terms of this journey, we would want to fit their discourse meaning into truth-conditional content but this is dictated by our initial appropriation of truth conditions for the meaning of an act of speech that is mutually agreed on by the interlocutors. This, of course, limits the discussion to cases without miscommunication. But even then, we can also ask about non-cognitive effects, feelings, and particularly emotions. These will have to go beyond the truth-conditional content. So, perhaps we can also differentiate slurs according to (iv) psychological effects or (v) social impact? Or even arrange them on (vi) a scale of offensiveness? After all, some slurs are prohibited while others can be more easily used as banter, especially about oneself, in an appropriate context. So, perhaps what is of interest is (vii) the extent to which their impact relies on the 'bad content' of the lexical entry rather than the context, situation, and attitudes. Relatedly, we can ask what is responsible for the offence: the linguistic content, situation, the attitude of the speaker, or a violation of the social norm (intended or not), or something else?

What has happened from the outset is a fragmentation of the field. Many focus on slurs, regarding them as a separate category and even debating whether it is appropriate

---

[112] See Potts 2007.  [113] See Kaplan 2008.

## 8.4 At a Crossroads with Ethical and Social Debates

to think about them in terms of semantic content. Slurs project strong lexical effects – hearing a word that is a near-homophone (similar-sounding) can also trigger strong emotions on some occasions. They carry expressive content, in view of conveying strong pejorative evaluation. But do they also carry descriptive content? And if so, what is it? Is it the content of the neutral counterpart (say, 'a person of [substitute nationality] origin' in the case of '[substitute slur for people of that nationality]'), or the neutral counterpart plus some expressive overlay?

Anderson and Lepore (2013: 26) pre-empt including slurs in theories of meaning. For them, 'slurs are *prohibited* words *not* on account of any content they get across, but rather because of relevant edicts surrounding their prohibition'. So, our journey through slurs could end here in that the follow-up questions are not theory-of-meaning questions: 'how words become prohibited, what's the relationship between their prohibition and their offense potential, and why is it sometimes appropriate to flout such prohibitions?' (*ibid.*). In this vein, Lepore and Stone add that a unified account of the interpretation of slurs is impossible: they form a heterogeneous and open-ended class that cannot be systematized.[114] But should we stop here? Yes and no. These final sections are intended as pointers to different offshoots, journeys that branch out into satellite areas but are still firmly rooted in questions about meaning in language and discourse. Bad language is definitely such a branch.

The class, to reiterate, is vast and diversified. Allan and Burridge focus on lexical items, or 'forbidden words'.[115] They talk about offensiveness and political correctness, individual censorship and institutional censorship, the role of social norms and conventions, as well as politeness/impoliteness effects of words that are considered taboo. They define taboos as words that normally cause offence or insult and group them into several categories such as (i) comparisons of people with animals (*pig, bitch, snake*); (ii) epithets derived from tabooed body organs (*asshole*), bodily effluvia (*shit*), and sexual behaviour (*wank*); (iii) dysphemistic epithets to do with physical characteristics (*fatty, baldy, carrot*); (iv) epithets ascribing mental subnormality (*idiot, cretin*); (v) sexist, racist, speciesist, classist, ageist, and other -*ist* dysphemisms (no need for examples here); slurs on character (*grump*), with some additional criss-crossing categories. Unsurprisingly, the lexicon is rich in these. Allan and Burridge offer a linguistic, including historical, analysis of an abundance per category. But an insightful lexical-semantic, including diachronic-semantic study can't solve all the questions with which we started. Most notably, it won't solve the question as to whether there is a distinction between intrinsically bad, offensive, dysphemistic lexical items and those that can easily be contextually appropriated to become 'good words'. There is no doubt that some cause deep uneasiness or even offence even if only mentioned, as in sentences along the pattern in (8.70).

(8.70)  '[racial slur]' has four letters.

---

[114] See Lepore and Stone 2018.
[115] See Allan and Burridge 2006, Chapter 3. Category labels adapted from there.

Predictably, the analysis of so many different 'forbidden words' shows that one size won't fit all and that sociopragmatics, as well as ethics and philosophy of law, all play a part in their understanding. One way out might be intentionalism combined with a bit of conceptual engineering. Keith Allan[116] advocates such an intentionalist stance: out of context, slurring expressions don't slur. They can only be *used to slur*, that is, be used with the perlocutionary intention to do so. He also adds that this calls for particular care in issuing speech acts so as not to slur inadvertently – for example by reporting on someone's speech act of slurring and quoting the slurring term in the report. Food for thought.

Now, if it is so difficult to fit all that bad words do in the lexicon, then perhaps we can fit it in the proposition pertaining to the sentence in which they occur? If the proposition is minimal, then, for the slurring meaning to be part of it, it would have to be in the lexicon – unless one can think of some 'forbidden structures' or 'forbidden resolution of indexical terms' that could be made the culprit. (More about this in a moment.) Let us begin with *descriptivism*. Hom's proposal, applied to racial epithets, places derogatory content within the lexical content. Derogatory content belongs to the semantics but it is bestowed by an 'external source', where '[t]he plausible candidates for the relevant external social practices that ground the meanings of racial epithets are *social institutions of racism*' (Hom 2008: 430). He represents the meaning of such epithets by embedding the neutral counterpart of the slur in the schematic predicate to the effect 'ought to be subjected to [substitute relevant discriminatory practices] due to being [substitute negative counterpart here]' that turns it into a slur.[117] Stated differently, there is a 'lexical marker of pejoration' (Hom and May 2013: 298) that functions like an operator on the neutral counterpart to yield a pejorative. He calls this view *combinatorial externalism* about meaning in that the semantic content is externally conferred by social practices and the epithet as such is socially constructed according to the above schema. It is a version of descriptivism in that in the truth-conditional representation it substitutes the description so constructed for the slur itself.

But is it really possible to substitute such a specific description for slurs? Or, rather, like in the case of descriptive theories of other types of expressions, is it the wishful thinking of a formal semanticist that does not withstand linguistic or psychological tests?[118] Moreover, the view does not extend to many other forms of offensive and derogatory speech – something that Hom picks up on later by allowing for a class of terms that operate through conversational implicature (NB: Hom distinguishes offence from derogation by dubbing the first subjective and the latter objective, in view of his proposed externalism).[119] He now proposes that expletives such as *Shit!* don't have truth-conditional content, and neither do expressive adjectives and adverbs (*damn cat*, *fucking great*).

---

[116] See Allan 2015.  [117] See Hom 2008, pp. 430–432.
[118] See here Cappelen and Dever 2019, Chapter 6 for a critical introduction and Cepollaro and Thommen 2019 for some formal tests.
[119] See Hom 2012.

On the other hand, expressive verbs and nouns, as in (8.71) and (8.72a), do have truth-conditional content.

(8.71)   When my cat doesn't get what he wants, he shits on the carpet.

(8.72a)  Nigel is a bastard.

It follows that they behave differently in such syntactic environments as negation, antecedent of a conditional, or propositional attitude reports. The content of 'a bastard' in a predicative position can be successfully negated, as in (8.72b).

(8.72b)  Nigel is not a bastard.

On the other hand, put in the position of an adjective, it often cannot, as in (8.73).

(8.73)   That bastard Conner was promoted. ?But probably he is not a bastard.
                                (from Potts 2005: 157, variation on Kaplan's original example)

But it has also been argued that slurs are neither true nor false *tout court*; they ought not to be evaluated using truth as a tool. As Richard (2008: 36) used to claim, 'sentence uses in which the user slurs say nothing true or false'. This is so because it is assumed that 'doing things with words' that are socially and emotionally reprehensible goes well beyond what truth conditions as a tool can be expected to be used for. How would the semantics of slurs work then? It has been proposed within semantic minimalism that a slur and its neutral counterpart share the same character (to reiterate, this is Kaplan's term for linguistic meaning) but one item is biased and derogatory. As Predelli (2013: 99) puts it, 'a slur's derogatory effects are achieved by virtue of truth-conditionally idle features of meaning'. But in order to agree we would have to accept, once again, the classic, counterintuitive conception of a proposition and be very pessimistic about what truth conditions can do. Other questions arise. What is, for example, a neutral counterpart for *whore*? Is it *sex worker*? And, would the counterpart remain 'neutral' if it were used pejoratively where the contextually induced offensive impact is strong? Food for thought again.

The positive side of a minimalist view is that slurs have meaning in the contextualist sense of what is said. They differ not only among themselves but also within registers of a single slur. As Richard more recently says, meanings are created in interaction, *in the common ground*, and the audience is expected to recognize the *presupposed* contempt. *The presuppositional account* is in fact one of the main players in the debate.[120] Schlenker tentatively proposes it for expressives at large, understood there as

*lexical items that carry a presupposition of a particular sort*, namely one which is *indexical* (it is evaluated with respect to context), *attitudinal* (it predicates something of the mental state of the agent of that content), and sometimes *shiftable* (the context of evaluation need not be the context of the actual utterance). (Schlenker 2007: 237)

---

[120] See Richard 2018. For arguments in favour of the presuppositional account, see also e.g. Cepollaro and Thommen 2019. They demonstrate that slurs project like presuppositions but the fact is sometimes obliterated by conceptual misunderstandings such as the one over descriptive vs. metalinguistic negation – concepts that we encountered in Section 4.5.2.

where shiftability is exemplified in (8.74).

(8.74)　Edith shouted that she never wanted to see that bitch Mary again.

On the other hand, since slurs have default derogatory senses, they can carry that sense to situations where they are not intended to offend, especially when their offensive meaning is so strong that it is *literally* there. So,

> In some populations, in some registers, the meaning of the sentence is *literally* made up of such things as the fact that those who use the words that occur in it ... think it acceptable to display such contempt. (Richard 2018: 167)

For example, can I always use an ethnic slur about myself when I assume I am in a setting where it will be taken humorously?[121] Note that the intention can misfire through misjudging the common ground and the very fact of uttering the term may inadvertently cause offence.

Be that as it may, the impact of slurs is to derogate, and leaving this out of their semantics simply doesn't seem the right thing to do. Or perhaps some slurs are 'slurs by lexicon' while others, such as newly coined slurs, say, focusing on an ethnic group's culinary habits, can just function as slurs on some occasions but not on others? Complex, multilexical slurs demonstrate this even better. Even within slurs, one size doesn't fit all. So, perhaps we can take one further step and instead of adapting the sense of 'literal' like Richard does (the term we effectively ditched in Section 8.1), allow that there are many different kinds of meaning that contribute to the proposition, and so to the truth-conditional content? In other words, the answer would be to analyse slurs not in terms of minimal propositions, or 'minimal propositions plus something else', but rather contextualist propositions. After all, we can harness propositions and truth conditions to do the job that all those important, practical issues make so pressing – like we have done before throughout this journey, equipped with functional propositions and truth conditions of conceptual representations. An additional benefit would be flexibility in addressing the question as to how, in virtue of what, 'bad language' offends, to which, again, there is no answer that fits all.[122]

This brings us to expressivism. Words such as *damn* or *bastard* are used in different linguistic and social environments with different senses. But what expressivism stresses about them is their *descriptive ineffability*: their emotional load cannot be adequately paraphrased. Chris Potts suggests that in a compositional account of meaning we should distinguish the truth-conditional content, presuppositions, and implicatures, but also add to this the *expressive dimension of meaning*. In (8.75), the expressive adjective *damn* does not contribute to the semantic content on this view but adds an expressive overlay. It adds the evaluation or emotional attitude conveyed by the speaker.

---

[121] We don't say much about humour in this journey, for the same reason that we had to leave out many other possible paths at this crossroads of applications, special uses of language, and so forth. For a comprehensive introduction to the linguistics of humour, see Attardo 2020. For a cross-disciplinary introduction to broadly understood 'language of humour' see Nilsen and Pace Nilsen 2019.

[122] On this question see the recent discussion in Diaz-Legaspe, Liu, and Stainton 2020, esp. p. 180.

(8.75)   The damn car broke twice last week.

Looked at from the perspective of information structure, *damn* does not contribute to at-issue content. On this account, expressive content is separate from descriptive content. Using his logic of conventional implicature,[123] Potts offers an elaborate formal compositional analysis of how expressives contribute to the overall meaning of the sentence, focusing on expressive adjectives (*damn* dog) and epithets (*jerk*). The account is modelled on his formal account of conventional implicatures in that expressives have some core properties in common with them.

While expressivism and descriptivism are often seen as two competing views, on closer inspection this is not the case. Part of the problem lies in the differences in researchers' interests. While some focus on predicative uses of expressives such as (8.72a), where they are undeniably in the at-issue position, others focus on their expressive roles in not-at-issue positions, such as (8.75). This can lead to terminological confusion: there can be *expressives* as lexemes, but also *expressive content* of a lexeme, where sometimes the latter is claimed to be all the content there is. But what is such purely expressive content? To take the example of slurs again, Robin Jeshion suggests that expressivism is too weak to capture their power to do more than just express a speaker's feeling of contempt:

Uses of slurs are so destructive in part because of their transpersonal normative power, their capacity to enjoin others in the same attitude. Expressivism cannot account for this insidious destructive power. (Jeshion 2018: 87)

She focuses on ethical expressivism (expressing contempt) but the underlying question is the same as in linguistic expressivism: more content is needed to adequately explain what slurs are and do. She proposes that this power to make others think of a group in a certain negative way is part of the meaning of the term that is additional to the basic function of picking out a group and expressing feelings.

If a journey through meaning has to lead anywhere, it has to suggest answers to be disputed or adopted. It seems that if we want to include an account of pejoratives, it is better to work with lexemes rather than functions. Making information structure dictate the object of study, as in Potts' expressivism, is a sophisticated intra-theoretic move in post-Montagovian formal semantics but, from the atheoretic perspective of words themselves, it throws the baby out with the bath water. We end up with *bastard₁* (at-issue) and *bastard₂* (not-at-issue) – not so unlike Montague's *believe₁* (*believe in* x) and *believe₂* (*believe that* p) to get formal semantics right. But words don't behave that way. Expressive content permeates all our talk and it is a matter of degree – the degree of this complex load with which people convey feelings and attitudes. Moreover, note that what Potts calls expressive adjectives and epithets can sometimes be used without much expressive content when they conform to a standard way of speaking for a community. On the other hand, expressive nouns

---

[123] See Potts 2005, Chapter 6.

and verbs (normally at-issue content) can convey an awful lot of emotions. As usual, the boundary is not as rigid: lessons were learned in the journey through said/implicated, literal/non-literal, semantic/pragmatic.[124] Perhaps the label 'expressives' is best consigned to the dustbin and we had better speak only of the expressive *role* of lexemes instead, remembering that they are not just 'grunts or facial contortions', as Geurts (2007: 209) sums up Potts' formal account tongue in cheek, but rather lexemes with content. As was discussed earlier, complex slurring expressions, including newly coined ones, reveal this fluidity of the descriptive/expressive boundary even more clearly in that they can offend in virtue of the coined epithet whose internal composition is not irrelevant.

This takes us back to speakers' commitments. There are commitments to the content (at-issue content) and commitments to the appropriateness of the way the speech act is formulated. Commitment to content appeared in our discussion of lying and misleading, while commitment to the 'way of putting it' permeates virtually all aspects of communication, but it is the study of politeness and offence where it is homed in on. Here, for example, Hess distinguishes *commitments at-issue*, which are assertoric commitments, from *commitments de lingua* – commitments to the appropriateness of expressions. He uses this distinction to explain how commitments can differ in properties. While assertoric commitment can easily be attributed to a third party, as in the case of reported speech in (8.76), linguistic commitment is entrenched. It 'sticks' to the speaker and is more difficult to shift, as B's reaction demonstrates.

(8.76)  A: I just talked to John this morning. He said that *that bastard Kaplan got promoted.* If it's true, then I can't believe that Regent's foolishness.

B: Oh, come on, what do you have against Kaplan?
(from Hess 2018: 29, variation on Kaplan's example)

All in all, to represent the meaning of 'bad language' in action is a challenge. Pejoratives are improper or offensive by default but (at least some of them) are not always so. By default, they are conventional, but there are also novel ways of slurring, or being offensive in general. Next, they may play a more, or less, central role in the information structure – with expressivism focusing on the 'less' or 'none' and descriptivism on the 'more'. They can convey many things, some of them easy to represent, others more elusive or more remote from what we want to call the meaning of a linguistic expression. Moreover, offence can be caused by expressions that are not offensive by default. How do such expressions fit in? There is no doubt that one size doesn't fit all – even within one category such as expletives or slurs. We could continue ad infinitum: the topic is an amalgam of lexical-semantic, syntactic, pragmatic, social, ethical, legal, and other interconnected issues. It is a journey in its own right, especially since 'bad language use' comprises more than just 'bad words'. What about, for example, expressions such as *female philosopher* or *male nurse*, or quoting male authors by surname but female ones by both first name and surname – a practice that

---

[124] For arguments against expressive/descriptive distinction see e.g. Geurts 2007 and Camp 2018.

used to be common even in academic papers? Such qualifications demonstrate that the speaker implicitly adheres to certain norms by which *philosopher* suggests a male, *nurse* a female and therefore accepts such senses as ordinary, unmarked.[125] But norms change, and they can also be made to change – a topic for the conceptual engineering briefly discussed in Stages 1 and 2, another cool area of philosophy of language that is on the rise.

**Suggested Further Reading**

*Metaphor*
Solving the 'meaning and metaphor' question requires browsing through approaches that focus on the use of metaphorical expressions, on the question of how they fit in the analysis of language as a system, as well as, as has become dominant, on the role of metaphor in cognition. It is best to start with a medley of texts that offer those diversified perspectives. As usual, references are given in footnotes but here is a (subjective!) starter selection: Cohen's 1993 [1979] 'The semantics of metaphor'; Searle's (1993 [1979]) 'Metaphor'; Davidson's (1984b [1978]) 'What metaphors mean'. For CMT see Lakoff and Johnson's (1980) *Metaphors We Live By*, or (1999) *Philosophy in the Flesh*, or Lakoff's (1993 [1979]) 'The contemporary theory of metaphor', and then Kövecses' (2020) *Extended Conceptual Metaphor Theory*. For an analysis of arguments against CMT, see Gibbs' (2017) *Metaphor Wars*. Good examples of truth-conditional semantic approaches are Leezenberg's (2001) *Contexts of Metaphor* and Stern's (2000) *Metaphor in Context*. Then, have a look at Carston's (2012b) 'Metaphor and the literal/non-literal distinction'. Comprehensive, textbook-style introductions include Kövecses' (2010 [2002]) *Metaphor: A Practical Introduction*; Ritchie's (2013) *Metaphor*; and contributions to Gibbs' (2008) *The Cambridge Handbook of Metaphor and Thought*.

*Speech Acts*
Start with the classics: Austin's (1975 [1962]) *How to Do Things with Words* and (1979 [1961]) 'Performative utterances'; Searle's (1996a [1965]) 'What is a speech act?'; (1996b [1975]) 'Indirect speech acts'; (1994 [1989]) 'How performatives work'; and/or (1969) *Speech Acts*. For a comprehensive introduction, see Sadock 2004. Then, Kissine 2012 for an introduction to illocutionary force assignment to utterances and Ruytenbeek 2021 for an introduction to indirect speech acts. For more recent work on speech acts, continue with essays of your choice in the anthology by Tsohatzidis (1994) (Dascal 1994 there is commendable on SAT and Gricean pragmatics); Vanderveken and Kubo 2001; and Fogal et al. 2018, remembering (i) the different uses that the concept of the speech act has been put to and (ii) the general disillusionment with the original preoccupation of speech-act theorists with (ii.a) the typology of the speech act and with (ii.b) the mapping from sentence form to illocutionary force (on which

---

[125] For a thought-provoking account of how such an implicit 'ordinary/special' 'normal, unmarked/marked' distinction operates and its social repercussions, see Zerubavel 2018.

detailed references were suggested as we moved along). On speech acts and intentionality, try Searle 1983 and Harnish 1990. On Austinian vis-à-vis Gricean approaches to meaning, see Witek 2022. Other core topics include the attempted formalization of speech acts and the history of speech acts, as well as their application in cross-cultural pragmatics – again, see footnotes.

*Commitment and Accountability*
Here the literature comes from very different disciplines, from ethics and philosophy of law on one end to linguistic pragmatics on the other. For pragmatic accounts of co-construction of meaning and joint accountability, start with Arundale 1999, 2010 and Elder and Haugh 2018.

For properties of assertoric speech see Goldberg's (2015) *Assertion*, then move to contributions of your choice to Brown and Cappelen (2011) and Moran (2018).

*Lying and Misleading*
Start with Stokke's (2018) excellent, comprehensive *Lying and Insincerity*. For some 'first-hand' experience continue with Saul's (2012) *Lying, Misleading, and What Is Said*, and for a very different view, Meibauer's (2014) *Lying at the Semantics–Pragmatics Interface*. Heffer's (2020) *All Bullshit and Lies?* offers a model of linguistic insincerity. Carson's (2010) *Lying and Deception* focuses on ethical values in relation to insincerity, including withholding information, in private and public settings. For a super-brief overview of the topic, go to Chapters 3–4 of Cappelen and Dever 2019.

*Politeness*
Start with the introductory Kádár and Haugh 2013; Terkourafi 2012; contributions to the *Palgrave Handbook of Linguistic (Im)politeness* (Culpeper, Haugh, and Kádár 2017), followed by some first-hand experience of seminal approaches: Brown and Levinson's (1987) *Politeness: Some Universals in Language Usage*; Fraser's (1990b) 'Perspectives on politeness'; Watts' (2003) *Politeness*; or Culpeper's (2011) *Impoliteness: Using Language to Cause Offence*. For a cross-section of the field, browse through articles in the *Journal of Politeness Research*.

*'Bad Language'*
Cappelen and Dever's (2019) *Bad Language* is a very brief and introductory but broad-in-scope introduction to various forms of misusing language. The brevity impacts somewhat on the clarity of the description of the views in Chapter 6, so follow up with first-hand accounts of your choice referenced as we moved along. Then, try Hom's (2010) 'Pejoratives' and the classification there. While reading, think how the proposals intertwine and how the enormous variability of the devices and strategies needs to be taken into consideration. For an in-depth linguistic, including historical, account of taboo and censored language, see Allan and Burridge's (2006). Follow by selected contributions to Allan's (2019) *Oxford Handbook of Taboo Words and Language*. For examples of first-hand views on slurs, see Chapter 1 of Richard's (2008) *When Truth*

## 8.4 At a Crossroads with Ethical and Social Debates

*Gives Out*; Anderson and Lepore's (2013) 'Slurring words'; Schlenker's (2007) 'Expressive presuppositions'; and Hom and May's (2013) 'Moral and semantic innocence'. Then, contributions to Sosa (2018) and to the symposium on slurs in *Analytic Philosophy* 54.4 (2013). For expressivism, start with Potts' (2007) 'The expressive dimension' and peer commentaries there. Remember that the field spans many areas of research, including lexical semantics, pragmatics, sociolinguistics, philosophy of language, ethics (and within it different sub-areas of ethics), so different sources may have very different objectives and use very different concepts.

Then, as usual, follow references to more detailed and/or advanced sources in the footnotes.

# Stage 9   Conclusion: The Future of Meaning?

We can get a grasp on what meaning is and how it works in discourse when we (i) approach it as the outcome of various modalities (channels, sources) through which it is conveyed in discourse; (ii) allow for its dynamic characteristics and joint construction by the participants; and (this is important) (iii) adopt stringent procedures to make sure that *talking and thinking about meaning* are not as fuzzy as the terminological disputes over 'meaning' suggest. Hence the starting point of this journey was the assumption that we have to combine the insights of linguistic semantics, pragmatics, and philosophy, and within them ideas about words and concepts, sentence structures, conceptual structures, intentions and conventions in communication, as well as psychological, social, and ethical considerations, to name the main contributors. These, of course, come with their own methods, so I have given here an example of how one might try to calibrate them in order to proceed in this 'positively eclectic' way. Arguably, such positive eclecticism is the only way to get as full a picture as possible out of the myriad ground-breaking ideas that semantics, pragmatics, and philosophy are rife with.

We have travelled through many seminal, often ground-breaking, approaches to various aspects of meaning and have done so in an organized way. We travelled through them with the idea in mind that the reader may want to use them in their own journey through meaning – either close to or very different from mine. So, the tools were assumed, and partly demonstrated, to be malleable. The history of semantics has proved that truth conditions are immensely flexible and we can use them not only in the way that early twentieth-century logicians and subsequently natural-language semanticists used them, but also apply them to thoughts and contextualist propositions, including the proposition that captures the main communicated meaning that we called a functional proposition. In this way, the discussions of ideas about meaning included here could play a dual role: as introductions to them, but also as steps on a journey with a clear aim in sight.

Asking about the philosophical foundations of meaning was crucial in this journey from the start. Foundational questions have to be asked first, even by beginners in the field: What is the nature of meaning in language? How are linguistic structures related to conceptual structures? How are they related to the physical world? Metasemantics, or the metaphysics of meaning, or what Stalnaker popularized as 'foundational semantics'[1] is therefore where beginners should start in order to understand meaning for themselves; it is certainly not just a sophisticated higher-level perspective for

---

[1] See Stalnaker 1997.

advanced, ageing scholars, as it is often taken to be. Put simply, since a linguistic expression has meaning, there has to be something somewhere that acts as a foundation, a basis for this meaning, or as its *grounding* – be it the human mind, the external world with its objects and situations, social reality, or a mixture of these. The theories of meaning that we have travelled with differ in such foundations, and it is important to remember that, as a result, the meanings they attach to technical terms such as 'reference', 'content', 'proposition', 'convention', or 'intention' may differ too. That is why the metatheory of meaning (metasemantics and metapragmatics) is normally so strictly separated from the theory of meaning (semantics and pragmatics). (NB: 'metapragmatics' is still an ambiguous term: here it *doesn't* stand for speakers' metadiscursive, reflexive awareness, as it sometimes does.[2]) An advantage of a journey through different theories that in addition has a clear goal is that we can see the differences in such foundations and do something about it. For instance, if truth-conditional semantics provides fantastic opportunities for formalization but does not apply to cognitive representations, we can make it do so by taking the tools (truth conditions) and reapplying them to such representations – a move begun by Gricean intention-based pragmatics and also in a very different way by Montagovian intensional semantics. Problems encountered on the way are then solved by some other revised concepts, such as that of the compositionality of such conceptual representations (rather than, traditionally, sentences).

In this way, we can avoid the common traps found in introductions: fragmentation into semantics, pragmatics, and philosophy of language that are often offered in separate introductions, but also, within each, introducing a bundle of different, disconnected views, all of them with something that seems right, but without fitting into a story with a path through that jungle. This can be an infuriating experience, spoiling all the fun. The only way to study meaning is *always to have a view* – open to revisions of course, but always a view to which one is temporarily committed – from the beginning of one's own journey, when the brain is free from indoctrinations, superstitions, and other shackles. So, the aim of this journey was not only to introduce seminal views and ideas but also to put them into some coherent unfolding picture, where at every turn one can learn and tick off what one finds justified to adopt and wants to further develop, but learn and put aside, or treat with scepticism, all the rest. The more questioning the better for the journey: there is nothing more uninspiring than ready answers.

What is the future of meaning? That depends on answers to some big questions. Yuval Noah Harari, in his international bestseller *Homo Deus: A Brief History of Tomorrow*, paints a picture of a possible future of humanity in which it is assumed as an incontrovertible dogma that living organisms, and therefore also humans, are algorithms.[3] Likewise, any forms of organized activity are also algorithmic. Somewhat unexpectedly, the question 'Are organisms algorithms?' appears to be an important question to debate at the end of this journey because it will allow us to delimit meaning and its provenance: is it just human meaning we are talking about, and if so, will it be replaced by something else when the assumed scientific paradigms change? Harari points out that people used

---

[2] For an introduction to metasemantics and metapragmatics, see Jaszczolt 2022.    [3] See Harari 2017.

to invest knowledge, meaning, and power with deities and scriptures – or, at least, used to search for them outside in the cosmos, like the ancient Babylonians who scrutinized the starry skies to foretell the future. With the rise of humanism in the eighteenth century, humans started to search for wisdom within themselves. But now, he surmises, we may be on the brink of relinquishing humanism and searching for wisdom in algorithms. If humans produce algorithms that can function better than them, that are better than 'the biological algorithms', and that can function independently of humans as regards decision-making, then consciousness, and the *concepts* that humans invented to systematize and understand the information available to them (such as those used in this journey through meaning), will only be of interest as a subjective net that humans throw on the world. They will have the status of a merely human-specific way, one of many, of getting a grasp on reality. This human-specific conceptual net is not a novel idea in the history of philosophy, but what is important here is that *such concepts may disappear with humans* – unless, of course, the non-biological life we invent 'evolves' to share our thoughts, with feelings and emotions and the ways they are structured and grounded. That is, unless these appear as emergent characteristics, by-products of their data processing. That is often a tacit hope. For example, the robot in Ian McEwan's novel *Machines Like Me and People Like You*[4] develops compassion and a sense of social justice as a result of processing large amounts of information (while humans happily sleep at night).

So, how is all this (only partly informed) speculation important for meaning? For Plato, thoughts were abstract objects, external to humans, existing in a 'third realm', separate from the external world of our sensations as well as from the internal world of our consciousness. For contemporary psychology, thoughts are processes internal to the mind, or ideas produced by such mental processes. Meaning is the material that the human mind (or brain, depending on the kind of discourse) uses in thinking and in 'giving orders' to the relevant body parts to communicate these thoughts. Even if our journey through meaning remains ambivalent on the question as to whether meaning is in the mind or in the world, it would have to be *in the human take on the world*: it is the way in which we organize information.

Harari (2017: 76) adds a disclaimer that his speculation is only 'the future of the past', based on limited facts – on what has occurred so far. But the degree of probability of the vision is not what interests us here. What interests us is how to place human meaning in the context of what is 'other than human': the world of current micro-level physics, or the world of progressing deep learning in AI. Harari ends his 'history of tomorrow' with the following three questions:

1. Are organisms really just algorithms, and is life really just data processing?
2. What's more valuable – intelligence or consciousness?
3. What will happen to society, politics and daily life when non-conscious but highly intelligent algorithms know us better than we know ourselves?

(Harari 2017: 462)

---

[4] See McEwan 2019.

We don't know, but throughout this journey through meaning we have been consistently moving away from meaning as an abstract concept, and from semantic representation of natural-language sentences as abstract objects, to representations as conceptual structures, meaning that is 'thought' and then 'conveyed'. Repeatedly, this appeared to be the best available option not only when formal tools from artificial languages of logic did not quite fit, but also when sentence meaning itself did not fit what the uttering of this sentence conveyed in discourse. And then, of course, we have to consider larger chunks than uttered sentences and sentence fragments.

The answer to Question 1 is difficult because we have a human, 'insider's' perspective on organisms and as such we treat their emergent properties as real – and among them consciousness, thought, and meaning. Questions 2 and 3 did not concern us directly but they flag an important point, namely that intelligence may be dissociable from the human idea of meaning that linguistics and philosophy so ardently pursue. Even if, in the future, non-biological organisms operate on the principle that meaning is best arrived at through systematization of language use derived from big data (those organisms' big data), there is nothing to suggest that those organisms won't at the same time operate on principles that are *analogous* to these encountered in this journey through human meaning. That is, *their* meaning may be very much like *our* meaning – meaning that we, humans, impose on the world through our mental architecture, mental operations, and as such also through the choices we make that can have social, political, and various other consequences. In order to survive and be successful, every kind of organism has to be savvy about what we broadly call rationality. And it is precisely rationality that permeates the composition of the real, dynamic, situated, discourse meaning that the journey was about.

# References

Abbott, Barbara. 2010. *Reference*. Oxford: Oxford University Press.
Aikhenvald, Alexandra Y. 2004. *Evidentiality*. Oxford: Oxford University Press.
Aitchison, Jean. 1989. *The Articulate Mammal: An Introduction to Psycholinguistics*. London: Routledge. Third edition.
Alexander, Larry and Michael Moore. 2020. 'Deontological ethics'. In Edward Zalta (ed.), *Stanford Encyclopedia of Philosophy* (online). plato.stanford.edu/entries/ethics-deontological/ [accessed 5 August 2021].
Allan, Keith. 1971. 'A note on the source of *there* in existential sentences'. *Foundations of Language* 7: 1–18.
Allan, Keith. 1980. 'Nouns and countability'. *Language* 56. 541–567.
Allan, Keith. 2000. 'Quantity implicatures and the lexicon'. In Bert Peeters (ed.), *The Lexicon–Encyclopedia Interface*. Oxford: Elsevier Science, pp. 169–217.
Allan, Keith. 2001. *Natural Language Semantics*. Oxford: Blackwell.
Allan, Keith. 2015. 'The reporting of slurs'. In Alessandro Capone, Ferenc Kiefer, and Franco Lo Piparo (eds.), *Indirect Reports and Pragmatics: Interdisciplinary Studies*. Cham: Springer, pp. 211–232.
Allan, Keith (ed.). 2019. *The Oxford Handbook of Taboo Words and Language*. Oxford: Oxford University Press.
Allan, Keith and Kate Burridge. 2006. *Forbidden Words: Taboo and the Censoring of Language*. Cambridge: Cambridge University Press.
Almog, Joseph and Paolo Leonardi (eds.). 2009. *The Philosophy of David Kaplan*. Oxford: Oxford University Press.
Altshuler, Daniel, Terence Parsons, and Roger Schwarzschild. 2019. *A Course in Semantics*. Cambridge, MA: MIT Press.
Ameka, Felix K. and Marina Terkourafi. 2019. 'What if . . .? Imagining non-Western perspectives on pragmatic theory and practice'. *Journal of Pragmatics* 145: 72–82.
Anderson, Luvell and Ernie Lepore. 2013. 'Slurring words'. *Noûs* 47: 25–48.
Ariel, Mira. 1990. *Accessing Noun-Phrase Antecedents*. London: Routledge.
Ariel, Mira. 2002a. 'Privileged interactional interpretations'. *Journal of Pragmatics* 34: 1003–1044.
Ariel, Mira. 2002b. 'The demise of a unique concept of literal meaning'. *Journal of Pragmatics* 34: 361–402.
Ariel, Mira. 2004. 'Most'. *Language* 80: 658–706.
Ariel, Mira. 2010. *Defining Pragmatics*. Cambridge: Cambridge University Press.
Ariel, Mira. 2016. 'Revisiting the typology of pragmatic interpretations'. *Intercultural Pragmatics* 13: 1–35.

Ariel, Mira. 2019. 'Different prominences for different inferences'. *Journal of Pragmatics* 154: 103–116.

Ariel, Mira and Caterina Mauri. 2019. 'An "alternative" core for *or* '. *Journal of Pragmatics* 149: 40–59.

Arundale, Robert B. 1999. 'An alternative model and ideology of communication for an alternative to politeness theory'. *Pragmatics* 9: 119–153.

Arundale, Robert B. 2010. 'Constituting face in conversation: Face, facework, and interactional achievement'. *Journal of Pragmatics* 42: 2078–2105.

Arundale, Robert B. 2013. 'Conceptualizing "interaction" in interpersonal pragmatics: Implications for understanding and research'. *Journal of Pragmatics* 58: 12–26.

Arundale, Robert B. 2020. *Communicating and Relating: Constituting Face in Everyday Interacting*. Oxford: Oxford University Press.

Asher, Nicholas. 2011. *Lexical Meaning in Context: A Web of Words*. Cambridge: Cambridge University Press.

Asher, Nicholas. 2016. 'Discourse semantics'. In Maria Aloni and Paul Dekker (eds.), *The Cambridge Handbook of Formal Semantics*. Cambridge: Cambridge University Press, pp. 106–129.

Asher, Nicholas and Alex Lascarides. 1998. 'The semantics and pragmatics of presupposition'. *Journal of Semantics* 15: 239–300.

Asher, Nicholas and Alex Lascarides. 2003. *Logics of Conversation*. Cambridge: Cambridge University Press.

Asher, Nicholas and Alex Lascarides. 2013. 'Strategic conversation'. *Semantics & Pragmatics* 6: 1–62.

Atlas, Jay D. 1977. 'Negation, ambiguity, and presupposition'. *Linguistics and Philosophy* 1: 321–336.

Atlas, Jay D. 1979. 'How linguistics matters to philosophy: Presupposition, truth, and meaning'. In Choon-Kyu Oh and David A. Dinneen (eds.), *Syntax and Semantics,* Vol. 11: Presupposition. New York: Academic Press, pp. 265–281.

Atlas, Jay D. 1989. *Philosophy Without Ambiguity: A Logico-Linguistic Essay.* Oxford: Clarendon Press.

Atlas, Jay D. 2005. *Logic, Meaning, and Conversation: Semantical Underdeterminacy, Implicature, and Their Interface*. Oxford: Oxford University Press.

Atlas, Jay D. 2006. 'A personal history of linguistic pragmatics 1969–2000'. Paper presented at the *Jay Atlas – Distinguished Scholar Workshop*, University of Cambridge.

Atlas, Jay D. 2012. 'Negation'. In Keith Allan and Kasia M. Jaszczolt (eds.), *The Cambridge Handbook of Pragmatics*. Cambridge: Cambridge University Press, pp. 351–376.

Attardo, Salvatore. 2020. *The Linguistics of Humor: An Introduction*. Oxford: Oxford University Press.

Austin, J. L. 1975. *How to Do Things with Words*. Oxford: Oxford University Press. Second edition. First published in 1962.

Austin, John L. 1979. 'Performative utterances'. In John L. Austin, *Philosophical Papers*. Oxford: Clarendon Press, pp. 233–252. Third edition. First published in 1961.

van der Auwera, Johan. 1997a. 'Conditional perfection'. In Angeliki Athanasiadou and René Dirven (eds.), *On Conditionals Again*. Amsterdam: John Benjamins, pp. 169–190.

van der Auwera, Johan. 1997b. 'Pragmatics in the last quarter century: The case of conditional perfection'. *Journal of Pragmatics* 27: 261–274.

van der Auwera, Johan and Vladimir A. Plungian. 1998. 'Modality's semantic map'. *Linguistic Typology* 2: 79–124.

# References

Bach, Emmon. 1981. 'On time, tense, and aspect: An essay in English metaphysics'. In Peter Cole (ed.), *Radical Pragmatics*. New York: Academic Press, pp. 63–81.
Bach, Kent. 1987. *Thought and Reference*. Oxford: Clarendon Press.
Bach, Kent. 1992. 'Intentions and demonstrations'. *Analysis* 52: 140–146.
Bach, Kent. 1994a. 'Semantic slack: What is said and more'. In Savas L. Tsohatzidis (ed.), *Foundations of Speech Act Theory: Philosophical and Linguistic Perspectives*. London: Routledge, pp. 267–291.
Bach, Kent. 1994b. 'Conversational impliciture'. *Mind and Language* 9: 124–162.
Bach, Kent. 1995. 'Remark and reply. Standardization vs. conventionalization'. *Linguistics and Philosophy* 18: 677–686.
Bach, Kent. 2000. 'Quantification, qualification and context: A reply to Stanley and Szabó'. *Mind and Language* 15: 262–283.
Bach, Kent. 2001. 'You don't say?' *Synthese* 128: 15–44.
Bach, Kent. 2006. 'The excluded middle: Semantic minimalism without minimal propositions'. *Philosophy and Phenomenological Research* 73: 435–442.
Bach, Kent and Robert M. Harnish. 1979. *Linguistic Communication and Speech Acts*. Cambridge, MA: MIT Press.
Bar-Lev, Zev and Arthur Palacas. 1980. 'Semantic command over pragmatic priority'. *Lingua* 51: 137–146.
Barker, Chris and Pauline Jacobson (eds.). 2007. *Direct Compositionality*. Oxford: Oxford University Press.
Barwise, Jon and Robin Cooper. 1981. 'Generalized quantifiers in natural language'. *Linguistics and Philosophy* 4: 159–219.
Beaver, David I. 1997. 'Presupposition'. In Johan van Benthem and Alice ter Meulen (eds.), *Handbook of Logic and Language*. Oxford: Elsevier Science, pp. 939–1008.
Beaver, David I. 2001. *Presupposition and Assertion in Dynamic Semantics*. Stanford, CA: CSLI Publications.
van Benthem, Johan and Alice ter Meulen (eds.). 1985. *Generalized Quantifiers in Natural Language*. Dordrecht: Foris.
Berlin, Brent and Paul Kay. 1969. *Basic Color Terms: Their Universality and Evolution*. Berkeley, CA: University of California Press.
Bertolet, Rod. 1994. 'Are there indirect speech acts?'. In Savas L. Tsohatzidis, (ed.), *Foundations of Speech Act Theory: Philosophical and Linguistic Perspectives*. London: Routledge, pp. 335–349.
Birner, Betty J. 2018. *Language and Meaning*. London: Routledge.
Black, Max. 1962. 'Metaphor'. In *Models and Metaphors: Studies in Language and Philosophy*. Ithaca, NY: Cornell University Press, pp. 25–47.
Black, Max. 1993. 'More about metaphor'. In Andrew Ortony (ed.), *Metaphor and Thought*. Cambridge: Cambridge University Press, pp. 19–41. Second edition. First published in 1977 in *Dialectica* 31.
Blakemore, Diane. 2002. *Relevance and Linguistic Meaning: The Semantics and Pragmatics of Discourse Markers*. Cambridge: Cambridge University Press.
Blok, Peter I. and Kurt Eberle. 1999. 'What is the alternative? The computation of focus alternatives from lexical and sortal information'. In Peter Bosch and Rob van der Sandt (eds.), *Focus: Linguistic, Cognitive, and Computational Perspectives*. Cambridge: Cambridge University Press, pp. 105–120.

Blome-Tillmann, Michael. 2008. 'Conversational implicature and the cancellability test'. *Analysis* 68: 156–160.

Blum-Kulka, Shoshana. 1987. 'Indirectness and politeness in requests: Same or different?'. *Journal of Pragmatics* 11: 131–146.

Blutner, Reinhard. 1998. 'Lexical pragmatics'. *Journal of Semantics* 15: 115–162.

Blutner, Reinhard and Henk Zeevat (eds.). 2004. *Optimality Theory and Pragmatics*. Basingstoke: Palgrave Macmillan.

Boër, Steven I. and William G. Lycan. 1976. The myth of semantic presupposition'. Bloomington, IN: Indiana University Linguistics Club.

Borg, Emma. 2004. *Minimal Semantics*. Oxford: Clarendon Press.

Borg, Emma. 2012. *Pursuing Meaning*. Oxford: Oxford University Press.

Borg, Emma. 2019. 'Explanatory roles for minimal content'. *Noûs* 53: 513–539.

Borg, Emma and P. J. Connolly. 2022. 'Exploring linguistic liability'. In Ernie Lepore and David Sosa (eds.), *Oxford Studies in Philosophy of Language*, Vol. 2. Oxford: Oxford University Press, pp. 1–26.

Bosch, Peter and Rob van der Sandt (eds.). 1999. *Focus: Linguistic, Cognitive, and Computational Perspectives*. Cambridge: Cambridge University Press.

Brandom, Robert. 1994. *Making It Explicit*. Cambridge, MA: Harvard University Press.

Braun, David. 2015. 'Indexicals'. In Edward Zalta (ed.), *Stanford Encyclopedia of Philosophy* (online). plato.stanford.edu/entries/indexicals/ [accessed 17 March 2021].

Brentano, Franz. 1973. *Psychology from an Empirical Standpoint*. Transl. by A.C. Rancurello, D.B. Terrell, and L.L. McAlister. London: Routledge & Kegan Paul. First published in 1874 as *Psychologie vom empirishen Standpunkt*. Leipzig: Duncker and Humblot. Second edition in 1924. Leipzig: Felix Meiner.

Brown, Gillian and George Yule. 1983. *Discourse Analysis*. Cambridge: Cambridge University Press.

Brown, Jessica and Herman Cappelen (eds.). 2011. *Assertion: New Philosophical Essays*. Oxford: Oxford University Press.

Brown, Penelope and Stephen C. Levinson. 1987. *Politeness: Some Universals in Language Usage*. Cambridge: Cambridge University Press.

Buckner, Cameron and James Garson. 2019. 'Connectionism'. In Edward Zalta (ed.), *Stanford Encyclopedia of Philosophy* (online). plato.stanford.edu/search/searcher.py?query=connectionism [accessed 7 May 2021].

Bultinck, Bert. 2005. *Numerous Meanings: The Meaning of English Cardinals and the Legacy of Paul Grice*. Oxford: Elsevier.

Bunt, Harry. 2006. 'Mass expressions'. In Keith Brown (ed.), *Elsevier Encyclopedia of Language and Linguistics*. Oxford: Elsevier, pp. 530–534. Second edition.

Büring, Daniel. 1999. 'Topic'. In Peter Bosch and Rob van der Sandt (eds.), *Focus: Linguistic, Cognitive, and Computational Perspectives*. Cambridge: Cambridge University Press, pp. 142–165.

Büring, Daniel. 2016. *Intonation and Meaning*. Oxford: Oxford University Press.

Bybee, Joan, Revere Perkins, and William Pagliuca. 1994. *The Evolution of Grammar: Tense, Aspect, and Modality in the Languages of the World*. Chicago, IL: University of Chicago Press.

Callender, Craig (ed). 2011. *The Oxford Handbook of Philosophy of Time*. Oxford: Oxford University Press.

Camp, Elisabeth. 2006. 'Metaphor and what is said'. *Mind and Language* 21: 280–309.

# References

Camp, Elisabeth. 2018. 'A dual act analysis of slurs'. In David Sosa (ed.), *Bad Words: Philosophical Perspectives on Slurs*. Oxford: Oxford University Press, pp. 29–58.

Cann, Ronnie. 1993. *Formal Semantics: An Introduction*. Cambridge: Cambridge University Press.

Cann, Ronnie, Ruth Kempson, and Eleni Gregoromichelaki. 2009. *Semantics: An Introduction to Meaning in Language*. Cambridge: Cambridge University Press.

Capone, Alessandro. 2006. 'On Grice's circle (a theory-internal problem in linguistic theories of the Gricean type)'. *Journal of Pragmatics* 38: 645–669.

Capone, Alessandro. 2009. 'Are explicatures cancellable? Towards a theory of the speaker's Intentionality'. *Journal of Intercultural Pragmatics* 6: 55–84.

Caponetto, Laura. 2020. 'Undoing things with words'. *Synthese* 197: 2399–2414.

Cappelen, Herman. 2018. *Fixing Language: An Essay on Conceptual Engineering*. Oxford: Oxford University Press.

Cappelen, Herman and Josh Dever. 2018. *Puzzles of Reference*. Oxford: Oxford University Press.

Cappelen, Herman and Josh Dever. 2019. *Bad Language*. Oxford: Oxford University Press.

Cappelen, Herman and John Hawthorne. 2009. *Relativism and Monadic Truth*. Oxford: Oxford University Press.

Cappelen, Herman and Ernie Lepore. 2005. *Insensitive Semantics: A Defense of Semantic Minimalism and Speech Act Pluralism*. Oxford: Blackwell.

Carlson, Gregory. 2011. 'Genericity'. In Claudia Maienborn, Klaus von Heusinger, and Paul Portner (eds.), *Semantics: An International Handbook of Natural Language Meaning*, Vol. 2. Berlin: De Gruyter Mouton, pp. 1153–1185.

Carnap, Rudolf. 1956. *Meaning and Necessity: A Study in Semantics and Modal Logic*. Chicago, IL: University of Chicago Press. Second edition. First published in 1947.

Carruthers, Peter. 1996. *Language, Thought and Consciousness: An Essay in Philosophical Psychology*. Cambridge: Cambridge University Press.

Carson, Thomas. 2010. *Lying and Deception: Theory and Practice*. Oxford: Oxford University Press.

Carston, Robyn. 1988. 'Implicature, explicature, and truth-theoretic semantics'. In Ruth M. Kempson (ed.), *Mental Representations: The Interface Between Language and Reality*. Cambridge: Cambridge University Press, pp. 155–181.

Carston, Robyn. 1993. 'Conjunction, explanation and relevance'. *Lingua* 90: 27–48.

Carston, Robyn. 1994. 'Conjunction and pragmatic effects'. In Ron E. Asher (ed.), *The Encyclopedia of Language and Linguistics*. Oxford: Pergamon Press, pp. 692–698.

Carston, Robyn. 1996. 'Metalinguistic negation and echoic use'. *Journal of Pragmatics* 25: 309–330.

Carston, Robyn. 1998a. 'Informativeness, relevance and scalar implicature'. In Robyn Carston and Seiji Uchida (eds.), *Relevance Theory: Applications and Implications*. Amsterdam: John Benjamins, pp. 179–236.

Carston, Robyn. 1998b. 'Negation, "presupposition" and the semantics/pragmatics distinction'. *Journal of Linguistics* 34: 309–350.

Carston, Robyn. 1998c. 'Postscript (1995) to Carston 1988'. In Asa Kasher (ed.), *Pragmatics: Critical Concepts*, Vol. 4. London: Routledge, pp. 464–479.

Carston, Robyn. 2001. 'Relevance theory and the saying/implicating distinction'. *UCL Working Papers in Linguistics* 13: 1–34.

Carston, Robyn. 2002. *Thoughts and Utterances: The Pragmatics of Explicit Communication*. Oxford: Blackwell.

Carston, Robyn. 2007. 'How many pragmatic systems are there?'. In Maria J. Frápolli (ed.), *Saying, Meaning and Referring: Essays on François Recanati's Philosophy of Language*. Basingstoke: Palgrave Macmillan, pp. 18–48.

Carston, Robyn. 2012a. 'Word meaning and concept expressed'. *Linguistic Review* 29: 607–623.

Carston, Robyn. 2012b. 'Metaphor and the literal/non-literal distinction'. In Keith Allan and Kasia M. Jaszczolt (eds.), *The Cambridge Handbook of Pragmatics*. Cambridge: Cambridge University Press, pp. 469–492.

Casasanto, Daniel and Lera Boroditsky. 2008. 'Time in the mind: Using space to think about time'. *Cognition* 106: 579–593.

Cepollaro, Bianca and Tristan Thommen. 2019. 'What's wrong with truth-conditional accounts of slurs'. *Linguistics and Philosophy* 42: 333–347.

Chalmers, David J. 2006. 'The foundations of two-dimensional semantics'. In Manuel García-Carpintero and Josep Macià (eds.), *Two-Dimensional Semantics*. Oxford: Clarendon Press, pp. 55–140.

Chierchia, Gennaro. 2004. 'Scalar implicatures, polarity phenomena, and the syntax/pragmatics interface'. In Adriana Belletti (ed.), *Structures and Beyond: The Cartography of Syntactic Structures*, Vol. 3. Oxford: Oxford University Press, pp. 39–103.

Chierchia, Gennaro and Sally McConnell-Ginet. 2000. *Meaning and Grammar: An Introduction to Semantics*. Cambridge, MA: MIT Press. Second edition. First published in 1990.

Chomsky, Noam. 2003. 'Reply to Ludlow'. In Louise M. Anthony and Norbert Hornstein (eds.), *Chomsky and His Critics*. Oxford: Blackwell, pp. 287–295.

Church, Alonzo. 1940. 'A formulation of the simple theory of types'. *Journal of Symbolic Logic* 5: 56–68.

Ciardelli, Ivano, Jeroen Groenendijk, and Floris Roelofsen. 2019. *Inquisitive Semantics*. Oxford: Oxford University Press.

Clark, Billy. 2013. *Relevance Theory*. Cambridge: Cambridge University Press.

Clark, Herbert. 1996. *Using Language*. Cambridge: Cambridge University Press.

Coecke, Bob, Mehrnoosh Sadrzadeh, and Stephen Clarke. 2010. 'Mathematical foundations for a compositional distributional model of meaning'. *Linguistic Analysis* 36: 345–384.

Cohen, Ariel. 1999. 'How are alternatives computed?'. *Journal of Semantics* 16: 43–65.

Cohen, L. Jonathan. 1971. 'Some remarks on Grice's views about the logical particles of natural language'. In Yehoshua Bar-Hillel (ed.), *Pragmatics of Natural Languages*. Dordrecht: D. Reidel, pp. 50–68.

Cohen L. Jonathan. 1986. *The Dialogue of Reason: An Analysis of Analytical Philosophy*. Oxford: Clarendon Press.

Cohen, L. Jonathan. 1993. 'The semantics of metaphor'. In Andrew Ortony (ed.), *Metaphor and Thought*. Cambridge: Cambridge University Press, pp. 58–70. Second edition. First published in 1979.

Cohen, L. Jonathan. 1999. 'Holism: Some reasons for buyer's remorse'. *Analysis* 59: 63–71.

Cole, Peter (ed.). 1981. *Radical Pragmatics*. New York: Academic Press.

Comrie, Bernard. 1976. *Aspect*. Cambridge: Cambridge University Press.

Comrie, Bernard. 1985. *Tense*. Cambridge: Cambridge University Press.

Connolly, Andrew C., Jerry A. Fodor, Lila R. Gleitman, and Henry Gleitman. 2007. 'Why stereotypes don't even make good defaults'. *Cognition* 103: 1–22.

Corazza, Eros. 2004. *Reflecting the Mind: Indexicality and Quasi-Indexicality*. Oxford: Clarendon Press.
Cremers, Alexandre and Emmanuel Chemla. 2016. 'A psycholinguistic study of the exhaustive readings of embedded questions'. *Journal of Semantics* 33: 49–85.
Crimmins, Mark. 1992. *Talk about Beliefs*. Cambridge, MA: MIT Press.
Crimmins, Mark and John Perry. 1989. 'The prince and the phone booth: Reporting puzzling beliefs'. *Journal of Philosophy* 86: 685–711.
Culicover, Peter W. and Ray Jackendoff. 2005. *Simpler Syntax*. Oxford: Oxford University Press.
Culpeper, Jonathan. 2011. *Impoliteness: Using Language to Cause Offence*. Cambridge: Cambridge University Press.
Culpeper, Jonathan, Michael Haugh, and Dániel Z. Kádár (eds.). 2017. *The Palgrave Handbook of Linguistic (Im)politeness*. London: Palgrave Macmillan.
Cumming, Sam. 2019. 'Names'. In Edward Zalta (ed.), *Stanford Encyclopedia of Philosophy* (online). plato.stanford.edu/entries/names/ [accessed 17 March 2021].
Cummins, Chris. 2015. *Constraints on Numerical Expressions*. Oxford: Oxford University Press.
Cummins, Chris and Napoleon Katsos (eds.). 2019. *The Oxford Handbook of Experimental Semantics and Pragmatics*. Oxford: Oxford University Press.
Curtiss, Susan. 1977. *Genie: A Psycholinguistic Study of a Modern-Day 'Wild Child'*. New York: Academic Press.
Dancygier, Barbara and Eve Sweetser. 1997. '*Then* in conditional constructions'. *Cognitive Linguistics* 8: 109–136.
Dascal, Marcelo. 1994. 'Speech act theory and Gricean pragmatics: Some differences of detail that make a difference'. In Savas L. Tsohatzidis (ed.), *Foundations of Speech Act Theory: Philosophical and Linguistic Perspectives*. London: Routledge, pp. 323–334.
Davidson, Donald. 1980a. 'The logical form of action sentences'. In Donald Davidson, *Essays on Actions and Events*. Oxford: Clarendon Press, pp. 105–122. First published in 1967 in Nicholas Rescher (ed.), *The Logic of Decision and Action*. Pittsburgh: University of Pittsburgh Press.
Davidson, Donald. 1980b. 'The individuation of events'. In Donald Davidson, *Essays on Actions and Events*. Oxford: Clarendon Press, pp. 163–180. First published in 1969 in Nicholas Rescher (ed.), *Essays in Honor of Carl G. Hempel*. Dordrecht: D. Reidel.
Davidson, Donald. 1984a. *Inquiries into Truth and Interpretation*. Oxford: Clarendon Press.
Davidson, Donald. 1984b. 'What metaphors mean'. In *Inquiries into Truth and Interpretation*. Oxford: Clarendon Press, pp. 245–264. First published in 1978 in *Critical Inquiry* 5.
Davidson, Donald. 1997. 'On saying that'. In Peter Ludlow (ed.), *Readings in the Philosophy of Language*. Cambridge, MA: MIT Press, pp. 817–831. First published in 1968–69 in *Synthese* 19.
Davis, Wayne A. 1998. *Implicature: Intention, Convention, and Principle in the Failure of Gricean Theory*. Cambridge: Cambridge University Press.
Davis, Wayne A. 2007. 'How normative is implicature?' *Journal of Pragmatics* 39: 1655–1672.
Dayal, Vaneeta. 2016. *Questions*. Oxford: Oxford University Press.
Deemter, Kees van. 1998. 'Ambiguity and idiosyncratic interpretation'. *Journal of Semantics* 15: 5–36.
Dekker, Paul. 2012. *Dynamic Semantics*. Dordrecht: Springer.

Del Pinal, Giuillermo. 2016. 'Prototypes as compositional components of concepts'. *Synthese* 193: 2899–2927.
Del Pinal, Giuillermo. 2018. 'Meaning, modulation, and context: A multidimensional semantics for truth-conditional pragmatics'. *Linguistics and Philosophy* 41: 165–207.
Dennett, Daniel C. 1993. *Consciousness Explained*. London: Penguin Books. First published in 1991.
DeRose, Keith. 1992. 'Contextualism and knowledge attributions'. *Philosophy and Phenomenological Research* 52: 913–929.
DeRose, Keith. 2009. *The Case for Contextualism: Knowledge, Skepticism, and Context*, Vol. 1. Oxford: Clarendon Press.
Dever, Josh. 2013. 'The revenge of the semantics-pragmatics distinction'. *Philosophical Perspectives* 27: 104–144.
Diaz-Legaspe, Justina, Chang Liu, and Robert J. Stainton. 2020. 'Slurs and register: A case study in meaning'. *Mind and Language* 35: 156–182.
Diller, Anthony. 1996. 'Thai and Lao Writing'. In Peter T. Daniels and William Bright (eds.), *The World's Writing Systems*. New York: Oxford University Press, pp. 457–466.
Dinges, Alexander. 2018. Knowledge, intuition and implicature'. *Synthese* 195: 2821–2843.
Donnellan, Keith S. 1996. 'Reference and definite descriptions'. In Aloysius P. Martinich (ed.), *The Philosophy of Language*. Oxford: Oxford University Press, pp. 231–244. Third edition. First published in 1966 in *Philosophical Review* 75.
Dowty, David R. 1979. *Word Meaning and Montague Grammar: The Semantics of Verbs and Times in Generative Semantics and in Montague's PTQ*. Dordrecht: D. Reidel.
Dowty, David R. 1986. 'The effects of aspectual class on the temporal structure of discourse: Semantics or pragmatics?' *Linguistics and Philosophy* 9: 37–61.
Dowty, David R. 2007. 'Compositionality as an empirical problem'. In Chris Barker and Pauline Jacobson (eds.), *Direct Compositionality*. Oxford: Oxford University Press, pp. 23–101.
Dowty, David R., Robert E. Wall, and Stanley Peters. 1981. *Introduction to Montague Semantics*. Dordrecht: D. Reidel.
Ducrot, Oswald. 1972. *Dire et ne pas dire*. Paris: Hermann.
Dummett, Michael. 1991. 'The relative priority of thought and language'. In Michael Dummett, *Frege and Other Philosophers*. Oxford: Clarendon Press, pp. 315–324.
Dynel, Marta. 2015. 'Intention to deceive, bald-faced lies, and deceptive implicature: Insights into *Lying at the Semantics/Pragmatics Interface* '. *Intercultural Pragmatics* 12: 309–332.
Eckardt, Regine. 1999. 'Focus with nominal quantifiers'. In Peter Bosch and Rob van der Sandt (eds.), *Focus: Linguistic, Cognitive, and Computational Perspectives*. Cambridge: Cambridge University Press, pp. 166–186.
van Eijck, Jan. 2006. 'Discourse Representation Theory'. In Keith Brown (ed.), *Encyclopedia of Language and Linguistics*, Vol. 3. Oxford: Elsevier, pp. 660–668. Second edition.
van Eijck, Jan and Hans Kamp. 1997. 'Representing discourse in context'. In Johan van Benthem and Alice ter Meulen (eds.), *Handbook of Logic and Language*. Oxford: Elsevier Science, pp. 179–237.
Elbourne, Paul. 2005. *Situations and Individuals*. Cambridge, MA: MIT Press.
Elbourne, Paul. 2011. *Meaning: A Slim Guide to Semantics*. Oxford: Oxford University Press.
Elder, Chi-Hé. 2019. *Context, Cognition and Conditionals*. Basingstoke: Palgrave Macmillan.

Elder, Chi-Hé. 2021. 'Speaker meaning, commitment and accountability'. In Michael Haugh, Dániel Z. Kádár, and Marina Terkourafi (eds.), *The Cambridge Handbook of Sociopragmatics*. Cambridge: Cambridge University Press, pp. 48–68.

Elder, Chi-Hé and Michael Haugh. 2018. 'The interactional achievement of speaker meaning: Toward a formal account of conversational inference'. *Intercultural Pragmatics* 15: 593–625.

Elder, Chi-Hé and Kasia M. Jaszczolt. 2016. 'Towards a pragmatic category of conditionals'. *Journal of Pragmatics* 98: 36–53.

Elder, Chi-Hé and Eleni Savva. 2018. 'Incomplete conditionals and the syntax-pragmatics interface'. *Journal of Pragmatics* 138: 45–59.

Enç, Mürvet. 1996. 'Tense and modality'. In Shalom Lappin. (ed.), *The Handbook of Contemporary Semantic Theory*. Oxford: Blackwell, pp. 345–358.

Escandell-Vidal, Victoria. 1996. 'Towards a cognitive approach to politeness'. In Kasia M. Jaszczolt and Ken Turner (eds.), *Contrastive Semantics and Pragmatics*, Vol. 2: Discourse Strategies. Oxford: Elsevier Science, pp. 629–650.

Escandell-Vidal, Victoria. 1998. 'Politeness: A relevant issue for relevance theory'. *Revista Alicantina de Estudios Ingleses* 11: 45–57.

Evans, Gareth. 1985a. 'Pronouns, quantifiers, and relative clauses'. Parts 1 and 2. In Gareth Evans, *Collected Papers*. Oxford: Clarendon Press, pp. 76–175. First published in 1977 in *Canadian Journal of Philosophy* 7.

Evans, Gareth. 1985b. 'Pronouns'. In Gareth Evans, *Collected Papers*. Oxford: Clarendon Press, pp. 214–248. First published in 1980 in *Linguistic Inquiry* 11.

Evans, Gareth. 1985c. 'Understanding demonstratives'. In Gareth Evans, *Collected Papers*. Oxford: Clarendon Press, pp. 291–321. First published in Herman Parret and Jacques Bouveresse (eds.), *Meaning and Understanding*. Berlin: Walter de Gruyter.

Evans, Nicholas and Stephen C. Levinson. 2009. 'The myth of language universals: Language diversity and its importance for cognitive science'. *Behavioral and Brain Sciences* 32: 429–492.

Everett, Daniel. 2006. 'Don't count on it'. Interview with Daniel Everett. *Scientific American Mind*, October/November 2006.

Everett, Daniel. 2012. *Language: The Cultural Tool*. London: Profile Books.

Faller, Martina. 2019. 'The discourse commitments of illocutionary reportatives'. *Semantics and Pragmatics* 12: 1–46.

Fauconnier, Gilles. 1985. *Mental Spaces: Aspects of Meaning Construction in Natural Language*. Cambridge, MA: MIT Press.

Fauconnier, Gilles. 1997. *Mappings in Thought and Language*. Cambridge: Cambridge University Press.

Feldman, Jerome. 2010. 'Embodied language, best-fit analysis, and formal compositionality'. *Physics of Life Reviews* 7: 385–410.

Fillmore, Charles J. 1985. 'Frames and the semantics of understanding'. *Quaderni di Semantica* 6: 222–254.

Fine, Kit. 2020. *Vagueness: A Global Approach*. Oxford: Oxford University Press.

von Fintel, Kai and Lisa Matthewson. 2008. 'Universals in semantics'. *The Linguistic Review* 25: 139–201.

Firth, John R. 1957. *Papers in Linguistics 1934–53*. Oxford: Oxford University Press.

Fodor, Jerry A. 1975. *The Language of Thought*. New York: Thomas Y. Crowell.

Fodor, Jerry A. 1994. *The Elm and the Expert: Mentalese and Its Semantics*. Cambridge, MA: MIT Press.

Fodor, Jerry A. 1998. *Concepts: Where Cognitive Science Went Wrong*. Oxford: Clarendon Press.

Fodor, Jerry A. 2008. *LOT 2: The Language of Thought Revisited*. Oxford: Clarendon Press.

Fodor, Jerry A. and Ernest Lepore. 1992. *Holism: A Shopper's Guide*. Oxford: Blackwell.

Fogal, Daniel, Daniel W. Harris, and Matt Moss (eds.). 2018. *New Work on Speech Acts*. Oxford: Oxford University Press.

Forbes, Graeme. 1990. 'The indispensability of *Sinn*'. *Philosophical Review* 99: 535–563.

Forbes, Graeme. 1997. 'How much substitutivity?'. *Analysis* 57: 109–113.

Fox, Chris and Shalom Lappin. 2005. *Foundations of Intensional Semantics*. Oxford: Blackwell.

Fraser, Bruce. 1990a. 'An approach to discourse markers'. *Journal of Pragmatics* 14: 383–395.

Fraser, Bruce. 1990b. 'Perspectives on politeness'. *Journal of Pragmatics* 14: 219–236.

Fraser, Bruce. 1999. 'What are discourse markers?'. *Journal of Pragmatics* 31: 931–952.

Frege, Gottlob. 1956. 'The thought: A logical inquiry'. *Mind* 65: 289–311. Transl. by A. M. and Marcelle Quinton. First published in 1918–19 as 'Der Gedanke'.

Frege, Gottlob. 1997a. 'On sense and reference'. In Peter Ludlow (ed.), *Readings in the Philosophy of Language*. Cambridge, MA: MIT Press, pp. 563–583. First published as 'Über Sinn und Bedeutung' in 1892. Translation first published in Peter T. Geach and Max Black (eds.). 1952. *Translations from the Philosophical Writings of Gottlob Frege*. Oxford: B. Blackwell.

Frege, Gottlob. 1997b. *Begriffsschrift*: A formula language of pure thought modelled on that of arithmetic'. Part 1, §§1–12. Transl. by Michael Beaney. In Michael Beaney (ed.), *The Frege Reader*. Oxford: Blackwell, pp. 47–78. Originally published in 1879 as 'Begriffsschrift, eine der arithmetischen nachgebildete Formelsprache des reinen Denkens'.

Frege, Gottlob. 1997c. *The Foundations of Arithmetic: A Logico-Mathematical Investigation into the Concept of Number*. Introduction. Transl. by Michael Beaney. In Michael Beaney (ed.), *The Frege Reader*. Oxford: Blackwell, pp. 84–91. Originally published in 1884 as *Die Grundlagen der Arithmetik, eine logisch mathematische Untersuchung über den Begriff der Zahl*.

Frege, Gottlob. 1997d. *Grundgezetze der Arithmetik*, Vol. 1. Preface. Transl. by Michael Beaney. In Michael Beaney (ed.), *The Frege Reader*. Oxford: Blackwell, pp. 194–208. Originally published in 1893.

Fricker, Miranda. 2007. *Epistemic Injustice: Power and the Ethics of Knowing*. Oxford: Oxford University Press.

Fukushima, Saeko. 1996. 'Request strategies in British English and Japanese'. In Kasia M. Jaszczolt and Ken Turner (eds.), *Contrastive Semantics and Pragmatics,* Vol. 2: Discourse Strategies. Oxford: Elsevier Science, pp. 671–688.

García-Carpintero, Manuel. 2020. 'On the nature of presupposition: A normative speech act account'. *Erkenntnis* 85: 269–293.

García-Carpintero, Manuel and Josep Macià (eds.). 2006. *Two-Dimensional Semantics: Foundations and Applications*. Oxford: Oxford University Press.

Garfinkel, Harold. 1967. *Studies in Ethnomethodology*. Englewood Cliffs, NJ: Prentice Hall.

Garmendia, Joana. 2018. *Irony*. Cambridge: Cambridge University Press.

Gauker, Christopher. 2019. 'Against the speaker-intention theory of demonstratives'. *Linguistics and Philosophy* 42: 109–129.

Gazdar, Gerald. 1979. *Pragmatics: Implicature, Presupposition, and Logical Form*. New York: Academic Press.

Geach, Peter T. 1962. *Reference and Generality*. Ithaca, NY: Cornell University Press.
Geeraerts, Dirk. 2010. *Theories of Lexical Semantics*. Oxford: Oxford University Press.
Geeraerts, Dirk and Hubert Cuyckens (eds.). 2007. *The Oxford Handbook of Cognitive Linguistics*. Oxford: Oxford University Press.
Geis, Michael L. and Arnold M. Zwicky. 1971. 'On invited inferences'. *Linguistic Inquiry* 2: 561–566.
Genovesi, Chris. 2020. 'Metaphor and what is meant: Metaphorical content, what is said, and contextualism'. *Journal of Pragmatics* 157: 17–38.
Geurts, Bart. 1998a. 'The mechanisms of denial'. *Language* 74: 274–307.
Geurts, Bart. 1998b. 'Presuppositions and anaphors in attitude contexts'. *Linguistics and Philosophy* 21: 545–601.
Geurts, Bart. 1998c. 'Scalars'. In Petra Ludewig and Bart Geurts (eds.), *Lexikalische Semantik aus kognitiver Sicht*. Tübingen: Gunter Narr, pp. 95–117.
Geurts, Bart. 1999. *Presuppositions and Pronouns*. Oxford: Elsevier Science.
Geurts, Bart. 2007. 'Really fucking brilliant'. *Theoretical Linguistics* 33: 209–214.
Geurts, Bart. 2009. 'Scalar implicature and local pragmatics'. *Mind and Language* 24: 51–79.
Geurts, Bart. 2010. *Quantity Implicatures*. Cambridge: Cambridge University Press.
Geurts, Bart. 2018. 'Convention and common ground'. *Mind and Language* 33: 115–129.
Geurts, Bart. 2019. 'Communication as commitment sharing: Speech acts, implicatures, common ground'. *Theoretical Linguistics* 45: 1–30.
Geurts, Bart and Rob van der Sandt. 1999. 'Domain restriction'. In Peter Bosch and Rob van der Sandt (eds.), *Focus: Linguistic, Cognitive, and Computational Perspectives*. Cambridge: Cambridge University Press, pp. 268–292.
Geurts, Bart and Rob van der Sandt. 2004. 'Interpreting focus'. *Theoretical Linguistics* 30: 1–44.
Geurts, Bart, David E. Beaver, and Emar Maier. 2020. 'Discourse Representation Theory'. In Edward Zalta (ed.), *Stanford Encyclopedia of Philosophy* (online). plato.stanford.edu/entries/discourse-representation-theory/ [accessed 7 March 2021].
Gibbs, Raymond W. (ed.). 2008. *The Cambridge Handbook of Metaphor and Thought*. Cambridge: Cambridge University Press.
Gibbs, Raymond W. 2017. *Metaphor Wars: Conceptual Metaphors in Human Life*. Cambridge: Cambridge University Press.
Gibbs, Raymond W., Jr. and Jessica F. Moise. 1997. 'Pragmatics in understanding what is said'. *Cognition* 62: 51–74.
Ginzburg, Jonathan. 1995. 'Resolving questions, I'. *Linguistics and Philosophy* 18: 459–527.
Ginzburg, Jonathan. 2012. *The Interactive Stance: Meaning for Conversation*. Oxford: Oxford University Press.
Ginzburg, Jonathan and Ivan A. Sag. 2000. *Interrogative Investigations: The Form, Meaning, and Use of English Interrogatives*. Stanford, CA: CSLI.
Giora, Rachel. 2003. *On Our Mind: Salience, Context, and Figurative Language*. Oxford: Oxford University Press.
Giora, Rachel. 2012. 'The psychology of utterance processing: Context vs salience'. In Keith Allan and Kasia M. Jaszczolt (eds.), *The Cambridge Handbook of Pragmatics*. Cambridge: Cambridge University Press, pp. 151–167.
Giora, Rachel, Shir Givoni, and Ofer Fein. 2015. 'Defaultness reigns: The case of sarcasm'. *Metaphor and Symbol* 30: 290–313.

Givón, Talmy. 1983a. 'Topic continuity in discourse: An introduction'. In Talmy Givón (ed.), *Topic Continuity in Discourse: A Quantitative Cross-Language Study*. Amsterdam: John Benjamins, pp. 1–41.

Givón, Talmy. 1983b. 'Topic continuity in spoken English'. In Talmy Givón (ed.), *Topic Continuity in Discourse: A Quantitative Cross-Language Study*. Amsterdam: John Benjamins, pp. 343–363.

Givón, Talmy (ed.). 1983c. *Topic Continuity in Discourse: A Quantitative Cross-Language Study*. Amsterdam: John Benjamins.

Givón, Talmy. 1993. *English Grammar: A Function-Based Introduction*, Vol. 1. Amsterdam: John Benjamins.

Givón, Talmy. 2005. *Context as Other Minds: The Pragmatics of Sociality, Cognition and Communication*. Amsterdam: John Benjamins.

Goffman, Erving. 1967. *Interaction Ritual: Essays on Face-to-Face Behavior*. New York: Anchor Books.

Goldberg, Sanford C. 2011. 'Putting the norm of assertion to work: The case of testimony'. In Jessica Brown and Herman Cappelen (eds.), *Assertion: New Philosophical Essays*. Oxford: Oxford University Press, pp. 175–195.

Goldberg, Sanford C. 2015. *Assertion: On the Philosophical Significance of Assertoric Speech*. Oxford: Oxford University Press.

Goldberg, Sanford C. 2020. *Conversational Pressure: Normativity in Speech Exchanges*. Oxford: Oxford University Press.

Goldin-Meadow, Susan and Ming-Yu Zheng. 1998. 'Thought before language: The expression of motion events prior to the impact of a conventional language model'. In Peter Carruthers and Jill Boucher (eds.), *Language and Thought: Interdisciplinary Themes*. Cambridge: Cambridge University Press, pp. 26–54.

Gómez Txurruka, Isabel. 2003. 'The natural language conjunction *and* '. *Linguistics and Philosophy* 26: 255–285.

Green, Georgia M. 1996. 'Ambiguity resolution and discourse interpretation'. In Kees van Deemter and Stanley Peters (eds.), *Semantic Ambiguity and Underspecification*. Stanford, CA: CSLI, pp. 1–26.

Gregoromichelaki, Eleni and Ruth Kempson. 2016. 'Joint utterances and the (split-)turn taking puzzle'. In Alessandro Capone and Jacob L. Mey (eds.), *Interdisciplinary Studies in Pragmatics, Culture and Society*. Cham: Springer, pp. 703–743.

Grice, Paul. 1989a. 'Meaning'. In Paul Grice, *Studies in the Way of Words*. Cambridge, MA: Harvard University Press, pp. 213–223. First published in 1957, in *Philosophical Review* 66.

Grice, Paul. 1989b. 'Logic and conversation'. In Paul Grice, *Studies in the Way of Words*. Cambridge, MA: Harvard University Press, pp. 22–40. First published in 1975 in Peter Cole and Jerry L. Morgan (eds.), *Syntax and Semantics*, Vol. 3. New York: Academic Press.

Grice, Paul. 1989c. 'Further notes on logic and conversation'. In Paul Grice, *Studies in the Way of Words*. Cambridge, MA: Harvard University Press, pp. 41–57. First published in 1978 in Peter Cole (ed.). *Syntax and Semantics*, Vol. 9. New York: Academic Press.

Grice, Paul. 1989d. 'Indicative conditionals'. In Paul Grice, *Studies in the Way of Words*. Cambridge, MA: Harvard University Press, pp. 58–85. First published in 1967 in Paul Grice, *Logic and Conversation*. William James Lectures, Harvard University.

Grice, Paul. 1989e. 'Utterer's meaning and intentions'. In Paul Grice, *Studies in the Way of Words*. Cambridge, MA: Harvard University Press, pp. 86–116. First published in 1969 in *Philosophical Review* 78.

# References

Groenendijk, Jeroen and Martin Stokhof. 1982. 'Semantic analysis of *wh*-complements'. *Linguistics and Philosophy* 5: 175–233.

Groenendijk, Jeroen and Martin Stokhof. 1991. 'Dynamic Predicate Logic'. *Linguistics and Philosophy* 14: 39–100.

Grosz, Barbara J. and Candace L. Sidner. 1998. 'Lost intuitions and forgotten intentions'. In Marilyn A. Walker, Aravind K. Joshi, and Ellen F. Prince (eds.), *Centering Theory in Discourse*. Oxford: Clarendon Press, pp. 39–51.

Grosz, Barbara J., Aravind K. Joshi, and Scott Weinstein. 1995. 'Centering: A framework for modelling the local coherence of discourse'. *Computational Linguistics* 21: 203–225.

Gumperz, John J. and Stephen C. Levinson (eds.). 1996. *Rethinking Linguistic Relativity*. Cambridge: Cambridge University Press.

Gundel, Jeanette K. 1996. 'Relevance theory meets the givenness hierarchy: An account of inferrables'. In Thorstein Fretheim and Jeanette K. Gundel (eds.), *Reference and Referent Accessibility*. Amsterdam: John Benjamins, pp. 141–153.

Gundel, Jeanette K. 1998. 'Centering theory and the givenness hierarchy: Towards a synthesis'. In Marilyn A. Walker, Aravind K. Joshi, and Ellen F. Prince (eds.), *Centering Theory in Discourse*. Oxford: Clarendon Press, pp. 183–198.

Gundel, Jeanette K. 1999. 'On different kinds of focus'. In Peter Bosch and Rob van der Sandt (eds.), *Focus: Linguistic, Cognitive, and Computational Perspectives*. Cambridge: Cambridge University Press, pp. 293–305.

Gundel, Jeanette K., Nancy Hedberg, and Ron Zacharski. 1993. 'Cognitive status and the form of referring expressions in discourse'. *Language* 69: 274–307.

Haegeman, Liliane. 1991. *Introduction to Government and Binding Theory*. Oxford: Blackwell.

Halliday, Michael A. K. 1967. 'Notes on transitivity and theme in English. Part 2'. *Journal of Linguistics* 3: 199–244.

Halliday, Michael A. K. 1994. *An Introduction to Functional Grammar*. London: Arnold. Second edition. First published in 1985.

Hamblin, C. L. 1958. 'Questions'. *Australasian Journal of Philosophy* 36: 159–168.

Hamblin, C. L. 1971. 'Mathematical models of dialogue'. *Theoria* 37: 130–155.

Hamm, Fritz, Hans Kamp, and Michiel van Lambalgen. 2006. 'There is no opposition between Formal and Cognitive Semantics'. *Theoretical Linguistics* 32: 1–40.

Hampe, Beate (ed.). 2017. *Metaphor: Embodied Cognition and Discourse*. Cambridge: Cambridge University Press.

Hampton, James A. and Martin L. Jönsson. 2012. 'Typicality and compositionality: The logic of combining vague concepts'. In Markus Werning, Wolfram Hinzen, and Edouard Machery (eds.), *The Oxford Handbook of Compositionality*. Oxford: Oxford University Press, pp. 385–402.

Harari, Yuval Noah. 2017. *Homo Deus: A Brief History of Tomorrow*. London: Vintage. First published in Hebrew in 2015.

Harnish, Robert M. 1990. 'Speech acts and intentionality'. In Armin Burkhardt (ed.), *Speech Acts, Meaning and Intentions: Critical Approaches to the Philosophy of John R. Searle*. Berlin: W. de Gruyter, pp. 169–193.

Harris, Zellig. 1954. 'Distributional structure'. *Word* 10: 146–162.

Haugh, Michael. 2007. 'The co-constitution of politeness implicature in conversation'. *Journal of Pragmatics* 39: 84–110.

Haugh, Michael. 2008. 'The place of intention in the interactional achievement of implicature'. In Istvan Kecskes and Jacob Mey (eds.), *Intention, Common Ground and the Egocentric Speaker-Hearer*. Berlin: Mouton de Gruyter, pp. 45–85.

Haugh, Michael. 2009. 'Intention(ality) and the conceptualisation of communication in pragmatics'. *Australian Journal of Linguistics* 29: 91–113.
Haugh, Michael. 2013. 'Speaker meaning and accountability in interaction'. *Journal of Pragmatics* 48: 41–56.
Haugh, Michael and Kasia M. Jaszczolt. 2012. 'Speaker intentions and intentionality'. In Keith Allan and Kasia M. Jaszczolt (eds.), *The Cambridge Handbook of Pragmatics*. Cambridge: Cambridge University Press, pp. 87–112.
Heffer, Chris. 2020. *All Bullshit and Lies? Insincerity, Irresponsibility, and the Judgment of Untruthfulness*. Oxford: Oxford University Press.
Hegarty, Michel. 2016. *Modality and Propositional Attitudes*. Cambridge: Cambridge University Press.
Heim, Irene. 1988. *The Semantics of Definite and Indefinite Noun Phrases*. New York: Garland.
Heim, Irene. 1990. 'E-type pronouns and donkey anaphora'. *Linguistics and Philosophy* 13: 137–177.
Heim, Irene. 1992. 'Presupposition projection and the semantics of attitude verbs'. *Journal of Semantics* 9: 183–221.
Heim, Irene and Angelika Kratzer. 1998. *Semantics in Generative Grammar*. Oxford: Blackwell.
Heritage, John. 1984. *Garfinkel and Ethnomethodology*. Cambridge: Polity Press.
Hess, Leopold. 2018. 'Perspectival expressives'. *Journal of Pragmatics* 129: 13–33.
Hintikka, Jaakko. 1962. *Knowledge and Belief: An Introduction to the Logic of the Two Notions*. Ithaca, NY: Cornell University Press.
Hirschberg, Julia B. 1991. *A Theory of Scalar Implicature*. New York: Garland Publishing.
Hobbs, Jerry R. 1979. 'Coherence and coreference'. *Cognitive Science* 3: 67–90.
Hobbs, Jerry R. 1990. *Literature and Cognition*. Stanford, CA: CSLI.
Holmes, Janet. 1995. *Women, Men and Politeness*. London: Longman.
Hom, Christopher. 2008. 'The semantics of racial epithets'. *Journal of Philosophy* 105: 416–440.
Hom, Christopher. 2010. 'Pejoratives'. *Philosophy Compass* 5: 164–185.
Hom, Christopher. 2012. 'A puzzle about pejoratives'. *Philosophical Studies* 159: 383–405.
Hom, Christopher and Robert May. 2013. 'Moral and semantic innocence'. *Analytic Philosophy* 54: 293–313.
Horn, Laurence R. 1984. 'Toward a new taxonomy for pragmatic inference: Q-based and R-based implicature'. In Deborah Schiffrin (ed.), *Georgetown University Round Table on Languages and Linguistics 1984*. Washington, DC: Georgetown University Press, pp. 11–42.
Horn, Laurence R. 1985. 'Metalinguistic negation and pragmatic ambiguity'. *Language* 61: 121–174.
Horn, Laurence R. 1988. 'Pragmatic theory'. In Frederick J. Newmeyer (ed.), *Linguistics: The Cambridge Survey*, Vol. 1: Linguistic Theory: Foundations. Cambridge: Cambridge University Press, pp. 113–145.
Horn, Laurence R. 1989. *A Natural History of Negation*. Chicago, IL: University of Chicago Press.
Horn, Laurence R. 1992. 'The said and the unsaid'. *Ohio State University Working Papers in Linguistics* 40 (SALT II Proceedings): 163–192.
Horn, Laurence R. 1996. 'Presupposition and implicature'. In Shalom Lappin (ed.), *The Handbook of Contemporary Semantic Theory*. Oxford: Blackwell, pp. 299–319.

Horn, Laurence R. 2000. 'From *if* to *iff*: Conditional perfection as pragmatic strengthening'. *Journal of Pragmatics* 32: 289–326.

Horn, Laurence R. 2004. 'Implicature'. In Laurence R. Horn and Gregory Ward (eds.), *The Handbook of Pragmatics*. Oxford: Blackwell, pp. 3–28.

Horn, Laurence R. 2006. 'The border wars: A neo-Gricean perspective'. In Klaus von Heusinger and Ken Turner (eds.), *Where Semantics Meets Pragmatics: The Michigan Papers*. Oxford: Elsevier, pp. 21–48.

Horn, Laurence R. 2012. 'Implying and inferring'. In Keith Allan and Kasia M. Jaszczolt (eds.), *The Cambridge Handbook of Pragmatics*. Cambridge: Cambridge University Press, pp. 69–86.

Horn, Laurence R. 2019. 'First things first: The pragmatics of "natural order"'. *Intercultural Pragmatics* 16: 257–287.

Horn, Laurence R. 2020a. 'Neg-raising'. In Viviane Déprez and M. Teresa Espinal (eds.), *The Oxford Handbook of Negation*, E-book. Oxford: Oxford University Press. DOI: 10.1093/oxfordhb/9780198830528.013.45.

Horn, Laurence R. 2020b. 'Negation and opposition: Contradiction and contrariety in logic and language'. In Viviane Déprez and M. Teresa Espinal (eds.), *The Oxford Handbook of Negation*, E-book. Oxford: Oxford University Press. DOI: 10.1093/oxfordhb/9780198830528.013.1

Horn, Laurence R. and Heinrich Wansing. 2020. 'Negation'. In Edward Zalta (ed.), *Stanford Encyclopedia of Philosophy* (online). stanford.edu/entries/negation/ [accessed 21 February 2021].

Husserl, Edmund. 1970. *Logical Investigations*. Transl. by J. N. Findlay. London: Routledge & Kegan Paul. First published in 1900–1901 as *Logische Untersuchungen*. Halle: Max Niemeyer.

Ismael, Jenann T. 2016. *How Physics Makes Us Free*. Oxford: Oxford University Press.

Jackendoff, Ray. 1990. *Semantic Structures*. Cambridge, MA: MIT Press.

Jackendoff, Ray. 2012. *A User's Guide to Thought and Meaning*. Oxford: Oxford University Press.

Jacobson, Pauline. 2014. *Compositional Semantics: An Introduction to the Syntax/Semantics Interface*. Oxford: Oxford University Press.

Jacobson, Pauline. 2018. 'Some people think there is Neg raising, and some don't: Neg raising meets ellipsis'. *Linguistic Inquiry* 49: 559–576.

Jäger, Gerhard. 1999. 'Topic, focus, and weak quantifiers'. In Peter Bosch and Rob van der Sandt (eds.), *Focus: Linguistic, Cognitive, and Computational Perspectives*. Cambridge: Cambridge University Press, pp. 187–212.

Jary, Mark. 1998. 'Relevance theory and the communication of politeness'. *Journal of Pragmatics* 30: 1–19.

Jary, Mark and Mikhail Kissine. 2014. *Imperatives*. Cambridge: Cambridge University Press.

Jaszczolt, Kasia M. 1996. 'Reported speech, vehicles of thought, and the horizon'. *Lingua e Stile* 31: 113–133.

Jaszczolt, Kasia M. 1997. 'The Default *De Re* Principle for the interpretation of belief utterances'. *Journal of Pragmatics* 28: 315–336.

Jaszczolt, Kasia M. 1999. *Discourse, Beliefs, and Intentions: Semantic Defaults and Propositional Attitude Ascription*. Oxford: Elsevier Science.

Jaszczolt, Kasia M. 2002a. 'Against ambiguity and underspecification: Evidence from presupposition as anaphora'. *Journal of Pragmatics* 34: 829–849.

Jaszczolt, K. M. 2002b. *Semantics and Pragmatics: Meaning in Language and Discourse*. London: Longman.

Jaszczolt, Kasia M. 2005. *Default Semantics: Foundations of a Compositional Theory of Acts of Communication*. Oxford: Oxford University Press.

Jaszczolt, Kasia M. 2007. 'Variadic function and pragmatics-rich representations of belief reports'. *Journal of Pragmatics* 39: 934–959.

Jaszczolt, Kasia M. 2008. 'Psychological explanations in Gricean pragmatics and Frege's legacy'. In Istvan Kecskes and Jacob Mey (eds.), *Intentions, Common Ground, and Egocentric Speaker-Hearer*. Berlin: Mouton de Gruyter, pp. 9–44.

Jaszczolt, Kasia M. 2009a. *Representing Time: An Essay on Temporality as Modality*. Oxford: Oxford University Press.

Jaszczolt, Kasia M. 2009b. 'Cancellability and the primary/secondary meaning distinction'. *Intercultural Pragmatics* 6. 259–289.

Jaszczolt, Kasia M. 2010. 'Default Semantics'. In Bernd Heine and Heiko Narrog (eds.), *The Oxford Handbook of Linguistic Analysis*. Oxford: Oxford University Press, pp. 193–221.

Jaszczolt, Kasia M. 2012a. 'Cross-linguistic differences in expressing time and universal principles of utterance interpretation'. In Luna Filipović and Kasia M. Jaszczolt (eds.), *Space and Time in Languages and Cultures: Linguistic Diversity*. Amsterdam: John Benjamins, pp. 95–121.

Jaszczolt, Kasia M. 2012b. 'Propositional attitude reports: Pragmatic aspects'. In K. Allan and K. M. Jaszczolt (eds.), *The Cambridge Handbook of Pragmatics*. Cambridge: Cambridge University Press, pp. 305–327.

Jaszczolt, Kasia M. 2012c. '"Pragmaticising" Kaplan: Flexible inferential bases and fluid characters'. *Australian Journal of Linguistics* 32: 209–237.

Jaszczolt, Kasia M. 2013a. 'First-person reference in discourse: Aims and strategies'. *Journal of Pragmatics* 48: 57–70.

Jaszczolt, Kasia M. 2013b. 'Temporality and epistemic commitment: An unresolved question'. In Kasia M. Jaszczolt and Louis de Saussure (eds.), *Time: Language, Cognition, and Reality*. Oxford: Oxford University Press, pp. 193–209.

Jaszczolt, Kasia M. 2016. *Meaning in Linguistic Interaction: Semantics, Metasemantics, Philosophy of Language*. Oxford: Oxford University Press.

Jaszczolt, Kasia M. 2018a. 'Time, perspective and semantic representation'. *Language and Cognition* 10: 26–55.

Jaszczolt, Kasia M. 2018b. 'Pragmatic indexicals'. In Minyao Huang and Kasia M. Jaszczolt (eds.), *Expressing the Self: Cultural Diversity and Cognitive Universals*. Oxford: Oxford University Press, pp. 260–286.

Jaszczolt, Kasia M. 2019a. 'Semantics/pragmatics boundary disputes'. In Claudia Maienborn, Klaus von Heusinger and Paul Portner (eds.), *Semantics Interfaces*. Berlin: De Gruyter Mouton, pp. 368–402. First published in 2012 in Claudia Maienborn, Klaus von Heusinger and Paul Portner (eds.), *Semantics: An International Handbook of Natural Language Meaning*, Vol. 3. Berlin: De Gruyter Mouton.

Jaszczolt, Kasia M. 2019b. 'Rethinking being Gricean: New challenges for metapragmatics'. *Journal of Pragmatics* 145: 15–24.

Jaszczolt, Kasia M. 2020. 'Human imprints of real time: From semantics to metaphysics'. *Philosophia* 48: 1855–1879.

Jaszczolt, Kasia M. 2021a. 'Functional proposition: A new concept for representing discourse meaning?' *Journal of Pragmatics* 171: 200–214.

Jaszczolt, Kasia M. 2021b. 'Default Semantics'. In Mark Aronoff (ed.), *Oxford Bibliographies in Linguistics*. New York: Oxford University Press (online).

Jaszczolt, Kasia M. 2022. 'Metasemantics and metapragmatics: Philosophical foundation of meaning'. In Piotr Stalmaszczyk (ed.), *The Cambridge Handbook of the Philosophy of Language*. Cambridge: Cambridge University Press, pp. 139–156.

Jaszczolt, Kasia M. 2023. 'Post-Gricean pragmatics for intercultural communication'. In Istvan Kecskes (ed.), *The Cambridge Handbook of Intercultural Pragmatics*. Cambridge: Cambridge University Press, pp. 11–39.

Jaszczolt, Kasia M. In press. 'Does human time really flow? Metaindexicality, metarepresentation, and basic concepts'. In K. M. Jaszczolt (ed.), *Understanding Human Time*. For Oxford Studies of Time in Language and Thought. Oxford: Oxford University Press.

Jaszczolt, Kasia M. and Lidia Berthon. In press. 'Negotiation and joint construction of meaning (or why health providers need philosophy of communication)'. In Sarah Bigi and Maria Grazia Rossi (eds.), *A Pragmatic Agenda for Healthcare*. Amsterdam: John Benjamins.

Jaszczolt, Kasia M. and Minyao Huang. 2017. 'Monsters and *I*: The case of mixed quotation'. In Paul Saka and Michael Johnson (eds.), *The Semantics and Pragmatics of Quotation*. Cham: Springer, pp. 357–382.

Jaszczolt, Kasia M. and Roberto B. Sileo. 2021. 'Pragmatics and grammar as sources of temporal ordering in discourse: The case of *and* '. In Fabrizio Macagno and Alessandro Capone (eds.), *Inquiries in Philosophical Pragmatics*. Cham: Springer, pp. 53–81.

Jaszczolt, Kasia M. and Ken Turner (eds.). 2003. *Meaning through Language Contrast*, Vol. 2. Amsterdam: John Benjamins.

Jaszczolt, Kasia M. and Maciej Witek. 2018. 'Expressing the self: From types of *de se* to speech-act types'. In Minyao Huang and Kasia M. Jaszczolt (eds.), *Expressing the Self: Cultural Diversity and Cognitive Universals*. Oxford: Oxford University Press, pp. 187–222.

Jaszczolt, Kasia M., Eleni Savva, and Michael Haugh. 2016. 'The individual and the social path of interpretation: The case of incomplete disjunctive questions'. In Alessandro Capone and Jacob L. Mey (eds.), *Interdisciplinary Studies in Pragmatics, Culture and Society*. Cham: Springer, pp. 251–283.

Jeshion, Robin. 2018. 'Slurs, dehumanization, and the expression of contempt'. In David Sosa (ed.), *Bad Words: Philosophical Perspectives on Slurs*. Oxford: Oxford University Press, pp. 77–107.

Johnson, Mark. 1987. *The Body in the Mind: The Bodily Basis of Meaning, Imagination, and Reason*. Chicago, IL: University of Chicago Press.

Johnson-Laird, Philip N. 1983. *Mental Models: Towards a Cognitive Science of Language, Inference, and Consciousness*. Cambridge: Cambridge University Press.

Johnson-Laird, Philip N. and Marco Ragni. 2019. 'Possibilities as the foundation of reasoning'. *Cognition* 193 (online). doi.org/10.1016/j.cognition.2019.04.019 [accessed 22 February 2019].

Jurafsky, Daniel and James H. Martin. 2014. *Speech and Language Processing*. Harlow: Pearson Education. Second edition.

Jurafsky, Daniel and James H. Martin. 2016. 'Vector semantics'. For: Daniel Jurafsky and James H. Martin. *Speech and Language Processing*. Third edition. Draft of 7 November 2016.

Kádár, Dániel Z. and Michael Haugh. 2013. *Understanding Politeness*. Cambridge: Cambridge University Press.

Kamp, Hans. 1990. 'Prolegomena to a structural account of belief and other attitudes'. In C. Anthony Anderson and Joseph Owens (eds.), *Propositional Attitudes: The Role of Content in Logic, Language, and Mind*. Stanford, CA: CSLI Publications, pp. 27–90.

Kamp, Hans. 2003. 'Temporal relations inside and outside attitudinal contexts'. Paper presented at *Where Semantics Meets Pragmatics* workshop, LSA Summer School, University of Michigan, July 2003.

Kamp, Hans. 2019. 'Tense and aspect in Discourse Representation Theory'. In Robert Truswell (ed.), *The Oxford Handbook of Event Structure*, E-book. Oxford: Oxford University Press. DOI: 10.1093/oxfordhb/9780199685318.001.0001.

Kamp, Hans and Barbara Partee. 1995. 'Prototype theory and compositionality'. *Cognition* 57: 129–191.

Kamp, Hans and Uwe Reyle. 1993. *From Discourse to Logic: Introduction to Modeltheoretic Semantics of Natural Language, Formal Logic and Discourse Representation Theory*. Dordrecht: Kluwer.

Kamp, Hans and Uwe Reyle. 2011. 'Discourse Representation Theory'. In Claudia Maienborn, Klaus von Heusinger, and Paul Portner (eds.), *Semantics: An International Handbook of Natural Language Meaning*, Vol. 1. Berlin: De Gruyter Mouton, pp. 872–923.

Kant, Immanuel. 1990. *Critique of Pure Reason*. Transl. by Norman Kemp. London: Macmillan. First published in 1781 as *Kritik der reinen Vernunft*. Riga: Johann Friedrich Hartknoch.

Kaplan, David. 1989a. 'Demonstratives: An essay on the semantics, logic, metaphysics, and epistemology of demonstratives and other indexicals'. In Joseph Almog, John Perry, and Howard Wettstein (eds.), *Themes from Kaplan*. New York: Oxford University Press, pp. 481–563.

Kaplan, David. 1989b. 'Afterthoughts'. In Joseph Almog, John Perry, and Howard Wettstein (eds.), *Themes from Kaplan*. New York: Oxford University Press, pp. 565–614.

Kaplan, David. 2008. 'The meaning of *ouch* and *oops*'. Howison Lecture in Philosophy, University of California at Berkeley, 25 April 2008. www.youtube.com/watch?v=iaGRLlgPl6w [accessed 29 March 2021].

Kapogianni, Eleni. 2022. 'Types and definitions of irony'. In Piotr Stalmaszczyk (ed.), *The Cambridge Handbook of the Philosophy of Language*. Cambridge: Cambridge University Press, pp. 622–638.

Karttunen, Lauri. 1973. 'Presuppositions of compound sentences'. *Linguistic Inquiry* 4: 169–193.

Karttunen, Lauri. 1976. 'Discourse referents'. In James McCawley (ed.), *Syntax and Semantics*, Vol. 7. New York: Academic Press, pp. 363–385.

Karttunen, Lauri. 1977. 'Syntax and semantics of questions'. *Linguistics and Philosophy* 1: 3–44.

Katz, Jerrold J. and Jerry A. Fodor. 1963. 'The structure of a semantic theory'. *Language* 39: 170–210.

Katz, Jerrold J. and Paul M. Postal. 1964. *An Integrated Theory of Linguistic Descriptions*. Cambridge, MA: MIT Press.

Kay, Paul. 1996. 'Intra-speaker relativity'. In John J. Gumperz and Stephen C. Levinson (eds.), *Rethinking Linguistic Relativity*. Cambridge: Cambridge University Press, pp. 97–114.

Kearns, Kate. 2011. *Semantics*. Basingstoke: Palgrave Macmillan. Second edition.

Keenan, Edward L. 1996. 'The semantics of determiners'. In Shalom Lappin (ed.), *The Handbook of Contemporary Semantic Theory*. Oxford: Blackwell, pp. 41–63.

Kehler, Andrew. 2002. *Coherence, Reference, and the Theory of Grammar*. Stanford, CA: CSLI.

Kehler, Andrew and Hannah Rohde. 2013. 'A probabilistic reconciliation of coherence-driven and centering-driven theories of pronoun interpretation'. *Theoretical Linguistics* 39: 1–37.

# References

Kehler, Andrew, et al. 2008. 'Coherence and coreference revisited'. *Journal of Semantics* 25: 1–44.

Keller, Charles M. and Janet D. Keller. 1996. 'Imaging in iron, or thought is not inner speech'. In John J. Gumperz and Stephen C. Levinson (eds.), *Rethinking Linguistic Relativity*. Cambridge: Cambridge University Press, pp. 115–129.

Kempson, Ruth M. 1975. *Presupposition and the Delimitation of Semantics*. Cambridge: Cambridge University Press.

Kempson, Ruth M. 1979. 'Presupposition, opacity, and ambiguity'. In Choon-Kyu Oh and David A. Dinneen (eds.), *Syntax and Semantics*, Vol. 11: Presupposition. New York: Academic Press, pp. 283–297.

Kempson, Ruth M. 1986. 'Ambiguity and the semantics–pragmatics distinction'. In Charles Travis (ed.), *Meaning and Interpretation*. Oxford: B. Blackwell, pp. 77–103.

King, Jeffrey C. 2001. *Complex Demonstratives: A Quantificational Account*. Cambridge, MA: MIT Press.

King, Jeffrey C. 2014. 'Speaker intentions in context'. *Noûs* 48: 219–237.

King, Jeffrey C. and Jason Stanley. 2005. 'Semantics, pragmatics, and the role of semantic content'. In Zoltán Gendler Szabó (ed.), *Semantics versus Pragmatics*. Oxford: Oxford University Press, pp. 111–164.

King, Jeffrey C., Scott Soames, and Jeff Speaks (eds.). 2014. *New Thinking about Propositions*. Oxford: Oxford University Press.

Kissine, Mikhail. 2012. 'Sentences, utterances, and speech acts'. In Keith Allan and Kasia M. Jaszczolt (eds.), *The Cambridge Handbook of Pragmatics*. Cambridge: Cambridge University Press, pp. 169–190.

Kissine, Mikhail. 2013. *From Utterances to Speech Acts*. Cambridge: Cambridge University Press.

Koenig, Jean-Pierre. 1993. 'Scalar predicates and negation: Punctual semantics and interval interpretations'. *Chicago Linguistic Society* 27. Part 2: *The Parasession on Negation*, pp. 140–155.

Koike, Dale A. 1994. 'Negation in Spanish and English suggestions and requests: Mitigating effects?'. *Journal of Pragmatics* 21: 513–526.

Korta, Kepa and John Perry. 2011. *Critical Pragmatics: An Inquiry into Reference and Communication*. Cambridge: Cambridge University Press.

Kövecses, Zoltán. 2010. *Metaphor: A Practical Introduction*. Oxford: Oxford University Press. Second edition. First edition published in 2002.

Kövecses, Zoltán. 2020. *Extended Conceptual Metaphor Theory*. Cambridge: Cambridge University Press.

Krahmer, Emiel and Kees van Deemter. 1998. 'On the interpretation of anaphoric noun phrases: Towards a full understanding of partial matches'. *Journal of Semantics* 15: 355–392.

Kratzer, Angelika. 1989. 'An investigation into lumps of thought'. *Linguistics and Philosophy* 12: 607–653.

Kratzer, Angelika. 2009. 'Making a pronoun: Fake indexicals and windows into the properties of pronouns'. *Linguistic Inquiry* 40: 187–237.

Kratzer, Angelika. 2012a. 'Conditionals'. In Angelika Kratzer, *Modals and Conditionals*. Oxford: Oxford University Press, pp. 86–108. First published in 1991 in Arnim von Stechow and Dieter Wunderlich (eds.), *Semantics: An International Handbook of Contemporary Research*. Berlin: De Gruyter.

Kratzer, Angelika. 2012b. 'What *must* and *can* must and can mean'. In Angelika Kratzer, *Modals and Conditionals*. Oxford: Oxford University Press, pp. 4–20. First published in 1977 in *Linguistics and Philosophy* 1.

Kratzer, Angelika. 2012c. 'The notional category of modality'. In Angelika Kratzer, *Modals and Conditionals*. Oxford: Oxford University Press, pp. 27–69. First published in 1981 in Hans J. Eikmeyer and Hannes Rieser (eds.), *Words, Worlds, and Contexts*. Berlin: De Gruyter.

Krifka, Manfred. 1999. 'At least some determiners aren't determiners'. In Ken Turner (ed.), *The Semantics/Pragmatics Interface from Different Points of View*. Oxford: Elsevier Science, pp. 257–291.

Kripke, Saul. 1980. *Naming and Necessity*. Oxford: B. Blackwell. Second edition. First published in 1972 in Donald Davidson and Gilbert Harman (eds.), *Semantics of Natural Language*. Dordrecht: D. Reidel.

Kripke, Saul. 1996. 'A puzzle about belief'. In Aloysius P. Martinich (ed.), *The Philosophy of Language*. Oxford: Oxford University Press, pp. 382–410. Third edition. First published in 1979 in Avishai Margalit (ed.), *Meaning and Use*. Dordrecht: D. Reidel.

Kripke, Saul. 1997. 'Speaker's reference and semantic reference'. In Peter Ludlow (ed.), *Readings in the Philosophy of Language*. Cambridge, MA: MIT Press, pp. 383–414. First published in 1977 in *Midwest Studies in Philosophy* 2.

Kuboň, Petr. 2004. 'Topic, focus and some aspects of the semantics of discourse'. In Hans Kamp and Barbara Partee (eds.), *Context-Dependence in the Analysis of Linguistic Meaning*. Amsterdam: Elsevier, pp. 209–220.

Van Kuppevelt, Jan. 1996. 'Inferring from topics: Scalar implicatures as topic-dependent inferences'. *Linguistics and Philosophy* 19: 393–443.

Labov, William. 1973. 'The boundaries of words and their meanings'. In Charles-James N. Bailey and Roger W. Shuy (eds.), *New Ways of Analyzing Variation in English*. Washington, DC: Georgetown University Press, pp. 340–373.

Lakoff, George. 1970. 'A note on vagueness and ambiguity'. *Linguistic Inquiry* 1: 357–359.

Lakoff, George. 1987. *Women, Fire, and Dangerous Things: What Categories Reveal about the Mind*. Chicago, IL: University of Chicago Press.

Lakoff, George. 1993. 'The contemporary theory of metaphor'. In Andrew Ortony (ed.), *Metaphor and Thought*. Cambridge: Cambridge University Press, pp. 202–251. Second edition. First edition published in 1979.

Lakoff, George. 1996. *Moral Politics: What Conservatives Know That Liberals Don't*. Chicago, IL: University of Chicago Press.

Lakoff, George. 1999. 'Cognitive models and prototype theory'. In Eric Margolis and Stephen Laurence (eds.), *Concepts: Core Readings*. Cambridge, MA: MIT Press, pp. 391–421. First published in Ulric Neisser (ed.) 1987. *Concepts and Conceptual Development: Ecological and Intellectual Factors in Categorization*. Cambridge: Cambridge University Press.

Lakoff, George and Mark Johnson. 1980. *Metaphors We Live By*. Chicago, IL: University of Chicago Press.

Lakoff, George and Mark Johnson. 1999. *Philosophy in the Flesh: The Embodied Mind and Its Challenge to Western Thought*. New York: Basic Books.

Lakoff, George and Mark Turner. 1989. *More than Cool Reason: A Field Guide to Poetic Metaphor*. Chicago, IL: University of Chicago Press.

Lakoff, Robin. 1973. 'The logic of politeness; or, minding your p's and q's'. *Papers from the 9th Regional Meeting, Chicago Linguistic Society*, pp. 292–305.

Lambrecht, Knud. 1994. *Information Structure and Sentence Form: Topic, Focus, and the Mental Representations of Discourse Referents*. Cambridge: Cambridge University Press.

LaPorte, Joseph. 2016. 'Rigid designators'. In Edward Zalta (ed.), *Stanford Encyclopedia of Philosophy* (online). plato.stanford.edu/entries/rigid-designators/ [accessed 8 March 2021].

Larson, Richard and Peter Ludlow. 1997. 'Interpreted logical forms'. In Peter Ludlow (ed.), *Readings in the Philosophy of Language*. Cambridge, MA: MIT Press, pp. 993–1039. First published in 1993 in *Synthese* 95.

Larson, Richard and Gabriel Segal. 1995. *Knowledge of Meaning: An Introduction to Semantic Theory*. Cambridge, MA: MIT Press.

Lascarides, Alex and Nicholas Asher. 1993. 'Temporal interpretation, discourse relations and commonsense entailment'. *Linguistics and Philosophy* 16: 437–493.

Lascarides, Alex and Matthew Stone. 2009. 'A formal semantic analysis of gesture'. *Journal of Semantics* 26: 393–449.

Lascarides, Alex, Anne Copestake, and Ted Briscoe. 1996. 'Ambiguity and coherence'. *Journal of Semantics* 13: 41–65.

Lasersohn, Peter. 2005. 'Context dependence, disagreement, and predicates of personal taste'. *Linguistics and Philosophy* 28: 643–686.

Lasersohn, Peter. 2009. 'Relative truth, speaker commitment, and control of implicit arguments'. *Synthese* 166: 359–374.

Lasersohn, Peter. 2012. 'Contextualism and compositionality'. *Linguistics and Philosophy* 35: 171–189.

Lasersohn, Peter. 2017. *Subjectivity and Perspective in Truth-Theoretic Semantics*. Oxford: Oxford University Press.

Lassiter, Daniel. 2017. *Graded Modality: Qualitative and Quantitative Perspectives*. Oxford: Oxford University Press.

Laurence, Stephen and Eric Margolis. 1999. 'Concepts and cognitive science'. In Eric Margolis and Stephen Laurence (eds.), *Concepts: Core Readings*. Cambridge, MA: MIT Press, pp. 3–81.

Laycock, Henry. 2006. 'Mass nouns, count nouns, and non-count nouns: Philosophical aspects'. In Keith Brown (ed.), *Elsevier Encyclopedia of Language and Linguistics*. Oxford: Elsevier, pp. 534–538. Second edition.

Leech, Geoffrey. 1983. *Principles of Pragmatics*. London: Longman.

Leech, Geoffrey. 2014. *The Pragmatics of Politeness*. Oxford: Oxford University Press.

Leezenberg, Michiel. 2001. *Contexts of Metaphor*. Oxford: Elsevier Science.

Lepore, Ernest and Kirk Ludwig. 2000. 'The semantics and pragmatics of complex demonstratives'. *Mind* 109: 199–240.

Lepore, Ernie and Matthew Stone. 2015. *Imagination and Convention: Distinguishing Grammar and Inference in Language*. Oxford: Oxford University Press.

Lepore, Ernie and Matthew Stone. 2018. 'Pejorative tone'. In David Sosa (ed.), *Bad Words: Philosophical Perspectives on Slurs*. Oxford: Oxford University Press, pp. 132–154.

Leslau, Wolf. 1995. *Reference Grammar of Amharic*. Wiesbaden: Harrassowitz.

Leslie, Sarah-Jane and Adam Lerner. 2016. 'Generic generalizations'. In Edward Zalta (ed.), *Stanford Encyclopedia of Philosophy* (online). plato.stanford.edu/entries/generics/ [accessed 9 March 2021].

Levinson, Stephen C. 1983. *Pragmatics*. Cambridge: Cambridge University Press.

Levinson, Stephen C. 1987. 'Minimization and conversational inference'. In Jef Verschueren and Marcella Bertuccelli-Papi (eds.), *The Pragmatic Perspective: Selected Papers From the 1985 International Pragmatics Conference*. Amsterdam: John Benjamins, pp. 61–129.

Levinson, Stephen C. 1995. 'Three levels of meaning'. In F. R. Palmer (ed.), *Grammar and Meaning: Essays in Honour of Sir John Lyons*. Cambridge: Cambridge University Press, pp. 90–115.

Levinson, Stephen C. 1996. 'Frames of reference and Molyneux's question: Crosslinguistic evidence'. In Paul Bloom et al. (eds.), *Language and Space*. Cambridge, MA: MIT Press, pp. 109–169.

Levinson, Stephen C. 1997. 'From outer to inner space: Linguistic categories and non-linguistic thinking'. In Jan Nuyts and Eric Pederson (eds.), *Language and Conceptualization*. Cambridge: Cambridge University Press, pp. 13–45.

Levinson, Stephen C. 2000. *Presumptive Meanings: The Theory of Generalized Conversational Implicature*. Cambridge, MA: MIT Press.

Levinson, Stephen C. 2003. *Space in Language and Cognition: Explorations in Cognitive Diversity*. Cambridge: Cambridge University Press.

Levinson, Stephen C., Sotaro Kita, Daniel B. M. Haun, and Björn H. Rasch. 2002. 'Returning the tables: Language affects spatial reasoning'. *Cognition* 84: 155–188.

Levinson, Stephen C., Sérgio Meira, and The Language and Cognition Group. 2003. '"Natural concepts" in the spatial topological domain – adpositional meanings in crosslinguistic perspective: An exercise in semantic typology'. *Language* 79: 485–516.

Lewis, David. 1970. 'General semantics'. *Synthese* 22: 18–67.

Lewis, David. 1973. *Counterfactuals*. Oxford: Blackwell.

Lewis, David. 1979. 'Attitudes *de dicto* and *de se* '. *Philosophical Review* 88: 513–543.

Lewis, David. 1991. 'Scorekeeping in a language game'. In Steven Davis (ed.), *Pragmatics: A Reader*. Oxford: Oxford University Press, pp. 416–427. First published in 1979 in *Journal of Philosophical Logic* 8.

Lewis, David. 2002. *Convention: A Philosophical Study*. Cambridge, MA: Harvard University Press. First published in 1969.

Liang, Percy and Christopher Potts. 2015. 'Bringing machine learning and compositional semantics together'. *The Annual Review of Linguistics* 1: 355–376.

Locher, Miriam A. and Richard J. Watts. 2008. 'Relational work and impoliteness: Negotiating norms of linguistic behaviour'. In Derek Bousfield and Miriam A. Locher (eds.), *Impoliteness in Language: Studies on Its Interplay with Power in Theory and Practice*. Berlin: De Gruyter Mouton, pp. 77–99.

Ludlow, Peter. 2000. 'Interpreted logical forms, belief attribution, and the dynamic lexicon'. In Kasia M. Jaszczolt (ed.), *The Pragmatics of Propositional Attitude Reports*. Oxford: Elsevier Science, pp. 31–42.

Ludlow, Peter. 2003. 'Referential semantics for I-languages?'. In Louise M. Anthony and Norbert Hornstein (eds.), *Chomsky and His Critics*. Oxford: Blackwell, pp. 140–162.

Ludlow, Peter. 2014. *Living Words: Meaning Underdetermination and the Dynamic Lexicon*. Oxford: Oxford University Press.

Ludlow, Peter. 2018. 'Descriptions'. In Edward Zalta (ed.), *Stanford Encyclopedia of Philosophy* (online). plato.stanford.edu/entries/descriptions/ [accessed 17 March 2021].

Ludlow, Peter and Stephen Neale. 1997. 'Indefinite descriptions: In defense of Russell'. In Peter Ludlow (ed.), *Readings in the Philosophy of Language*. Cambridge, MA: MIT Press, pp. 523–555. First published in 1991 in *Linguistics and Philosophy* 14.

Lyons, Christopher. 1999. *Definiteness*. Cambridge: Cambridge University Press.

Lyons, John. 1977. *Semantics* (2 volumes). Cambridge: Cambridge University Press.

Lyons, John. 1995. *Linguistic Semantics: An Introduction*. Cambridge: Cambridge University Press.

Macagno, Fabrizio. 2020. 'How can metaphors communicate arguments?'. *Intercultural Pragmatics* 17: 335–363.

Macagno, Fabrizio. 2022. 'Ignoring qualifications as a pragmatic fallacy: Enrichments and their use for manipulating commitments'. *Languages* 7, 3 (online). www.mdpi.com/journal/languages [accessed 28 May 2022].

McCawley, James D. 1993. 'Contrastive negation and metalinguistic negation'. In Lise M. Dobrin, Lynn Nichols, and Rosa M. Rodriguez (eds.), *Papers from the 27th Regional Meeting of the Chicago Linguistic Society 1991. Part 2: The Parasession on Negation*, pp. 189–206.

McEwan, Ian. 2019. *Machines Like Me and People Like You*. London: Jonathan Cape.

MacFarlane, John. 2005. 'Making sense of relative truth'. *Proceedings of the Aristotelian Society* 105: 321–339.

MacFarlane, John. 2011. 'Relativism and knowledge attributions'. In Sven Bernecker and Duncan Pritchard (eds.), *Routledge Companion to Epistemology*. London: Routledge, pp. 536–544.

MacFarlane, John. 2014. *Assessment Sensitivity: Relative Truth and Its Applications*. Oxford: Oxford University Press.

McGrath, Matthew and Devin Frank. 2018. 'Propositions'. In E. Zalta (ed.), *Stanford Encyclopedia of Philosophy* (online). plato.stanford.edu/entries/propositions/ [accessed 7 August 2022].

Machery, Edouard. 2009. *Doing without Concepts*. Oxford: Oxford University Press.

Machery, Edouard. 2015. 'By default: Concepts are accessed in a context-independent manner'. In Eric Margolis and Stephen Laurence (eds.), *The Conceptual Mind: New Directions in the Study of Concepts*. Cambridge, MA: MIT Press, pp. 567–588.

McLaughlin, Brian and Karen Bennett. 2018. 'Evidentiality'. In Edward Zalta (ed.), *Stanford Encyclopedia of Philosophy* (online). plato.stanford.edu/entries/supervenience/ [accessed 16 January 2021].

McTaggart, John McT. E. 1934. 'The unreality of time'. In *Philosophical Studies*. London: Edward Arnold, pp. 110–131. First published in 1908 in *Mind* 17.

Mahon, James Edwin. 2019. 'Classic philosophical approaches to lying and deception'. In Jörg Meibauer (ed.), *The Oxford Handbook of Lying*. Oxford: Oxford University Press, pp. 13–31.

Manne, Kate. 2019. *Down Girl: The Logic of Misogyny*. Penguin Books.

Mao, LuMing R. 1994. 'Beyond politeness theory: "Face" revisited and renewed'. *Journal of Pragmatics* 21: 451–486.

Margolis, Eric and Stephen Laurence (eds.). 1999. *Concepts: Core Readings*. Cambridge, MA: MIT Press.

Margolis, Eric and Stephen Laurence. 2007. 'The ontology of concepts: Abstract objects or mental representations?' *Noûs* 41: 561–593.

Margolis, Eric and Stephen Laurence (eds.). 2015. *The Conceptual Mind: New Directions in the Study of Concepts*. Cambridge, MA: MIT Press.

Marsh, Jessica. 2018. 'Why say it that way? Evasive answers and politeness theory'. *Journal of Politeness Research* 15: 55–76.

Matthewson, Lisa. 2006. 'Temporal semantics in a superficially tenseless language'. *Linguistics and Philosophy* 29: 673–713.

Mauri, Caterina and Johan van der Auwera. 2012. 'Connectives'. In Keith Allan and Kasia M. Jaszczolt (eds.), *The Cambridge Handbook of Pragmatics*. Cambridge: Cambridge University Press, pp. 377–401.

Meibauer, Jörg. 2014. *Lying at the Semantics–Pragmatics Interface*. Berlin: Mouton de Gruyter.
Meibauer, Jörg. 2019a. 'What is an indirect speech act?'. *Pragmatics and Cognition* 26: 61–84.
Meibauer, Jörg (ed.). 2019b. *The Oxford Handbook of Lying*. Oxford University Press.
Meier, Emar. 2016. 'Attitudes and mental files in Discourse Representation Theory'. *Review of Philosophy and Psychology* 7: 473–490.
Merchant, Jason. 2004. 'Fragments and ellipsis'. *Linguistics and Philosophy* 27: 661–738.
Merchant, Jason. 2010. 'Three types of ellipsis'. In François Recanati, Isidora Stojanovic, and Neftalí Villanueva (eds.), *Context-Dependence, Perspective and Relativity*. Berlin: De Gruyter Mouton, pp. 141–192.
Michaelson, Eliot. 2016. 'The lying test'. *Mind and Language* 31: 470–499.
Michaelson, Eliot and Marga Reimer. 2019. 'Reference'. In Edward Zalta (ed.), *Stanford Encyclopedia of Philosophy* (online). plato.stanford.edu/entries/reference/ [accessed 17 March 2021].
Mill, John Stuart. 1872. *An Examination of Sir William Hamilton's Philosophy*. London: Longmans, Green, Reader, and Dyer. Fourth edition.
Mill, John Stuart. 1959. *A System of Logic: Ratiocinative and Inductive*. London: Longmans. Eighth edition. First published in 1843.
Milsark, Gary. 1977. 'Toward an explanation of certain peculiarities of the existential construction in English'. *Linguistic Analysis* 3: 1–29.
Montague, Richard. 2002. 'The proper treatment of quantification in ordinary English'. In Paul Portner and Barbara H. Partee (eds.), *Formal Semantics: The Essential Readings*. Oxford: Blackwell, pp. 17–34. First published in Jaakko Hintikka, J. M. E. Moravcsik, and Patrick Suppes (eds.). 1973. *Approaches to Natural Language. Proceedings of the 1970 Stanford Workshop on Grammar and Semantics*. Dordrecht: D. Reidel.
Moran, Richard. 1997. 'Metaphor'. In Bob Hale and Crispin Wright (eds.), *A Companion to the Philosophy of Language*. Oxford: Blackwell, pp. 248–268.
Moran, Richard. 2018. *The Exchange of Words: Speech, Testimony, and Intersubjectivity*. Oxford: Oxford University Press.
Mulkern, Ann E. 1996. 'The game of the name'. In Thorstein Fretheim and Jeanette K. Gundel (eds.), *Reference and Referent Accessibility*. Amsterdam: John Benjamins, pp. 235–250.
Müller, Ralph-Axel. 2009. 'Language universals in the brain: How linguistic are they?' In Morten H. Christiansen, Christopher Collins, and Shimon Edelman (eds.), *Language Universals*. Oxford: Oxford University Press, pp. 224–252.
Mulligan, Kevin. 1987. 'Promisings and other social acts: Their constituents and structure'. In *Speech Act and Sachverhalt: Reinach and the Foundations of Realist Phenomenology*. Dordrecht: M. Nijhoff, pp. 29–90.
Musolino, Julien. 2004. 'The semantics and acquisition of number words: Integrating linguistic and developmental perspectives'. *Cognition* 93: 1–41.
Nagel, Thomas. 1986. *The View from Nowhere*. Oxford: Oxford University Press.
Neale, Stephen. 1990. *Descriptions*. Cambridge, MA: MIT Press.
Nelson, Michael. 2019. 'Propositional attitude reports'. In Edward Zalta (ed.), *Stanford Encyclopedia of Philosophy* (online). plato.stanford.edu/entries/prop-attitude-reports/ [accessed 4 February 2021].
Nicolle, Steve and Billy Clark. 1999. 'Experimental pragmatics and what is said: A response to Gibbs and Moise'. *Cognition* 69: 337–354.
Nilsen, Don L. F. and Alleen Pace Nilsen. 2019. *The Language of Humor: An Introduction*. Cambridge: Cambridge University Press.

Noveck, Ira. 2018. *Experimental Pragmatics*. Cambridge: Cambridge University Press.
Noveck, Ira A. and Dan Sperber (eds.). 2004. *Experimental Pragmatics*. Houndmills: Palgrave Macmillan.
Ogden, Charles K. and Ivor A. Richards. 1960. *The Meaning of Meaning*. London: Routledge & Kegan Paul. Tenth edition. First published in 1923.
Palmer, Frank R. 2001. *Mood and Modality*. Cambridge: Cambridge University Press. Second edition.
Parikh, Prashant. 2010. *Language and Equilibrium*. Cambridge, MA: MIT Press.
Parsons, Terence. 1990. *Events in the Semantics of English: A Study in Subatomic Semantics*. Cambridge, MA: MIT Press.
Partee, Barbara H. 1995. 'Lexical semantics and compositionality'. In Lila R. Gleitman and Mark Liberman (eds.), *An Invitation to Cognitive Science*, Vol. 1: Language. Cambridge, MA: MIT Press, pp. 311–360. Second edition.
Partee, Barbara H. 1999. 'Focus, quantification, and semantics–pragmatics issues'. In Peter Bosch and Rob van der Sandt (eds.), *Focus: Linguistic, Cognitive, and Computational Perspectives*. Cambridge: Cambridge University Press, pp. 213–231.
Partee, Barbara H. 2004. 'Some structural analogies between tenses and pronouns in English'. In Barbara H. Partee, *Compositionality in Formal Semantics: Selected Papers by Barbara H. Partee*. Oxford: Blackwell, pp. 50–58. First published in 1973 in *Journal of Philosophy* 70.
Pavlidou, Theodossia. 1994. 'Contrasting German–Greek politeness and the consequences'. *Journal of Pragmatics* 21: 487–511.
Pearson, Hazel. 2013. 'A judge-free semantics for predicates of personal taste'. *Journal of Semantics* 30: 103–154.
Pederson, Eric et al. 1998. 'Semantic typology and spatial conceptualization'. *Language* 74: 557–589.
Peeters, Bert. 2000. 'Setting the scene: Some recent milestones in the lexicon–encyclopedia debate'. In Bert Peeters (ed.), *The Lexicon–Encyclopedia Interface*. Amsterdam: Elsevier, pp. 1–52.
Peleg, Orna and Rachel Giora. 2011. 'Salient meanings: The whens and wheres'. In Kasia M. Jaszczolt and Keith Allan (eds.), *Salience and Defaults in Utterance Processing*. Berlin: De Gruyter Mouton, pp. 35–51.
Pelletier, Francis J. and Nicholas Asher. 1997. 'Generics and defaults'. In Johan van Benthem and Alice ter Meulen (eds.), *Handbook of Logic and Language*. Oxford: Elsevier Science, pp. 1125–1177.
Peräkylä, A. 1997. 'Conversation analysis: A new model of research in doctor–patient communication'. *Journal of the Royal Society of Medicine* 90: 205–208.
Perry, John. 1979. 'The problem of the essential indexical'. *Noûs* 13: 3–21.
Perry, John. 1997. 'Frege on demonstratives'. In Peter Ludlow (ed.), *Readings in the Philosophy of Language*. Cambridge, MA: MIT Press, pp. 693–715. First published in 1977 in *Philosophical Review* 86.
Perry, John. 2001. *Reference and Reflexivity*. Stanford, CA: CSLI Publications.
Perry, John. 2009. 'Directing intentions'. In Joseph Almog and Paolo Leonardi (eds.), *The Philosophy of David Kaplan*. Oxford: Oxford University Press, pp. 187–207.
Peters, Stanley and Dag Westerståhl. 2006. *Quantifiers in Language and Logic*. Oxford: Clarendon Press.
Pinker, Steven and Ray Jackendoff. 2009. 'The components of language: What's specific to language, and what's specific to humans'. In Morten H. Christiansen, Christopher Collins,

and Shimon Edelman (eds.), *Language Universals*. Oxford: Oxford University Press, pp. 126–151.

Pino, Bernardo and Bernardo Aguilera. 2018. 'Machery's alternative to concepts and the problem of content'. *Erkenntnis* 83: 671–691.

Poggi, Francesca and Alessandro Capone (eds.). 2017. *Pragmatics and Law: Practical and Theoretical Perspectives*. Cham: Springer.

Popper, Karl R. 1959. *The Logic of Scientific Discovery*. London: Hutchinson. First published as *Logik der Forschung* in 1934.

Portner, Paul H. 2005. *What Is Meaning? Fundamentals of Formal Semantics*. Oxford: Blackwell.

Portner, Paul. 2009. *Modality*. Oxford: Oxford University Press.

Portner, Paul. 2018. *Mood*. Oxford: Oxford University Press.

Portner, Paul and Barbara H. Partee (eds.). 2002. *Formal Semantics: The Essential Readings*. Oxford: Blackwell.

Potts, Christopher. 2005. *The Logic of Conventional Implicatures*. Oxford: Oxford University Press.

Potts, Christopher. 2007. 'The expressive dimension'. *Theoretical Linguistics* 33: 165–198.

Potts, Christopher. 2012. 'Conventional implicature and expressive content'. In Claudia Maienborn, Klaus von Heusinger, and Paul Portner (eds.), *Semantics: An International Handbook of Natural Language Meaning*, Vol. 2. Berlin: De Gruyter Mouton, pp. 2516–2535.

Potts, Christopher. 2015. 'Presupposition and implicature'. In Shalom Lappin and Chris Fox (eds.), *The Handbook of Contemporary Semantic Theory*. Oxford: John Wiley & Sons, pp. 168–202.

Predelli, Stefano. 2005a. *Contexts: Meaning, Truth, and the Use of Language*. Oxford: Clarendon Press.

Predelli, Stefano. 2005b. 'Painted leaves, context, and semantic analysis'. *Linguistics and Philosophy* 28: 351–374.

Predelli, Stefano. 2011. 'I am still not here now'. *Erkenntnis* 74: 289–303.

Predelli, Stefano. 2013. *Meaning without Truth*. Oxford: Oxford University Press.

Predelli, Stefano. 2014. 'Kaplan's three monsters'. *Analysis* 74: 389–393.

Prinz, Jesse J. 2012. 'Regaining composure: A defence of prototype compositionality'. In Markus Werning, Wolfram Hinzen, and Edouard Machery (eds.), *The Oxford Handbook of Compositionality*. Oxford: Oxford University Press, pp. 437–453.

Prior, Arthur N. 1957. *Time and Modality*. Oxford: Clarendon Press.

Prior, Arthur N. 1967. *Past, Present and Future*. Oxford: Clarendon Press.

Prior, Arthur N. 1968a. *Papers on Time and Tense*. Oxford: Clarendon Press.

Prior, Arthur N. 1968b. 'Now'. *Noûs* 2: 101–119.

Prosser, Simon and François Recanati (eds.). 2012. *Immunity to Error through Misidentification*. Cambridge: Cambridge University Press.

Pulvermüller, Friedemann. 2002. *The Neuroscience of Language: On Brain Circuits of Words and Serial Order*. Cambridge: Cambridge University Press.

Pulvermüller, Friedemann. 2010. 'Brain-language research: Where is the progress?' *Biolinguistics* 4: 255–288.

Pulvermüller, Friedemann. 2012. 'Meaning and the brain: The neurosemantics of referential, interactive, and combinatorial knowledge'. *Journal of Neurolinguistics* 25: 423–459.

Pustejovsky, James. 1995. *The Generative Lexicon*. Cambridge, MA: MIT Press.

Putnam, Hilary. 1975. 'The meaning of "meaning"'. In Hilary Putnam, *Mind, Language and Reality*. Philosophical Papers, Vol. 2. Cambridge: Cambridge University Press, pp. 215–271.

First published in Keith Gunderson (ed.), *Language, Mind and Knowledge*. Minnesota Studies in the Philosophy of Science, Vol. 7. Minneapolis: University of Minnesota Press.

Quine, Willard V. O. 1972. 'Quantifiers and propositional attitudes'. In Ausonio Marras (ed.), *Intentionality, Mind and Language*. Urbana, IL: University of Illinois Press, pp. 402–414. First published in 1956 in *Journal of Philosophy* 53.

Raffman, Diana. 2014. *Unruly Words: A Study of Vague Language*. Oxford: Oxford University Press.

Rayo, Augustín. 2013. 'A plea for semantic localism'. *Noûs* 47: 647–679.

Recanati, François. 1981. 'On Kripke on Donnellan'. In Herman Parret, Marina Sbisà, and Jef Verschueren (eds.), *Possibilities and Limitations of Pragmatics*. Amsterdam: John Benjamins, pp. 593–630.

Recanati, François. 1988. 'Rigidity and direct reference'. *Philosophical Studies* 53: 103–117.

Recanati, François. 1991. 'The pragmatics of what is said'. In Steven Davis (ed.), *Pragmatics: A Reader*. Oxford: Oxford University Press, pp. 97–120. First published in 1989 in *Mind and Language* 4.

Recanati, François. 1993. *Direct Reference: From Language to Thought*. Oxford: Blackwell.

Recanati, François. 1996. 'Domains of discourse'. *Linguistics and Philosophy* 19: 445–475.

Recanati, François. 2000. 'Opacity and the attitudes'. In Alex Orenstein and Petr Kotatko (eds.), *Knowledge, Language and Logic: Questions for Quine*. Dordrecht: Kluwer, pp. 367–406.

Recanati, François. 2002a. 'Unarticulated constituents'. *Linguistics and Philosophy* 25: 299–345.

Recanati, François. 2002b. 'Does linguistic communication rest on inference?'. *Mind and Language* 17: 105–126.

Recanati, François. 2004. *Literal Meaning*. Cambridge: Cambridge University Press.

Recanati, François. 2005. 'Literalism and contextualism: Some varieties'. In Gerhard Preyer and Georg Peter (eds.), *Contextualism in Philosophy: Knowledge, Meaning, and Truth*. Oxford: Clarendon Press, pp. 171–196.

Recanati, François. 2007. Reply to Carston 2007. In Maria J. Frápolli (ed.), *Saying, Meaning and Referring: Essays on François Recanati's Philosophy of Language*. Basingstoke: Palgrave Macmillan, pp. 49–54.

Recanati, François. 2010. *Truth-Conditional Pragmatics*. Oxford: Clarendon Press.

Recanati, François. 2012a. 'Contextualism: Some varieties'. In Keith Allan and Kasia M. Jaszczolt (eds.), *The Cambridge Handbook of Pragmatics*. Cambridge: Cambridge University Press, pp. 135–149.

Recanati, François. 2012b. 'Pragmatic enrichment'. In Gillian Russell and Delia Graff Fara (eds.), *The Routledge Companion to Philosophy of Language*. New York: Routledge, pp. 67–78.

Recanati, François. 2012c. 'Compositionality, flexibility, and context dependence'. In Markus Werning, Wolfram Hinzen, and Edouard Machery (eds.), *The Oxford Handbook of Compositionality*. Oxford: Oxford University Press, pp. 175–191.

Recanati, François. 2016. 'Indexical thought: The communication problem'. In Manuel García-Carpintero and Stephan Torre (eds.), *About Oneself: De Se Thought and Communication*. Oxford: Oxford University Press, pp. 141–178.

Reichenbach, Hans. 1948. *Elements of Symbolic Logic*. New York: Macmillan.

Reid, Thomas. 1788. *Essays on the Active Powers of Man*. Edinburgh: John Bell and G.G.J. & J. Robinson.

Reimer, Marga. 1995. 'Performative utterances: A reply to Bach and Harnish'. *Linguistics and Philosophy* 18: 655–675.

Richard, Mark. 1990. *Propositional Attitudes: An Essay on Thoughts and How We Ascribe Them*. Cambridge: Cambridge University Press.
Richard, Mark. 2008. *When Truth Gives Out*. Oxford: Oxford University Press.
Richard, Mark. 2018. 'How do slurs mean?'. In David Sosa (ed.), *Bad Words: Philosophical Perspectives on Slurs*. Oxford: Oxford University Press, pp. 155–167.
Richards, Ivor A. 1936. *The Philosophy of Rhetoric*. Oxford: Oxford University Press.
Riemer, Nick. 2010. *Introducing Semantics*. Cambridge: Cambridge University Press.
Ritchie, L. David. 2013. *Metaphor*. Cambridge: Cambridge University Press.
Roberts, Craige. 2014. 'Indexicality: *de se* semantics and pragmatics'. Ms, Ohio State University. www.asc.ohio-state.edu/roberts.21/Roberts.Indexicality.pdf [accessed 16 March 2021].
Rohrer, Tim. 2007. 'Embodiment and experientialism'. In Dirk Geeraerts and Hubert Cuyckens (eds.), *The Oxford Handbook of Cognitive Linguistics*. Oxford: Oxford University Press, pp. 25–47.
Rooth, Mats. 1996. 'Focus'. In Shalom Lappin (ed.), *The Handbook of Contemporary Semantic Theory*. Oxford: Blackwell, pp. 271–297.
Rosch, Eleanor. 1975. 'Cognitive representation of semantic categories'. *Journal of Experimental Psychology, General* 104: 193–233.
Ross, John Robert. 1967. *Constraints on Variables in Syntax*. PhD dissertation, MIT.
Ross, John Robert. 1970. 'On declarative sentences'. In R. A. Jacobs and P. S. Rosenbaum (eds.), *Readings in English Transformational Grammar*. Waltham, MA: Ginn & Co., pp. 222–272.
Rothstein, Susan. 2004. *Structuring Events: A Study in the Semantics of Lexical Aspect*. Oxford: Blackwell.
Rothstein, Susan. 2017. *Semantics for Counting and Measuring*. Cambridge: Cambridge University Press.
Rovelli, Carlo. 2018. *The Order of Time*. London: Allen Lane. Transl. by Erica Segre and Simon Carnell. First published in 2017 as *L'ordine del tempo*. Milan: Adelphi Edizione SPA.
Rumelhart, David E. and James L. McClelland (eds.). 1986. *Parallel Distributed Processing: Explorations in the Microstructure of Cognition*, Vol. 1. Cambridge, MA: MIT Press.
Russell, Bertrand. 1956. 'The philosophy of logical atomism'. In Bertrand Russell, *Logic and Knowledge. Essays 1901–1950*. London: George Allen & Unwin, pp. 175–281. First published in 1918–19 in *The Monist* 28–29.
Russell, Bertrand. 1962. *The Problems of Philosophy*. London: Oxford University Press. First published in 1912. London: Williams and Norgate.
Russell, Bertrand. 1996. 'On denoting'. In Aloysius P. Martinich (ed.), *The Philosophy of Language*. Oxford: Oxford University Press, pp. 199–207. Third edition. First published in 1905 in *Mind* 14.
Russell, Bertrand. 1997. 'Descriptions'. In Peter Ludlow (ed.), *Readings in the Philosophy of Language*. Cambridge, MA: MIT Press, pp. 323–333. Originally published in 1919 in *Introduction to Mathematical Philosophy*. London: George Allen and Unwin, pp. 167–180.
Ruytenbeek, Nicolas. 2021. *Indirect Speech Acts*. Cambridge: Cambridge University Press.
Sacks, Harvey, Emmanuel A. Schegloff, and Gail Jefferson. 1974. 'A simplest systematics for the organization of turn-taking for conversation'. *Language* 50: 696–735.
Sadock, Jerry M. 1984. 'Whither radical pragmatics?'. In Deborah Schiffrin (ed.), *Georgetown University Round Table on Languages and Linguistics 1984*. Washington, DC: Georgetown University Press, pp. 139–149.
Sadock, Jerry M. 2004. 'Speech acts', In Laurence R. Horn and Gregory Ward (eds.), *The Handbook of Pragmatics*. Oxford: Blackwell, pp. 53–73.

# References

Saeed, John I. 2016. *Semantics*. Chichester: Wiley-Blackwell. Fourth edition.
Sainsbury, Mark. 2014. 'Fishy business'. *Analysis* 74: 3–5.
Salmon, Nathan. 1986. *Frege's Puzzle*. Cambridge, MA: MIT Press.
van der Sandt, Rob A. 1988. *Context and Presupposition*. London: Croom Helm.
van der Sandt, Rob A. 1992. 'Presupposition projection as anaphora resolution'. *Journal of Semantics* 9: 333–377.
van der Sandt, Rob A. 2012. 'Presupposition and accommodation in discourse'. In Keith Allan and Kasia M. Jaszczolt (eds.), *The Cambridge Handbook of Pragmatics*. Cambridge: Cambridge University Press, pp. 329–350.
Saul, Jennifer. 1997. 'Substitution and simple sentences'. *Analysis* 57: 102–108.
Saul, Jennifer. 2002. 'What is said and psychological reality; Grice's project and relevance theorists' criticisms'. *Linguistics and Philosophy* 25: 347–372.
Saul, Jennifer. 2007. *Simple Sentences, Substitution, and Intuitions*. Oxford: Oxford University Press.
Saul, Jennifer. 2012. *Lying, Misleading, and What Is Said: An Exploration in Philosophy of Language and Ethics*. Oxford: Oxford University Press
de Saussure, Ferdinand. 1983. *Course in General Linguistics*. Transl. by R. Harris. London: Duckworth. First published as *Cours de linguistique générale* in 1916. Paris: Éditions Payot.
Savva, Eleni. 2017. *Subsentential Speech from a Contextualist Perspective*. PhD thesis, University of Cambridge.
Sayre-McCord, Geoff. 2012. 'Metaethics'. In Edward Zalta (ed.), *Stanford Encyclopedia of Philosophy* (online). plato.stanford.edu/entries/metaethics/ [accessed 5 August 2021].
Schiffer, Stephen. 1987. *Remnants of Meaning*. Cambridge, MA: MIT Press.
Schiffer, Stephen. 1992. 'Belief ascription'. *Journal of Philosophy* 89: 499–521.
Schiffer, Stephen. 1993. 'Actual-language relations'. In James E. Tomberlin (ed.), *Language and Logic, 1993. Philosophical Perspectives Series 7*. Atascadero, CA: Ridgeview, pp. 231–258.
Schiffer, Stephen. 1994. 'A paradox of meaning'. *Noûs* 28: 279–324.
Schiffer, Stephen. 1996. 'The hidden-indexical theory's logical-form problem: A rejoinder'. *Analysis* 56: 92–97.
Schiffer, Stephen. 2003. *The Things We Mean*. Oxford: Clarendon Press.
Schiffrin, Deborah. 1987. *Discourse Markers*. Cambridge: Cambridge University Press.
Schlenker, Philippe. 2003. 'A plea for monsters'. *Linguistics and Philosophy* 26: 29–120.
Schlenker, Philippe. 2007. 'Expressive presuppositions'. *Theoretical Linguistics* 33: 237–245.
Schlenker, Philippe. 2019. 'Gestural semantics: Replicating the typology of linguistic inferences with pro- and post-speech gestures'. *Natural Language and Linguistic Theory* 37: 735–784.
Schroeter, Laura. 2017. 'Two-Dimensional Semantics'. In Edward Zalta (ed.), *Stanford Encyclopedia of Philosophy* (online). plato.stanford.edu/entries/two-dimensional-semantics/ [accessed 16 March 2021].
Schurz, Gerhard. 2012. 'Prototypes and their composition from an evolutionary point of view'. In Markus Werning, Wolfram Hinzen, and Edouard Machery (eds.), *The Oxford Handbook of Compositionality*. Oxford: Oxford University Press, pp. 530–553.
Searle, John R. 1969. *Speech Acts: An Essay in the Philosophy of Language*. Cambridge: Cambridge University Press.
Searle, John R. 1979a. 'Referential and attributive'. In John Searle. *Expression and Meaning: Studies in the Theory of Speech Acts*. Cambridge: Cambridge University Press, pp. 137–161. First published in *The Monist* 62.
Searle, John R. 1979b. 'A taxonomy of illocutionary acts'. In *Expression and Meaning: Studies in the Theory of Speech Acts*. Cambridge: Cambridge University Press, pp. 1–29. First

published in 1975 in Keith Gunderson (ed.), *Language, Mind and Knowledge. Minnesota Studies in the Philosophy of Science*, Vol 7. University of Minnesota Press.

Searle, John R. 1983. *Intentionality. An Essay in the Philosophy of Mind*. Cambridge: Cambridge University Press.

Searle, John R. 1990. 'Collective intentions and actions'. In Philip R. Cohen, Jerry Morgan, and Martha E. Pollack (eds.), *Intentions in Communication*. Cambridge, MA: MIT Press, pp. 401–415.

Searle, John R. 1991. 'Response: Meaning, intentionality, and speech acts'. In Ernest Lepore and Robert van Gulick (eds.), *John Searle and His Critics*. Oxford: Basil Blackwell, pp. 81–102.

Searle, John R. 1993. 'Metaphor'. In Andrew Ortony (ed.), *Metaphor and Thought*. Cambridge: Cambridge University Press, pp. 83–111. Second edition. First published in 1979 in John R. Searle. *Expression and Meaning: Studies in the Theory of Speech Acts*. Cambridge: Cambridge University Press.

Searle, John R. 1994. 'How performatives work'. In Robert M. Harnish (ed.), *Basic Topics in the Philosophy of Language*. New York: Harvester Wheatsheaf, pp. 74–95. First published in 1989 in *Linguistics & Philosophy* 12.

Searle, John R. 1996a. 'What is a speech act?' In Aloysius P. Martinich (ed.), *The Philosophy of Language*. Oxford: Oxford University Press, pp. 231–244. Third edition. First published in 1965 in Max Black (ed.), *Philosophy in America*. Ithaca: Cornell University Press.

Searle, John R. 1996b. 'Indirect speech acts'. In Aloysius P. Martinich (ed.), *The Philosophy of Language*. Oxford: Oxford University Press, pp. 168–182. Third edition. First published in 1975 in Peter Cole and Jerry L. Morgan (eds.), *Syntax and Semantics*, Vol. 3: Speech Acts. New York: Academic Press.

Searle, John R. and Daniel Vanderveken. 1985. *Foundations of Illocutionary Logic*. Cambridge: Cambridge University Press.

Segal, Gabriel M. A. 2000. *A Slim Book about Narrow Content*. Cambridge, MA: MIT Press.

Shanon, Benny. 1976. 'On the two kinds of presuppositions in natural language'. *Foundations of Language* 14: 247–249.

Shapiro, Stewart. 2006. *Vagueness in Context*. Oxford: Clarendon Press.

Shklovsky, Kirill and Yasutada Sudo. 2014. 'The syntax of monsters'. *Linguistic Inquiry* 45: 381–402.

Siewierska, Anna. 2004. *Person*. Cambridge: Cambridge University Press.

Sileo, Roberto and Kasia M. Jaszczolt. 2021. 'Towards a conceptual-semantic model of cross-sentential anaphora'. *Cambridge Occasional Papers in Linguistics* 13: 63–97.

Simons, Mandy, Judith Tonhauser, David Beaver, and Craige Roberts. 2010. 'What projects and why'. In *Proceedings of SALT* 20, pp. 309–327.

Smith, Barry. 1984. 'Ten conditions on a theory of speech acts'. *Theoretical Linguistics* 11: 310–330.

Smith, Barry. 1990. 'Towards a history of Speech Act Theory'. In Armin Burkhardt (ed.), *Speech Acts, Meaning and Intentions: Critical Approaches to the Philosophy of John R. Searle*. Berlin: Walter de Gruyter, pp. 29–61.

Smith, Barry. 1999. 'Truth and the visual field'. In Jean Petitot et al. (eds.), *Naturalizing Phenomenology: Issues in Contemporary Phenomenology and Cognitive Science*. Stanford, CA: Stanford University Press, pp. 317–329.

Smith, Nicholas J. J. 2008. *Vagueness and Degrees of Truth*. Oxford: Oxford University Press.

Soames, Scott. 1997. 'Direct reference, propositional attitudes, and semantic content'. In Peter Ludlow (ed.), *Readings in the Philosophy of Language*. Cambridge, MA: MIT Press, pp. 921–962. First published in 1987 in *Philosophical Topics* 15.

Soames, Scott. 2014. 'Cognitive propositions'. In Jeffrey C. King, Scott Soames, and Jeff Speaks (eds.), *New Thinking about Propositions*. Oxford: Oxford University Press, pp. 91–124.

Soames, Scott. 2019. 'Propositions as cognitive acts'. *Synthese* 196: 1369–1383.

Sosa, David (ed.). 2018. *Bad Words: Philosophical Perspectives on Slurs*. Oxford: Oxford University Press.

Spector, Benjamin and Yasutada Sudo. 2017. 'Presupposed ignorance and exhaustification: How scalar implicatures and presuppositions interact'. *Linguistics and Philosophy* 40: 473–517.

Sperber, Dan and Deirdre Wilson. 1995. *Relevance: Communication and Cognition*. Oxford: Blackwell. Second edition. First edition published in 1986.

Sperber, Dan and Deirdre Wilson. 2012. 'Pragmatics, modularity and mindreading'. In Deirdre Wilson and Dan Sperber, *Meaning and Relevance*. Cambridge: Cambridge University Press, pp. 261–278. First published in 2002 in *Mind and Language* 17.

Srioutai, Jiranthara. 2006. *Time Conceptualization in Thai with Special Reference to $d_1ay_1^{II}$, $kh_3oe$:$y$, $k_1aml_3ang$, $y_3u$:[I] and $c_1a$*. PhD thesis, University of Cambridge.

Stainton, Robert J. 2006. *Words and Thoughts: Subsentences, Ellipsis, and the Philosophy of Language*. Oxford: Clarendon.

Stalnaker, Robert C. 1973. 'Presuppositions'. *Journal of Philosophical Logic* 2: 447–457.

Stalnaker, Robert C. 1997. 'Reference and necessity'. In Bob Hale and Crispin Wright (eds.), *A Companion to the Philosophy of Language*. Oxford: Basil Blackwell, pp. 534–554.

Stalnaker, Robert C. 1999a. *Context and Content: Essays on Intentionality in Speech and Thought*. Oxford: Oxford University Press.

Stalnaker, Robert C. 1999b. 'Indicative conditionals'. In Robert C. Stalnaker, *Context and Content: Essays on Intentionality in Speech and Thought*. Oxford: Oxford University Press, pp. 63–77. First published in 1975 in *Philosophia* 5.

Stalnaker, Robert C. 1999c. 'Assertion'. In Robert C. Stalnaker, *Context and Content: Essays on Intentionality in Speech and Thought*. Oxford: Oxford University Press, pp. 78–95. First published in 1978 in *Syntax and Semantics* 9.

Stalnaker, Robert C. 1999d. 'Pragmatic presuppositions'. In Robert C. Stalnaker, *Context and Content: Essays on Intentionality in Speech and Thought*. Oxford: Oxford University Press, pp. 47–62. First published in 1974 in Milton K. Munitz and Peter K. Unger (eds.), *Semantics and Philosophy*. New York: New York University Press.

Stalnaker, Robert C. 2008. *Our Knowledge of the Internal World*. Oxford: Oxford University Press.

Stalnaker, Robert C. 2011. 'Conditional propositions and conditional assertions'. In Andy Egan and Brian Weatherson (eds.), *Epistemic Modality*. Oxford: Oxford University Press, pp. 227–248.

Stalnaker, Robert C. 2014. *Context*. Oxford: Oxford University Press.

Stanley, Jason. 2000. 'Context and logical form'. *Linguistics and Philosophy* 23: 391–434.

Stanley, Jason. 2002. 'Making it articulated'. *Mind and Language* 17: 149–168.

Stanley, Jason. 2007. 'Postscript'. In Jason Stanley, *Language in Context: Selected Essays*. Oxford: Clarendon Press, pp. 248–260.

Stanley, Jason and Zoltán Gendler Szabó. 2000. 'On quantifier domain restriction'. *Mind and Language* 15: 219–261.

Stanley, Jason and Timothy Williamson. 1995. 'Quantifiers and context-dependence'. *Analysis* 55: 291–295.

Steedman, Mark. 1997. 'Temporality'. In Johan van Benthem and Alice ter Meulen (eds.), *Handbook of Logic and Language*. Oxford: Elsevier Science, pp. 895–938.

Stenius, Erik. 1967. 'Mood and language-game'. *Synthese* 17: 254–274.

Stern, Josef. 2000. *Metaphor in Context*. Cambridge, MA: MIT Press.

Sternau, Marit et al. 2015. 'Levels of interpretation: New tools for characterizing intended meanings'. *Journal of Pragmatics* 84: 86–101.

Stojnić, Una, Matthew Stone, and Ernest Lepore. 2017. 'Discourse and logical form: Pronouns, attention and coherence'. *Linguistics and Philosophy* 40: 519–547.

Stojnić, Una, Matthew Stone, and Ernest Lepore. 2020. 'Pointing things out: In defense of attention and coherence'. *Linguistics and Philosophy* 43: 139–148.

Stokke, Andreas. 2018. *Lying and Insincerity*. Oxford: Oxford University Press.

Stotts, Megan Henricks. 2020. 'Toward a sharp semantics/pragmatics distinction'. *Synthese* 197: 185–208.

Strawson, Peter F. 1964. 'Intention and convention in speech acts'. *Philosophical Review* 73: 439–460.

Strawson, Peter F. 1997. 'On referring'. In Peter Ludlow (ed.), *Readings in the Philosophy of Language*. Cambridge, MA: MIT Press, pp. 335–359. First published in 1950 in *Mind* 59.

de Swart, Henriëtte. 1998. *Introduction to Natural Language Semantics*. Stanford, CA: CSLI.

Szabó, Zoltán Gendler. 2000. 'Compositionality as supervenience'. *Linguistics and Philosophy* 23: 475–505.

Szabó, Zoltán Gendler. 2018. 'What is a quantifier?'. *Analysis* 78: 463–472.

Szabó, Zoltán Gendler. 2020. 'Compositionality'. In Edward Zalta (ed.), *Stanford Encyclopedia of Philosophy* (online). plato.stanford.edu/entries/compositionality/ [accessed 29 August 2020].

Szabó, Zoltán Gendler and Richmond H. Thomason. 2019. *Philosophy of Language*. Cambridge: Cambridge University Press.

Szabolcsi, Anna. 2010. *Quantification*. Cambridge: Cambridge University Press.

Talmy, Leonard. 1985. 'Lexicalization patterns: Semantic structure in lexical forms'. In Timothy Shopen (ed.), *Language Typology and Syntactic Description*, Vol. 3: Grammatical Categories and the Lexicon. Cambridge: Cambridge University Press, pp. 57–149.

Talmy, Leonard. 1996. 'The windowing of attention in language'. In Masayoshi Shibatani and Sandra A. Thompson (eds.), *Grammatical Constructions: Their Form and Meaning*. Oxford: Oxford University Press, pp. 235–287.

Talmy, Leonard. 2000. *Toward a Cognitive Semantics* (2 volumes). Cambridge, MA: MIT Press.

Tanaka, Hiroako. 2012. 'Scalar implicature in Japanese: Contrastive *wa* and intersubjectivity'. Paper presented at the First International Conference of the American Pragmatics Association (AMPRA 1), Charlotte, North Carolina.

Tannen, Deborah. 1994. *Gender and Discourse*. Oxford: Oxford University Press.

Tarski, Alfred. 1933. *Pojęcie prawdy w językach nauk dedukcyjnych*. Warsaw: Towarzystwo Naukowe Warszawskie.

Tarski, Alfred. 1952. 'The semantic conception of truth'. In Leonard Linsky (ed.), *Semantics and the Philosophy of Language*. Urbana, IL: University of Illinois Press, pp. 13–47. First published in 1944 in *Philosophy and Phenomenological Research* 4.

Terkourafi, Marina. 2012. 'Politeness and pragmatics'. In Keith Allan and Kasia M. Jaszczolt (eds.), *The Cambridge Handbook of Pragmatics*. Cambridge: Cambridge University Press, pp. 617–637.

Van Tiel, Bob, Ira Noveck, and Mikhail Kissine. 2018. 'Reasoning with "some"'. *Journal of Semantics* 35: 757–797.

Tiersma, Peter M. and Lawrence M. Solan. 2012. *The Oxford Handbook of Language and Law*. Oxford: Oxford University Press.

Tonhauser, Judith. 2011. 'Temporal reference in Paraguayan Guaraní, a tenseless language'. *Linguistics and Philosophy* 34: 257–303.

Tonhauser, Judith, David Beaver, Craige Roberts, and Mandy Simons. 2013. 'Toward a taxonomy of projective content'. *Language* 89: 66–109.

Tonhauser, Judith, David I. Beaver, and Judith Degen. 2018. 'How projective is projective content? Gradience in projectivity and at-issueness'. *Journal of Semantics* 35: 495–542.

Toosarvandani, Maziar. 2016. 'The temporal interpretation of clause chaining in Northern Paiute'. *Language* 92: 850–889.

Traugott, Elizabeth Closs. 2004. 'Historical pragmatics'. In Laurence R. Horn and Gregory Ward (eds.), *The Handbook of Pragmatics*. Oxford: Blackwell, pp. 538–561.

Traugott, Elizabeth Closs. 2012. 'Pragmatics and language change'. In Keith Allan and Kasia M. Jaszczolt (eds.), *The Cambridge Handbook of Pragmatics*. Cambridge: Cambridge University Press, pp. 549–565.

Travis, Charles. 2006. 'Psychologism'. In Ernest Lepore and Barry C. Smith (eds.), *The Oxford Handbook of Philosophy of Language*. Oxford: Clarendon Press, pp. 103–126.

Travis, Charles. 2008a. 'Pragmatics'. In Charles Travis, *Occasion-Sensitivity: Selected Essays*. Oxford: Oxford University Press, pp. 109–129. First published in Bob Hale and Crispin Wright (eds.). 1997. *A Companion to the Philosophy of Language*. Oxford: B. Blackwell.

Travis, Charles. 2008b. *Occasion-Sensitivity: Selected Essays*. Oxford: Oxford University Press.

Truswell, Robert (ed.). 2019. *The Oxford Handbook of Event Structure*, E-book. Oxford: Oxford University Press. DOI: 10.1093/oxfordhb/9780199685318.001.0001.

Tsohatzidis, Savas L. (ed.). 1994. *Foundations of Speech Act Theory: Philosophical and Linguistic Perspectives*. London: Routledge.

Ungerer, Friedrich and Hans-Jörg Schmid. 1996. *An Introduction to Cognitive Linguistics*. London: Longman.

Vallesi, Antonino, Malcolm A. Binns, and Tim Shallice. 2008. 'An effect of spatial-temporal association of response codes: Understanding the cognitive representations of time'. *Cognition* 107: 501–527.

Vanderveken, Daniel. 1990a. *Meaning and Speech Acts*, Vol 1: Principles of Language Use. Cambridge: Cambridge University Press.

Vanderveken, Daniel. 1990b. 'On the unification of Speech Act Theory and formal semantics'. In Philip R. Cohen, Jerry Morgan, and Martha E. Pollack (eds.), *Intentions in Communication*. Cambridge, MA: MIT Press, pp. 195–220.

Vanderveken, Daniel. 1991. *Meaning and Speech Acts*, Vol 2: Formal Semantics of Success and Satisfaction. Cambridge: Cambridge University Press.

Vanderveken, Daniel. 1994. 'A complete formulation of a simple logic of elementary illocutionary acts'. In Savas L. Tsohatzidis (ed.), *Foundations of Speech Act Theory: Philosophical and Linguistic Perspectives*. London: Routledge, pp. 99–131.

Vanderveken, Daniel and Susumu Kubo (eds.). 2001. *Essays in Speech Act Theory*. Amsterdam: John Benjamins.

Vendler, Zeno. 1967. *Linguistics in Philosophy*. Ithaca, NY: Cornell University Press.

Venhuizen, Noortje J., Johan Bos, Petra Hendriks, and Harm Brouwer. 2018. 'Discourse semantics with information structure'. *Journal of Semantics* 35: 127–169.

Viebahn, Emanuel. 2020a. 'Ways of using words: On semantic intentions'. *Philosophy and Phenomenological Research* 100: 93–117.

Viebahn, Emanuel. 2020b. 'Lying with presuppositions'. *Noûs* 54: 731–751.

Walker, Marilyn A., Aravind K. Joshi, and Ellen F. Prince (eds.). 1998. *Centering Theory in Discourse*. Oxford: Clarendon Press.

Watts, Richard J. 2003. *Politeness*. Cambridge: Cambridge University Press.

Weiner, Matthew. 2006. 'Are all conversational implicatures cancellable?'. *Analysis* 66: 127–130.

Weissman, Benjamin and Marina Terkourafi. 2019. 'Are false implicatures lies? An empirical investigation'. *Mind and Language* 34: 221–246.

Werning, Markus, Wolfram Hinzen, and Edouard Machery (eds.). 2012. *The Oxford Handbook of Compositionality*. Oxford: Oxford University Press.

Westerståhl, Dag. 1985. 'Determiners and context sets'. In Johan van Benthem and Alice ter Meulen (eds.), *Generalized Quantifiers in Natural Language*. Dordrecht: Foris, pp. 45–71.

Westerståhl, Dag. 2019. 'Generalized quantifiers'. In Edward Zalta (ed.), *Stanford Encyclopedia of Philosophy* (online). plato.stanford.edu/entries/generalized-quantifiers/ [accessed 21 February 2021].

Whorf, Benjamin L. 1956. 'Science and linguistics'. In John B. Carroll (ed.), *Language, Thought and Reality: Selected Writings of Benjamin Lee Whorf*. Cambridge, MA: MIT Press. 207–219.

Wierzbicka, Anna. 1985. 'Different cultures, different languages, different speech acts: Polish vs. English'. *Journal of Pragmatics* 9: 145–178.

Wierzbicka, Anna. 1991. *Cross-Cultural Pragmatics: The Semantics of Human Interaction*. Berlin: Mouton de Gruyter.

Wierzbicka, Anna. 1996. *Semantics: Primes and Universals*. Oxford: Oxford University Press.

Wierzbicka, Anna. 2003. *Cross-Cultural Pragmatics: The Semantics of Human Interaction*. Berlin: Mouton de Gruyter. Second edition. First published in 1991.

Wierzbicka, Anna. 2014. *Imprisoned in English: The Hazards of English as a Default Language*. Oxford: Oxford University Press.

Williamson, Timothy. 1994. *Vagueness*. London: Routledge.

Williamson, Timothy. 2020. *Suppose and Tell: The Semantics and Heuristics of Conditionals*. Oxford: Oxford University Press.

Wilson, Deirdre. 1975. *Presuppositions and Non-Truth-Conditional Semantics*. London: Academic Press.

Wilson, Deirdre and Robyn Carston. 2019. 'Pragmatics and the challenge of "non-propositional" effects'. *Journal of Pragmatics* 145: 31–38.

Wilson, Deirdre and Dan Sperber. 2012a. 'Truthfulness and relevance'. In Deirdre Wilson and Dan Sperber (eds.), *Meaning and Relevance*. Cambridge: Cambridge University Press, pp. 47–83. First published in 2002 in *Mind* 111.

Wilson, Deirdre and Dan Sperber (eds.). 2012b. *Meaning and Relevance*. Cambridge: Cambridge University Press.

# References

Wilson, Robert A. and Lucia Foglia. 2015. 'Embodied cognition'. In Edward Zalta (ed.), *Stanford Encyclopedia of Philosophy* (online). plato.stanford.edu/entries/embodied-cognition/ [accessed 21 February 2021].

Wiltschko, Martina. 2021. *The Grammar of Interactional Language*. Cambridge: Cambridge University Press.

Winograd, Terry. 1972. 'Understanding natural language'. *Cognitive Psychology* 3: 1–191.

Witek, Maciej. 2022. 'An Austinian alternative to the Gricean perspective on meaning and communication'. *Journal of Pragmatics* 201: 60–75.

Wittgenstein, Ludwig. 1958. *Philosophische Untersuchungen/Philosophical Investigations*. Oxford: B. Blackwell. Second edition. First published in 1953.

Wittgenstein, Ludwig. 1980. *Remarks on the Philosophy of Psychology/Bemerkungen über die Philosophie der Psychologie*, Vol. 1. Transl. by G. E. M. Anscombe. Oxford: Blackwell.

Wittgenstein, Ludwig. 1984. 'The language of sense data and private experience I, II'. Notes taken by Rush Rhees of Wittgenstein's lectures, 1936. *Philosophical Investigations* 7: 1–45, 101–140.

Wittgenstein, Ludwig. 1988. *Wittgenstein's Lectures on Philosophical Psychology 1946–47*. Edited by Peter T. Geach. New York: Harvester Wheatsheaf.

Zerubavel, Eviatar. 2018. *Taken for Granted: The Remarkable Power of the Unremarkable*. Princeton, NJ: Princeton University Press.

Zufferey, Sandrine, Jacques Moeschler, and Anne Reboul. 2019. *Implicatures*. Cambridge: Cambridge University Press.

Zwicky, Arnold M. and Jerrold M. Sadock. 1975. 'Ambiguity tests and how to fail them'. In John P. Kimball (ed.), *Syntax and Semantics*, Vol. 4. New York: Academic Press, pp. 1–36.

# Index

absolute tense, 135
abstraction operator (lambda operator (λ)), 72–73
abstractions, 62
accenting, 228
accommodation, 226–229
accountability, 331, 333–334, 336
adequacy
   criterion of, 15, 158, 164
adjectives
   classes, 65
   numerals as, 125
adjustment, 271
adverbial clauses, conditionals as, 95
adverbials, and focus, 222–223
adverbs, as temporal locators, 134
advising, 321
AI (artificial intelligence), 1
Aikhenvald, Alexandra, evidentiality, 153
alethic modality, 147
algorithms, humans as, 361–362
Allan, Keith, 249, 352
Allan, Keith and Kate Burridge, 351
alternative semantics (Rooth), 220–221
ambiguity
   in conjunctions, 80
   in definite descriptions, 192–194
   in negation, 103–108
   in numerals, 125–126, 127–129
   in word senses, 37–38
   logical form, 50–51
   necessity for translations to logical forms, 53–54
   of *or*, 89–90
   semantic, 261
ambiguity tests, 103–105
ambiguous logic, 37
ambiguous semantic representations, 37
Ameka, Felix K. and Marina Terkourafi, 242
Amharic language, monster contexts, 208–209
analytic sentences, 46
   logical form, 48–49
anaphora
   in presupposition, 226, 228–229
   Scale of Accessibility, 184–185
   temporal, 137–138
anchors, 159–160
Ancient Greek language, subjunctive, 150
*and*
   absence in some languages, 109
   ambiguity, 80
   meanings, 80
   multiple meanings, 87–88
   temporal ordering, 86–87
Anderson, Luvell and Ernie Lepore, 351
anglocentricity
   of Grice's maxims, 242
   of politeness maxims, 342
antecedents, linked with consequents, 95
applications, 295
Approbation maxim, 342
Aquinas, Thomas, 35
Ariel, Mira, 123, 277, 315
   anaphor scales, 184–185
Ariel, Mira and Caterina Mauri, 90
Aristotle, 53, 98, 299, 301, 334
   existential operators, 106
art, non-linguistic thought, 33
Arundale, Robert B., 252, 332–333, 347
Asher, Nicholas, 37
Asher, Nicholas and Alex Lascarides, 84–85, 251
   rhetorical relations, 229
aspectual distinctions, 133–134
assertion, 329–330
   lying as type of, 339
assignment functions, 72
assumptions, 4–5, 243
   compositionality as, 66
   methodological and ontological, 275–276
A-theory, 142, 143
at-issue content, 233–234, 247–248, 355, 356
Atlas, Jay, 105, 262
   semantic underdetermination, 106–107
   semantics–pragmatics interface, 107–108
Atlas, Jay and Ruth Kempson (Atlas–Kempson thesis), 261

## Index

atomism, 25
attention theory, 86
attitude reports, 154–164
attitudes, beliefs based on, 14
Augustine, 333, 338
Austin, John L., 96, 262, 316, 318–319, 325
automatic indexicals, 204
Availability Principle (Recanati), 265

Bach, Emmon, 131
Bach, Kent, 287
   referential intention, 240
   semantics/pragmatics boundary, 282–284
Bach, Kent and Robert M. Harnish, 240
background beliefs, 231
background knowledge, 254
backward-looking centres, 217
bad language, 349–357
bald-faced lies, 339
banter, 343, 350
Barwise, Jon and Robin Cooper, generalized quantifiers, 117
basic categories, 68
Beaver, David, 233
belief operators, 208–209
beliefs
   context sensitive, 162
   *de re* vs. *de dicto*, 156–158, 159
   in possible worlds, 158
   regarding proper names, 162–163
   theories, 160–161
biconditionals, 93–94
binary distinctions, 132–133
binary features, 23
binding theory
   of presupposition, 225, 227–229
biscuit conditionals, 96
bi-uniqueness, 25
blends, 309
Blutner, Reinhard and Henk Zeevat, 258
Borg, Emma, 287, 334
   *Minimal Semantics*, 285
Bosanquet, Bernard, 98
'bottom-up' approach, 1
bouletic modality, 148
bound variables, 201
boundaries, 313–314
bounding, of quantifiers, 122
Brentano, Franz, 317
broad content, 25
Brown, Penelope and Stephen C. Levinson, 343, 345–346, 348
B-theory, 142
Bühler, Karl, 317
bullshitting, 338, *see also* lying

Camp, Elisabeth, 301
cancellability, 255, 274, 279–281
   of implicature, 244–245
cancellation, and metaphor, 300
Cappelen, Herman, 29
Cappelen, Herman and Ernie Lepore, 287
   *Insensitive Semantics*, 285–286
Cappelen, Herman and Josh Dever, 349
Carnap, Rudolf, 69
Carnapian propositions, 7
Carruthers, Peter, natural language for thinking, 35
Carson, Thomas, 340
Carston, Robyn, 83, 84, 102, 243, 262
   explicature, 264–265
   literality, 291
   metaphor, 304
   pragmatic enrichment, 263–264
cataphora, 179
categorial grammars, 67–68
causal (-historical) theory of reference, 185
c-commanding, 168
centering theory, 217–218
Central Meaner, 277
Chalmers, David J., 207
character
   and literalness, 294
   vs. content, 205, 304
Chierchia, Gennaro, 287–288
child-directed speech, 210
Chomsky, Noam
   generative grammar, 5
   universal grammar, 33
Church, Alonzo, lambda operator ($\lambda$), 73
Ciardelli, Ivano, Jeroen Groenendijk, and Floris Roelofsen, 57
Cicero, 299
Clark, Herbert, 332, 333
co-construction of meaning, 333, 358, *see also* joint construction of meaning
coding time (time of utterance), 199
cognitive approach to metaphor, 307–312
cognitive defaults (CDs), 274, 276
cognitive linguistics, 11, 108
cognitive propositions, 7–8
cognitive reality, 74–76
   of logical forms, 55–56
   of meaning, 5
Cohen, Jonathan, 83, 264
   cancellation, 300
coherence, 86, 217, 218
co-indexing, 219
collective intentions, 332
collective reading, 124
comment vs. topic, 216
commissive speech act, 336, *see also* promising
commitment, 301, 335–336, 356
common ground, 243

and politeness, 344
communicated content, 238, 241, 247
communication
 definition, 252
 theory, 251
communication acts, 57
communicative intention vs. informative intention, 240
communicative presumption, 240
communicative principle, 256–257
comparison theory, 299–300
complementary clauses, 154
complex concepts, 24
complex demonstratives, 211
componential analysis, 23–24, *see also* lexical decomposition
compositional structure, 24
compositionality, 63–67, 160, 271
 implicature vs. utterance, 273
compositionality principle, 14
 and prototypes, 29–31
computational linguistics, 20, 126
computational semantics, 37
concepts
 definition, 21
 family resemblance, 22
 hierarchies of, 28
 lexical decomposition, 22–23
 one-to-one correspondence with objects, 25
 ontology, 32
 prototypes, 27–31
 shared information, 21–22
 speaker knowledge, 25
conceptual atomism, 24
conceptual engineering, 3, 29
Conceptual Metaphor Theory (CMT), 298
conceptual structures, 11, 12
 of *or*, 90
 universalism, 109–110
conceptualization of metaphor, 297–298, 307–312
conditional perfection, 94
conditional reasoning, 22
conditionals, 92–97
 as adverbial clauses, 95
 as politeness markers, 96
 incomplete, 96–97
 link between antecedents and consequents, 95
Conjoint Co-constituting Model of Communication (Arundale), 252, 332, 347
conjunction, 79–88
 dynamic, 179
 temporal ordering, 81–82
connectionism, 35–36, 277
connectives, 77
 and implicature, 245
 biconditional (equivalence), 93–94
 conditionals, 92–97

conjunction, 79–88
conventional implicature, 247
discourse connectives, 78
disjunction, 88–92
linguistic variation, 108–110
natural language vs. metalanguage, 77–78
negation, 97–108
pragmatic inferences, 110, 262–263
temporal ordering, 81–82
types, 78–79
Connolly, Andrew C., Jerry A. Fodor, Lila R. Gleitman, and Henry Gleitman, 30
connotative expressions, 185
conscious pragmatic inference (CPI), 274
consequentialism, 334
consequents, linked with antecedents, 95
constatives, 318
construction *in situ*, 304
content, 9, 25, 252, 349, 350–351, 354–355
 accountability for, 337
 at-issue, 233–234, 247–248, 355, 356
 communicated, 238, 241, 247
 derogatory, 352
 descriptive, 299, 355
 explicit, 266–267, 280, *see also* what is said
 expressive, 232–233, 248, 352–357
 in context, 123, 189, 289, 324
 in interrogatives, 57
 in proper names, 187–188
 information, 85, 216, 300
 literal, 327
 metaphorical *see* metaphor
 negation, 101–103
 of connectives, 83, 247, 262–263, 264
 of indexicals, 197–198, 204–205, 210
 pragmatic, 38, 82
 primary, 10–11, 275, 281, *see also* merger representations (Σ)
 propositional, 8–11, 317, 319, 322, 325, 347
 semantic, 24, 31, 277–278, 281–286
 truth-conditional, 260–262, 266–268, 283, 350, 353
 vs. character, 205, 304
context
 in defining words, 18–19
 in dynamic sematics, 167–168
 in place deixis, 199
 in presupposition, 225
 in prototypes, 30–31
 metaphorical extension, 305
 of indexicals, 198, 202–207
context dependence, 194
contextual cancellation, 279
contextual satisfaction theory, 225
contextualism, 267, 281–282, 283–284, 288
 about meaning vs. about knowledge attributions, 267

contextualism (cont.)
  and Default Semantics, 277–278
  in speech acts, 324
  in the semantics/pragmatics debate, 289
contextually referential expressions, 182–183
continuous–habitual distinction, 133
continuum of referentiality, 183–184
contradictions, 47–48, 104
contradictories, 98
contraries, 98–99
conventional implicature, 247–249
conventional metaphor, 294, 302, 306–307
conventionalized speech acts, 327–328
conventions, 249–251
Conversation Analysis (CA), 332
conversational background, 148–149
conversational contract, 348
conversational implicature, 238, 241, 247
Conversational Pressure (Goldberg), 337
conversational repair, 279
cooperation principle, 217
Cooperative Principle, 241–249
Corazza, Eros, 210
coreference, 186–187
correlates, 6
correspondence theory of truth, 44
counterfactuals, 94
covert politeness, 348
Crimmins, Mark, 160
criterion of adequacy, 15, 158, 164
Croft, William, 32
cross-cultural variation
  in politeness, 342, 343, 345–346
  in speech acts, 329
crossed readings, 103–104
cross-linguistic variation
  criticism of Grice's maxims, 242
  demonstratives, 184
  place deixis, 199
Culpeper, Jonathan, 348

Daubert, Johannes, 317
Davidson, Donald, 45, 139–140, 163, 305
Davis, Wayne, 248–249, 253
*de re* beliefs vs. *de dicto* beliefs, 156–158, 159
de Saussure, Ferdinand
  signifiers, 2
  structuralism, 26
deaccented focus, 220
default interpretations, 334
Default Semantics, 66, 110, 178, 273–275
  and theories of time, 143
defining words, difficulties of, 18–19
definite descriptions
  ambiguity in, 192–194
  as referring expressions, 41–42
  definition, 185

degrees of informativeness, 183–184
  semantics of, 189–197
  vs. proper names, 191
definites, 181
degree of contextual contribution, 279
degrees of informativeness, 183–184
deictic verbs, 199
deixis
  and non-deictic uses, 201
  categories, 198–202
  related to indexicality, 197–198
  tense as, 134–135
Del Pinal, Giuillermo, 30, 37
demonstratives
  cross-linguistic differences, 184
  disambiguation, 204
Dennett, Daniel, 277
  language and thought, 34
denotation, 40, 180
deontic modality, 147–148
deontological meaning, 333–335
derived categories, 68
derogatory content, 352
DeRose, Keith, 340
descriptive content, 299, 355
descriptivism, 186–188, 299, 352
determiners, numerals as, 125
Dever, Josh, 289
direct reference view, 41, 185, 187, 214
direct speech acts, distinction from indirect speech acts, 328
directing intention, 203
direction of fit, 323, 326
directly referential expressions, 182
discourse coherence, 217, 218
discourse connectives, 78
discourse deixis, 200, 201
Discourse Representation Structures (DRSs), 117
  conditions, 174–176
  Construction Rules, 173–176
  for distinguishing ambiguities, 125–126
  representing natural language, 126
  subordinate, 176
  truth conditions, 177
Discourse Representation Theory (DRT), 117, 124
  donkey sentences, 170–171
  dynamic semantics, 167
  multi-sentence discourses, 173–178
  related to B-theory of time, 143
  Segmented (SDRT), 84, 178, 250
discourse topic *see* topic
discourses
  in Discourse Representation Theory (DRT), 173–178
  in Dynamic Predicate Logic (DPL), 178–180
  temporality in, 141–142
discretionary indexicals, 204

disjunction, 49, 88–92
　as epistemic possibility, 108
dispositional modality, 148
disquotational principle, 163
distributive reading, 124
diversity, 5
division of linguistic labour, 25
domain of quantification, 286
domains, 315
donkey sentences, 168–172, 201
Donnellan, Keith, definite descriptions, 192, 193
Dowty, David, compositionality, 66
dual theory, 31, 38
duality of use of negation, 101–102
Ducrot, Oswald, 242
duplex condition, 118, 119, 126
dynamic conjunction, 179
dynamic existential quantifier, 171–172
dynamic implication, 171–172
dynamic meaning, 76, 335
dynamic modality, 148
dynamic pragmatic approach, 252, 337
Dynamic Predicate Logic (DPL), 168
　donkey sentences, 171
　multi-sentence discourses, 178–180
dynamic semantics, 167
　changing context, 167–168
　presupposition in, 226
dynamic situations, 131
dynamic verbs, 131–132

Elder, Chi-Hé and Eleni Savva, 96–97
Elder, Chi-Hé and Kasia Jaszczolt, 96
Elder, Chi-Hé and Michael Haugh, 252, 332, 334–335
embodied cognition, 307
embodiment, 24–25
empathetic deixis, 199
encyclopedic knowledge vs. linguistic knowledge, 18, 19
enriched proposition, 263–266
entailment vs. presupposition, 100–101, 225–226
epistemic modality, 147–148, 151–152
　time as, 144
epistemic necessity, 153
Equilibrium Semantics, 250
equivalence, 93
essential condition, 319
ethnomethodology, 333, 335
E-type anaphora, 169
evaluation, 295
Evans, Gareth, 203
　E-type anaphora, 169
Evans, Nicholas and Stephen Levinson, recursion, 109
evasiveness, 345
events
　logical form, 139–142
　vs. processes, 131
Everett, Daniel, 129
evidentiality, 153
exclusive disjunction, 89
existential presupposition, 100
existential quantifiers (∃), 51, 53, 106
experiential hypothesis, 307
explanandum (explananda), 239
　definition, 12
explanans (explanantia), 239
　definition, 12
expletives, 350, 352
explicature, 263–265, 280
explicit cancellation, 279
explicit content, 266–267, 280, *see also what is said*
expressive content, 232–233, 248, 352–357
extended conceptual metaphor theory (extended CMT), 310
extensional semantics, 69
extensions, relationship with intensions, 69–72
externalism, 15, 16

face, saving, 343–344
face-threatening acts (FTAs), weightiness of, 344–347
factive verbs, 227
factivity, 155–156, 231
fake indexicals, 210
false presuppositions, 338
falsifiability, 258
family resemblance, 22
Fauconnier, Gilles, 309
faultless disagreement, 214
felicity conditions, 319
*fiat* boundaries, 313
Fillmore, Charles, 32
first-order logic, 52
Firth, John, 20
fixing, 267
fluid characters, 256
focus, 220–223
Fodor, Jerry, 19
　atomism, 25
　bi-uniqueness, 25
　compositionality, 29
　conceptual atomism, 24
　Mentalese, 34
　representational theory of mind, 35
forbidden words, 349–357
foregrounding, 207, 277
formal tools, inclusion of pragmatics, 237–238
forward-looking centres, 217
Fox, Chris and Shalom Lappin, 71
frames, 28
Fraser, Bruce, 348
free enrichment, 268

Frege, Gottlob, 13
  compositionality, 64
  descriptivism, 186
  indexicals, 202–203
  on psychologism, 259
  'On Sense and Reference', 71
  on the compositionality principle, 14
  presupposition, 224
  sense, 69
  sense vs. reference, 26
Fregean propositions, 7
French language, subjunctive, 149
Fricker, Miranda, 337
functional indexicals, 214
functional proposition, 10–11, 275, 281, *see also* merger representations (Σ)
future conditionals, truth conditions, 94
future studies, 360–363
future tense, as modality, 151

game theory, 250, 332
Garfinkel, Harold, 333, 335
Gauker, Christopher, indexicals, 204
Gazdar, Gerald, 253, 262
Geach, Peter, 168
Geis, Michael and Arnold Zwicky, 94
generalized conversational implicatures (GCIs), 123, 245, 246, 254–256
generalized quantifiers, 117, 124
  numerals as, 124–130
generative grammar, 5
generative lexicon, 37
generative power, 109
generics, as definite descriptions, 189
'Genie', 33
Genovesi, Chris, 301
Geurts, Bart, 103, 129, 228, 356
  commitment, 335–336
  conventions, 250
Gibbs, Raymond, 312
Giora, Rachel, 289
  literalness, 293
Givenness Hierarchy, 184, 215, 217
Givón, Talmy, 216
glue logic, 84–85
Goldberg, Sanford, 329–330, 337
'grab-bag' approach (Rayo), 31, 37, 270
graded salience hypothesis, 289, 293
grammatical role hierarchy, 218
Grice, Paul, 262
  cancellability, 279–280
  conventional implicature, 247–249
  conventions, 249–251
  cooperation principle, 217
  Cooperative Principle, 241–249
  criticisms of, 241, 242, 251–252, 253
  implicature, 240–241
  incomplete utterances, 91
  intention in communication, 238–240
  meanings of *and*, 87–88
  metaphorical meaning, 303
  Modified Occam's Razor, 80, 82
  on definition of meaning, 2
  politeness, 341–343
  scalar expressions, 123
  temporal ordering, 83
  untruthfulness, 340
Groenendijk, Jeroen and Martin Stokhof, 168
Grosz, Barbara, Aravind Joshi, and Scott Weinstein, 218
growing block view, 143
Gundel, Jeanette, 183
Gundel, Jeanette, Nancy Hedberg, and Ron Zacharski, 183–184
Guugu Yimithirr language, connectives, 109

habitual–continuous distinction, 133
Halliday, Michael, 216
  information structure, 216
Hamm, Fritz, Hans Kamp, and Michiel van Lambalgen, 177
Harari, Yuval Noah, 1, 361–362
Harnish, Robert M., 320
Haugh, Michael, 333–334, 347
'heap' paradox, 38
Heffer, Chris, 340
Heim, Irene, 168, 225
  donkey sentences, 170
Heritage, John, 335
hermeneutical injustice, 337
Hess, Leopold, 356
'Hey, wait a minute!' (HWAM) test, 230
hidden indexical theory, 160–161
hierarchies of concepts, 28
Hintikka, Jaakko, 158
Hobbes, Thomas, 333
Hockett, Charles, 216
holism, 26
Hom, Christopher, 352
*Homo Deus* (Harari), 361–362
honorifics, 198
  as indexicals, 212
Horn, Laurence, 287
  contradictories, 98
  implicature vs. implying, 244
  natural order, 83
  negation, 101
  on the semantics–pragmatics interface, 3
  pragmatic strengthening, 99
  Q- and R-principles, 253
*How to Do Things with Words* (Austin), 316
human meaning, 1–2, 12–13
humans as algorithms, 361–362
Hume, David, 317, 333

humour, 354
Husserl, Edmund, 67, 317, 322, 333
   intentionality, 320

Idealized Cognitive Models (ICMs), 28
identity of indiscernibles, 155
identity of sense anaphora, 200
identity tests, 103–104
*if*, absence in some languages, 109
I-heuristic, 253, 254
illocutionary acts, 318
illocutionary force, 321–326
illocutionary logic, 322
illocutionary-informative intention, 240
image schemas, 308, 309
immunity to error through misidentification (IEM), 213
imperatives, 326
   illocutionary force, 322
   truth conditions in logical forms, 56–57
imperfective–perfective distinction, 133
implication, 92–93, 96
   dynamicity, 179
   in presupposition, 225
implicatum, 241
implicature, 240–241
   and connectives, 245
   and politeness, 347
   as primary meaning, 272–274
   calculability, 245
   cancellability, 244–245
   conventional, 247–249
   debate, 256
   lying through, 340
   non-conventionality, 245
   non-detachability, 245
   scalar, 245–247, 287–288
   vs. implying, 244
impliciture, 283
impoliteness, 348
inanimate objects, indexicals, 209
inchoatives, 131
inclusive disjunction, 88–89
incomplete conditionals, 96–97
incomplete descriptions, 191–192
incomplete utterances, 91–92
inconstancy under substitution, 104
indefinite descriptions, 195–197
indexical expressions, 267
indexicalism, semantic, 287
indexicality
   of time, 143
   related to deixis, 197–198
indexicals, 269–270
   content vs. character, 205
   context, 202–207
   in propositions, 9–10

Kaplan's list, 204–206
Kaplan's monster contexts, 208–215
   narrow vs. wide, 204
   pure vs. demonstrative, 202
   temporal, 138
indicatives, 326
   illocutionary force, 322
indirect speech acts (ISAs), 327–330
   as mark of power, 346
   distinction from direct speech acts, 328
indiscernibility of identicals, 155
individual constants, 51
individual variables, 52
inferences in negation, 101
inferential evidentiality, 153
inferential system (IS), 274
infinite sequences, 212
information content, 85, 216, 300
information structure, 215, 216, 250
   and focus, 223
informative intention vs. communicative intention, 240
informativeness, strength of, 194
injustice, 337–338
inquisitive semantics, 57
insensitive semantics, 285–286
insincerity, 338–341
   out of politeness, 341
institutional speech acts, 325
intended and recovered meaning, 273
intensional contexts, 14–15, 16, 158–159
intensions, 58, 63, 69
   relationship with extensions, 69–72
intentionality
   of speech acts, 320–321
   strength of, 194
intentions, 274
   and conventions, 249–251
   communicative vs. informative, 240
   indexicals, 204
interaction theory, 300
Interpersonal Rhetoric (Leech), 343
interpretation, 59
   in Discourse Representation Structures (DRSs), 173–174
interpreted logical forms, 162
interrogatives, 326
   illocutionary force, 322
   truth conditions in logical forms, 56–57
   using disjunction as a politeness marker, 90–91
intersective adjectives, 65
intonation, in negation, 99
irony, 243, 280, 295, 343

Jackendoff, Ray, 75
Japanese language
   deixis, 200

Japanese language (cont.)
　honorifics, 212
　theme vs. rheme, 215
Jary, Mark and Mikhail Kissine, 329
Jaszczolt, Kasia M., 109
　'being Gricean', 257
　compositionality, 66
　Default Semantics, 66, 110, 178, 275
　literalness, 292–293
Jaszczolt, Kasia M. and Lidia Berthon, 335, 337
Jaszczolt, Kasia M. and Roberto B. Sileo, 86–87
Jaszczolt, Kasia M., Eleni Savva, and Michael Haugh, 91–92
Jeshion, Robin, 355
Johnson, Mark, 308
joint construction of meaning, 332–338,
　*see also* co-construction of meaning
judgement fields, 313–314
jussive, 150

Kamp, Hans, 65, 168
　Discourse Representation Theory (DRT), 117
Kamp, Hans and Uwe Reyle, 137, 159
Kant, Immanuel, 107
　embodied cognition, 307
　theory of mind, 24
Kaplan, David
　character, 294
　direct reference, 185
　expletives, 350
　expressive content, 232
　indexicals, 202, 203–204, 205–206
　monster contexts, 208–215
　proper names, 41, 188
Karttunen, Lauri, 225
Kemp, Hans and Barbara Partee, 29–30
Kempson, Ruth, 102, 262
　semantic underdetermination, 106
King, Jeffrey, indexicals, 204
kinship terms, as deixis, 199
knowledge base, 37
Koenig, Jean-Pierre, 128
Kövecses, Zoltán, 310–311, 315
Kratzer, Angelika, 95, 210
　modality, 148–149
Kripke, Saul
　definite descriptions, 193
　proper names, 41, 162–163, 185–186
Kuboň, Petr, 220

Labov, William, prototypes, 27–28
Lakoff, George, 32
　ambiguity tests, 104, 105
　cognitive semantics, 272
　Idealized Cognitive Models (ICMs), 28
　metaphor, 297
　political metaphor, 311

Lakoff, George and Mark Johnson, 312
　embodied experience, 24–25
　metaphor, 298, 307, 309
Lakoff, Robin, 342
lambda abstraction, 73
lambda conversion, 73–74
lambda operator (λ), 72–73
Langacker, Ronald, 32
language acquisition, and thought, 33
language variation
　connectives, 108–110
　demonstratives, 184
　numerals, 129–130
　place deixis, 199
language, and thought, 33–36
Larson, Richard and Peter Ludlow, 162
Lascarides, Alex and Nicholas Asher, 84, *see also* Asher, Nicholas and Alex Lascarides
Lascarides, Alex, Anne Copestake, and Ted Briscoe, 105
Lasersohn, Peter, 214, 272
Leech, Geoffrey, 342–343
Leezenberg, Michiel, 305
legal cases, interpretations of *or*, 89
Leibniz's Law, 155
lekton, 271
Lepore, Ernie and Matthew Stone, 86, 218, 351
Levinson, Stephen, 83
　generalized implicatures, 246
　heuristics, 253–255
　implicature debate, 256
　presumptive meanings, 274, 275
Lewis, David
　accommodation, 226
　game theory, 250
lexical decomposition, 22–23
lexical semantics, 36
lexicon–encyclopedia interface, 18, 19
lexicon–pragmatics interface, 36–39
liability, 334
Liang, Percy and Christopher Potts, 65
linguistic knowledge vs. encyclopedic knowledge, 18, 19
linguistic relativity, 33
literal content, 327
literal meaning, 291–296
locutionary acts, 318
'Logic and conversation' (Grice), 83
logical forms, 48, 115–116
　definition, 48–49
　events, 139–142
　illocutionary force, 322–323
　metalanguage in, 48–57
　modality, 146–148
　of definite descriptions, 191
　of tense, 135–139
Ludlow, Peter and Stephen Neale, 194–195

lying, 229–230, 338–341
*Lying and Deception* (Carson), 341
*Lying, Misleading, and What Is Said* (Saul), 339

m[inimal]-literalness, 292
m[inimal]-non-literalness, 292
Macagno, Fabrizio, 334
MacFarlane, John, relativism about truth, 214
Machery, Edouard, 38, 39
*Machines Like Me and People Like You* (McEwan), 2, 362
Mandarin Chinese language, numerals, 130
Manner maxim, 241
　anglocentricity, 242
Manning, Elizabeth, 211
mapping relations, 20
mapping, metaphorical, 308–310
Maricopa language, connectives, 109
Marsh, Jessica, 345
Marty, Anton, 317
matching procedures (Tarski), 45
Maurice vs. Judd case, 39
maxims (Grice's), 241–243
　alternatives, 252–254
　of politeness, 341–343
McCawley, James, 103
McEwan, Ian, 2, 362
McGrath and Frank, 8
McTaggart, John M. E., 142, 143
meaning
　captured in logical forms, 54–55
　definitions, 2
　dynamic, 167
　implicature as primary, 272–274
　in terms of semantics, pragmatics, and philosophy, 3
　inferred, 236
　objective reality, 5
　problems with defining, 236–237
　psychological reality, 5
　strengthening, 94
'Meaning' (Grice), 238
*Meaning of Meaning, The* (Ogden and Richards), 15
Meibauer, Jörg, 329, 339
mental representations, 35
　and truth conditions, 46
mental spaces, 28
mental structures, 11, 12
Mentalese, 19, 34
mentalistic theories, 11, 13
　visual images, 21
mereology, 313
merger representations (Σ), 275–277
meronymy, 313
metaethics, 329
metalanguage
　connectives, 77–78
　in logical forms, 48–57
　representing quantifiers, 116–122
　selecting, 63
metalinguistic negation, 101–102, 229
metanegotiation of meaning, 337
metaphor, 243, 291
　as secondary meaning, 304
　as speaker meaning, 301
　blends, 309
　cognitive approach, 307–312
　comparison theory, 299–300
　conventional, 294, 302, 306–307
　debate, 312–316
　identifying, 296
　in Relevance Theory, 303
　interaction theory, 300–301
　literalness, 292, 305
　'made as if to say', 303
　mapping, 308–310
　metaphorical extension, 305
　political, 311
　purpose, 305
　studies of, 297
　subjectivism, 297–298
*Metaphors We Live By* (Lakoff and Johnson), 298, 309
metaphysical modality, 147
metapragmatics, examples, 3
metasemantics, 3, 6, 360–361
metavariables, 136, 172
methodological assumption, 275–276
M-heuristic, 253, 254
Mill, John Stuart
　inference, 242
　proper names, 185–186
Milsark, Gary L., 121
minimal meaning, 315
minimal proposition, 282
Minimal Semantics (Borg), 285
minimalism, 284–286, 287
　literalness, 294–295
miscommunication, 10, 243–244, 274, 331, 337
misleading, 338–340
mistaken descriptions, 192
modal logic, 146–148
modality
　and mood, 149–150
　and temporality, 151–154
　as relational expression, 148–149
　epistemic, 147–148
　future tense as, 151
　tense regarded as, 151
models, and possible worlds, 59–62
model-theoretic semantics, 60
modes of presentation, 161–162
Modesty maxim, 342
Modified Occam's Razor (Grice), 80, 82, 87, 245

modulation, 267–272, 275, 291
monotonicity, 119–121
monster contexts (Kaplan), 208–215
Montague semantics, 323
Montague, Richard, 45, 60, 65, 69, 272
  generalized quantifiers, 117
  semantics as a mirror of syntax, 5
mood
  and modality, 149–150
  definitions, 149–150
*Moral Politics* (Lakoff), 311
Moran, Richard, 337
*most*, interpretations of, 123–124
Mostowski, Andrzej, 117
moving spotlight view, 143
multi-sentence discourses
  in Discourse Representation Theory (DRT), 173–178
  in Dynamic Predicate Logic (DPL), 178–180
Munich phenomenologists, 317

*Naming and Necessity* (Kripke), 185
natural language
  and thought, 33–36
  connectives, 77–78
  problems with quantifiers, 112–113
  quantifiers, 115
  represented by DRSs, 126
natural meaning, 238
natural order, 83
negation
  ambiguity, 103–108
  and focus, 220
  connective as, 97–108
  dynamicity, 179
  echoic use, 102–103
  inferences in, 101
  intonation in, 99
  metalinguistic, 101–102, 229
  *Neg*-raising, 98–99
  not negating a proposition, 99–102
  of presuppositions, 229
  pragmatic aspects, 261
  truth values of, 97–98
negative face, 343
negative polarity items (NPIs), 102
negative politeness, 344
  cultural differences, 346
negotiation, 332–338
*Neg*-raising, 98–99
neo-classical theory, 31
neo-Gricean approaches, 256
neuropragmatics, 310
neuroscience of meaning, 5
neurosemantics, 20, 310
non-connotative expressions, 185
non-declaratives, 318

non-linguistic cues, in indirect speech acts (ISAs), 328
non-linguistic utterances, 239
non-literality, 284
non-monotonic presuppositions, 226
non-natural meaning, 238, 239
normative approach, 3, 337–338
Northern Paiute language
  relative tenses, 145
nouns, as indexicals, 210–211
Noveck, Ira, 89–90
numerals
  ambiguity in, 125–126, 127–129
  and focus, 222
  as generalized quantifiers, 124–130
  linguistic variation, 129–130
  scalar implicature, 246
  universalism, 129–130

objectifying acts, 317
objective reality of meaning, 5
objectivity, 13
off-record face-threatening acts, 344–345
offence, 356–357
Ogden, Charles K. and Ivor A. Richards, 15
on record face-threatening acts, 344
'On Sense and Reference' (Frege), 13, 71
one-place predicates, 51
ontological assumption, 276
open sentences, 52
operative interpreting, 333
operative meaning, 334–335
Optimality Theory (OT), 258
*or*
  absence in some languages, 108
  ambiguity, 89–90
  as a politeness marker, 90–92
  conceptual structure, 90
  inclusive or exclusive, 88–89
ordinary language philosophy, 16, 316
ostensive definition, 25
overt politeness, 348

p[rimary]-literalness, 292
Palmer, Frank R., 153
Paraguayan Guaraní language, tenseless, 145
parallel distributed processing models, 36, *see also* connectionism
paratones, 217
Parikh, Prashant, 250
Parsons, Terence, 65, 139–140
Partee, Barbara, 65
  conjunctions, 87
  indexicals, 138
particularized conversational implicatures (PCIs), 245
past of narration, 134

perfective–imperfective distinction, 133
performatives, 318
perlocutionary acts, 319
  and illocutionary force, 322
Perry, John, 160
  indexicals, 202–203, 204
person deixis, 198–199
Pfänder, Alexander, 317
phenomenology, 317
Philosophical Investigations (Wittgenstein), 316
*Philosophy in the Flesh* (Lakoff and Johnson), 307
Pirahã language, numerals, 129
place deixis, 199
Plato, 139, 158, 362
pleonastic propositions, 8, 161
Polish language
  aspectual distinction, 133–134
  fake indexicals, 210
  requests, 322
  subjunctive, 149
politeness, 273, 341–343
  covert, 348
  cross-cultural differences, 342, 343, 345–346
  face-threatening acts (FTAs), 344–347
  implicatures, 347
  strategic but subconscious, 348
  studies of, 348
politeness markers
  conditionals as, 96
  *or* as, 90–92
political correctness, 29
political metaphor, 311
Port Royal logic, 139
Portner, Paul, mood, 150
positive face, 343
positive politeness, cultural differences, 346
possible worlds, 19
  and modality, 146–147
  and models, 59–62
  belief in, 158
  definition, 58
  proper names, 188
  truth conditions, 58–59
post-propositional implicature, 256
potential (or putative) implicature, 254, 279
Potts, Christopher, 233, 350
  conventional implicature, 247–248
  expressivism, 354–356
pragmatic content, 38, 82
pragmatic strengthening, 98–99
pragmatically modulated sentence, 271
pragmatics, 3, 236
  and lexical semantics, 37
  captured in logical forms, 55
  of connectives, 110
pragmatics–lexicon interface, 36–39

pragmatics/semantics boundary, 282–284, 288–290
  minimalism, 284–286
pragmatics–semantics interface, 3–4, 255, 260–261
Prague school, 215
pre-conceptual experiences, 308
Predelli, Stefano, 210, 295, 353
predicate logic, 51–52
  quantifying expressions, 112–113
  representing conventional implicature, 247–249
predicates, 181
predicates of personal taste, 214
preference order, 229
preparatory conditions, 319
Present Perfect Continuous, 136
presentism, 143
presumptive meanings, 246, 274, 275
presupposition, 99–100, 206, 223–231
  vs. entailment, 100–101
presupposition pool, 217
presuppositions
  false, 338
  in DRT, 126
  of existence, 106
primary content, 10–11, 275, 281, *see also* merger representations ($\Sigma$)
primary meaning
  implicature as, 272–274
  vs. secondary meaning, 280–281
primary pragmatic processes, 264
primitive characters, 294
principle of compositionality, 14
Prior, Arthur, 135
private inferences, 335
private language, 35
privative opposites, 104
privileged interactional interpretation, 277
processes vs. events, 131
projection line, 227–228
projection problem, 231
projective content, 230–231, 353
  and at-issueness, 233–234
  and expressive content, 232–233
  types, 234
promising, 317, 319, 321, 336
pronouns
  as deixis, 198
  as referring expressions, 41
  conceptualization, 212
  disambiguation, 204
  indexicality, 197
  lazy use, 200
proper names, 41
  as referring expressions, 185–189
  need for intensions, 71
  propositional attitude reports, 162–163
  sticking to referents, 203
  vs. definite descriptions, 191

proportion problem, 170
propositional attitude reports, 14, 45, 65, 154–164, 190
propositional concept, 8, 206
propositional content, 8–11, 317, 319, 322, 325, 347
propositional logic, 49–50
propositional modality, 153
propositional radicals, 282
propositions, 6
  as intensions, 69
  Carnapian, 7
  cognitive, 7–8
  definition, 6–7
  Fregean, 7
  functional, 10–11, 275, 281, see also merger representations (Σ)
  indexicals in, 9–10
  language and thought, 36
  pleonastic, 8
  Russellian, 7
  singular vs. general, 193
  truth values, 58–59
prototypes, 27–31
provisional interpreting, 333
psychological reality of meaning, 5
psychologism, 259
publicly available inferences, 335
Pulvermüller, Friedemann, 20
punctual semantics, 128
punning effect (zeugma), 104–105
puns, 295
pure indexicals, 212–213
Pustejovsky, James, generative lexicon, 37
putative (or potential) implicature, 244, 254
Putnam, Hilary, 15
  division of linguistic labour, 25

Q-principle, 253
Q-heuristic, 253, 254
Quality maxim, 241, 243
quantificational force, 149
quantifiers, 51–54
  and focus, 221–222
  and presupposition, 228
  generalized, 124
  in natural language, 115
  in predicate logic, 112–113
  numerals as generalized quantifiers, 124–130
  quirks of interpretation, 122–124
  represented in metalanguage, 116–122
  restrictions, 113–114
  strong vs. weak, 121
Quantity maxim, 241, 242
  and tautology, 243
question under discussion (QUD), 233–234
Quine, W. V. O., 25, 155
Quintilian, 299

R-principle, 253
radial structures, 28
radical pragmatics, 107, 261, 262
radical semantic minimalism, 283
radical semantics, 288
radical view, 278–279, 291
radicals, 282
Ramsey, Frank, 139
rationality principle, 238
Rayo, Augustín, 37
  'grab bag' approach, 31, 270
Recanati, François, 114, 288
  compositionality, 271
  contextualism, 267
  explicature, 264–265
  literality, 292–293
  modulation, 267–269
  Subjective Reference View, 194
  Truth-Conditional Pragmatics, 271
receiving time (time of the recovery of the information by the hearer), 199
recursion, 109
reference
  vs. sense, 14, 71, 186, 202–203
reference, definition, 40–41
referential approach, 12, 13–14, 39
  limitations, 39–40
referential intention, 240
referentialist view, 299
referring, 40
referring expressions, 41
  and topic, 216
  definite descriptions as, 41–42, 196–197
  proper names as, 41, 185–189
  types, 180–185
regularity, 5
Reichenbach, Hans, 137–138, 139
Reid, Thomas, 317, 333
Reinach, 317, 321
Relation maxim, 241, 242
relational expressions, modals as, 148–149
relations vs. sense, 26
relative tenses, 145
relativism about truth, 214
relativity vs. universalism, 22–23
Relevance Theory (Sperber and Wilson), 252, 256–259, 273
  explicatures, 264
  metaphor, 303, 315
repair, 279
representational theories, 11, 13
  visual images, 21
representational theory of mind (Fodor), 35
requests, 322, 327, 336
responsibility, avoiding, 273
restrictions, 113–114, 148
restrictors, 95

resultatives, 131
rheme vs. theme, 215–216
rhetorical cooperativity, 251
rhetorical relations, 229
Richard, Mark, 162, 353, 354
Richards, I. A. and Max Black, 299
Roberts, Craige, 233
Rooth, Mats, 220–221, 228
Rosch, Eleanor
    hierarchies of concepts, 28
    prototypes, 27
Ross, John Robert 'Haj', 200
Rothstein, Susan, 129
Russell, Bertrand, 180
    concepts, 25
    definite descriptions, 190
    descriptivism, 186–187
    existential operators, 106
    indefinite descriptions, 195
    on proper names, 41
    presupposition, 224
    theory of types, 63
Russellian propositions, 7

Sainsbury, Mark, Maurice vs. Judd case, 39
salience, 293
Salmon, Nathan, 162
Sapir, Edward and Benjamin L. Whorf, 23
satisfaction conditions, 323
saturation, 267, 268, 269
Saul, Jennifer, 71, 339
scalar expressions, 123
scalar implicature, 245–247, 287–288
Scale of Accessibility, 184–185
schemas, 308, 309
Schiffer, Stephen, 8, 67, 160, 161
Schlenker, Philippe, 208, 353
scope principle, 264, 265
Searle, John R., 300, 316
    classification of speech acts, 326
    collective intentions, 332
    definite descriptions, 193
    indirect speech acts (ISAs), 327
    intentionality, 320
    metaphor, 301–302
    social acts, 321
Searle, John R. and Daniel Vanderveken, 319, 322, 324
secondary meaning, 304
    vs. primary meaning, 280–281
secondary pragmatic processes, 264
Segmented Discourse Representation Theory (SDRT), 84, 178, 250
semantic ambiguity, 261

semantic content, 24, 31, 277–278, 281–286, *see also* content
    negation, 101–103
semantic difference, 104
semantic fields, 27
semantic indexicalism, 114, 287
semantic innocence, 163–164
semantic primitives, 23
semantic types, 69
    reading, 70
semantic underdetermination, 37, 106–108, 128, 261–262, 282, 284
semantics, 1, 3
    captured in logical forms, 54–55
    changing context in, 167–168
    dynamic, 167
    of definite descriptions, 189–197
semantics/pragmatics boundary, 282–284, 288–290
    minimalism, 284–286
semantics–pragmatics interface, 3–4, 255, 260–261
sense, 26, 37
    and intension, 69
    and the punning effect, 104–105
    conventions, 249–251
    enriched, 83, 85
    modulation, 267–272, 275, 291
    of connectives, 78, 87–88
    of proper names, 41, 185
    vs. reference, 14, 71, 186, 202–203
sense extension, 268, 292
sense-generality, 37, 106–108, 128, 261–262, 282, 284
sensorimotor apparatus, 307
sensorimotor thought, 33
sentences, 6
set operator (lambda operator ($\lambda$)), 72–73
set theory, 118–119
Shanon, Benny, 230
signifiers, 2
Simons, Mandy, 233
Simons, Mandy et al., 233, 234
sincerity conditions, 319, 330
situation of discourse (SD), 274
situations, 131–133
    temporality of, 130–131
slurs, 350–356
Smith, Barry, 313–314
Soames, Scott, 162, 189
    cognitive propositions, 7–8
social deixis, 198, 200–201
social interaction, speech acts as, 320–321
social operations of the human mind, 317
social, cultural and world knowledge defaults (SCWDs), 274, 275, 276
society and culture (SC), 274
sociopragmatics, focus on speech acts, 324
solitary operations of the human mind, 317

*some*
   interpretations of, 122–123
   scalar implicature, 246
Spanish language, place deixis, 199
speaker intentions, 240, 243–244, 274
   and conventions, 249–251
   in definite descriptions, 193
   indexicals, 204
   metaphor as, 301
   truth conditions, 46
speaking on a topic, 217
Speech Act Theory (SAT), 150, 278, 316–319
   illocutionary force, 321–326
   indirect speech acts (ISAs), 327–330
speech acts
   classification, 325–326
   conventionalized, 327–328
   cross-cultural differences, 329
   institutional, 325
   intentionality vs. social interaction, 320–321
   labelling, 325
Sperber, Dan and Deirdre Wilson, 240, 252, 256–259, 262, 303, *see also* Wilson, Deirdre and Dan Sperber
   institutional speech acts, 325
Stalnaker, Robert C., 95, 225, 360
   indexicals, 206–207
standard minimalist views, 287
Stanley, Jason, 113–114, 286
Stanley, Jason and Zoltán Gendler Szabó, 286, 287
states of affairs, 7, *see also* propositions
stative verbs, 131
stereotypical features, 27–31
stereotypical modifiers, 30
Stern, Josef, 304
Stoicism, 316
Stokke, Andreas, 339
Stotts, Megan Henricks, 286
Strawson, Peter, 100, 180, 262
   definite descriptions, 193
   presupposition, 224
strengthening, 94, 267
structuralism, 16, 26–27
sub-intentions, 239–240
subjectivity, 13
subjunctive, 149
   in English, 150
subordinate Discourse Representation Structures (DRSs), 176
subsective adjectives, 65
substitutivity, 154–155, 156
suggestion, 324
supervenience, 152
Swahili language
   tense, 145
symmetry, 122
syntactic constraint, 273

syntactic types, reading, 70
synthetic sentences, 46
   logical form, 49
*System of Logic* (Mill), 185
Szabó, Zoltán, compositionality, 66

t[ype]-literalness, 292
taboo expressions, 349–357
tactfulness, 273
Tamil language, connectives, 109
Tannen, Deborah, 346
Tarski, Alfred, matching procedures, 45
tautology, 46–47, 243
temporal anaphora, 137–138
temporal ordering, 81–82
   of *and*, 86–87
temporality, 130–131
   and modality, 151–154
   in Default Semantics, 276–277
   in discourse, 141–142
   intervals vs. instants, 138–139
   semantic representation, 134–135
   truth conditions, 140–141
tense
   absence in some languages, 145
   absolute, 135
   and temporal ordering, 86–87
   deictic expressions, 134–135, 198, 200
   future tense as modality, 151
   indexicals, 138
   logic, 135–139
   mismatched with time, 144
   optional in some languages, 144–145
   regarded as modality, 151
   relative, 145
testimonial injustice, 337
Thai language
   honorifics, 212
   tense, 144–145
*that*-clauses, 154
theme vs. rheme, 215–216
theory of mind (Kant), 24
theory of types, 63
thought, and natural language, 33–36
three-place predicates, 51
time
   mismatched with tense, 144
   theories, 142–144
time deixis, 199–200
time metaphors, 146
token-referential expressions, 182
Tonhauser, Judith, 233
'top-down' approach, 1
topic, 215–218
   vs. comment, 216
topic framework, 217
translation principle, 163

translations to logical forms, 53–54
transparency, 156
Traugott, Elizabeth Closs, 306
Travis, Charles, speaker intentions, 46
Trust-Related Untruthfulness in Situated Text (TRUST), 340
truth conditions, 44, 45
  and definite descriptions, 192–193
  and focus, 220–223
  and logical forms, 56–57
  and possible worlds, 58–59
  matching procedures (Tarski), 45
  of Discourse Representation Structures (DRSs), 177
  of future conditionals, 94
  of utterances, 262
  propositional logic, 49–50
  speaker intentions, 46
  temporality, 140–141
truth values, 44, 46–48, *see also* lying
  as extensions, 69
  conjunction, 79
  of negation, 97–98
  of presuppositions, 226
truth-conditional approach, 12
truth-conditional content, 260–262, 266–268, 283, 350, 353
Truth-Conditional Pragmatics (Recanati), 114, 271, 273, 275
  radical view, 278
Turing, Alan, 33
Twin Earth thought experiment (Putnam), 15
two-dimensional semantics, 206–207
two-place predicates, 51
type-referential expressions, 182
type-shifting, 66
type-theoretic language, 54, 67–69
typicality scale, 27–28

unarticulated constituents, 268–269
underdetermination, 37, 106–108, 128, 261–262, 282, 284
uniqueness condition, 190
universal grammar, 33
universal quantifiers, 52
universalism
  of conceptual structures, 109–110
  of numerals, 129–130
  vs. relativity, 22–23
universals, 13
unselective binding, 170
Upriver Halkomelen language, connectives, 108–109
use theory, 16

utterances, 6
'Utterer's meaning and intentions' (Grice), 239

vagueness, 38, 48, 53, 303, *see also* ambiguity
Van der Auwera, Johan and Vladimir A. Plungian, 153
van der Sandt, Rob, 228
  anaphors, 228
  preference order, 229
  presupposition, 225–227
Vanderveken, Daniel, 323, *see also* Searle, John R. and Daniel Vanderveken
variation *see* language variation
vector semantics, 20
Vendler, Zeno, verb classifications, 132
Venus, thought of as both Morning and Evening Star, 13–14
verbs, classification, 131–132
Viebahn, Emanuel, indexicals, 204
Vietnamese language, honorifics, 212
visual images, as mental representations of meaning, 21
vivid present, 134, 144
von Fintel, Kai and Lisa Matthewson, 110

Wari language, disjunction, 108
Watts, Richard J., 348
weightiness of an FTA, 345–346
Weissman, Benjamin and Marina Terkourafi, 340
*what is said*, 238, 241, 265–266
  and implicatures, 266–267
  vs. *what is meant*, 282–284
'Whose meaning?' question, 257, 273
Wierzbicka, Anna, 242
Williams syndrome, 33
Wilson, Deirdre, 102, 262
Wilson, Deirdre and Dan Sperber, 243, 303, *see also* Sperber, Dan and Deirdre Wilson
Wittgenstein, Ludwig, 22, 262, 291
  language of mental representations, 35
  meaning as use, 316
word meaning and sentence structure (WS), 274, 278
word senses
  ambiguity in, 37–38
  difficulties with defining, 18–19
  generative lexicon, 37
world knowledge (WK), 37, 274

*zeugma* (punning effect), 104–105
Zwicky, Arnold and Jerrold Sadock, 104
  ambiguity, 103